REVIEWS FOR

'IN THE SHADOW OF EMPIRES'
The historic Vlad Dracula, the events he shaped and the events that shaped him.

Congratulations, I'm impressed by your emphatic understanding of Vlad's personality, and by a very well written and interesting book.
- Tudor Sălăgean, Directorul Muzeului Etnografic, Cluj-Napoca -

Finally. Fantastic book. Packed with information, easy to ready, well-researched & well organized. Finally a Vlad book not written for teenagers, and not based on biased historical slanders. My other historical obsessions usually have countless sources publicized, more than enough to feed my hunger for knowledge: Vlad Dracula is entirely different, it's nearly impossible (and for me nearly painful) to find competent info on him. Jens clearly has a great interest in providing what history buffs adore: the truth behind the legends. Much of his info comes from personal experience & in-depth study, and his collective research is worthy of respect. If you've been searching for a fact-driven book dedicated to the complex subject of Vlad Dracula III, I highly recommend this one.
- Reader from US -

I really enjoyed this book, very well written and equally as well researched. You're told the facts and where these are questionable they're given to you clearly stated as being sourced from legend. This is a book I'll return to again and again and I especially loved the end, tips for the tourist visiting Romania, brilliant touch.
- Reader from UK -

The author not only assembled all available information but he also guided the reader through the exciting process of gaining an understanding of why things happened. Somehow he managed to achieve a perfect balance of being passionate about the subject and at the same time to refrain from speculating too much (and only when necessary - due to lack of data). Great work that managed to completely change that little that I "knew" about this historical figure.
- Reader from US -

THE CONQUEROR'S ENEMIES

A biography of Fatih Sultan Mehmed told through the stories of his enemies

Sir Jens

Copyright © 2013 Sir Jens

Estate copyright © 2026 Donna Schwarz-Nielsen

All rights reserved.
ISBN: 9780957647220

Also by Sir Jens:

In the Shadow of Empires
ISBN: 9780957647206

For Lady Donna Elizabeth, whose Sisyphean task it is to Anglify my ramblings and ensure that I occasionally interact socially with things other than dusty books while - at the same time - she fights for my attention with long-dead rulers of obscure lands.

TABLE OF CONTENTS

Foreword 1

Overview of Key People 5

Part 1 - The Conqueror's Empire 25

   1 - The Ottoman Empire, Setting the Scene 27

   2 - The Conqueror's World 39

Part 2 - The Byzantine Empire 47

   3 - Birth, Decline, Crusades and Reconquest 49

   4 - Deadly Neighbours 75

Part 3 - Troublesome Kindsmen 117

   5 - The Seljuks 119

   6 - The Karamanids 127

   7 - The White Sheep 141

   8 - The Empire of Trebizond 155

Part 4 - The Maritime States of Italy 165

   9 - Italy and the Maritime States 167

   10 - Venice 173

   11 - Genoa 213

Part 5 - The Balkans **255**

   12 - The Bulgarian Empires 257

   13 - Hungary 291

   14 - The Buffer States 341

      Serbia 343

      Bosnia 363

      Wallachia 379

      Moldavia 399

   15 - Albania 413

Part 6 - The Pope and the Crusader Knights **435**

   16 - The Pope 437

   17 - The Crusader Knights 603

   18 - The Ottoman Empire after Mehmed II 617

Notes and Index **619**

   Notes 621

   Index 623

Appendixes **649**

   A - Overview of Key Military Encounters 651

   B - Consolidated Timeline 659

EMPIRE

An extensive group of states or countries ruled over by a single monarch, an oligarchy, or a sovereign state.

- Oxford Dictionaries -

FOREWORD

Sultan Mehmed II, given the moniker 'Fatih' (The Conqueror) was one of the most colourful and charismatic sultans of the Ottoman Empire.

Though it would be his great-grandson, Suleiman I, whom historians would give the moniker 'The Magnificent' (even though his contemporaries would call him 'Kanuni' - 'The Lawgiver') and under whom the Ottoman Empire would experience its golden age, it was Fatih Sultan Mehmed who once and for all cemented the empire's position as a super-power in both Asia Minor and Europe.

Of course the one achievement that Mehmed II is best known for is the Conquest of Constantinople in 1453, but his thirty years rule was a period of constant conflict and confrontation aimed at both expanding and consolidating the Empire's borders.

Several books have been written about Mehmed II, first among them Franz Babinger's *"Mehmed the Conqueror and his Time"*, with a more recent addition being John Freely's *"The Grand Turk"*. As is natural, these books - being dedicated biographies - are centred on Mehmed II and the Ottoman Empire, they are, in other words *'Mehmed-centric'*.

Having read these and many other, books and articles on the subject of Mehmed II and having written a book (*In the Shadow of Empires*) about the historic Vlad III Dracula - one of Mehmed II's contemporaries and enemies - I started thinking that there are so many interesting cameo-appearances in the story of Mehmed II, Vlad III Dracula being only one of those, that it would be worth trying to tell the story of Mehmed II's enemies; who they were, why they were his enemies and how the confrontations came and went.

Another reason to do this is that the classic approach of writing a biography in chronological order does not work so well when it comes to Mehmed II. He simply had so many conflicts, with so many enemies, spread over so many separate incidents, that a chronological approach diffuses the picture of his enemies into a lot of small fragments, never really providing the bigger picture and leaving you wondering why he did what he did when he did.

Through this approach a web is spun that even though it sets out to not be Mehmed-centric, anyway ends up with Mehmed II in the centre, thus telling both a string of interesting stories about Mehmed II's enemies and at the same time telling the story of Mehmed II in a way very different from the way it has been told before.

Like in my previous book I try to tell the story in a narrative form that, though factual, reads more like a story than a history-lesson. I hope that this will give a less academic audience the urge to read a story that is at the same time exciting, gruesome, and poetic, and which still affects the way our world looks today.

Though the parts and chapters of this book are of course interconnected through overlapping people and events, each part, or chapter, can be read on its own. If for instance you have a special interest in Venice, then Chapter 10 can be read in isolation. The exception to this rule is Mehmed II and the Ottomans, their story is told in fragments relevant to the main subject of each chapter. That said, to get the full picture you should of course rather read it all.

I appreciate when reading a book with as many people and names as is the case in this book, it is easy to get a bit lost and find yourself flipping back and forth to rekindle your memory as to whom is whom and so forth! That is normal, and it applies to the writing process as much as it does to the reading process. As I cannot reduce the number of people involved in history, what I have done is try to differentiate as much as possible.

Many of the people in this book have historic records which mention their names in their local language, Greek and Latin as a minimum. There is thus the possibility to choose. I have made that choice to try to not have fifteen people called '*Stefan*', but rather have say five called '*Stefan*', five called '*Stephen*' and five called '*Stjepan*'. Furthermore, I have tried to use full titles such as '*Stefan II*' even when it is obvious from the context who that particular '*Stefan*' is.

I have also included an **Overview of Key Individuals** at the front of the book, so you do not find this tool only after you have struggled through the book without it. Furthermore, I have inserted a table with a **Critical Timeline** in front of each chapter (except Chapter 9 and 18), to provide an outline of the key events of that chapter in chronological order. At the back of the book there is also an **Index** as well as an **Overview of Key Military Encounters** and an appendix with a **Consolidated Timeline**. Hopefully, you will find that these tools reduce the potential confusion.

Finally, a word on writing a book which spans more than a millennium. When I set out, I knew what I wanted to do and I had a rough outline of the composition of the book. Some of the subject I knew well, some I knew a little and some I did not know anything about apart from the fact that they needed to be in the book as they emerge as enemies of the Conqueror. Thus, armed with a plan it is always an unknown how much material is really there to write about. In this case the answer is absolute lots of it.

Indeed, there is so much material about the subjects covered by this book that it has been a matter not of finding enough material but rather of filtering the material and decide which would finally end up in the book and make some hard choices about wonderful material which simply could not fit in.

It does not matter who you are and how neutral you are in your views. When you write about history it always gets an angle, a little tweak here and there - your fingerprint - and I hope that what I have selected for this book and the way I have chosen to present it does these compelling stories justice.

Sir Jens

Foreword

OVERVIEW OF KEY INDIVIDUALS

The following is an overview in alphabetic order of the key individuals mentioned in this book.

Adalbert

King of Italy 950 - 963. Son of Berengar II.

Adrian I

Pope 772 - 795.

Adrian II

Pope 867 - 872.

Adrian III

Pope 884 - 885.

Adrian IV

Pope 1154 - 1159.

Ageltrude

Empress of the Romans 891 - 894. Mother of Lambert II.

Agilulf

King of the Lombards 590 - 616.

Aistulf

King of the Lombards 749 - 756.

Alaattin Ali of Karaman

Ruler of Karaman 1361 - 1398. Son-in-law of Murad I.

Alaric

King of the Visigoths 395 - 410.

Albert II

King of Hungary 1437 - 1439.

Alboin

King of the Lombards 560 - 572.

Alexander II

Pope 1061 - 1073.

Alexander III

Pope 1159 - 1181.

Alexandru I (of Moldavia)

Voivode of Moldavia 1400 - 1432. Son of Roman I.

Alexandru I Aldea

Voivode of Wallachia 1432 - 1436. Son of Mircea I.

Alexandru II

Voivode of Moldavia 3 times between 1449 and 1455. Son of Ilias I.

Alexios I Komnenos

Emperor of Byzantium 1081 - 1118.

Alexios I of Trebizond

Co-founder and ruler of the Empire of Trebizond 1204 -1222.

Overview of Key Individuals

Alexios II Komnenos

Emperor of Byzantium 1180 - 1183. Son of Manual I Komnenos.

Alexios III Angelos

Emperor of Byzantium August 1195 - 1203. In charge of defending Constantinople against the Fourth Crusade.

Alexius Angelus

As Alexius IV Angelus Emperor of Byzantium August 1203 - January 1204. The nominal subject of the Fourth Crusade's conflict with the Byzantine Empire. Son of Isaac II Angelos.

Alfonso V of Aragon

King of Aragon and Naples 1416 - 1458.

Alfonso VII of Castile

King of Castile 1127 - 1157.

Al-Kamil

Sultan of Egypt 1218 - 1238.

Alp Arslan

Sultan of the (Great) Seljuk Empire 1063 - 1072. Nephew of Tuğrul.

Amadeus VI

Count of Savoy 1343 -1383.

Amalasuntha

Regent and Queen of Italy 526 - 534. Daughter of Theodoric the Great.

Anacletus II

Anti-Pope 1130 - 1138.

Anastasios II

Emperor of Byzantium 713 - 715.

Anastasius III

Pope 911 - 913.

Anastasius Bibliothecarius

Chief Archivist of the (Roman) Church. Possibly anti-pope. †878.

András I of Hungary

King of Hungary 1046 - 1060.

András II of Hungary

King of Hungary 1205 - 1235. Son of Béla III.

András III of Hungary

King of Hungary 1290 - 1301. Great Grandson of Stefan II.

Andronikos I Komnenos

Emperor of Byzantium 1182 - 1185. Last of the Komnenos dynasty to rule Byzantium.

Andronikos II Palaiologos

Emperor of Byzantium 1282 - 1328.

Andronikos III Palaiologos

Emperor of Byzantium 1321 - 1341. Son of Michael IX Palaiologos.

Andronikos IV Palaiologos

Emperor of Byzantium 1376 - 1379

Arnulf of Carinthia

Emperor of the Romans 896 - 899. The illegitimate son of Carloman of Bavaria.

Overview of Key Individuals

Árpád

Ruler (Prince) of the Magyars 895 - 907.

Attila

King of the Huns 434 - 453.

Avitus (Eparchius Avitus)

Emperor of Rome 455 - 456.

Baibars

Sultan of Egypt 1260 - 1277.

Baldwin II of Jerusalem

King of Jerusalem 1118 - 1131.

Baldwin of Flanders

Count of Flanders 1194 - 1205. Emperor of the Latin Empire of Constantinople (as Baldwin I of Constantinople) 1204 - 1205. Co-leader of the Fourth Crusade.

Basarab I

Founder and Voivode of Wallachia c.1310 - 1352.

Basarab II

Voivode of Wallachia 1442 - 1443. Son of Dan II.

Basarab III Laiotă

Ruler of Wallachia five times between 1473 and 1477. Son of Dan II.

Basil II

Emperor of Byzantium 976 - 1025.

Bayezid I

Sultan of the Ottoman Empire 1389 - 1402. Died a prisoner of Timur in 1403. Son of Murad I.

Bayezid II

Sultan of the Ottoman Empire 1481 - 1512. Son of Mehmed II.

Béla II

King of Hungary 1131 - 1141.

Béla III

King of Hungary 1172 - 1196. Son of Geza II.

Béla IV

King of Hungary 1235 - 1270. Son of András II.

Belisarius

Commander of the Byzantine Army 527 - 559.

Benedict I

Pope 575 - 579.

Benedict III

Pope 855 - 858.

Benedict IV

Pope 900 903.

Benedict VI

Pope 972 - 973.

Benedict VIII

Pope 1012- 1024. Son of Gregory I of Tusculum.

Overview of Key Individuals

Benedict IX

Pope 932 - 944, 945 and 947 - 948.

Benedict XI

Pope 1303 - 1304.

Benedict XIII

Anti-Pope 1394 - 1423.

Berengar I

Emperor of the Romans 915 - 924.

Berengar II

King of Italy 950 - 963.

Bernard of Clairvaux

Abbot of Clairvaux 1115 - 1153.

Bogdan II

Voivode of Moldavia 1449 - 1451. Son of Alexandru I.

Boniface I

Pope 418 - 422.

Boniface II

Pope 530 - 532.

Boniface III (Pope)

Pope 607.

Boniface IV

Pope 608 - 615.

Boniface VI

Pope for 15 days in 896.

Boniface VII

Anti-Pope 974, 980 - 981 and 984 - 985.

Boniface VIII

Pope 1294 - 1303.

Boniface IX

Pope 1389 - 1404.

Boniface of Montferrat

Marques of Montferrat 1183 - 1207. Co-leader of the Fourth Crusade. King Boniface I of the Kingdom of Thessalonica 1204 - 1207.

Boris I of Bulgaria

Khan of Bulgaria 852 - 889. Son of Presian I.

Callixtus II

Pope 1119 - 1124.

Çandarlı Halil Pasha

Grand Vizier to Murad II and Mehmed II 1439 - 1453. Executed by Mehmed II immediately following the Conquest of Constantinople.

Carloman I

King of the Franks 768 - 771. Co-ruler with Charlemagne.

Celestine I

Pope 422 - 432.

Celestine III

Pope 1191 - 1198.

Celestine V

Pope 1294.

Overview of Key Individuals

Cem

Contender for the Ottoman throne. †1495. Son of Mehmed II.

Charlemagne

King of the Franks, Emperor of the Romans 768 - 814. Son of Pepin the Short.

Charles I of Hungary (Charles Robert of Anjou)

King of Hungary 1308 - 1342.

Charles I of Naples (Charles of Anjou)

King of Naples 1266 - 1285, King of Sicily 1266 - 1282, King of Albania 1272 - 1285, Prince of the Morea 1278 - 1285.

Charles II of Hungary (Charles III of Naples)

King of Hungary 1385-1386.

Charles II of Naples (Charles of Salerno)

King of Naples 1285 - 1309. Son of Charles I of Naples.

Charles of Valois

Count of Valois 1284 - 1325. Son of Philip III of France.

Charles the Bald

Emperor of the Romans 875 - 877. Son of Louis the Pious.

Charles the Fat

Emperor of the Romans 881 - 888.

Clement III

Anti-Pope 1084 - 1100.

Clement III

Pope 1187 1191.

Clement IV

Pope 1265 - 1268.

Clement V

Pope 1305 - 1314. Moved the papacy to Avignon.

Clement VI

Pope 1342 - 1352.

Cleph

King of the Lombards 572 - 574.

Coloman

King of Hungary and Croatia 1095 - 1116. Son of Géza I.

Conrad II

Holy Roman Emperor 1027 - 1039.

Conrad III

King of Germany 1138 - 1152.

Conrad IV

King of Germany 1250 - 1254. Son of Frederick II.

Conradin

King of Sicily 1254 - 1268. Son of Conrad IV.

Constance of Sicily

Queen of Sicily 1194 1198.

Constantine (Pope)

Pope 708 - 715.

Overview of Key Individuals

Constantine II

Anti-Pope 768 - 769.

Constans II

Emperor of Byzantium 641 - 668.

Constantine IV

Emperor of Byzantium 668 - 685.

Constantine V

Emperor of Byzantium 741 - 775. Son of Leo III.

Constantine VII

Emperor of Byzantium 913 - 959. Son of Leo VI.

Constantine XI Palaiologos

Emperor of Byzantium 1448 - 1453. Son of Manuel II Palaiologos. Last emperor of Byzantium.

Constantine the Great

Roman Emperor 306 - 337. First Christian emperor of Rome and founder of Constantinople.

Constantine Tikh

Tsar of Bulgaria 1257 - 1277.

Crescentius II

Patricius Romanorum (de-facto ruler of Rome). †998.

Damasus I

Bishop of Rome (Pope) 366 - 384.

Dan I

Voivode of Wallachia 1383 - 1386. Son of Radu I.

Dan II

Voivode of Wallachia 5 times between 1420 and 1431. Son of Dan I.

Dante Alighieri

Florentine poet and leader of the 'White Guelphs'. 1265 - 1321.

David Komnenos

Co-founder and ruler of the Empire of Trebizond 1202 - 1212.

David Megas Komnenos

Emperor of Trebizond 1459 - 1461. Last emperor of the Empire of Trebizond.

Desiderius

(Last) King of the Lombards 756 - 774.

Dimitri Progoni

Lord of Arbanon (Albania) 1208 - 1216. Son of Progon.

Đurađ Branković

Ruler (Despot) of Serbia 1427 - 1456.

Edmund Plantagenet ('Crouchback')

Son of Henry III of England. Claimant to the throne of Sicily. †1296.

Eleutherius

Exarch of Ravenna 616 - 619.

Elizabeth of Bosnia

Queen Consort of Hungary 1353-1382. Mother of Mary of Hungary.

Overview of Key Individuals

Emeric

    King of Hungary 1196 - 1204. Son of Béla III.

Enrico Dandolo

    Doge of Venice 1192 - 1205. Commercial and operational brain behind the Fourth Crusade.

Ertugrul Bey

    Head of the Kai tribe? - 1281.

Eugene III

    Pope 1145 - 1153.

Eugene IV

    Pope 1431 - 1447.

Felix II

    Bishop of Rome (Anti-Pope) 355 - 357.

Ferdinand I of Aragon (Naples)

    King of Naples 1458 - 1494. Son of Alfonso V of Aragon.

Flavius Aetius

    Roman Consul and General 432 - 454.

Formosus

    Pope 891 - 896.

Frederick I 'Barbarossa'

    Holy Roman Emperor 1155 - 1190.

Frederick II

    Holy Roman Emperor 1220 - 1250. Son of Henry VI

Frederick II of Sicily

    King of Sicily 1296 - 1337.

Frederick III

    Holy Roman Emperor 1452-1493.

Gavril Radomir of Bulgaria

    Tsar of Bulgaria 1014 - 1015. Son of Samuel of Bulgaria.

Gedik Ahmed Pasha

    Commander of the Ottoman invasion of Italy. †1482.

Genseric

    King of the Vandals 428 - 477.

George Kastrioti

    See '**Skanderbeg**'.

Gerard Thom (Blessed Gerard)

    Founder of the Religious Order of St. John (Knights Hospitaller). †1120.

Géza I

    King of Hungary 1074 - 1077. Son of Béla I.

Géza II

    King of Hungary 1141 - 1162. Son of Béla II.

Giovanni Giustiniani Longo

    Genoese nobleman and military commander. In charge of the Genoese relief force to Constantinople in 1453. Subsequently appointed commander of the Byzantine land forces during the Ottoman siege and conquest.

Overview of Key Individuals

Giuliano Cesarini

    Papal Legate to Hungary 1442 - 1444.

Godfrey III

    Margrave of Tuscany. †1069.

Gregory I

    Pope 590 - 604.

Gregory I of Tusculum

    Count of Tusculum 961 - 1012.

Gregory II

    Pope 715 - 731.

Gregory III

    Pope 731 - 741.

Gregory V

    Pope 996 - 999.

Gregory VI

    Anti-Pope 1012.

Gregory VI

    Pope 1045 - 1046.

Gregory VII

    Pope 1073 - 1085.

Gregory VIII

    Pope 1187.

Gregory VIII

    Anti-Pope 1118 - 1121.

    Pope 1227 - 1241.

Gregory XII

    Pope 1406 - 1415.

Guy of Tuscany

    Margrave of Tuscany 915 - 929.

Guy II

    Duke of Spoleto 880 - 883.

Guy III

    Duke of Spoleto 883 - 894.
    Emperor of the Romans 891 - 894.

Güneri of Karaman

    Ruler of Karaman 1277 - 1300.
    Brother of Mehmed I of Karaman.

Henry II

    Holy roman Emperor 1014 - 1024.
    Son of Henry II of Bavaria.

Henry III

    King of Germany and Holy Roman Emperor 1028 - 1056.

Henry IV

    King of Germany and Holy Roman Emperor 1053 - 1105. Son of Henry III.

Henry V

    King of Germany and Holy Roman Emperor 1111 - 1125. Son of Henry IV.

Henry VI

    Holy Roman Emperor 1191 - 1197. Son of Frederick I 'Barbarossa'

Henry VII

    King of Italy and Holy Roman Emperor 1311 - 1313.

Overview of Key Individuals

Heraclius

    Emperor of Byzantium 610 - 641.

Hilarius

    Pope 461 - 468.

Honorius

    Emperor of Rome 395 - 423.

Honorius I

    Pope 625 - 638.

Honorius II

    Anti-Pope 1061 - 1064.

Honorius II

    Pope 1124 - 1130.

Honorius III

    Pope 1216 - 1227.

Hormisdas

    Pope 514 - 523.

Ibrahim II of Karaman

    Ruler (Grand Karaman) of the Karaman beylik 1424 - 1464.

Innocent II

    Pope 1130 - 1143.

Innocent III

    Anti-Pope 1179 - 1180.

Innocent III

    Pope 1198 - 1216. Instigator of the Fourth Crusade.

Innocent IV

    Pope 1243 - 1254.

Innocent VI

    Pope 1352 - 1362.

Innocent VII

    Pope 1404 - 1406.

Irene of Athens

    Empress of Byzantium 797 - 802.

Isaac II Angelos

    Emperor of Byzantium August 1185 - 1195 and 1203 - 1204. Ousted and blinded by his brother Alexios III Angelos, reinstated during the Fourth Crusade.

Isidore of Kiev

    1385 - 1463. Metropolitan of Kiev and Cardinal. Ambassador from the Pope to Constantinople 1452 - 1453.

Ivan Alexander

    Tsar of Bulgaria 1331 - 1371

Ivan Asen II of Bulgaria

    Tsar of Bulgaria 1218 - 1241. Son of Ivan Asen I.

Ivan Asen III of Bulgaria

    Tsar of Bulgaria 1279 - 1280. Son of Mitso Asen.

Ivan Vladislav of Bulgaria

    Tsar of Bulgaria 1015 - 1018. Last Tsar of the First Bulgarian Empire.

Ivaylo of Bulgaria

    Tsar of Bulgaria 1278 - 1279.

Overview of Key Individuals

Ivan Šišman

Tsar of Bulgaria 1371 - 1395. Son of Ivan Alexander.

Ivan Sratsimir

Tsar of Bulgaria 1356 - 1396 (with interruptions). Son of Ivan Alexander.

Jahan Shah

Ruler of the Black Sheep (Kara Koyunlu) 1436 - 1467. Son of Qara Yusuf.

Janos Hunyadi

Also known as "The White Knight". Hungarian nobleman, politician and military commander 1407 - 1456.

Joanna I of Naples

Queen of Naples 1414 - 1435.

Joanna II of Naples

Queen of Naples 1343 - 1382.

John I Tzimiskes

Emperor of Byzantium 969 - 976.

John III

Pope 561 - 574.

John III Doukas Vatatzes

Emperor of Nicaea 1221 - 1254.

John IV Laskaris

Emperor of Nicaea 1258 - 1261.

John V Palaiologos

Emperor of Byzantium 1341 - 1376, 1379 - 1390 and 1390 - 1391. Son of Andronikos III Palaiologos.

John VI

Pope 701 - 705.

John VIII

Pope 872 - 882.

John VIII Palaiologos

Emperor of Byzantium 1425 - 1448. Son of Manuel II Palaiologos.

John IX

Pope 898 - 900.

John X

Pope 914 - 928.

John XII

Pope 955 - 964. Son of Alberic II.

John XIII

Pope 965 - 972.

John XIX

Pope 1024 - 1032.

John XXII

Pope 1316 - 1334.

John Crescentius

Consul (de-facto ruler of Rome 1002 – 1012).

John Kantakouzenos

Major Domestic (Chief Minister) to Andronikos III Palaiologos 1321-1341. Emperor of Byzantium as John VI Kantakouzenos 1347 - 1354.

Justin I

Emperor of Byzantium 518 - 527.

Overview of Key Individuals

Justinian I

    Emperor of Byzantium 527 - 565

Justinian II

    Emperor of Byzantium 685 - 695 and 705 - 711. Son of Constantine IV.

Kasım

    Prince of Karaman. Son of Ibrahim II of Karaman.

Kayqubad I

    Sultan of the Seljuk Sultanate of Rum 1220 -1237.

Kormisosh of Bulgaria

    Khan of Bulgaria 737 - 754.

Krum

    Khan of Bulgaria app.800 - 814.

Kulin

    Ban of Bosnia 1167 - 1204.

Ladislaus IV

    King of Hungary 1272 - 1290. Son of Stefan V.

Ladislaus V

    King of Hungary 1301 - 1305.

Ladislaus of Naples

    King of Naples 1386 - 1389, 1399 - 1414. Son of Charles III of Naples.

Lambert II

    Emperor of the Romans 892 - 898. Son of Guy III.

Laurentius

    Anti-Pope 498 - 506.

Lazar Hrebeljanović

    Knez of (Moravian) Serbia 1393 - 1389.

Leo I

    Pope 440 - 461.

Leo III (Pope)

    Pope 795 - 816.

Leo III (Emperor)

    Emperor of Byzantium 717 - 741.

Leo IV (Pope)

    Pope 847 - 855.

Leo IV (the Kazar)

    Emperor of Byzantium 775 - 780.

Leo V (Pope)

    Pope 903 - 904.

Leo V (the Armenian)

    Emperor of Byzantium 813 - 820.

Leo VI (Pope)

    Pope 928 - 929.

Leo VI (the Wise)

    Emperor of Byzantium 886 -912.

Leo VII

    Pope 936 - 939.

Leo VIII

    Anti-Pope 963 - 964. Pope 963 - 964.

Overview of Key Individuals

Leo IX

    Pope 1048 - 1054.

Leontios

    Emperor of Byzantium 695 - 698.

Libius Severus

    Emperor of Rome 461 - 465.

Liutprand

    King of the Lombards 712 - 744.

Lothair I

    Emperor of the Romans 817 - 855. Son of Louis the Pious.

Lothair II

    King of Lotharingia 855 - 869. Son of Lothair I.

Lothair II

    Emperor of the Romans 1133 - 1137.

Louis I of Hungary

    King of Hungary 1342 - 1382. Son of Charles I.

Louis I of Anjou

    King of Naples 1382 - 1384. Son of

Louis II

    Emperor of the Romans 850 - 875. Son of Lothair I.

Louis II of Naples

    King of Naples 1389 - 1399. Son of Louis I of Anjou.

Louis III of Anjou

    Duke of Anjou 1417 - 1434. Son of Louis II of Naples.

Louis IV (the Bavarian)

    King of the Germans, later Holy Roman Emperor 1314 - 1347.

Louis VII of France

    King of France 1131 - 1180.

Louis IX of France

    King of France 1226 - 1270.

Louis the Blind

    Emperor of the Romans (as Louis III) 901 - 905.

Louis the Pious

    Emperor of the Romans 813 - 840. Son of Charlemagne.

Lucius III

    Pope 1181 - 1185.

Manfred of Sicily

    King of Sicily 1258 - 1266. Son of Frederick II.

Manuel I Komnenos

    Emperor of Byzantium 1143 - 1180.

Manuel II Palaiologos

    Emperor of Byzantium 1391 - 1425. Son of John V Palaiologos.

Mara Brancovic

    Also known as "Mara Hatun", wife of Murad II 1435 - 1451. Daughter of Đurađ Branković.

Overview of Key Individuals

Maria Palaiologina Kantakouzene

Empress of Bulgaria 1269 - 1279.

Marinus I

Pope 882 - 884.

Martin I

Pope 649 - 655.

Martin IV

Pope 1281 - 1285.

Martin V

Pope 1417 - 1431.

Marozia

'Senatrix' of Rome. Alleged mother of Pope John XI. †937.

Mary

Queen of Hungary 1382-1385 and 1386-1395. Daughter of Louis I.

Matej Ninoslav

Ban of Bosnia 1232 - 1250.

Matilda of Tuscany

Margravine of Tuscany 1076 - 1115.

Matthew Kantakouzenos

Emperor of Byzantium 1353 - 1357. Son of John Kantakouzenos.

Matthias I (Corvin)

King of Hungary 1458 0 1490. Son of Janos Hunyadi.

Mehmed I

Sultan of the Ottoman Empire 1413 - 1421. Son of Bayezid I.

Mehmed II of Karaman

Bey of Karaman 1402 - 1423. Son of Alaattin Ali of Karaman.

Mehmed II

Given the moniker "Fatih" (The Conqueror), sultan of the Ottoman Empire 1451 - 1481. Son of Murad II.

Mesih Pasha

Commander of the Ottoman invasion of Rhodes 1480. †1501.

Michael I

Emperor of Byzantium 811 - 813.

Michael III

Emperor of Byzantium 842 - 867.

Michael VIII Palaiologos

Emperor of Nicaea 1259 - 61, Emperor of Byzantium 1261 -1282. Conqueror of the Latin Empire of Constantinople.

Michael IX Palaiologos

Co-emperor of Byzantium 1294 - 1320 with his father Andronikos II Palaiologos.

Michael Asen I

Tsar of Bulgaria 1246 1256. Son of Ivan Asen II.

Michael Shishman of Bulgaria

Tsar of Bulgaria 1323 - 1330.

Miltiades (St.Miltiades)

Bishop of Rome (Pope) 311 - 314.

Overview of Key Individuals

Mircea I

Ruler (founder) of Wallachia 1386 - 1418. Given the moniker "Cel Batran" (The Elder).

Mircea II Dracula

Voivode of Wallachia c. 1436 - 1436. Son of, and co-ruler with, Vlad II Dracul.

Mitso Asen of Bulgaria

Tsar of Bulgaria 1256 - 1257.

Muhammad (Abū al-Qāsim Muḥammad ibn ʿAbd Allāh ibn ʿAbd al-Muṭṭalib ibn Hāshim)

Founding Prophet of Islam †632.

Murad I

Ruler of the House of Osman 1361 - 1389, First Ottoman Sultan 1386. Son of Orhan.

Murad II

Sultan of the Ottoman Empire 1421 - 1451. Son of Mehmed I.

Mutimir

Knez of Serbia 850 - 890. Son of Vlastimir.

Nefise

Daughter of Murad I. Wife of Alaattin Ali of Karaman.

Nero (Nero Claudius Caesar Augustus Germanicus)

Emperor of Rome 54 - 68.

Nicholas I

Pope 858 - 867.

Nicholas II

Pope 1059 - 1061.

Nicholas IV

Pope 1288 - 1292.

Nicholas V

Anti-Pope 1328 - 1330.

Nicholas V

Pope 1447 - 1455.

Niccolo da Canale

Commander of the Venetian fleet during the Conquest of Negroponte 1470.

Nikephoros I

Emperor of Byzantium 802 - 811.

Odoacer

Germanic tribal leader and Roman General. The de-facto ruler of the Western Roman Empire 475 - 491.

Olybrius

Emperor of Rome 472.

Orhan

Ruler of the House of Osman 1324 - 1361. Son of Osman.

Osman

Head of the Kai tribe 1281 - 1324, founder of "The House of Osman".

Otto I

King of Germany and Emperor of the Romans 936 - 973.

Overview of Key Individuals

Otto II

King of Germany and Emperor of the Romans 973 - 983. Son of Otto I.

Otto III

King of Germany and Holy Roman Emperor 983 - 1002. Son of Otto II.

Otto IV

King of Germany and Holy Roman Emperor 1198 - 1215.

Paschal I

Pope 817 - 824.

Paschal II

Pope 1099 - 1118.

Paschal III

Anti-Pope 1164 - 1168.

Paul I

Pope 757 - 767.

Paul II

Patriarch of Constantinople 642 - 653.

Paul II

Pope 1464 - 1471.

Pepin the Short

King of the Franks 752 - 768.

Petar Svačić

King of Croatia 1093 - 1097.

Peter I of Bulgaria

Emperor of Bulgaria 927 - 969. Son of Simeon I

Peter I of Cyprus

King of Cyprus (titular King of Jerusalem) 1358 - 1369.

Peter III of Aragon

King of Aragon 1276 - 1285, King of Valencia 1276 - 1285, King of Sicily 1282 - 1285.

Petronius Maximus

Emperor of Rome 455.

Petru II

Voivode of Moldavia 1375 - 1391.

Petru III

Voivode of Moldavia 1444 - 1457 with interruptions. Son of Alexandru I.

Philip II

King of France 1180 - 1223. Son of Luis VII.

Philip IV

King of France 1285 - 1314.

Philip V

King of France 1316 - 1322.

Philip of Swabia

King of Germany 1198 - 1208.

Philip the Good

Duke of Burgundy 1417 - 1467.

Overview of Key Individuals

Philippikos Bardanes

Emperor of Byzantium 711 - 713.

Pir Ahmed

Ruler (grand Karaman) of Karaman 1465 - 1468. Son of Ibrahim II of Karaman.

Pius II

Pope 1458 - 1464.

Qara Iskander

Ruler of the Black Sheep (Kara Koyunlu) 1420 - 1436. Son of Qara Yusuf.

Radivoj

Anti-King of Bosnia 1432 - 1435. Son of Stjepan Ostoja.

Radu II

Voivode of Wallachia 4 times between 1421 and 1427. Son of Mircea I.

Radu III (cel Frumos)

Voivode of Wallachia 1462 - 1475 with interruptions. Son of Vlad II Dracul.

Ricimer

Supreme Commander of the Army of the Western Roman Empire 457 - 472.

Richard I (Lionheart)

King of England 1189 - 1199. Son of Henry II.

Robert of Anjou

King of Naples 1309 - 1343. Son of Charles II of Naples.

Robert Guiscard

Duke of Apulia 1057 - 1085.

Roger II of Sicily

King of Sicily 1130 - 1154.

Rollo

Founder 'Duke' of Normandy. †931.

Romulus Augustus

Emperor of Rome 475 - 476.

Rudolf I

King of Germany 1273 - 1291.

Saladin (Ṣalāḥ ad-Dīn Yūsuf ibn Ayyūb)

Sultan of Egypt and Syria 1171 - 1193. Founder of the Ayyubid dynasty.

Samuel Aba

King of Hungary 1041 - 1044.

Samuel of Bulgaria

Tsar of the (first) Bulgarian Empire 997 - 1014.

Selim I

Sultan of the Ottoman Empire 1512 - 1520. Son of Bayezid II.

Sergius I

Pope 687 - 701.

Sergius II

Pope 844 - 847.

Overview of Key Individuals

Sergius III

Pope 904 - 911.

Sergius IV

Pope 1009 - 1012.

Sigismund of Hungary (Luxemburg)

Holy Roman Emperor 1433 - 1437, King of Hungary 1387 - 1437.

Silverius

Pope 536 - 537. Son of (Pope) Hormisdas.

Simon Peter (Saint Peter)

Christian apostle and first Bishop of Rome (Pope) †64.

Simplicius

Pope 468 - 483.

Sinucello della Rocca, (Giudice de Cinarca)

Ruler of Corsica 1245 - 1301.

Skanderbeg (Iskender Bey)

Born in 1405 as **George Kastrioti**. Albanian nobleman educated at the Ottoman court and elevated to general in the Ottoman army. Changed sides in 1443 and returned to Albania where he successfully led a revolt against the Ottomans that would last more than two decades. †1468.

Simeon I of Bulgaria

Khan of Bulgaria 893 - 927.

Solomon I

King of Hungary 1063 - 1074. Son of András I.

Stefan I (of Hungary)

King of Hungary 997 - 1038. Son of Géza of Hungary.

Stefan II (of Hungary)

King of Hungary 1116 - 1138. Son of Coloman.

Voivode of Moldavia 1433-1447. Son of Alexandru I.

Stefan (II) Nemanjić

Grand Prince (later King) of Serbia 1196 - 1228. Son of Stefan Nemanja.

Stefan III (the Great) of Moldavia

Voivode of Moldavia 1457 - 1504. Son of Bogdan II.

Stefan V

King of Hungary 1270 - 1272. Son of Béla IV.

Stefan Dragutin

King of Serbia 1276 - 1282. Son of Stefan Uroš I.

Stefan Lazarević

Prince/Despot of Serbia 1389 - 1427. Son of Lazar Hrebeljanović.

Stefan Nemanja

Grand Prince of Serbia 1166 - 1196.

Stefan Uroš II Milutin

King of Serbia 1282 - 1321. Son of Stefan Uroš I.

Stefan Uroš IV Dušan

King (later Emperor) of Serbia 1331 - 1355. Son of Stefan Uroš III Dečanski.

Stefan Uroš V

Emperor of Serbia 1355 - 1371. Son of Stefan Uroš IV Dušan.

Stefan Vladislav I

King of Serbia 1234 0 1243. Son of Stefan II.

Stephen II

Pope 752 - 757.

Stephen III

Pope 767 - 772.

Stephen V

Pope 885 - 891.

Stephen VI

Pope 896 - 897.

Stjepan I

Ban of Bosnia 1287 - 1314. Son of Prijezda I.

Stjepan II

Ban of Bosnia 1314 - 1353. Son of Stjepan I.

Stjepan Dabiša

King of Bosnia 1391 - 1395.

Stjepan Tomaš

King of Bosnia 1443 - 1461.

Stjepan Tomašević

Despot of Serbia 1459. King of Bosnia 1461 - 1463. Son of Stjepan Tomaš.

Stjepan Tvrtko I

Ban of Bosnia 1353 - 1377. King of Bosnia 1377 - 1391.

Suleiman I

Given the monikers "Kanuni" ('The Lawgiver) and "The Magnificent", sultan of the Ottoman Empire 1520 - 1566. Great-grandson of Mehmed II.

Sylvester I

Bishop of Rome (Pope) 314 - 335.

Sylvester II

Pope 999 - 1003.

Sylvester III

Pope 1045.

Symmachus

Pope 498 - 514.

Taksony of Hungary

Ruler of Hungary 955 - c. 970. Son of Zoltán.

Telerig of Bulgaria

Khan of Bulgaria 768 - 777

Tervel of Bulgaria

Khan of Bulgaria 695 - 715. Son of Asparukh of Bulgaria.

Theodahad

King of Italy 534 - 536.

Overview of Key Individuals

Theodelinda

    Queen of the Lombards 589 - 616.

Theodora

    Empress of Byzantium 527 - 548.

Theodora (Senatrix)

    Wife of Theophylact I. 'Senatrix' of Rome. †916.

Theodore I Lascaris

    Emperor of the Empire of Nicaea 1208 0 1221. The kingpin in the restoration of the Byzantine Empire following the fall of Constantinople during the Fourth Crusade.

Theodore II

    Pope 897.

Theodore II Laskaris

    Emperor of Nicaea 1254 - 1258.

Theodore Komnenos Doukas

    Ruler of Epirus 1215 - 1230 and of Thessalonica 1224 - 1230.

Theodore Svetoslav of Bulgaria

    Tsar of Bulgaria 1300 - 1322. Son of George I.

Theodoric (the Great)

    Ruler of the Ostrogoths. Viceroy of the Western Roman Empire 491 - 526.

Theodoric I

    King of the Visigoths 418 - 451.

Theodoric II

    King of the Visigoths 453 - 466. Son of Theodoric I.

Theodosios III

    Emperor of Byzantium 715 - 717.

Theodosius I

    Emperor of Rome 379 - 395.

Theodosius II

    Emperor of Byzantium 402 - 450.

Theophanu

    Empress of the Romans 972 - 991. Mother of Otto III.

Theophylact I

    Count of Tusculum? - 924/925.

Timur (Tamerlane)

    Turco-Mongolian warlord. Founder and ruler of the Timurid Empire (1370) - 1405.

Tomasina Morosini

    Mother of András III of Hungary. †1300.

Urban II

    Pope 1088 - 1099. Instigator of the First Crusade and the Crusade movement.

Urban IV

    Pope 1261 - 1264.

Urban V

    Pope 1362 - 1370.

Urban VI

Overview of Key Individuals

Pope (in Rome) 1378 - 1389.

Uroš I

Grand Prince of Serbia 1112 - 1145.

Uroš II

Grand Prince of Serbia 1145 - 1161. Son of Uroš I.

Valentian III

Emperor of Rome 425 - 455.

Vigilius

Pope 537 - 555.

Victor IV

Anti-Pope 1138.

Victor IV

Anti-Pope 1159 - 1164.

Vitalian

Pope 657 - 672.

Vlad II Dracul

Ruler of Wallachia 1436 - 1447. Son of Mircea I.

Vlad III Dracula

Ruler of Wallachia 1447, 1456-1462 and 1476. Son of Vlad II Dracul.

Vlad IV Călugărul

Voivode of Wallachia multiple times between 1481 and 1495. Son of Vlad II Dracul.

Vladislav II

Voivode of Wallachia 1447 - 1456 (with interruptions). Son of Dan II.

Vlastimir

Knez (Prince) of Serbia 836 - 850.

Vukan Nemanjić

Grand Prince of Serbia 1202 - 1204. Son of Stefan Nemanjić.

Wenceslaus IV

King of Bohemia 1378 - 1419, King of the Germans 1376 - 1400.

William II of Holland

Anti-King of Germany 1247 - 1256.

Wladyslaw III

King of Poland 1434 - 1444, King of Hungary 1440 - 1444. Killed in battle against Murad II at Varna.

Zeno

Emperor of Byzantium 474 - 491.

PART 1

THE CONQUEROR'S EMPIRE

1 - THE OTTOMAN EMPIRE, SETTING THE SCENE
2 - THE CONQUEROR'S WORLD

Part 1 - The Conqueror's Empire

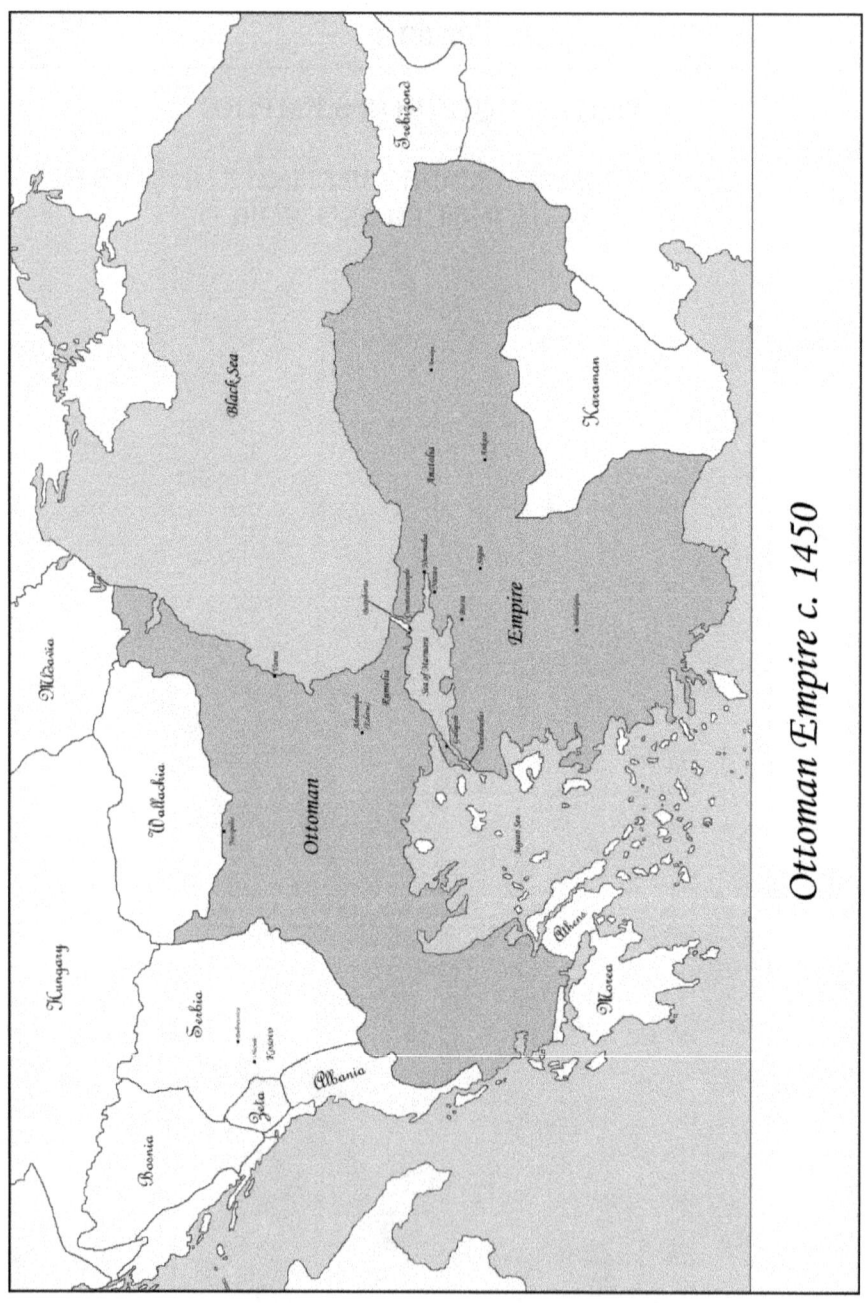

1 - THE OTTOMAN EMPIRE, SETTING THE SCENE

Part 1 - The Conqueror's Empire

CRITICAL TIMELINE

Year	Event	Involved Parties
Early 1200s	Kai tribe arrives in eastern Anatolia	Ottomans
1237	Sultanate of Rum disintegrates	Seljuks Ottomans
1281	Osman becomes leader of Kai tribe	Ottomans
1300	Kai tribe becomes known as '*House of Osman*'	Ottomans
1302	Ottomans beat Byzantines at Nicomedia	Byzantium Ottomans
304	Byzantines beat Ottomans at Philadelphia	Byzantium Ottomans
1324	Orhan becomes leader of Ottomans	Ottomans
1326	Ottomans conquer Bursa	Ottomans
1329	Ottomans defeat Byzantines at Pelekanon	Byzantium Ottomans
1352	Ottoman mercenaries at Gallipoli peninsula	Byzantium Ottomans
1354	Ottomans annex town of Gallipoli	Byzantium Ottomans
1361	Murad I becomes leader of Ottomans	Ottomans
1365	Ottomans conquer Adrianople (Edirne)	Byzantium Ottomans
1381	Battle of Dubravnica	Ottomans Serbia
1386	Battle of Pločnik	Ottomans Serbia
1386	Murad I becomes 'Sultan'	Ottomans
1389	First Battle of Kosovo. Bayezid I becomes Sultan	Ottomans Serbia
1394	Building of Anadoluhisarı. Siege of Constantinople	Byzantium Ottomans
1396	Battle of Nicopolis	Ottomans Bulgaria Hungary France Venice Knights Hospitaller
1402	Battle of Ankara. Beginning of Ottoman Interregnum	Ottomans Timurids
1413	Mehmed I becomes Sultan. End of Ottoman Interregnum	Ottomans
1416	Battle of Gallipoli	Venice Ottomans
1421	Murad II becomes Sultan	Ottomans

1 - The Ottoman Empire, Setting the Scene

To most casual observers of fifteenth century history the Ottoman Empire was an established super-power in both Anatolia (Asia-minor) and south-eastern Europe, a view that has some credence with the advantage of hindsight with which historians are blessed, but to the contemporary political observer the Ottoman Empire was a much more fragile, perhaps even vulnerable, entity; a power that might well be up and coming, but which still had to fight for its basic survival and integrity.

As incredible as it may sound, and at least according to Ottoman tradition, the Ottoman Empire originated from 400 tents in a refugee camp outside Ankara. In the early thirteenth century, the Kai tribe of Turkoman nomads, like many of their fellow tribes, had been pushed west by the Mongols and eventually they arrived in eastern Anatolia, which at that time was part of the Seljuk Sultanate of Rum (see Chapter 5).

Having first been given refuge in Ahlat in eastern Anatolia, part of the tribe - counting 400 tents - moved on to a temporary camp outside of Ankara, effectively a refugee camp from where they were recruited to act as scouts and skirmishers by the Seljuk Sultan, Kayqubad I. Led by Ertugrul Bey they followed the Seljuk army to western Anatolia and distinguished themselves in battle to such an extent that they were granted use of the town of Söğüt and its surrounds.

Following Sultan Kayqubad I's death in 1237, and with Mongol hordes pushing in from the east, the Sultanate of Rum started to disintegrate, leaving eastern Anatolia under Mongol control and western Anatolia as a patchwork of small '*beyliks*' (similar to a principality, but ruled by a Bey), like the one led by Ertugrul Bey, loosely connected through religion (Islam), language (Turkish) and their nominal allegiance to the remains of the Sultanate of Rum.

Ertugrul Bey died, in his nineties, in 1281, leaving leadership of the tribe to his son Osman.

Osman had ambitions (according to folklore he even had a visionary dream, foreseeing future glory), and he expanded the tribe's area considerably through a combination of dynastic marriages and outright military annexation of the surrounding towns, fortifications and beyliks. Around the year 1300 Osman officially made his growing state independent of the last, nominal, remains of the Sultanate of Rum, by minting his own coins, the privilege of a sovereign ruler, and the tribe started to become known as '*Osmanlı*' in Turkish and '*Ottomans*' in the West.

The Ottoman expansion eventually brought them into contact with the remaining Byzantine possessions in north-western Anatolia (see Chapter 4), resulting in skirmishes and sieges. The Ottomans defeated the Byzantines outside Nicomedia (modern day Izmit) in 1302, but were beaten by Catalan mercenaries in Byzantine service at Philadelphia (modern day Alaşehir) in 1304. Despite these token efforts to protect the Byzantine interests, the Ottomans gradually expanded their territory, their next main target being the city of Bursa, which they besieged for seven years.

By 1324 Osman, suffering from gout, handed over leadership to his son Orhan, the last instruction from father to son being to finally capture Bursa and bury his father there. Orhan did just that in 1326, the Ottoman army now having grown to around 20,000 strong, and Bursa became the capital of what was becoming a considerable, ever expanding, nation state.

With a solid base, and a powerful army at hand, Orhan continued his father's expansion policy and gradually grew the state in all directions. This brought the Ottomans on to the edge of the sea and the Byzantine port-towns of Nicaea (modern day Iznik) and Nicomedia on the coast of the Sea of Marmara.

The Byzantines once again sent an army out to defend their possessions, but the Ottomans defeated the Byzantine army at Pelekanon (near Nicomedia) in 1329, and soon after annexed Nicaea and Nicomedia, expanding their territory to the sea and making them neighbours with the Byzantines lands in Europe, albeit across the Sea of Marmara and the narrow crossing points at the Dardanelles in the south and the Bosporus in the north. This military expedition was effectively the last time the Byzantine Empire tried to defend its remaining possessions in Anatolia, leaving the door open for further Ottoman expansion, soon to engulf most of western Anatolia.

The Byzantine Empire was rife with internal political rivalry, members of the ruling dynasty challenging each other for power over the increasingly weak state. One such internal conflict flared up in 1352 between John VI Kantakouzenos and his son Matthew on one side and John V Palaiologos on the other.

Desperately seeking allies, John V Palaiologos turned to the Ottomans across the narrow sea. An Ottoman army was ferried across the strait at the Dardanelles (on Genoese ships) and given military headquarters in the fortress of Çimpe at the narrowest point of the strait.

The Ottoman army fought alongside Venetian troops to subdue Rumelia (Thrace), eventually helping John V Palaiologos to gain control of the crumpling empire.

The deal with the Ottomans was that they would not occupy any of the cities or fortresses they helped to subdue, but in the end, it was nature which provided them with a perfect pretext for consolidating their newfound presence in Europe.

In 1354 the city and fortress of Gallipoli was devastated by an earthquake and abandoned by its inhabitants. The Ottomans quickly moved in from neighbouring Çimpe, rebuilding and refortifying the city and castle. When rebuked for having broken the agreement, their argument was that Gallipoli had not been conquered, but that the Ottomans had simply repopulated and rebuilt the abandoned area. Opportunistic as is was the fact was that the Byzantines had no military muscle to force the issue and the Ottomans started to consolidate their position in Europe.

The area of 'Rumelia', loosely defined as modern day European Turkey and Northern Greece, and named from the Byzantines' own name for Constantinople; *'Rum'* or *'Rome'*, reflecting their claim as the legitimate heirs of the Roman Empire, had fallen into general upheaval and political chaos as the Byzantine Empire had effectively imploded in the wake of decades of civil war. The Byzantines did not have the resources to bring the area back under control, but the Ottomans did.

Gradually the Ottomans expanded their territory in Rumelia from the Gallipoli peninsula to cover most of Rumelia, leaving only Constantinople itself and its immediate surroundings under Byzantine control.

In 1361 the Ottoman throne had passed to Orhan's son Murad I, and by 1365 the Ottomans had annexed the city of Adrianople, renamed it to Edirne, and made it capital of the Ottoman territories in Europe.

Murad I was a warlike man and he quickly grasped the opportunity for further expansion into Bulgaria and northern Greece. In 1386 he elevated himself to Sultan, effectively declaring the Ottoman state an empire proper and he took further initiatives with important and long-lasting consequences.

Murad I consolidated, and institutionalized, the Ottoman policy of multi-cultural and multi-religious tolerance. The Christian World was characterized by strict religious conformity where "heretics" - whether individuals or groups - were subject to persecution and death and ethnic minorities were subject to differentiated treatment and pogroms. The Ottomans, however, deployed a very different social model.

The growing Ottoman Empire was not a single homogenous population, despite being referred to as *'Turks'* by the Western World. The expansion over large areas on two continents meant that the Ottoman Empire embraced a range of religions, cultures and ethnic groups. There were of course Muslims, a group in itself split by factions and mystic minorities, but also many Christians, mainly Orthodox of Greek origins, and Jews.

Rather than trying to make the conquered populations conform to Turco-Islamic culture and religion, ethnic and religious groups were given a large amount of autonomy and freedom to continue their style of life. As long as they lived by the law of the lands, paid their taxes and provided soldiers to the Sultan, they were treated with a live-and-let-live attitude that in many cases gave people a significantly freer existence than they had been used to under former rulers. This inspired a genuine loyalty to the new Empire that would be instrumental in making the Ottoman Empire a unified political entity for centuries to come.

Part 1 - The Conqueror's Empire

Historians have coined the phrase *'Pax Ottomana'*, inspired by *'Pax Romana'*, to describe the peace and security experienced by the population inside the Ottoman Empire, the same way some fifteen hundred years before the Roman Empire had guaranteed their population similar as long as they stayed within the laws of the Empire. In comparison the *'Pax Dei'*, or 'Peace of God', which had been dictated by the Catholic Church since late in the tenth century, had turned out to be mainly ineffective in western Europe, as manifested by the constant wars and upheaval which rendered a concerted Christian response to the Ottoman expansion practically impossible.

Another initiative taken by Murad I was the recruiting of Christian boys, who at a young age would be brought to live in the Ottoman Empire and educated - in modern terms possibly "brainwashed" - into fierce loyalty to the Sultan himself. This system, known as Devşirme, would supply not only capable and impartial civil servants but also the formation of 'the new corps' or *'yeni çeri'*, known as Janissaries in the Christian World. These troops, unassociated with any internal political factions and loyal only to the Sultan himself, would gradually grow to become not only the Sultan's personal household troops but also the Ottoman army's crack infantry troops. It is highly likely that Murad I was inspired by the Byzantine Emperor's Varangian Guard, his personal 'Viking' bodyguard, paid mercenaries from Scandinavia with no interest in internal politics and loyal only to their paymaster.

Lastly, Murad I initiated the Timariot system by which a landholding (Timar) was given to a keeper (Timariot) on the condition that the land was kept and farmed in times of peace and that the Timariot supplied a set number of troops when the Sultan so demanded. Based on the Western European feudal system, but improved in terms of central control, the key difference was that the Timariot system kept ownership of the land with the state, so although loyal service could ensure that the use (and proceeds) of the land was inherited on the Timariot's death, the state could take the land back at any given time. It would serve the Ottoman Empire for centuries, enabling the Sultan to assemble significant armies in a very short period of time.

Towards the end of the fourteenth century, Murad I started pushing into Serbia (see Chapter 14). After initial setbacks at the Battle of Dubravnica in 1381 and the Battle of Pločnik in 1386, the Ottomans eventually overcame the Serbian army at the (First) Battle of Kosovo in 1389. Serbia was being turned into a vassal-state, paying tribute to the Ottomans, and Albania (see Chapter 15), with the exception of a Venetian enclave on the Adriatic coast, was fully annexed into the Ottoman Empire.

An incursion into Wallachia (see Chapter 14), the southern part of modern day Romania, was unsuccessful in terms of conquest, but ended in agreement with its ruler, Mircea I, that Wallachia, like Serbia would pay an annual tribute to the Ottomans. This establishment of vassal-states on the

1 - The Ottoman Empire, Setting the Scene

border to Hungary would cause constant conflict over the next century and a half.

Though successful at the (First) Battle of Kosovo, Sultan Murad I did not live to enjoy his victory. He was killed by a Serbian prisoner immediately after the battle, passing the throne to his grown up son Bayezid I, who on accession to the throne had his younger brother, Yakub, strangled, a way to secure against dynastic instability that gradually would become both the norm and the law.

Bayezid I quickly followed up on his father's military successes, finally annexing Bulgaria and northern Greece into Ottoman provinces following the Battle of Nicopolis in 1396 after which he turned his attention to the city of Constantinople.

The problem which had arisen - and which would not be finally solved for another six decades - was the fact that the Ottoman Empire now was split over two continents, separated by water, and those waters were not controlled by the Ottomans.

Control of the waters of the Eastern Mediterranean Sea belonged to Venice and Genoa (see Chapters 10 and 11), the two competing Italian merchant states, whose fleets of warships had long since replaced the Byzantine fleet. This meant that passage between the two parts of the empire was relying on Christian ships, based in the natural harbour of the Golden Horn at Constantinople. The Ottomans originated from nomadic horsemen and even though the people in their new costal possessions had added some ship-building and seafaring capabilities, they were literally centuries behind the Italians when it came to building, maintaining and operating an effective navy.

Bayezid I saw this problem, and he did two things about it. First he built a fortress, known as Anadoluhisarı (The Anatolian Castle), on the Anatolian side of the Bosporus to provide some protection during transport of Ottoman troops across the narrow strait north of Constantinople. Secondly, he laid siege to Constantinople.

The siege started in 1394 and sparked off a concerted Christian response to the Ottoman expansion. Following appeals for help from the Byzantine Emperor, Manuel II Palaiologos, a 'crusade' against the Ottomans was organised, fielding an army consisting of Hungarians, Wallachian, Germans and French soldiers supported by a (rather lacklustre) Venetian fleet and under the overall command of Sigismund, King of Hungary.

The Christian army marched to relieve Constantinople, and Bayezid I marched to meet them at Nicopolis in northern Bulgaria. They met on 25 September 1396, and the Ottomans destroyed the Christian army in a battle that would see the end of Christian unity against the Ottomans for fifty years.

With his back thus free, Bayezid I returned to the siege of Constantinople, but despite his successes in the western part of the Empire, all was not well in the East.

Part 1 - The Conqueror's Empire

In the two centuries since the Ottomans arrived as refugees in eastern Anatolia, the Seljuk Sultanate of Rum had collapsed, and eastern Anatolia had developed into a patchwork of Turco-Mongol beyliks keeping Ottoman expansion at bay, mostly because the Ottomans were too busy in the west to explore further ambitions in the East.

As the fourteenth century turned into the fifteenth century, Timur (Tamerlane), a Turco-Mongolian warlord with an ambition to re-establish the Mongol Empire, though this time as a Muslim state, consolidated large parts of former Mongol territories into the Timurid Empire, another warlike and quickly expanding empire reaching from Afghanistan to Anatolia and including all of Persia. Timur allied himself with some of the easternmost Ottoman beyliks and they rose against Ottoman sovereignty.

The Ottomans abandoned the siege of Constantinople and went to war to protect their eastern border where they were solidly beaten at Ankara in 1402. Indeed, Sultan Bayezid I was taken prisoner and subsequently died a prisoner of Timur.

Some of Bayezid I's sons were also taken prisoners, but three of them were free and soon all three established themselves as his successor, in what would become known as the Ottoman Interregnum period.

Bayezid I's oldest son, Suleyman, set up his capital in Edirne, controlling the Ottoman territories in Europe. The second son, Isa, set up capital in Bursa and controlled parts of western Anatolia. Finally another son, Mehmed, set up in Amasya in northern-central Anatolia, where he ruled over parts of eastern Anatolia as a vassal of Timur.

This situation was of course not viable for any extended period of time and gradually the brothers fought it out between them.

First Isa and Mehmed fought over Anatolia, with Mehmed as the eventual winner. Isa fled to the independent beylik of Karaman (see Chapter 6) in south-eastern Anatolia where he was subsequently assassinated by Mehmed's henchmen.

On the request of Mehmed, Timur then released yet another of Bayezid's sons, Musa, who went into alliance with his brother, Mehmed.

With Mehmed now controlling Anatolia, Suleyman crossed the sea from Europe and went to war with Mehmed. Though Suleyman was initially successful, and managed to expel Mehmed from most of Anatolia, Musa had crossed the Black Sea with another army and now attacked Suleyman from the rear, forcing him to go back to Europe to fight it out with Musa.

Musa eventually prevailed and Suleyman was executed, leaving Musa in control of the Ottoman possessions in Europe and Mehmed in control of Anatolia.

Musa now turned his attention to the Byzantine Empire, which had supported Suleyman. He laid siege to Constantinople, who turned to Mehmed for assistance. In a weird twist of fate, Mehmed's Ottoman troops now garrisoned Constantinople and held off Musa's army, even when

Mehmed had to go back to Anatolia to fight off revolt there and then return back to Europe.

Mehmed supported by the vassal-state of Serbia, in 1413 eventually defeated Musa, who was killed in the decisive battle, leaving Mehmed in full control of the Ottoman Empire as Sultan Mehmed I.

Amazingly, and despite the fact that the Ottoman Empire for more than a decade was engulfed in near-disintegration and civil war, there were no concerted attempts from the Christian states in the west to take advantage of the situation.

As we shall see, the Christian World was simply split into too many factions, caught between religious, secular and commercial conflicts of interests, to form a united front against the Ottomans. If such unity had been found, then it is highly likely that the Ottomans would have been expelled from Europe, but such was not to be.

The victorious son finally became Sultan Mehmed I in 1413 and spent the eight years of his reign consolidating and reuniting the Ottoman Empire, so much so that he would become known as 'the second founder of the Empire'.

The Timurid Empire had fallen into disunity on the death of Timur in 1405, and the territories lost in eastern Anatolia were soon back under Ottoman control. With no concerted effort from the Christian states to push the western boundaries of the Empire, Mehmed I had an easy job regaining the initiative and ensuring that the Ottoman borders were back to what they had been before his father's fatal confrontation with Timur.

One episode from Mehmed I's reign is worth mentioning, as it had consequences beyond his reign. Mehmed I had not forgotten the Ottoman dilemma regarding safe crossing of the seas between Anatolia and Europe. His father had built the Anadoluhisarı castle on the Bosporus to protect Ottoman crossings, but Mehmed I started to develop an Ottoman navy proper.

Based in Gallipoli the Ottomans secretly built a fleet manned by a combination of Ottomans and foreigners, scraped together from renegades, mercenaries and pirates.

When a Venetian fleet approached Gallipoli in 1416 on a diplomatic mission, their signal for parley was mistaken for a signal to attack and the Ottoman fleet sailed out to meet them. Despite the enthusiasm of the Ottomans and their hired help, they were destroyed by the experienced Venetians. Following the battle the Venetians executed all non-Ottoman prisoners as an example to others that helping the Ottomans in their naval ambitions was totally unacceptable. This accidental battle effectively put an end to any concerted attempts to deploy an Ottoman navy for nearly forty years hence.

Part 1 - The Conqueror's Empire

On Mehmed I's death in 1421, he was succeeded by his son Murad, who became Sultan Murad II. This handover of power was, however, far from smooth.

First a throne-pretender claiming to be Murad II's uncle Mustafa, another of Bayezid's sons, with support from Constantinople, landed in Rumelia and took control of the European part of the Ottoman Empire. He then crossed to Anatolia where Murad II showed his first capability as a military commander and defeated Mustafa's army. Mustafa himself was executed.

To punish the Byzantines for their involvement, Murad II now laid siege to Constantinople, but had to break it off when his own younger brother, also called Mustafa, with support from both Constantinople and some of the Anatolian beyliks launched an attack at Bursa.

Murad II defeated the young Mustafa in 1422 and Mustafa was executed. He was only thirteen years of age and really just a pawn in someone else's power game.

There were no more pretenders to the throne, and Murad II now began a thirty-year reign that even though violent was not per se aggressive.

Murad II was an inherently peaceful man, who was keenly interested in philosophy and mystic religion. He preferred to keep things status quo, but aggressive neighbours, now finally sensing the weakness of the Ottoman Empire, would repeatedly force him to defend his borders, something he did successfully and to such an extent that he was seen by most observers as a warrior-sultan despite the fact that he really did little but defend his realm when provoked.

Apart from his temporary abdication between 1444 and 1446, to which we shall return, he ruled for thirty years until he passed away in February 1451, supposedly having suffered a fit while in a state of drunkenness, a state not uncommon to him as he did not deny himself earthly pleasures.

1 - The Ottoman Empire, Setting the Scene

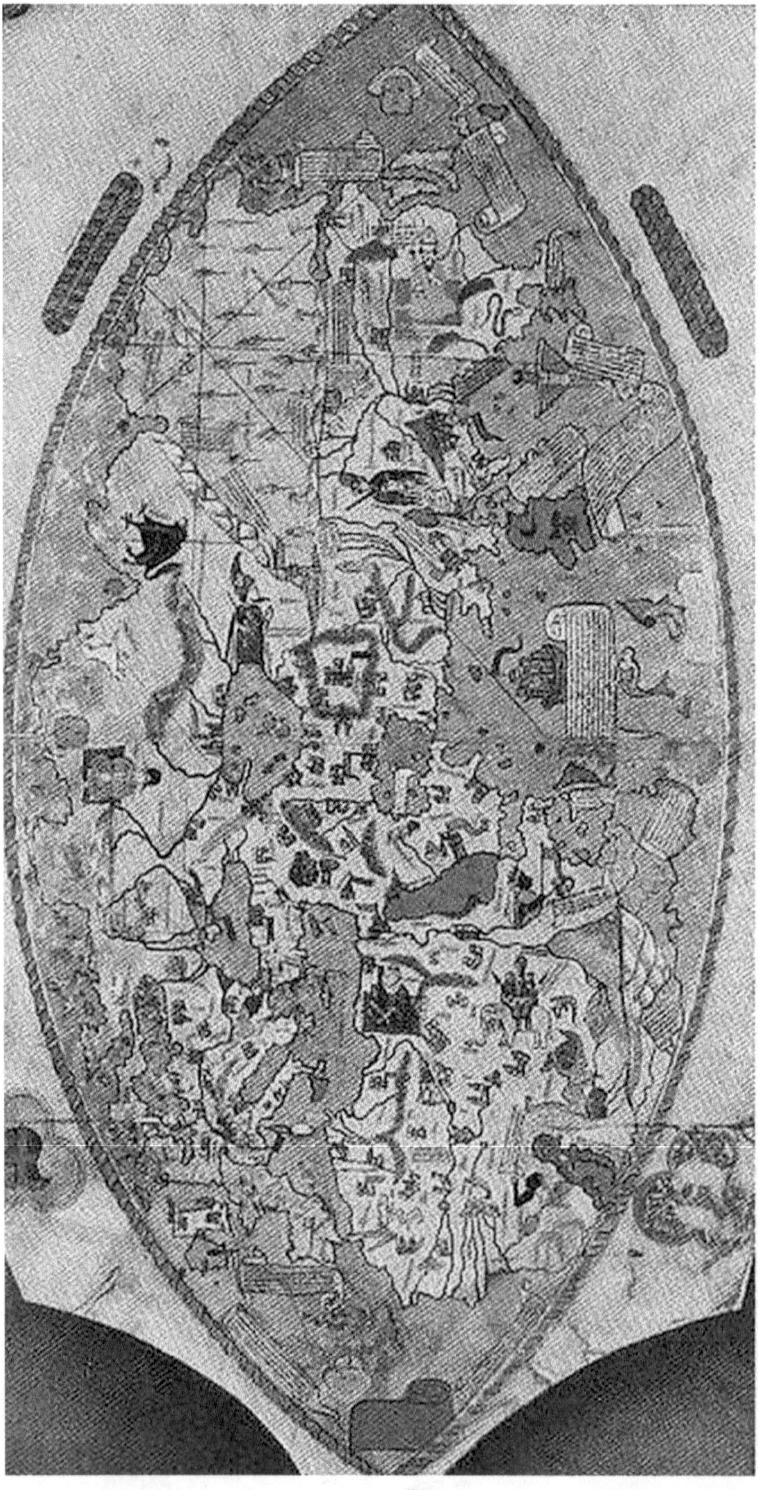

Part 1 - The Conqueror's Empire

Genoese Map of the World c. 1457

2 - THE CONQUEROR'S WORLD

Part 1 - The Conqueror's Empire

CRITICAL TIMELINE

Year	Event	Involved Parties
1432	Birth of Mehmed II	Ottomans
1437	Prince Ahmed dies	Ottomans
1443	Prince Ali is assassinated	Ottomans
1443	The Long Campaign	The Pope Hungary Poland Serbia Wallachia Ottomans
1444	Battle of Varna	The Pope Hungary Poland Ottomans
1444	Sultan Murad II abdicates	Ottomans
1446	Sultan Murad II returns to power	Ottomans
1448	Second Battle of Kosovo	Hungary Serbia Ottomans
1451	Start of Sultan Mehmed II's reign	Ottomans

2 - The Conqueror's World

Mehmed II was the third son of Sultan Murad II and was not from the outset of his life destined to become sultan.

His mother was Hüma, a servant or slave of sultan Murad II and from the few mentions of her name in historic sources most likely a non-Muslim. That did not, however, affect Mehmed's potential claim to the throne as any son born to the Sultan was considered a full-born heir.

According to Islamic Law the Sultan could have four wives, but as many concubines as he pleased. The official marriages were mostly used to form political alliances and, in some cases, entirely so.

An example of one such political marriage is one of Sultan Murad II's wives, Mara, daughter of Đurađ Branković, the ruler of Serbia. After Murad II's death she returned to Serbia, and it was proposed that she re-married the Byzantine Emperor to cement ties between Serbia and Byzantium. Whereas the proposed union did not happen (as Mara herself refused the proposal), the interesting thing is that in the letter sent to the Emperor it is said about Mara that she was '*The wife of a very powerful monarch and she, it is generally believed, did not sleep with him*'.

By the time Mehmed was born in 1432 his father already had two sons, Ahmed and Ali, the later rumored as being the favourite of his father. Both his older brothers however died young.

Ahmed died, in unclear circumstances but probably from sickness, in 1437 and Ali was assassinated in 1443. His assassin is known, a nobleman named Kara Hizin Pasha, but his motives were never revealed. He did not just kill Ali though, but also his two infant sons, effectively wiping out any possible challenge to the throne from both Ali and his descendants. Though it was Mehmed who stood to benefit from this gruesome murder, it is unlikely that he, at the age of eleven, should be behind it and, as we shall soon see, neither did he have a particularly strong group of supporters at this time whom could have masterminded the pre-emptive murder of his brother.

Whatever the motive behind Ali's assassination, Mehmed now became first in line for the throne, despite the fact that his relationship with his father was rather tense.

Mehmed was a difficult child and youth, who resisted education until he was finally, literally, beaten into submission. He subsequently became an enthusiastic student of history, but there was little in his younger years that pointed to his later merits as a scholar, poet, and warlord.

Having grown up mainly outside the court in Edirne, he was recalled after his brother's death, in order that he could receive the necessary insight in matters political.

Immediately following his return, his father, Sultan Murad II, set off to meet a combined Christian army that had successfully marched through Serbia and Bulgaria, aiming at Edirne itself. The Christian army was in the end stopped by the onset of winter and had to slug it back to Hungary giving up all the territory it had gained. The experience, however, put hope in Christian hearts that they could possibly defeat the Ottoman army in Europe.

Murad II came back to Edirne, but immediately had to leave for Anatolia where there was once again trouble on the eastern border (see Chapter 6). This time he left, twelve year old, Mehmed behind in Edirne as official regent of his European possessions, even though it was the grand vizier, Çandarlı Halil Pasha, who was the de-facto regent.

Though Murad II was only gone for three months, several incidents happened during Mehmed's short period as regent, incidents which would create tension and unrest and have consequences beyond the incidents themselves.

One incident was the appearance of a mystic Shiite missionary, who caught the attention of the young prince Mehmed. The missionary upset the (Sunni) religious establishment, not least the mufti, Fahreddin, who had Çandarlı Halil Pasha, the grand vizier, on his side.

Through trickery they managed to apprehend the heretic preacher, but he escaped and sought refuge at the royal palace, protected by Prince Mehmed. After a short stand-off Mehmed however had to give him back to the authorities, where he, despite the Ottoman policy of religious freedom, was quickly condemned and burned alive. This did no good to the relationship between Mehmed and Çandarlı Halil Pasha.

Another episode was a mutiny by the Janissaries, who demanded a pay increase, though their real bone of contention was more with Mehmed's personal advisor, a eunuch called Sihabeddin Pasha, than with Mehmed himself. Though on this occasion Mehmed did manage to protect his advisor, he had to concede to a salary increase after the Janissaries had started a fire which amongst other things burned down the central bazaar in Edirne.

Luckily, Murad II was soon back from Anatolia to relieve his son from his somewhat compromised position as regent. He did not stay long though as the Christian armies were once again on the march, fuelled by what they saw as a successful campaign the year before (despite the fact that at the end of the campaign they had lost all the ground they had previously won).

Led by the young King Wladyslaw III of Poland and the veteran Hungarian commander Janos Hunyadi, a substantial Christian army had set out along the coast of the Black Sea, once again aiming for Edirne and Rumelia.

The armies met at Varna (in Bulgaria), where the Ottomans dealt a crushing blow to the Christian's ambitions of throwing them out of Europe. Not only did they win the hard-fought battle, but they killed King Wladyslaw

III in the process as well as the Pope's warlike representative; cardinal Cesarini.

Murad II again returned to Edirne and in December he decided to abdicate and leave the throne for his twelve year old son, though in practical terms the Empire would once again be run by a council lead by the grand vizier Çandarlı Halil Pasha. Exactly why he did that is still puzzling historians, but no matter his reasons, he retired to Manisa and left Mehmed and his advisers in charge.

Even though, compared to his first short regency, Mehmed's next reign was more successful, mainly gauged from the fact that there were no violent revolts, he was not popular; with the army in particular. Whereas his father was a jovial man with great respect for the army and of course considerable military experience and merit to win that respect back, Mehmed was turning into a young man with somewhat haughty and forbidding manners, with little respect for anyone and no military experience on which to build a respectful relationship with the army.

Also, Mehmed's relationship with the grand vizier, Çandarlı Halil Pasha, was strained. He was starting to show an increased level of independence, questioning Halil Pasha's dispositions. In particular, he had started to develop a plan for the conquest of Constantinople, something that Çandarlı Halil Pasha would not endorse.

Finally, Çandarlı Halil Pasha called Murad II back, under the pretext of unrest in southern Greece, and Murad II grudgingly answered his call and returned to Edirne, and the throne, in the autumn of 1446. Though Prince Mehmed took his father's return gracefully it no doubt did not exactly endear him any further to Çandarlı Halil Pasha.

In 1448, Janos Hunyadi was once again in the field with a Hungarian army. Murad II gave battle to the Hungarians in Kosovo, where the massively outnumbered Hungarian army was routed. Prince Mehmed saw his baptism of fire in this battle and fought with the rank and file of Anatolian troops on the Ottoman right flank, vastly improving his rapport with the army.

After this defeat, known as the Second Battle of Kosovo, the Christian states were pacified and Murad II returned to Edirne where he spent his last years in relative peace until his death in 1451, as mentioned earlier.

With Sultan Murad II's death, Mehmed became Sultan Mehmed II and he immediately showed that he had learned from the past. Without much ceremony he had his only surviving half-brother, an infant boy named Ahmed, murdered so as to avoid any of the civil wars and intrigues that had weakened the Empire during both his grandfather's and father's accession to the throne.

Later on, he would make the act of fratricide a matter of law with the words *'Whichever of my sons inherits the sultan's throne, it behoves him to kill his brothers in the interest of world order'*.

Mehmed's choice of the words '*world order*' was not an accident. As far as Mehmed was concerned 'the world' was the Ottoman Empire and even though that may not actually be entirely true, he had a plan to make it so!

But what did 'the world' look like from Mehmed's perspective?

First and foremost, it did not look like our world. Christopher Columbus was only born in the same year Mehmed came to power and his 'discovery' of the Americas was still more than fifty years in the future as was the birth of Copernicus, with Tycho Brahe following nearly another decade later. So as far as anyone was concerned, the Earth was flat, it was at the centre of the Universe, the Sun and the Moon moved around the Earth and the centre of the world was Jerusalem.

Mehmed's worldview would probably be similar to the view presented in the Genoese map from 1457 seen at the beginning of this chapter. The world went from the British Isles in the west through to China/Japan in the east, with Scandinavia and Russia in the north and Africa being the southernmost landmass. It was speculated that you could sail south of Africa in order to get to India and China, but it was only actually proven late in the fifteenth century.

Missing from the worldview were the Americas and Australia as well as the Poles, even though tales of land further to the west was widespread in northern Europe as vague memories of Viking settlers in Greenland and Newfoundland.

The Ottoman Empire itself, in 1451, was a patchwork of cultures and religions strung together over more than a century of expansion and annexation.

The core Ottoman territory in north-western Anatolia had long since been extended south and east, effectively putting the entire westernmost part of Anatolia under solid Ottoman control. To the south-east was the Karaman beylik (see Chapter 6), ruled by the Grand Karaman, Ibrahim II, who would regularly take advantage of any perceived Ottoman weakness and raid Ottoman territories.

To the east, the Ottoman territories in Anatolia met with the 'White Sheep' (see Chapter 7), the heirs to the western Timurid territories, remaining free of Ottoman dominance since Timur's incursion in the early part of the fifteenth century even though most parts of eastern Anatolia itself had been gradually recovered under Mehmed's father Murad II. At the top of eastern Anatolia, on a stretch of Black Sea coast, was the Empire of Trebizond (see Chapter 8), a grand name for a small former Byzantine territory centred on and around the city of Trebizond.

On the European side of the Empire the Ottoman possessions included all of Bulgaria, most of northern and eastern Greece and of course Rumelia, the area surrounding the Byzantine capital of Constantinople, now an isolated enclave in a state of decline far removed from its former glory.

2 - The Conqueror's World

The southernmost Greek peninsula of Peloponnese, also known as Morea, was one of the few remaining Byzantine possessions, split into two small states ruled by brothers of the Byzantine emperor. This area was troublesome as the rulers of Morea were not slow to exploit any Ottoman weaknesses and consistently would try to re-impose Byzantine dominance in mainland Greece, as often as not assisted by Albanians.

Albania had been all but lost to partisans under the warlord Skanderbeg, though regular fighting took place and the frontiers were fluidly defined.

The Ottoman Empire did not have direct a border to the Hungarian Empire, the closest and most aggressive Catholic state. Instead a range of smaller states, namely Bosnia, Serbia, Wallachia and Moldavia (see Chapter 14), made up a convenient 'buffer zone' between the two empires. As we shall see, both empires would consistently try to exert their influence over these buffer-states, leading to constant upheaval and conflict.

Though small in geographical terms, costal enclaves and Islands under the control of Italian city-states, Venice and Genoa in particular, played dominant roles in the area. This was mainly due to the fact that the Ottomans were not traditional seafarers and had yet to catch up in terms of both naval technology and the establishment of a sizeable navy, whereas the Italians had been seafarers for centuries and their warships ruled supreme in the seas surrounding the Ottoman Empire. We meet them in Part 4.

It should be understood that the borders between the Ottoman Empire and its neighbours were not fixed. The Ottomans came from a stock of nomadic horsemen, and this culture included raiding neighbouring territories for livestock, whether cattle, women or slaves. The Ottomans had kept up this tradition, and the borders of the Empire were constantly subject to raids by Ottoman raiding parties. On land they would come sweeping in on horseback, loot, burn and disappear. At sea they would come as pirates, Ottoman or otherwise (in particular Catalan), who raided coastal settlements and islands. Though not officially operated by the Ottoman state, they were tolerated, sometimes even encouraged by the Empire, as long as they stayed off raiding Ottoman possessions.

Though there were plenty of hostile neighbours around, none of them were in a position to pose a major or immediate threat to Mehmed II's empire and furthermore they did not feel a particular need for aggression, as they did not see Mehmed himself as a clear and present danger.

Indeed, most outside observers saw Mehmed II as a young and inexperienced boy, unpopular with his own army and people and even somewhat simpleminded. Compared to his highly respected and competent father, he was seen as a weak and non-threatening ruler, a rather spoiled youth who '*Led a dissipated life amid wine and women*' according to one contemporary observer.

Mehmed II himself confirmed these opinions by, immediately following his accession to the throne, sending out peaceful signals to all and sundry, re-confirming existing peace and trade treaties.

Most potential enemies were more than happy for peace to reign, as they all had their own issues to deal with, and congratulations, assurance of peaceful intentions, embassies and rich gifts came in from near and far, including Wallachia, Chios, Lesbos, Genoa, The Knights of Rhodes, Venice, Serbia, the monks on Mount Athos, Ragusa, Hungary and, of course, Constantinople.

One observer, the Venetian Giacomo de Languschi, however had a different and, as it turned out, far more correct, opinion of Mehmed II. He wrote:

'The sovereign, the Grand Turk Mehmed Bey, is well built, of large rather than medium stature, expert at arms, of aspects more frightening than venerable, laughing seldom, full of circumspection, endowed with great generosity, obstinate in pursuing his plans, bold in all undertakings, as eager for fame as Alexander of Macedonia.'

He continues:

'He speaks three languages, Turkish, Greek and Slavic. He is of great pains to learn the geography of Italy and to inform himself of the places where Anchises and Aeneas and Antenor landed, where the seat of the Pope is and that of the Emperor and how many kingdoms there are in Europe. He possesses a map of Europe with the countries and provinces. He learns of nothing with greater interest and enthusiasm than the geography of the world and military affairs; he burns with desire to dominate; he is a shrewd investigator of conditions. It is with such a man that we Christians have to deal.'

And he concludes:

'Today, he says, the times have changed, and declare that he will advance from East to West as in former times the Westerners advanced into the Orient. There must, he says, be only one empire, one faith and one sovereignty in the world.'

Giacomo de Languschi was the odd one out, but history would show that he was right and the general policy of appeasement towards Mehmed II would turn out to work as well as it did with Hitler nearly 500 years later. But let us leave Mehmed II for now and continue the story through the stories of his enemies.

PART 2

THE BYZANTINE EMPIRE

3 - BIRTH, DECLINE, CRUSADES AND RECONQUEST
4 - DEADLY NEIGHBORS

Part 2 - The Byzantine Empire

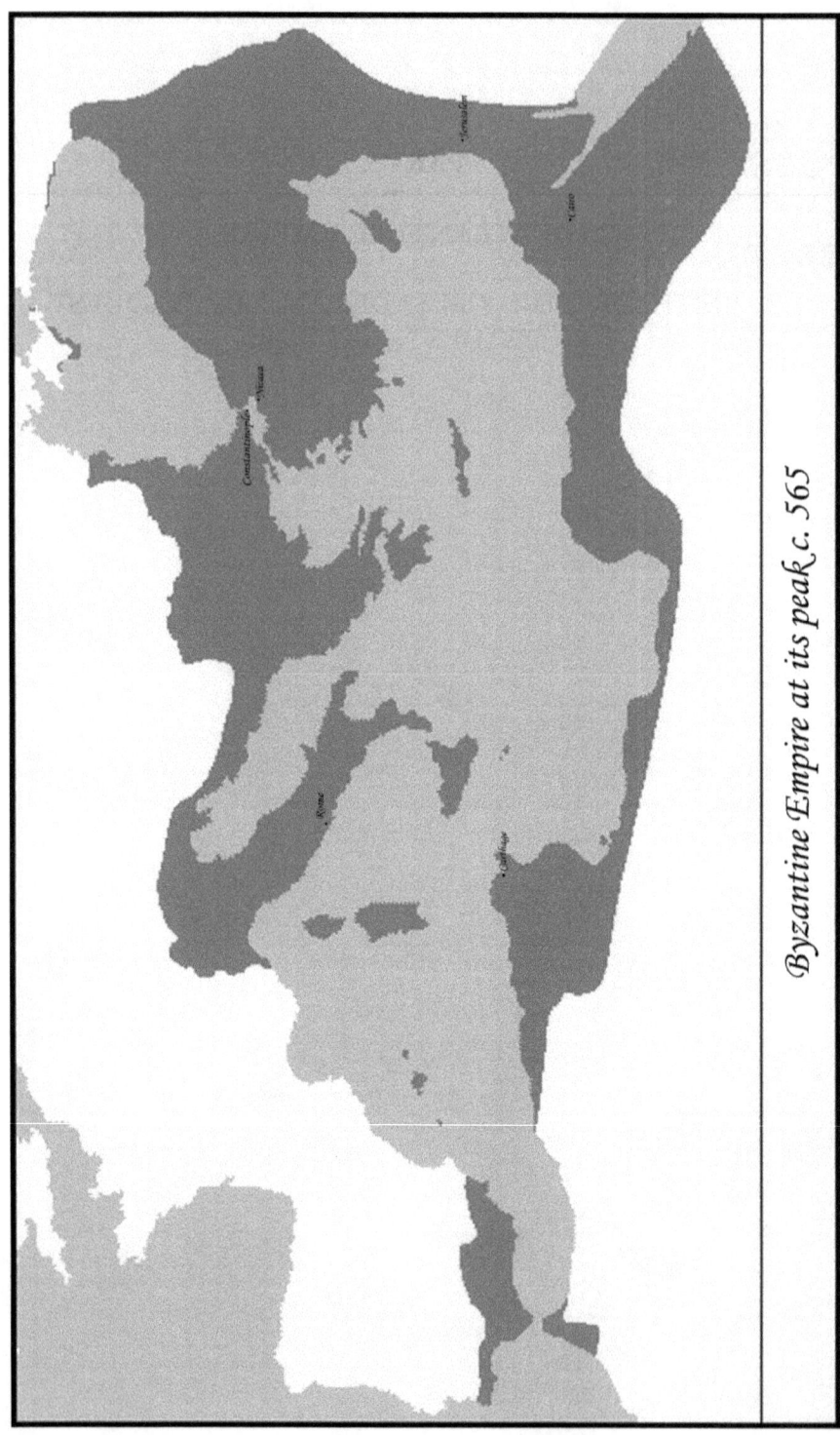

Byzantine Empire at its peak c. 565

3 - BIRTH, DECLINE, CRUSADES AND RECONQUEST

Part 2 - The Byzantine Empire

CRITICAL TIMELINE

Year	Event	Involved Parties
324	Constantinople is founded	Rome Byzantium
674	Muslim siege of Constantinople	Byzantium Muslim Caliphate
717	Muslim siege of Constantinople	Byzantium Muslim Caliphate
1054	East-West Schism of the Christian Church	Rome Byzantium
1071	Battle of Manzikert	Byzantium Seljuks
1081	Alexios I Komnenos becomes emperor	Byzantium
1095	Pope Urban II calls for 'crusade'	Byzantium Western Europe
1099	The First Crusade (conquest of Jerusalem)	Byzantium Western Europe Seljuks Egypt
1187	Egyptian reconquest of Jerusalem	Egypt Crusader States
1204	Fourth Crusade. Sack of Constantinople	Byzantium Venice Western Europe Latin Constantinople
1208	Theodore I becomes Emperor of Nicaea	Empire of Nicaea
1221	John III Doukas Vatatzes becomes Emperor of Nicaea	Empire of Nicaea
1246	Nicaea conquers Thessaloniki	Empire of Nicaea Latin Constantinople
1254	Theodore II Laskaris becomes Emperor of Nicaea	Empire of Nicaea
1258	The infant Theodore II Laskaris becomes Emperor of Nicaea	Empire of Nicaea
1259	Michael VIII Palaiologos becomes co-Emperor of Nicaea	Empire of Nicaea
1261	Reconquest of Constantinople	Latin Constantinople Byzantium Empire of Nicaea Venice Genoa
1274	Partly annexation of Morea	Byzantium Naples
1274	Reunification of the Christian Church	The Pope Byzantium
1282	Sicilian Vespers	Naples Aragon Byzantium
1282	Andronikos II Palaiologos becomes Emperor of Byzantium	Byzantium

3 - Birth, Decline, Crusades and Reconquest

When the story of the Roman Empire is told, it normally ends in the fifth century with the Goth's taking of Rome itself or with the last emperor, Romulus Augustus, being deposed by the barbarian Odoacer. That, however, is not correct.

True, the 'Western Roman Empire' collapsed, but the eastern part of the Roman Empire lived on, even though historians over time would name it the Byzantine Empire as it morphed into its own Greek speaking identity.

At the height of its power the Byzantine Empire was one of the biggest empires the world has seen, and through its more than 1,000 years of existence also one of the most long-lived.

It emerged as a reaction to Rome's fading status as the capital of the Roman Empire in the early part of the fourth century AD. The Emperor, Constantine the Great, having himself won the crown after yet another devastating civil-war, decided to build a new capital city from which to rule his vast, though somewhat disintegrating, empire.

Having originally considered both Sofia or a new capital raising like a phoenix from the remains of Troy, he eventually settled on the small city of Byzantium, conveniently located at the tip of a peninsula, protected by the sea on three sides, positioned right where the Black Sea and Mediterranean trade routes naturally met at the bottom of the Bosporus Strait and with a large natural harbour in the Golden Horn inlet on the north side of the city.

Constantine effectively tore the old, rather stagnant and insignificant, city down and built a new city befitting its status as an Imperial Capital. That said, Constantinople, as it was now renamed, initially only shared its status of capital with Rome, and only became the sole capital of the remaining Roman Empire in the beginning of the fifth century.

Constantine spared no expense in building his new city. He built a royal palace and a hippodrome (a chariot racing track), with an imperial box connected to the palace as had become custom among Roman emperors. The city was equipped with colonnaded fora, public buildings, and baths as well as a number of Christian churches, Constantine being the first officially Christian Roman emperor.

To demonstrate the superiority and vastness of the Empire, he had ancient monuments brought from all corners of the Empire and displayed in the new city, not least of which was on the spine (central barrier) of the Hippodrome. They included (the upper part of) an obelisk removed from Carnac in Egypt, a 'Serpent Column' in bronze brought in from Delphi and a statue of a donkey and driver taken from a shrine (marking Augustus' victory over Mark Antony) in Actium. To make sure he was not entirely forgotten in

Rome, he had the Arch of Constantine built outside the Coliseum there as well.

Through the fifth and sixth centuries, with Rome overrun by 'barbarians' and Constantinople reigning supreme as the capital, the Empire managed to regain many of the territories in the west that had gradually been lost with the decline of the western part of the Roman Empire and managed to also expand onto the north-coast of Africa, effectively forming a complete circle of influence around the Mediterranean Sea while also dominating the southern part of the Black Sea.

The new Empire, referred to as 'Byzantine' by historians from the original town of that name, was now the true heir to the Roman Empire and even though it was now by all means 'Greek' rather than 'Roman', with Greek spoken rather than Latin, the citizens still referred to themselves as 'Romans' and Constantinople was referred to as 'Rome', or 'Rum', with the lands inside the immediate influence of the city itself referred to as 'Rumelia'.

Pressure, however, mounted on the vast borders and gradually the Empire started to shrink. Even though initial attempts at conquest by the Sassanids of Persia in the sixth century were mainly reversed, the Empire was exhausted and could offer little resistance when the new Muslim Caliphate started expanding northwards from the Arab Peninsula in the seventh century. In a prolonged war that would last 400 years, the Byzantines and the Arabs fought for control, with the Arabs eventually controlling the Middle East, North Africa and Spain while the Byzantines stubbornly held onto Anatolia and their remaining European possessions.

Twice during this extended war, the Arabs tried to conquer Constantinople. First, they came in 674 and besieged the city for five years. They were eventually ousted when the Byzantine navy attacked their winter harbour and used 'Greek fire' from ship-mounted nozzles to burn the Arab fleet. The remaining army was then hit by bad weather on their crossing back to Anatolia and those that made it back were ambushed by Byzantine troops.

This was the first major military setback the emerging Muslim Caliphate had experienced, and it sent reverberations through time, namely the strong desire for revenge and proof that nothing would stand in the way of Muslim world-domination.

In 717 the Arabs were back, so determined to succeed that they even brought their own crops which they planted outside the walls of Constantinople. They were, however, not prepared for an unusually cold winter, which gradually decimated the army and the food supplies. When the Arab relief fleet, bringing much needed food supplies, was surprised by the Byzantine fleet and burned, and the army reinforcements marching from Syria were ambushed and destroyed by Byzantine troops in Anatolia they had no option but to abandon the siege and retreat.

The Byzantine Empire, contrary to the original Roman Empire, was an empire built on culture and religion rather than raw military might. Though they had armies, they could not muster the seemingly endless quantities of well-trained legions that the Roman Empire could put in the field in its day, so in the centuries following, the Byzantine Empire gradually lost most of its European possessions, apart from parts of Greece and Rumelia to the forming and expanding new Christian nation states of western Europe and the Bulgarian Empire in the Balkans. This formation of a new post-Roman, Christian, western Europe brought with it not only conflict over land, but also conflict over religion.

Dating back to Christianity's official acceptance as the religion of the Roman Empire in the fourth century, there were five traditional 'sees', or bishop's seats, located in Rome, Constantinople, Jerusalem, Antioch and Alexandria. The conquest of the Muslims in the seventh century meant that three of these, Jerusalem, Antioch and Alexandria, had been removed from Christian influence, leaving only the Sees in Rome and Constantinople.

As the Roman Empire became the Byzantine Empire, and shifted from Latin to Greek, the church in Rome remained Latin, in language and culture. During the last centuries of the first millennium a divide started to develop with the new western European states adhering to the Latin version, as overseen by Rome, whereas the eastern European states adhered to the Greek version, as overseen by Constantinople.

Conflict developed, with the Greek language being forbidden in areas under the influence of Rome and Latin being forbidden in areas influenced by Constantinople and, ultimately, exploded in 1054 when the Christian church officially split into two separate churches, the Catholic Church based in Rome and the Orthodox Church based in Constantinople.

But this was far from the only major challenge that the Byzantine Empire faced in the eleventh century.

Originating from the area around what we today know as Kazakhstan, the Seljuk Turks had converted to Islam and soon overran both Persia and eastern Anatolia, spilling down along the coast of Palestine as far as the border to Egypt.

Watching the Seljuk Turks' continued push westwards, the Byzantine Emperor Romanos IV Diogenes decided to march east to meet them. The resulting Battle of Manzikert on 26th August 1071 became a disaster for the Byzantines, and started a period of slow, but constant, decline that would last for nearly another four centuries.

The Byzantine army was defeated, although not destroyed, and the Byzantine Emperor himself taken prisoner. He was, however, released after only a week of, most civilized, captivity by the Seljuk Sultan Alp Arslan.

Militarily the defeat at Manzikert was limited, but it led to three decades of internal conflicts and civil war in the Byzantine Empire, so even though the Seljuk Turks had not per se flooded into (undefended) Anatolia immediately following the Battle of Manzikert, they soon started to move westwards, and with the Byzantines fighting each other, rather than Seljuks, by the end of the eleventh century Anatolia - with the exception of some coastal areas - had in practical terms been taken over as part of the Great Seljuk Empire.

Some stability had started to return to the Byzantine Empire with the emergence of Emperor Alexios I Komnenos (1081-1118), but without financial or military capability he could only watch with increasing concern as the Anatolian heartlands slipped out of Byzantine control, and so he finally did the nearly unspeakable; in 1095 he asked the Pope in Rome for help.

What emperor Alexios I Komnenos wanted from Pope Urban II was soldiers, preferably experienced mercenaries, and he hoped that the Pope would realize the inherent threat from the emerging Muslims, put their differences aside and open his purse. What he got was something completely different, he got a crusade!

The Pope was in Piacenza when he received the Emperor's ambassador and a council was called to take place in Clermont in November that same year, to discuss the Emperor's petition.

The Council of Clermont was so big that it was held outdoors, and Urban II was well prepared. He had prepared a sermon in which he urged all and sundry to go to the aid of the Christians against the Muslims, retake "the Holy Land" and promised absolution for all participants.

It is impossible to guess what exactly Urban II expected would happen, he probably hoped for some of the many knights idling around Europe - creating trouble and unrest because they had little else to do - to volunteer, which meant he would not have to pay for the exercise. What he got was a popular movement that would last 200 years.

Rather than the well-organised, and paid-for, army which Emperor Alexios I Komnenos had hoped for to arrive at Constantinople, he got a massive host of rag-tag volunteers. Most were ordinary people (generally classified as 'peasants'), full of religious zeal but with no organization, arms or military experience. Some were knights and other hopefuls, with some arms and some military experience and a few were organised fighting units, led by ambitious (mainly Norman) lords.

They did have one thing in common though; they all expected to be fed and maintained by the Byzantine Emperor, so plundering their way down through eastern Europe, arriving in disparate groups, they camped outside the gates of Constantinople.

The Byzantine Emperor did not know what to do with them. This was not what he had asked for or expected, and he had few resources with which to maintain the hundreds of thousands of 'crusaders' now on his doorstep.

Eventually, some kind of command-structure emerged and the Emperor negotiated a deal in which he would assist with supplies and transport to his best ability on the condition that the 'army' moved on into Anatolia, gave war to the Seljuks and ultimately did so in his name, implicit that all lands conquered would be Byzantine possessions once more.

3 - Birth, Decline, Crusades and Reconquest

When Pope Urban II called for people to 'take the cross' (the word 'crusade' being a label added later by historians), and go to fight the infidels, he had no particular ambitions over and above stopping the Muslim advance towards Europe. Though he did use the word 'Jerusalem' as a metaphor, there is no historic evidence that he actually meant the city of Jerusalem itself.

The zealous crusaders, however, took it literally and they set out to re-conquer Jerusalem, long lost to the initial advance of the Muslim Caliphate in the seventh century. Fighting their way through Anatolia, the peasant-armies were generally slaughtered by the Seljuks, but the, by now better organised, military army advanced through Anatolia, swung south into the Palestine and eventually, after much hardship, conquered Jerusalem itself. This endeavour was assisted by internal conflict amongst the Seljuks after the death of the ruler Malik-Shah I, which left the defenders weakened.

Along the way parts of the army broke off the main host and established themselves in enclaves around some of the major cities.

The end result was the establishment of several new 'Latin' (i.e. European/Catholic) nation states; the Kingdom of Jerusalem, the County of Tripoli, the Principality of Antioch and the County of Edessa.

Forgotten were all promises to return the conquered lands to the Byzantines, even though the Emperor did take the opportunity to fall in behind the crusader army and solidify his control over some of the coastal areas in north-western Anatolia.

Though the Seljuk Empire (as covered in Chapter 5) continued to exist for another two centuries and would consistently fight with the Latin invaders, it never regained its former glory, and eventually dissolved, split into smaller independent states.

For the Byzantines this meant a period of relative stability. Though the central and eastern parts of Anatolia were lost forever, there was no organised pressure on their remaining possessions, so they could occupy themselves with their favourite pastimes; trade, diplomacy, political intrigue and civil war.

Jerusalem remained in Christian hands for nearly a hundred years. Conquered at the end of the First Crusade in 1099, it fell to the armies of Saladin in 1187. An attempt to retake it between 1189 and 1192 (known as the Third Crusade) was unsuccessful in terms of the city itself. And a new attempt (the Fourth Crusade) was called for by Pope Innocent III in 1198.

The Fourth Crusade started with a clear goal; to invade Egypt and move north to re-conquer Jerusalem. It turned into one the most bizarre events in history, pitching Christians against Christians and the original goal lost to commercial and political intrigue.

It started well enough, in a crusading kind of sense, in that a leadership structure was defined, men were recruited and transport arranged. The latter, as it turned out, becoming the defining issue of the campaign.

We shall come back to the city state of Venice in Chapter 10, but in short; Venice operated the most successful state-controlled merchant fleet in the world at the beginning of the thirteenth century. It was thus to Venice that the leaders of the Fourth Crusade came with a request for transport of the army-to-be.

The estimate was that the army needed transport for 33,000 men and 4,500 horses, an enterprise that was unsurpassed in terms of size and the underlying logistics. Even the Venetians struggled to accommodate the request, but eventually put a price on it; 94,000 marks, the equivalent of twenty-five tons of silver, plus half the spoils of the campaign.

That was an enormous sum of money, but not unreasonable, as the Venetians to facilitate the task had to effectively cease trading for a two-year period and put everything they had into the enterprise. The deal was struck, the Venetians started building and organizing and the crusader leaders went away to muster their army and raise the funds.

The deal was that the fleet would set off in June 1202, and at the agreed time the Venetians were ready. There was, however, no crusader army.

Through the summer of 1202 the army started to arrive and camp outside Venice itself. By August it was complete, except it was around half the estimated size, and the money available to pay the Venetians finally came to 60,000 Marks, 34,000 Marks short of the agreed price.

A stand-off ensued, the crusader army effectively being held hostage in camps on outlying islands off Venice, but eventually a new deal was struck, this time not on the basis of religious zeal, but purely on commercial terms; one way or another the Venetians were going to make up their losses or face ruin.

The Venetians agreed to put the remaining payment on hold, on the condition that it was repaid from spoils of the campaign before any spoil was given to the crusaders, and also that the crusader armies would assist Venice in their own mini-campaign once they were underway. The crusaders had no options but to agree, and finally in October 1202 the fleet set sail down the Adriatic Sea.

Heading the expedition was Boniface of Montferrat and Baldwin of Flanders, on behalf of the crusader Army, the Venetian Doge (elected chief-of-state) Enrico Dandolo on behalf of the Venetians and two bishops (Martin of Paris and Conrad of Halberstadt) to represent the Church.

And it was in the Adriatic Sea that the next chapter of the Fourth Crusade would develop. Venice had a long-standing disagreement with the city of Zara on the Dalmatian coast, a city that much to Venice's regret was independent and, currently, under the protection of the Hungarian king.

The Pope had actually anticipated that Venice may take the opportunity to make war on Zara, and had specifically forbidden it under threat of excommunication, but this was kept quiet to the rank and file.

Moving down the Dalmatian Coast, the fleet made several stops, each designed to impose Venetian sovereignty, and finally they broke through the maritime defences of Zara and unloaded the army before its walls.

The crusader army, set out to conquer Jerusalem, however now found themselves laying siege to another Christian city in the hinterlands of Europe, but with no other options they played along with the Venetians. Eventually, and after much internal unrest between the crusaders and the Venetians, Zara surrendered and was looted. When the Pope heard about it he excommunicated the whole enterprise, of which he himself was the spiritual overlord, but again this was kept secret and not communicated to the rank and file.

With winter now approaching, it was decided to stay in Zara and start afresh in spring.

While the crusade was going nowhere, in January 1203 a small embassy arrived with an offer to the Venetians and the crusaders alike. Nominally it was from Philip of Swabia, King of the Germans, but it concerned his brother-in-law, the Byzantine 'prince' Alexius Angelus.

Alexius Angelus' father, Isaac II Angelos, had been ousted as emperor by his own brother, Alexios III Angelos, in the ongoing game of thrones in which the Byzantines had occupied themselves during the last, relatively peaceful, century.

Alexius Angelus thus believed to have a rightful claim to the throne, and he was, according to Philip of Swabia's ambassadors, well-liked by the people who would not only welcome him back, but proactively assist in his accession to the Byzantine throne should he appear before the gates of Constantinople.

As good as that sounded, it was hardly enough to secure the support of the crusader army, the Venetians, or indeed the Pope, but there was more on offer. Cleverly, well understanding the predicament of the crusader enterprise, there was a promise of no less than 200,000 Marks in cash, 10,000 soldiers for a year and - to please the Pope - a further promise to put Byzantium back under spiritual leadership by the Pope.

The offer was simply too good to refuse.

Some of the crusaders had had enough and simply upped and left, for home or by their own means towards the Holy Land, most, however, stayed, and in April 1203 the fleet moved again, this time towards Constantinople to undertake the simple, but highly profitable, enterprise of putting Alexius Angelus onto the throne of Byzantium. After a short stay on Corfu, they eventually arrived in the waters outside Constantinople on 24 June 1203.

The crusaders unloaded on the Asian shore across from the city itself and now waited for the city's population to open the gate and welcome their rightful emperor as they had been led to believe would be the case. Nobody came, except an embassy from the Emperor expressing his confusion as to their intent and purpose.

An attempt to show Alexius Angelus to his adoring populace, by rowing him up and down before the seawalls of the city, was equally unsuccessful, and only resulted in shouts from the walls of the city, denying any recognition of Alexius Angelus or his claim. The seemingly easy enterprise was turning out to be a very different affair.

Once again, the crusade was effectively stranded. The plan was to get Alexius Angelus installed on the throne, get his army organised and the promised cash handed over and be on their way again by September. Furthermore, the communication to the Pope that Byzantium was once again under his spiritual leadership would surely result in a waiver of the previous (secretly kept) excommunication and a revival of the original spiritual purpose of the expedition. The reality was different, very different indeed.

There were two options available; to move the crusade on, or to attack and try to force the issue. With only three weeks of supplies at hand and no cash to pay for anymore, moving on was not really an option at all, so they decided to stay and fight.

The ill-fated crusade had now turned into a farce. Already excommunicated, the crusader army, destined to retake Jerusalem for Christianity, now stood before the walls of one of the most important cities in Christendom.

And these walls were intimidating to say the least. They spanned the whole circumference of the city. On three sides they faced the sea and on the western side a massive land-wall ran from the Sea of Marmara in the south through to the Golden Horn in the north. Despite tens of attempts over the city's nearly thousand years of history, no one had successfully conquered Constantinople.

The natural harbour of the Golden Horn had been barred by means of a chain drawn from the city itself to the township of Galata on the northern shore of the Golden Horn and this became the first target of the attack on the city.

The crusader army launched an attack on Galata, aiming for the fortified tower that held the mechanism for the chain across the Golden Horn. The defenders were simply not prepared as the Emperor still did not believe in, or expect, an actual attack to be forthcoming. A battle raged to and from, but eventually the Galata Tower was taken and the chain lowered, allowing the Venetian fleet to enter the Golden Horn, a key strategic point in the Venetian plan.

The next stage of the plan was to attack the city in a pincer move on both the land and seawalls. The reason for the latter was that the seawalls were significantly lower and less heavily defended than the land-walls, simply because there was a limit to how many troops could be landed on the narrow stretches of beach in front of the walls.

The crusader army was thus ferried across the Golden Horn, still with little organised resistance from the Byzantines, and put up camp in front of the northern part of the land-wall, right outside the Emperor's palace at Blachernae, itself partly integrated into the defensive walls.

In the meantime, the idea that would turn out to make the difference between this and the many other previous, failed, attempts to scale the walls of Constantinople was put into motion.

Basically, the idea was to utilize the relatively low height of the seawalls in combination with the relatively tall height of the Venetian freight ships. Simply put, the Venetians installed hinged drawbridges in the mast of the taller ships, engineered to unfold onto the seawalls, that is if you could get close enough to do so.

From a purely military viewpoint the whole enterprise was madness fed by desperation. Constantinople had a population of up towards 500,000 people, many of whom could be relied upon for defensive service on the walls. In addition, the Emperor's standing army counted some 30,000 troops, roughly three times as many as the dwindling crusader army. Though the Venetians held the sea, and thus could cut the city off from supplies, with only three weeks of supplies at hand to feed the crusader army, it was unlikely that the city could be starved into surrender.

The political situation was, however, a different matter all-together. A strong, determined and warlike emperor could have put up a unified defence, even an offensive, and no doubt have repelled the attack. Alexios III Angelos, however, was not such a man. He had as good as ruined the Empire, spending lavish sums on palaces and gardens, leaving the Byzantine territories in Rumelia undefended and effectively lost to renegade Bulgarians. In the initial phases of the attack by the crusader army and the Venetian fleet, he sat as a spectator rather than a participant, still as if not really believing that the city was under attack.

Thus, the attackers, with a nothing-to-loose attitude, met the defenders led by a spineless monarch, and battle ensued.

The attack on the land-walls went badly. Though the crusader army tried to scale the walls, they were quickly repelled by the Byzantine defenders. The crusader army simply did not have the numbers to make an impression.

It went better by the seawall in the Golden Horn though. Despite initial setbacks, the Venetians eventually managed to get close enough to the walls with their tall ships to drop the improvised landing bridges from the masts, resulting in, mainly Venetian, soldiers running directly onto the top of the seawalls. The ill organised defenders gave way, and the attackers started to occupy the towers along the wall. When they penetrated into the city, fighting broke out between the tightly packed, wooden, buildings and a fire broke out. It spread with explosive speed and soon made fighting impossible. The Venetians withdrew to their newly conquered seawall and the defenders withdrew back towards the city centre and the land-wall, the by now massive and out-of-control fire separating the two sides.

With the city on fire and the enemy within the gates, Emperor Alexios III Angelos finally snapped out of his inactivity and decided to confront the crusader army in front of the land-wall. He assembled his considerable army and marched out to meet the enemy.

Lined up in front of each other, the Byzantine army, 30,000 strong, vastly outnumbered the crusader army of perhaps 10,000. The crusader army had the Golden Horn behind them and the land-walls on their left flank, left with nowhere to run.

The crusader commanders ordered as slow tactical withdrawal towards the Golden Horn, but the desperate soldiers refused to follow orders and instead started to advance on the enemy. Once again, an experienced and warlike commander of the Byzantine army would have seen the enemy's ranks breaking up and would have started an all-out, and no doubt decisive, attack, but Alexios III Angelos simply turned the Byzantine army around and marched it back inside the protective walls.

That night, realizing that all was lost, Emperor Alexios III Angelos gathered as much gold as he could lay his hands on and disappeared into the night, leaving the Byzantine Empire without an emperor, the capital city burning and the enemy both at, and inside, the gates.

The population, woke up to a sudden power vacuum, and they reacted by releasing the absconded Emperor's (blinded) brother, the former emperor and the father of Alexius Angelus, Isaac II Angelos and reinstating him to the throne of Byzantium.

Messages were sent to the crusaders and a meeting was arranged. The crusaders outlined the promises they had been given to the new Emperor, who first bluntly told them it was impossible. The Empire simply did not have the funds, and the population was likely to riot in case the Church reverted to the Catholic denomination. However, after some time arguing the case, Emperor Isaac II Angelos realized that he had no option but to agree, so oaths were taken and a charter signed, now making the deal between the Venetians, the crusader army and the Byzantine Empire final and legal. Another condition was added, namely that his son Alexius Angelus would be crowned as co-emperor, so a ceremony took place on 1 August 1203 in Hagia Sophia, making him Alexius IV Angelus.

It seemed as if the Fourth Crusade had finally turned its bad fate around. The army was withdrawn to the area north of the Golden Horn, where it was well supplied, and the soldiers were free to move around the city. The Venetians were paid all their back-payments (now amounting to 86,000 Marks) and the crusader army was also given money so they could catch up with back payments of the troops. Messages were sent to the Pope, confirming his new authority over the Byzantines, with the implied expectation that he would now withdraw the previous excommunication of the crusader army before it was even made known to the troops.

But alas, the situation was not as good as it seemed. Alexius IV Angelus, with no support from his father, was fighting a desperate battle to keep his promises. Out of gold, he started to melt down the city's treasures. Churches were plundered and monuments melted down. Finally, he tried to win some time by offering the crusaders to stay till March 1204, rather than leaving in September 1203, with an additional prize of 100,000 Marks for the Venetians and all expenses paid for the crusader army. There was some mumbling, but eventually the deal was agreed.

However, there was ever deepening tension between the, predominantly Greek, population of Constantinople and the, predominantly French, crusaders. A skirmish broke out late August, resulting in a new fire, this time covering nearly 1/4 of the city, creating an enormous, charred scar, dividing the city into two. The crusaders withdrew to their camp outside the city, the Venetians hauled up their ships for maintenance, and the locals did their best to patch up their city, while the newly appointed (co-) emperor Alexius IV Angelus went on an expedition to regain control of some of the areas outside the city of Constantinople itself.

This lull lasted till November 1203, when Alexius IV Angelus returned to the city. He had completed a very successful expedition, had secured support from cities various in Rumelia and had taken the opportunity to take all their gold.

Where Alexius IV Angelus had left the city as a somewhat insecure co-emperor, he returned with the mindset of a confident ruler. His father was put aside from government, all but in name, and his attitude towards the crusaders, camped across the Golden Horn, had cooled considerably now that he felt he could rely more on the support of his own populace. Whereas he continued to send food, he hesitated and eventually completely stopped sending cash.

The increasingly hostile population of Constantinople supported this move, they had come to the stage where they would see the crusaders leave sooner rather than later, but the Venetians, in particular, were not happy. Discussions were had, embassies sent and ultimately Alexius IV Angelus met with the aging and blind Venetian Doge Enrico Dandolo. The meeting took place with Enrico Dandolo sitting in a boat in the Golden Horn and the Emperor standing on the beach. After an exchange it which it became clear that Alexius IV Angelus had no intentions of paying the Venetians anything any time soon, Dandolo called him amongst other things a *'Contemptible boy'* and told him that *'We hauled you out of the dung heap, and we will drop you back in it'*.

This diplomatic breakdown started a range of violent confrontations around the Golden Horn, mostly brawling with no clear advantage won by either side apart from an opportunity to vent some frustration.

The Byzantines were, however, becoming better organized. What started as rabble had turned into a well organised 'resistance movement' and they clearly realized that the strength of the crusaders was their ships. Without ships they would be stuck across the Golden Horn, with no way out except by the grace of the Byzantines. Consequently, the Greeks tried to burn the Venetians ships twice, both times using fireships sent across the Golden Horn when the wind was favourable, and both times only narrowly avoided through quick acting Venetian sailors.

The skirmishes continued into the early weeks of 1204, both opposing parties launching attacks, the crusaders using fire as a means to their ends, leaving even larger parts of the city as burnt-out ruins. The Emperor kept melting down more and more of the public monuments and collected more and more taxes, but he did not organize a concerted military response to the Latin attacks, still holding the door open in case he would need to once again rely on the crusaders for support.

Towards the end of January, the situation became too heated to contain. The Byzantine population gathered in Hagia Sophia where they demanded from the nobility that a new emperor be appointed. With no candidates coming forth for this rather doomed position, the mob selected their own candidate; a young nobleman named Nicholas Kannavos, and appointed him emperor.

Alexius IV Angelus' response to this was to once again call on the crusaders, but his 'unpatriotic' conversations were witnessed by an ambitious nobleman and courtier, Alexios Doukas, nicknamed "Mourtzouphlos" who seized the moment.

On 27th January, Mourtzouphlos roused the Emperor, under threat of a palace revolt, to follow him into 'safety' in the middle of the night, only for Alexius IV Angelus to be chained and thrown in jail. The following morning Mourtzouphlos emerged in the Palace in full imperial regalia, supported by the army and the Varangian Guard. In two weeks Byzantium had gone from uneasy co-regency between father and son to no less than four emperors; one in jail, one blind and quickly aging, one appointed by the people and contained in Hagia Sophia and one sitting in the Blachernae Palace with the apparent support of the army. That situation would not last long.

On 2 February Mourtzouphlos had the Varangian Guard storm Hagia Sophia, were the population did not put up a fight when their 'emperor' was apprehended and decapitated. On 5th February 1404, Mourtzouphlos had himself declared emperor as Alexios V Doukas. Sometime in between, the aging Isaac II Angelos had 'conveniently' died, from age, grief or, very likely, poison.

With a populist agenda, including the return to the Orthodox rite, Mourtzouphlos now broke the last links with the crusaders. He stopped the food supply, forcing the crusaders to organize foraging expeditions as far away as the coast of the Black Sea. During one such expedition, on 6 February, Mourtzouphlos ambushed the crusaders, but he was beaten back and his banner, and a holy relic of the Virgin taken and subsequently mockingly shown to the people of Constantinople by the crusaders.

On 7 February there were negotiations, and the crusaders demanded that Mourtzouphlos should step down and reinstate Alexius IV Angelus, as well as the Byzantines should pay huge reparations and submit to the Pope's authority.

Mourtzouphlos reacted by having Alexius IV Angelus murdered the following day. This was quickly followed by an honourable state-funeral, though nobody inside or outside the city had any doubts as to who was responsible for Alexius IV Angelus' death.

Having dealt with the last obvious threat to his rule, Mourtzouphlos escalated the stakes by telling the crusaders that they needed to vacate his land or they would be killed. This ultimatum removed any remaining illusion that there was a deal still to be had, and it left the crusaders with range of unattractive options.

They could simply turn around and go home, but the shame on the crusaders and the financial losses to the Venetians, not to mention the fact that technically they had been excommunicated by the Pope, made it a non-option. They could attempt to go to the Holy Land as originally planned, but in reality, this was not an option either as they had no resources with which to supply and pay for the expedition. The last and only viable option was to storm Constantinople and take what they had been promised.

There were all kind of moral issues connected to this choice, but the crusader clerics were consulted and concluded that since Constantinople had, briefly, been put back under the control of the papacy, and had now in a deliberate act once again refused the 'true faith' and returned to the Orthodox rites, the city was, technically, an enemy of the Church. Thin as it was, the argument was enough to convince the crusaders that, even though Constantinople was not Jerusalem, it was as good an alternative as could be found.

For all intents and purposes, it was the same battle that had already been fought the year before, which now was to be fought again. Both sides thus knew what to expect and they both made improvements to suit their respective needs. The Venetians installed nets on their ships to catch missiles from catapults and drew vinegar covered hides over the hulls to prevent fire. The Byzantines had high wooden stockades, gradually leaning outwards installed on top of the dangerously low seawalls and gateways bricked up to isolate the various sections of the seawalls and contain a breach.

While preparations went on during March 1204, the crusaders sat down to agree what would happen after they took the city. In outline they agreed that the Venetians would have all the booty until all debts, presently amounting to 150,000 Marks had been paid, after which the spoils would be evenly shared. A committee of six Venetians and six crusaders would appoint a new emperor, and the crusader army would stay in Constantinople for a year to secure the new rule. Furthermore, it was agreed that the new regime would not allow trade with anyone who was at war with Venice, securing an immensely profitable de-facto monopoly for Venetian trade in and out of Constantinople.

On 8 April 1204, the Latins attacked. Contrary to emperor Alexios III Angelos, responsible for the lacklustre defence the previous year, Mourtzouphlos understood that this was a battle for life or death, so he had organised the defence as well as possible and personally commanded the Byzantines from a vantage point on the highest hill in Constantinople.

The attack was, as expected, similar to before, but with an organized defence and winds from the south that kept blowing the crusader-ships away from the walls, ultimately the attack had to be stopped, and the crusaders withdrawn.

The crusaders now prepared for one last attempt. They tied their ships together two-by-two, so they could attack two towers at the same time. They also boosted the morale of the troops by a big mass in which the clergy had further developed the moral high-ground by declaring that because the Byzantines had murdered their own lord (Alexius IV Angelus) they were in fact worse than the Jews, indeed they were enemies of the Lord God. In a few weeks the theologians had turned an ally into first the equivalent of Jerusalem and now to the enemies of the Lord God himself.

With the improved tactics and the new boost to morale the crusaders attacked again on 12 April. The new tactics of tying the ships together turned out to be successful as, combined with a shift in the wind to drive the ships closer to the wall; it enabled several towers to be taken, even though they only made up isolated enclaves. They did however enable the attackers to raise their banners on the contested towers, further driving their compatriots on.

A small group of crusaders made it to the foot of one of the walls, under constant barrage of stones and other missiles, and discovered a bricked-up door. Breaking it down, they managed to make a hole big enough for a man to get through and once the first man was through, the enemy waiting inside simply panicked and ran, allowing for a steady stream of crusaders to enter through the opening.

The Emperor himself launched a counterattack but basically had to stop when he realized that he was alone! Soon the crusaders had control of a large section of the seawall and opened the gates to allow further troops, now on horseback, into the city.

The Byzantines fought the intruders house by house, street by street and eventually the attackers decided to start yet another fire to drive the defenders back. With the crusaders settling on the beaches and inside the seawall and the Byzantines leaving the city by the tens of thousands through the land-wall, 12 April ended with, once again, the enemy inside the walls and the contestants separated by fire.

During the night Emperor Mourtzouphlos tried to regroup the defenders, but he ultimately had to realize that the city was lost and fled on a fishing boat. He eventually sought refuge with the previous emperor Alexios III Angelos, who himself had fled the city under similar circumstances the year before.

On the morning of 13th April, what remained of the Byzantine nobility met in Hagia Sophia and appointed a new emperor, a nobleman named Constantine Lascaris. He refused to wear the imperial robes, in order to secure his eventual escape, left Hagia Sophia, addressed the population with an urge to take up arms, realized it was futile and fled by boat to Anatolia within hours of his appointment.

What remained of the nobles in Constantinople now decided that instead of appointing a new emperor from their own ranks, they might as well pre-empt the inevitable and appoint someone from the crusader-army. Their choice fell on Boniface of Montferrat, of whom they had seen the most during past negotiations with the invaders.

Subsequently they gathered a parade of nobles, citizens, and Varangian Guards, fully equipped with icons and holy relics, which would traditionally greet a new emperor, and marched down to the invaders at the seawall.

The crusaders, preparing for another day of hard-fought street-by-street battle could not believe their eyes, or the situation, and reluctantly started to follow the procession back towards the centre of the city and Hagia Sophia.

Instead of armed resistance, the population was lining the streets, hailing the new emperor as was tradition, but the crusaders were so mentally prepared for war, that they simply could not readily adapt to this new and unexpected situation.

The soldiers started to help themselves to food and goods from traders and soon the situation developed from a peaceful procession to theft and plunder and then, like a wildfire, to full scale sacking of the city.

Murder, mayhem, rape and plunder engulfed the city. The population could not put up any kind of organized defence, so the crusaders had a free hand.

Holy relics were broken into pieces; precious stones were rudely cut from their settings. Anything made of valuable metals were chopped up into carry-size pieces. When the supply of the most obviously valuable items ran out, anything made of bronze or copper was pried free and cut up for later smelting down as ore or coinage.

Churches, public buildings, and private homes were looted and the defenceless population terrorized and murdered. The crusaders had been told by their own prelates that the population of Constantinople was the enemies of the Lord God, so they were treated accordingly.

Apart from securing some of the most valuable treasure for themselves, the crusader leaders were in no position to stop the soldiers in their lust for blood and booty and in just five days the pride of Christianity, the city that was the rightful heir to the Roman Empire was reduced to burning rubble, stripped of all its treasure, much of which predated the city itself.

Once things calmed down, the crusader leaders managed to restore some central control, mainly for the purpose of securing as much booty as possible was collected centrally so it could be distributed according to their own pre-arranged scheme. The Venetians got their 150,000 Marks and another 100,000 Marks was made available for distribution between the Venetians and the crusaders. It is estimated that booty worth 600,000 Marks simply 'disappeared' as private booty.

Of course, the Byzantines' election of Boniface of Montferrat as emperor was ignored, and instead the agreed upon committee was formed to elect a new emperor. Though Boniface of Montferrat was a candidate, the Venetians vetoed his appointment as, as an Italian, he was perceived to have too close ties to some of Venice's enemies and competitors. With the Venetian Doge being out of the competition due to his old age and frail constitution, the final choice was the other crusader leader Baldwin of Flanders.

Baldwin was, however, not appointed as Emperor of Byzantium. Instead it was decided to create a fresh start with a new empire named the Latin Empire of Constantinople, so on 16th May 1204 Baldwin was crowned, in Hagia Sophia, as Baldwin I of Constantinople.

Large parts of the Byzantine Empire were now split between various factions. Boniface of Montferrat established himself as King Boniface I of the Kingdom of Thessalonica, controlling the north-eastern side of the Greek peninsula, though nominally under the suzerainty of Emperor Baldwin I. Other exotic nation states emerged in the Greek hinterlands and on the islands of the Aegean Sea in the ensuing 'free-for-all'; the Megaskyrate of Athens and Thebes, the Triarchy of Euboea, the Principality of Morea, the Marquisates of Boudonitza and Salona to mention some, but before the spoils were divided between crusaders, opportunistic adventurers and pirates, the Venetians had their pick.

As we shall see further in Chapter 10, the Venetians had interest not in land but in seaports, so they secured for themselves the Island of Crete (which they formally bought from Boniface of Montferrat), and the (port) cities of Hellespont, Modon and Coron on the Greek coast in addition to a string of smaller island that made up strategic waypoints on the trade routes between the East and the West. Furthermore, they were granted three eights of Constantinople itself, including the natural harbour of the Golden Horn.

The Venetians had thus become the real winners of the Fourth Crusade, now effectively and exclusively controlling the sea-ways, and thus the trade, of the eastern Mediterranean Sea and the access to the Black Sea.

Despite the loss of Constantinople and most of the areas in Europe, the Byzantine Empire had, however, not completely disappeared.

Though the small Byzantine province of Trebizond on the Black Sea coast in north-eastern Anatolia had nominally broken free of The Byzantine

Empire a few weeks before the final fall of Constantinople, and had morphed into the Empire of Trebizond (as per Chapter 8), the Despotate of Epirus, covering the western side of the Greek peninsula remained under Greek control.

The last, in desperation, appointed Byzantine Emperor, Constantine Lascaris, had fled Constantinople on the verge of the city's fall and after only a few hours as emperor. He settled in the city of Nicaea in north-western Anatolia, as did his brother Theodore Lascaris and eventually such other remains of the Byzantine nobility and army that had made it out of Constantinople.

Constantine Lascaris had had enough of being emperor, but his brother, Theodore became the de-facto leader of what remained of devastated Byzantine Empire. He did, however, nor immediately become emperor, as there were contenders to the throne in the form of David Komnenos in Trebizond and Manuel Maurozomes, a Byzantine nobleman who had set himself up in the neighboring province in Anatolia. With the Latins busy fighting the Bulgarians for dominance of Greece and the Balkans (the new emperor Baldwin I being killed in battle in 1205 and Boniface I befalling the same fate in 1207) and the Seljuk Turks in disarray, Theodore took what remained of the Byzantine army and defeated both his competitors and what little Latin resistance was at hand to carve out the Empire of Nicaea, of which he was crowned emperor, as Theodore I, in 1208 by the new - appointed by himself - Patriarch of the Orthodox Church.

In the following years, Theodore I fought off further pressure from both the Latin states and the Seljuk Sultanate of Rum (the latter having allied themselves with the former emperor Alexios III Angelos) consolidating his new empire which started in the north by the Black Sea and wound its way southwest through Anatolia, ending at the coast between Smyrna and Halicarnassus on the west coast. Compared to the former glory of the Byzantine Empire it was not much, but it was a lifeline and it would prove to be enough to keep the Empire alive for another 250 years.

Theodore I married his daughter Irene Laskarina to one of his successful generals, John Doukas Vatatzes, and made him his appointed successor and on Theodore I's death in 1221. John became emperor John III Doukas Vatatzes.

Theodore I's family did not like the way John III had been chosen over Theodore I's immediate family, so a small revolt broke out, but it was quickly suppressed and John III began a reign that would last for more than three decades and would be instrumental in the resurrection of the Byzantine Empire.

As it turned out Theodore I had chosen his successor well. John III understood both warfare and diplomacy, and he effectively worked his way into every crack and weak spot in his enemies' defences.

The Latin Empire of Constantinople had supported the Lascaris family in their revolt against John III, and following John III's victory had to concede territory to him in Anatolia. Sensing they were weak, John III moved on Europe, where he initially conquered Adrianople, though he had to concede the city to Theodore Komnenos Doukas, the ruler of the Epirus, who in the meantime had overrun and annexed the Kingdom of Thessalonica, originally formed by Boniface I in the aftermath of the Fourth Crusade. Only some twenty years after the fall of Constantinople, the heirs to the Byzantine Empire, though disunited, once again were in control of western Anatolia and most of Greece.

A few years later Theodore Komnenos Doukas was captured by the Bulgarians, removing the most immediate competition to John III in Greece and he made an alliance with the Bulgarians against the Latin Empire of Constantinople.

The alliance was cemented by the marriage between John III's son (the later Theodore II Laskaris) and Elena, a daughter of Ivan Asen II, the ruler of Bulgaria.

Taking the opportunity of Ivan Asen II's death in 1241 to take over the Bulgarian's possessions in Greece, John III maintained pressure on the Latin Empire of Constantinople and the Empire of Epirus. In 1246 John III conquered Thessaloniki and in 1248 he nominally gained control over Epirus, though effective control would elude him.

Though the heirs to the Byzantine Empire were still united in name only and were yet to finally fight it out between themselves for final supremacy, they had now effectively isolated Constantinople to the city itself and its immediate surroundings, s situation which would repeat itself 200 years later.

On John III's death in 1254 his son Theodore II Laskaris was appointed emperor (though he was only nominally crowned in 1255). Theodore II Laskaris had to fight the Bulgarians for his possessions in Greece, but successfully fought them off and further consolidated the Nicaean possessions in Europe. Theodore II Laskaris (like his father) had epilepsy and died from a stroke on 16 August 1258, leaving behind as heir his, only seven-year-old, son; John IV Laskaris.

Due to John IV Laskaris' status as a minor a regent was appointed. Apart from nominal participation of the Patriarch it fell to George Mouzalon an autocrat of humble origins elevated to high office by Theodore II Laskaris.

The nobles did not like Theodore II Laskaris's elevation of George Mouzalon and other civil servants of modest origins, so they staged a palace coup headed by one of their own; Michael Palaiologos.

On 25th August George Mouzalon was assassinated and Michael Palaiologos appointed as regent. By November he was appointed despot and by 1 January 1259 as co-emperor Michael VIII Palaiologos. Effectively this ended the Lascaris dynasty and started the Palaiologos dynasty which would last till the final death of the Byzantine Empire 200 years later.

Michael VIII Palaiologos was ambitious, not only personally, but also on behalf of his country. He felt the time was right to re-establish the Byzantine Empire and he started warfare in Europe.

He once again confronted the troublesome Empire of Epirus, which had rebelled since its submission to Nicaean supremacy in 1248. The Nicaeans were initially successful, forcing the ruler of Epirus to flee, but he was soon back with support from an Italian mercenary army and pushed the Nicaeans back.

Even though the campaign against Epirus had not been entirely successful, Michael VIII Palaiologos decided it was time to start making a move on Constantinople. He concluded an alliance with Genoa, fierce rivals to Venice, according to which the Genoese would supply a small fleet with which to attack Constantinople from the sea in support of a land-attack.

In July 1261 he sent a small expeditionary force of 800 men, under command of his general Alexios Strategopoulos, to sniff around Constantinople and spy on the city's defences.

Through locals, Alexios Strategopoulos gained intelligence that the Latin army and the Venetian fleet had left the city to strike at the island of Kefken, a Nicaean possession off the Black Sea coast.

Hardly believing his luck and well aware of the risk should the intelligence be false or the Latin army return, on the evening of 25 July Alexios Strategopoulos moved his small force closer to the land-walls of Constantinople, hiding in a monastery close to the Selymbria Gate.

The following day a small band of his soldiers passed through the walls by means of a secret passage pointed out by the locals and managed to open the gates. The Nicaeans risked everything and stormed in. Though the guards put up some token resistance, they were so taken by surprise that the invaders soon found themselves in control of the land-wall. The situation was a complete reverse of the collapse of the Byzantine defense against the crusaders in 1204, where the breakthrough of a small force had sent the defenders into a state of panic that led to the loss of the city.

Rumors soon reverberated through the city that it had been invaded and panic spread. Even the Emperor, Baldwin II, literally caught napping, believed the rumors and fled to the harbor. As it happened, the Venetian fleet returned just in time, but with the city in a state of panic all they could do was to load as many panic-stricken citizens as possible (including the Emperor and the nobility) and take them to safety.

Practically without a fight, Constantinople was back in the hands of the Greeks, and on 25 August 1261 Michael VIII Palaiologos entered through the Golden Gate to have himself crowned as Emperor of Byzantium.

To secure his position he had eleven-year-old John IV Laskaris, left behind in Nicaea, blinded and his own infant son, Andronikos Palaiologos, appointed nominal co-regent. John IV Laskaris was later placed in a monastery to live out his life as monk until his death in 1305.

The city that Michael VIII Palaiologos took over was a mere shadow of its former glory. The population, estimated to at least 400,000 at the time of the Fourth Crusade was reduced to some 35,000. Little had been done to rebuild the city, ravaged by fire and looting. The impressively sounding Latin Empire of Constantinople really was little but a puppet regime serving the Venetians. The Venetians in turn were only interested in the safe harbour of the Golden Horn and enough supplies to keep their fleet operational, so they had little interest in spending any money on rebuilding the city.

Michael VIII Palaiologos started a repopulation program which gradually built the population up to around 70,000, a level it never managed to go above in the remaining time of the Byzantine Empire. He also did his best to rebuild the damaged city, spending as much money as could be found on restoring as much as the former glory as was possible. Churches were rebuilt, public buildings likewise and the growing population was set to clean up the mess that was left from nearly six decades of neglect.

Politically Michael VIII Palaiologos had ambitions over and above Constantinople. Though the city was immensely important in terms of the legitimacy of his reign as emperor (the ruler of Epirus had in 1227 declared himself Emperor of Byzantium, but without Constantinople had not been recognized as such by anyone) it only constituted a small part of the former empire which had been cut to pieces following the Fourth Crusade.

Though Epirus had nominally been under Nicaean suzerainty since 1248, and thus should make up a part of the re-established Byzantine Empire, in reality it had long since revolted. They were to be brought back into the fold, but first Michael VIII Palaiologos had his eyes on the southernmost part of the Greece, the peninsula of Peloponnese, or Morea as it was known at the time.

The peninsula had been turned into a Latin state, under the name of the Principality of Morea following the Fourth Crusade. Having flourished during the first half of the thirteenth century, it had become involved in the ongoing conflicts between Nicaea and Epirus, eventually leading to the capture of its prince, William II of Villehardouin, by the Nicaeans.

After the Nicaeans capture of Constantinople and the resurrection of the Byzantine Empire, William II of Villehardouin officially recognized emperor Michael VIII Palaiologos as overlord, and so was released and returned to Morea as Byzantine governor.

Once back in the Morea, and its capital city of Mistra, he met up with Baldwin II of Constantinople, recently himself ousted by Michael VIII Palaiologos. They decided to rebel, and Michael VIII Palaiologos sent an army against them.

Twice, in 1263 and 1274, did the Moreans hold out against the armies of Byzantium but out of resources to fight another battle they declared themselves under the lordship of Charles I of Naples, who in the meantime had conquered the Kingdom of Sicily. Byzantine ambitions on the Morea

3 - Birth, Decline, Crusades and Reconquest

had to be put on hold, though the Byzantines from now on held the eastern part of the peninsula as the Despotate of Morea.

This was not Michael VIII Palaiologos' only military defeat; indeed he had little luck in matters military following his incredible luck in the reconquest of Constantinople.

His armies were defeated in 1275 when attacking the west coast of Greece, though his new navy, consisting of 80 ships, was successful. He was also defeated later in the 1470s when he tried to take advantage of a power vacuum in Bulgaria.

He was more successful as a diplomat, although one big diplomatic move was very badly received at home.

Michael VIII Palaiologos' great fear was that the Pope would support moves to re-establish the lost Latin states. Isolated former rulers were bad enough on their own, as was the case in the Morea, but unified and with papal blessing they would be potentially lethal. If you cannot beat them join them so Michael VIII Palaiologos decided to offer the Pope what he wanted the most, reunion between the Western and Eastern Churches.

The details were hammered out in Lyon in 1274 and were met with violent opposition at home and never implemented in practice, but it kept the Pope placated for now.

His diplomatic masterpiece was, however, his involvement in 'the Sicilian Vespers'.

In short; Charles I of Naples, King of Naples, Sicily and overlord of the Principality of Morea (the eastern part of the peninsula) had ambitions to re-establish the Latin states on his own and with himself as emperor. Controlling most of Italy now with a foothold in Greece, he was dangerous, probably the only really dangerous Latin force threatening the Byzantine Empire.

Though the Byzantine Empire did not have the resources to meet Charles I of Naples in battle, Michael VIII Palaiologos instead played his enemies.

Through his wife's dynastic claim, Peter III of Aragon contested Charles I' of Naples's rule in Sicily and when a revolt broke out in Sicily around Easter of 1282, Peter III was considering his options. He was however, soon convinced to intervene, when he was promised no less than 60,000 Gold Ducats by Michael VIII Palaiologos to cover his expenses. Peter III of Aragon invaded, took Sicily for himself and killed off Charles I of Naples' plans for a resurrection of the Latin states.

As much of a diplomatic victory as this was for Michael VIII Palaiologos - who in his memoires wrote *'Should I dare to claim that I was God's instrument to bring freedom to the Sicilians, then I should only be stating the truth'* - it came at significant long-term cost to the Byzantine Empire. To pay for this and the consolidation of his European defences in general, Michael VIII Palaiologos started to scale down the army in Anatolia, reduce their pay and increase their taxes. Though the effect was not immediate, he effectively started leaving the back-door open for the Turcoman tribes of western Anatolia.

At the end of 1282 Michael VIII Palaiologos died and the throne went to his son (and for the last ten years his co-regent), Andronikos II Palaiologos.

3 - Birth, Decline, Crusades and Reconquest

Part 2 - The Byzantine Empire

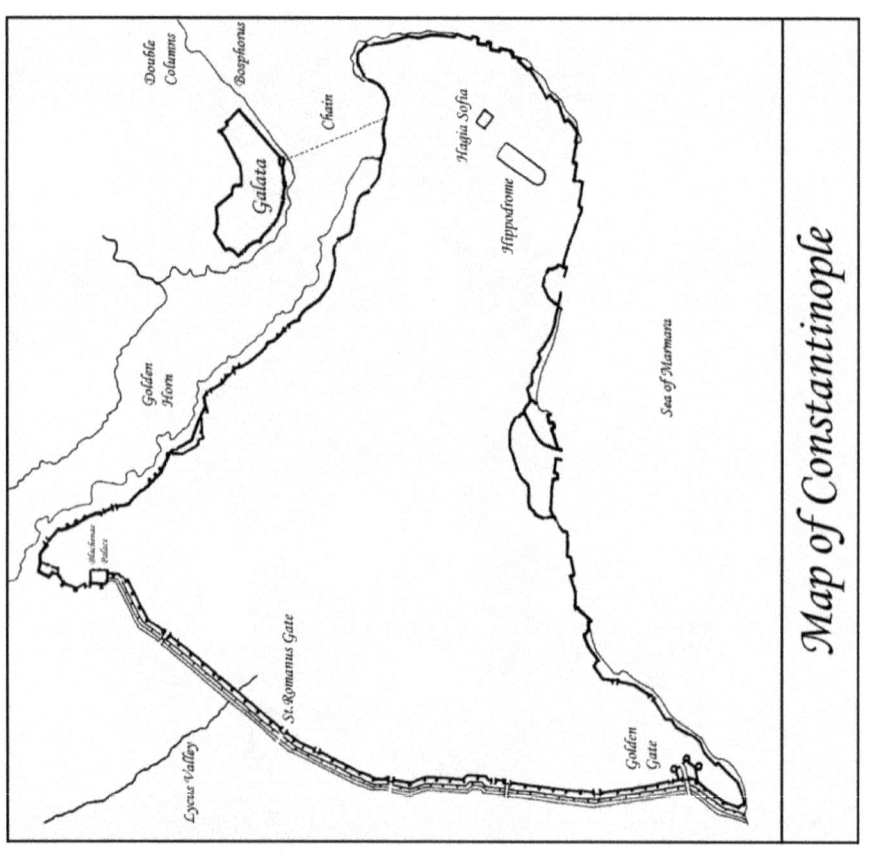

4 - DEADLY NEIGHBORS

CRITICAL TIMELINE

Year	Event	Involved Parties
1282	Andronikos II Palaiologos becomes Emperor of Byzantium	Byzantium
1285	Dismantling of the Byzantine fleet	Byzantium
1302	Defeat to the Ottomans outside Nicomedia	Byzantium Ottomans
1304	Catalan mercenaries defeat Ottomans at Philadelphia	Byzantium Ottomans
1326	Bursa falls to the Ottomans	Byzantium Ottomans
1328	Andronikos III Palaiologos becomes Emperor of Byzantium	Byzantium
1329	Battle of Pelekanon	Byzantium Ottomans
1331	Ottoman annexation of Nicaea	Byzantium Ottomans
1337	Ottoman annexation of Nicomedia	Byzantine Ottomans
1337	Byzantine control of Epirus	Byzantium Empire of Epirus
1341	John V Palaiologos becomes Emperor of Byzantium	Byzantium
1342	Civil war in Byzantium	Byzantium
1348	John VI Kantakouzenos becomes co-Emperor of Byzantium (end of civil war)	Byzantium
1352	Civil war in Byzantium Ottoman mercenaries are given quarters at Çimpe.	Byzantium Ottomans
1354	John V Palaiologos becomes Emperor of Byzantium (end of civil war)	Byzantium
1354	Ottoman mercenaries re-populate and rebuild town of Gallipoli after earthquake	Byzantium Ottomans
1365	Ottoman conquest of Adrianople (Edirne)	Byzantium Ottomans
1369	Emperor John V Palaiologos is held at Venice	Byzantium Venetians
1371	Byzantium agrees to pay annual tribute to expanding Ottoman Empire	Byzantium Ottomans
1386	Murad I becomes 'Sultan'	Ottomans
1389	First Battle of Kosovo. Bayezid I becomes Ottoman Sultan	Ottomans Serbia
1390	Ottoman annexation of Philadelphia	Byzantium Ottomans
1391	Manuel II Palaiologos becomes Emperor of Byzantium	Byzantium
1394	Ottoman siege of Constantinople	Byzantium Ottomans

Year	Event	Involved Parties
1396	Battle of Nicopolis	Ottomans Bulgaria Hungary Venice
1399	Emperor Manuel II Palaiologos travels through Europe support	Byzantium
1402	Battle of Ankara. Start of Ottoman Interregnum	Ottomans Timurids
1403	Emperor Manuel II Palaiologos returns to Constantinople	Byzantium
1403	Byzantium supports Suleiman in Ottoman war of succession	Byzantium Ottomans
1411	Musa defeats Suleiman and besiege Constantinople	Byzantium Ottomans
1412	Mehmed I defends Constantinople and defeats Musa	Byzantium Ottomans
1413	Mehmed I becomes Ottoman Sultan and ends Ottoman Interregnum	Ottomans
1415	Rebuilding of the Hexamilion Wall	Byzantium
1421	Murad II becomes Ottoman Sultan	Ottomans
1421	Byzantium supports Mustafa against Murad II	Byzantium Ottomans
1422	Ottoman siege of Constantinople and Thessaloniki	Byzantium Ottomans
1423	Thessaloniki ceded to Venice	Byzantium Venice
1424	Byzantines renew annual tribute to Ottomans	Byzantium Ottomans
1425	John VIII Palaiologos becomes Emperor of Byzantium	Byzantium
1430	Byzantium takes full control of Morea	Byzantium
1430	The Ottomans conquer Thessaloniki	Ottomans Venice
1437	Emperor John VIII Palaiologos goes to Rome	Byzantium The Pope
1439	The Christian Churches are (nominally) reunited	Byzantium The Pope
1440	King Wladyslaw III of Poland becomes King of Hungary	Hungary Poland
1443	The Long Campaign	The Pope Hungary Poland Serbia Wallachia Venice Ottomans

Part 2 - The Byzantine Empire

Year	Event	Involved Parties
1444	Battle of Varna	The Pope Hungary Poland Ottomans
1446	Ottoman suppression of Morea	Byzantium Ottomans Despotate of Morea
1448	Second Battle of Kosovo	Ottomans Hungary Wallachia
1448	Constantine XI Palaiologos becomes Emperor of Constantinople	Byzantium
1451	Start of Sultan Mehmed II's reign	Ottomans
1452	Ottomans build the Boğaz Kesen castle	Ottomans Byzantium
1453	Conquest of Constantinople	Byzantium Ottomans
1461	Final Ottoman annexation of Morea	Ottomans Despotate of Morea

4 - Deadly Neighbours

The Byzantine Empire inherited by Andronikos II Palaiologos in 1282 was not in a good state. Admittedly, having an empire to inherit in the first place was just short of a miracle, but the Empire was for all intents and purposes bankrupt.

The unsuccessful military campaigns of his father, the heavy investment in fortification in Europe and the large sum of money invested in the Sicilian Vespers had left the coffers of the Empire empty.

To restore some order taxes were increased, former tax exemptions removed and the new Byzantine fleet, built at great expense by his father was dismantled. His father had long since re-engaged with Venice, whose loyalty was to profit, not to who happened to be residing in Constantinople, so Andronikos II Palaiologos, by dismantling his fleet now became dependent on Venice and Genoa for protection of its maritime interests, just the way Byzantium had depended on the Italians in the decades leading up to the Fourth Crusade.

None of this was popular, austerity seldom is, but Andronikos II Palaiologos had an ace up his sleeve with which to placate the population; he once again officially broke with the Catholic Church and reinstituted the Orthodox Church.

Being a diplomat rather than a warrior, Andronikos II Palaiologos entered into a range of dynastic inter-marriages involving both himself and his children. Through a cabal of alliances cemented by marriages, he effectively removed the remaining threats to his empire from Europe, but like his father before him, his focus on Europe meant that his borders in Anatolia became increasingly fragile and finally collapsed.

As covered in Parts 1 and 3, Turcoman tribes on the western frontier of the crumbling Seljuk Sultanate of Rum had established their own beyliks towards the end of the thirteenth century, and in western Anatolia the Osmanli, or Ottomans, had emerged as the strongest and dominant force.

Led by Osman, the Ottoman expansion eventually brought them into contact with the Byzantine possessions in western Anatolia, resulting in skirmishes and sieges.

Due to the cost-cutting started by Michael VIII Palaiologos and continued by his son, Andronikos II Palaiologos, the Byzantine army in Anatolia was weak and could not stand against the Ottomans, who gradually annexed larger and larger parts of Byzantine territory, forcing scores of Byzantine refugees west and eventually across the straits to safety in Constantinople.

By 1294, the Emperor's oldest son had been crowned co-regent under the name Michael IX Palaiologos and in 1302 he led a campaign into Anatolia to teach the Ottomans a lesson. His army significantly outnumbered the Ottoman army, so the Ottoman avoided direct battle, instead harassing the Byzantines and continuing their raids on Byzantine lands, to which a large army could not move fast enough to react. Eventually the Byzantine army was dissolved, and Michael IX Palaiologos made his way home.

Before Michael IX Palaiologos reached Constantinople, his father Andronikos II Palaiologos had sent a significantly smaller replacement army to Anatolia, with the specific task of protecting the city of Nicomedia. The Ottomans were happy to give battle to this smaller force and - led by Osman himself - beat it soundly outside Nicomedia on 27 July 1302.

The Byzantines next hired a Catalan band of mercenaries which, under the nominal command of Michael IX Palaiologos, beat an Ottoman army outside of Philadelphia (modern day Alaşehir), but the victory was not instrumental in removing the Ottoman threat and gradually they absorbed the Byzantine territories. By 1326 they had secured Bursa and by the late 1320s they stood on the coast of the Sea of Marmara from where they could see Constantinople itself.

In the meantime, the Byzantine Empire had fallen back on its old habits, internal strife and civil war.

Michael IX Palaiologos' son, Andronikos Palaiologos (born 1297), the de-facto heir to the throne was a wild youth, surrounding himself with likewise sons of the aristocracy. By accident he caused the death of his brother Manuel in 1320, which caused his father to step down from the throne and soon thereafter die.

Emperor Andronikos II Palaiologos did not look upon his grandson's actions with favour. Indeed, he disowned him, and Andronikos Palaiologos fled the city. As he was popular with the young nobility, he gathered support and started a revolt. First he managed to be accepted back as co-emperor, and finally he forced his grandfather, Andronikos II Palaiologos, to step down and leave the throne to him as Andronikos III Palaiologos.

After unsuccessful military adventures in Bulgaria, Andronikos III Palaiologos, who enjoyed hunting and warfare and left administrative matters to his grand domestic John Kantakouzenos, decided that it was time to go and face the Ottomans, now threatening the last remaining Byzantine possessions in Anatolia; the port-towns of Nicaea and Nicomedia.

The largest army he could raise was 4,000 men strong and it was a trivial matter for the Ottoman army to send them packing after a short skirmish outside Nicomedia in June 1329 (known as the Battle of Pelekanon). The army had to retreat back to Constantinople and this was the last Byzantine military expedition into Anatolia. The Ottomans now had a free hand and by 1337 they had annexed Nicaea (the cradle of the re-birth of the Byzantine Empire) and Nicomedia. With the exception of a few small enclaves, like

4 - Deadly Neighbours

Philadelphia which held on until 1390, Anatolia was lost to the Byzantine Empire.

Unsuccessful in the East, Andronikos III Palaiologos was more successful in the West, where he utilized yet another succession crisis in Epirus to finally secure western Greece to the Empire. He also instigated various administrative and legal reforms and even tried to build the Byzantine Fleet back up, though this never materialized.

In 1341 Andronikos III Palaiologos died, leaving his under-aged son, John V Palaiologos, under the regency of his Major Domestic, and trusted friend, John Kantakouzenos.

Despite John Kantakouzenos' clear lack of personal ambition for the throne, a group led by the Empress Dowager, the Patriarch and Alexios Apokaukos, an influential courtier and general, started to form in opposition to his regency.

While John Kantakouzenos was away with the army to deal with a rebellion in Greece, the group stages a coup, declaring John V Palaiologos emperor with themselves as regents and commanded the disbandment of the army.

The army had no appetite for the coup-makers and instead declared John Kantakouzenos as emperor. As if the Byzantine Empire did not have enough problems as it was, this threw the Empire into yet another civil war, this time lasting no less than six years.

Money was scarce and what could be looted or pawned was. The Empress Dowager pawned the Byzantine crown jewels for 30,000 Ducats to the Venetians. The pawn was never redeemed and would later cause her son significant embarrassment.

Soldiers were equally hard to get, so both parties sought allies. John V Palaiologos, or rather the coup-makers, allied themselves with the Bulgarians and Kantakouzenos allied himself with the Serbians and also had maritime support from the Beylik of Aydin a Turcoman beylik (around modern day Izmir) as of yet not under Ottoman control.

The battle raged to and fro, initially with the coup-makers as the dominant force, but gradually Kantakouzenos took the initiative. During the war the Bey of Aydin had been forced to go back to Anatolia to defend his own territories, but Kantakouzenos replaced them with a contingent of Ottomans supplied by the Ottoman bey, Orhan, son of Osman.

The coup-makers eventually surrendered in 1348 and John Kantakouzenos could victoriously enter the city where he was crowned a co-emperor as John VI Kantakouzenos.

The civil war had completely devastated the already near-ruined state, not just by emptying the coffers but also as the Bulgarians and Serbians had helped themselves to large territories from where they simply could not be removed. The Ottomans, however, returned to Anatolia.

The deal dictated by John VI Kantakouzenos on his enemy's surrender was that he would act as senior emperor for a period of ten years after which John V Palaiologos would become a full equal.

In this deal, Kantakouzenos' son, Matthew, had been overlooked. Matthew Kantakouzenos had acted as military commander in his father's army during the civil war and would, like many others, have preferred a clean cut with the Palaiologos and the establishment of a new dynasty. That would, of course, have put him in line for the Byzantine crown. To placate him and get him out of Constantinople, he was given governorship of western Greece.

Attempts to regain the territories lost to the Serbians were mainly unsuccessful and the consequences of the Black Death and an unnecessary military conflict with Genoa further led the Byzantine Empire down the road of ruin.

With John V Palaiologos now coming of age, he was given Matthew's territories in western Greece and Matthew was moved to eastern Greece. Like two young lions they eyed each other off.

Finally in 1352 the peace broke. John V Palaiologos attacked Matthew Kantakouzenos, assisted by Venetian and Serbian troops. John VI Kantakouzenos came to his son's assistance, but to muster a force that could match the Serbians supporting John V Palaiologos he once again relied on the Ottoman troops of Orhan.

Whereas the civil wars of Byzantium were not leaving significant marks in history, John VI Kantakouzenos' alliance with the Ottomans would turn out to dramatically change world-history.

There was as such, no reason to suspect that the Ottomans could not be trusted. They had been sent back to Anatolia after their initial assistance to John VI Kantakouzenos in 1348 and the terms for their assistance were clearly agreed.

The Ottomans were given military headquarters in the fortress of Çimpe on the Gallipoli peninsula and it was agreed that whereas they could keep their loot, they were to abandon any territories, cities and fortresses taken on behalf of the Byzantines.

Militarily the Ottoman alliance was a success. The Ottoman forces beat the Serbs fighting for John V Palaiologos in October 1352, and he had to temporarily flee to the island of Tenedos.

John V Palaiologos then came back, first with an unsuccessful attempt at Constantinople in early 1353, but then secured Genoese support which enabled him to finally force the surrender of John VI Kantakouzenos at the end of 1354. John VI Kantakouzenos abdicated and withdrew to a monastery.

During the conflict, John VI Kantakouzenos had appointed his son Matthew as co-emperor, and Matthew held out until 1357 where he was captured by John V Palaiologos' Serbian allies and sold to the Emperor for

4 - Deadly Neighbours

ransom. After two years of imprisonment, and having abdicated, he was allowed to join his younger brother, Manuel, in the Morea. John V Palaiologos was now finally established as sole Emperor of Byzantium, but there was trouble ahead for the victorious emperor.

While busying themselves with civil war, the Byzantines had turned their back on the Ottomans camped at Çimpe. In 1354 the neighbouring city of Gallipoli had been devastated by an earthquake and deserted by its citizens. The Ottomans took the opportunity to re-build the damaged city and its fortress, ferrying over increasing numbers of Ottoman and starting to settle on the Gallipoli peninsula.

It is very possible that the Ottomans originally intended to go home after their services had been paid for, but seeing the chaos ensuing in the Byzantine territories and how Bulgarians and Serbs seemed to help themselves to land, they changed their minds and decided to seize the opportunity.

When finally the Emperor got around to accusing the Ottomans of having broken their agreement to give all conquered cities and territories back to the empire, they truthfully, but somewhat tongue-in-cheek, responded that they had not broken the agreement as Gallipoli had not been conquered but abandon and all they had done was rebuild and repopulate. As transparent as this was, the Byzantines had no military power with which to force the issue, so the Ottomans now had a strategic bridgehead in Europe.

And the Ottomans did not waste much time. They quickly started annexing first the Gallipoli peninsula and then gradually moved across Rumelia and northern Greece. Starting out as convenient allies, they had now become a serious threat.

So much so that emperor John V Palaiologos started to ask other Christian states for help. He even started travelling round Europe to proactively convince other Christian rulers in the area to come to his, and Christianity's, assistance, but his pleads were fruitless. Indeed, passing through Venice in 1369, he was imprisoned for the debts owed to Venice over the Crown Jewels pawned by his mother.

In the meantime, the Ottomans advanced steadily. By 1365, now under the leadership of Orhan's son, Murad I, the Ottomans had conquered Adrianople, renamed it to Edirne and made it their European capital.

By 1371 they were the de-facto masters of Rumelia, northern Greece and large parts of Bulgaria, and emperor John V Palaiologos had to accept the nominal suzerainty of the Ottomans and agree to pay an annual tribute. Humiliating as it was, this alliance actually served the Emperor well, as the Ottomans came to his assistance when his oldest son, and subsequently his grandson tried to overthrow him.

John V Palaiologos finally died in 1391 having nominally ruled for fifty years. He left behind him the sorry remains of the reborn Byzantine Empire. Constantinople was sealed off as a disparate enclave consisting of the city itself and its immediate surroundings. The only other part left of the Byzantine Empire was the Despotate of the Morea, covering half of the Peloponnese peninsula hundreds of kilometres to the south-west.

A few years before the death of Emperor John V Palaiologos, in 1386, Murad I had declared himself Sultan, There was no more pretence, the Ottomans were now a powerful and ambitious empire in their own right.

Swarming across Serbia, having by now effectively overrun Bulgaria, the Ottomans met with the Serbian army at Kosovo in 1389. The battle was bloody and decisive. Despite both armies being more or less annihilated in the battle, the Serbians had no more resources to call up whereas the Ottomans could rebuild with fresh troops from Anatolia.

Sultan Murad I died during or immediately following the battle, and his son Bayezid I took over where his father had left off.

Serbia was formally subdued and forced to pay tribute, though as we shall see in Chapter 14 it would persist to cause trouble. Bulgaria was simply mopped up and turned into an Ottoman province as was the case with Albania and northern Greece and by 1394 Sultan Bayezid I was ready to deal with Constantinople.

As covered in Chapter 1, the immediate problem that Bayezid I had with Constantinople was not the Byzantines themselves. Though they used all opportunities to plot against the Ottomans they were rather toothless. The problem was the harbour in the Golden Horn and its strategic position.

The emerging Ottoman Empire was now split across two continents with the traditional, and still expanding, core territories in Anatolia and the quickly growing territories in Europe. To get from one part of the state to the other the Ottomans needed to be able to freely cross between the two continents, and to do that they needed control of the seas at the natural crossing-points at Bosporus and Gallipoli.

As also covered in Chapter 1, the Ottomans had little naval tradition, and though they were gradually acquiring some naval skills from the populations along the coastlines they were annexing, such knowledge was worth little if they could not put a fleet at sea without it being destroyed by a much stronger adversary.

The Sea of Marmara was, like most of the eastern part of the Mediterranean Sea completely dominated by Italian fleets, in particular by Venice and Genoa. Though these trading cities were as often as not at loggerheads with each other (as covered further in Part 4), they nevertheless had full control of the Seas. The critical strategic harbour for control of the Sea of Marmara - and thus critical for the Ottoman's capability to cross freely across their empire - was Constantinople.

To provide some protection for the crossing Ottomans, Bayezid I built a fortress, known as Anadoluhisarı (The Anatolian Castle), on the Anatolian side of the Bosporus Strait north of Constantinople. He then laid siege to Constantinople.

4 - Deadly Neighbours

The siege started in 1394 and once again the Byzantine Emperor, now Manuel II Palaiologos, asked the other Christian states for help. Contrary to previous futile attempts at getting help, this time the Christian World was starting to appreciate the dangers caused by the Ottoman expansion in Europe.

An army was assembled consisting of Hungarians, Wallachian, Germans and French soldiers supported by a (rather lacklustre) Venetian fleet and under the overall command of Sigismund, King of Hungary.

The Christian army marched along the Danube River, with the Venetians in support, aiming to relieve Constantinople by attacking the Ottomans from the back.

Bayezid I had, however, good intelligence so he marched to meet the Christian army, with support also from his new vassals in Serbia. On 25 September 1396 the two armies met at Nicopolis in northern Bulgaria, where the Christian troops were performing a somewhat half-hearted siege of the, Ottoman-held, fortress.

Though exact figures vary significantly, as is the case in most accounts from the period, historians generally believe that the Ottoman forces outnumbered those of the Christians. To an extent this difference could be levelled out by the Christian forces' heavy cavalry, in this particular case consisting mainly of French knights.

The Christian army was, however, handicapped by a rather cavalier attitude to the whole situation, first allowing the Ottomans to come much to close before they were discovered and secondly seeing the French knights ignoring their battle orders and pursuing a feigned Ottoman retreat which led to their destruction.

The Christian army was essentially annihilated, Sigismund of Hungary himself narrowly escaped in a fishing boat to reach the Venetian ships which had played no role in the battle itself.

Following the battle, any remaining resistance in Bulgaria fizzled out and Bulgaria was once and for all Ottoman. It would take another fifty years before another concerted Christian attempt at facing the Ottoman expansion in Europe.

Bayezid I went back to the siege of Constantinople, but whereas he effectively sealed off the city from the landside he could not stop the city from being supplied from the sea, and he did not have the means or technology to make an impression on the massive Byzantine land-walls.

In 1399 emperor Manuel II Palaiologos once again tried to raise awareness of the Ottoman issue with other Christian rulers. Having exhausted any further local options by the defeat of the Christian army at Nicopolis, Manuel II Palaiologos left the Empire in the hands of his nephew John (VII) Palaiologos, who had himself tried to replace John V Palaiologos during a brief coup in 1390.

His travels took Manuel II Palaiologos as far away as England and Denmark, but despite receiving some 1,500 soldiers from France, his efforts were basically fruitless. On his return he painlessly regained the throne from his nephew.

Though the situation was not as such desperate for the Byzantines, they were effectively locked into their city, only capable of moving to and from by means of Venetian and Genoese ships. As was an integral part of Byzantine way of life they prayed for a miracle, and a miracle they got, though it was probably of a nature they did not exactly expect.

Far away east of Constantinople, on the eastern border of the Ottoman Empire in Anatolia, a new empire was emerging. Timur, also known as Tamerlane, a Turco-Mongolian warlord with an ambition to re-establish the Mongol Empire, consolidated large parts of former Mongol territories into the Timurid Empire, another warlike and quickly expanding empire reaching from Afghanistan to Anatolia and including all of Persia. As the fourteenth century merged into the fifteenth century, Timur allied himself with some of the easternmost Ottoman beyliks and they rose against Ottoman sovereignty.

Bayezid I could not afford to allow his eastern borders to start crumbling, so the siege of Constantinople, not going anywhere fast, was abandoned and the Ottoman army moved across to Anatolia, marching east to meet Timur.

The two armies collided on 20 July 1402 and the Ottomans, though supported by contingents of Serbs and Albanians were decisively beaten. Sultan Bayezid I initially made his escape but was surrounded and taken prisoner by Timur, as was some of his sons.

As covered in Chapter 1, this led to the Ottoman Interregnum Period in which Bayezid I's sons fought each other for over a decade over the throne of the Ottoman Empire.

Emperor Manuel II Palaiologos, having got rid of any immediate threat from the Ottomans, took the opportunity to regain some of the areas lost to the weakened Ottomans, focusing on coastal areas on either side of the Sea of Marmara and on the city of Thessaloniki. He also took the opportunity to rebuild the Hexamilion Wall, a defensive wall dating back to the fifth century, reaching more than six miles across the Isthmus of Corinth, a narrow land-bridge which connects the Morea (Peloponnese) peninsula with the Greek mainland. This latter activity showed that Manuel II Palaiologos was under no illusion when it came to further Ottoman aggression; they may well be weak at the moment, but it was not going to last.

However, following centuries of Byzantine tradition for intermingling, Manuel II Palaiologos also got involved in the Ottoman civil war. He supported Suleyman, the son of Bayezid I who was in control of the European side of the Ottoman Empire. It is uncertain whether Manuel II Palaiologos did so of his own free will or whether he simply did not have a choice, but in any case, his support of Suleyman caught the ire of Musa,

Suleyman's brother who had defeated and killed Suleyman and now controlled the European side of the empire.

Musa decided to besiege Constantinople and Manuel II Palaiologos called upon the help of Musa's brother, Mehmed, who now controlled the Anatolian part of the Ottoman Empire.

As bizarre as it was, ten years after the Ottomans had laid siege to Constantinople, one group of Ottoman troops now helped defend Constantinople against another group. Ultimately Mehmed was victorious and the Interregnum Period ended with Mehmed's crowning as Sultan Mehmed I in 1413.

Sultan Mehmed I ruled for eight years in which he mainly focused on rebuilding the Ottoman Empire, retaking the territories lost in the East and consolidating Ottoman authority over other areas which had seized the opportunity to revolt. Emperor Manuel II Palaiologos and the Byzantine Empire thus had a quiet time in which to take a deep breath and pray for the best while preparing for the worst.

Another of Bayezid I's sons, Mustafa, had not been directly involved in the civil war between his brothers, but had remained in captivity. He either died in captivity or was released after the death of Timur in 1405. If he was released, he simply disappeared.

But once the civil war had been settled, a person claiming to be Mustafa reappeared in Rumelia, proposing that his brother, Mehmed, should share the throne. Mehmed I, having fought a civil war for eleven years had no such intentions, but rather than having his alleged brother killed, as other emerging sultans had done before him, he allowed Mustafa to live under the protection of the Byzantine Emperor, but under house arrest, on the island of Lemnos. To Sultan Mehmed I, this was a good solution, and he could move on with the job of rebuilding his empire. For Manuel II Palaiologos it was an ace up the sleeve.

When Sultan Mehmed I died in 1421, Emperor Manuel II Palaiologos decided to play the card in a manner worthy of a Byzantine emperor. He released Mustafa - who was in the Emperor's debt for having saved his life - and supported him with troops and money in a challenge to the official heir to the Ottoman throne, Mehmed I's only eighteen year old son Murad II.

It was a wild gamble from Manuel II Palaiologos, but it nearly paid off. Mustafa established himself in Edirne and started gathering local support. Murad II sent an expeditionary force across from Anatolia, but once in Rumelia it deserted to Mustafa.

Confident that he had enough support to press on, Mustafa then crossed over to Anatolia, but this time large parts of his troops deserted to Murad II. He fled back to Rumelia, but Murad II gave chase, caught him and had him hanged like a common criminal. The Emperor's gamble had failed, and he had not exactly impressed the new Ottoman sultan by his deeds. In the

Ottoman annals, Mustafa is known as 'False Mustafa' as he was not officially recognized for being who he claimed to be.

To punish the Byzantine Emperor, Murad II decided to continue what his predecessors had started; a siege of Constantinople.

Once again Manuel II Palaiologos tried intrigue as a weapon, this time allying himself with some of the remaining semi-independent beyliks in western Anatolia and supporting a revolt in Bursa, nominally rallying around Murad II's younger brother, thirteen year old Mustafa.

Murad II broke off the siege, returned to Anatolia where he relatively easily defeated and subsequently executed, his brother. As punishment, what little autonomy had been given to the Anatolian beyliks was withdrawn and they were fully integrated into the Ottoman Empire.

This time the Emperor's gamble had actually paid off, as the siege of Constantinople was lifted and Murad II stared to concentrate on issues other than the Byzantines. His borders were under threat from the Bey of Karaman, rebellious Albanians and others who were now suddenly becoming aware that perhaps all was not well in the Ottoman Empire. Once again, the Byzantines had bought themselves some time.

Manuel II Palaiologos took the opportunity to once again seek support from other Christian states, but none was found, the most obvious ally being Hungary which, however, was involved in dynastic wars in Bohemia and had no resources to start a fight with the Ottomans. As a consequence, Manuel II Palaiologos in 1424 renewed the agreement to pay tribute to the Ottomans. He died the year after.

The new emperor of the Byzantine Empire, Manuel's son John VIII Palaiologos had successfully taken part in the defence of Constantinople during the Ottoman siege in 1422 and was as a consequence popular amongst the population. He would subsequently manage to change that.

The 1420s was a mixed bag for the Byzantines. They successfully managed to get the whole peninsula of the Morea under Byzantine control, inviting down settlers from Albania. This with the exception of the coastal cities of Modon and Coron, held by the Venetians since the aftermath of the Fourth Crusade. The Morea was held as a Despotate, split between John VIII Palaiologos' brothers; Constantine (XI), Demetrios, and Thomas Palaiologos.

They had less luck with Thessaloniki, the strategically important coastal city, on the north-western coast of Greece which had been put back under Byzantine control by Manuel II Palaiologos during the Ottoman Interregnum. It was being managed by Manuel II Palaiologos' brother, Andronikos Palaiologos, but with the Ottomans regaining their strength it was not to last. In 1422 - parallel with the Ottoman siege of Constantinople - they also laid siege to Thessaloniki, and Andronikos Palaiologos soon realized that with the capital under siege, and effectively cut off from rendering any assistance, his best choice was to hand the city over to Venice, always on the lookout for strategically placed ports. The Venetians in turn had to surrender the town to the Ottomans by 1430.

At the beginning of the 1430s The Byzantine Empire thus effectively consisted of the city of Constantinople with its immediate surroundings and the Despotate of the Morea, disparate enclaves separated by landmasses mainly controlled by the Ottomans and sea controlled by Venice and Genoa. The Byzantine army was in a sorry state and decimated to mainly garrison Constantinople rather than equipped to fight any battles proper.

Sultan Murad II had little time to worry about Constantinople. He was at war with Venice and otherwise occupying himself with re-asserting Ottoman control of the Balkans, where in particular the Serbians and Albanians still caused trouble in the wake of the Ottoman Interregnum.

John VIII Palaiologos was, however, under no illusions as to whether there would be more trouble with the Ottomans once they had secured their borders, so like others before him he went to western Europe to seek assistance.

In 1437 he appointed his brother Constantine, one of the Despots of the Morea, as regent and went on a mission to secure support for his ailing empire. Having learned from his predecessors' failure to secure any meaningful support he decided to play the last card in the deck, the religious independence of Byzantium.

Rather than visiting individual Christian rulers, each busy with their own conflicts, often with each other, he went to the only unifying force to be reckoned with in western Europe, the Pope, and he went to offer him what the Pope wanted most, control of the souls in the Orthodox Church.

Pope Eugene IV had his own troubles to deal with, his authority being challenged by many of the princes of Europe. He needed something to bolster his authority, so when John VIII Palaiologos appeared on his doorstep offering the Orthodox Church, Eugene IV quickly appreciated the value of this and in 1439 the Council of Florence ratified the renewed union of the Catholic and the Orthodox Churched under the supremacy of the Pope.

As much as this was meant to secure the Pope's support of the Byzantine Empire, little difference did it make, indeed if anything, it managed to further weaken the Byzantine Empire from within.

Fact of the matter was that Pope Eugene IV had little influence over the rulers of western Europe. He had himself been ousted from Rome and had an anti-Pope - supported by some of the most powerful western European rulers - to deal with as well. As we shall see shortly, his influence only reached as far as some rulers in eastern Europe, and it was not enough.

What really undermined the Byzantine Empire was, however, the reaction of its own population. The Byzantine people were deeply religious and deeply faithful to their own Orthodox mother-church, so when John VIII

Palaiologos returned to Constantinople in 1440 and tried to enforce the new union, he was less than successful.

Led by the charismatic Bishop Mark of Ephesus, who as the only Orthodox bishop had refused to sign the Treaty of Florence, the Byzantine population simply refused to accept, or implement, the unification. John VIII Palaiologos, who up until then had been a popular emperor, fell from public grace and, though he managed to hold on to nominal power, he effectively lost any real influence, casting the Byzantine Empire into an ungovernable state.

The Pope was somewhat more successful in his efforts. Though he had lost any real influence over the western European rulers, he still found resonance for his call for a 'crusade' against the Ottomans amongst rulers in eastern Europe.

King Wladyslaw III of Poland had in 1440 taken over the Hungarian crown due to a power vacuum in the wake of the death of Sigismund of Hungary in 1437. He was not everyone's favourite choice so he had something to prove. When the Pope called for crusaders, Wladyslaw III seized the opportunity to gain both papal support for his reign and to prove himself.

In the summer of 1443 Wladyslaw III assembled an army of Polish, Hungarian and Serbian soldiers. He was the nominal leader, although the true commander of the army was the veteran Janos Hunyadi, assisted by another veteran, the disposed Serbian Despot Đurađ Branković. Representing the Pope was Cardinal Guiliano Cesarini.

The army, consisting of some 30,000 soldiers crossed the Danube river close to the Serbian (but Ottoman held) capital of Smederevo and continued south. It took (and plundered) Sofia and then continued south, its target being the Ottoman capital of Edirne.

The Ottomans did not put forward their main army to counter the approaching army. It had been busy that same summer fighting an incursion by Ibrahim II, the Bey of Karaman, and Murad II had only just himself returned, with the main army remaining in Anatolia.

Though local Ottoman garrisons put up as much resistance as they could, the Christian army simply ploughed through all resistance, capturing Ottoman territories and fortifications with relative ease.

As the 'crusaders' came closer to Edirne, the Ottomans barred their way through the mountains by felled trees and contested their passage through the well protected passes.

Murad II finally started to gather the main host of the Ottoman army, but before it came to a decisive battle the Christian advance stopped by itself. Winter was approaching and the Christian supply lines, under constant attack from Ottoman forces which had remained behind the advancing army, had become impractically long. The army got as far as the town of Panagyurishte in southern Bulgaria when a bitterly cold winter and lack of supplies forced it to turn around.

The Ottomans picked at the rear of the retreating army but were fought off. When reaching Serbia, it considered whether to camp for the winter and start the campaign again come spring, but the lack of supplies finally forced the decision to return home.

The expedition, named 'The Long Campaign', was considered a great success, despite the fact that the Ottoman army tracking behind the retreating Christen army soon restored all the conquered territories and fortifications to Ottoman control.

Despite the lack of any real gains, the expedition had shown that the Ottomans were vulnerable, not least so when their forces were split between the eastern and western parts of their empire.

Not missing an opportunity to take advantage of the Sultan's predicament, the Palaiologos brothers in the Morea had started an incursion into Greece and Albania and, despite suing for peace in 1443, Ibrahim II of Karaman, had not given up on his ambitions to pick at the Ottomans in south-eastern Anatolia.

Murad II countered by coming to terms with Đurađ Branković, giving him back the throne of Serbia as an Ottoman vassal, and by sending peace envoys to King Wladyslaw III.

A peace treaty was concluded in the summer of 1444, promising peace for a ten year period and making small concessions on behalf of the Ottomans, such as waiver of the tribute paid by Vlad II Dracul, Voivode of Wallachia, and reconfirmation of Đurađ Branković's rule in Serbia.

With the Hungarians seemingly pacified, Murad then turned his attention back to Ibrahim II in Anatolia who had once again rebelled, possibly encouraged to do so by the Hungarians.

Amongst the first to congratulate the young King Wladyslaw III on his return from the previous year's campaign had been ambassadors from Byzantium, and they were also first to inform the King of the Ottoman army's move to Anatolia. Peace treaty apart, the opportunity simply seemed too good to miss.

Thus ignoring the peace treaty with the Ottomans, the Christians once again assembled an army, this time securing support from a Venetian fleet which would guard the crossing-points between Anatolia and Europe, preventing the Ottoman army from returning to Europe, and which would also meet the Christian army at Varna on the Bulgarian Black Sea coast with supplies, minimizing the size of the supply train the army had to rely on. Additional troops were also promised by the Byzantine Emperor John VIII Palaiologos, once again sensing that fortune may swing his way.

It was a good plan, executed at the perfect time. Its failure was due to the duplicity of the Italian city-states.

While Murad II was busy in Anatolia, a Venetian led fleet went to block the strait at the Dardanelles and the Christian army started their march, this time moving down along the Bulgarian Black Sea coast.

Murad had left his son, Mehmed, in charge in Edirne, and it was clear that he neither had the capability or the resources to put up a meaningful fight against a well organised and determined Christian army. This was the time! The Ottomans could be expelled from Europe and Byzantium could be relieved.

The Ottoman garrisons along the Bulgarian coast put up a spirited defence, delaying the Christian army's progress, buying time for Murad II who in the meantime hastened to conclude his conflict with Ibrahim II, concluding a peace treaty in which Ibrahim II even supplied Murad II with troops. Murad II then rushed to the Dardanelles. When he got there, he found the crossing point blocked by the Venetian fleet.

Marching his army north to the Bosporus, Murad II now used the weakness of the Italians; gold. He offered the Venetian and Genoese ships posted in and around Constantinople a gold piece for each Ottoman soldier landed in Europe, and soon his army was ferried across by more than willing Italian ships. The Venetian fleet was in the meantime incapable of interfering, as it had been hit by storms and could not proceed up through the Sea of Marmara, which also meant it could not proceed to the Black Sea with supplies for the Christian army. That, at least, was the story that the Venetians stuck to after the events that followed.

Murad II now had his army, intact and ready for battle on European soil and he hastened first to Edirne, where his son had lost all real control of the city, and then on to meet the Christians.

Emperor John VIII Palaiologos saw which way the wind was blowing and made no attempts to send troops to reinforce the Christian army; now at Varna waiting for the Venetian's to bring supplies.

On 10 November 1444, the two armies faced each other outside Varna. The Christian army counted some 30,000 troops, who were facing the main Ottoman army of some 100,000.

For the Christians, the battle was a rout, leaving both King Wladyslaw III and Cardinal Guiliano Cesarini dead. King Wladyslaw III's head was first impaled on a lance and shown in triumph at the battlefield and later put in a cask of honey and sent to Edirne as a symbol of the Sultan's victory.

The remaining Christian troops were harassed through their flight north, and very few survived. The Hungarian veteran commander, Janos Hunyadi, made it across the Danube river to Wallachia, where Voivode Vlad II Dracul took him prisoner, probably to impress the Sultan. He did, however, soon release him and Janos Hunyadi would live to fight again.

Amongst the first to congratulate the Sultan on his victories and offer him rich gifts was, not surprisingly, the Byzantine Emperor John VIII Palaiologos.

4 - Deadly Neighbours

As I have mentioned before, Sultan Murad II was not inherently a warlike man. His aim was to consolidate and defend the Ottoman territories, pretty much as they had looked before the disastrous defeat of his grandfather, Bayezid I, to Timur in 1402. True, his military exploits had been tremendous successful, and his troops had raided as far as the coast of the Adriatic Sea, but his main concerns had been to secure the Empire's borders.

With the defeat of the Christian army at Varna, and with peace seemingly assured in the East, his objective had essentially been achieved. There was trouble in southern Greece, and the former Ottoman general Iskender Bey, now known as Skanderbeg, had returned to his native Albania and started a revolt against the Ottomans, but for now these were more irritants than imminent threats.

Consequently, returning from Varna in the autumn of 1444, Murad II decided to abdicate his throne in favour of his son and heir, Mehmed, although it was really to a council lead by the Grand Vizier Çandarlı Halil Pasha.

The relationship between Prince Mehmed and Çandarlı Halil Pasha was fragile. The young prince was starting to develop his own view of things, including an urge to besiege Constantinople, and the elder statesman, who was known for being a friend of the Byzantines, would have nothing of it.

Mehmed signed a peace treaty with Venice, whom the Venetians duly insisted had to be ratified by his father, and the next two years passed in relative peace.

Towards the end of 1446 matters, however, came to a head between Mehmed and Çandarlı Halil Pasha and the latter decided to, secretly, call back Murad II from his retirement, the pretext being the actions of the Palaiologos brothers in the Morea.

While Murad II was busy with more important matters such as Karaman and Hungary, the Palaiologos brothers had started an offensive north into Greece, subduing the Duchy of Athens, the territories of south-western Greece, ruled by Duke Nerio II Acciaioli as a vassal of the Ottomans.

When asked to vacate, the Palaiologos brothers replied by demanding an independent Greek state from the Morea to Thermopalyi. Enough was enough, and Grand Vizier Çandarlı Halil Pasha used this as a pretext to get Murad II back and engaged.

On Murad II's return his son Mehmed was moved to a position as governor in Anatolia, and Murad II retook the reins. Even though it was late in 1446 and later than one would normally start a military campaign, he decided to move out and march on the troublesome despots of the Morea.

Hearing of the approaching Ottoman army, the Greeks quickly withdrew, giving Murad II a basically uncontested march along the Greek east coast as far as the Isthmus of Corinth, the small land-bridge connecting mainland Greece and the Morea.

The Hexamilion Wall across the narrow isthmus had been reinforced by Emperor Manuel II Palaiologos at the beginning of the fifteenth century and the Palaiologos brothers had further improved it, believing it to be an as good as impenetrable defence. Under normal circumstances that was possibly true or the wall was at least sufficiently difficult to get through to deterring the Ottomans in not wasting thousands of lives trying.

But the situation was not normal; indeed, the situation was to mark a dramatic change in the art of European warfare.

Firearms had gradually been introduced into Europe through the fourteenth and fifteenth century, the Ottoman Janissary corps recently being issued with muskets.

Cannon had also been introduced, and both the Hungarians and Germans were master cannon-makers, but impressive as the cannon were, by 1446 they had mainly been used against massed infantry. They were not powerful enough to break down walls from a distance, or so it was believed. Murad II's attack on the Hexamilion Wall in 1446 changed that perception.

Without much publicity, Murad II had engaged foreign cannon-makers, most likely from the Saxon trader cities in southern Transylvania. The task they had been given was simple; to make cannon powerful enough to break down a wall from a safe distance.

There is some doubt as to whether the Ottoman cannon were transported down the Greek coast, probably following the marching army by ship, or whether the cannon were cast on the spot from raw materials transported with the army (as would certainly be the case ten years later), but once the army was settled on the northern side of the Hexamilion Wall, with the rebellious Greeks hiding on the south side believing themselves safe, Murad II had his new cannon set up and starting firing at the wall.

It took the new cannon three days to make significant breaches in the wall, and on 10 December the Ottomans stormed through the gaps and routed the defending Greeks.

The main cities were sacked, villages burned and thousands of people taken as slaves. The Palaiologos brothers fled and were preparing to leave the peninsula by ship when Murad II turned his army north and marched towards home, having razed the defences behind him.

Ambassadors from the Despots caught up with him, and he gave them control of the Morea back, but as tribute-paying vassals of the Ottomans. What little fighting-spirit was left in the Byzantine Empire was quickly fizzling out and Murad II's new military technology would in less than a decade later spell doom for the imperial capital itself.

The following year was peaceful, the Ottomans resting after the late campaign of 1446, but in 1448 Murad II was keen to deal with the last fire burning in his empire; Albania.

4 - Deadly Neighbours

Skanderbeg had had significant success in rallying the Albanians, and they were consistently keeping the Ottomans at bay, fighting guerrilla warfare rather than facing the numerically superior Ottomans in staged battles.

Murad II set out for Albania in the spring of 1448 but had little success. The Albanians retreated into the mountains in front of the Ottoman army and then reappeared, attacking the Ottoman supply lines. Though the Ottomans held most of the fortresses, the Albanians held the countryside and, in particular, the mountains. Having secured the fortresses on the eastern border of Albania, Murad II withdrew to Sofia, eventually aiming for a return to Edirne.

Murad II's reliance on Hungary being effectively pacified after their defeat at Varna in 1444, turned out to be false. The experienced politician and warlord Janos Hunyadi still had a fight in him, and he had been looking for allies.

Nobody readily appeared under the Hungarian banner though. The Serbian ruler Đurađ Branković, finally back in Serbia after his peace deal with the Ottomans from 1444, had no appetite for a war. The Pope, now Nicholas V, was a lover of art and science, and did not have the same motivation for dominance as his predecessor. The Venetians were licking their wounds after years of war and were quite happy to leave things as they were. The only support that Hungary could rely on was from Skanderbeg's Albanians.

Undeterred, Janos Hunyadi put the Hungarian army in the field, supported by German mercenaries and Wallachian horsemen sent by the reluctant Wallachian Voivode, Vladislav II (sometime referred to as Dan).

Due to Đurađ Branković's refusal to participate, the marching army considered Serbia as hostile area and thus pillaged their way south through the country.

Murad II heard of their approach, probably from Đurađ Branković, and instead of going home he marched his army to Kosovo, the scene of a similar battle in 1389, which had seen the death of his great-grandfather and namesake, Murad I.

In a battle which, untypically, unfolded over three days, the Hungarians gave it their everything against the numerically superior Ottomans. Whereas Murad II had developed the use of cannon to break down walls, the Hungarians had developed the use of 'wagenburgs'; wagons armed with culverins, small cannon with a limited range but lethal against massed infantry.

The Hungarians also hoped for assistance from Skanderbeg, assistance that could have well tipped the balance of the battle, but Skanderbeg never came, held up by a combination of Ottoman rearguard and Serbians.

In the end the Hungarians were overrun by sheer numbers. Janos Hunyadi and Voivode Vladislav II were intercepted by Đurađ Branković on their way home and only released for ransom towards the end of the year.

Though victorious, the Ottoman loses were significant, and Murad II had no inclination, or capability, to follow up on his victory. He took the army back to Edirne, including his son Mehmed, who had seen his first military action during the battle.

While they were holed up by Đurađ Branković, Janos Hunyadi and the voivode of Wallachia's fates were unknown and Murad II saw an opportunity to put a pliant ruler on the throne in Wallachia. Vladislav II had taken the throne the year before with support from Janos Hunyadi and by murdering his predecessor, Vlad II Dracul.

Sultan Murad II had in 1443 entered into a renewed peace and vassalage agreement with Vlad II Dracul and had, as was common practice, taken two of Vlad II Dracul's sons, Vlad and Radu, as hostages.

After their father's murder, they had stayed at the Ottoman court and Murad II now sent the older, Vlad Dracula, to Wallachia with a contingent of Ottoman troops to fill the apparently vacant throne. Vlad was received with suspicion but was crowned as Vlad III Dracula. His reign ended two months later, in December 1448, when Vladislav II and Janos Hunyadi reappeared and the young pretender to the throne quickly left with his small contingent of Ottoman troops.

Of more lasting impact was the death of the Byzantine Emperor John VIII Palaiologos, who died on 13 October 1448. John VIII Palaiologos did not leave any sons, so he had appointed as his heir his younger brother, Constantine, one of the troublesome despots of the Morea.

Constantine's accession to the throne was difficult, and illustrates how weak, and to some extent dependant on the Ottomans, the Byzantine Empire had become.

Constantine's brother Demetrius tried to take Constantinople by force, and with neither party really in a position to press the issue, deputations were sent to Murad II to settle the matter. After all, in principle the Byzantine Empire was a vassal of the Ottomans.

Murad II ruled in favour of Constantine, who was crowned in Mistra in the Morea and sent by (Catalan) ship to Constantinople. Constantine XI Palaiologos would be the last Emperor of Byzantium.

Murad II, now followed by his son Mehmed, started a new campaign against Albania in 1450, using mortars against the fortress at Krujë. The fortress, however held, supplied by Venetians who also supplied the Ottomans. Towards winter the Ottomans turned around and went back to Edirne with little accomplished. The Christian World, needing something to celebrate, rejoiced. The new Emperor in Byzantium stayed silent.

On 3 February 1451, Sultan Murad II died at Edirne. He was succeeded by his son Mehmed, who immediately had his only, infant, brother strangled. Mehmed was not intent on entertaining any of the troubles that his father had experienced, but as before the Byzantine Emperor had his own candidate for the Ottoman throne at hand.

4 - Deadly Neighbours

Inside the walls of Constantinople, the Emperor maintained an Ottoman 'prince', Orhan, grand-child to one Suleyman, himself a son of Bayezid I. Orhan was thus second-cousin to Sultan Mehmed II, and though his claim to the throne was weak, he was nevertheless a prince of the blood.

Mehmed II could not readily get to Orhan, so instead provided the Emperor with a generous annual allowance for Orhan's upkeep, on the understanding that the Emperor would not try to use Orhan as the rallying point against Mehmed II.

As covered in Chapter 2, the western world took a deep sigh of relief on Mehmed II's accession to the Ottoman throne, considering him weak and unpopular and Mehmed II himself confirmed this impression by readily re-confirming peace agreements to all and sundry.

The Bey of Karaman, Ibrahim II, once again sensed that he had an opportunity to claim western Anatolia so, possibly encouraged by the Byzantines, he launched an attack and in the summer of 1451 the new sultan was marching his troops eastwards to meet the challenge. Once again, the Karamans withdrew and a peace agreement was made, but Mehmed II's return became the start of the end of the Byzantine Empire.

While Mehmed II was on his way back through Anatolia, ambassadors came from the Emperor Constantine XI Palaiologos. They informed Çandarlı Halil Pasha, who Mehmed II had kept on as grand vizier, that the allowance for Prince Orhan had not been paid. They furthermore demanded that it be doubled, or they would support Orhan's claim to the throne.

Çandarlı Halil Pasha verbally abused the ambassadors, but once the news reached Mehmed II, he held his tongue and promised to deal with the issue once he was back in Edirne. Once back, he did. He took away the allowance altogether.

Mehmed II's return was, however, not without problems, and again acted as a catalyst to what would follow. On reaching the crossing point at the Dardanelles, he found that the strait was blocked by Christian ships, and he had, like his father before him, to redirect the army north and finally cross over the Bosporus.

These two events were symptomatic of the troubles of the Byzantine Empire. Political intrigue and difficulties in moving between the two parts of the Ottoman Empire were old issues, but like his forefathers Mehmed II realized that they needed to be dealt with. And there was a further issue with Constantinople.

To run an empire costs money, lots of money, not least when an army constantly has to be kept at the ready. The Ottoman Empire lay right in the middle of the extremely lucrative trading routes between the East and the West, but despite this, the Ottomans made little money from it as Venetian and Genoese ships simply circumvented the Ottomans.

Goods from the East would come to Black Sea ports such as Trebizond and sail down the Bosporus, pass through the Dardanelles on to safe ports controlled by the Italians. Goods from the West would follow the opposite route. At no point did they need to land in Ottoman ports and the Ottomans, consequently, were left out in terms of taxes and profit.

It all came together for Mehmed II. These three key issues could be solved by one single solution: conquest of Constantinople.

Control of Constantinople would mean no more political intrigue, safe passage across the water secured by the harbour in the Golden Horn, which would also control the access through and from the Black Sea and thus the capability to demand taxes of passing traders.

The sieges of Constantinople attempted by Mehmed II's immediate successors had been half-hearted affairs. They did not actually aim at taking the city, merely at keeping the Byzantines inside the walls.

Mehmed's siege was going to be different. It was going to be big, it was going to be spectacular, and it was going for the jugular. No more containment, the target was conquest and the end of the Byzantine Empire. The problems however were twofold.

Firstly, as long as Constantinople could be supplied by sea, it was practically impossible to starve it into submission.

Secondly, without a fleet of tall ships, like those deployed during the Fourth Crusade, the sea walls of Constantinople were impossible to breach, and the land walls had never been breached by military power. Mehmed found solutions for both problems.

Despite their ambitions for naval power being suppressed by the Italians, controlling the seas from Gibraltar to the Black Sea, the Ottomans had over the preceding decades built up some naval capability. From wharfs in their coastal possessions, not least around Gallipoli, they had launched galleys, rowed by Christian slaves of whom there was plenty supply. Though they had not tried to challenge the fleets of Venice or Genoa, they had become frequent visitors to outlying island and coastal town, which would be raided, though officially the pirates were not in Ottoman service. Mehmed now initiated a scheme of accelerated ship building and outfitting in the ports of the Gallipoli peninsula and the Anatolian coast. The Ottomans might not be able to match the Italians in technology, skill and experience, but there was something to say for quantity.

Then, having seen enough of the problem of crossing between the two parts of his empire, he started to build a castle. He built it on the Bosporus, across from the Anadoluhisarı castle built by his great-grandfather, Bayezid I.

In principle he built it on Byzantine land, but when the Byzantines protested, they were told to go away. The Emperor slammed the gates of Constantinople from the inside.

Mehmed II designed the castle himself, and all available resources were put to build it. It was completed in four months and sixteen days. He equipped it, and the older fortress on the other side of the narrow passage, with cannon and they started to stop the ships coming through the strait.

Nothing was allowed into Constantinople and everything else was taxed. The locals called the Bosporus 'the Throat', Mehmed II named his new castle Boğaz Kesen, 'the Throat cutter'. It was August 1452; the clock was ticking for the Byzantine Empire.

The Italians were far from happy with Mehmed II's actions, suddenly imposing control on their trade on the Black Sea. Towards the end of 1452 a small fleet of three Venetian ships coming from the Black Sea decided to sail straight through the two castles and unload their goods at Constantinople. Two went through, the third was sunk by a straight hit from a cannon. Its crew and captain, named Antonnio Erizzo, were captured and brought in front of the Sultan. The crew were beheaded and the Captain impaled. One sailor was allowed free to tell the tale.

With control of the Bosporus and a fleet being built, Mehmed II could now focus on the task of actually conquering Constantinople. He believed that his father's destruction of the Hexamilion Wall five years prior was the key. He needed cannon, big cannon, cannon capable of doing damage to the massive walls of Constantinople.

Sometime during that period, a 'Hungarian' (which probably means a Saxon from Transylvania) by the name of Urban had presented himself to the Sultan with a claim that he could build cannon that could blast *'the walls of Babylon itself'*. He had originally approached Emperor Constantine XI Palaiologos, but the Byzantine Emperor had little use for wall-blasting cannon and no funds to build them with. His interest was in smaller wall-mountable cannon, so Urban continued on and offered his services to the Sultan.

What was offered by Urban was exactly what Mehmed II needed. The walls of the Hexamilion Wall were made of paper compared with the walls of Constantinople.

The land-walls, stretching from the Sea of Marmara in the south to the Golden Horn in the north, had originally been built by Emperor Theodosius II (emperor of Byzantium 408 - 450), but had of course been renovated and extended in the 1,000 years since.

By the mid fifteenth century the walls were organised in a three-tier structure.

Seen from the perspective of the invader, the first thing to pass was a moat, though it was mostly not filled with water and thus was a 'ditch' rather than a moat as such. Twenty meters wide and up to ten meters deep, the bank closest to the wall was furthermore guarded by a one and a half meters crenellated wall.

The wall on the bank of the moat was followed by a twenty meters wide 'terrace' connecting it to the outer wall. This wall was 2 meters thick at the base and reached a height of between eight and nine meters. Behind crenellations at the top was another terrace, some ten meters wide, connecting it to the inner wall. The outer wall had towers at every fifty or

Part 2 - The Byzantine Empire

Cross-cut of Constantinople's Land-walls

sixty meters, placed at intervals between the towers of the inner wall. These towers were ten to twelve meters tall.

The inner wall was between four and a half and six meters thick and rose to a height of twelve meters. It had ninety-six towers, each reaching between fifteen and twenty meters in height.

There were nine gates in the walls, and an unknown number of smaller posterns, some bricked up, some kept available. The land-walls of Constantinople were, in one word: formidable.

The one thing the walls had against them was that they were basically solid, even though the inner wall did have a layer of mortar, made from lime and crushed bricks, for protection against earthquake.

Solid walls had been built for centuries and were effective against all known siege weapons. They were, however, not very effective against cannon.

The velocity of a cannonball is such that when it meets a solid wall, the wall shatters. To prevent that, later walls were built with a flexible core of rubble, which absorbs some of the energy from the cannonball, and they were also often covered with dirt, which in itself would dampen the effect of the projectile.

But the walls of Constantinople were not built for cannon fire. Even worse, when the Byzantines attempted to put their own cannon on the walls in defence against the Ottomans, the walls started to crack as they could not properly absorb the vibration from the firing cannon.

On the other side of the equation, the problems Mehmed II had were twofold.

First, he needed cannon that in sheer power were powerful enough to break down the walls of Constantinople. To make dents in the walls was not enough, he needed breaches.

Secondly, the cannon needed to be able to do so from a distance that was safe from counter-fire from Constantinople. Here, the Byzantines had the advantage, as their cannon would be mounted on the top of a wall, and thus be able to shoot further than the Ottoman cannon on the ground.

Urban claimed he had the solution the sultan was looking for; a gun bigger than any gun built before. With nothing to lose, Mehmed gave Urban a free hand at the cannon foundry in Edirne and, no doubt understanding that his life depended on it, Urban went to work.

Urban first built cannon for Mehmed II's new fortress on the Bosporus, capable of firing stone balls weighing up 300 kg, but Urban was aiming further, much further. The cannon he had in mind for the walls of Constantinople would be capable of shooting stone balls weighing 750 kg, would be double the size of the cannon in the fortress and would have to be moveable.

In January 1453 Urban was done. His contraption was transported by means of fifty yoke of oxen and 700 men, and that was barely enough to move the monster cannon. It was placed outside the Sultan's Palace, the population of Edirne was warned not to panic and Urban loaded the cannon, which was a logistic challenge in its own right.

The firing could be hard for miles and filled the city with black smoke. When the smoke cleared it turned out that the projectile had gone for a full mile and had ploughed itself nearly two meters into the ground. Mehmed II had his cannon.

Urban built several smaller cannon, in their own right 'superguns', though smaller than the monster, now called the 'Basilica' Cannon. These were supplemented by a range of lighter guns to finally form fifteen batteries, capable of firing balls weighing between 100 and 750 kg, the latter being Urban's masterpiece. With his cannon sorted, Mehmed was ready to move as soon as spring came.

The logistic effort put forth by the Ottomans had of course not been undetected in Constantinople. Mehmed II's intentions were clear from the moment he started building the 'Throat Cutter' castle, and Emperor Constantine XI Palaiologos once again called for help.

Constantinople itself had never recovered from the devastating effects of the Fourth Crusade, 250 years previous. Where at that time it had housed between 400,000 and 500,000 people, in the middle of the fifteenth century it housed less than 50,000. With a city built for 500,000 occupied by less than ten percent of that, one contemporary observer described it as a series of villages, separated by fields, housed inside a common wall. That common wall was some twenty kilometres long, a third of that being the land wall. A count of the able-bodied defenders came to the depressing number of 4,773 locals and around 200 foreigners.

The only immediate response came from the Vatican. Once again, the Pope, now Nicholas V, sensed that the Byzantines were in such dire straits that they could be forced to agree to the unification of the two churches. In May 1452 he sent Cardinal Isidore of Kiev and 200 archers, paid for by the Pope.

Cardinal Isidore arrived in October 1452 and his message to the Byzantines was clear; accept union of the churches under the sovereignty of the Pope, and the Pope will help you. With no other choice Emperor Constantine XI Palaiologos agreed and Catholic mass was called in Hagia Sophia, the 1,000 years old central church of the Orthodox faith.

Though as a whole the Byzantine population at first accepted the union, on the assumption that it would mean the imminent arrival of significant military reinforcements from the Pope, not everybody was convinced. An anti-union party formed around the very outspoken monk Gennadius Scholarius, who preached heresy, damnation and the end of the world in Constantinople.

Despite the Pope's appeal to the Christian monarchs of Europe, no soldiers appeared, and the anti-unionists grew in strength until eventually the majority of the population turned and boycotted mass in Hagia Sophia, attending instead Orthodox mass in one of the many other churches in the city. Gennadius Scholarius himself withdrew from the public debate and focused on prayer in a monastery.

The European states were generally involved in either war with each other or internal revolt and none of them dared leave home and come to the assistance of Constantinople.

The only real potential ally was Hungary, but even they had their own internal issues, the regent Janos Hunyadi being replaced by the thirteen year old King Ladislaus Posthumous and the nobles fighting it out for the de-facto regency.

Janos Hunyadi did however approach the Byzantines in 1452, though it is unclear if he did so as an individual or representing the Hungarian King. Whether one or the other, he demanded control of two of the last remaining Byzantine fortresses, Misivri (modern day Nesebar) on the west coast of the Black Sea and Silivri on the Sea of Marmara. The Byzantines refused, and by the time they changed their mind in early 1453, the two fortresses had already been captured by the Ottoman vanguard.

Hunyadi's argument was that he needed strongholds from which to house troops, his appetite for a long march through the Balkans to meet the Ottomans obviously somewhat dampened after the defeats at Kosovo and Varna. Ulterior motives may have been for either Janos Hunyadi himself or the Hungarians to secure two valuable seaports before all was lost. Either way, there was no support from the Hungarians forthcoming either.

The last powerful ally to be found be the Italian merchant states, in particular Venice and Genoa. Venice were reluctant to do anything proactively, they did not want to upset the Ottomans and they were no particular friends of Emperor Constantine XI Palaiologos, who during his time as despot in the Morea had caused them much grief and who had a clear preference for Genoa, having given the Genoese use of the Galata suburb on the north side of the Golden Horn.

Genoa was also reluctant, not least as their substantial population in Galata would be in a very precarious situation should they upset the Ottomans, but they did support a small expeditionary force of 700 mercenaries commanded, and officially paid for, by Giovanni Giustiniani Longo. As was the style of Genoa, Giovanni Giustiniani-Longo's relief force was in concept a private, rather than state, expedition. The Genoese force arrived in Constantinople in January 1453 and Emperor Constantine XI Palaiologos subsequently appointed Giovanni Giustiniani-Longo commander of the Byzantine land forces.

In February 1453, a number of Venetian ships managed to sneak away from Constantinople at night, carrying on them some 700 soldiers, so the net effect of the help received from the Italian merchant states really came to zero.

At the last count, Constantinople was able to raise some 9,000 fighting men, 6,000 locals and 3,000 foreigners, having also received some, unofficial, help from the Genoese population in Galata. Many of the fighting men were untrained volunteers, few had any battle experience.

Against them stood the full might of the Ottoman army, the size of which is given by contemporary sources as anywhere between 165,000 and 400,000, but which was probably closer to 80,000 fighting men and numerous logistic personnel and camp followers. But the army was not alone.

Mehmed II had learned from his forefather's and their aborted attempts to take Constantinople. As long as the city could be re-supplied with men and provisions from the sea, it could hold out longer than the besieging army.

Having shut down the sea-route from the Black Sea, Mehmed II needed to seal off the route through the Sea of Marmara. An obvious choice would have been to also seal off the passage at the Dardanelles in the south, but Mehmed II was clever enough to understand that such a move, at that time, would likely tip the balance of the Italian merchant states' neutrality, so he did something else.

Over the preceding decades, the Ottomans had gradually built themselves a fleet, harboured along the Gallipoli peninsula and the west coast of Anatolia. The fleet consisted of war galleys, fast, sleek and low vessels, driven mainly by oars. They had not previously put an assembled fleet to sea and had not sought to provoke a staged sea battle. It therefore came as a surprise when at the beginning of April 1453 their assembled fleet, counting upwards of 200 ships of varying size appeared in the Sea of Marmara, and anchored three kilometres up the Bosporus, at a place called 'the Double Columns', approximately where the Dolmabahçe Palace is situated today. Mehmed meant to block the access to Constantinople by sheer numbers of naval vessels,

The Byzantines in response had the great chain suspended across the Golden Horn, where they kept their small fleet composed of the few Byzantine warships and a mixture of foreign ships that had been trapped in the harbour and pressed into service. All in all, the Byzantine fleet consisted of thirty-seven ships, most of them high-sided merchant ships. Before it got to this naval stand-off, Mehmed II had, however, been busy.

He had already, towards the end of 1452, sent an expeditionary force to the Morea in southern Greece. Their task was to engage and hold the forces of the despots of the Morea, the brothers of Emperor Constantine XI Palaiologos, so no reinforcements could come to Constantinople from there.

Then in February 1453 he started to move in Rumelia. A vanguard commanded by Karaja Bey started to besiege the few remaining fortresses and defensive towers still under Byzantine control on the coasts of the Blacks Sea, the Sea of Marmara and the Bosporus. Most just surrendered, some were taken by force, and a few were, simply put, under containment to be dealt with later.

At the same time army-engineers started to build and reinforce roads from Edirne to Constantinople, a stretch of some 200 kilometres, and the gigantic cannon, including the 'Basilica Cannon' slowly started to move. It took sixty oxen and 200 men to move the monster piece at a speed of four kilometres per day.

Then, on 23 March 1453, sultan Mehmed II set out from Edirne ahead of his army, and the fleet started to move towards the Sea of Marmara. On 2 April, the army was forming before the walls of Constantinople, even though the cannon had still not arrived. On 6 April, the smaller guns were in place and by 11 April all the cannon had arrived and been set up.

Mehmed II lined his army up outside the land walls, covering the whole stretch from the Sea of Marmara to the Golden Horn, but he had two particular points of interest.

The last northern part of the land wall had been modified and extended outwards, at a right angle, and a new single wall built without a protective moat. Here was placed considerable amounts of artillery aiming at the single wall and the right-angle joining point of the walls.

In the middle of the land wall was a small valley, the Lycus valley, with a stream running under the land walls. This was a natural centre point, and Mehmed II put up his tent and the biggest of the cannon here on a hill called Maltepe, across from the St. Romanus Gate.

The defenders, with too few men to defend the whole length of the walls, left the sea walls lightly defended, the Golden Horn being sealed off and the walls towards the Sea of Marmara posing little threat as the seas were too rough for ships to come close enough to unload troops.

Instead, the defence was concentrated on the land wall, in particular on the two weaker spots mentioned above. With the Ottoman fleet unable to enter the Golden Horn, the Ottomans had to come over or through the land walls, a quest never before achieved by a besieging army.

Despite the investment in cannon, Mehmed II still believed that going over the walls was a realistic option. Accordingly, a small, somewhat unorganized attack was started before the artillery was in place, but it was thrown back by a sortie from the defenders.

While waiting for the artillery and in preparation for a bigger more concerted attack, the Ottomans started to fight skirmishing battles against defending sorties, the purpose being to gradually fill the moat with stones and timber at strategic points. Whereas the defenders were reasonably successful in their sorties, and took several Ottoman prisoners, they also took loses and finally had to stop the sorties as, contrary to the Ottomans, they could not afford the loss of fighting men. Instead, they fought from the walls, affecting massive losses on the Ottomans by means of arrows, small firearms and anything they could throw at them.

Parallel to this effort, Ottoman sappers started to dig a tunnel towards the wall, aiming to get under the wall and undermine it with a massive blast.

Once the smaller cannon were in place they started to bombard the walls, but as expected they had little effect. Once the big cannon were in place that changed.

On 12 April, a day-long bombardment was started and Mehmed II's new super-guns soon started to show their effect. They shattered the walls and towers in a way never seen before and the concept of siege warfare had simply changed forever.

While the fight for dominance of the moat continued, the Ottoman cannon started to break down whole sections of the walls, in particular in the single wall in the north and around the St. Romanus Gate.

The bombardment continued for seven days. It could be heard in Anatolia, and felt through the planks of the ships in the Golden Horn. Every night the defenders filled up the holes with a combination of timber, stone debris and earth and covered the improvised repairs by cowhides to avoid the Ottomans setting them on fire.

On the evening of 18 April Mehmed II decided that the wall was damaged enough for a full-scale attack. His decision was partly based on a rumour that a Hungarian army was on its way to relieve the besieged city, a rumour started due to an embassy from Janos Hunyadi informing the Sultan that a peace agreement made between them in 1451 was no longer valid, as he did no more act as regent and the new king did not recognize the agreement. As it turned out, there was no Hungarian army on its way.

Starting the attack two hours after sunset, the Ottomans concentrated their effort at new breaches in the wall by the St. Romanus Gate. They came with everything they had, battering rams, attack towers, ladders and foot soldiers, tens of thousands of foot soldiers.

But it was not enough. After four hours of all-out assault, the Ottomans had to retreat, the breaches were not big enough, they were too easy to defend against the small number of soldiers that could pass through them and the traditional attack with battering rams, attack towers and ladders simply did not make an impact on the massive walls.

Mehmed II started the bombardment again, but he had lost the 'Basilica Cannon'. Being fired seven times per day, the enormous gun became immensely hot and gradually started to develop small hairline cracks. Urban warned against using it further, but Mehmed II insisted. Eventually it burst, killing and wounding many, some say including Urban, though this has never been verified. It was put back together by means of metal-bands but burst again beyond repair. The slightly smaller super-guns were however holding, and their effect was devastating.

At the same time as the attack on the land walls, Mehmed II started the naval war. His fleet left its anchoring point in the Bosporus and went to

4 - Deadly Neighbours

attack the Byzantine fleet, anchored in a line across the Golden Horn to protect the chain that had been drawn across the narrow entry.

Though the Ottoman fleet outnumbered the Byzantine fleet, the defenders had one, determining, advantage, height.

The Ottoman galleys were low in the water and difficult to manoeuvre in the choppy seas. The defending fleet was mainly tall merchant ships, so the attackers were attacking upwards and the defenders were defending downwards, giving significant advantage to the defenders who could bombard the attackers with arrows, spears and anything else that could be thrown, while the attackers could make little impression once at close quarters. The Ottoman galleys had small cannon mounted, but they were so small that they could not make an impression on the sturdy hulls of the merchant ships.

After a fierce battle, the Ottomans finally gave up and returned to their base. Mehmed II's attempt at settling matters fast had failed. He had been defeated on land and at sea. And it would get worse.

Failing to raise any voluntary military support, the Pope had in March paid for three (Genoese) ships loaded with provisions and men. They had left for Constantinople, but not arrived there before the siege had begun. Along the way they had met up with a fourth ship, this one from Constantinople, crewed by Italians, and full of corn purchased in Sicily.

On the morning of 20 April, only a day after the unsuccessful Ottoman attacks, they came within sight of Constantinople, having passed through the Dardanelles unchallenged. It was time to see if the sheer number of Ottoman ships could prevent supplies from reaching the city.

Once the ships were sighted, Mehmed II personally rode down to the fleets anchoring point at the Double Columns to tell his admiral to *'take the sailing ships and bring them to me, or never come back alive.'*

So, a hundred or more galleys set off to stop four merchantmen, seemingly an uneven fight, but once again the significant difference in height, the manoeuvrability of the bigger ships riding on a southern wind and the significant experience of the Italian sailors gave the defenders the advantage.

The small merchant fleet simply ignored the Ottomans demands for them to stop, and elegantly swung left from the Sea of Marmara to make it through to the Golden Horn, the Byzantine ready to lower the chain for just long enough for them to pass.

The Ottoman galleys fired arrows and cannonballs at the larger ships but were met by a fierce shower of arrows and other missiles coming back. They tried to get close enough to board the merchantmen, or set fire to their sails, but could not manoeuvre fast enough in the turbulent waters.

Just as the merchantmen seemed to be unstoppable, the wind dropped. The merchantmen, having ridden on a southern breeze that carried them straight to where they wanted to go, suddenly came to a stop, starting to drift pass the entry to the Golden Horn and giving the advantage to the oar-powered galleys.

The Ottoman fleet was everywhere, attacking the motionless merchant ships from all sides, men were crawling up anchor cables or ropes attached to grappling hooks. The defenders were dropping stones from cranes to sink the lightly built galleys. Barrages of missiles were interchanged.

The defenders held for three hours. Then they managed to bring their ships alongside each other and tie them together, creating a massive fighting platform with fewer sides to attack, but they were still drifting past their destination and would gradually run out of men and ammunition.

Then the wind returned and the merchantmen, after four hours of relentless fighting, rode into the Golden Horn under the never-ending applause of the Byzantines, lining the walls.

Mehmed II himself had ridden down to the beach on the northern side of the Golden Horn to shout a mix of encouragement and threats to his troops, drifting closer and closer to his position. When he realized the battle was lost, he *'whipped up his horse and rode away'*.

In the style that would become trademark for Mehmed II, he now threw himself into a frenzy of activity. He needed to regain the initiative, and he needed to establish his authority unless his army should fall apart as a consequence of the recent defeats.

First to deal with was his admiral, Baltaoglu. Mehmed II rode to the Double Columns and demanded to know how the admiral had failed to stop the merchant ships despite his clear supremacy in numbers.

The admiral, himself wounded in one eye during the battle, tried to explain the simple facts, but Mehmed II would have none of it. He ordered the admiral impaled.

The assembled nobles and high ranking military commanders begged for mercy, and Mehmed II changed the judgment to confiscation of all the admirals possessions (to be distributed between the Janissaries), dismissal and a 100 lashes, which were administered on the spot.

Having re-established his authority, Mehmed II now called his war council to discuss a peace proposal from the Byzantine Emperor who was now feeling the battle was swinging to his advantage.

Mehmed II's grand vizier, his old adversary, Çandarlı Halil Pasha, led a party of the council believing that it was time for peace. Another party, led by Zaganos Pasha, believed that Çandarlı Halil Pasha loved Greek gold too much, and that the assault should continue. Strangely enough Çandarlı Halil Pasha was of old Ottoman blood and Zaganos Pasha was a convert Greek.

In the end it was decided to continue, and Mehmed II had a plan at hand, which he had been preparing on the quiet and which now came to an explosive execution.

Anticipating that it could turn out to be impossible to get through the naval defences at the mouth of the Golden Horn, engineers had been

4 - Deadly Neighbours

working behind the Galata Township, invisible to the Byzantines and in the eyes of the Genoese in Galata simply preparing a road. They were, however, up to something entirely different.

If the Ottoman fleet could not get into the Golden Horn through the water, they would have to come over land. Mehmed II planned to move part of the fleet across from the Bosporus, behind Galata, and into the Golden Horn behind the Byzantine fleet. In the way was a 65 meter ridge, and it was here that the engineers had been gradually preparing the surface so on Mehmed II's orders, which he gave on 21 April - probably even before he went to deal with the admiral and the council - wooden rolls were placed on the new surface, and a small Ottoman ship was pulled out of the water in the Bosporus and literally rolled over the ridge and into the waters of the Golden Horn. It required a massive amount of manpower, but that was something the Ottomans were never short of.

As the first smaller ship got on its way, more, and bigger, vessels followed and the Byzantines knew nothing of it until, on the morning of Sunday 22 April Ottoman ships started to drop into the Golden Horn next to the walls around the Galata township.

Vulnerable to attacks by the Byzantine fleet, Mehmed II had in parallel with the operation of moving the ships also moved a battery of cannon to the water's edge so the Ottoman fleet inside the Golden Horn had cover for any pre-emptive strikes.

This time it was Emperor Constantine XI Palaiologos who held council. The appearance of the Ottoman fleet, now counting seventy vessels, in the Golden Horn opened a new front on the sea walls, a front the defenders could not afford to spare their meagre resources on. Various options were discussed. In the end it was decided to use the same strategy the Byzantines had attempted against the Venetians in 1203, to burn the enemy fleet.

It was left with the Venetian commander of the fleet to prepare the attack. Basically, two merchant vessels would be kitted out with sacks of wool hanging over the hull to be able to withstand cannon fire. They would protect two smaller vessels equipped with nozzles shooting 'Greek fire', which could close on the Ottoman fleet and set it alight.

First the Genoese did not want to participate, then they changed their minds, causing a four-day delay, but finally, on 28 April, everything was ready and in the middle of the night they set off quietly, travelling the mile or so toward the Ottoman fleet.

The Ottomans were, however, prepared. One of the (Venetian) attacking vessels advanced too far forward and was shot to pieces. The merchant ships designed to draw fire ended up stuck in the middle of a chaotic withdrawal and had to spend two hours fighting off the collective Ottoman fleet before finally the two parties broke away from each other.

The end result was that the Ottoman fleet was intact and Italian pride severely dented. The Ottomans had won their first naval encounter, a small victory, but of great importance to morale.

Forty of the soldiers from the sunken ship were captured by the Ottomans. The following day they were impaled in full view of the Byzantine defenders.

Not to be outdone, Emperor Constantine XI Palaiologos ordered that 260 Ottoman prisoners, taken during the fights for the moat, be taken to the walls and hung in view of the Ottomans.

The failed night-attack on the Ottoman fleet meant that the two Italian factions started blaming each other. The Genoese blamed the Venetians for not following the plan and breaking the line for personal glory. The Venetians blamed the Genoese for having revealed the plan to the Ottomans, probably through their community in the Galata Township.

And indeed, the Galata Township was in a very precarious situation. Officially Genoa was neutral, so Mehmed II was not waging war on Galata. However, most of the inhabitants were sympathetic to the defenders, and provided whatever help they could smuggle across Golden Horn out of sight of the Ottomans. Their situation would become even more precarious over the following weeks.

First the defenders decided that further attacks on the Ottoman fleet were futile. Instead, they pulled a couple of big cannon down to a gate in the water wall and started firing across the water at the Ottoman fleet, initially having some success and sinking a few Ottoman ships. The Ottomans moved their ships out of range of the Byzantine guns and countered by three of their own guns, trying to take out the Byzantine guns, which in turn tried to take out the Ottoman guns. None of the parties, however, could do any damage to each other. The Byzantine guns were protected by a wall and the Ottoman guns by an earthen bank. Nevertheless, the duel continued for ten days.

On 5 May Mehmed II introduced a new strategy: mortars. He wanted to be able to aim for the Byzantine fleet from behind the Galata Township. For this he needed guns with a very high but not necessarily very long, trajectory, so his engineers came up with a basic mortar, capable of hitting the Byzantine ships from behind the Galata Township.

The mortars were an immediate success, forcing the Byzantine fleet to take cover under the Galata walls, effectively preventing it from moving. The only ship sunk was, however, a Genoese trading ship belonging to a trader from Galata.

Precision was not the main strength of Mehmed II's new mortars, so when the Byzantine fleet moved closer to Galata, so did the Ottoman fire, with the inevitable result that houses and people in Galata were hit. The Genoese complained to the sultan, and were told to go away, with the promise that their losses would be compensated.

4 - Deadly Neighbours

As April became May, it was clear that the Byzantine fleet presented no more danger in the Golden Horn, so Mehmed II had a pontoon-bridge built, ready to be pulled across the Golden Horn, close to the land wall, enabling fast movement of troops, cannon and supplies across the waterway.

While the warring parties battled for supremacy on the water, the land war moved on. The cannon bombardment had intensified after 21. April and large parts of the walls were shot out, with the defenders desperately filling the holes as well as they could during the night.

There were problems with the big guns, another one cracked and they all showed signs of wear, but Mehmed II ordered that the bombardment continue, he had no intentions of letting the defenders have any rest.

At the end of April Mehmed II ordered another attack on the walls, not so much to make a real run for it, as to wear down the defenders. As before, there were heavy losses on both sides. The Ottomans could afford that; the defenders could not.

Inside the walls things were getting somewhat desperate. With the threat of an attack coming from the Golden Horn, the defenders were now spread thin. They got little rest, as the days were spent preventing the Ottomans getting to the walls and the nights were spent repairing the damaged walls. Furthermore, food was running out.

Mehmed II was aware of this, probably through spies in Galata and he deliberately continued a war of attrition, constantly launching attacks, some small, some larger, some during the day and some during the night and all the time maintaining the barrage from the cannon.

On the night of 6 May he ordered that the cannon continue firing through the night, preventing the defenders from repairing the damaged walls. On the night of 7 May he ordered an all-out attack, concentrating around the area of the St. Romanus Gate, the area where he had now also concentrated the cannonade.

The battle was fierce, the Ottoman coming in great numbers and with much noise, the defenders desperately fighting for their lives, their city and their empire. At the end of it the attack was repelled, twice, but the defenders were so exhausted that they could only do makeshift repairs on the inside of the damaged walls before they collapsed.

By 12 May, a breach had developed at the junction with the single wall at the northern part of the wall. That evening Mehmed II ordered another night attack. This time the attackers managed to get inside the walls and were only repelled after Emperor Constantine XI Palaiologos himself went to the front and boosted the morale of the defenders. The defences were holding, but the attacks got closer and closer to success.

On 19 May Mehmed II tried something else. In the dark of night, the Ottomans had erected several gigantic siege-towers on the edge of the moat. They were so tall that they overlooked the fighting platforms on the Byzantine walls. At the bottom they had hatches, enabling the Ottomans to dig inside the tower and throw the earth into the moat in front, gradually filling it up. Causeways covered by hide and camel skin went back to the Ottoman trenches, allowing the Ottomans to pass freely to and from the towers with men and materials.

Gradually they filled the moat, and by nightfall a tower placed in front of the Charisius Gate had made such progress that it could be rolled over the moat and onto the defending wall. Inside the tower a number of fighting platforms were connected by ladders, which could be re-used to cover the last distance between the tower and the walls. It was archaic, even in the fifteenth century, but it seemed to work.

The defenders had to do something, and do it fast, before hordes of Ottoman soldiers infiltrated the walls, so they prepared barrels of gunpowder, fused them up, lit them, and simply dumped them towards and under the approaching tower.

The tower was tipped over, with great loss of life, the now exposed survivors were bombarded with the obligatory storm of missiles from the walls. Mehmed II called a halt to proceedings and the other towers were abandoned and eventually burned by sorties from the walls.

The towers were ultimately not successful, but once again Mehmed had shown that he could come up with a plan and execute it in secrecy and with speed, fully utilizing the vast resources at his disposal.

Mining operations - started early in the siege and continued throughout - were also showing to be ineffective. The miners had gotten under the wall several times, in some cases even digging several meters along the wall and undermining it, but in all cases, they had been detected by the defenders (using barrels of water on the ground to detect underground activity).

The defenders dug countermines, intercepting the Ottoman mines, and the Ottoman miners were killed by collapse of the mines or underground hand-to-hand combat, the defenders using portable nozzles spraying Greek fire. Like the siege-towers, it was close, very close, but not enough.

Having tried everything else, Mehmed II now concentrated the cannon fire on the middle of the wall around the St. Romanus Gate. This section of the wall had been under intense bombardment from the outset of the siege and was in a state of rubble and makeshift repairs.

The bombardment was now extended to continue round the clock, giving the defenders no room to make repairs.

On 26 May Mehmed II once again called his war council. Both sides of the conflict were exhausted and had taken great loses. There were false rumours of both an Italian relief fleet and a Hungarian relief army. Morale was waning, supplies were running out. Something had to happen. Like before, the Ottomans needed to decide whether to give up or press for a result.

The same discussion as the previous month took place between the same two factions in the council, and again Mehmed II decided to stay and try to

4 - Deadly Neighbours

finish what he had started. The Ottoman army was told to prepare for a final assault in the next few days.

Inside the walls the renewed activity in the Ottoman camp could only be interpreted in one way, an attack was coming, and also here did they understand that this was the defining moment. If they repelled the Ottomans once more, they would break the siege, alternatively, all was lost.

The following days were spent on preparation and coordination. The Ottoman plan was simple; attack along as far a stretch of the land wall as possible to draw out the defenders. The fleet would circle the sea walls in order to draw as many defenders away from the land wall as possible. The main attack, however, would be at the St. Romanus Gate.

The walls around the St. Romanus Gate had been constantly bombarded and massive breaches had appeared. Despite the defender's best effort to repair them, they were widening at an alarming rate. A ricocheting fragment from a cannon ball had hit the Byzantine commander, the Genoese Giovanni Giustiniani Longo, and he was carried off the walls. Without his coordination and motivation, the defenders were in an even worse state.

On the evening of 28th May Giovanni Giustiniani Longo was back on the walls, weakened, but present and still in command of the essential central part of the wall.

At one thirty in the morning of 29th May, the Ottoman cannon finally stopped. Instead of cannonballs came foot soldiers, once again tens of thousands of them, the majority aiming for the breaches in the wall around the St. Romanus Gate.

The first wave consisted of irregulars; mainly untrained Christians pressed into service and their attack was designed to wear down the defenders. The irregulars were easily replaceable, expendable, but useful. Behind them roamed Military Police, ordered to kill anyone who turned back and ran. There was only one way, and it was forward. Their attack lasted two hours until the sad remains were allowed to move back.

The next wave consisted of well trained and equipped heavy infantry from Anatolia. Their attack lasted another two hours. They managed to penetrate to within the outer wall but could not put enough soldiers through the gaps in the wall to hold their position. Ultimately, after another two hours of intense fighting this wave was also turned back.

The Ottoman loses were appalling, the pile of their own dead being one of the hindrances they now had to negotiate in their attempt to reach the wall. Throughout this wave of attack, Mehmed II had ordered the bigger cannon to continue to fire directly at the walls in an attempt to widen the breaches, killing both defenders and his own troops in the process.

Mehmed II now only had one attack-wave left, the toughest, best trained and best equipped troops, including the Janissaries. 5,000 strong they were immediately ordered forward, led by Mehmed II himself as far as the moat. It was make or break time.

And it nearly did not work. Once again, the defenders gave it everything they had and more. Ottoman troops penetrated the wall but were thrown back. Ottoman attackers on the walls were cut down. Missiles flew from both sides, the cannon kept firing hitting friend and foe. Smoke enveloped the battlefield, but slowly, ever so slowly, did the Ottomans start to give. The battle was swinging in the way of the defenders.

On the northern part of the wall, the Ottomans were not making any major impression but maintained pressure to spread out the Byzantine defenders. Indeed, the battle was so relatively one-sided that the defenders could make sorties, using a small door, called the Circus Gate, hidden between overlapping sections of the wall.

After one of these sorties, the gate was not closed properly, and a band of Ottoman attackers noticed the open door. They entered, gained access to one of the towers where they were subsequently isolated and killed. They did however manage to raise the Ottoman flag on the tower, sending a shockwave down the wall. The defenders, thinking that the wall had been breached, lost their morale. The attackers, thinking likewise, renewed their push forward, once again turning the initiative their way.

Giovanni Giustiniani Longo was wounded again. He needed medical attention, best administered on his ship in the Golden Horn. A gate was opened in the inner wall to allow the wounded commander through, and the Genoese fighting men took the opportunity to follow their leader and sneak away towards the relative safety of their ships.

Panic now struck all along the defensive line. Defenders were trying to retreat back behind the inner wall, but with the exception of the gate from which Giovanni Giustiniani Longo and the Genoese had disappeared, all the gates were locked. Commanders tried to rally their men to once again push the attackers off the ramparts, but the battle was lost.

Ottoman troops poured into the breaches, sending the remaining defenders into an all-out escape through the one open gate. The Ottomans took tower by tower, placing their own flag on top, and opened the gates of the massive land walls from the inside, letting in more of their comrades.

By six o'clock, as dawn broke, it was all over. Mehmed II's strategy had worked. Emperor Constantine XI Palaiologos personally defended his city till the end. He was killed in the last big push, never leaving the front line.

As was custom, the city was given to the conquering army for three days. What had been rebuilt of the greatest city in Christianity since the sack of the Fourth Crusade 250 years earlier was ripped apart. The buildings belonged to the Sultan, but anything that could be carried away, living or otherwise, could be taken, and so it was.

Though, on the Sultan's orders, the buildings were left intact, the population at large was led away to slavery. Constantinople, the capital of the biggest and most powerful Christian empire was left behind as a smoking, empty shell when the Ottoman army disengaged. Mehmed II stayed until 21

June, after which he returned to Edirne, already making plans for what to do with his new treasure.

Constantinople was renamed as Istanbul, and a few years later took over as the, single, capital of the Ottoman Empire. The city was rebuilt, little of the former capitals monuments and buildings remaining, and Mehmed II would throughout the rest of his rule seek to repopulate it by forcefully moving people from conquered cities to Istanbul, creating the foundation for the multi-culture and multi-ethnic city that Istanbul still is today.

Those - and they were the majority - in the Christian World who had considered Mehmed II a weak, possibly simpleminded, sultan, a shadow of his impressive father, now had to rethink. Mehmed II had shown them differently, and his burning ambition for a worldwide empire had to be taken seriously.

But the fall of Constantinople did not necessarily mean the end of the Byzantine Empire. Constantinople had fallen to the crusaders 250 years previous and yet the Empire had risen again from the ashes, at that time growing out from Nicaea in Anatolia.

This time the remaining part of the Empire was to be found in the Morea, held by the late Emperor Constantine XI Palaiologos' two brothers, Demetrios, and Thomas Palaiologos.

As a reaction to Mehmed II's Conquest of Constantinople, the Palaiologos brothers feared that they were next and planned to flee for Italy. They however lost the confidence of the locals, fearing Ottoman revenge, and had to change their plans, stay, and face a revolt. They ultimately had to ask Mehmed II for help, and the Ottoman commander in the area came to their assistance.

Despite this, a new revolt broke out. This time Mehmed II came to an understanding directly with the revolting nobles, who agreed to pay tribute directly to the Ottomans. Though reinstated, by the end of 1454 the Palaiologos brothers were mere shadow rulers.

That however did not mean an end to their ambitions. In 1458 Thomas Palaiologos attacked both Demetrios and the Ottoman's garrison, throwing the peninsula into a state of chaos. Demetrios appealed to Mehmed II, who once again intervened and secured a peace and reconciliation agreement. That lasted a few months until Demetrios attacked Thomas.

Mehmed II now had had enough. In 1460 he marched on the Morea and once and for all put it under Ottoman control. A few die-hard fortifications lasted until 1461 before they were taken, but the last remains of the Byzantine Empire had been crushed.

The only Greek settlement left in the Ottoman hinterlands was the Empire of Trebizond, which is covered in the Chapter 8 as that had not been part of the Byzantine Empire since the Fourth Crusade some 250 years prior.

As a closing remark on Mehmed II's conflict with the Byzantine Empire, it is interesting that the Conquest of Constantinople, one of the biggest, most spectacular, famous and important land-battles in history was not about the land that was conquered, as it was per se insignificant, but about controlling the seas.

By the Conquest of Constantinople Mehmed II had both secured his capability to move troops and ordinary people alike between the European and Asian sides of his empire, and he had started the slow but steady course towards a challenge on the Italian merchant state's monopoly on the seaways.

When he conquered Constantinople, and his soldiers gave him the moniker 'Fatih', 'the Conqueror', he had ruled for two years and was twenty-one years old. He would rule for another twenty-eight years, few of which were not defined by military conflict.

PART 3

TROUBLESOME KINSMEN

5 - THE SELJUKS
6 - THE KARAMANIDS
7 - THE WHITE SHEEP
8 - THE EMPIRE OF TREBIZOND

Part 3 - Troublesome Kinsmen

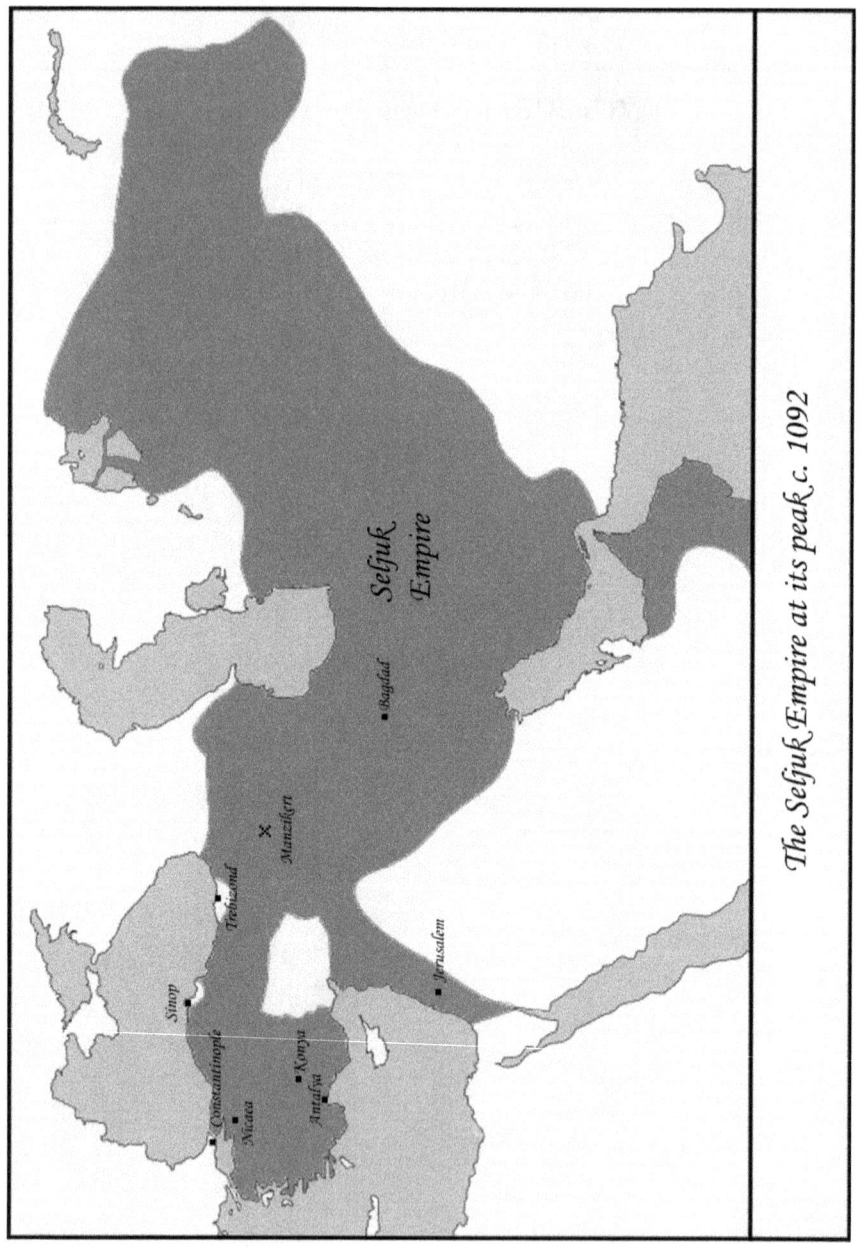

The Seljuk Empire at its peak c. 1092

5 - THE SELJUKS

CRITICAL TIMELINE

Year	Event	Involved Parties
700s	Oguz Yabgu State develops in central Asia	Oguz Yabgu State
977	The Ghaznavids take control of Persia	Persia
985	The Seljuk clan converts to Islam and splits from Oguz Yabgu State	Oguz Yabgu State Seljuks
1055	Seljuks capture Persia and end the Ghaznavid dynasty	Seljuks Persia
1055	Tuğrul becomes 'Sultan' of the Great Seljuk Empire	Seljuks
1063	Alp Arslan becomes Seljuk Sultan	Seljuks
1068	Romanus IV Diogenes becomes Emperor of Byzantium	Byzantium
1069	Byzantine campaign in eastern Anatolia	Byzantium Seljuks
1071	Battle of Manzikert	Byzantium Seljuks
1072	Malik-Shah I becomes Seljuk Sultan	Seljuks
1077	The Seljuk Sultanate of Rum splits from the Great Seljuk Empire	Seljuks
1092	Malik-Shah I die. Civil war follows	Seljuks
1099	First Crusade	Byzantium Western Europe Seljuks Egypt
1147	Second Crusade	Seljuks Western Europe
1192	Third Crusade	Seljuks Germany
1207	Seljuks conquer Antalya	Byzantium Seljuks
1214	Seljuks conquer port-town of Sinop	Byzantines Seljuks
1243	Mongols conquer Seljuk Sultanate	Seljuks Mongols

5 - The Seljuks

Throughout this book I use the expression 'Ottoman' rather than 'Turk' or 'Turkish.' That is on purpose and because I believe that there is a distinct difference.

True, the original Osmanlı were Turks, or of 'Turkoman' origins to be even more precise, but the Ottoman Empire soon grew to cover large areas populated by people with other than Turkish background, so by using the words 'Turk' or 'Turkish' we effectively cut off a very large part of the growing empire's population.

Similarly, there were large Turkish/Turkoman populations which were not part of the Ottoman Empire and if we call the Ottomans 'the Turks', we ignore this fact. However, for most casual observers these Turkoman enemies of the Empire are somewhat fuzzy entities, but in this part, we will change that perception and cover the Conqueror's own kinsmen and how and why they became his enemies.

To start the tale, we need to envisage Anatolia at the onset of the second millennium AC.

The area had for millennia been under the influence of Greek culture and language. For centuries it had been in first Roman, then Byzantine possession, providing a mainly stable and peaceful environment in which people could live and prosper, as could art and culture.

The push from the Arab-Islamic armies of the seventh and eight centuries had been held by the Byzantine army at an uneasy, ragged, borderline along the Taurus Mountains in south-eastern Anatolia, so most people in Anatolia spoke Greek and they were predominantly Christians.

North-east of Anatolia, in central Asia, nomadic tribes of Mongol origins, had for centuries wandered, migrated, and intermixed with the populations they encountered. They had settled in tribal areas, so called khanates, ruled by a Khan. This is not dissimilar to the way Europe, after the fall of the western Roman Empire, had formed into a patchwork of principalities and small kingdoms.

Occasionally a particularly strong khanate would dominate its neighbours, creating small empires, ruled by a 'Khan of Khans'.

Sometime in the eighth century, a khanate called the Oguz Yabgu State had developed in an area between and north of the Caspian and Aral seas, in modern terms covering parts of Kazakhstan, Uzbekistan and Turkmenistan. Crucially, to the south, they were bordering the (Muslim) Caliphate of Persia.

The Oghuz Yabgu State was surrounded by similar khanates, and when not occupied by internal strife, they would fight their neighbours for land and supremacy. Again, in this context, the khanates of central Asia were no different from the principalities and kingdoms of Europe.

From time to time, they would also get involved in hostilities with the powerful Persians and the Persians took many Turkmen slaves who were pressed into service in the army. At the end of the tenth century, a revolt by the slave army took control in Persia, creating the Ghaznavids Dynasty, bringing significant Turkman influence into Islamic culture.

And that influence worked both ways, as some Turkmen tribes outside Persia converted to Islam, though they had originally been Buddhists.

One such tribe, originating from the Oghuz Yabgu State, was the Seljuk tribe, named after its founder Seljuk. The tribe separated from the Oghuz Yabgu State and started moving south. Under Seljuk's son, Tuğrul, it reached Persia where in 1055, having beaten the Persian army off, ended the Ghaznavids Dynasty, and set themselves up in Baghdad as a major force to be reckoned with.

The Caliph in Bagdad (the spiritual head of Islam was more than happy to see the last of the Ghaznavids Dynasty and gave Tuğrul his daughter and the title of 'Sultan', possibly an existing honourable title, but for the first time used on coins issued by Tuğrul. His budding empire would become known as the Great Seljuk Empire.

On Tuğrul's death in 1063, he was, after the almost obligatory civil war, succeeded by his nephew Alp Arslan.

Alp Arslan had imperial ambitions, and soon conquered Armenia and Georgia. He then turned his eyes towards the Byzantine Empire.

During the late part of the 1060s the Seljuks started to cross over the border to the Byzantine Empire in eastern Anatolia and gradually move west. The Byzantine Empire was impacted by yet another succession-crisis following the death of emperor Constantine X Ducas in 1067 and had little to offer in terms of resistance, but finally (co-) emperor Romanus IV Diogenes was appointed in 1068 and started to reform and rebuild the ailing Byzantine army.

A contemporary source described the Byzantine army of the time as an army '*of Macedonians and Bulgars and Cappadocians and Uzes and other foreigners who happened to be about*' and added that they were '*bent over by poverty and distress and were deprived of armour. Instead of swords and other military weapons they were bearing hunting spears and scythes*'.

The Emperor's mercenary army campaigned in Anatolia with little success in 1068 - 1069 and went back in 1071 where, after playing cat and mouse, the two armies finally met at Manzikert on 26 August. The Seljuks not only beat the Byzantine army but also took Emperor Romanos IV Diogenes prisoner. Though Arp Arslan treated the Emperor with all due respect, and released him after a week of pleasantries, the Battle of Manzikert had broken the back of Byzantine resistance and Alp Arslan allowed his military commanders a free hand to proceed westwards and carve out their own territories which they could rule under his suzerainty.

And so, the Seljuks started a migration westward. First came raiders and then settlers. With little Byzantine resistance they got as far as the coast of the Sea of Marmara, even though the Byzantines did manage to take the western part of Anatolia back over the next few decades.

When Alp Arslan died in 1072, his empire fell to his son, Malik-Shah I under whose rule it further expanded until it bordered China in the East and the Byzantine Empire in the West. On Malik-Shah I's death in 1092 the empire, however, started to fall apart due to several candidates to the throne, and eventually it split into several smaller pieces.

The Byzantine Emperor's call for help from his fellow Christians resulted in the First Crusade in 1098-1099. It came at a time where the Seljuk Empire was in disarray and it meant the loss (from Seljuk control) of Syria and Palestine as well as important cities in Anatolia.

Even though pieces of the former, short-lived, empire still hung on to some kind of unity for a few more decades, the Great Seljuk Empire had effectively imploded the same way empires before and after having torn themselves apart due to issues of succession. By 1156 the Great Seljuk Empire was no more, but it left behind a patchwork of Turkmen states, ruled by their own 'bey' (and thus gradually taking on the name 'beyliks' rather than khanates).

The First Crusade and the Byzantine army following in its wake however eventually retook the westernmost areas and gradually a state known as 'The Seljuk Sultanate of Rum', headed by Kilij Arslan I, formed around the town of Konya in central Anatolia.

To its north-east it had another ambitious beylik, the Danishmends ruled by Malik Ghazi in Sivas. Together these two Seljuk rulers effectively pulled the armies of The Second Crusade apart in 1147.

Once any further risks from crusader armies were eliminated, they started fighting each other for dominance, a fight that would last seven decades and end with the Sultanate of Rum annexing the Danishmends, as well as the territories to their immediate south-east, known as Little Armenia, making the Seljuk Sultanate of Rum the dominant player in central and eastern Anatolia.

Having fought off the armies of the Third Crusade in the 1190s, by 1207 the Seljuk's captured the Mediterranean port-town of Antalya from the Byzantines and in 1214 the Black Sea port-town of Sinop. In the same year they made the Empire of Trebizond on the Black Sea a vassal. We shall cover the Empire of Trebizond separately at the end of this part.

These were the years immediately following the Fourth Crusade and the ousting of the Byzantine rulers from Constantinople. As covered in Part 2, the Byzantines started to reform around Nicaea, so by the middle of the thirteenth century Anatolia was effectively split into three north-south belts;

in the west was a narrow band controlled by the Latin Empire of Constantinople, west of the middle was a band under the control of the Byzantines in Nicaea and from the middle and eastwards was a band controlled by the Seljuk Empire of Rum.

The Byzantines regained control of Constantinople and the westernmost part of Anatolia in 1261, but the Byzantine Empire was weak and preoccupied by their own issues in Rumelia, Greece and Bulgaria, leaving Anatolia free for the Seljuk tribes to still move west. As covered in Part 1, one of these tribes eventually developed into the Ottomans, initially carving out their territory in north-westernmost Anatolia.

By that time, the Seljuk Empire of Rum itself had, however, effectively disintegrated. They had been annexed by the Mongols in 1243, but the beyliks that formed in the west were far removed from central control and finally the Empire just ceased to exist in any real form, being split into the patchwork of beyliks covering Anatolia that would eventually spurn off the mighty Ottoman Empire. But the Ottomans were not the only strong nation to emerge from the ashes of the Seljuk Sultanate of Rum.

5 - The Seljuks

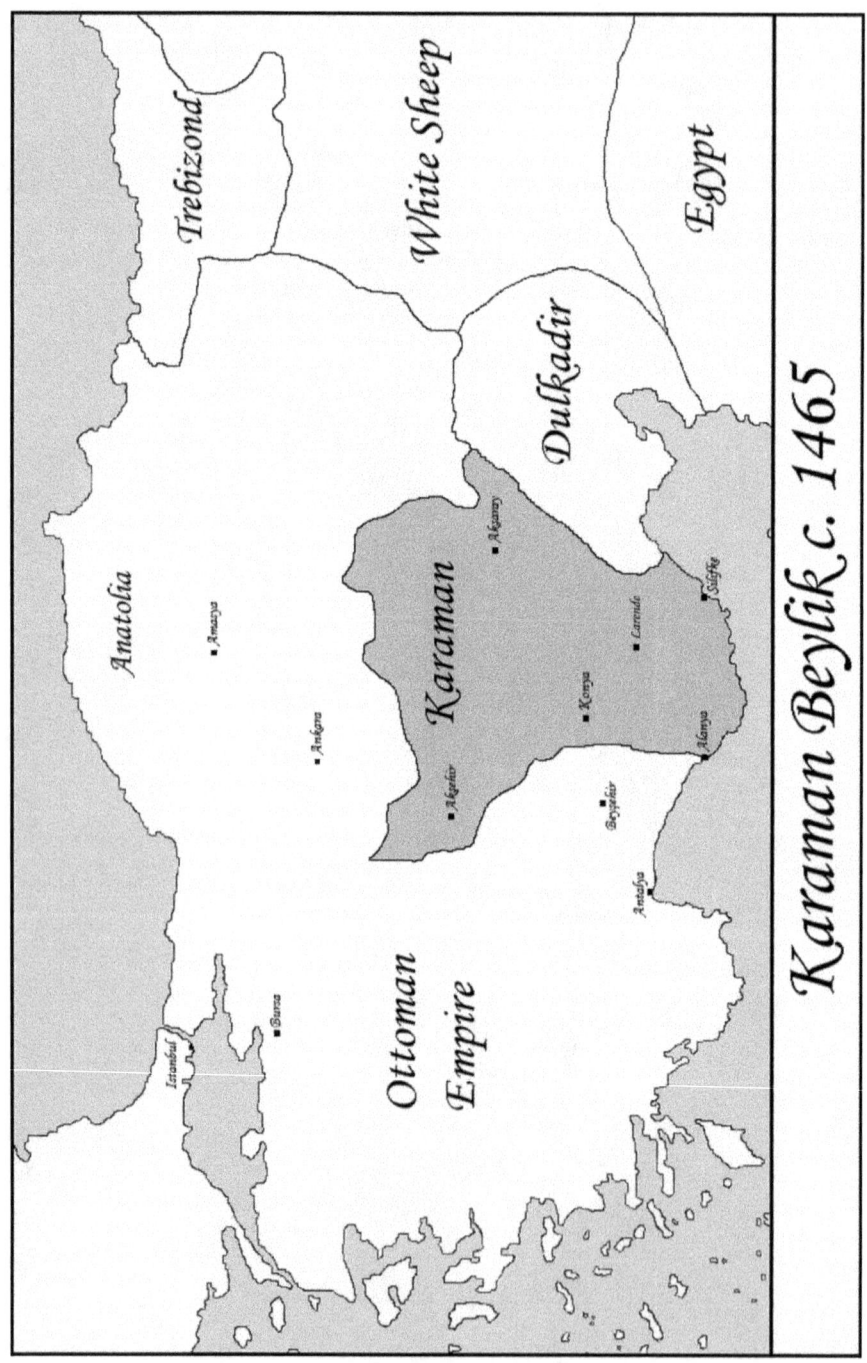

6 - THE KARAMANIDS

Part 3 - Troublesome Kinsmen

CRITICAL TIMELINE

Year	Event	Involved Parties
Early 1200s	Afshar tribe arrive at Sivas	Afshars / Seljuks
1239	Afshars revolt	Afshars / Seljuks
1243	Mongol invasion creates opportunity for Afshars under Kerîmeddin Karaman Bey	Afshars / Seljuks
1262	Mehmed I becomes Bey of Karaman	Karamanids
1277	Karamanids occupy Konya	Karamanids / Mongols / Egypt
1277	Güneri becomes Bay of Karaman	Karamanids
1294	Karamanids conquer Antalya	Karamanids / Byzantium
1300	Mahmut becomes Bey of Karaman	Karamanids
1308	Karamanids conquer Konya	Karamanids / Seljuks
1352	Musa returns to power after long internal battle for power	Karamanids
1356	Suleyman becomes Bey of Karaman	Karamanids
1361	Alaattin Ali Becomes Bey of Karaman	Karamanids
1386	Karamanids occupy, then lose, Beyşehir	Karamanids / Ottomans
1390	Renewed attempt at annexing Ottoman territories	Karamanids / Ottomans
1398	Ottomans take Konya. Alaattin Ali executed	Karamanids / Ottomans
1402	Mehmed II becomes Bey of Karaman	Karamanids / Mongols
1414	Seljuks surrender former Ottoman territories	Karamanids / Ottomans
1421	Murad II becomes Ottoman Sultan	Ottomans
1421	Seljuk attempt on Antalya. Mehmed I is killed. Bengi Ali becomes Bey of Karaman	Karamanids / Ottomans
1424	Ibrahim II becomes Bey of Karaman with Ottoman support	Karamanids / Ottomans
1433	Karamanids take Beyşehir	Karamanids / Ottomans
1435	Ottomans re-take Beyşehir	Karamanids / Ottomans
1437	Karamanid siege of Amasya	Karamanids / Ottomans
1443	Karamanids revolt (Long Campaign)	Karamanids / Ottomans
1444	Karamanids revolt (Battle of Varna)	Karamanids / Ottomans
1448	Karamanid invasion of Cilicia	Karamanids / Egypt

6 - The Karamanids

Year	Event	Involved Parties
1451	Mehmed II becomes Ottoman Sultan	Ottomans
1451	Karamanids revolt. Mehmed II's first campaign in Anatolia. Karaman agrees to pay tribute	Karamanids Ottomans
1456	Egypt re-take Cilicia	Karamanids Egypt
1462	Karamanid war of succession	Karamanids
1464	Ibrahim II dies	Karamanids
1465	Pir Ahmed becomes Bey of Karaman as Ottoman vassal	Karamanids Ottomans
1468	Ottoman campaign in Karaman	Karamanids Ottomans
1469	Ottoman campaign in Karaman. Pir Ahmet flees to the White Sheep. Ottomans annex Karaman	Karamanids Ottomans White Sheep
1471	Ottoman mop-up campaign in Karaman	Karamanid Ottomans
1472	Ottoman mop-up campaign Karaman. Pir Ahmet attempts invasion.	Karamanids Ottomans White Sheep
1474	Final purge of Karamanid nobility	Karamanids Ottomans

Part 3 - Troublesome Kinsmen

6 - The Karamanids

Like the Kai tribe, which would eventually become the Ottomans, the Afshar tribe migrated in front of the Mongol invasion and first appeared in the area around Sivas in the Seljuk Sultanate of Rum in the early parts of the thirteenth century.

Also like the Kai, they went into the service of the Seljuk Sultan Kayqubad I, but contrary to the Kai tribe, which had moved west, the Afshar tribe stayed in the East and participated in a revolt against the Seljuk Empire instigated by a preacher named Baba Ishak in 1239.

Led by Nûre Sûfi, the Afshars eventually moved to the region of the western Taurus Mountains in south-eastern Anatolia and under Nûre Sûfi's son, Kerîmeddin Karaman Bey, they utilized the power vacuum caused by the Mongol invasion of the Seljuk Sultanate of Rum to carve out a small beylik of their own, centred around the town of Larende (modern day Karaman).

Conflict followed, the Karamanids (as they would now be known) expanding into Seljuk territories, but the Seljuks - by now assisted by their Mongol overlords - regaining control.

In 1262 Kerîmeddin Karaman Bey died and was succeeded by his son Mehmed I of Karaman. Like his father before him, he tried to utilize the gaps that emerged in the wake of the crumbling Seljuk Sultanate of Rum and Mongol attempts to reassert their authority.

Another player who had started to emerge in the area was the Mamluk Empire of Egypt, itself a dynasty of Turkman origins and which at that time held Palestine and Syria. Led by Baibars, the Mamluks had by now as good as thrown the crusaders out of Syrian and Palestine and they were competing with the Mongols for control of Syria and the eastern coast of the Mediterranean Sea.

In 1277 the Mamluks moved on Anatolia, where they routed the Mongol army that came to meet them. Mehmed I of Karaman; no friends of the Mongols, had allied himself with the Mamluks and for a short period of time in the summer of 1277 managed to capture Konya, the old Seljuk capital, where he inserted a puppet Sultan of Rum, and had himself appointed as Vizier.

The new regime only lasted a month as the Mamluks, with no real desire for an occupation of Anatolia, withdrew and the Mongols quickly reasserted their authority, killing Mehmed I of Karaman in the process.

Mehmed I of Karaman was succeeded by his younger brother Güneri of Karaman who continued his brother's policies of pursuing cracks and gaps in the Seljuk/Mongol authority and with pretty much the same result of gains followed by loses, even though he successfully annexed the port-town of Antalya in 1294, after it had already been lost from Mongol control.

On the death of Güneri of Karaman in 1300, he was succeeded by his brother Mahmut of Karaman, who initially did not involve himself in any armed conflict. An opportunity, however, presented itself in 1308, when the death of the Seljuk Sultan Mesut II created yet another power vacuum, which Mahmut of Karaman utilized to once again capture the old Seljuk capital of Konya. There were no more Sultans of the Seljuk Empire of Rum, their time had run out.

Like strong nations and empires before and after, once the most immediate threat from the outside had been removed, the attention shifted to an internal power struggle.

Mahmut of Karaman was succeeded by one of his sons, Musa, who was eventually overthrown by his own brother Ibrahim, supported by Mamluk troops. Ibrahim for a period of time left the throne for his other brother Halil but came back and on his death around 1350 left the throne to his son Ahmed.

Ahmed was killed that same year in battle with the Mongols -, who in the meantime had long since utilized the unrest in Karaman to take back Konya - and he was in turn succeeded by his brother Şemseddin who was poisoned in 1352 (it is believed by another of his brothers), which saw Musa back on throne he had lost to his brother Ibrahim twenty years prior. Follow it if you can!

On Musa's death in 1356, he was succeeded by Suleyman of Karaman, a son of Halil, but he was assassinated in 1361 on behest of the bey of a neighbouring beylik.

Suleyman of Karaman was succeeded by his brother Alaattin Ali of Karaman, who ruled for thirty-seven years, re-establishing stability and, important for this story, starting a love-hate relationship with the Ottomans that would last a century.

In the aftermath of the Seljuk Empire of Rum, the Ottomans had, as covered in Chapter 1, gradually expanded their territories in all directions. Most of western and central Anatolia was now under Ottoman control, with new Ottoman territories developing in Rumelia, Bulgaria and Greece.

Leaving out some smaller beyliks on the western coast of Anatolia, the one big chunk of central Anatolia which was not under Ottoman control was the Beylik of Karaman, which eventually annexed a range of smaller neighbouring beyliks, forming a unified beylik controlling the south-eastern part of central Anatolia.

The two states were on a clear collision course for dominance, but conflict was initially avoided as Alaattin Ali of Karaman was married to Nefise, a daughter of the Ottoman Sultan Murad I.

While Murad I was busy in Europe, eventually appointing himself Sultan in 1386 and Alaattin Ali of Karaman was occupied by the dominance of his neighbours, all was well and peaceful.

In 1386 Alaattin Ali of Karaman decided to expand his territories to also include the Ottoman held town, and fortress, of Beyşehir, probably on the assumption that Murad I, following defeat at the hands of the Serbians at the Battle of Pločnik, had no capacity to react.

In this Alaattin Ali of Karaman was however wrong and Murad I appeared with an Ottoman army and beat Alaattin Ali of Karaman in battle outside of Konya.

This was an important occasion, as it was the first time the Ottomans took their new, modernized, well-organised and to some extent 'westernized' army to battle against a major 'tribal' army, mainly consisting of horse-mounted bowmen, fighting the same way their ancestors had done for centuries.

The victorious Ottomans could well have taken the decision to annex the Karaman beylik, but the intervention of Nefise resulted in Murad I withdrawing on the condition that the old borders were re-established.

Once again inspired by an apparent weakening of the Ottomans, this time in connection with Murad I's death at Kosovo in 1389, Alaattin Ali of Karaman again invaded Ottoman territories.

As was the case in his previous attempt, he had miscalculated the strength and speed of the Ottomans, and in 1390 he was facing the Ottoman army, now under Bayezid I. A quickly formed alliance with Kadi Burhan al-Din, the ruler of the Eretnids beylik in easternmost Anatolia, probably saved him this time around as Bayezid I decided to once again leave the beylik on the condition that the old borders, also agreed in 1386, were restored.

At this time a new powerhouse, in the form of Timur, was starting to emerge in the east, and when Timur was seeking allies in Anatolia, Alaattin Ali of Karaman was quick to take the offer. Thinking he now had some protection, he went to war with his previous ally Kadi Burhan al-Din, but was soon forced to retreat as Timur had no interest in any direct confrontation in Anatolia as of yet.

But Alaattin Ali of Karaman was not done yet. Once again thinking that the Ottomans were exhausting their capacity, having recently fought a major battle against a Christian army at Nicopolis in Bulgaria, he decided to move against them again. This time the target was Ankara.

Once again, he had miscalculated the Ottomans, and in particular Bayezid I, who was becoming known as 'the Thunderbolt' for his capability to move his army with amazing speed between theatres of conflict. In 1398 Bayezid I was back, and this time he was not interested in Alaattin Ali of Karaman's assurances of peace. Bayezid I took Konya, executed Alaattin Ali of Karaman and put the Karaman beylik under Ottoman control, something his father, Murad I, should have done twelve years prior.

That would have probably spelt the end of the Karaman beylik, like so many other beyliks which succumbed to Ottoman supremacy, had it not been for the abovementioned Timur.

While Bayezid I had Alaattin Ali of Karaman executed, he spared his two sons, Mehmed and Bengi Ali. He took them prisoners and held them at Bursa.

When Timur continued to seek rebellious allies in eastern Anatolia, Bayezid I reacted and mobilized his army to meet Timur. In the ensuing battle outside Ankara in 1402, the Ottomans were solidly beaten and Bayezid I taken prisoner. This led to ten years of Ottoman Interregnum as covered in Chapter 1.

Immediately following the Ottoman defeat at Ankara, Timur's army went on to occupy the Ottoman Anatolian capital of Bursa, and Mehmed and Bengi Ali of Karaman were set free. Given their father's previous alliance with Timur, Mehmed was reinstated in Karaman as Mehmed II of Karaman, with all the Beyliks former territories and some additional, former Ottoman, territories granted by Timur.

The following decade was one of confusion in Anatolia, the Ottomans fighting it out over the succession of Bayezid I and the Timurids doing the same following the death of Timur.

During this power vacuum, Mehmed II of Karaman took the opportunity to both consolidate his own rule and furthermore invade parts of the Germiyan beylik in western Anatolia, a beylik formerly under Ottoman suzerainty.

But once Mehmed I emerged as the new Sultan of the Ottoman Empire, he soon started to put his house back in order. In 1414 Mehmed II of Karaman was forced to surrender all territories outside the old (1386) borders to the Ottomans, and when he transgressed the year after he was arrested and he was only released on a solemn promise to keep the peace. He did so until 1421.

Mehmed II of Karaman now looked east, picking a fight with the neighbouring Dulkadir beylik, but as they were vassals of the Mamluks of Egypt, he soon found himself in jail once more, this time in Cairo. Once again he was released due to a change of ruler, this time the Mamluk Sultan, and thus found himself back in Karaman by 1421, when Sultan Mehmed I died and the Ottoman throne went to his son Murad II.

As covered in Chapter 1, the accession of Murad II was not without complications, with no less than two pretenders - supported by the Byzantines - challenging Murad II for the throne. Mehmed II of Karaman seized the moment and took the Mediterranean port-town of Antalya, likely assuming that there were more important things going on in the Ottoman Empire than the defence of this faraway town.

His assumption was possibly correct, but as it turned out Antalya was perfectly capable of defending itself, and Mehmed II of Karaman was killed during the siege.

Power in Karaman was grabbed by Mehmed II's brother, Bengi Ali, but Mehmed II's son, Ibrahim, sought assistance from the Ottomans and with their help defeated Bengi Ali and took the throne as Ibrahim II of Karaman in 1424.

Despite their assistance, Ibrahim II of Karaman was not loyal to the Ottomans. Indeed, like his predecessors, he tried to utilize their periods of apparent weakness to further his own ambitions, but contrary to his predecessors he looked for allies beyond his own immediate surroundings.

Ibrahim II of Karaman had seen, as was the case of the Christians, and in particular the Hungarians, that whereas the Ottomans were seemingly unbeatable in isolation, their weak point was the size of their empire, and their incapability to fight on two fronts at the same time.

Ibrahim II thus from the very outset of his reign started to open diplomatic channel to various Western powers, in particular the Hungarians, the Italians (Venice and Genoa) and the Pope himself, as often as not with the Byzantines as middlemen.

The exact chronological order of the following twenty years now becomes somewhat blurred.

Ibrahim II of Karaman married an (unnamed) sister of Sultan Murad II, which went some way to secure peace with the Ottomans, the same way his ancestor Alaattin Ali of Karaman's marriage to a daughter of Mehmed I had gone some way to secure peace decades before.

According to some sources, Sultan Murad II led a campaign against Ibrahim II of Karaman in 1435, to retake the town of Beyşehir (taken by Ibrahim II of Karaman in 1433); other sources do not mention this. Similarly, some sources cover Ottoman support to other of Ibrahim II of Karaman's enemies in 1437, apparently to make Ibrahim II of Karaman give up a siege of the (Ottoman) town of Amasya.

All sources, however, agree that the relationship between the Karamanids and the Ottomans continued to be one of constant tension, even though no actual hostilities are reported between 1437 and 1443.

'The Long Campaign' of the Hungarians in 1443, however, changed things. As covered in Part 2 and further in Part 5, the advance of a major Christian army deep into Ottoman territories in the winter of 1443 raised hopes that perhaps the Ottomans could be thrown out of Europe after all. Not least as the Ottoman's lack of a major military response was mainly due to the fact that they had their army in the field in Anatolia, moving against Ibrahim II of Karaman who had once more risen against the Ottomans.

Though he was quickly pacified, and Murad II eventually managed to get his army back to Europe, the fact that the Ottomans could be stretched thin did not go unnoticed in Hungary.

It is unknown whether Ibrahim II of Karaman was in league with the Hungarians in 1443, but it is rather clear that when he rebelled again in 1444 it was very much in cooperation with the Hungarians, who at the same time started to move against the Ottomans in Europe, spurred on by the preceding year's relative successful campaign (the Long Campaign). The theory was that the Ottomans could not fight two major battles at the same time, and it nearly proved to be true.

As it happened, Ibrahim II of Karaman did not have the military resources to do real battle with the Ottomans, so when Murad II ignored the danger from the Hungarians (possibly believing that the peace agreement he had signed with them in the spring was worth the paper it was written on) and fielded the Ottoman army in Anatolia, Ibrahim II of Karaman quickly decided to make peace, and even offered Murad II to supplement his troops with Karamanid troops.

This quick settlement was the key reason why Murad II could return his army to Europe fast enough to meet and destroy the Christian army at Varna, but the incident had proven the danger of having the Karamanids sitting in the Ottoman hinterlands, always on the lookout for an opportunity and clearly in cohorts with the Christians. Murad II did not have the time to deal with it at that time, but the lesson would not be wasted on his son, Mehmed II.

When Murad II had to choose a wife for his son and heir, Mehmed, he decided on a daughter of the Bey of Elbistan, an independent beylik to the immediate east of Karaman, possibly hoping that he would win an ally who could both keep an eye on Ibrahim II of Karaman and possibly even intervene on behalf of the Ottomans should the Karamanids transgress further.

As it happened, Ibrahim II of Karaman seemed to have learned his lesson and not provoke Murad II further. Instead, in 1448, he invaded Cilicia, to the south-east of his own domains, despite this area being under Mamluk (Egyptian) suzerainty. He would later have to give it back after Mamluk intervention in 1456.

In the meantime, Murad II had died in 1451, leaving the Ottoman throne to his son Mehmed II. As covered in Chapter 2, the general assumption was the Mehmed II was a weak and not very popular. Ibrahim II of Karaman subscribed to this opinion and he took the opportunity to help himself.

This time the scheme was grander than before, and he allied himself with several beyliks under Ottoman rule, urging them to support him in re-establishing the independent beyliks of central Anatolia. In the meantime, he attacked Ottoman possessions in the immediate surroundings of the Karaman beylik.

It is unclear what he expected, but if he expected a lame and un-concerted response from a weak an unpopular Sultan, he was wrong, very wrong.

Mehmed II initially trusted the matter to his Anatolian commander, and then soon after fired him due to lack of activity. He moved the responsibility to his governor of Anatolia, and then he made his own way to Anatolia to head up the army.

The rebellious beyliks disappeared from the alliance like dew in the morning sun, and when Ibrahim II of Karaman realized that he was facing a properly organised Ottoman army led by the Sultan himself, and there were no signs of weakness or discord, he sent ambassadors to Mehmed II, begging forgiveness.

Mehmed II forgave his wayward uncle, but only after Ibrahim II of Karaman had promised to pay annual tribute, declared that his rule in the first place should be considered a gift from (his brother-in-law) Sultan Murad II and furthermore promised one of his daughters to Mehmed II.

Mehmed II now returned to Europe to deal with Constantinople. Though some speculate that Ibrahim II of Karaman's 1451 uprising was encouraged by the Byzantines, in an attempt to recreate the pincer-movement previously attempted in 1444 - and also this time relying on a Hungarian army to move in Europe - this is not very likely.

First of all the hopes for a Hungarian army moving against Mehmed II were minimal, and secondly Ibrahim II of Karaman had previously proven that he was more than capable of creating trouble on his own initiative.

He had, however, finally also learned his lesson in terms of Mehmed II and did not provoke him further but paid his annual tribute as agreed. It is unclear if any of his daughters actually married Mehmed II.

Ibrahim II of Karaman had seven sons, Ishak, Pir Ahmet, Kasım, Karaman, Nure Sufi, Alaeddin and Suleyman. The oldest, Ishak, was the son of a mistress, whereas the others were born in wedlock, possibly by the sister of Murad II, but Ibrahim II of Karaman may well have had more than one wife.

In any case, as he was getting older, around 1462, Ibrahim II of Karaman decided to appoint Ishak as his successor, causing his remaining sons to put him under siege in Konya in order to change his mind. Though he managed to escape, he died in 1464, leaving behind him all the necessary ingredients for an internal battle for succession.

And that battle was not long in the coming. The nominated successor, Ishak, stayed in the Mediterranean town of Silifke (where he was governor), whereas his brother Pir Ahmet, set himself up in Konya, each ruling part of the beylik.

Other brothers were given land in Ottoman territories from (their cousin) Mehmed II, and one fled to seek refuge with the Mamluks in Egypt.

Ishak now sought the support of Uzun Hasan, the ruler of the White Sheep, whom we shall cover in more detail in the following chapter. With his help he managed to beat Pir Ahmed and take control of all of Karaman, according to Mamluk sources as a vassal of the Mamluks.

Pir Ahmed had fled to the Ottomans, and when Ishak sought Mehmed II's approval of his rule, as technically Karaman was now an Ottoman vassal, Mehmed II refused and instead sent an army in support of Pir Ahmed, which beat the army of Ishak and reinstated Pir Ahmed in Konya, this time ruling the entire beylik.

Ishak fled to Uzun Hasan, but had left his family behind, and was not in a position to move further without putting their lives in danger. He died soon after of unknown causes.

But Pir Ahmed's bid for the throne had not been without cost. He had to give the town of Akşehir and Beyşehir to Mehmed II, and renew his oaths of vassalage.

What happened next is again covered in some uncertainty. What is known is that the Ottomans came back to Karaman sometime within the 1468 to 1469 timeframe, most likely on two separate occasions. The exact pretext for clamping down on their own vassal is also unclear, but it would be a good bet that Mehmed II simply had had enough of the notoriously rebellious Karamanids, and that he in particular did not like their flirting with Uzun Hasan, with whom he had plenty of problems already.

Another explanation given is that Mehmed II was planning a campaign on the Mamluks of Egypt, who had their own crisis of succession, and that his attack on the Karamanids was as reaction to Pir Ahmed refusing to participate, as a consequence of which the campaign had to be cancelled.

I personally find that a less plausible explanation as a campaign against the Mamluks was a major undertaking with potential long-term consequences, and not something that would have been cancelled just because the Karamanids would not participate.

In any case, the Ottomans came back and cleaned up. Pir Ahmed, and his brother Kasım fled to Uzun Hasan and Karaman was annexed into the Ottoman Empire with Mehmed II's young son Mustafa as governor. On Mehmed II's orders, all the artisans and artists of Konya and Larende were rounded up and sent to various parts of Greece, Serbia and Bosnia.

Small rebellious enclaves in the towns of Silifke, Alanya and Aksaray were brought under control in 1471 and 1472 in separate expeditions. Mehmed II had the entire population of Aksaray forcefully moved to Istanbul, to a quarter in the city that is still named after them.

In 1472 Pir Ahmed and Kasım followed Uzun Hasan on an incursion into Anatolia, and for a short time they made a play for recapturing Karaman. As covered in the next chapter, Uzun Hasan's forces were beaten by Mehmed II in 1473, and Pir Ahmed died in the year following.

In 1474 Prince Mustafa, Governor of Karaman, died and it was feared that the locals may use this as an opportunity to revolt. The Ottoman Vizier Gedik Ahmed Pasha negotiated with the local nobility and managed to quell any aspirations to rebel. In celebration, he invited the nobility to a banquet, at which they were systematically murdered.

6 - The Karamanids

The Karamanids, the kinsmen of the Ottomans, had made themselves enemies of The Conqueror. As a consequence, they ceased to exist.

Part 3 - Troublesome Kinsmen

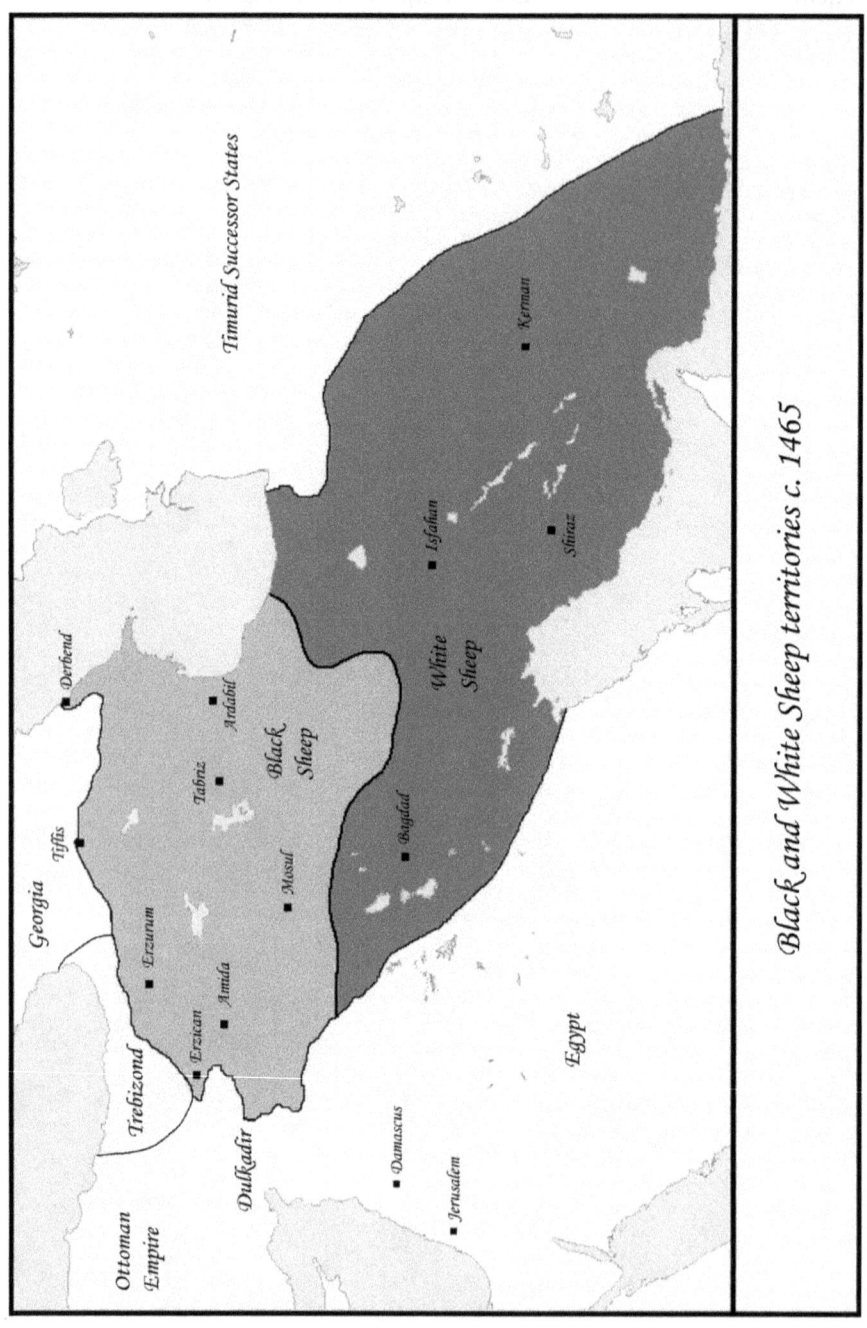

Black and White Sheep territories c. 1465

7 - THE WHITE SHEEP

Part 3 - Troublesome Kinsmen

CRITICAL TIMELINE

Year	Event	Involved Parties
1404	Timur dies	Timurids
1408	Timurid attack on Black Sheep	Timurids, Black Sheep
1410	Timurid attack on Black Sheep	Timurids, Black Sheep
1420	White Sheep attempt to invade Black Sheep	White Sheep, Black Sheep
1429	Timurids put Abu Sa'id in control of Black Sheep, but Qara Iskander retain the leadership	Timurids, Black Sheep
1435	Qara Osman dies and war of succession follows in the White Sheep beylik	White Sheep
1436	Timurids put Jahan Shah in control of Black Sheep	Timurids, Black Sheep
1440	Black Sheep attempt invasion of Georgia	Black Sheep, Georgia
1444	Black Sheep attempt invasion of Georgia	Black Sheep, Georgia
1447	Jahan Shah takes control of all Black Sheep territories	Black Sheep, Persia
1447	Prolonged war starts between White Sheep and Black Sheep	White Sheep, Black Sheep
1451	War between White Sheep and Black Sheep ends	White Sheep, Black Sheep
1453	Uzun Hasan becomes Bey of the White Sheep	White Sheep
1459	David Megas Komnenos becomes Emperor of Trebizond	Trebizond
1460	Uzun Hasan puts ultimatum to Mehmed II	White Sheep, Ottomans, Trebizond
1461	Ottomans conquer Empire of Trebizond	Ottomans, Trebizond
1463	Venice proposes alliance with White Sheep	White Sheep, Venice
1464	White Sheep assist in revolt in Karaman	White Sheep, Ottomans, Karamanid
1467	War between White and Black Sheep see White Sheep conquer Black Sheep territories	White Sheep, Black Sheep
1469	White Sheep provides shelter for Karamanid refugees	White Sheep, Karamanids
1471	Alliance between White Sheep and Venice	White Sheep, Venice
1472	White Sheep incursions in Trebizond and Karaman	White Sheep, Ottomans, Karamanids

7 - The White Sheep

Year	Event	Involved Parties
1472	Christian fleet raid in Mediterranean and Aegean Sea	Venice The Pope Naples Knights Hospitaller
1473	Battle of Otlukbeli. Ottomans annihilate White Sheep army	White Sheep Ottomans
1473	Venetian artillery-support for White Sheep is returned to Venice	White Sheep Venice
1474	Uzun Hasan's son revolt	White Sheep
1478	Uzun Hasan dies. After war of succession Ya'qub becomes Bey	White Sheep
1490	Ya'qub dies and the White Sheep dissolve in following war of succession.	White Sheep

Part 3 - Troublesome Kinsmen

7 - The White Sheep

When the empire-founder Timur died in 1404 his hastily built empire did not last long. The almost obligatory fight for succession meant that his empire was soon to split into smaller pieces.

In an area south-west of Lake Van, in south-easternmost Anatolia, was a beylik called the White Sheep (Aq Qoyunlu), which had been granted lands by Timur and after his death continued as an independent state. To put it in modern terms, their territory covered parts of south-easternmost Turkey, north-western Syria, and north-eastern Iraq.

To their immediate north-west, and stretching north towards the easternmost coast of the Black Sea was a beylik/khanate called the Black Sheep (Kara Qoyunlu), which had re-formed after having been previously conquered by Timur. The Black Sheep controlled, in modern terms, Armenia, Azerbaijan, north-western Iran (Persia), parts of eastern Turkey and most of Iraq.

Put together, these two beyliks formed the easternmost border of the Ottoman Empire, itself having re-establish control of its territories in eastern Anatolia following Timur's death.

At the beginning of the fifteenth century the ruler of the Black Sheep was Qara Yusuf, who had fled his territories during Timur' invasion, but had successfully returned from refuge in Egypt and re-established the state following Timur's death.

Qara Yusuf successfully defended Azerbaijan from an attempted conquest by the remaining Timurids in 1408 and in 1410 repelled a similar attempt from the Sultan of Baghdad (who was caught and executed), putting Qara Yusuf also in control of Iraq and Persia as far as Baghdad.

At the same time the White Sheep were ruled by Qara Osman, who had sided with Timur and managed to hold on to his territory, but with his beylik effectively surrounded by the Ottomans, the Karamanids, the Mamluks and the Black Sheep, he had no room to expand.

When the leader of the Black Sheep, Qara Yusuf, died in 1420 and his sons started fighting each other for the throne, the White Sheep tried to invade, but two of Qara Yusuf's sons, Qara Iskander and Ispend fought them off.

Having also fought off an invasion attempt by the Timurids, Qara Iskander and Ispend then fought each other, with Qara Iskander as the winner, even though Ispend continued to rule in Baghdad. In 1429 the Timurids came back, this time for a short period of time placing Qara Iskander's brother, Abu Sa'id, on the throne, but Qara Iskander fought back and ultimately executed his brother.

Part 3 - Troublesome Kinsmen

The Timurids were however not that easily beaten, they tried again in 1436, this time using Qara Iskander's only remaining brother, Jahan Shah, as their champion, This time they were more successful as Jahan Shah managed to defeat Qara Iskander, who in the end was murdered by his own son. You could not make it up!

Though the years under Jahan Shah were generally a peaceful and prosperous time for the Black Sheep, he did try twice, in 1440 and 1444, to invade Georgia, but with little success. In 1447 his brother, Ispend, died, and Jahan Shah took the opportunity to retake Baghdad and gain control of the whole Black Sheep state.

In the meantime, the ruler of the White Sheep, Qara Osman, had died in 1435, with the inevitable war of succession following in the wake of his death. Over the next twenty-two years there were no less than four rulers. During this period the White Sheep and the Black Sheep were in regular conflict, most seriously in a prolonged war between 1447 and 1451, which left both states exhausted, but did not bring any gains or losses to either party.

It is worth noticing that in these same decades, the Ottomans were busy expanding and consolidating their territories in Europe, and that the infighting between their easternmost neighbours meant that the Ottomans did not have to worry about them for the time being.

In 1453 the throne of the White Sheep was taken over by Uzun Hasan, a strong and determined ruler, and the status quo started to change.

As a side remark, both Jahan Shah and Uzun Hasan were married to princesses of Trebizond, the Hellenistic pocket empire to which we shall return in the following chapter.

Uzun Hasan had ambitions that went beyond those of his forefathers, ambitions that were along the lines of re-establishing the former glory of the Great Seljuk Empire, and to do that he needed to fight it out with the Black Sheep and the Ottomans.

Realizing that taking on the Ottomans was a task probably beyond his own capabilities, he very early on established diplomatic contact with Venice, the perceived strongest and most determined enemy of the Ottomans. He was here most likely assisted by his (Christian) relatives in Trebizond.

In 1463 the Venetians, through their ambassador Lazzaro Querini, tried to talk Uzun Hasan into attacking the Ottomans, and thus force Mehmed II to divert troops from Europe to Anatolia, but Uzun Hasan did not agree with the plan, fearing that a war with the Ottomans would invite an attack from the Black Sheep. Before he could take on the Ottomans, he needed his back free.

And the conflict was not long in coming. Having eyed each other off for decades, with the occasional open conflict, and now with two strong leaders, the White Sheep and the Black Sheep went to war.

7 - The White Sheep

In 1467 Jahan Shah marched on the White Sheep. He met little resistance but soon found out that the reason for that was that Uzun Hasan had gone round him and was now raiding in Black Sheep territory with a 12,000-man strong cavalry troop.

Jahan Shah turned around, and the two rulers now exchanged emissaries, trying to find a peaceful solution. That, however, turned out to be impossible, as Uzun Hasan would not accept the demands of Jahan Shah, the latter probably seeing himself as the dominant player.

Eventually Jahan Shah had to accept the demand from his own army to break off the campaign and seek winter-quarters, which they did, but on 11 November. Uzun Hasan and the White Sheep caught the Black Sheep army unaware in their winter-quarters and defeated them, killing Jahan Shah.

Uzun Hasan could now merge the Black Sheep territories with his own, though it took him a year to round up resistance and capture and execute Jahan Shah's son and successor Hasan Ali who was supported by the Timurid Khan Abu Sa'id Mirza. The Black Sheep had been, literally, eliminated and the White Sheep now formed the easternmost border with the Ottoman Empire.

But the White Sheep's success came at a price. They had long been allied, in a communal stance against the Ottomans, with the Empire of Trebizond, an alliance cemented by Uzun Hasan's marriage to a sister of the Emperor John IV Komnenos. When John IV Komnenos died in 1459 he was succeeded by his brother David Megas Komnenos, who contrary to his wise brother did not have the patience to allow his allies to build up their strength.

Instead David Megas Komnenos started to develop fantastic schemes to form alliances against the Ottomans, involving several rulers of western Europe, the Venetians, the Pope and Uzun Hasan and his White Sheep.

As part of his scheme, he decided to stop paying the annual tribute of 3,000 gold pieces to the Ottomans, agreed by his brother John IV Komnenos in 1456. Or rather he managed to convince Uzun Hasan to intercede on his behalf.

Uzun Hasan thus sent an ambassador to Mehmed II in the beginning of 1460, asking for the Empire of Trebizond to be released from its tribute. But it did not stop there. Uzun Hasan had decided to add some demands of his own, namely that the Ottoman Sultan would honour a tribute (consisting of 1,000 horse blankets, and a similar amount of turbans, cloth and carpets), allegedly agreed by his grandfather Mehmed I, and also give Uzun Hasan the central Anatolian territory of Cappadocia, which Uzun Hasan claimed to have been granted by the Emperor of Trebizond as his wife's dowry.

Mehmed II's response is quoted in various versions, none of them polite, but his most likely answer was that he himself personally would come and settle the issue of tribute in the coming year, and so he did.

In 1461 Mehmed II set out with a coordinated manoeuvre between a fleet in the Black Sea and the army led by himself overland in Anatolia. After a stop in Sinop, where a troublesome bey was brought under final Ottoman control, Mehmed II marched south-east towards the White Sheep. His vanguard captured the border-fortress at Koylu Hisar and the Ottoman army marched on into White Sheep territory. Here they were met by a delegation led by Uzun Hasan's (Christian born) mother and other dignitaries. They assured Mehmed II of Uzun Hasan's peaceful intentions, and they were sent back with a promise that Mehmed II would not attack the White Sheep, on the explicit condition that they stayed out of his conflict with the Empire of Trebizond.

As we shall see in the next chapter, Mehmed II now turned around and went to conquer the Empire of Trebizond, his original destination, and Uzun Hasan, not ready for a full on confrontation with the Ottomans, had to sit by and watch while his ally, and kinsmen, were annexed into the Ottoman Empire.

Soon negotiations with Venice were resumed and in 1471 a new Venetian ambassador, Caterino Zeno, whose wife was a niece of Uzun Hasan's (Trebizond born) wife, arrived at Uzun Hasan's court in Tabriz.

Uzun Hasan had already started to once more provoke the Ottomans. In 1464 he provided military support to Ishak in his bid for the throne of Karaman (see Chapter 6), and after the Ottoman Conquest of Karaman in 1469 he had given refuge to Pir Ahmed and Kasım, the last of the ruling house of Karaman. None of these provocations had, however, met a meaningful response from Mehmed II.

This time it was different. Uzun Hasan made it clear to the Venetians that whereas he had plenty of cavalry and archers; he lacked *'everything needed to attack the enemy from a distance and to capture cities'*, in other words Uzun Hasan needed artillery and firearms in general. His army was a traditional Turkmen army, consisting mainly of bowmen on horses, mixed with lancers and swordsmen, probably something he had picked up from his Hellenistic allies. It was, however, not a modern army of that time's standard, something that eventually proved decisive.

In May 1472 Uzun Hasan escalated the provocations. First, he supported a nephew of the last Emperor of Trebizond in an attempt to re-take the lost empire. This attempt was, however, fought off by the Ottoman garrison in the town of Trebizond, assisted by the timely arrival of an Ottoman fleet of nine galleys and twenty-five sailing ships.

Next, he moved further south, into Karaman, only just brought under Ottoman control in the preceding year. In this campaign his troops went in support of Pir Ahmed and his brother Kasım, the two princes of Karaman who had fled to him after the Ottoman campaign of 1469.

Through the summer they laid waste to large areas in Karaman with a sizeable expeditionary force of probably 50,000 men. Mehmed II commanded his governor in Karaman, his son Mustafa, to counter the attack. Mustafa commanded around 60,000 troops and the two armies met in

August 1472 outside Beyşehir. The Ottomans were victorious. The commander of the White Sheep forces was captured and sent to Istanbul, but the two princes of Karaman managed to escape again. Pir Ahmed went back to Uzun Hasan and Kasım took refuge in the fortress at Silifke, from where he was to be expelled the following year in the last Ottoman clean-up expedition in Karaman.

During the same year, and in line with the alliance between Uzun Hasan and Venice, an 'Italian' fleet had emerged in the Aegean Sea. This fleet had been put together by not only ships from Venice, but also ships paid for by the Pope and ships from the King of Naples and the Knights of Rhodes. The Pope's contribution of eighteen galleys (out of a total of eighty-five) was the best he could do, having failed to raise any interest for a new 'crusade' from the rulers of Western Europe, despite him sending ambassadors to France, Burgundy, England, Spain, Germany, Poland and Hungary.

The fleet anchored at Rhodes, a long-established meeting point for envoys between Uzun Hasan and the Christians. When no emissaries arrived, they moved on to attack Antalya, but the town was well defended, so they returned to Rhodes, this time to find emissaries from Uzun Hasan. The message from Uzun Hasan was the same as before, he needed artillery and men to handle it, something the fleet could do nothing about.

The fleet then commenced a string of attacks on various coastal towns, ending up with a notorious sack of Smyrna. The fleet should now have pushed through the Sea of Marmara and attacked the Ottoman Fleet at Istanbul, which would have disrupted Mehmed II's preparations for a campaign against Uzun Hasan and thus would have been useful, instead they resorted to grand-scale piracy and with the onset of winter all but the Venetian contingent sailed home.

That was the total amount of assistance that Uzun Hasan received from his Christian allies, as the following year the Venetian fleet, although staying in the area, did not get further involved with fighting the Ottomans as they were kept in place to support Venetian interests in a strife of succession that had broken out with the death of the King of Cyprus.

In September 1472 news started to trickle in to Istanbul about Uzun Hasan's expeditionary forces laying waste to large parts of central Anatolia as far as Ankara, the Ottoman garrisons being destroyed in front of them. The messages also said that the main White Sheep army was still inside their own border, but that it was the strength of 100,000, with yet another 100,000 to join it.

Intercepted messengers revealed that Uzun Hasan had all intentions of making war on the Ottomans, that he had alliances with both Venice and Hungary and that all three parties intended to attack at the same time. Mehmed II had no time to speculate, he needed to react, and as was his style he reacted with great speed and determination.

Mehmed II had been away from Istanbul due to an outbreak of plague, but he now returned and threw himself into the task at hand. Wooden docks were built to accommodate the loading of troops and all available seagoing vessels were pressed into service, ferrying the Rumelian army, assembled at Edirne, across the Bosporus to Üsküdar on the Anatolian side.

The expedition started badly. A storm broke out in the Istanbul area, sinking several ships loaded with supplies for the army, wreaking havoc on the army's camp and leaving the army without food for four days. Once the storm subsided, supplies were brought across to the army and they marched to Amasya in north-central Anatolia where they camped for the winter and Mehmed II's sons, Bayezid and Mustafa, joined them.

To provide an idea of how multi-cultural the Ottoman Empire, and thus the Ottoman army, had become, it is worth mentioning that the army, all in all counting 190,000, of which probably 100,000 were actually front-line fighting men, consisted of men from Rumelia, Greece, Bulgaria, Anatolia, Wallachia, Albania and Serbia. Many of these were (Orthodox) Christians.

In March 1473 the Ottoman army, unmolested by the enemy during winter, set out east. They followed a line through Tokat, Niksar, Koylu Hisar and Şebinkarahisar, finally arriving in the vicinity of Erzincan in north-eastern Anatolia.

In the meantime Uzun Hasan had also started moving, and in July he sent letters to the King of Hungary and the Holy Roman Emperor to *'set fire and flame to the European territories of the Ottomans'*. Whether the letters were ever received is unknown, what is known is that neither the Hungarians, nor the Germans made any moves against the Ottomans in Europe. If Uzun Hasan though that he was just one part of a concerted pincer move on the Ottomans, he was wrong.

Uzun Hasan reached the area of Erzincan at the end of July, positioning himself in the mountains, looking down onto the Ottoman army's camp across the Euphrates River.

On 4 August a young Ottoman commander, Hass Murad, a protégé of Mehmed II and commanding the Rumelian army, decided to gain glory, so he crossed the river and attacked. His troops were surrounded by the White Sheep and had to withdraw with the loss of 12,000 men, including Hass Murad himself.

Mehmed II was furious, and for a short time seems to have lost the will to go through with the campaign. He ordered the army to withdraw and head for Trebizond, most likely to continue west and go home.

Uzun Hasan was, however, not intent on letting the Ottomans withdraw without a fight, a position strongly supported by the Venetian ambassador Caterino Zeno. But Uzun Hasan decided to try diplomacy first, so he sent a letter to Mehmed II in which he demanded that he should withdraw, hand over the former Empire of Trebizond to its rightful ruler (his wife's uncle), give the Beylik of Sinop to his sister's sons and give the Karaman beylik back to his nephews (Pir Ahmed and Kasım). Should Mehmed II refuse, then Uzun Hasan would consider him his enemy!

To add insult to injury, Uzun Hasan's ambassador also brought a sack of millet, with the message that should the Sultan not accept the terms, then Uzun Hasan's troops would be as numerous as the grains. Mehmed II responded by having the millet poured on the ground in front of a flock of chickens, with the message that '*as quickly as these chickens have devoured the sack of millet my Janissaries will deal with his men, who may be skilled at herding goats but not at fighting*'.

Further diplomacy would have been wasted, and Mehmed II's comment had touched a raw nerve, namely the difference between the Turkoman army, still mainly fighting the way Turkomen had fought for centuries - their main force being light horse-archers - and the battle hardened Ottoman army, having adopted the latest technology and the fighting doctrines of the time.

The Ottoman army stayed and on 11 August Uzun Hasan attacked, suddenly, on the Ottoman right flank. The Ottomans quickly got organized and gave battle.

Now the difference between the two armies started to show. The Ottomans had artillery and firearms, which caused massive losses on the attackers. Furthermore, they were extremely well organised and drilled, having fought countless battles in the preceding years.

After a battle - known as the Battle of Otlukbeli - that lasted eight hours, and which saw Uzun Hasan's youngest son, Zeynel, killed, the Ottomans had routed the White Sheep, killed 10,000 and taken their camp and baggage train. Thousands of prisoners were taken, most killed in the days following the battle, but 3,000 were selected for following the Ottoman army on its march home, 400 being killed every day until the supply ran out. This was not necessarily Mehmed II's own idea, but rather a replication of a similar approach by Marcus Licinius Crassus after his final defeat of the rebellious slaves under Spartacus in 71 BC. Then the message was to not rebel against the Roman Empire, in 1473 it was a similar message to other would-be enemies of Ottoman Conqueror Sultan.

Mehmed II was of a mind to press home his victory and move on to invade the White Sheep territories, but his grand vizier managed to talk him out of it with sound advice that it would be practically impossible to hold the territory after the main army's retreat.

Ironically, the Venetians had actually finally decided to send artillery to Uzun Hasan, and launched a shipment consisting of six large cannon, ten medium sized and thirty-six smaller ones. The shipment, trusted to one Giosafat Barbaro, left Venice in February 1473, but several stops were made along the way to visit the rulers of various islands, and when the fleet finally arrived in Cyprus at the end of March, they could not proceed further as the Ottomans had control of the Anatolian coast and blocked all possible land routes to the White Sheep capital of Tabriz. The supply of artillery was later re-routed, as Venice had use of it elsewhere.

Though thoroughly beaten, Uzun Hasan had not given up his dreams of a concerted attack on the Ottomans, and the Venetians were quick in reassuring him of their support, though they did absolutely nothing in practical terms.

In 1474 Uzun Hasan's son, Ugurlu Mehmed rebelled against him and though the rebellion was put down, Uzun Hasan had lost his appetite for a fight. As was typical of the times, Ugurlu Mehmed fled to the Ottoman court, where he was not only well received, but was given a daughter of Mehmed II in marriage.

Uzun Hasan died in 1478, and his death meant the beginning of a fight between his remaining sons. Eventually one of the sons, Ya'qub, prevailed and ruled for twelve years. On his death his sons fought each other, gradually pulling the state apart from the inside. At this time Ugurlu Hasan's son, Ahmad-beg, a grandson of Mehmed II also appeared in the mix, and finally the state was split up, until a new dynasty, the Safavids, re-united it. The White Sheep were gone and the Safavids ruled Persia for more than 200 years.

7 - The White Sheep

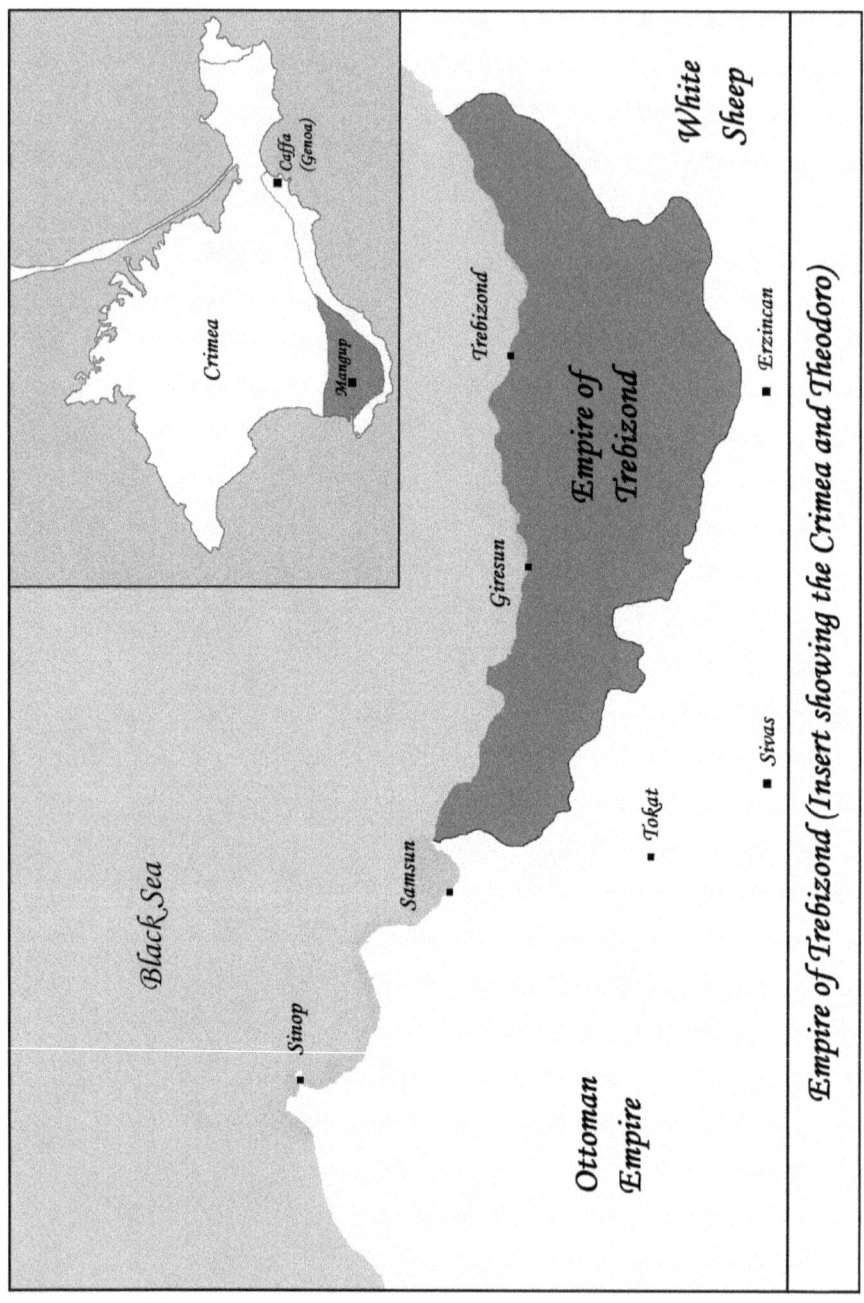

Empire of Trebizond (Insert showing the Crimea and Theodoro)

8 - THE EMPIRE OF TREBIZOND

CRITICAL TIMELINE

Year	Event	Involved Parties
1071	Seljuks capture Trebizond following Battle of Manzikert	Byzantium Seljuks
1080s	Byzantines recapture Trebizond. Theodore Gabras becomes governor.	Byzantium Seljuks
1091	Theodore Gabras marries Mariam of Georgia	Byzantium Georgia
1091	Theodore Gabras' attempt to rescue his son means he is dismissed in Trebizond	Byzantium
1185	Rusudan escaped to Georgia with her sons Alexios and David Komnenos	Byzantium Georgia
1204	Fourth Crusade. Alexios and David Komnenos invade Trebizond and declare independence	Byzantium Trebizond
1205	Trebizond expel Seljuk attack on Sinop	Trebizond Seljuks
1206	David Komnenos lays siege to Nicomedia. Nicaea receives help from Constantinople	Trebizond Constantinople Nicaea
1206	Trebizond expel Seljuk attack on Sinop	Trebizond Seljuks
1208	David Komnenos lays siege to Nicomedia. Nicaea receives help from Constantinople	Trebizond Constantinople Nicaea
1212	David Komnenos dies as a monk	Trebizond Constantinople
1214	Seljuks take Sinop	Trebizond Seljuks
1258	Mongols overrun Persia. Trebizond becomes endpoint on Silk Route	Trebizond Mongols
1291	Pope Nicholas IV forbids trade with Muslims. Enclave granted to Genoa	The Pope Trebizond Genoa
1319	Enclave granted to Venice	Trebizond Venice
1344	Papal trade-ban expires	The Pope
1452	Mehmed II cuts off Black Sea route with Boğaz Kesen castle on the Bosporus Strait	Ottomans
1456	Ottoman expeditionary force at Trebizond forces annual tribute to be agreed	Trebizond Ottomans
1459	David Megas Komnenos becomes Emperor of Trebizond	Trebizond
1460	Uzun Hasan forward ultimatum to Ottomans on behalf of Trebizond	Trebizond Ottomans White Sheep
1461	Ottomans conquer Empire of Trebizond	Trebizond Ottomans
1463	David Megas Komnenos is executed in Istanbul	Trebizond Ottomans
1475	Ottomans annex Theodoro in Crimea	Ottomans

8 - The Empire of Trebizond

The Empire of Trebizond, which we have already encountered in the previous chapter, does not really belong in this part of this book called '*Troublesome Kinsmen*', but it does not belong anywhere else either as it really was an anachronism. I have thus chosen to place it here because this is where it fits the best, both in terms of geography and context.

The Empire of Trebizond was a very grand name for a small coastal stretch of land on the south-east coast of the Black Sea, placing it in the north-eastern part of Anatolia. Its main city was Trebizond (modern day Trabzon), its second city being Giresun, app. 175 kilometres west of Trebizond. Its claim to imperial status really came from the fact that the Empire of Trebizond also claimed suzerainty over the Principality of Theodoro, a small enclave on the Crimean peninsula, squeezed in between the Genoese possessions on the coast and the Tatars of the Khanate of Crimea in the hinterlands. On an on-and-off basis it would also claim suzerainty of the Beylik of Sinop, to its immediate west, but as time went by this beylik was at the same time paying tribute to the Ottoman Empire, and its exact loyalties were dubious.

The areas controlled by the Empire of Trebizond were originally Byzantine and controlled by a Byzantine provincial governor, occasionally given the title of Dux (Duke).

In the 1080s the Seljuk Turks temporarily conquered the Trebizond province, but it was taken back by the Byzantines, commanded by a Byzantine noble named Theodore Gabras.

Theodore Gabras set himself up in Trebizond as a semi-independent ruler for a few years as the Byzantine Emperor, Alexios I Komnenos, had enough to do with holding his crumbling empire together, finally calling for help from the Pope and thus (unaware) instigating the First Crusade.

Theodore Gabras was, however, called back to Constantinople in the late 1080s, and although he was re-appointed to the seat as regional governor, this time as Dux of Trebizond, the Emperor kept his eldest son, Gregory, as a de-facto hostage to ensure his loyalty.

Gregory was engaged to the Emperor's niece, but when Theodore Gabras (re-) married to a princess from Georgia, who in turn was related to the (imperial) Komnenos family, the twist and turns of Byzantine law prescribed that the alliance between Gregory and the house of Komnenos was now considered to be too closely related and the engagement was called off.

Theodore Gabras was not happy with this, and on a visit to Constantinople he tried to smuggle Gregory out of the city and take him with him back to Trebizond. The Emperor - realizing that this was the prelude to a revolt - managed to capture Theodore Gabras and Gregory and bring them back to Constantinople. Even though Theodore Gabras continued to serve as a successful commander in the Byzantine army, he was never sent back to Trebizond, and for a century there were no further attempts at revolt.

For nearly a century thereafter, the Komnenos dynasty ruled Byzantium. Finally, they were overthrown in 1185, the last Komnenos to rule in Constantinople being Andronikos I Komnenos. Though, per se, irrelevant to the story, but to give an insight into the perils of Byzantine power-play, his successor, Isaac II Angelos handed him over to the mercy of the city-mob. They tied him to a post, and for three days he was beaten and abused by all and sundry. During this time his right hand was cut off, his teeth and hair were pulled out, one of his eyes was gouged out, and boiling water was thrown in his face. Finally, he was taken to the Hippodrome where he was hung by the feet between two pillars and two soldiers competed as to whose sword could penetrate his body the deepest. Finally, his body was torn apart.

The Komnenos family originated from the Black Sea area and Andronikos I Komnenos' son, Manuel, was married to Rusudan, a daughter of George III of Georgia. Though Manuel was blinded, and probably killed, when his father fell from grace, his wife managed to escape to Georgia, bringing with her their two infant sons: Alexios and David.

Isaac II Angelos was himself overthrown (and blinded) by his brother, Alexios III Angelos, in 1195. His son, also called Alexios, fled to the safety of the court of Philip of Swabia, his brother-in-law. It was from here, and promoted by Philip of Swabia, that Alexios Angelos in 1402 emerged as the champion of the Fourth Crusade, as covered in more detail in Chapter 3.

In the meantime, the Komnenos brothers, Alexios and David, had grown up and when it became clear that Constantinople was under threat of being overrun by the crusader army and their Venetian puppet-masters, they struck.

George III of Georgia had died and left the throne to his daughter Tamar, the sister of Rusudan Komnenos, and thus the aunt of the two young Komnenos brothers. With her help, and Georgian troops, Alexios and David moved on Trebizond, which was easily overrun, and while Alexios remained in the city of Trebizond, his brother David continued west along the coast, subduing the territories as far east as Heraclea Pontica (modern day Karadeniz Ereğli).

The brothers met little resistance, as they were to some extent considered 'locals', the family originating from the area, and the population had little confidence in the fate of Constantinople, still entangled in the complex power-games of the Fourth Crusade.

At the same time they claimed suzerainty over the small Byzantine enclave of Theodoro on the Crimean peninsula, an area so isolated that they would accept any protection they could get, and a few weeks before the final fall of Constantinople in the summer of 1204, and the (temporary) end of the

Byzantine Empire, the brothers declared the Empire of Trebizond as independent.

Alexios became emperor as Alexios I of Trebizond, and though he co-ruled with his brother David, David never took on an imperial title himself. There may have been a reason for that as follows.

As also covered in Part 2, the Byzantine Empire was officially dispersed into a range of exotic 'Latin' states, and much of the rest was taken by pirates and fortune-hunters, but several 'Byzantine' territories remained.

The Despotate of Epirus, covering the western side of the Greek peninsula, remained under Greek control, Theodore Lascaris had set himself up in Nicaea, and the Komnenos brothers had now established the Empire of Trebizond. Furthermore, Manuel Maurozomes, a Byzantine nobleman had also set himself up in central Anatolia with the support of the Seljuk Sultan, who was his son-in-law.

Someone had to take the lead and be the rallying-point for Byzantine resurgence and whereas Manuel Maurozomes soon gave up and withdrew to the Seljuk court, David Komnenos and Theodore Lascaris were the two most obvious candidates.

As Theodore Lascaris was carving out the Empire of Nicaea, David Komnenos laid down his own claim of being the established Byzantine leader and in 1206 he laid siege to Nicomedia, part of Theodore Lascaris' pocket-empire.

Theodore Lascaris pushed David Komnenos back, and he himself then laid siege to David's town of Heraclea Pontica. David Komnenos now appealed for help from the Latin Emperor in Constantinople, who laid siege to Nicomedia, forcing Theodore Lascaris to lift the siege and return west.

The same scenario played out again in 1208, David once again seeking assistance from the Latin Emperor and thus forcing Theodore Lascaris to break his siege.

The details now become sketchy, but Theodore Lascaris was finally successful, and David had to flee to the Latin Emperor. He in turn may not have had much appetite for having a Byzantine throne-pretender on the loose and may well have used the centuries-old tradition of neutralizing political enemies by forcing them into monastic service.

However, he ended up there, David Komnenos died on Mount Athos in 1212, having taken the monkish name of Daniel. There was one less contender for the throne of a resurgent Byzantium and David's brother Alexios I now ruled the Empire of Trebizond alone.

While David Komnenos had been busy trying to live out his imperial ambitions on a grander scale, Alexios I of Trebizond had (probably with the help of Georgian troops) successfully defended the city of Trebizond against attacks from the Seljuk Empire of Rum in 1205 and 1206.

In 1214 the Seljuks came back, and this time they succeeded in taking the city of Sinop, moving the Empire of Trebizond's border east and also forming a wedge between the two Greek empires of Nicaea and Trebizond.

With the borders now settled, the Komnenos started a dynasty that would last for more than 250 years, a dynasty that would understand how to use diplomacy at a level only surpassed, if even, by Byzantium itself.

For all intents and purposes, the new empire should have been mopped up by one of the Muslim states that dominated in eastern Anatolia in the preceding centuries. The Seljuk Sultanate of Rum, the Mongols, the Timurids, the Black Sheep, the White Sheep and, of course, the Ottomans were but the biggest players who came and went in the immediate vicinity of the Empire of Trebizond, and yet they maintained their independence. How? is a relevant question and the answer is a complex mosaic which brings us from Persia to Italy.

In 1258, half a century after the Empire of Trebizond had been founded, the Mongols overran Persia, taking Baghdad. The Mongols were difficult to deal with and erratic in their politics, so the trade routes between the East and the West now shifted their route to avoid Mongol held territories.

The city of Trebizond had always been a port-town, serving the local hinterland, but now it suddenly found itself at the end of the 'Silk Route', wares from the Orient flooding into its harbour and merchant ships from the West massing at its docks. For a small and politically insignificant state they made a lot of money, a whole lot of money.

Four decades later Acre, the last surviving Crusader State in the Holy Land, fell to the Mamluks, effectively ending the Age of Crusades and wiping out Christian influence in the Middle East. The Pope, Nicholas IV, reacted by issuing a ban on trade with the Mamluks, a ban that would stand for fifty years and gradually be extended to cover trade with the whole Muslim World.

The lively trade that had taken place through ports in Egypt and Palestine suddenly ceased, and emphasis was shifted from the eastern Mediterranean to the Black Sea.

And here Trebizond was ideally placed. Not only was it already geographically established as an endpoint of the Silk Route, but there was a second factor in play. The Empire of Trebizond was Orthodox, not Catholic. It was religiously tied to the Patriarch in Constantinople, not the Pope in Rome and so they could freely trade with whom they wanted, no matter what the Pope in Rome thought about it.

Thus Trebizond could trade with the Muslims and the, predominantly Italian, traders could trade with Trebizond, making even more money for the local middlemen.

Initially the merchants from Genoa were given priority, provided with a walled township facing the port similar to the colony they had at Galata across from Constantinople. When they became too involved in internal politics, not to mention regular brawls with the local population, their influence was cut down by the establishment of a similar Venetian enclave in 1319.

On this basis it was simply not good business for the neighbouring Muslim states to absorb the Empire of Trebizond, there was too much money to be made from the passing trade caravans, and furthermore the rulers of Trebizond were not afraid to share in their wealth.

Rather than taking a hostile stance towards their Muslim neighbours, successive rulers of Trebizond embraced them. When the time was right for such, they paid generous tributes. At other times they made sure that ambassadors carried lavish gifts, but first and foremost they traded in princesses.

The stereotypical medieval dynasty would be more concerned about male than female offspring, but the Komnenos of Trebizond understood the principle of forming dynastic relations better than most.

Blood is thicker than water, and forming an extended family, reaching into the dynasties of their powerful neighbours, was the name of the game, and so princesses from Trebizond became a commodity.

Rulers of the Seljuk Empire of Rum, Karaman, The Black Sheep and the White Sheep were all given princesses from Trebizond. Over time famed for their beauty, and with each princess coming with a hefty dowry, they assured that the Muslim rulers got a good share in the riches of Trebizond. In addition, the Komnenos kept up their family ties with Georgia, interchanging princes and princesses over time.

It is worth noticing that when Uzun Hasan approached Sultan Mehmed II with his peace proposal in 1473, as described in the previous chapter, his territorial demands were all backed up by references to his family ties with the various rulers that had been deposed by Mehmed II.

Though the papal ban on trade with the Muslim World expired in 1344, Trebizond continued to be an important port for the East-West trade and though the Komnenos dynasty had its own share of intrigue and infighting - they were after all children of Byzantium - it maintained control and was in no immediate danger. That is, until Mehmed II decided differently.

As covered in Chapter 4, Mehmed II blocked off the sea-routes to the Black Sea in 1452 in preparation of his siege of Constantinople. His new 'Throat Cutter' castle on the Bosporus now controlled the all-important route between the Mediterranean Sea and the Black Sea, and though the odd ship would still pay the fees and make its way to Trebizond, the trade dried up, as did the revenues. All was, however, not lost.

After Mehmed II had conquered Constantinople, he started a campaign that would gradually see the Ottomans annexing all the Italian trading colonies in the Black Sea. It would strangle the remaining Italian trade in the Black Sea, forcing trade, and revenue, to go through Ottoman ports. But that was not necessarily the end of Trebizond, an independent state, not subject to Venice or Genoa.

Part 3 - Troublesome Kinsmen

What really killed the Empire of Trebizond was the megalomania of its last ruler, and namesake of its founder, David Megas Komnenos.

After the Conquest of Constantinople, having learned from the Fourth Crusade that if left alone the Byzantine Empire could well re-emerge, in 1456, while he himself was busy in front of Belgrade (as covered in Chapter 14), Mehmed II sent an expeditionary force to Trebizond, commanded by Hızır Pasham, the Ottoman Governor of Amasya.

The Ottoman army soon penetrated through to the suburbs of the city, but plague had broken out in the city itself, and they were hesitant to move any further. The Emperor of Trebizond, realizing that he had no military response (his total armed capability by a contemporary observer being assessed as 4,000 men) approached the Ottomans with an offer of an annual tribute, effectively making the Empire of Trebizond a vassal state of the Ottomans. The offer was accepted, although Mehmed II raised it from the proposed 2,000 to 3,000 gold pieces annually. As far as Mehmed II was concerned, the remote Greek enclave in Trebizond would not cause any more problems and he had bigger fish to fry.

When John IV Komnenos died in 1459 he left a minor son and heir, but the nobility did not want a regency, they preferred an experienced leader. Consequently John IV Komnenos' brother, David Megas Komnenos took the throne.

John IV Komnenos had already started negotiations with various Western states, the Pope and the unavoidable Italian trader-states, regarding an anti-Ottoman league, also including his 'kinsmen' Uzun Hasan and Ibrahim II of Karaman. Though embassies were exchanged and bold statements were made, nothing had actually materialized, but David Megas Komnenos decided to throw himself actively into this project, seeing it as the Empire's salvation from Ottoman dominance.

Despite the lack of practical progress, David Megas Komnenos felt that the Empire of Trebizond had gathered so much support that they could shake off the yoke of the Ottomans and in 1460 he decided to tell the Sultan that no more tribute would be forthcoming. Or rather he decided to talk Uzun Hasan of the White Sheep into relaying the message to Mehmed II as a demonstration of the powerful allies the Empire of Trebizond could rely upon.

I have described this embassy in some detail in the previous chapter, but the end result was that Mehmed II came to the conclusion that the Komnenos rulers in Trebizond could not only not be trusted in terms of their loyalty, but that they obviously fostered schemes of rebellion in which they could very well end up being the crucial 'missing link' between the East and the West.

Mehmed II had promised the ambassadors to deal with the issue the following year, so in 1461 he marched his army east. As described in the previous chapter, he first entered the territories of Uzun Hasan's White

8 - The Empire of Trebizond

Sheep, in order to ensure that they understood that any assistance rendered to their kinsmen in Trebizond would be considered an act of war, a war that Uzun Hasan was not ready for.

While Mehmed II led the land army to the White Sheep, an Ottoman fleet - having already secured the, somewhat shaky, loyalty of the Beylik of Sinop - had landed at Trebizond and put the city under siege.

When Mehmed II arrived, the Ottoman army had already taken the suburbs of the city and negotiations had begun. Though Mehmed II would have preferred an outright military conquest, he allowed the negotiations to continue and ultimately the Empire surrendered, on the condition that David Megas Komnenos and his family would not be harmed.

The Ottomans now annexed the Empire of Trebizond and kept their promise to David Megas Komnenos who was issued with a valuable estate in Rumelia providing him with an annual income of 300,000 silver pieces.

The Empire of Trebizond, yet another state which decided to make itself an enemy of Mehmed II the Conqueror, had ceased to exist, and yet the story does not end there.

David Megas Komnenos' family ties with Uzun Hasan continued to be utilized, either by David himself or by someone conspiring against him. A letter between David and Uzun Hasan was brought to Mehmed II's attention in 1463, allegedly outlining a plan to send one of David's sons into hiding with Uzun Hasan, to be used as a rallying point for a re-conquest of Trebizond.

The letter was possibly a forgery, but that did not help David any. He was arrested, as was the other male members of his family, and on 1 September 1463 he was beheaded with three of his sons and a nephew. His youngest son, George, was spared because of his young age. He later converted to Islam but subsequently fled to his remaining family in Georgia.

The legacy of the princesses of Trebizond lived on as one of David Megas Komnenos' daughters, Anna, joined the Sultan's harem.

Another legacy of the Empire of Trebizond that lived on was the small Principality of Theodoro on the Crimean peninsula. It was ruled by Alexander Komnenos, who in the style of Trebizond had a sister who was married to the Voivode of Moldavia. The Principality was a part of the Empire of Trebizond (indeed the only reason why the state would be termed an 'empire) even though they also paid tribute to the Tatar Crimean Khanate, their powerful neighbours to the north. They were in constant conflict with the Genoese, who had positioned themselves on most of the coastal areas around the southern rim of the peninsula, but otherwise lived a rather unremarkable existence.

In 1475 Mehmed II came for the Genoese, and their central port of Caffa. While there he happened to take prisoner the Tatar Khan who, after being taken to Istanbul, agreed to pay tribute as an Ottoman vassal.

Mehmed II occupied and took the Genoese possessions, and while he was at it laid siege to Mangup, the capital of the Principality of Theodoro. After a six month siege the city fell, and the Principality was, along with the Genoese territories, annexed into the Ottoman Empire.

PART 4

THE MARITIME STATES OF ITALY

9 - ITALY AND THE MARITIME STATES
10 - VENICE
11 - GENOA

Part 4 - The Maritime States of Italy

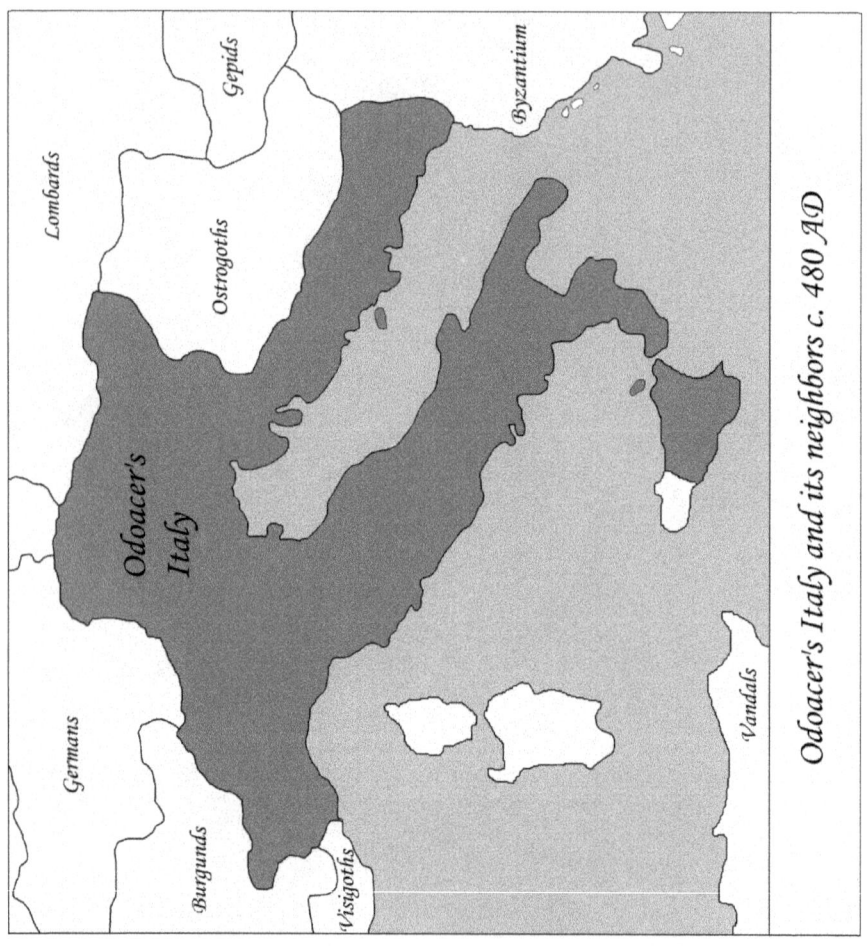

9 - ITALY AND THE MARITIME STATES

Before we go into a more detailed description of the two dominant Maritime States, Venice and Genoa, we need to spend a little time defining what a Maritime State is and in particular the 'Italian' Maritime States that dominated the Mediterranean and Black Sea in the fifteenth century.

I deliberately put the word 'Italian' inside inverted commas, as the concept of Italy was very different in the fifteenth century than it is today, the nation state we now know as 'Italy' only coming into existence in 1861.

After the break-down of the (Western) Roman Empire in the fifth century, the Italian peninsula was the regular recipient of foreign invaders.

First came 'the Germans' identified in the shape of Odoacer, a 'German' chief who ousted the last emperor of the (Western) Roman Empire in 476. Or at least so the most common story goes. In reality, Odoacer was a high-ranking soldier in the Roman army, and though he did participate in the ousting of the Emperor, Romulus Augustulus, he ruled as the de facto ruler behind the nominal Emperor, Julius Nepor, and on his death under the nominal suzerainty of the Emperor in Byzantium.

Odoacer's road to power was thus not as the head of a big migration of 'Germans' streaming into Italy even though that is what it sounds like when the story is normally told. That kind of mass-migration was reserved for the next force to rule Italy, the Ostrogoths.

But we need to stay with Odoacer for a moment, as we need to expand our definition of Italy some from the nice geographically defined peninsula we know as Italy today. Odoacer's 'Italy' went north-east into what is today parts of Austria and made a 180 degrees turn and expanded down the east coast of the Adriatic Sea, covering the south-western parts of (modern day) Slovenia, Croatia, Montenegro and Albania, ending pretty much directly across from the south-easternmost point of the Italian peninsula. Directly east of these Dalmatian possession was the territories of the Ostrogoths.

Goths had started to appear in the Roman Empire in the fourth century. Originally they came from north of the Danube River, but they were gradually forced south by the expanding Huns, and a tribe known as the Visigoth ended up literally stranded on the north side of the Danube River, with the Huns approaching from the north and the Byzantines guarding the southern shore.

The Byzantines allowed the Visigoths to cross the river, and a love-hate relationship developed in which the Byzantine army gradually became populated by more Visigoths than indigenous Byzantines, with the inevitable potential for king-making and political intrigue.

At the death of the Byzantine Emperor Theodosius I in 395, the Visigoths rose up and although the revolt was nominally put down, the Visigoth chief Alaric (referred to as King by his own people) ruled supreme in the eastern Balkans, regularly parading his army outside the walls of Constantinople itself.

In 401 Alaric, however, decided to turn his attention on the western part of the Roman Empire, assembled his people and led them north of the Adriatic Sea. First they went to Italy, where they sacked Rome in 410, and then they turned north and settled in southern Gaul and eventually penetrated into Portugal and Spain.

The other main gothic tribe, the Ostrogoths, had not fled with the Visigoths, but had stayed north of the Danube River as vassals to the Hun. On the death of Attila (the Hun) in 452, the Hunnish Empire broke down, and the Ostrogoths established themselves first along the Danube and then came across the river and moved south-west into the south-western parts of the Balkans, bordering the Dalmatian possessions of Odoacer's Italy to the west and the Byzantine Empire to the east.

For two decades the Ostrogoths regularly raided east into the Byzantine Empire, to such an extent that the parts of the Balkans closest to the Ostrogoths were starting to become depopulated.

The Byzantine emperor, Zeno, had tried to turn the two leaders of the Ostrogoths; both called Theodoric, against each other but without success. One of them was killed by accident anyhow, and then Zeno came up with a piece of brilliant diplomacy, possibly one of the finest pieces of Byzantine trickery conceived.

Instead of trying to beat the Ostrogoths, he offered the (remaining) chief the Western Empire, in reality meaning Italy. As mentioned above, Italy was de-facto ruled by Germans who paid only nominal obedience to Byzantium and Zeno now offered that if Theodoric could take Italy, then he could be Viceroy of The West, paying only homage to Zeno himself.

The offer was too good to refuse so in 488 Theodoric took his people with him and disappeared into Italy from where they removed the ruling Germans and put themselves in power, accepting that the Byzantine Emperor was their over-lord, but otherwise minding their own business, ruling Italy from Ravenna.

Emperor Zeno had with one smart move both rid his empire of the Ostrogoth raiders and regained Italy to the Empire, although on his death in 491 the Ostrogoth's suppression of Italy had not yet completed.

The bliss did not last long though. Theodoric, known as Theodoric the Great, turned out to be a very good ruler, managing to keep a balance between the local 'Romans' and the ruling Goths, his successors did not master this art, and after his death in 526, the Roman nobles, the 'political class', and the Goths, the 'military class', started to clash, leading to unrest

9 - Italy and the Maritime States

and succession issues. Finally, in 535, the Byzantine Emperor, Justinian I, intervened.

Having recently secured victories in North Africa, the Byzantines moved on Italy and even though the war initially went their way, it took nearly twenty years to finally suppress the Ostrogoths.

The Byzantine victory was what is known as a 'pyrrhic victory', a victory that has exhausted you to a point where nothing is actually achieved and another victory on the same terms may lead to your ultimate defeat. In other words, the Byzantines were exhausted and worse, Italy had been depopulated to an extent that meant that it fell into decline.

Justinian I died in 565, and only three years later Italy was partly lost to the Byzantine Empire.

This time the invaders were 'Lombards', another Germanic tribe which had gradually moved from the southern parts of Scandinavia to (modern day) Austria and who simple wandered into the depopulated peninsula.

The Italian peninsula was now divided between Lombard possessions in the north and the north-west and a long stretch along the east coast, mixed with the remaining Byzantine possessions.

For the next 200 years, there was relative peace in Italy. Not that there was not conflict of course, the Lombards and the Byzantines would have it out with each other and various would-be-invaders would knock on the door, but things stayed pretty much as was.

Then in 774 northern and central Italy was conquered by Charlemagne (Charles I), who was crowned as the first Holy Roman Emperor by the Pope (see also Chapter 16), leaving the southern part of the peninsula as a combination of Byzantine and Lombard control and creating a broad band in the middle ruled by the Pope as its temporal lord.

In the following centuries, the Pope and the Holy Roman Emperor would regularly fight it out over control of central and northern Italy, gradually leading to the formation of a range of city-states, whose loyalty would swing one way or the other depending on the situation.

The final big entry was in the middle of the eleventh century, when the Normans came. Initially Norman mercenaries were hired by the various parties in Italy, including the Pope, but news soon reached home to Normandy (in northern France) that the southern part of the country was in disarray and Normans started to arrive, not as a concerted conquest, as would be the case when the Normans went to England in 1066, but as a gradual take-over, leaving southern Italy in Norman control at the end of the century and once and for all removing the last Byzantine influence on the peninsula.

The Normans even had designs on crossing the Adriatic Sea and move on Constantinople, but that is a different story which we shall come back to in the next chapter.

Eventually southern Italy united into first the Kingdom of Sicily and, when Sicily seceded in 1282 following the Sicilian Vespers (see Chapter 4), the Kingdom of Naples.

Parallel to all this the rest of Europe had also changed dramatically. Nation states had formed; some of them similar to what we know today, others more fragmented, but one important thing had happened, all of western Europe had become Christian.

Although history shows that Christianity is not in itself a guarantor of peace between people or nations - indeed Christianity, or the definition of Christianity, would in itself cause plenty of wars and unrest in the centuries to follow - it did create some communality, and first and foremost a single authority in the shape of the Pope.

Not that the Pope had ultimate control, indeed as we shall see in Chapter 16 the papacy was in continuous war with Europe's secular rulers for supremacy, but nevertheless the single religion created a base for relative peace, and with peace came prosperity.

That prosperity meant that famers could farm their fields without the risk of their crops being burned or confiscated by warring parties and that craftsmen could develop their skills over an uninterrupted period of time. It also meant that goods could be transported to be exchanged with other goods, and gradually goods started to flow through Europe, on the rivers and by land-routes across mountain passes.

A similar trend had started in the East, caravans making their way westwards from as far away as China, however there was a problem with the two streams of goods meeting and being exchanged.

The part of the world between the East and the West, central Asia and Russia, was not stable. It was not Christian and it was not Muslim, the two defining 'civilizations', rather it was populated by 'heathens', and the weather conditions were often adverse to overland travel. There thus was no practical land-route connecting the two parts of the world, but there was a sea-route.

Goods could be transported, by river or over land, to the nearest practical sea-port, which could be thousands of miles away, but if you could get your goods to a sea-port on the Black or Mediterranean Seas, ships would connect the East and the West, bringing goods to and from and creating an ever increasing interchange of goods between the extremes of the known world.

From the perspective of Europe, when you transported goods from Western Europe or the Balkans, the natural end-point, the best suited seaports, were in northern Italy or on the Dalmatian coast.

So goods started to arrive in northern Italian sea-ports like Venice and Ancona (at the north-eastern side of the peninsula), Genoa and Pisa (on the north-western side of the peninsula), and because of the political map even as far south as Gaeta and Amalfi on the south-western coast. Goods from the Balkans came to Ragusa (modern day Dubrovnik) on the eastern shore of the Adriatic Sea.

Through all the turmoil of medieval Italy, these port-cities developed into independent city-states, moving goods between the Christian World in Europe and the Muslim World in North Africa, Egypt, the Middle East and Anatolia, and as far northeast as the Black Sea.

As was the case with the Empire of Trebizond (see Chapter 8), these city-states did not necessarily have the military strength to withstand a concerted conquest-attempt by one of the larger players in the area, but they were useful, too useful, so they were mainly left alone to do what they did best; trade.

Over time, two dominant players developed, Venice and Genoa, both situated at the top of the Italian Peninsula, Venice to the east and Genoa to the west, both located at natural shipping points for goods coming to or from Western Europe and both developing maritime trade into a fine art.

Their approach was, however, very different, and in the following chapters we shall cover the story of each of them and see how they became enemies of the Conqueror.

Part 4 - The Maritime States of Italy

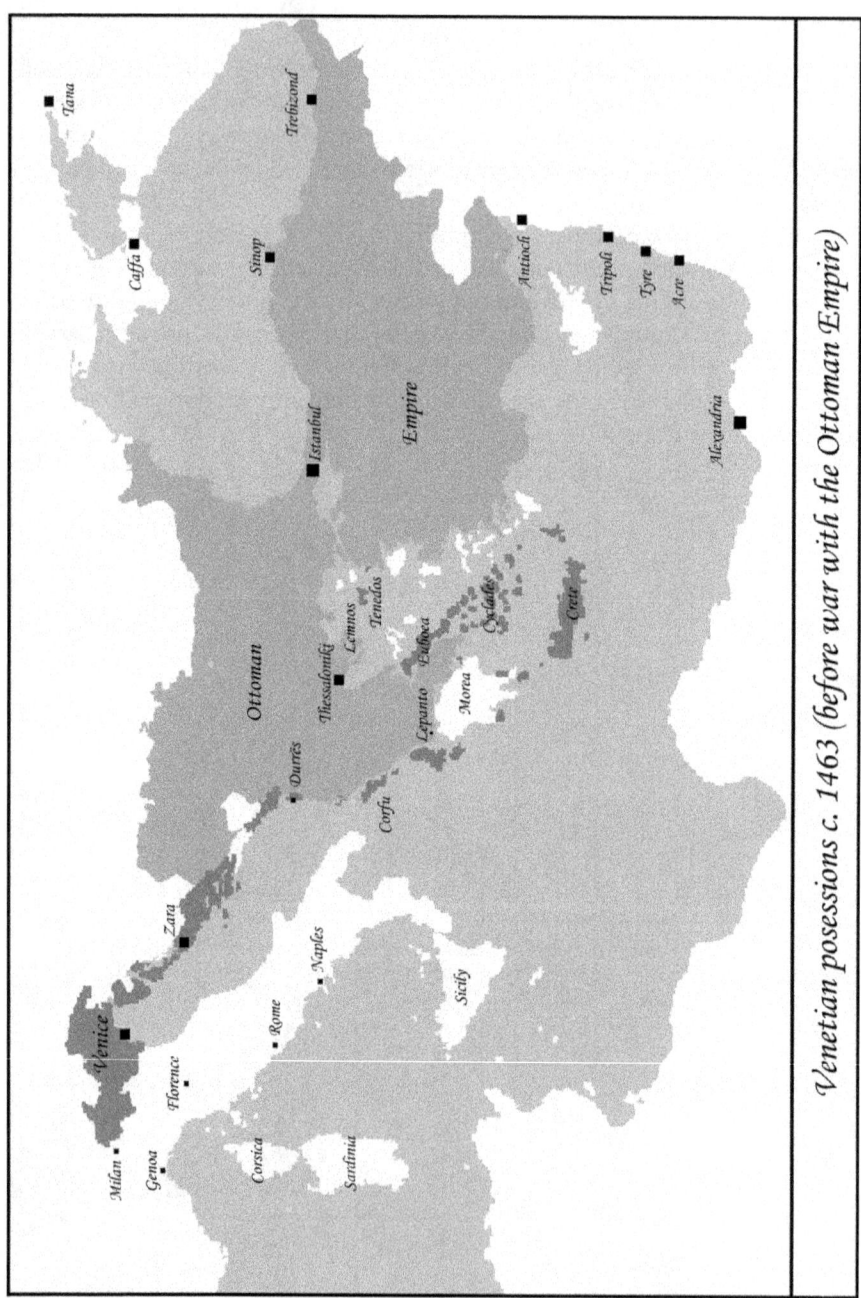

Venetian posessions c. 1463 (before war with the Ottoman Empire)

10 - VENICE

Part 4 - The Maritime States of Italy

CRITICAL TIMELINE

Year	Event	Involved Parties
500s	First mention of Venice in written sources	Venice
803	*Pax Nicephori* states that Venice remains part of Byzantium	Venice Byzantium
1000	Venice granted status as *Dux Dalmatiae* by Byzantium	Venice Byzantium
1081	Battle with Normans off Corfu	Venice Normans
1082	Venice given exclusive trading rights in the Byzantine Empire	Venice Byzantium
1083	Venetian retake Durrës and Corfu from Normans	Venice Normans
1084	Battle with Normans off Corfu	Venice Normans
1099	First Crusade	Venice Western Europe
1111	Pisa given trading rights in Byzantine Empire	Venice Byzantium Pisa
1122	Venetian attack on Byzantine Empire	Venice Byzantium
1123	Trading rights in the Kingdom of Jerusalem	Venice Jerusalem
1126	Restoration of 1082 trading rights in Byzantine Empire	Venice Byzantium
1156	Genoa given trading rights in Byzantine Empire	Byzantium Genoa
1171	Genoese settlement in Constantinople attacked. Venetians are arrested and attack Byzantine Empire. Venetians expelled from Constantinople	Venice Byzantium Genoa
1179	Venetians allowed back in Constantinople in limited numbers	Venice Byzantium
1182	Attack on Latins in Constantinople	Venice Byzantium Genoa Pisa
1185	Venice officially returns to Constantinople	Venice Byzantium
1204	Fourth Crusade. Venice becomes *Dominante*	Venice Byzantium
1250	Sacking of Venetian quarters in Acre	Venice Genoa
1255	Venetian fleet attacks Acre and Tyre	Venice Genoa
1258	Venice and Genoa do battle in Acre	Venice Genoa

Year	Event	Involved Parties
1261	Reconquest of Constantinople	Venice, Genoa, Byzantium
1265	Genoa is expelled from Constantinople	Genoa, Byzantium
1267	Genoa is invited back to Constantinople	Genoa, Byzantium
1268	Venice is invited back to Constantinople	Venice, Byzantium
1291	Acre is lost to Egypt	Egypt, Jerusalem
1296	Venetian attack on Constantinople	Venice, Genoa, Byzantium
1297	Genoese attack on Constantinople	Venice, Genoa, Byzantium
1298	Venetian attack on Constantinople	Venice, Genoa, Byzantium
1299	Peace settlement	Venice, Genoa
1302	Venetian attack on Constantinople	Venice, Byzantium
1324	Papal ban on trade with Muslims	The Pope, Venice, Genoa
1325	Venice acquires trading rights at Tana	Venice, Golden Horde
1343	Mongol attack on Tana and Caffa	Venice, Genoa, Golden Horde
1344	Papal trade-ban expires	The Pope, Venice, Genoa
1346	Mongol attack on Caffa. Black Death	Venice, Genoa, Golden Horde
1347	Venetians back in Tana	Venice, Golden Horde
1348	Black Death reached Europe	Venice, Genoa
1351	Venetian attack on Constantinople	Venice, Genoa, Byzantium
1352	Naval battle off Constantinople	Venice, Genoa, Pisa
1354	Naval battle off Pylos	Venice, Genoa

Part 4 - The Maritime States of Italy

Year	Event	Involved Parties
1355	Peace agreement	Venice, Genoa
1369	Emperor John V Palaiologos offers the island of Tenedos to Venice	Venice, Genoa, Byzantium
1376	Venice once again granted Tenedos	Venice, Genoa, Byzantium
1380	Battle of Chioggia	Venice, Genoa
1381	Settlement over Tenedos	Venice, Genoa
1423	Venice granted Thessaloniki	Venice, Byzantium
1430	Venice loses Thessaloniki to Ottomans. Venice gain trade rights in Ottoman Empire	Venice, Ottomans
1444	Venice participates in campaign leading to Battle of Varna	Venice, Hungary, Ottomans
1446	Venice and Ottomans renew trade agreement	Venice, Ottomans
1447	Ottoman attack on Morea leaves Venetian possessions untouched	Byzantium, Ottomans
1448	Venetians supply Ottomans and Albanians in Albania	Venice, Ottomans, Albania
1450	Venetians supply Ottomans and Albanians in Albania	Venice, Ottomans, Albania
1452	Mehmed II cuts off Black Sea route with Boğaz Kesen castle on the Bosporus Strait	Ottomans
1453	Ottoman conquest of Constantinople, Venetians ships and troops leave before the battle.	Ottomans, Byzantium, Venice
1453	Venetians granted trade rights in Ottoman Empire	Venice, Ottomans
1458	Mehmed II pays impromptu visit to Negroponte. Ottomans enforce tribute on Duchy of Naxos	Venice, Ottomans
1462	Ottoman siege of Lepanto. Ottomans fortify Dardanelles	Venice, Ottomans
1463	Ottomans occupy Argos. Venice declares war on Ottoman Empire	Venice, Ottomans
1463	Venice proposes alliance with White Sheep	Venice, White Sheep
1463	Venetians retake Argos. Ottoman counter-offensive in Morea. Hungarian attack on Bosnia	Venice, Ottomans, Hungary

10- Venice

Year	Event	Involved Parties
1464	Ottoman counter-offensive in Bosnia. Venetian attack on Lesbos. 'Crusader' alliance breaks down when the Pope dies	Venice Ottomans The Pope Hungary
1466	Venice takes Imroz, Thasos and Samothrace and lays siege to Athens	Venice Ottomans
1467	Ottoman siege of Durrës. Ottoman raiders in Croatia	Venice Ottomans Albania
1468	Venice takes control of Krujë	Venice Ottomans
1469	Ottoman raiders in Dalmatia. Venetian raids in Morea	Venice Ottomans
1470	Ottomans conquer Euboea	Venice Ottomans
1471	Alliance between White Sheep and Venice	Venice White Sheep
1472	Christian fleet raid in Mediterranean and Aegean Sea	Venice
1473	Venetian artillery-support for White Sheep is returned to Venice	Venice White Sheep
1474	Ottoman siege of Shkodër	Venice Ottomans
1475	Ottoman attacks on Lepanto, Lemnos and Naxos.	Venice Ottomans
1476	Siege of Krujë	Venice Ottomans
1477	Ottoman raiders reach outskirts of Venice	Venice Ottomans
1478	Ottomans take Krujë. Ottoman raiders outside Venice. Siege of Shkodër	Venice Ottomans
1479	Peace agreement between Venice and Ottoman Empire	Venice Ottomans

Part 4 - The Maritime States of Italy

10- Venice

I mentioned in the beginning of this book that the Ottomans, according to folklore, emerged from 400 tents in a refugee camp. Their (probably) most persistent enemy, the Republic of Venice, also came from very humble beginnings.

Venice was not really a 'city', or even a town in the traditional sense. Instead, it was a collection of low-lying islands and sandbanks which were gradually converted into a city by means of houses built on wooden stakes, interlaced by canals and connecting bridges. Fortifications were added over time, forming a confusing complex serving one very specific purpose, maritime trade.

The first mention of Venice is from the sixth century, where a Byzantine traveller mentions them for three things in particular; their strange dwellings *'across the surface of the water'*, their richness - due to the rich salt-deposits they were mining at the delta formed by the River Po River's confluence into the Adriatic Sea -, and the structure of their society, in which everyone was equal and there was no feudal structure the way it was common in the Christian World.

Of course, a feudal structure is based on landholding, and since Venice was not 'land', but consisted of sea, which was claimed for the purpose of dwellings, harbours and, eventually, fortifications, the Venetians were different from the outset.

With no land, and thus no agricultural production, they had to trade for food with what they had, salt and fish, so they were always dependent on their capability to transport those goods by water. First they travelled up the rivers of northern Italy, but soon they developed their ships to enable them to venture further afield, down the coasts of the Adriatic Sea and eventually to the eastern ports of Greece, Anatolia, the Middle East, North Africa and Egypt as well as ports on the Atlantic coast of Europe.

These trips brought an abundance of 'exotic' goods, which again could be exchanged in Europe, so over the years Venice became a natural place of exchange of goods, streaming down into the city from northern Europe and streaming back up again when ships arrived from faraway shores in the East. But there were problems.

The first problems were close to home. As much as the Adriatic Sea was the perfect sea-corridor, offering relative shelter even though it could be subject to foul weather on occasions, it was not only the home of the Venetians, it was also the home of many others.

Maritime States were also developing in Ancona and Rugusa, across from each other halfway down the Adriatic Sea, and there were pirates, mainly from Croatia, hiding in the multitude of coves and bays along the eastern coast of the Adriatic Sea.

So, trading ships were not enough, they needed protection and Venice started to build men-of-war, creating convoys with a combination of naval and trading vessels. As we shall see later, they eventually changed this strategy for one of more proactive domination.

A second problem was that of long-distance seafaring itself. We most often envisage medieval sea voyages as the ocean-crossing sailing ships of the late fifteenth and sixteenth century, like Christopher Columbus or Bartolomeu Dias, but in the centuries prior naval technology was not developed for this kind of point-to-point travel. Rather a voyage between points A and B consisted of a number of short 'hops', staying close to the coast and stopping at several ports along the way to take on supplies, exchange goods and take shelter from or foul weather. In addition, this method also meant that if you encountered pirates, which was common, you only needed to outrun them to the nearest safe port.

To effectively run an operation between Venice and the ports in the East, they needed safe harbours along the way. Such harbours, including of course the central harbour of Constantinople, could be supplied by the Byzantine Empire, so where most other Italian cities, and city-states, gradually trickled away from Byzantine suzerainty, Venice stayed in the Byzantine fold, made official in the '*Pax Nicephori*' the peace agreement of the early ninth century defining the borders between the Western and Eastern Roman Empires.

This made Venice special in another way as well, as they were "Catholic" rather than "Orthodox", recognizing the Pope in Rome as their spiritual head, while recognizing the Emperor in Constantinople as their secular lord. To their fellow Italians they were renegades and freebooters, to the Byzantines they were "Latins," but as long as they were profitable the Venetians themselves cared little for what others thought.

As the Byzantine Empire started to crumple and could no longer guarantee the safety of the shores and ports that the Venetians needed, a new strategy was required. The first target was the Adriatic Sea.

At the turn of the first Millennium (and covered in Chapter 12) a new strong Bulgarian state (referred to as the First Bulgarian Empire) had developed in the north-eastern Balkans, gradually pushing back Byzantine control. When they managed to reach Dyrrachium (modern day Durrës) on the Adriatic Sea's eastern shore the Byzantine emperor, Basil II, decided that he needed help and he made the Venetians an offer.

What Basil II offered was for the Venetians to take effective control of the Adriatic Sea and its eastern shores, ruling it as they saw fit, as a protectorate of the Byzantine Empire.

For the Byzantines it meant that they could concentrate their diminishing naval forces somewhere else, and for the Venetians it opened up the opportunity to expand their home lagoon at the top of the Adriatic Sea to include the whole of the Adriatic Sea.

The Venetian Dodge, Pietro II Orseolo, did not hesitate but immediately accepted and on Ascension Day of the Year 1000 he led a big fleet out of Venice and down the Adriatic Sea where he soon got the official acceptance of the, Greek speaking, coastal towns on the east coast, happy to receive 'imperial' protection. They stopped just north of Ragusa, which remained independent for the time being.

Now free to do as he pleased, Doge Orseolo took his fleet to the Neretva River, which, together with some outlying islands, was the main centre for the Croatian pirates to which Venice had for a long time been paying protection-money to secure safe passage in the Adriatic Sea.

The Venetians stormed the pirate strongholds and effectively put an end to piracy in the Adriatic Sea. Having started out as salt panners, the Venetians were now, and with official imperial sanction, 'Dux Dalmatiae', Lords of Dalmatia.

The annexation of the Dalmatian east coast created a model for Venetian expansion, which would be repeated at a much larger scale in the centuries to come, but before we move forward, it is worth discussing the Venetian model of 'colonization'.

Venice was, as previously mentioned, different due to their equality of their (male) citizens. They had an elected Representative of 200 citizen, and further upper councils which changed over time, but all served to first elect and then control the appointed Doge, the Head of State. Of course, 'equality' was then, as now, a relative term. Some citizens lived rather typical, or by our terms, 'poor', lives, whereas others became immensely rich, and thus powerful in both politics and every-day life.

The model which made Venice strong and powerful was one based on the absolute authority of the State. It was a kind of early fascism, without the need for a vanguard or a revolution.

The State owned everything, including the trading ships, and whereas it was left to individuals, or groups of individuals, to rent the ships and perform the actual trading, the individual was always subject to the State and performing the State's business before his own. The State collected taxes on everything, through a complex system of laws, and whereas individuals were free to make their own fortunes, it was only after the State had taken its cut.

On the other hand, the State provided protection, in the form of warships, escorts and safe harbours. And these safe harbours were the real key to Venetian success.

At the turn of the first millennium most of the harbours around the eastern part of the Mediterranean Sea were not as such under Venetian control, but in each of them there was a Venetian 'colony', taking care of the Venetian State's interests and headed by a representative of the State. He could be called rector, consul, bailo or dux, but no matter what he was called, he represented the State in all local matters, whether in regard to the host-country or amongst the Venetians themselves.

The Venetians were, however, not alone. There were traders from other cities, not least Genoa and Pisa. Each merchant-city had their own quarters in the host city, and often local conflicts and skirmishes broke out, spilling over into conflict with the locals, as often as not already irritated by the haughty attitude of the 'Latins'.

With the de-facto annexation of the 'Greek' cities on the eastern Dalmatian coast, Venice now started a new model. The cities became 'Venetian', with a fortress, soldiers, naval vessels, and a Venetian governor applying the (Venetian) law. And the word 'city' is not chosen randomly, as the Venetian interest was indeed that, the city, or rather the port with the attached city providing the necessary underlying infrastructure.

Venice had no lust for land, a fact in which they set themselves apart from practically any other empire. They could have taken possessions on the hinterlands, but they satisfied themselves with narrow stretches of land, often just a few kilometres inland. The value of a city was the access it created to the sea because Venice's empire was the sea, not the land.

Similarly, they had no intentions on cultural colonization. The people who happened to live in the cities they annexed were useful as workers or soldiers, and of course as taxpayers, but their spiritual and cultural lives had no interest to the Venetians. People could believe what they wanted and live like they wanted as long as they served their purpose.

With the Adriatic Sea now secure, Venetian trade flourished. They had to share in the spoils with others, in particular the Genoese and the Pisans and, importantly, the Byzantines would only allow them, and everybody else, as far as Constantinople. Access to the Black Sea was reserved for Byzantium itself and goods coming to or from the Black Sea had to be exchanged at Constantinople, ensuring a massive income for the Byzantine Empire who had their own complex taxes. What they did not have, however, was a sizeable navy. They used to, but over the centuries they had been worn financially down by warfare, constantly engaging in either civil war or the protection of their crumpling borders and the Byzantine navy had become too expensive to maintain. Instead, they started to rely on the Italians, in particular Venice and Genoa, to protect Byzantine interests at sea. This situation meant that the Byzantine Empire, strongly driven by its religious and cultural values, became increasingly dependent on states that believed only in profit, and gave but lip-service to religious or cultural values. Eventually it had to go wrong.

At first it went well though, in particular for the Venetians. Goods flowed and even though trade had to be shared with the other maritime states, there was wealth enough to be shared. But in the 1080s events changed for the better for the Venetians.

10- Venice

In the previous chapter I mentioned the Normans who, in the latter half of the eleventh century, had started to annex southern Italy for themselves. By 1071 they had conquered Bari, the last remaining Byzantine city in Italy, a year later Palermo, breaking Saracen hold on Sicily and four years later they took the last Lombard possession, Salerno. With all of southern Italy in hand, they started to develop even bigger ambitions, ambitions which included the Byzantine Empire itself.

The idea was not as far flung as it may seem. The cities of southern Italy, now in Norman control, were not 'Italian' in the sense we would understand it today, rather they were 'Greek, in that the population spoke Greek and were subject to the Orthodox Church. The Normans had thus conquered a true part of the Byzantine Empire, and the Byzantines had not put up much of a fight.

Realizing that the Normans were becoming a real threat, in 1074 the Byzantine emperor, Michael VII Doukas, in 1074 tried to tie them into a dynastic bond by offering his son and co-emperor, the infant Constantine, to Olympias, a far from infant daughter of Robert Guiscard, Duke of Apulia and de-facto ruler of southern Italy.

Robert Guiscard took the bait and the opportunity to become father-in-law to the future Emperor of Byzantium, so the girl was sent off to Constantinople, where she was renamed Helena. Here she was to await Constantine growing to marriageable age, while she herself was being educated in all things Byzantine. But it was not to be.

Michael VII Doukas was overthrown in 1078, and the marriage contract was annulled. Helena was parked in a convent and her father Robert Guiscard had the perfect 'casus belli' for an attack on Constantinople. If he could not get to Constantinople by means of diplomacy, he would just have to get there by means of military force.

Robert Guiscard started to prepare for war, but before he could even start his campaign the new Byzantine emperor, Nikephoros III Botaneiates, had been overthrown by his own general, Alexios I Komnenos, so Robert Guiscard had all reason to believe that he was setting out against a weak and divided Byzantine Empire, which could be subdued by a determined and powerful enemy.

In May of 1081 his preparations were done, and he set out with his fleet for Corfu. The Byzantine garrison on Corfu surrendered to the Normans without a fight, but then it got more difficult.

A terrible storm destroyed part of the Norman fleet, and then the Venetians did their job of protecting the Adriatic Sea by destroying more of Robert Guiscard's fleet. Undeterred he did, however, manage to get his army across to the mainland where he put Durazzo (modern day Durrës in Albania) under siege.

Contrary to the Byzantines on Corfu, the garrison in Durazzo did not surrender to the Normans, but held out in the knowledge that Emperor

Alexios I Komnenos was now in the field with an army, marching to relieve the besieged city.

By mid-October, the Byzantine army reached Durazzo and three days later they attacked the Normans. It is worth mentioning, because it gives a picture of how confused the political situation really was, that the Norman army, apart from the Normans themselves, included Saracens recruited from Sicily and 'Greeks' recruited in southern Italy. Against them stood a Byzantine army which had lost its core at Manzikert ten years earlier and now was a mix of Byzantines, Seljuks hired in Anatolia and the Varangian Guard, the Emperor's bodyguard, which by now consisted nearly entirely of Englishmen, Anglo-Saxons with no love lost for the Normans who had invaded their home-country fifteen years prior.

The battle was hard fought, but the Normans held the day, not least helped by the Emperor's 7,000 Seljuk archers abandoning the battlefield. Alexios I Komnenos had to withdraw, but he had not left the matter to be settled entirely by his own military intervention.

Durazzo held on until February 1082, after which Robert Guiscard could march on to Kastoria in northern Greece. Here, however, Emperor Alexios I Komnenos' diplomatic efforts caught up with the Normans.

Robert Guiscard had a nephew, Abelard, whom he had dispossessed, and who had taken refuge in Constantinople. Alexios I Komnenos had now provided him with sufficient gold to return to Italy and raise a revolt while Robert Guiscard was away on his campaign in Greece. At the same time Henry IV, King of the Germans, was intent on removing Pope Gregory VI and crowned as Emperor of the Romans, so he needed little convincing - and 360,000 Byzantine gold pieces - to start a campaign in Italy. This took him to the gates of Rome, forcing the Pope to request help from Robert Guiscard.

The Norman leader had to return home and leave the army in the care of his brother, Bohemund, who kept advancing west, but in the spring of 1083 he was beaten by the Byzantine army at Larissa in western Greece and had to withdraw to Kastoria. Beaten by the Byzantines, without the leadership of Robert Guiscard and unpaid, the Norman army now fell apart and started to drift towards home. Bohemund himself set off to Italy to raise more money, but the remaining Normans quickly surrendered and then once again the Venetians got involved and retook both Durrës and Corfu, leaving the Normans with a few outlying islands and a small strip of Albanian coast - but they were not yet done.

Robert Guiscard had in the meantime got things back under control at home, and had taken the opportunity to 'relieve' Rome, which was sacked by its Norman 'rescuers'. He thus sailed for Greece again in the autumn of 1084. His fleet of 150 ships was attacked by a Venetian fleet and beaten twice in three days, but when the battle was seemingly over, Robert Guiscard counterattacked, causing Venetian losses of more than 10,000 men. He retook Corfu and landed in Greece, but here, like large parts of his army, he was hit by typhoid and died in July 1085. The Normans withdrew to Italy, their challenge for the Byzantine Empire gone.

Whereas these events were just a speck on the canvas in the larger context of the Byzantine Empire, their importance was major for Venice. The Venetians had stood up for the Empire, though admittedly they themselves had little appetite for Norman control of the southern access to the Adriatic Sea. They had consistently attacked the Norman fleets and had, in the end, taken major damage, but their compensation was plentiful.

In 1082 Emperor Alexios I Komnenos rewarded the Venetians with their biggest prize. They were given the right to trade freely, and exempt from tax, in the Byzantine Empire, the only exception being the Black Sea, and not only that, but they were given this right on an exclusive basis, they were granted monopoly, dealing a serious blow to their competitors.

A truly golden age started for the Venetians. Their traders flocked to Byzantine cities such as Athens, Salonika, Thebes, Antioch and Ephesus and to harbours such as Modon and Coron on the southern tip of the Morea. And of course, they went to Constantinople, the Venetian colony growing to 12,000 and occupying the key part of the Golden Horn.

The Byzantines had, with the exception of the Black Sea trade, left their entire trade in the hands of Venice, who had also effectively taken over the role of the Byzantine navy, which had fallen into decline due to the Empire's constant lack of funds (to fund the campaign against the Normans, emperor Alexios I Komnenos had to confiscate all church treasure).

The First Crusade brought further opportunities, the Venetians assisting in the conquest of the coastal cities of Syria in the later stages of the campaign and in 1123 assisting the Kingdom of Jerusalem in their fight against the Fatimid Egyptians, obtaining virtual autonomy in the cities of the Kingdom.

But as much as both fortune and the Empire favoured Venice, the Byzantine population at large did not. They did not like the Venetians, who in their eyes were arrogant, a law unto their own, morally vulgar, and well in the process of buying up the best properties in Constantinople. And then they were, of course, Catholics.

Within three decades the Venetians had become such a nuisance, and so powerful, that the only way to bring them back under some kind of control was to break their monopoly, so in 1111 the Pisans were given trading rights in Constantinople. The Venetians complained, the Byzantines stalled and in 1118 the Emperor, Alexios I Komnenos, died and was replaced by his son John II Komnenos.

As was custom, the Venetians asked John II Komnenos to re-confirm the trading rights given to them in 1082, but the new Emperor refused. He believed that there was more money to be made by the Empire in a free-trade environment.

The Venetians were furious and in 1122 they attacked the Byzantine Empire, their fleet plundering the Byzantine islands of Corfu, Rhodes, Chios, Samos, Lesbos and Andros and furthermore occupying the island of Cephalonia. The Emperor realized that it cost the empire more to be at war with the Venetians than to let them have their trading rights, so in 1126 he re-confirmed the 1082 agreement, though the Pisans were allowed to stay in Constantinople.

In 1156 the right to trade in Constantinople was extended to the Genoese and the three leading Italian merchant-states now had their own quarters in Constantinople, leading to constant brawling and violence. Mini trading-wars began under the eyes of the local Greeks, who got more and more tired of the troublesome Italians and in 1171 the situation exploded.

The Genoese had been given the township of Galata on the north side of the Golden Horn, and early in 1171 it was attacked by a mob, burned and looted. Though the perpetrators were never identified, the locals had no doubt that the Venetians were behind it, so in a concerted and well executed move, all Venetians on Byzantine soil were arrested, their goods, property and ships confiscated. Amongst the 10,000 Venetians arrested in Constantinople alone was Enrico Dandolo who, as Doge, would lead the Venetians in the Fourth Crusade some thirty years later.

The Venetians reacted the only way they knew how, forced an emergency loan on their citizens and sailed with a fleet of 120 ships, led by Doge Vitale Michiel, against Constantinople. But they only got as far as Euboea on the eastern side of the Greek peninsula, where they were met by Byzantine ambassadors, urging them to halt hostilities and send ambassadors to Constantinople, where the Emperor invited them to negotiate a solution satisfactory to both parties.

Always weighing the cost of options against each other, the Venetians agreed and sent their ambassadors while the fleet anchored on the island of Chios. The ambassadors came back in the spring with no result, having realized that the Byzantine Emperor wanted nothing but to stall, but by then plague had broken out in Chios and killed most of the Venetians, leaving the survivors weak and demoralized.

The Venetians headed home, where the population accused the Doge of both falling into a classic Byzantine trap and bringing plague to the mother city, so he was deposed and murdered by a mob in the street. For fourteen years diplomatic contact between the Venetians and the Byzantines was severed, though a treaty in 1179 allowed Venetians back in Constantinople in limited numbers.

Strangely this may have saved many Venetians from being slaughtered when in 1182 the overthrow of the under-aged Emperor Alexios II Komnenos led to public uprising and a flash mob let go of all the anger against the 'Latins' which had built up over the years. Tens of thousands of

Latins were indiscriminately murdered in Constantinople, most of them Genoese and Pisans.

By the late 1180s the Venetians were once again back in Constantinople, but the Byzantine Empire was deeply troubled by civil wars and ultimately the situation once again erupted, this time leading to the unlucky events of the Fourth Crusade.

I have gone through the Fourth Crusade in some detail in Chapter 3, as it was such a momentous event for the Byzantine Empire that I feel it belongs in that part of this book, but as I also mention at the end of that chapter, the consequences for the Venetians were equally enormous.

Up to this point the Venetians had had to use Byzantine ports once they were out of the Adriatic Sea, with the Adriatic ports even in principle held by the Venetians on behalf of the Byzantines. Being the de-facto winners of the Fourth Crusade, they now got to pick what they wanted, and what they wanted was dominance, clear dominance.

The Venetians were given 3/8 of Constantinople itself, choosing the central part around Hagia Sophia and the area stretching from there down to the Golden Horn, where they took possession of the dock area. But as important as their new possessions in Constantinople were, with the implicit monopoly, the real prize was the port-cities and islands leading from the East to the West.

Venice was given as possessions all of Western Greece, but they only took possession of the port-city of Durrës, leaving the hinterlands to become the Empire of Epirus (see Chapter 3). They furthermore took possession of Corfu (from where they had to expel Genoese pirates), Gallipoli (which they failed to fortify), Crete (which they bought from Boniface of Montferrat for 5,000 gold Ducats and had to spend four years clearing of Genoese pirates), Modon and Coron on the south side of the Morea and the Cyclades, a scattering of islands in the Aegean Sea, south-west of the Greek mainland and north of Crete. Originally, they were also given Adrianople (modern day Edirne), but it is not a port-town so they had no interest in it and it was reallocated to someone else.

The new port-towns were fortified and became imperial outposts, as the Republic of Venice had now in one swift move become an empire, though an unusual empire, an empire of the sea.

So great was the extent of their new possessions that they, over and above simply just occupying some of them, broke their principle for expansion in two cases.

One such case was Crete, where they took possession of the whole island rather than just its ports, leading to two centuries of unhappy rule, which saw no less than twenty-seven uprisings. Venice was not set up for ruling land or any major number of colonial subjects.

The other case was the Cyclades. There were simply too many island and with the possession of Crete, and a colony on the island of Euboea off the

Greek west coast (the island was now in the possession of six Lombard families), they did not need the Cyclades as such. What they did need was to keep the sea free of (mainly Genoese) pirates, so they did something very untypical, and indeed Genoese in concept, and offered them to individual Venetian adventurers on the condition that they cleared them out and held them. This time not for Venice but for themselves, and first and foremost kept the sea-lanes free of pirates. This led to the formation of a range of small island-states, waging war on each other, but at most times staying loyal to Venice and fulfilling their purpose.

Another major bonus for Venice was now that they effectively ruled Constantinople; they also had access to the Black Sea, the last morsel that the Byzantines had kept to themselves. Up until now all goods to and from the Black Sea had to be traded through Constantinople, with Byzantine middlemen, but now the Venetians had a free hand.

This new situation of course made Venice the big player, so much so that they became known as the *'Dominante'*, the dominant one, because that was exactly what they were.

The big losers were Pisa and Genoa who in the same swift move which had seen Venice win an empire had seen Pisa and Genoa lose a big part of their trade on the East. They could still trade in the Crusader States and Egypt, but the exotic goods coming along the Silk Road had been lost, at least in terms of direct trade.

Because of the organizational model deployed by Genoa, which was very different from the one deployed by Venice, and to which we shall return in the following chapter, Genoese traders were quite capable of turning their peaceful pursuit of trade into the less peaceful pursuit of piracy, so they started to harass Venetian traders wherever they could be found.

And it was not only at sea the citizens of the two competing states met. Genoa had been involved in the crusading movement even earlier than Venice, and they considered the ports of Acre and Tyre, on the Syrian coast, as their key ports in the East. With Constantinople and the Black Sea trade in the hands of Venice these ports became even more important for the Genoese, even though they had to tolerate that Venetian traders were also allowed to have colonies there.

In 1250, after nearly forty years of Venetian dominance in the Eastern Mediterranean and semi-official Genoese pirates taking every opportunity to share in the spoils, the tension and immense hatred between the two flowed over.

I have described the incident in more detail in Chapter 11, but in short, a simple brawl between a Venetian and a Genoese caused the sacking of the Venetian quarters in Acre.

The Venetians then sent a fleet to Acre in 1255, which took both Acre and neighbouring Tyre. A Genoese fleet arrived in Acre in 1258, as did a new Venetian fleet and soon the two fleets met, while the warring parties were also battling it out inside the city. The Venetians were victorious in the aftermath the Genoese were expelled from Acre and the many prisoners the Venetians had taken were paraded in St. Mark's Square and only released after the direct intervention of the Pope. The Venetians had made their dominant position even more dominant.

But the Genoese were not done yet. They were soon back in Palestine and they had seen the weakness of the Latin Empire of Constantinople, and the resurgence of the quickly expanding Empire of Nicaea consolidating their dominance in Greece, so it was here they found their ally who would be the key to breaking the Venetian monopoly.

I have covered the Reconquest of Constantinople, and the resurrection of the Byzantine Empire in Chapter 3, and the way it evolved Genoa gets little mention, but that is only because Constantinople was reconquered by chance. The bigger plan was to launch a combined assault from land and sea, with a Genoese fleet of fifty ships making up the naval assault force.

Despite the fact that this fleet never came to play a role in the reconquest, the new Emperor fulfilled his part of the deal; the Genoese in all issues that mattered were to replace the Venetians. They would take over their quarters in Constantinople, trade tax free across the Empire, have the right to self-governing colonies and take formal ownership of Euboea and Crete, two islands which, should truth be told, were not the Emperor's to give as they were no longer part of the Byzantine Empire. That trading on the Black Sea was included was a given, providing Genoa with better terms than ever before in the East.

This represented a complete reversal for Venice as well. The *'Dominante'* was now suddenly not only not dominant, they were if anything the 'Missing'. In the years that followed, the Venetians and the Genoese fought it out whenever they had the occasion. The battles were mainly won by Venice, but the Genoese got theirs back through increased piracy and their favoured status in Constantinople. That is, until they lost that.

It took only three years for Genoa to lose its prize. Genoese by the thousands had flooded into Constantinople, and the old tensions between the locals and the 'Latins' were soon rekindled. What got the Emperor to react was, however, that the leader of the Genoese settlement, the Podestà, was found to be conspiring with the King of Sicily to reconstitute the lost Latin Empire of Constantinople, so in 1265 the Genoese were expelled.

Needing friends however, the Emperor recalled them in 1267, this time housing them across from the city itself in the township of Galata and in 1268 the Venetians were invited back in as a counterweight. The Emperor made it clear to both that from now on they would have to share.

And although they did share, and really there was enough for everyone, peace lasted less than thirty years. The preamble was the loss of the remaining Crusader States. In 1291 the Mamluk Egyptians had taken and destroyed Acre, Tyre, Sidon, Beirut and Haifa, putting an end to the Christian presence in Palestine born from the First Crusade.

Even though neither of the two rivalling city-states was shy of trading with the Mamluks, the fight for supremacy only got more intense with the safe harbours of the Syrian coast taken out.

A new intense war started, this time focusing on the Black Sea and in 1296 (as one of several battlegrounds) the Venetians attacked the Genoese in Galata. Not wanting war on his doorstep, the Emperor put the imperial garrison in defence of the Genoese, causing the Venetians to turn their fire on Constantinople itself.

The following year the roles were reversed. The local Genoese attacked the Venetian quarter, destroying their official buildings and killing the leading Venetians.

This of course made the Venetians come back the following year, this time delivering a letter to the Emperor demanding compensation for the damage caused by his 'encouragement' of the Genoese (as if they needed any), before setting fire to an imperial galley and sailing back to Venice with a shipload of Genoese prisoners.

The next year, 1299, Venice and Genoa signed a peace treaty, leaving the Byzantine emperor out, so in 1302 the Venetians came back to Constantinople, This time they set fire to all Byzantine buildings in range and then withdrew to the island of Prinkipo in the Sea of Marmara. That island was full of Greek refugees from Anatolia (seeking refuge from the emerging Ottoman beylik) whom the Venetians threatened to kill if they did not get their compensation. The Emperor caved in, the Venetians were paid off and had all their rights confirmed.

In 1324 a papal ban, originally from 1291 and covering only the Mamluk Egyptians, became absolute and covered trade with the Muslim World at large. This put further pressure on the Black Sea trade, where the Genoese had gradually taken the lead, not least through their well-positioned colony at Caffa.

In response to the new challenges the Venetians approached the Khan of the Golden Horde and got his permission to open a new colony at Tana on the Sea of Azov in the north-westernmost corner of the Black Sea. This was a perfect spot at the mouth of the River Don, providing easy access to the Russian river-system. The Genoese maintained a small subsidiary colony there as well and so the new Venetian settlement became a major issue for them. Again, the Venetians had outmanoeuvred them and they were not pleased.

But as we have seen was too often the case, the advantage did not last long as pride and greed soon caught up with the Venetians again. As was the case elsewhere, both the Venetians and the smaller number of Genoese soon started to act as if they owned the place. They cheated on the taxes they paid the Khan, they took taxes off others, they fought with each other, and they treated the locals with utter contempt.

In 1341 the Khan died and his successor's view on the Latins was less friendly. In 1343 a dispute between a local nobleman and a Venetian led to murder and when the Venetians asked the Genoese to stand with them in defence the Genoese instead plundered as much local loot as they could and sailed off to Caffa. The Khan attacked and destroyed the Tana settlement, sending the surviving Venetians as refugees to Caffa.

That Caffa was next on the Khan's list was clear, and when he arrived in the winter of 1343 the Genoese and Venetians did for once stand together and held him off. The siege was relieved by a fleet arriving in 1344, but the destruction of Tana and the siege of Caffa had led to a near-stop of trade.

With trade with the Muslims banned by the Pope and trade on the Black Sea as good as frozen, people in the West started to go hungry.

As a consequence, the Pope started to lift his ban, and the Venetians and Genoese tried to force the Khan into submission by a trade embargo. The Khan in turn went back to lay siege to Caffa until in 1346 the Mongols started to die from what was to become known as the Black Death.

The Mongols catapulted their dead across the walls of Caffa in an attempt to spread the disease, in which they were successful but in vain as their army had been wiped out.

With the Mongols gone trade resumed, but goods were not the only thing that was now brought home from the Black Sea. By December 1347, the Plague was in Constantinople and in Venice and Genoa by January 1348. By the end of the 1350s it had halved the population of Europe changing society for ever.

But despite the setbacks caused by the Black Death competition continued and the Venetians were back in Tana by 1347, with a new concession from the Khan. The Genoese responded by occupying a Byzantine castle on the Bosporus (this after having burned the Byzantine Emperor's new fleet in the Golden Horn) from where they could control the access to the Black Sea. The stage was set for more war.

A range of alliances were formed, involving the Aragonese in Sicily (on the side of Venice) and the emerging Ottomans (on the side of Genoa), and in 1351 the Venetians once more went back to Constantinople and burned the Genoese settlement in Galata, forcing the Byzantine Emperor onto their side of a conflict he would rather be without.

Venice had, in the dying moments of the Latin Empires in the East, annexed a third of the island of Euboea off the Greek west coast and in response to the attack on Galata a Genoese armada laid siege to the fortress at Oreoi. The Duchy of Athens (controlled by the remnants of a Catalan mercenary band which had caused chaos in Greece in the early part of the century) went overland in support of the Venetians, and the arrival of a Catalan fleet finally brought an end to the siege.

By the following year, 1352, the Venetians had also dragged Pisa into the conflict. The Pisans had previously suffered defeat in the hands of the Genoese and were keen to rekindle their interests in the Eastern Mediterranean.

A combined Venetian and Pisan fleet met with a Genoese fleet outside Constantinople, and even though the Genoese won the day, and the Venetians had to withdraw, it was a battle which seriously decimated both the warring nation's fleets, already reduced by the sheer lack of potential troops due to the death-toll of the Black Death.

In 1354 the Genoese beat the Venetians in a naval battle outside Pylos on the Greek southwest coast and finally they had both had enough. A peace agreement was signed in 1355, resetting status quo. Both maritime states were exhausted.

During this war between Venice and Genoa, both parties had taken active part in supporting factions in the on-going civil war for control of Constantinople. The civil war had developed in the wake of the death of Emperor Andronikos III Palaiologos and is covered in Chapter 4. It was the same conflict which saw the Ottomans establishing themselves in Europe. During the conflict the Empress Dowager, Anne, had pawned the Byzantine Crown Jewels to the Venetians for 30,000 ducats and this transaction would eventually lead to the next phase of the war between Venice and Genoa.

In 1369 the Byzantine Emperor, John V Palaiologos set off to Italy to discuss a Church Union with the Pope. Having completed his business in Rome he called on Venice, who had asked him to come and discuss the issue of the Crown Jewels and the spiralling interest on the loan. With not even enough money to continue his travels home, the Emperor offered the Venetians the island of Tenedos situated in a strategic position just south of the entry into the Dardanelles. In exchange he was to be given the Crown Jewels, six war galleys and 25,000 ducats in cash, of which 4,000 were payable immediately to help him out of his most immediate financial difficulties.

The Venetians accepted, but it did not go as easy as that. Tenedos was being administered by John V Palaiologos' son, Andronicus, who with the promise of support from Genoa refused to hand the island over to Venice. Finally, John V Palaiologos had to be bought out of de-facto arrest by the Venetians by his other son, Manual, who came to his aid with enough cash to settle matters with the Venetians - for now.

A sequence of other events led to the arrest and imprisonment of Andronicus and in 1376 the Venetians informed John V Palaiologos that they were still keen on the original deal, this time offering 30,000 ducats on top of the return of the Crown Jewels.

John V Palaiologos agreed but had once again underestimated the Genoese. Well unhappy about the prospect of the Venetians controlling the island, and the possible implications on their control of access through the Dardanelles, they engineered Andronicus' escape and supported him in an alliance with the Ottomans, in their turn promised to regain control of Gallipoli.

In 1376 Andronicus ousted John V Palaiologos and ceded Tenedos to the Genoese, but once again it all went wrong and the Byzantine governor refused his orders and instead gave the island over to Venice.

Venice then supported John V Palaiologos in a countercoup and the civil war raged on until 1381.

During this chain of events, sparked off by control of Tenedos, the Venetians and Genoese had taken the opportunity to fight it out with each other in a range of sea-battles, initially with Genoa as the most successful party but ultimately with the Genoese fleet destroyed by the Venetians in the Battle of Chioggia, a battle which was the culmination of a siege of Venice itself.

The war left both states crippled and they finally made peace in 1381, a peace in which they agreed to share use of Tenedos. This time the peace would last, not because they had any love for each other, but because they were both exhausted and would soon see bigger challenges, not least in the form of the Ottomans.

However, for a few more decades Venice would prosper, indeed it would expand to its largest size ever. The situation in the Balkans and Greece had become so chaotic in the wake of the Ottoman expansion and the de-facto collapse of Byzantine control that cities simply started to offer themselves to Venice, perceived to be the only state powerful enough to provide real protection.

Venice was picky, only selecting the prize pieces that fitted their imperial model, but gradually they took possession of the vast majority of cities and ports on the Dalmatian coast, including the island of Corfu, a string of ports on the coast of Greece and, finally, gained full control of the island of Euboea, the biggest island in the Aegean. As far as the Venetians were concerned, the Ottomans could do what they wanted in the hinterlands, as long as the trading routes remained free.

As has been discussed previously, the Ottomans were having problems connecting the eastern and western parts of their growing empire. They had to be able to cross between Anatolia and Europe, the two narrowest points being at the Dardanelles in the south and the Bosporus in the north. Both straits were easily controlled by Venetian, or Genoese, fleets, the Ottomans having little to match them in terms of naval capacity.

When sultan Bayezid I built the Anadoluhisarı castle on the west coast of the Bosporus in the 1390s, the Venetians just frowned. The castle was only useful for close protection of Ottoman transport ships and did not represent any real danger in terms of control of the strait. Shortly after the Ottomans had their own problems after the defeat by Timur, and for three decades they were occupied by their own internal conflict and the subsequent consolidation.

Although the Ottomans supported the operation of a rough fleet of pirates, harassing the traders and the islands and coasts of Greece, the first real conflict between Venice and the Ottomans did not develop until 1423, in the reign of Sultan Murad II.

The issue of contention was Thessaloniki, the strategically important coastal city, on the north-western coast of Greece. The city had been re-annexed by the Byzantines during the Ottoman Interregnum Period, but Sultan Murad II saw it as an Ottoman possession which needed to be brought back into the Empire. In 1422 he laid siege to both Constantinople and Thessaloniki and the Byzantine governor, Andronikos Palaiologos, brother to Emperor Manuel II Palaiologos, soon realized that he could not hold the city or expect any relief from Constantinople.

In line with what other cities had done in the preceding decades, he offered the city to the Venetians, to whom it fitted very nicely into their network of ports. On the assumption that the Ottomans could not muster enough naval capacity to match the Venetians, they accepted, and in 1423 added Thessaloniki to their possessions.

But they had underestimated the Ottomans tenacity. Despite fresh defenders ferried in from Venice, the Ottomans maintained the siege, even when the siege of Constantinople had long since been lifted.

The Venetians tried to divert Murad II's attention by supporting an offensive by the Bey of Aydın, on the west coast of Anatolia, but Murad quickly counter-attacked and put the beylik under Ottoman control once and for all.

The Venetians had calculated that Thessaloniki was easy pickings, but the expense of keeping it defended started to mount and the city was gradually depopulated, supplies running short and the Ottomans maintaining their siege. In 1430 Venice cut its losses. The Ottomans stormed the city, and the Venetians simply let it go.

A peace treaty was agreed between the Ottomans and the Venetians, both promising to respect each other's territories and the Venetians were granted rights to trade throughout the Ottoman Empire.

From here on the Venetians mainly maintained a live-and-let-live attitude towards the Ottomans until they were reluctantly drawn into support of the ill-fated Christian campaign in 1444, culminating in the Battle of Varna. I have covered this in Chapters 2 and 4, but to recap the Venetians were responsible for two things; one to prevent the Ottoman army's crossing from Anatolia to Europe; two to re-supply the Christian army off the coast of Bulgaria. They failed to do both.

Whereas the presence of a Venetian fleet did prevent Sultan Murad II from crossing at the Dardanelles, he found plenty 'Italian' vessels prepared to ferry the Ottoman army across at the Bosporus. The Venetians blamed the Genoese, and the Genoese blamed the Venetians, but Murad II got his army across, once again highlighting the danger to the Ottomans of not having control of the crossing points.

The Venetian fleet was then hit by a storm, preventing it from proceeding up through the Sea of Marmara and reaching the Christian army at Varna. At least that was their story, which they maintained when accused by the Pope of having abandoned the Christian cause.

Despite the Pope's anger, the Venetians signed a new peace agreement with the Ottomans in 1446, basically confirming the treaty of 1430, but the agreement is interesting because it was negotiated with Murad II's son, Mehmed, left to rule the Empire during Murad II's temporary abdication. The Venetians, however, did insist that the agreement was underwritten by Murad II himself, which it was on Murad II's return later that year.

In 1447 Murad II attacked the Morea, but left the Venetian ports alone. In 1448 and again in 1450 he was in Albania, where the Venetians happily supplied both the Ottomans and the Albanians with whatever they needed from their coastal possessions.

Venice's appeasement strategy seemed to be paying off despite lively Ottoman pirate-activity in the Aegean Sea. Officially this was not a state-sponsored operation, and the Venetians turned a blind eye to it.

In January 1451 Murad II died and everything changed forever.

The new sultan, Mehmed II, was perceived to be weak and unpopular. He immediately renewed all existing peace and trade agreements with Venice as well as everybody else, and the general assessment was that he did not represent any clear and present danger. This assessment was sound given the available information, but it was nevertheless wrong, very wrong indeed.

Mehmed II had, despite strong refusal of education in his younger days, developed into a student of history and military strategy and he had had the opportunity to study, first hand, the problems encountered by his father, Murad II, and for that matter his predecessors before him.

The Ottoman Empire was vulnerable to simultaneous attacks on the eastern end western fronts, not least so because they did not have a reliable mechanism for ferrying their army across between Anatolia and Europe.

Murad II had experienced this problem in 1444, running the risk of not being able to counter the Christian army moving down along the Black Sea coast and Mehmed II himself soon experienced the same problem on his return from his first campaign in Anatolia in 1451.

On top of that Mehmed II had imperials ambitions that went beyond those of his father. Mehmed II was not satisfied to maintain status quo; he had his designs on world-dominance and that could not be achieved without naval dominance and significant revenues - both the domain of the Italian merchant-states.

It was with this in mind that Mehmed II built the 'Throat Cutter' castle on the Bosporus in 1452 and then proceeded with his Conquest of Constantinople the year following.

Two years into his reign, Mehmed II now controlled the strategic port in Constantinople, soon to be renamed Istanbul, and had full control of the access to the Black Sea, turning the latter into an Ottoman lake in which he could further develop his fleet without having to worry about the Italians.

Throughout the Conquest of Constantinople the Venetians stayed out of the conflict. A vote had been put to the Venetian Senate to completely abandon Constantinople, but that was rejected. Instead, a fleet of two-armed transports and fifteen galleys were equipped and sent to patrol in the Sea of Marmara, but their instructions were clear: to assist any Christians in need but to avoid confrontation with the Ottomans.

The Venetian's approach to Mehmed II's aggression was, true to their nature, entirely pragmatic. The Pope may well worry about the fate of Christianity, and the Venetians had provided him with promises of a loan to finance further papal assistance, but the Venetians cared about the future of their trade, not the future of the faith.

Fact of the matter was that the shifty relationship between Venice and the Byzantine emperors was not good for business. They never knew where they had the Byzantines, whom in the eyes of the Venetians seemed to have an inherent preference for Genoa.

The Ottomans may not be Christians, but they were more pragmatic in their approach to religion than was the Byzantines, and they were far more stable as state.

Also the lessons learned at Thessaloniki in 1430 clearly showed that even if the Venetians had intervened in the Conquest of Constantinople by sea, the overwhelming force of the Ottoman army at the city's gates would have made the defence of the city a very costly and ultimately impossible affair. The only thing that could have possibly saved Constantinople was a combined operation of relief from the sea and a considerable army coming overland, but as there was no army coming, a singular naval effort would have been ultimately useless.

So, the Venetians stayed quiet. A few Venetian galleys and their crews, caught inside the Golden Horn at the commencement of hostilities, were pressed into service. At the end of the battle they narrowly made their escape - with greatly reduced crews, but full of Venetian refugees -and reached the Venetian settlement on Euboea with news of the fall of Constantinople.

From Euboea the news soon reached the mother-city and it is in the spirit of Venetian mentality when a contemporary observer reports that the Venetian reaction of grief was due to *'the death of a father, a son or a brother, or for the loss of their property'*

But the Venetians were not hesitant in picking up the pieces. Before the end of the year the Venetian ambassador, Bartolomeo Marcello, had arrived at Mehmed II's court. He carried an official apology for the Venetian involvement, however sparse, in the defence of Constantinople and had no harsh words to say about the fact that the Ottomans had slaughtered many Venetians, including the Venetian bailo, in the days following the conquest.

The Venetians policy now paid off, and the Venetians had all their former rights and privileges confirmed.

They were free to trade throughout the Ottoman Empire, as was the Ottomans in the domains of Venice. The 'tax' for the Venetian possessions in Albania was reconfirmed as was Venice's ownership of the island of Euboea. Finally, the Venetians were granted permission to re-establish their colony in Istanbul, Bartolomeo Marcello himself becoming the first bailo.

As a safeguard the Venetians also concluded an agreement of alliance with Ibrahim II of Karaman, just in case they should need a friend in the East, but for a few years peace reigned between the Ottomans and the Venetians. Trade flowed as did money.

An extraordinary episode occurred in 1458. Mehmed II had, as per Chapter 4, been campaigning in the Morea. On his way back he first visited, recently annexed, Athens, and then he did something highly unorthodox. He sent messengers to the Venetian bailo in Negroponte, on the island of Euboea, that he intended to visit.

It was rare that rulers visited each other, normally all communication was through embassies, and it was virtually unheard of that a ruler should decide on visiting a colony of another sovereign state. But Mehmed II was not conventional.

The Venetian bailo, Paolo Barbarigo, had to make a quick decision, so he let it be known that Mehmed II was welcome. And so, he arrived in the beginning of September, escorted by 1,000 horsemen. The population of Negroponte received him with apprehension and palm branches in hand and Mehmed made idle conversation, rode through the town and went on his way. Twelve years later he would be back under less amicable circumstances.

In the years since the peace agreement with Venice was signed in 1453, Mehmed II was busy with his main pursuit; war; but as of yet not against Venice. Indeed, Mehmed had systematically eroded the Genoese possessions in the East, making Venice's position even stronger, but ultimately the two dominant players, Venice dominating the seas and the Ottomans dominating on land, had to clash, and when the clash came it came in style.

What troubled Venice was the Ottoman suppression of Bosnia in 1463 (see Chapter 14). Bosnia had long been a convenient buffer-zone, keeping the Ottomans away from the upper parts of the Adriatic Sea. With Ottoman dominance in Bosnia this suddenly changed and there was clear and present danger of the Ottomans taking possession of the east coast of the Adriatic Sea and even marching overland towards Italy, Venice being the first place they would reach.

There had been early warnings. The agreement between Venice and the Ottomans had specifically included also the Duchy of Naxos, the conceptually independent, but in reality Venetian, group of islands in the

Cyclades also mentioned earlier. Despite this the Ottomans demanded, and obtained, a tribute from the Duchy in 1458, but the Venetians decided to take that one on the chin and move on.

The 'casus belli', when it came, was a detail blown up by the general situation.

In 1462 a runaway slave, serving the Ottoman commander of Athens, sought refuge in the Venetian colony in Coron. Here he converted to Christianity and, according to popular believe, shared the 100,000 silver ducats he had stolen from his master with the Venetian mayor. The Ottomans asked the slave to be handed over, and the Venetians refused on the strength of him being a Christian.

Normally something like that would be solved through diplomacy and money, but this time it started a range of events on the side of the Ottomans. In late 1462 the unsatisfied governor of Athens laid siege to the Venetian fortress of Lepanto, which only just held out.

At the same time the Mehmed II, no doubt as per a previous plan, started to build fortresses on either side of the Dardanelles, the same model he had deployed in the Bosporus, but now threatening to control the access to the Sea of Marmara in its entirety.

In April 1463, the Ottomans attacked and occupied Argos, a Venetian city on the east coast of the Morea. The city was taken by treason, an Orthodox priest with a deep hatred of the Catholic Venetians opens a gate for the besiegers. Other Ottoman troops laid waste to Venetian possessions around Lepanto and Methoni on the western side of the Morea.

The writing was on the wall, and the Venetians had to make a decision; stand and fight or risk the Ottomans roll up their empire in the East.

After a brief discussion in the Venetian Senate, they reached a decision and on 28 July 1463 the Venetians declared war on the Ottoman Empire.

Their strategic targets were twofold; to make it clear to Mehmed II that violation of their territory would not be tolerated and, always with profit in mind, to take possession of the entire Morea peninsula.

From Mehmed II's perspective the strategic target was equally clear; world-domination, which in turn meant subjection of western Europe, which in turn could only be achieved with superiority, or at least a level playing field, at sea.

The Venetians had repeatedly refused to participate in 'crusades' but now found themselves at the other end of the equation. They appealed to Florence, an emerging merchant state which had flourished due to a good relationship with Mehmed II (based on the fact that they made their extensive intelligence service available to him), but Florence would only go as far as offering their citizens in Istanbul free passage home should they so wish.

The Pope, Pius II, however saw the opportunity to start another crusade, so he brokered a deal between Venice, Hungary, Albania (in rebellion under

Skanderbeg) and Philip the Good, Duke of Burgundy, and the only western ruler outside the immediate area with an appetite for a crusade.

The alliance agreed their strategic objective as driving the Ottomans from Europe, simple as that. Then they agreed how they would split the area between them; Venice would get the Morea and western Greece (Epirus), Hungary would get Bulgaria, Serbia, Bosnia and Wallachia including its former possessions on the Black Sea. There would be a new pocket-state in Constantinople ruled by the remaining nobles of the Palaiologos dynasty. Albania would be expanded to include Macedonia. All set, the only thing remaining was to kick the Ottomans out.

It can be assumed that Mehmed II would have soon heard of the alliance and its pre-allocation of his European territories, as well as its negotiations with Uzun Hasan, the Karamanids and even the Tatars of the Crimea. He was probably not too overly worried.

The Venetians struck first. With a sizeable fleet under the command of Alvise Loredano and a mercenary army under the command of Bertoldo, margrave of Este, they laid siege to, and retook, Argos.

Their next target was Corinth, and to prevent the Ottomans from coming to its assistance they first refortified the Isthmus of Corinth by rebuilding the Hexamilion Wall, which had been torn down after Murad II shot it to pieces in 1446.

An army of 30,000 workmen completed the work in two weeks. This time they were prepared for the Ottoman cannon, so the wall itself was equipped with cannon, ditches and no less than 136 watchtowers, all built from stone left on the site.

And so the siege of Corinth began, but it did not turn out to be a success. The key assault on 20 October did not go well. The Venetian mercenary army took massive loses, its commander, Bertoldo of Este, was mortally wounded. In the end the siege was lifted and the army transferred partly to the Hexamilion Wall and partly to the Venetian port of Nafplio where the fleet was at anchor.

In the meantime, the Ottomans had been approaching from the north. An expeditionary force under Turahanoğlu Ömer Bey had arrived at the Hexamilion Wall in September but hastily withdrew to a safe distance when it started to rain cannonballs. They camped and sent for reinforcements, which came in the shape of the Grand Vizier Mahmud Pasha.

In messages to Mahmud Pasha, Turahanoğlu Ömer Bey had informed him to proceed with care as the wall was defended by a large army and 2,000 cannon. That was, however, probably rather exaggerated!

They did not have to worry though. The defeat at Corinth, the approach of Ottoman reinforcements and the outbreak of dysentery amongst the Venetian army made the replacement commander, Bettino de Calzina, decide to withdraw from the Hexamilion Wall and regroup at Nafplio.

Thus, when Mahmud Pasha, despite the advice from his colleague, approached the Hexamilion Wall he found it abandoned, and the Ottomans took the opportunity to once more dismantle it.

With the Hexamilion Wall reduced to rubble, the Ottomans continued to once again take Argos with relative ease and then proceeded to Nafplio. With the Venetian army massed inside the city it proved a harder nut to crack, and when a Venetian sortie left the Ottomans with severe loses, they withdrew.

But whereas the heavily fortified city of Nafplio was holding out, the hinterlands of the Morea were practically undefended and soon fell to the Ottomans. Anyone who had declared for the Venetians quickly changed their minds, and the Ottoman troops reached as far as the walls of the Venetians fortresses at Coron and Modon on the south coast. With the onset of winter the Ottomans, however, withdrew, leaving a governor in complete control of the peninsula as before. The Venetian effort had come to nothing.

It had gone somewhat better in the north. The Hungarian King, Matthias Corvin, had led an army into Bosnia in September 1463. They met little resistance from the Ottomans who had not made any defences in the open country and who had only left small garrisons behind when the army had marched south towards the Morea.

The Hungarian army soon recovered the capital, Jajce, even though the citadel held out till December. In addition the Hungarians took possession of more than sixty locations, some fortified some not, and when the King returned victorious to his capital on Christmas Day, Bosnia and the Duchy of Herzegovina had been claimed back under Hungarian suzerainty.

But the Hungarian success did not last long. Furious over the loss of his newly acquired territories, Mehmed set out for Bosnia again in 1464 and the end result of the campaign was that the Ottomans regained significant parts of Bosnia, but the Hungarians still held Jajce and other fortifications in the north, just enough to ensure that an Ottoman incursion into Hungary itself could be checked. In isolation that was a success, but it was a far cry from kicking the Ottomans out of Europe.

At the same time as the Ottomans and Hungarians fought over Bosnia, the early part of 1464 saw some Venetian success. Their army was still bogged down in Nafplio, where all it could achieve was to defend the city against the Ottoman expeditionary force that had otherwise suppressed the Morea peninsula. The navy, however, was more active.

Alvise Loredano had taken his fleet to the island of Lemnos in the Aegean Sea. The island had been given to govern by Demetrios Palaiologos, brother of the last Emperor of Byzantium, when the Ottomans had annexed the Morea in 1460. By 1464 it had, however, de-facto been taken over by a Greek pirate who, on the arrival of the Venetian fleet soon realized his predicament and assisted the Venetians in taking over the island.

The Venetians then changed the command of their naval operations and gave it to Orsato Giustiniano, who proceeded to lay siege to the island of

Lesbos, which the Ottomans had taken from Genoa in 1462 (see the following chapter). The siege had lasted for six weeks when on 18 May a substantial Ottoman fleet, counting some 150 ships, appeared under the command of Mahmud Pasha. The Venetian commander, his fleet consisting of only 32 galleys, decided to call it a day and withdraw to Euboea with 300 Ottoman prisoners and as many Christians from Lesbos as they could carry.

Giustiniano brought the Venetian fleet back to Lesbos in June, but once again had to abandon the siege. The fact was that the Venetian land army had been destroyed in the campaign in the Morea and naval blockade alone simply did not do the trick. On the fleet's return to Modon, Giustiniano died.

The new Venetian commander, Iacopo Loredano took the fleet out again, but did little but cruise around in the Aegean Sea. At length the fleet cast anchor close to the entry to the Dardanelles where they achieved a small moral victory. One of their ships set sail and entered the Dardanelles, recently fortified by Mehmed II. The bombardments from the Ottoman forts cost fifteen of his men their lives, but he succeeded to turn around and return to the fleet under full sails. It was, no doubt, courageous, but once again not exactly a major step towards winning the war and removing the Ottomans from Europe.

Back in the Morea a new Venetian mercenary army had arrived in Modon, under the command of Sigismondo Malatesa. The army made an incursion north, retook a few fortresses and laid siege to Mistra. Once again intelligence of an approaching Ottoman army saw an end to the siege and the Venetians withdrew to Nafplio, reinforcing the depleted Venetian army there.

While at least some military effort was forthcoming in Greece and Bosnia, events in Italy were farcical. As part of the agreement between Venice and the Pope, a new crusade was to be called and both the Pope and the Venetian doge, Cristoforo Moro were obliged to participate in person.

The Venetian doge was doubtful, to say the least, as the expedition was to be under papal command, and he was in no great hurry to take a newly equipped fleet to Ancona where the crusaders were going to meet.

With undertones of the Fourth Crusade, the call did not prove to be as successful as hoped for, and rather than experienced men of war, the rabble which gradually started to trickle into Ancona consisted of opportunists and adventurers, demanding pay and food from the Pope. When both were slow in coming, they started to sell their weapons and return home.

By the time the, mortally ill, Pope arrived in Ancona on 19 July there was neither a crusader army, nor a fleet, and excuses came in from all and sundry as to why they could not contribute to the Pope's project. The merchant city of Ragusa went as far as falsely alerting the Pope to a massive Ottoman army approaching their city, tying up all their forces. The Pope sent them 400 archers and a shipload of grain in support.

On 12 August, the Venetian fleet finally arrived. On 15 August, the Pope died, On 18 August the Venetians left for home, where the crusader fleet was disarmed and put in storage.

As the year 1464 ended, the Ottoman reconquest of parts of Bosnia was the only true result and 1465 saw no major conflicts.

There were reciprocal raids across the Morea and the Venetian fleet still sailed around in the Adriatic Sea, but Mehmed II simply had no appetite for warfare that year. His army was tired after endless campaigns and he dismissed it, with rich gifts, and simply took a year off campaigning. His own, deteriorating health, also playing a role as he had developed both gout from his relentless campaigning and obesity from his good living as he was well known for his indulgences.

To keep things quiet Mehmed II initiated peace-negotiations with the Venetians and at the same time unleashed a flurry of false, and often contradictory, rumours about the state of affairs in the Ottoman Empire. The Venetians, eager for a quick resolution to the increasingly expensive war, took the peace negotiations seriously even though they consistently demanded to be given the Morea and insisted that all of Bosnia was to be given to Hungary, conditions which made it easy for Mehmed II to reject their demands, even though he in all likelihood had no intentions on peace in the first place.

Instead of war, Mehmed II occupied himself with the repopulation and redefinition of Istanbul and it was in this year that he started the construction of the Çinili Kösk, the Tiled Pavilion, to this day one of the iconic buildings of Istanbul.

In the Morea, bands of Venetian mercenaries mixed with locals were raiding the southern part of the peninsula, but that was the only land-based warfare that year.

After this sabbatical year, both Mehmed II and his army were ready for warfare again and, under extreme secrecy as far as their target was concerned, set out from Istanbul as early as February 1466. They were moving west, but their intended target was guessed as either of Albania, Bosnia, Belgrade or even Euboea.

The Venetians prepared for all eventualities, and it soon turned out that Mehmed II's target was Albania, partly occupied by Skanderbeg's rebels (see Chapter 15) and with Venetian ports on the Adriatic coast. Mehmed's specific target was the fortress at Krujë, Skanderbeg's main stronghold.

The Venetians immediately sent reinforcements to Krujë, assisting Skanderbeg's forces, and even though the Ottomans completely dominated the surrounding areas, they could not take the fortress.

Mehmed II left the siege to his local commander, Balaban Bey and proceeded to loot through the Albanian countryside, indiscriminately murdering and taken prisoners any locals that he encountered. Finally, he settled the army down at Elbasan on the Shkumbi River. On this strategic point in the middle of the country he built a fortress, probably on the foundations of an older fortification. He then turned around to spend the winter in Bulgaria, as plague had broken out in Istanbul.

In the southern theatre the Venetian fleet, now under the command of Vettore Cappello, had taken the islands of Imroz, Thasos and Samothrace after which it landed and laid siege to Athens.

Unable to take the Acropolis, the Venetians withdrew to Patras, where a small Venetian army was besieging the Ottomans. When an Ottoman relief force of 12,000 arrived, the Venetians were routed and Cappello, protecting the Venetian rearguard, marched back to Euboea, where he died the following spring.

Balaban Bey had stayed in front of Krujë and in early 1467, hard pressed by a relief force led by Skanderbeg himself, threw everything into a final attack on the fortress, getting himself killed in the effort. Without his leadership, and with the Sultan away, the Ottoman army started a chaotic flight towards Macedonia, taking heavy losses due to Albanian resistance fighters snapping at their heels.

The news of the new Ottoman fortress at Elbasan was very worrying to the Venetians, as it was only some 48 km from their port at Durrës and, situated on the Shkumbi River, provided direct access to the Adriatic Sea. With Venetian duplicity they asked Skanderbeg to drive the Ottomans out, while at the same time they refused to assist him, as they were trying to negotiate a peace agreement with Mehmed II.

Even without the Venetians, Skanderbeg did attack the new Ottoman fortress, but he could not take it and in the summer of 1467 Mehmed II came back to Albania. This time he went straight through to the Dalmatian coast where he raided the areas around (Venetian) Durrës and then went on to Krujë. No serious attempts were made to take either, but Mehmed II had made his point; anytime he so wanted to he could now, from his stronghold in Elbasan, move on the Adriatic coast, putting himself only 140 kilometres from Brindisi on the Italian coast.

To make the statement even clearer, Mehmed II had at the same time released bands of raiders further north along the Dalmatian coast in Bosnia and penetrating as far north as Zara in Croatia, only a two days march from Italy itself.

In Albania Skanderbeg had immediately, on the retreat of the Ottoman army, sought to regain control of the centre of the country, but in the winter of 1467 he fell ill with a fever and by 17 January 1468 he died.

Skanderbeg's death sent Albania into a spiral of succession issues and central control was lost. Venice, to protect its own interests, had to take control of the castle of Krujë, further adding to their increasing expenses. Once again, they sought a peace-agreement with Mehmed II, once again they failed.

Also in the beginning of 1468 the Hungarian King declared war on Bohemia (see Chapter 13), so with Skanderbeg out of the way and the Hungarians otherwise occupied, Mehmed II turned his attention away from Europe and went away to deal with the Karamanids as described in Chapter 6.

Early 1469 saw a serious outbreak of plague in Istanbul and during the year there were more Ottoman raids on the Dalmatian coast. The Venetians in turn raided the coastline of Greece and the Morea, their fleet now, crucially, under the command of Niccolo de Canale, but there was to be no major confrontations. Instead, Mehmed II spent 1469 building up the largest ever Ottoman fleet.

The war against Venice had always been about naval dominance, but so far, the Ottomans had not offered battle at sea. With the exception of the fleet sent to relive Lesbos in 1464, they had been staying north of the, strongly protected, Dardanelles with the Venetians staying south.

In 1452 Mehmed II had made the Black Sea an Ottoman lake when he built the 'Throat Cutter' castle on the Bosporus. In 1463 he had done the same with the Sea of Marmara when he fortified the Dardanelles. The next battle for dominance on the seas would be fought over the Aegean Sea, a defacto Venetian lake.

Whereas there were smaller Venetian ports on the east coast of the Morea and the islands of the Cyclades (the Duchy of Naxos) still remained loyal to Venice at the same time as they paid tribute to the Ottomans, the key Venetian possession in the Aegean was the island of Euboea, with its capital city of Negroponte.

Euboea is the second largest of the 'Greek' islands, only outsized by Crete. But contrary to Crete it is situated very close to the Greek mainland. Indeed, it lies parallel to the Greek east coast in a northwest to south-easterly direction only separated by what really is a flooded valley, which at its narrowest point separates the mainland and the island by only 38 meters.

The island is 150 kilometres long and varies in width from fifty km to six km. Approximately halfway down, on the west coast facing the mainland at the narrowest point of the separating strait, is the city of Negroponte (modern day Chalcis).

After 1453 Negroponte had gradually become the Venetian's de-facto replacement for Constantinople, acting as the centre for their trading activities in the Aegean, but navigation in the narrow strait was precarious.

The strait, known as the Euripus Strait, is subject to a combination of geological properties which means that the water flows at speeds up to twelve kilometres an hour, more than small ships could sail against, and the tide changes no less than four times a day, also causing the formation of vortexes during tidal reversals.

Negroponte had been a full Venetian colony since 1390 and the city was fortified with a wall and a considerable citadel. Halfway across the narrow gap to the mainland there was a fortified tower and from there were two drawbridges, one to the mainland and one to the island, controlling access to both the town and the island.

It was this bulwark of Venetian dominance in the Aegean which was next on Mehmed II's agenda, but to take it he needed a navy. Despite the narrowness of the strait, Euboea was still an island, and it required a navy to both land an army and, not least important, to keep it supplied as well as securing a retreat should that be necessary.

With control over the Black Sea and the Sea of Marmara, Mehmed II was free to build up an Ottoman navy and even though the Ottomans were still inferior in terms of technology and experience, they had enormous resources available. If they could not fight the Venetians on quality, they could fight them on quantity.

In early 1470 reports started to reach the Venetians of an enormous Ottoman fleet starting to assemble off Tenedos. Eyewitnesses reported that *'the sea is like a forest'* and estimated the Ottoman fleet at anywhere between 300 and 400 ships.

A reconnaissance squadron of ten ships was sent to gather further intelligence and as was typical for the Venetian perception of the relative strength of the two fleets they were under orders to not engage in battle if the Ottoman fleet counted more than sixty ships.

They soon realized that indeed it did, and they turned back west with a small Ottoman fleet in pursuit. The Venetians gave way and the Ottomans moved west, storming the island of Skiros on the way and then proceeding to raid coastal towns and fortifications on Euboea in preparation for the main assault.

The Venetian fleet, still commanded by Niccolo da Canale, at this time consisted of thirty-six galleys and six freight vessels. Outnumbered even by the Ottoman vanguard it had initially moved to sit at anchor off the southern tip of Euboea Island and subsequently moved to Crete where it was both resupplying and waiting for reinforcements to arrive from Venice. They were still waiting when the main Ottoman fleet arrived at Euboea.

Mehmed II's main fleet had finally started to move in early June, at the same time Mehmed II himself left Istanbul ahead of the army. The fleet made stops at Imroz, Lemnos and Skiros and arrived off Euboea on 15 June.

The Ottoman fleet brought a substantial landing force, at the time reported at 70,000 men but probably really a quarter of that size. The Sultan, arriving at the same time by land had double that amount, all in all an Ottoman assault force of up to 50,000 men. They also brought cannon, specifically made during spring for the campaign, and they brought another custom-made piece of equipment; a pontoon-bridge which could be placed over chained-together boats.

The Ottoman fleet settled and put the pontoon-bridge in place just south of the drawbridge, now pulled up and shut. They moved their cannon into place, and they started to pound the defensive walls. It was a trademark Mehmed II assault, a carbon-copy of the sieges of Constantinople and Belgrade, but improvised to the specific situation.

But contrary to both Constantinople and Belgrade, Venetian Negroponte was well prepared. The defences were in excellent shape, the troop contingent was sufficient, well equipped and highly motivated. And they too had cannon, initially deployed with some success as they blew away several Ottoman cannon and their crews. Their key advantage, however, was that they would only have to endure the Ottoman onslaught for a limited time before their fleet came to their relief. Or so they thought.

As per tradition, Mehmed II had offered the city to hand itself over without a fight, in which case, its citizens would be spared, even richly rewarded. The answer was not too overly polite, ending in a request that the sultan should *'go and eat pig's meat'*. At that point Mehmed II promised the city to his troops, on the proviso that they left nobody alive.

And so, the siege began, following the prescribed pattern. The Ottoman cannon assaulted the city walls day and night, in addition to which they hurled incendiary devices into the city itself, forcing the population to take shelter along the outer wall. As in Constantinople, the citizens did their utmost to repair the breaches in the walls caused by the Ottoman cannon, but with endless bombardments it was next to impossible to fill the gaps as quickly as they appeared.

The first Ottoman attempt at the walls came on 25 June but was unsuccessful. The next attack came on 30 June and was likewise. Both attacks, however, cost thousands of Ottomans their lives.

But Mehmed II had a trick up his sleeve. A detachment of Dalmatian mercenaries, or at least their leaders, had made contact with Mehmed II, offering to let the Ottomans in during the next assault, no doubt in exchange for rich rewards. The plot was, however, discovered and all was revealed when the coup-makers were tortured.

The Venetians now proceeded to set the signal agreed with Mehmed II, so when he ordered another attack on 5 July, it was on the assumption that the traitors on the inside would let the Ottomans in. No such thing happened, and again the Ottomans took significant losses. Mehmed II tried again on 8 July, but again without success.

Inside the walls, the situation was, however, getting desperate. The discovery of the coup and the following clean-up had let to internal fighting, leaving the defenders short of troops. Consequently, all boys over ten years of age were sent to the arsenal where 500 were selected; taught how to use a musket and put on the walls with a promise of two aspers for each Ottoman they shot.

Both parties now expected the imminent arrival of the Venetian fleet, so Mehmed II had a second bridge constructed north of the drawbridge as a first line of defence against an assault from the north. This turned out to be a good idea as, on the morning of 11 July, the Venetian fleet came rushing down the strait from the north.

Niccolo da Canale had finally realized that the reinforcements from Venice would not reach him in time so, reinforced by a few more ships from Crete, he had now returned to Euboea with what he had.

What he had to do was beat his way through the throng of Ottoman ships, destroy the two bridges and anchor in the harbour of Negroponte. This would both make a defining difference to the strength of the defence and at the same time cut off the Ottoman army located on the island itself from reinforcements and supplies.

What he did was move down at great speed till about a mile off the northernmost Ottoman bridge, where he brought the fleet to a halt. The problem was that Niccolo da Canale was an intellectual and a lawyer, and the way he now calculated the risk was with the mindset of a lawyer not a military commander. He simply estimated that the risk to his fleet, counting seventy-one ships, was too big to attempt an all-out breakthrough attempt.

In his fleet was a great galley, the battle-tank of the seas manned by Cretans, and they begged him to be allowed to make an attempt at breaking the Ottoman pontoon-bridges. Hesitantly Niccolo da Canale gave his permission, but as they had set off, he changed his mind and called them back.

The warring parties did not know what to do or how to react. The besieged had celebrated the sighting of the Venetian fleet with great elation, manning the walls and shouting to the Ottomans exactly what they intended to do with them. The Ottomans had as good as given up, the Sultan himself hastily preparing to leave the island before the escape-route was cut off.

With the Venetian fleet sitting impotently at anchor Mehmed II decided on one more push and in the early morning of 12 July they came again. This time they knew it was their last chance, and they gave it everything they had.

The defenders fought back with everything they had, but they felt that this time they could not hold the invaders off and they appealed to the Venetian fleet to intervene. A black flag was hoisted, a sign of extreme distress, but Niccolo da Canale did not move.

The Ottomans broke through the walls, but the Venetians defended every meter of every street until they - completely exhausted - surrendered.

Niccolo da Canale had finally started to move, but by the time he came close it was too late, Ottoman banners were waving on the walls and he simply turned around and, having trailed the Ottoman fleet back to the Dardanelles, went back to Venice.

The aftermath was bloody, very bloody. Mehmed II had sworn that the citizens of Negroponte would pay the full price of defiance, and it was under the pain of death forbidden the Ottoman soldiers to take live captives from the city. Such was Mehmed II's lust for blood that he had inspections done on the Ottoman galleys to ensure that captives had not been stowed away.

The fortified tower in the middle of the strait did not initially surrender, but when the commander was assured that his head was safe he too gave in. Mehmed II flew into a rage on this news, verbally insulting the commander who had given his word to the Venetian, but ultimately, he lived up to the promise made; the Venetian commander's head was saved and he was sawed in halves instead.

The many casualties caused to the Ottomans by the young recruits with their muskets were avenged. All males over the age of ten were rounded up. Counting some eight hundred they had had their hands tied behind their backs, were forced to kneel in a big circle in the town square and were then beheaded.

On his return to Venice Niccolo da Canale was arrested and tried for treason. Initially looking at a death-sentence, he was finally allowed to keep his life but banned from the city. The underlying reason for this remarkable judgment was that the Venetian senate simple accepted that they had appointed the wrong man for the job.

Despite attempts to form yet another unified Christian response to Mehmed II, nothing happened and Venice remained alone.

Already the end of 1470 and continuing into 1471, a year where no warfare took place between the parties, peace proposals started to flow between Venice and Istanbul. The parties were, however, so far from each other that it came to naught. Mehmed II now, in outline, wanted all the Venetian possessions in the Aegean (most of which he already occupied) and an additional annual tribute. Venice wanted Euboea back but was not willing to pay a lump sum for it.

The Venetians plotted to have Mehmed II murdered (a total of fourteen plots were conceived between 1456 and 1479) and had negotiations with the commander of the Ottoman fleet at the Dardanelles. Nothing came of it. The only one really listening to Venice was Uzun Hasan of the White Sheep.

I have covered the Venetian alliance with Uzun Hasan in Chapter 7, but in summary a small fleet of mainly Venetian ships raided various coastal towns in the summer of 1472, while Uzun Hasan made incursions into eastern Anatolia. With the onset of winter the fleet split up (small contingents from the Pope, Napoli and the Knights of Rhodes went home) and the Venetians wintered on the island of Cyprus.

On 8th June 1473, the King of Cyprus, James II, died. He left behind an infant son and his widow, Caterina Carnaro, a Venetian by birth.

Though the fleets from the Pope and Napoli did return in the summer of 1473, there was no coordinated effort against the Ottomans or in support of Uzun Hasan.

Instead, the Venetians, including a transport-fleet carrying artillery for Uzun Hasan, stayed in Cyprus where they ensured that Caterina Carnaro became regent after which they returned to Venice. Uzun Hasan had in the meantime been defeated by Mehmed II, so they took the artillery with them.

10- Venice

The infant King of Cyprus died in 1475, leaving Caterina Carnaro without an heir and in 1489 she signed Cyprus over to Venice. To an extent, Venice had found a replacement for Euboea, well situated for its trade with the coast of Palestine and the Mamluk Egyptians.

In 1474 Mehmed II stayed at home in Istanbul, mourning the death of his favourite son, Mustafa. Command of the army was given to Suleyman Pasha, the governor of Rumelia. His target was, once again, Albania but this time aiming straight for the Venetian town of Shkodër.

The Ottoman army marched through Serbia and Macedonia arriving in front of Shkodër in early May. 500 camels brought all the materials to found cannon on the spot and so they went to work. In a few days they had four large and a dozen smaller cannon ready, with which they started to bombard the citadel, situated high above the town.

Although the walls soon gave, the citadel had massive earthworks, which the cannon could not make much f an impression on. Negotiations to surrender the fort were fruitless so Suleyman Pasha decided to try an all-out attack which failed - at great cost of lives. When, false, rumours of a Venetian army's approach got to him he decided to withdraw.

Venice rejoiced, but those with an insight knew well that at best they had won some time.

The following year, 1475, the Ottomans were in the Black Sea, wiping out the last remnants of Genoese presence (see the following chapter) and in 1476 Mehmed II was campaigning in Moldavia and Wallachia.

While these bigger campaigns took place, the war with Venice moved on in a smaller scale. In the beginning of 1475 Mehmed II had offered a six-month truce, supposedly to negotiate a peace which never happened.

Once the truce had expired an Ottoman army marched on (Venetian) Lepanto on the south coast of Greece, but a Venetian relief fleet forced them to abandon the siege.

The Ottomans then attacked Lemnos, but were again chased off. They then proceeded to sack Naxos.

In Albania a new siege was taking place a Krujë, The besiegers were driven back, only to come back and counterattack. The Venetian troops were spread so thin that, even though the fortress held out, no concerted attempt could be done to relieve the besieged town.

Though Mehmed II himself refrained from campaigning in 1477, he kept the pressure up. In parallel to the bigger campaigns, Ottoman raiders had for years terrorized the populations of the north-western Balkans.

Ottoman raiding parties, sometime thousands strong, made incursions into Hungary, Croatia and Austria, carrying away loot and slaves. In September 1477 they nearly reached Venice itself.

The area of Friuli, effectively the hinterlands of Venice itself, was the Venetian territories Ottoman raiders would reach if they came through Croatia and that is exactly what they did.

1,000 horsemen strong and led by Iskender Bey, the Ottoman governor of Bosnia, the raiders cast aside any resistance and looted and burned their way along the north coast of the Adriatic Sea. The flames from their burning could be seen in Venice itself and in November the army was sent out to meet them. By the time the Venetian army reached the affected areas the raiders were long gone. The enemy was truly at the gates.

Venice now really needed peace, and negotiations were once again commenced. The more it became clear that the Venetians were becoming desperate, the more did Mehmed II tighten the screw. In May 1478, his demand was accepted by Venice, but before their decision could be communicated Mehmed II had already started to march on Albania.

Once again Iskender Bey was instructed to raid Friuli, which he did. This time he met more organised resistance, but nevertheless spread fear, the main purpose of the incursion.

The Ottoman vanguard now marched on Shkodër, the object for the abandoned siege of 1474. They arrived in early May.

Mehmed II went on a detour to Krujë, already under siege for a year. When the defenders, already desperate, saw the Sultan himself they decided to surrender under promise of safe conduct. Once they had surrendered and started leaving, they were rounded up and killed. Mehmed II now moved on to join the rest of the army at Shkodër where he arrived on 2 July.

The artillery, this time consisting of eleven great guns, started firing at the walls, smaller guns threw incendiary devices over the walls and on 22 July the first all-out attack took place. Though the attackers penetrated through the first line of defensive walls, they ultimately had to withdraw with heavy losses. A second attack on 27 July went likewise.

Mehmed II now left the siege and instead mopped up the last Albanian resistance in the area. With the onset of winter, he withdrew home followed by most of the army, leaving a small contingent to keep the besieged city of Shkodër isolated.

Though Shkodër still held out, the situation was desperate and Venice simply did not have anything else to throw at the Ottomans. In December 1478 Venice sent the experienced statesman Giovanni Dario to Istanbul. Very unlike the Venetian's normal approach, he had been given unlimited powers. His brief was to do what he could but make such concessions as were necessary to obtain lasting peace.

On 25 January 1479, an agreement was reached and it was not kind to Venice.

The Venetians had to cede Shkodër, Lemnos and the peninsula of Mani on the south coast of the Morea. In addition, the Ottomans were to keep the conquests of Krujë and Euboea. Financially the Venetians had to pay a one-off sum 100,000 ducats and an annual tax of 10,000 ducats for the privilege of allowing their trader's access to the Ottoman Empire.

It took two years to untangle all the ends left behind from fifteen years of war. The citizens and defenders of Shkodër were offered to stay, but all decided to leave, most settling in Cyprus. Prisoners were exchanged, populations changed masters and property was redistributed.

A review of the strategic objectives shows that Mehmed II got pretty much everything he wanted, the Venetians, and their allies, got nothing.

There would be no more conflict between Mehmed II and Venice. They had made themselves enemies of the Conqueror and they had barely survived. There would, however, be more warfare between Venice and the Ottoman Empire after Mehmed II's death.

Between 1499 and 1503 open warfare broke out again. By now the Ottoman fleet could match the power of Venice and the Venetian colonies at Durrës, Lepanto, Modon and Coron were lost.

In 1570 the Ottomans took Cyprus, but their fleet was subsequently defeated at Lepanto by a combined Venetian, Spanish and Papal fleet.

In 1669 Venice lost Crete to the Ottomans, but they succeeded in conquering the Morea, their original objective in the war with Mehmed II, in 1699. The Ottomans took the Morea back in 1715, but the Venetians repelled an Ottoman attempt at Corfu. This was the last hostilities between Venice and the Ottoman Empire.

Rapidly declining, the Republic of Venice was officially dissolved in 1797 and fell under the administration of Napoleonic France. It changed hands between France and Austria until, in 1866, it became part of the Kingdom of Italy.

Part 4 - The Maritime States of Italy

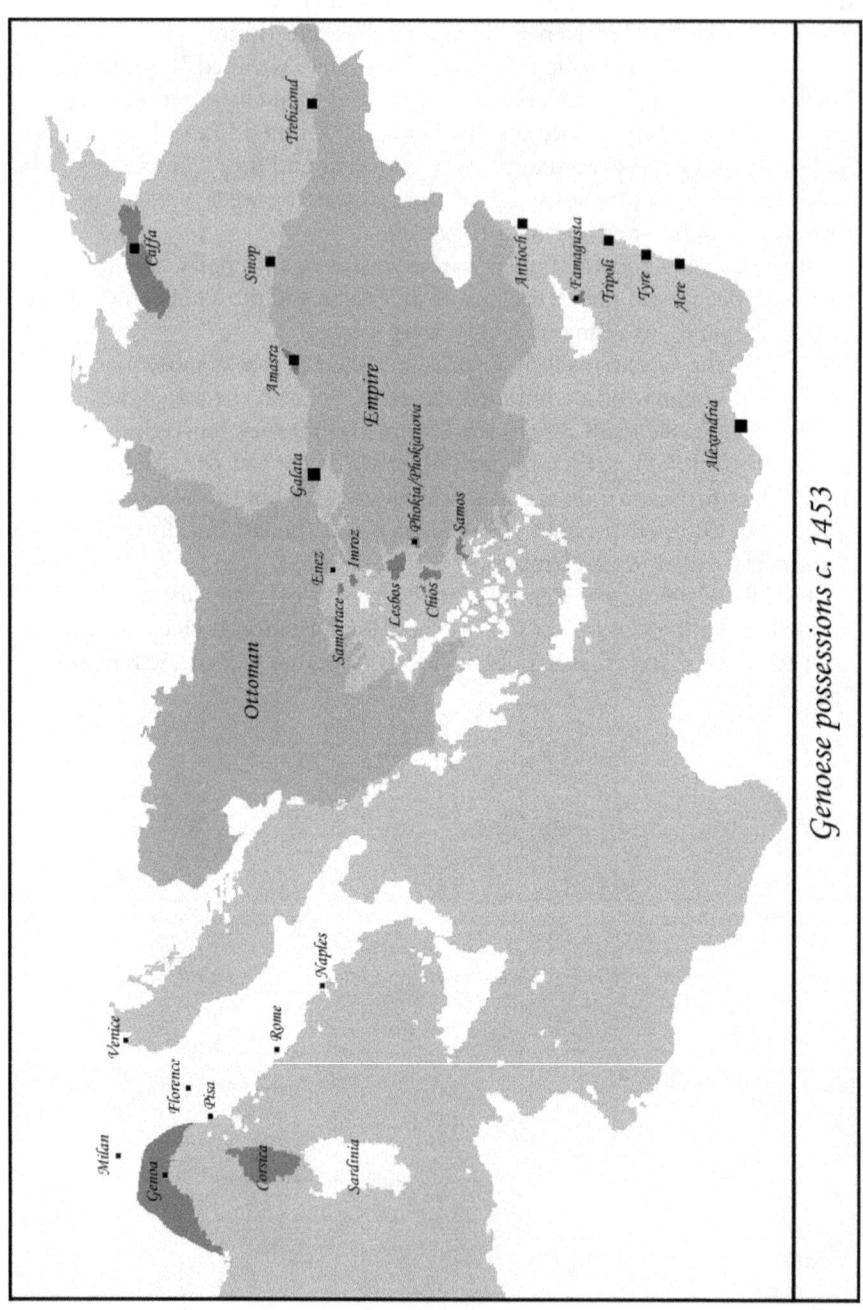

Genoese possessions c. 1453

11 - GENOA

Part 4 - The Maritime States of Italy

CRITICAL TIMELINE

Year	Event	Involved Parties
935	Saracen raid on Genoa	Genoa, Saracens
1016	Genoa and Pisa attack Saracens in Sardinia	Genoa, Pisa, Saracens
1034	Genoa and Pisa attack Bone in Algeria	Genoa, Pisa, Saracens
1050	Genoa attacks Sardinia	Genoa, Saracens
1060	Genoese traders reported in Egypt	Genoa, Egypt
1060s	Genoa at war with Pisa	Genoa, Pisa
1087	Genoa and Pisa attack Mahdia in Tunisia	Genoa, Pisa
1097	Genoa is early participant in the First Crusade	Genoa
1098	Second expedition to the Holy Land	Genoa
1100	Genoa become 'commune'	Genoa
1101	Grand Fleet leave for the Holy Land	Genoa
1103	Genoa barred from Egypt	Genoa, Egypt
1119	War begins with Pisa	Genoa, Pisa
1136	Genoese attack on Bougie in Algeria	Genoa, Saracens
1146	Naval battle off Almeria	Genoa, Saracens, Barcelona
1147	Conquest of Almeria	Genoa, Saracens, Barcelona
1148	Conquest of Tortosa	Genoa, Saracens, Barcelona
1159	Genoa obtain trade rights in Byzantine Empire	Genoa, Byzantium
1162	Genoese and Pisan clash in Constantinople	Genoa, Pisa
1165	War breaks out with Pisa	Genoa, Pisa
1171	Genoese settlement in Constantinople attacked. Venetians expelled from Constantinople	Genoa, Byzantium
1182	Attack on Latins in Constantinople	Genoa, Byzantium
1191	First foreign podestà appointed	Genoa

11 - Genoa

Year	Event	Involved Parties
1194	Genoa assists Henry VI in conquest of Sicily	Genoa Naples
1200	Genoa assists Philip of Swabia with invasion of Sicily	Genoa Naples
1204	Fourth Crusade. Genoa expelled from Constantinople	Genoa Byzantium Venice
1212	Frederick I visits Genoa. Peace agreed with Pisa	Genoa Pisa Roman Empire
1218	Genoa participates in Fifth Crusade	Genoa Roman Empire Egypt
1222	Pisans burn down Genoese quarters in Acre	Genoa Pisa
1237	Imperial ban on Genoa. Emperor Frederick II defeats Lombard League at Battle of Cortenuova	Genoa Roman Empire Lombard League
1240	Genoa besieged by imperial land troops and a Pisan navy	Genoa Roman Empire Pisa
1242	Naval battle with Pisa off Savona	Genoa Pisa
1243	Innocent IV becomes pope	The Pope
1244	The Pope goes into exile in Genoa	Genoa The Pope
1250	Sacking of Venetian quarters in Acre	Venice Genoa
1255	Venetian fleet attacks Acre and Tyre	Venice Genoa
1257	Peace with Pisa	Genoa Pisa
1258	Venice and Genoa do battle in Acre	Venice Genoa
1261	Reconquest of Constantinople	Venice Genoa Byzantium
1265	Genoa is expelled from Constantinople	Genoa Byzantium
1265	Naval battle off Trapani	Genoa Venice
1267	Genoa is invited back to Constantinople	Genoa Byzantium
1270	Peace with Venice	Genoa Venice
1272	War with Charles of Anjou	Genoa House of Anjou
1277	Peace with Charles of Anjou	Genoa House of Anjou

Year	Event	Involved Parties
1282	War breaks out with Pisa over Corsica	Genoa, Pisa
1284	Battle of Meloria. Genoa destroys Pisan fleet	Genoa, Pisa
1290	Pisan attack on Elba. Porto Pisano filled in, Corsica and Chios added to Genoese possessions.	Genoa, Pisa
1291	Acre is lost to Egypt	Egypt, Jerusalem
1291	Vandino and Ugolino Vivaldi leave to find India	Genoa
1296	Venetian attack on Constantinople	Genoa, Venice, Byzantium
1297	Genoese attack on Constantinople	Genoa, Venice, Byzantium
1298	Venetian attack on Constantinople. Naval battle off Curzola.	Genoa, Venice, Byzantium
1299	Peace settlement	Genoa, Venice
1303	Genoa transports the Grand Company of Catalans to Constantinople	Genoa, Byzantium
1307	Mongols Attack on Caffa	Genoa, Golden Horde
1308	Genoa abandons Caffa	Genoa, Golden Horde
1311	Genoa ceded to Henry VII	Genoa, Roman Empire
1313	Civil war following death of Henry VII	Genoa
1316	Genoa returns to Caffa	Genoa, Golden Horde
1329	Chios is lost to Byzantium	Genoa, Byzantium
1331	Peace agreement ends civil war. Genoa ceded to Naples	Genoa, Naples
1335	Naples expelled from Genoa	Genoa, Naples
1339	Public revolt in Genoa	Genoa
1343	Mongol attack on Tana and Caffa	Genoa, Venice, Golden Horde
1346	Genoa retake Chios	Genoa, Byzantium
1346	Mongol attack on Caffa. Black Death	Genoa, Venice, Golden Horde

Year	Event	Involved Parties
1348	Black Death reached Europe	Venice, Genoa
1348	Short conflict with Byzantium	Genoa, Byzantium
1350	Genoa, with Ottoman support, unleashes pirate fleet against Venice	Genoa, Venice, Ottomans
1351	Venetian attack on Constantinople	Genoa, Venice, Byzantium
1352	Naval battle off Constantinople	Venice, Genoa, Pisa
1354	Naval battle off Pylos. Genoa under protection of Milan	Genoa, Venice, Milan
1355	Genoa destroys Modon. Peace agreement. Lesbos becomes Genoese	Venice, Genoa
1356	Milan expelled from Genoa	Genoa, Milan
1369	Emperor John V Palaiologos offers the island of Tenedos to Venice	Genoa, Venice, Byzantium
1373	Genoese attack on Cyprus	Genoa, Cyprus
1376	Venice once again granted Tenedos	Genoa, Venice, Byzantium
1378	Naval battle off Anzio	Genoa, Venice
1379	Naval battle off Pola.	Genoa, Venice
1380	Battle of Chioggia	Genoa, Venice
1381	Settlement over Tenedos	Genoa, Venice
1396	Genoa ceded to France	Genoa, France
1403	Last freebooter-fleet leaves Genoa	Genoa
1409	French expelled from Genoa	Genoa, France
1420	Conflict over Corsica leads to Genoa being ceded to Milan	Genoa, Milan, Aragon
1431	Naval battle off Portofino	Genoa, Venice
1433	Peace with Venice	Genoa, Venice

Part 4 - The Maritime States of Italy

Year	Event	Involved Parties
1435	Milan expelled from Genoa	Genoa, Milan
1444	Genoese ships transport Murad II's army from Anatolia before the Battle of Varna	Genoa, Ottomans
1453	Unofficial Genoese support to Byzantium during Conquest of Constantinople	Genoa, Byzantium, Ottomans
1454	Ottomans demand tribute of Caffa	Genoa, Ottomans
1455	Failed Ottoman attack on Chios. Ottomans conquer Phokia and Phokianova.	Genoa, Ottomans
1456	Ottomans conquer Enez, Imroz and Samothrace	Genoa, Ottomans
1458	Genoa under French rule	Genoa, France
1459	Ottomans conquer Amasra	Genoa, Ottomans
1461	French expelled from Genoa	Genoa, France
1462	Ottomans conquer Lesbos	Genoa, Ottomans
1464	Genoa loses Famagusta	Genoa, Cyprus
1468	Genoa under Milanese rule	Genoa, Milan
1475	Ottomans conquer Caffa and Samos	Genoa, Ottomans

11 - Genoa

Where Venice gets mentioned as early as the sixth century, Genoa is practically a non-entity until the middle of the tenth century.

The town of Genoa is situated on the sea against a backdrop of mountains. It did make for a natural harbour, but the hinterland had little in terms of agricultural potential, or natural resources. The nearby rivers were not navigable, making transport further inland depend on overland routes, mainly by mule. Furthermore, the fishing was not that good and in the post-Roman centuries Genoa was little but a sleepy fishing-village slightly off the beaten track.

When we use the term 'Genoa' then, contrary to Venice, we are really talking about an area rather than just a city. Genoa is situated in Liguria, a coastal area spanning (in the Middle Ages) from (and including) Monaco in the west to Ventimiglia in the east. Eventually Genoa would control the whole area inside its republican structure. As Venice is situated at the top of the Adriatic Sea, so is Genoa situated on the top of the Ligurian Sea, leading south past the island of Corsica to the Tyrrhenian Sea, Sardinia, Sicily and the coast of North Africa.

And for Genoa, like Venice, it was all about location even though for Genoa it was also, to some extent, about its neighbours.

In the tenth century the west coast of Spain, the north coast of Africa and the island of Sicily were all in the hands of Saracens who were also raiding as far as Sardinia, Corsica and, importantly, Liguria.

It is in connection with such a raid that Genoa, for the first time, starts to appear in written sources, as it was subject to a raid by Saracens in 935. According to some sources it was left uninhabited for some period afterward, whereas according to other (later) sources the Genoese 'fleet' returned immediately following the raid, pursued the attackers and released the prisoners which had been taken. The later version is somewhat wishful.

In any case, it was the fact that there were Saracens in the neighbourhood that really made Genoa. The hinterlands behind the town were owned by local nobles and, not least, the Church. There was not that much arable land, but there were even fewer people to farm it, so very early in the history of Genoa a, well controlled and documented, system emerged in which land was rented out to free farmers.

As there was little to use the cash made from such deals for locally, it was invested in ships which set out to trade. Initially they would go to Corsica or Sardinia with a combination of olive oil and wine and return with other foodstuffs and salt, but they would most likely also trade for cash.

By 1016 Genoa had recovered enough from the raid in 935 to ally with Pisa in an attack on Saracens in Sardinia, and here starts the story of Genoa for real.

There were well established trading routes connecting Saracen settlements in Spain, North Africa, Sicily and Egypt and they ran not that far from Genoa. The Saracen traders were richly laden, so the Genoese simply became pirates, a pursuit they never really gave up.

In between piracy they started to frequent Saracen ports as traders, and it was not uncommon that a galley which set out from Genoa could play both roles on the same roundtrip, taking the opportunities as they came along.

By 1034, once again allied with Pisa, the Genoese raided the city of Bone (modern Annaba in Algeria) where, possibly for the first time, they started dealing in a commodity that would become a specialty; slaves.

In 1050 the Genoese were back in Sardinia, again raiding Saracen settlements and in 1060 there are records of Genoese traders in Egypt. Gradually they were moving further and further away from home, now also bringing home 'exotic goods' over and above foodstuff.

Around this time, Genoa also for the first time went to war with Pisa, a conflict which in itself is obscure and the reasons for which are assumed to be dominance of the ports on Sardinia. It is, however, the first taste we get of the rivalry between Pisa and Genoa which would last more than three centuries.

Pisa is located further down the west coast of Italy and is a significantly bigger city with a hinterland providing a range of natural trading goods. Pisa was thus, in the eleventh century, the bigger player in the Tyrrhenian Sea and thus both the most likely ally and enemy of Genoa.

In 1087 Pisa and Genoa were once again allied, this time in a raid on Mahdia in Tunisia, presumably with the Pisans playing the leading role as they were built up and battle hardened from having assisted the Normans in their conquest of Sicily in the years before.

Then at the end of the eleventh century everything changed for Genoa. The reason was the First Crusade.

The First Crusade was not from the outset a naval expedition. Quite on the contrary, the crusading armies arrived at Constantinople overland and then fought their way through Anatolia and Palestine. But once in Palestine, where they started to establish the Crusader States, they needed both supplies and naval support in order to take the port cities of Syria.

The bishops of Grenoble and Orange came to Genoa in 1097, preaching crusade, and eventually a small fleet of twelve galleys and one small ship, with probably a total of 1,200 men aboard, left Genoa in July 1097. The fleet arrived in the right place at the right time and offered its services to Bohemund of Taranto, would-be founder of the Principality of Antioch, as he was laying siege to that very city.

The fleet returned to Genoa in May 1098, a month before Antioch finally fell to the crusaders, but enough Genoese had been left behind to claim their spoils from Bohemund, who gave them part of the city and the right to live by their own rules in the Principality. All of a sudden Genoa had acquired trading-privileges which set them apart for the first time, and in 1098 they sent a new fleet, this time assisting in the final capture of Jerusalem.

In August 1100, a new 'grand' fleet of twenty-six galleys, four ships and 3,000 men left Genoa for the Holy Land. On their arrival they found that Bohemund of Taranto had been captured in battle and the Principality was ruled by his nephew Tancred. The Genoese were keen to ensure their privileges and Tancred confirmed them and in addition gave them 1/3 of the port of Solino and 1/3 of the port of Laodicea plus the promise of a similar share of any other ports they would help to conquer.

The fleet drifted down the coast and ended up in the service of King Baldwin I of Jerusalem, assisting in the capture of Arsuf and Caesarea after which the main part of the fleet returned home laden with booty.

A small contingent stayed behind, and they were later given more shares in towns and ports and the promise of 1/3 of any city or port conquered, when the King was assisted by fifty or more Genoese. A specific promise was made that the Genoese would receive 1/3 of Cairo once conquered, but things never got that far.

In the meantime, both Pisan and Venetian fleets had started to emerge in the theatre, but it was the Genoese who were there first and it was they who got the lion's share of the spoils.

In 1103 the sultan in Egypt had all Genoese in Alexandria arrested, as punishment for the Genoese effort during the crusade, a testament to the fact that by this time there was a critical mass of Genoese present in Egypt.

Back in Genoa the sudden success in the East forced a dramatic change. With 'Genoa' now suddenly being awarded land and privileges, they needed some kind of functioning government which went beyond the city and its immediate surrounds.

Technically Genoa was under the rule of the Roman (German) Emperor, at that time Henry V, but nobody had paid much attention to the rather unimportant city, which now started to take matters in their own hands.

Around the year 1100 Genoa formed a 'commune', a sworn association of citizens. It was to last for three years, ruled by six elected consuls. The commune represented Genoa in foreign political matters and became the de-facto government, guild and port-authority in one body.

Membership of the commune was essential at local level, as only members were allowed to trade, and at international level things were now being done in the name of the commune, rather than in the name of the Archbishop as had been the custom.

In 1119 Genoese pirates attacked a fleet of Pisan traders, leading to eleven years of war, though it was mainly fought as a succession of raids and pirate attacks rather than as staged battles. One of the key areas of contention between the two maritime states was dominance of Corsica, under the suzerainty of the Pope.

The problem was that the Pope had granted the right to appoint the Bishop of Corsica to the Bishop of Pisa, in effect giving Pisa preferred status on the island, but in 1120 the Genoese simply bribed the Pope and the Curia. A decision was made to revoke Pisa' rights of appointing the Bishop of Corsica, a decision backed up by a Papal Bull in 1123.

In the following decades the Genoese gradually took de-facto control of the whole area of Liguria, mainly by simply buying the local nobles off and including them in the commune and thus in the considerable wealth that trade was bringing.

Having secured Liguria, Genoese interests started to spread west along the French south coast, and agreements were made with the ports of Provence to favour Genoese traders, indeed, to not trade with their enemies, i.e. the Pisans.

As their dominance spread westwards, the Genoese started to take an interest in Spain, over and above harassing the local Saracen communities, an activity that also still took place in North Africa, a Genoese attack on Bougie (modern Béjaïa in Algeria) in 1136 being one such example.

The First Crusade had put new wind into the Reconquista, the effort to expel the Saracens from Spain, and in 1146 the Genoese gambled big by committing practically their entire fleet to assisting Alfonso VII of Castile and Ramon Berenguer IV, Count of Barcelona, in their attempt to take Almeria on the south-eastern coast of Spain. The Genoese initially fought the Saracens outside Almeria, a battle in which the Genoese were successful and had to be bought off.

Next year a Genoese fleet of 63 galleys and 164 other ships, carrying some 12,000 men, went back to Spain. This was a very large fleet and an expensive gamble, even though both Spanish rulers had contributed to the costs of preparing it. The potential reward was 1/3 of the conquered cities, Almeria and Tortosa (in Catalonia) being the targets for the campaign.

Almeria fell in October 1147, the Genoese taking an enormous amount of booty and slaves. The Genoese then moved to Barcelona to stay over winter.

By July 1448 they were in front of Tortosa, which fell on 30 December. This time terms were offered so the immediate reward was not as plentiful.

Now the Genoese did something which would become a model for their imperial expansion. Whereas the Venetians, as seen in the previous chapter, were putting great effort into governing all of its imperial territories directly from Venice, Genoa, having received 1/3 of Almeria and Tortosa, simply sold its rights.

This difference in business model was a key differentiator between the two maritime states which would become the dominant players in the

Mediterranean. In Venice the individual worked for the glory of the state, in Genoa the State worked for the glory of its individuals. In modern terms, if both Venice and Genoa were multinational corporations, then Venice would operate its international businesses as subsidiaries whereas Genoa would operate theirs as franchises.

Genoa's business model meant that the city did not have to pay for the upkeep or defences of the foreign territories, making them less capital-intensive, but as part of the deals were, that the new 'owners' would stay loyal to Genoa (the 'brand'), they maintained the advantages originally granted. It had the added advantage that the quick, mostly opportunistic, transformation of a Genoese trading ship to a pirate ship was purely a private matter. The state was at arm's length and could not be held responsible for its citizen's behaviour.

In the case of Almeria, it was rented for thirty years to Ottone Bonvillano, a Genoese noble. Tortosa was initially rented to a consortium, but in 1153 sold to the count of Barcelona.

Despite the apparent success of these campaigns in Spain, the fact of the matter was that they had not been profitable. The sheer cost of the operation (and the reduced trade, as almost all available ships and men were taking part in the campaign) simply overshadowed the rewards. Like the Venetians would experience fifty years later in connection with their big gamble on the Fourth Crusade, crusading was expensive business, but unlike the Venetian's conquest of Constantinople, Genoa simply had to lick its wounds and regroup.

By now the Genoese trade had become a much more complex business than when they originally set sails to trade for salt and foodstuff. A busy home industry had grown in Genoa and Liguria, processing goods brought in by the traders. In particular, the business of transforming wool, and later silk, into cloth was a booming business, keeping a large part of the city's women engaged in moneymaking pursuits and providing them with a level of independence which was rare for the times.

The Genoese specialty however was the concept of being 'first movers'. Simple in principle but hard to execute, the concept works on the fact that most profit is made the first time an item is sold on. The 'first mover' therefore buys goods from the port in which it is first brought to market and then moves it on to the first port in which it is in demand, making the first, and largest, profit in the supply chain.

This concept was perfectly suited for a state like Genoa with few goods of their own. A roundtrip from Genoa would thus possibly go along the coast of Provence, down the east coast of Spain, across to North Africa, along the coast to Egypt, then up along the coast of Palestine, round Anatolia into Constantinople and home via an assortment of ports on the coast of (Byzantine) Greece, Sicily and the west coast of Italy. Along this route the Genoese would seek to become 'first movers' buying and selling goods along the way, finally arriving in Genoa with an assortment of exotic goods and slaves, which European customers would increasingly come to Genoa to acquire or which could be used as seeding goods for the next trip, in its raw form or processed.

Trading and piracy trips were typically financed by a range of investors, each entering into a contract defining the investment and the repayment. A typical financial instrument was a 'sea loan' which provided an investment in cash and repayment of a fixed amount no more than one month after the ship's safe return. The potential gain was good, but the loan was only repayable on the ship's safe return, so if it failed to return the investment was lost.

By the late 1150s, the Byzantine Emperor, Manuel I Komnenos, was starting to realize the threat of the Normans in Sicily and southern Italy. At that time the Venetians and the Pisans were given preferential treatment in the Byzantine Empire, but the Emperor was keen to make friends.

In order to avoid the Genoese supporting the Normans, the Emperor granted them the same rights at the Pisans. This meant a reduction of 60% on their taxes, their safety guaranteed throughout the Empire and the rights to hire quarters in Constantinople. For the Genoese the circle was now complete, and they had once again managed to, if not outdo, then at least match the Pisans. It is worth noticing that the Byzantines actually agreed to pay the Genoese an annual amount of cash to enter into the agreement, that is how much they needed them aboard.

At the same time the Genoese reconfirmed their trading agreement with the Normans in Sicily, but they had not in either agreement promised to provide any military assistance, so they were free to negotiate trade agreements with whomever they saw fit.

Taking stock at around 1160, things looked good for the Genoese, even though they were influenced by several powerful states in their immediate surround.

The Holy Roman Emperor, Frederick I 'Barbarossa', was at odds with the papacy about secular authority, forcing the election of an anti-pope and a union between the papacy and the Normans in southern Italy. The Byzantines were still fighting to hold on to their last remaining possessions in Italy, and the Normans were doing their best to oust them. The Genoese literally sailed through it all.

A Genoese galley was at the time, on average, manned by 100 men, mostly, though not exclusively, free men hired to do a combination of jobs. Not unlike the Vikings coming out of Scandinavia a few centuries prior, the crew of a Genoese galley could man the oars, fight at sea (in defence or as pirates), unload and fight on land as well as act as individual traders, each man allowed a sea-bag worth of his own goods. Their contemporaries coined the phrase '*Ianuensis ergo marcator*' ('Genoese therefore a merchant') as

Genoese could be encountered everywhere, always looking for a deal to be had.

Staying out of the bigger political game, the Genoese had time and resources at hand to fight their own war; that of dominance, at this time primarily aimed at the old enemy Pisa, even though their growing appearance in the Byzantine Empire, not least in Constantinople, also brought them into direct contact with the Venetians.

War broke out in 1165, apparently following a Genoese attack on Pisan ships on the River Rhone, an important river providing access into western Europe from the top of Tyrrhenian Sea. The war raged on for more than a decade, the two states challenging each other at any given opportunity, but never entering into any decisive battles. The underlying question was about control of Sardinia, an imperial fiefdom, and in the end a peace was brokered which gave Pisa and Genoa defined areas of interest on the island.

In the same period there was trouble in Constantinople. In 1162 the rivalry between Pisa and Genoa spilled into a conflict in Constantinople where the Pisans, assisted by some Venetians, raided the Genoese quarters. The result was a temporary ban on Pisan and Genoese traders in Constantinople.

They were back soon enough though and in 1171 the Genoese colony was raided by a flash-mob. This time the confrontation was, probably rightfully so, blamed on the Venetians and the Emperor had all the Venetians in the Byzantine Empire arrested. Despite a Venetian effort to force the Emperor's hand by means of military intervention, the end result was that the Venetians were barred from the city until 1179, and then only allowed back at their own risk as diplomatic relations between Venice and Byzantium were only re-established in 1195.

When the Byzantine emperor, Manual I Komnenos, died in 1180, he left the throne to his son, Alexios II Komnenos. As Alexios II Komnenos was only eleven years old, his mother, Maria of Antioch, was appointed regent.

Maria of Antioch, as her name implies, was a descendant of the Latin rulers of Antioch and she was seen by the locals as overly supportive of the 'Latins', i.e. the Italian traders who had for centuries irritated the local population by their arrogance, wealth and, of course, perceived heresy.

The regency of Maria of Antioch was unpopular, and when she was challenged by Andronikos I Komnenos, a grandson of Emperor Alexios I Komnenos, the population soon backed the pretender, who in 1182 entered Constantinople ahead of a rebel army. It is very possible that agents of Andronikos I Komnenos had arrived before him to organize civil uprising, but unlikely that they would have directed it against the Latin population in isolation.

It was, however, the Latin population who caught the sharp end of the revolt. The anger against the Latins, hemmed up for decades, now erupted and tens of thousands of Italians, in particular Genoese and Pisans, were murdered regardless of gender or age. According to some sources thousands were sold as slaves to the Seljuks, but in any case, the Latin settlements in Constantinople were basically eradicated.

Though the Italians came back, it was in smaller numbers and the resentment towards the citizens of Constantinople was easily an underlying reason for the sack of Constantinople some twenty years later.

Towards the end of the century they Genoese and the Pisans again cooperated, this time in support of Emperor Henry VI, who through marriage was now King of Sicily but had to take possession of the island by force. As had become the norm, the Genoese and the Pisans were promised defined shares of specific cities and ports but, despite Henry VI being successful in the campaign, he negated on his promises, and the Genoese and Pisans had to leave without their promised possessions. Genoa and Pisa then started fighting each other again.

We now once again return to the Fourth Crusade. Several sources mention that the reason the Crusader leaders went to Venice to look for transport to Egypt was not that Venice per se was the preferred partner, indeed, they would have preferred Genoa, but the consistent warfare between Genoa and Pisa made Venice the better choice. World history would have been dramatically different had this not been the case.

However the Fourth Crusade evolved as it did and suddenly Genoa, and Pisa, were excluded from trade in many parts of the Byzantine Empire, for the next six decades split into the various Latin states, all under dominance of Venice. And to add insult to injury, Venice now also controlled the trade in the Black Sea, previously an exclusively Byzantine territory, putting Venice even further ahead.

This blow to free trade had a major impact on Venice's competitors, but more severely on Pisa as the Genoese were late arrivals in Constantinople and had always seen trade in Egypt and the Crusader States as the core of their trade in the East. In 1191 17% of Genoas trade came from the Byzantine Empire. By 1216 it had dropped to 0%. In the same time-span trade with the Crusader States, had risen from 20% to 32%.

As another compensating factor Genoa also had piracy to fall back on, and gains acquired through this channel are not included in the numbers quoted above.

Genoese pirates started to infest the eastern Mediterranean, now pounding on any Venetian ships they could get to, alternating with raids on Venetian colonies. Genoese pirates also occupied Crete, making it a year-long process for Venice to take possession of the island which they had purchased in the aftermath of the Fourth Crusade.

Apart from this there was little to do about the situation in Byzantium for the time being, so the Genoese took the opportunity to consolidate their position closer to home.

On the home front all was but calm. Over the closing decades of the twelfth century Genoa had experienced a range of civil unrest, Powerful families had emerged in and around the city, competing with each other for political dominance in the commune. Each family had followers and the result was violence and unrest.

By 1191 the problems had become so grave, with warring factions besieging each other's neighbourhoods inside the city itself, that the consuls decided to step aside and invite a foreigner to come in and rule the city for a set period of time, with the title of 'podestà'. This title was common in Italy, but mostly used for top officials and governors appointed by the Emperor. In the case of Genoa it was self-inflicted. Podestàs were appointed on and off in the following decades and centuries, the governing model swinging between consuls in time of internal peace and podestàs in times when the city became ungovernable by its own means.

Furthermore, Genoa's superiority over the Liguria region was not undisputed. Ligurian communities and towns, in particular on the edges of the area, were often in revolt against Genoa. Such revolts were as often as not 'sponsored' by Genoa's neighbours, Pisa in the east and Marseille in the west.

In terms of settling these (in the bigger picture minor) disputes there was little help to gain from the Roman Emperor, as Henry VI had died in 1197 leaving the Empire in chaos. That, however, was about to change.

After Henry VI's death, his empire had been split between competing factions. There were two nominal emperors, Otto IV and Philip of Swabia (the same Philip who introduced Alexius Angelus to Boniface of Montferrat and caused the Fourth Crusade to divert to Constantinople) and Henry VI's heir, the infant Frederick, who was holed up with his mother in Sicily.

The Genoese had sided with Philip of Swabia's party and had in 1200 assisted in an invasion of Sicily which put the heir to the Empire under Philip's control (and gave the Genoese preferred status in Sicily). At that time Philip was also favoured by the Pope, but that changed a year later when the Pope decided to change sides and support Otto IV. Just to give an example of how complex the situation was.

By 1208 the heir Frederick had come of age, and he immediately started to reunite the Roman Empire. The Pope feared him and confirmed Otto IV as Holy Roman Emperor in 1209. Then when Otto IV made a pre-emptive strike on Italy the Pope changed his mind and crowned Frederick, now Frederick II, in 1211.

Frederick II quickly regained control of southern Italy and by 1212 he started to march north to assert his authority in Germany. On his way he stopped in Genoa, the first emperor to ever do so.

Frederick II arrived on 1 May and stayed for nearly three months. Basically, he came for support and more precisely for money. While he was there peace was agreed with both Venice and Pisa and the Emperor confirmed the borders as before as well as Genoa's supremacy of the Liguria region. He also promised that he would repay the money forwarded to him by the Genoese. By July he moved on towards Germany.

The promises made to the Genoese were not the only promises made by Frederick II, indeed in his dealings with Pope Innocent III Frederick II had promised to go on a crusade once he had regained the crown of Germany, and the Pope started to prepare for the campaign.

At the Fourth Council of the Lateran it was decided to start the new crusade in 1217, but Pope Innocent III died in 1216 and the task was handed over to his successor Honorius III.

The Pope insisted that this crusade should be led by the Papacy, in order to avoid individual interests, like those of the Venetians during the Fourth Crusade, should divert their effort to retake Jerusalem. The initial campaign was thus led by the King of Hungary and the duke of Austria under the supreme command of the Pope.

Transported on Venetian ships the crusader army landed in Palestine in late 1217 and were initially successful, but the campaign was badly organised, and lack of siege equipment soon led to setbacks. When the King of Hungary became sick he decided to return home, which in turn made the other crusaders decide likewise, so by February 1218 the crusaders left Palestine with nothing achieved despite the fact that the Egyptians had already demolished the defences of Jerusalem as they did not want them to be inherited by the crusaders.

A new mixed army, containing a small element of Germans sent by Frederick II, landed in Egypt in June of 1218, laying siege to the coastal town of Damietta. This time the Genoese contributed with a considerable fleet, despite also having problems with rebellious cities in Liguria.

The crusaders, who had allied with the Seljuks in Anatolia to keep the Egyptians busy in Syria, were once again initially successful, taking the defensive tower in front of Damietta in August.

The Egyptian sultan, Al-Kamil, now offered favourable terms. In exchange for the crusaders lifting the siege of Damietta and leaving Egypt, he would re-establish the Kingdom of Jerusalem.

If common sense had prevailed the crusaders would have accepted this offer, but the papal legate, Pelagio Galvani, who was officially in charge, would not accept. He was convinced that Frederick II would arrive with reinforcements and that Egypt itself was up for grasps.

The crusader army thus continued the siege of Damietta and finally gained control of the harbour in November of 1220. By this time, a Dutch contingent had left in protest over Pelagio Galvani's decision.

Now infighting started as John of Brienne, regent for the under-aged rulers of the Latin Empire of Constantinople and the Kingdom of Jerusalem, claimed Damietta for himself. The papal legate disagreed and John of

Brienne also left the army. He was, however, back in 1221 and the army now marched on Cairo itself.

The campaign was a disaster. The Egyptians had in the meantime beaten off the Seljuks in Syria and could concentrate on the crusaders in Egypt and their knowledge of the terrain decided the outcome.

Rather than offering a pitched battle, the Egyptians held back and raided the crusader's supply lines until nature played its part. As the Egyptians knew would happen, the Nile overflowed cutting off the crusader's advance, and when it also spilled into a canal behind the crusaders they were trapped.

The crusaders started a slow withdrawal, marred by hostile terrain, lack of supplies and constant raids of Egyptian forces. Finally, a night attack by Al-Kamil forced the army to surrender.

The terms of the surrender were that Al-Kamil would release his prisoners, but the crusaders had to abandon Damietta. Finally, the crusaders sailed home with nothing achieved. They had managed to grasp defeat from the claws of victory.

The Genoese had no doubt hoped for new trade privileges, but nothing was achieved. Instead, the problems on the home-front continued, with skirmishes both inside the city and with its neighbours, including the powerful Milanese.

In the East it was 'business as usual' which also meant low level confrontation between Genoese and, in particular, Pisan traders. In 1222 the situation exploded in Acre, where the Pisans burned down the Genoese quarter.

Frederick II finally did go on crusade in 1228, where he negotiated a (temporary) return of Jerusalem to the Christians. Since Frederick himself was, however under excommunication from the Pope, and Jerusalem was soon lost again, this crusade was considered a political manifestation rather than a wholehearted effort on behalf of Frederick II. The Genoese, like most others, did not contribute to Frederick II's crusade.

When Frederick II was back from his adventures in Palestine he once again started to flex his muscles in Italy. During his absence, the Pope had taken the opportunity to conquer southern Italy and Frederick II immediately went to work to recover it. Once done, he started to throw his weight around in northern Italy.

In terms of Genoa, he tried to impose a 10% tax on their trade and also to enforce his selection of a podestà. In terms of other cities in the region, he demanded similar monetary contributions and a de-facto acceptance of his suzerainty. When Genoa refused Frederick II ordered all their citizens in the Roman Empire arrested and their goods confiscated.

The pressure from Frederick II led to the reformation of the 'Lombard League' an alliance of northern Italian states initially formed to counter similar moves from Frederick II's grandfather, Frederick I 'Barbarossa'.

The Lombard League refused Frederick II, who then invaded and finally defeated the army of the Lombard League in 1237. Although the league disintegrated, Frederick II insisted on unconditional surrender, which Milan and others denied him and eventually he had to abandon the conflict in 1238 and proceeded to invade the Papal States.

While Frederick II himself was campaigning elsewhere, his supporters continued the conflict in northern Italy. Instigated by Frederick II and his allies in Pisa, once again there was civil war in Liguria and the Genoese had their hands full with protecting their territory.

By 1240 the Genoese were being pressed both by land and sea, imperial forces were attacking in the north, and a Pisan fleet defeated a Genoese fleet. The situation was becoming somewhat critical, but a concerted effort on land stopped the imperial army and gradually the Pisan navy was pushed away from Genoa. At the end of 1242, the Genoese navy had trapped the Pisan navy at Savona, west of Genoa, one of the cities in revolt. Here fighting continued through the following years, but what really turned the tide in favour of Genoa was the election of a new pope in 1243.

Pope Innocent IV was Genoese. Even though he had long since left Genoa for Rome, he was by default favourable to his hometown and when a Genoese fleet in June of 1244 rescued the Pope and six cardinals from Civitavecchia on the west coast of Italy, the Pope risking capture by Frederick II, Genoa effectively had their own pope.

Innocent IV stayed in Genoa until October that year after which he went to Lyon. From there he excommunicated Frederick II and issued a range of bulls in favour of Genoa. The revolts in Liguria continued, but the Genoese now held the moral high ground.

Frederick II died in 1250 and his support in northern Italy collapsed. Genoa had once again weathered a serious crisis, this time the lucky choice of a pope helping them along.

During these difficult times the Genoese had of course not ceased to sail and trade. Peace with Venice had been established several times, the latest with the Pope as intermediary in 1250. Peace with Pisa was formally agreed to in 1257.

Peace with Venice did not last long though. I mentioned the conflict of 1258 in Chapter 10, but I will go into more detail here.

It started in 1250; the very year peace was officially declared between Genoa and Venice. The place was Acre, one of the few remaining ports in Palestine still in Christian hands.

It started, as such things do, with a rather low-key event. There was already tension between the two communities over the use of a church which was located between the Venetian and Genoese quarters. Then the Venetians claimed that a newly arrived Genoese ship was indeed a Venetian ship captured through piracy and then a brawl between a Venetian and a Genoese ended up with the Genoese dead.

Snap! A mob descended on the Venetian quarter, looted it, slaughtered the inhabitants, and then went on to sack the Venetian ships in the harbour.

The Venetians responded not in haste, but in force. A fleet of thirty-two galleys were equipped and left Venice. It arrived in front of Acre in 1255 and first crashed through the chain the Genoese had used to bar access to the harbour. Then they burned the Genoese galleys.

The Venetians now proceeded to neighbouring Tyre, where they repeated the exercise, this time taking the Genoese admiral and 300 Genoese citizens prisoners.

With the Genoese fleet out of play, they returned to Acre with their prisoners and this time they landed. An immense fight ensued, street by street, quarter by quarter, gradually dragging all the citizens of Acre into taking one side or the other. The Venetians gradually got the upper hand inside of the city, confining the Genoese to their own quarter, but a stalemate ensued. It was broken by the arrival of fresh troops.

Both cities had, over time, sent more ships from nearby colonies, but in 1258 they both sent new big fleets, the Genoese fleet consisting of forty galleys and four round ships, the Venetian fleet being of a similar size.

The Venetians got there first, further enforcing the Venetian dominance in the, by now, long running contest, but soon the Genoese fleet anchored outside the harbour of Acre, bringing hope of deliverance to the Genoese.

The ensuing battle took place both at sea and on land. While the Venetian fleet set out to meet the blockading Genoese, the Genoese citizens set out to attack the Venetians.

Despite an advantage in numbers the sea-battle went bad for the Genoese, very bad. Twenty-five galleys were destroyed and nearly 2,000 men were lost. With the sea-battle lost the spirit went out of the land-battle as well, and the Genoese surrendered.

In the aftermath the Genoese were expelled from Acre until, once again, papal intervention ensured the Genoese access to Acre and Tyre was restored.

It was becoming increasingly clear that the Latin Empire of Constantinople was a spent force, only held alive by the Venetians in Constantinople who treated the city pretty much as a personal possession.

For the Genoese this represented an opportunity to regain their position in Anatolia and Greece, so they decided to gamble on a winner, they gambled high and they gambled well.

Their choice was Michael VIII Palaiologos, the Emperor of Nicaea, simply put, the dominant Greek force in the region. It was a high gamble as even if the Genoese had picked a winner, the fact that they had sided with an Orthodox regent against a Catholic regent would get them into trouble with the Pope.

Forgotten were the original sins of the Fourth Crusade, where the Pope had excommunicated the participants for attacking another Christian state.

The papacy had long since reconciled itself with the fact that Constantinople, and the Latin states around it, were Catholic, so the Genoese proactively supporting a return to Orthodoxy was playing for high stakes. The potential prize, however, was worth it.

In late 1260 the Genoese sent ambassadors to Michael VIII Palaiologos and by April 1261 they had a deal. The Genoese would supply a fleet of up to fifty galleys, paid for by the Emperor. The fleet would be put in combat with all the Emperor's enemies except the Catholic Church itself.

The prize for Genoa was basically to take over the Venetian's position. They would be granted the Venetian quarters in Constantinople, free trade within the Empire, including the Black Sea. They were even granted the islands of Euboea and Crete, though these were now ruled by Venice and thus technically not the Emperor's to give to anyone.

When Michael VIII Palaiologos took Constantinople in July 1261 it was, however, by chance and coincidence and the Genoese never participated. They did of course hasten to Constantinople where the Emperor fulfilled his part of the deal as his fragile new empire needed all the help it could get. Fortune had indeed smiled on Genoa, who now had reversed the roles with Venice and with the rights to trade on the Black Sea had gained more than they had lost short of six decades earlier.

As a symbolical gesture the Genoese demolished the Venetian headquarters in Constantinople, shipped the stone back to Genoa and used it to build a church in commemoration of their triumph (in which they had not fired a single shot). As a similarly symbolic gesture the Pope, as expected, excommunicated the Genoese.

But as we have seen so often, fortune is a vain mistress. Back in Genoa there was trouble. The 'Captain of the People', Marino Boccanegra, was enormously unpopular and in 1262 he was ousted by a coup after which a new, foreign, podestà was called in to rule the city. In the meantime the Genoese fleet in the East did little but cruise up and down the Bosporus and the Sea of Marmara, where they did manage to repel a pirate fleet launched from Negroponte.

In 1263, the Byzantine Emperor however, needed their support when he went on a campaign in the Morea where William II of Villehardouin had allied himself with the disposed Latin Emperor Baldwin II of Constantinople.

A combined Byzantine and Genoese fleet set sail for Monemvasia on the south coast of the Morea, but before they got there they encountered a Venetian fleet heading north for Negroponte.

The Byzantine-Genoese fleet was superior in numbers with thirty-nine galleys and ten cutters against thirty-two Venetian galleys. But the Genoese captains were reluctant to give battle and risk their, privately owned, ships, so their attack on the Venetians was half-hearted, around half of the fleet sitting back and waiting. The result was a resounding victory for the Venetians, though the Genoese only lost the half of the fleet which actually took part in the hostilities.

Whereas the battle itself was not in any way conclusive, the Byzantine Emperor was less than happy with the Genoese effort. He actually paid the Genoese for their troubles, and he expected a full return on his investment.

The Emperor now dismissed the Genoese fleet for which he had no use if they did not want to fight. But there was also trouble with the Genoese in Constantinople itself.

The city which Michael VIII Palaiologos had taken over was in ruins, literally. The weak Latin Empire had not had the resources, or inclination, to rebuild Constantinople following the Fourth Crusade, so large parts of the city were still left as burned-out ruins. The population was down to 35,000, less than 10% of its size before the Fourth Crusade, and there was only so much tax to be gained from the rather destitute Byzantines.

The Emperor therefore depended on trade, and the associated taxes, to start rebuilding and maintaining his capital city, but since the Genoese had taken over from the Venetians, Genoese traders had flooded into Constantinople and effectively taken control of the city's trade.

Very quickly the old animosity between the locals and the Italians started to flare up and when in 1265 the leader of the Genoese settlement, the Podestà, admitted to be conspiring with the King of Sicily to reconstitute the lost Latin Empire of Constantinople, the Genoese were expelled.

This however left the Byzantine Empire with no allies, something they badly needed as the King of Sicily was still eyeing off Constantinople.

The death of Frederick II had left the Kingdom of Sicily, covering all of southern Italy and now ruled from Naples, in turmoil. Frederick II's son Manfred took control of the Kingdom from his nephew Conradin in 1258, but the Pope, who was the protector of Conradin, decided to intervene and went into alliance with Charles of Anjou who, with papal support, conquered the Kingdom of Sicily in 1266.

Charles of Anjou then went on to take Corfu and part of the Greek west coast and in 1267 he made his intentions clear by entering into a range of dynastic marriages and declaring his support for Baldwin II's attempts to retake the Latin Kingdom of Constantinople, an alliance which also included support from Venice.

In the meantime, the Genoese and the Venetians fought on. Genoese piracy had forced the Venetians to move in convoys, with a combination of traders and warships to protect them. In 1264 the Genoese scored a victory when they manage to lure the military escort away from the traders, which were looted by the Genoese.

In pure military matters the Venetians however prevailed. In 1265 the two fleets meet outside Trapani, on the north coast of Sicily, and once again the Genoese captains showed reluctance to fight when their ships were at risk.

By 1267 the Byzantine Emperor had once again realized that he needed allies, so a new deal was made with the Genoese, who were allowed back into Constantinople, this time with quarters across from the city, on the north shores of the Golden Horn in the area of Galata. As was customary they built themselves a defensive tower. In that same year the Pope nullified the excommunication, all was forgotten now that Charles of Anjou had shown to be a clear and present danger.

But this time the deal with the Genoese was not exclusive. The following year Venice was allowed back in as well, and it was made clear to both parties that there would be no more exclusivity. They would simply have to share. I did mention above that the Venetians were in an alliance with Charles of Anjou, but his annexation of Corfu and the Greek west coast had made the Venetians realize that it was too dangerous to help him further advance his ambitions.

The Genoese had less scruples. They happily concluded an agreement with Charles of Anjou which gave them right to trade all over the Kingdom of Sicily. They did, however, not grant him any military assistance.

While they were expelled from Constantinople, the Genoese had not been idle. The great prize they had won was trade on the Black Sea and for that they needed a base in the area. Luckily, the Venetians, having had monopoly for six decades since the Fourth Crusade, had made a settlement on the south coast of the Crimean peninsula, and the Genoese moved in and took over.

The main port in the new Genoese possession on the Black Sea was Caffa (modern day Feodosya in Ukraine), the westernmost endpoint on the Silk Road. Over the decades following the Genoese slowly but surely made themselves undisputed masters of the Black Sea, annexing the south coast of the Crimean peninsula from the Principality of Theodoro (part of the Empire of Trebizond, see Chapter 8), renaming it the Captainship of Gothia.

The ongoing war between Genoa and Venice officially came to an end in 1270, The peace was brokered by King Louis IX of France, not because he cared per se, but because he needed both Venice and Genoa to support him in his plans for a new crusade.

Louis IX had been on a crusade before, and in 1250 he was captured by the Egyptians and had to be ransomed. This time his target was also Egypt, but through Tunisia, or at least so his brother, Charles of Anjou, had convinced him, as he himself had vested interests in dominance on the north coast of Africa.

The crusader army of Louis IX landed on the north coast of Africa in July 1270. By August it had been joined by Charles of Anjou, but disease had quickly broken out in the crusader camp, probably from dirty water, and on 25 August Louis IX died.

The campaign continued albeit somewhat lacklustre, now under the de-facto command of Charles of Anjou, so when the Khalif of Tunis offered terms, which included free trading rights for the crusader states; that suited everybody just fine and the crusade came to an end. Commercially it was a success. In terms of regaining Jerusalem it did nothing. In terms of ensuring peace between Genoa, Pisa and Venice it worked for a while.

Once done with the crusade, Charles of Anjou started to show his teeth again. His allies in southern France and northern Italy started to push into Genoese territory, but their rather half-hearted efforts were beaten off by the Genoese.

Soon, however, Charles of Anjou needed Genoa, so all previous borders were reconfirmed and Genoa was asked to participate in a grand new scheme. Charles of Anjou had decided to make his final move on Constantinople, and he had already secured the support of the Pope and Venice. This time, however, the Genoese declared themselves neutral, but in reality, sent warning to the Byzantine Emperor. The scheme never materialized due to the Sicilian Vespers, after which Peter III of Aragon invaded Sicily. Genoa did not officially lend support to Peter III of Aragon, but it was well known that they did not have much love lost for Charles of Anjou.

What occupied the Genoese more than Charles of Anjou's imperial plans were, once again, Pisa, on this occasion their presence on Corsica.

Corsica had a colorful history itself, but towards the middle of the thirteenth century it was unified under Sinucello della Rocca, also known as Giudice de Cinarca (the judge of Cinarca). Sinucello della Rocca had allied himself with Genoa in 1258, but in 1282 he rebelled and declared himself - and thus Corsica - for Pisa.

This provocation was more than Genoa was prepared to accept, so they prepared for war, total war. Traders were barred from leaving the city after 1 August and fifty new galleys were built at the expense of the commune. The aim was to put an enormous fleet together and deal with Pisa once and for all.

Initially the Genoese sent an expeditionary force to Corsica, and subsequently laid siege to Porto Torres and Sassari in north-eastern Sardinia. They also established a blockade by the river Arno, the access-point to the Pisan port of Porto Pisano, and they unleashed their semi-official, army of pirates in the Mediterranean Sea.

The Genoese then proceeded to raid the island of Elba between Corsica and Italy after which they unleashed an attack on Porto Pisano, trying to provoke the Pisan fleet to battle.

The Pisans avoided a fight and when the Genoese fleet withdrew, they launched their own, unsuccessful attack on Genoa. Finally, the main Genoese fleet, consisting of ninety-three galleys and eight sailing-ships, laid siege to Porto Pisano, where the Pisan fleet was holed up.

The Genoese fleet appeared in front of Porto Pisano on 6 August 1284 and after three centuries of on and off warfare, what followed would be decisive.

The Genoese fleet positioned itself in two battlelines. The front line, commanded by Oberto Doria, was visible to the Pisans, the second line, commanded by Benedetto I Zaccaria was not.

The Pisans, hemmed in by their own harbour, came out to give battle in a single line. Though they evenly matched the first line of the Genoese fleet, the second Genoese line sailed round them and attacked them from the flank. The result was a resounding victory for Genoa.

The Pisans lost the majority of their fleet, half their army and their podestà, Alberto Morosini , was captured. The Genoese burned down part of Porto Pisano and withdrew with more than 9,000 prisoners.

The war did not end though, even if the result was by now predictable, not least given the amount of Pisan prisoners held by the Genoese. In 1285 the Genoese went, unopposed, to Porto Pisano where they destroyed one of the fortifications. Finally, in 1288, official peace was made.

The peace settlement was entirely in Genoa's favour. They got the Pisan possessions in northern Sardinia and Pisa renounced their interests in Corsica. The Genoese kept Elba and the Pisans had to pull down all their defences in Acre. The Pisans got their prisoners back.

This battle, known as the Battle of Meloria, spelled the end of Pisa. They tried vainly to re-conquer Elba in 1290 in response to which the Genoese filled in the port of Porto Pisano and symbolically covered the land with salt, a curse against re-inhabitation. Pisa never managed to regain their momentum, and they disappear from our story at this point. But even with Pisa out of the equation, the Genoese still had plenty to do.

Even though the Pisans had given up any claims on Corsica, its ruler Sinucello della Rocca had not given up his rebellion. He once again declared for Pisa, but they never came to his assistance. Instead, the Genoese came back and by the end of the century Sinucello della Rocca was in prison in Genoa and Corsica had effectively become a Genoese possession, which it remained until 1768. The new territory was immediately, and in line with Genoa's policies, rented out to a consortium of merchants.

Around the same time one of Genoa's own, Benedetto Zaccaria, pursued the time-honoured combination of pirate-trader in the East. Essentially a private operator, like others, he never forgot his loyalties so when he, in the later part of the thirteenth century, took possession of the island of Chios he added to the Genoese presence in the East, a presence which by that time matched that of Venice.

Things, however, did not go well in the East in general. The fragile crusader states, the remnants of the First Crusade, finally ceased to exist when the Mamluk Egyptians captured Acre, Tyre, Sidon, Beirut and Haifa in 1291.

As I have also mentioned in the previous chapter, the pressure caused by the loss of the crusader states, and thus the harbours of Syria, caused intense conflict between Genoa and Venice.

In 1296 the Venetians attacked the Genoese in the Galata. Trying to assert his authority, the Byzantine Emperor sided with the Genoese - nominally under his protection while in the city - and the Venetians turned their fire on the city itself.

The year after, Genoese in Galata attacked the Venetian quarter, destroying their official buildings and killing the leading Venetians.

The Venetians went back the following year, this time delivering a letter to the Emperor demanding compensation for the lack of protection of their citizens the year before but got nothing from him.

The Genoese now decided on a daring raid into the Adriatic Sea, Venice's own front yard.

On 9 September 1298 a Genoese fleet, commanded by Lamba Doria, met an equally sized Venetian fleet, commanded by Andrea Dandolo, off the island of Curzola, and for once the Genoese outsmarted the Venetians. Both parties suffered losses, but the Venetians most. They lost eighty-three of their ninety-five ships and 7,000 men were killed.

Enough was enough and both sites realized that further warfare would be ruinous. Peace was, once again, signed in 1299 with no concessions to either side. This time the peace would last for fifty years.

Protecting their trade in the East was not the only initiative taken in Genoa. A motion had several times been aired that the way to avoid trouble with Egypt, and for that matter the Byzantines and the Venetians, was to find a sea-route to India. In May 1291 two brothers, Vandino and Ugolino Vivaldi, left Genoa with two galleys to find India, bring back goods to trade and spread God's word, as they had on board two Franciscan friars. The two ships were last seen off Cape Chaunar on the Atlantic Coast of Africa. They were never heard of again. Although outside the scope of this story, it would be another Genoese, Christopher Columbus, who would eventually discover 'India' two centuries later.

Back in the East, the Genoese, as was their habit, offered their services when a band of Catalan mercenaries needed transport across the Bosporus. The mercenaries, under the command of one Roger de Flor, were hired by the Byzantine Emperor, Andronikos II Palaiologos, to help him fight the emerging Ottoman state in Anatolia.

Roger de Flor was a colourful person and the archetypical pirate and mercenary captain. Born in Brindisi he had, at a young age entered service on a galley belonging to the Knights Templar, and gradually worked his way up to become captain. Having rescued members of the Order from the fall of Acre he was accused of theft and dismissed. He ended up in Genoa, where he raised money to equip him for piracy.

When war broke out in Sicily, the Sicilian regent, Frederick, called on the services of Roger de Flor, who quickly assembled a band of mercenaries. They were from many places, but mostly from Catalonia, so they were generally referred to as Catalan mercenaries or 'the Grand company of Catalans'.

When hostilities ceased in Sicily in 1302, Roger de Flor sent a message to the Byzantine Emperor that for suitable payment (double their normal rate) he and his company were available - the Emperor accepted.

At that time the Byzantine army had all but ceased to exist, and what was left was mainly based on cheap, and ineffective, mercenaries, so Andronikos II Palaiologos saw the opportunity to get some real professional help.

The Genoese were hired to transport the mercenaries counting 2,500 men at arms, and their entourage of wives, mistresses, children and sundry, a total of 7,000 passengers.

Andronikos II Palaiologos could not get rid of them soon enough, so once again the Genoese were hired to transport them across the Sea of Marmara to Anatolia, where they successfully engaged the emerging Ottomans outside Philadelphia.

The relation with the Grand Company of Catalans, however, soon turned sour, as they had not been paid and they had also realized how weak the Byzantine Empire was and started fostering ideas of carving out their own state in western Anatolia.

The Emperor lured the Catalans back to Europe after they started to help themselves in Anatolia, once again relying on Genoese ships, and then had Roger de Flor assassinated while he was being hosted by the Emperor's son and co-regent, Michael IX Palaiologos.

The Catalans reacted by marching across the Byzantine territories in Europe, occupying the Gallipoli peninsula and the Duchy of Athens, leaving the countryside in flames wherever they went.

During this period, the Byzantine Emperor again relied on the Genoese to supply him with naval support, and though it never came to a major confrontation the Genoese secured the coastal cities for the Empire, also for their own good as the Catalans could not be trusted as business partners.

There was trouble in the Black Sea as well. The Mongol Khan, Toqta, had a problem with the Genoese capturing his subjects and selling them as slaves (to the Egyptians), so in 1307 he arrested all the Italians in the Crimea and laid siege to the Genoese settlement in Caffa.

Not capable of holding the city, the Genoese finally, in 1308, burned it down and abandoned it. It would be eight years until they re-established the relations with the Khan and returned to the city. At that time the new Khan, Öz-Beg, had made Islam the state-religion, which prevented the Genoese from selling (Muslim) slaves to the Egyptians.

Back in the mother-city the situation was chaotic. For centuries there had been a divide between the political party which supported the Pope and those who supported the Holy Roman Emperor, a divide fuelled also by commercial interests and political power. The unrest had resulted in several violent confrontations and changes to the political system, swinging between consuls, podestàs and 'captains of the people'.

In 1311, Henry VII, soon to be Holy Roman Emperor, arrived in Genoa. Like his predecessors he was trying to enforce his rule over Italy, but unlike them he insisted on a much more direct model of government. Where previously Genoa had been allowed to manage its own affairs, Henry VII insisted that the city be put under direct government by himself.

Under normal circumstances the Genoese would probably have rejected that and allied themselves with the other cities of northern Italy, but the internal political situation was so bad that they accepted and ceded the city to Henry VII for a period twenty years.

However, Henry VII died in 1313, having spent two years of constant fighting in Italy, and Genoa had lost its ruler. A new council was put together, and the city was once again under its own rule.

That turned out to be a disaster. Old hatreds flared up and the conflict turned into a proper civil war. Liguria was literally split into warring factions. The fleet was also divided, as were the colonies where, for instance, the citizens of Galata supported one party, but the same party was barred from Genoa itself. Mercenaries were hired to fight for both parties and various other rulers, like the Duke of Milan and the King of Sicily, were involved at times. Even the Ottomans were briefly involved when the civil war spilled over onto the Black Sea coast.

Genoese influence in Sardinia just slipped away, and the Genoese traders were left undefended from pirates as one half of the Genoese fleet was too busy fighting the other half.

In 1329 the population on the island of Chios, rose against the ruling, Genoese, Zaccaria family, and the Byzantine Emperor took the opportunity to reclaim the island into the Empire. He had by now built up a small Byzantine fleet as he could not rely on Genoa.

Finally in 1331 the warring parties had had enough. They met and made peace in Naples, while a Catalan fleet raided, defenceless, Liguria. The city was now officially under the suzerainty of Robert of Anjou, King of Naples, who established a 'rector' and a council of eight nobles and eight commoners. That model lasted for four years until new rivalry broke out, the King's men were ousted and the regime of a podestà reinstituted.

Fourteen years of civil war had nearly ruined Genoa. The colonies in Galata and Caffa were running their own affairs and trade had fizzled down to nearly northing.

The new regime now tried to re-establish the republic's finances, but their taxes became so unpopular that a popular uprising in 1339 ousted the regime and instead inserted a doge like in Venice. The people also burned the public records recording the State's debts, a symbolic rather than practical measure.

In the Black Sea the Venetians had set up a colony at Tana on the mouth of the River Don. The Venetians had secured an agreement with the Khan of the Golden Horde, and even though the new settlement was difficult to access due to low water, the Genoese also established a small sub-colony at Tana.

The trouble experienced by the Byzantine Emperor and others through the centuries now repeated itself in a new theatre. The Latins simply took over, cheated the Khan on his taxes, taxed foreign traders and conducted themselves as local lords.

When a fight between a Venetian and a local led to the death of the local, the new Khan had enough and he attacked Tana. The Venetians, with the most vested interests, wanted to stand and fight, but the Genoese took as much loot as they could get their hands on and withdrew to Caffa. A subsequent attack by the Khan sent the Venetians to Caffa as refugees.

When the Khan arrived in Caffa in the winter of 1343 the Venetians stood to fight with the Genoese and were eventually relieved by a Genoese fleet in 1344.

The Khan went back to lay siege to Caffa again the following year until in 1346 the Mongols just started to die from an unknown, but deadly, disease.

The Mongol army was wiped out by the disease, but before it got to that they had catapulted their dead across the walls of Caffa, infecting the defenders.

When in turn ships returned from Caffa, they brought with them the Black Death which would halve the population of Western Europe.

Before the disease reached Europe a typical private venture had left Genoa. In May 1346 a fleet sailed for the Aegean Sea. Its purpose was loosely defined, basically they were ready for piracy and anything else which may come their way. When they reached Negroponte they met another fleet, this one mainly Venetian.

The Venetians were on a crusade with Humbert II of Viennois and the Knights Hospitaller. Their target was Smyrna on the Anatolian coast and the Genoese were offered a chance to join them.

The Genoese however refused the offer heard a rumour that the crusader fleet may also take the opportunity to occupy Chios, so the Genoese sailed on to Chios, put it under siege, and took it in September.

In what was a classic Genoese manoeuvre, the Genoese freebooters then secured the island and returned home with whatever was not required for the island's defence. They then offered the island to the Republic, but as it had no money, the island was handed over to manage by the private cooperation which had financed the fleet on a twenty-year lease.

As everywhere else in Europe, Genoa was hard hit by the Black Death, which reached the city in 1348, but even the enormous loss of people could not keep the Genoese still. The size of their fleets, commercial or military, simply became smaller as did those of their enemies and the defined enemy now remained first and foremost Venice.

The Venetians resettled in Tana on the Black Sea in 1347 and the Genoese in order to protect their near-monopoly in the area spread out from their settlement in Galata and occupied a Byzantine fortress on the Bosporus.

The Byzantine Emperor, John VI Kantakouzenos, was less than impressed by this as he also had other problems with the Genoese. The Genoese in Galata had such a flair for business that most ships landing in Constantinople docked and traded, on the Genoese side of the Golden Horn. Indeed, the Genoese revenue on taxes and customs was seven times that of the Emperor, so he decided to lower the Byzantine taxes significantly to attract foreign ships to his side of the narrow strait.

The Genoese responded in August 1348 by sending an expedition across the Golden Horn, burning all the Byzantine ships they could find.

The locals responded in turn by bombarding the Genoese settlement in Galata with rocks and flaming bales, setting the Genoese warehouses on the harbour-front alight. After weeks of hostilities the matter was settled. The Genoese had realized that this was a battle they could not win, so they agreed to withdraw from the occupied areas on the Bosporus and pay the, always cash-strapped, Emperor compensation. But the troubles were only beginning.

The Genoese had no intentions of letting the Venetians gain foothold in the Black Sea and when they could not prevent them from passing through the Bosporus, they started to confiscate their ships in the Black Sea itself. Once again, the borderline between Genoese colonial politics and outright piracy was very, very, thin.

The Venetians responded by forming an alliance for the removal of Genoa, no less. They found allies in Aragon, Pisa and Byzantium, although the Venetians had to pay for half of the thirty Aragonese galleys which were put at their disposal. Genoa did not find any military allies; however, they did get support from the Ottoman beylik in Anatolia, who were only too happy to unleash their own pirates on the Venetians.

In the annals of history the war which followed is noted as beginning in 1350, but little happened until a Venetian fleet arrived in the Golden Horn in 1351, setting fire to the Genoese settlement in Galata.

The next big event also took place in Constantinople, on 13 February 1352 when Venetian and Genoese fleets met in the confluence of the Golden Horn and the Bosporus.

Given the time of year, the day was short and fighting only commenced in the afternoon. The weather conditions were adverse to manoeuvring; a condition strengthened by a strong wind from the south blowing against the current coming from the north down the Bosporus Strait.

The result was chaos, absolute chaos. Instead of a battle fought with orderly lines, the two opposing forces were simply thrown together. Visibility was limited and everybody shot at anything they could see, as often as not their own comrades in arms. Fights took place between individual ships or clusters of ships and when ships started to burn, the fire soon spread to other ships. This factor actually prolonged the battle, as it enabled fighting to continue in the dark. Finally, late in the evening, the two fleets disengaged.

The losses on both sides were horrendous. Wrecked ships and dead soldiers were floating everywhere; both forces being nearly destroyed. But the Venetians had to withdraw, leaving the Genoese in Galata and still in control of access to the Black Sea. The Byzantine Emperor had no option but to change sides. The Venetians now changed tactics.

As described in Chapter 4, Byzantium had only years before gone through a civil war and tension ran high between Matthew Kantakouzenos, the son of the Emperor, and John V Palaiologos, his son-in-law.

The Venetians now provided military support to John V Palaiologos and he attacked Matthew Kantakouzenos. This dragged the Emperor into the fight and - supported by Ottoman troops - he quelled the rebellion and banned John V Palaiologos to the island of Lemnos in 1353.

In March 1354, an earthquake hit the Gallipoli peninsula and reduced the town of Gallipoli to rubble. The Ottoman troops, still stationed there, took the opportunity to occupy the town and rebuild it. To populate it they ferried settlers across from Anatolia. The romantic Turkish version of this story is that people travelled across to Europe on rafts and anything else which would float. The reality is that they were ferried across by Genoese ships for a ducat per person, the Genoese not caring much about the cargo as long as they were being paid. A profitable deal on the day, it was ultimately the start of their own destruction.

The Venetians managed to get John V Palaiologos away from Lemnos and onto the mainland. In November he had reached Constantinople, where he was supported by the crowds and eventually also by Genoa. By December he had replaced John VI Kantakouzenos as Emperor of Byzantium.

In the meantime, in August 1354, the Venetians had also taken the war to the Genoese closer to home. A combined Venetian and Aragonese fleet beat a Genoese fleet off Sardinia, cutting off an important food-source for the city and forcing the Genoese to seek protection from the Duke of Milan.

The Duke of Milan had no interest in the Venetians overrunning Genoa, he was quite happy to divide and rule, so he asked Venice for peace. The Venetians, feeling they had the upper hand, refused absolutely.

As a consequence of Venice's refusal to have peace, the Duke of Milan assisted the Genoese in refitting their fleet, which moved on the Venetian colony in Modon where it practically destroyed the Venetian fleet.

Much to the regret of Genoa, the Duke of Milan now tried again and this time he succeeded. Peace was made, a somewhat uneasy peace, by which the

Sea of Azov, and thus the Venetian colony at Tana, was agreed to be no-go area for both parties for a period of three years. Not much had been achieved apart from near ruin of both warring parties. They did not learn much from it though; the hatred simply went too deep.

As a by-product of the war the new Byzantine Emperor gave the Island of Lesbos to a Genoese freebooter, Francesco Gattilusio as a reward for services rendered during the civil war. A somewhat strange outcome as the Emperor had won the war through assistance from Venice, but typical for the confused situation.

Back in Genoa the population soon became tired of the Milanese overlordship, so in 1356 they ousted the Milanese and appointed their own doge. Gratitude did not live long in Genoa, and neither would peace with Venice.

Exhausted the city now restarted to do what it did best, trade with a bit of piracy thrown in as and when it was opportune. Gradually it regained some of its strength, so much so that in 1373 it could send an expedition to Cyprus.

Once again it was small issue which was blown out of proportions. At the coronation of King Peter II of Cyprus in 1372, a fight broke out between the resident Genoese and Venetians about who should have preference, and the result was a raid on the Genoese quarter which led to losses in lives and property.

Led by a smaller vanguard, a substantial Genoese fleet and army arrived in Cyprus in the beginning of October and a week later it had taken Famagusta. Although it was less successful in subduing the rest of the island, Peter II had to sue for peace, and the Genoese were effectively given Famagusta. They were also given large sums of money in compensation, making the investors in the expedition, of which the state was but one, a huge profit. Genoa was back with a vengeance.

In the meantime, events unfolded which were outside of Genoa's control, but which would soon engulf them.

The Byzantine Emperor, John V Palaiologos, was looking for allies and in desperation he visited the Pope where he personally submitted to the Pope's authority, even though he could not submit on behalf of his empire. On his way back he was waylaid in Venice, where the Venetians wanted to talk to him about the Byzantine Crown Jewels which they had pawned for 30,000 ducats decades before.

The Emperor had no money, but the Venetians suggested a deal. They had realized that they could not oust the Genoese from Constantinople, but if they could control the island of Tenedos at the mouth of the Dardanelles, then they could control access to the Sea of Marmara, and thus block the Genoese.

The Venetians therefore suggested that they were given the island by the Emperor in lieu of the Crown Jewels and a substantial amount of cash. The deal suited the Emperor just fine, but he had not factored the Genoese reaction into the equation.

While John V Palaiologos was away his son Andronikos IV Palaiologos was acting as regent and there were several things he disagreed with his father about. One of these was the Venetian purchase of Tenedos, a position in which he was strongly - and possibly financially - encouraged by the Genoese community in Galata. The Emperor could agree what he wanted, Andronikos IV Palaiologos was not handing the island over and the deal between John V Palaiologos and the Venetians came to nothing.

On his return to Constantinople, John V Palaiologos was forced to assist the Ottomans militarily in Anatolia, but his son had had enough. In 1373 he revolted, was declared emperor and ousted his father. The revolt was quickly reversed and despite Sultan Murad I's insistence that Andronikos IV Palaiologos was blinded, he only lost one eye and was imprisoned.

The Venetians had not forgotten the deal they had struck with John V Palaiologos years prior, and with the Genoese having taken de-facto control of Cyprus they were back in Constantinople in 1376 offering the Emperor even more cash for Tenedos. Once again, he agreed.

This time the Genoese reacted by orchestrating Andronikos IV Palaiologos' escape from prison. He went to Murad I and asked for military assistance, for which he would get back the Gallipoli peninsula, taken from the Ottomans by Amadeus VI, Count of Savoy, a few years prior in an unassociated episode.

John V Palaiologos had nothing to use against the Ottomans, so Andronikos IV Palaiologos was soon back in Constantinople, once again replacing his father on the throne in 1377.

And once again the story twists. True to his word Andronikos IV Palaiologos ceded the Gallipoli peninsula to the Ottomans and the Island of Tenedos to the Genoese. But this time the Byzantine governor of Tenedos refused to hand it over to the Genoese. His motives can most likely be found in the fact that he shortly thereafter handed it over to Venice.

With the Genoese yet again in control of Constantinople and the Venetians in control of Tenedos, and the two parties not talking to each other, war was looming and it came the year after.

This time the Genoese were playing for keeps and they virtually surrounded Venice by allying with her neighbours; Hungary (now expanding to the Adriatic coast), Austria, Padua and Aquileia on the north-east coast of Italy.

Venice in turn allied with Milan, still smarting from the treatment they had received from the Genoese after they had bailed them out of their last conflict with Venice, and the King of Cyprus, who was keen to see the Genoese kicked out of Famagusta.

The first naval encounter went the way of Venice. Two expeditionary fleets - the Genoese counting ten galleys, the Venetian eleven, encountered each other outside Anzio on the Italian west coast in May 1378. The Venetians won the battle and destroyed half the Genoese fleet. It is telling to see how small the expeditionary fleets had become after the Black Death.

The Milanese enticed the population in Liguria to start the usual selection of local uprisings, but the Genoese managed to get a fleet of seventeen galleys off to the Adriatic Sea. The fleet wintered in Zara (at that time in Hungarian hands) and by spring it had grown to twenty-two galleys.

The Venetians responded by sending a fleet of twenty-one galleys against it. The two opponents met in May 1379 outside Pola and this time Genoa won the day, capturing fifteen Venetian galleys and nearly 3,000 prisoners.

The Venetian alliance had bought a mercenary army to attack Genoa from the north, but two could play that game so the Genoese paid them more and the army disappeared. Next the Genoese moved on Venice itself.

To understand the strategic positioning, we need to quickly look at the geography of Venice. Venice itself is situated inside a lagoon. On the southeastern side the lagoon opens towards the Adriatic Sea, but the opening is barred by three islands, moving north to south, Lido, Pellestrina and Chioggia. Access to the lagoon itself is thus only through the four narrow gaps between the islands and between the islands and the mainland.

Knowing that the Genoese were coming, the Venetians had closed off all but the southernmost access, by Chioggia, and removed all the buoys and other markers which marked the sailable routes through the shallow passages.

It was thus to Chioggia that the Genoese came, their fleet now consisting of forty-seven galleys, and by August 1379 the town and island was theirs. The Genoese were now twenty-five kilometres from Venice, which was blocked from the seaside and effectively surrounded on the landside by Genoa's allies. The majority of the Venetian fleet, under Carlo Zeno, was away from the area harassing Genoese traders in the East, so the Genoese, assisted by their allies had the advantage.

The situation was appreciated by the Venetians, and they sent out emissaries to negotiate peace, but the Genoese were not interested. This was their chance to crush Venice, taking the mother-city itself, and they wanted nothing but total victory, which they believed would present itself by starving the Venetians out.

Their position is understandable, knowing that they had the Venetians surrounded by land and sea and that the Venetian fleet was away, but they had not taken into account their own vulnerability, which was that 14,000 men, 4,000 of which were Genoese and the rest mercenaries, also required supplies and their own supply lines were thin and fragile. Furthermore, once inside the lagoon, their escape route could be cut off, and these were the two soft spots that the Venetians utilized.

First the Venetians started to raid the Genoese from inside the lagoon. Contrary to the Genoese, the Venetians did not need buoys and markers, they knew their way through the canals and passages, so they consistently pestered the besiegers and, more importantly, interrupted their supply lines from the mainland.

By December the Genoese had to send for supplies all the way from Apulia at the extreme other end of the Adriatic Sea as their local supply lines were being cut off. At this time their ally, Francesco Carrara, lord of Padua, suggested that he take over command of Chioggia and the Genoese fleet disengage so as to not be cut off, but again the Genoese refused, apparently because they had started to mine the local salt-works. Whether this was the reason or not, they stayed and it would cost them dearly.

In late December, the Venetians launched a major assault from inside the lagoon. Although they did not take Chioggia, and probably had no ambitions to do so either, they managed to sink enough ships in the remaining open access point to effectively close off the Genoese's access to the sea. The besiegers had become the besieged, and when the Venetian fleet under Carlo Zeno returned in January 1380 and placed itself outside Chioggia, the manoeuvre was complete.

The Genoese now launched several attempts to resupply their troops, but the Venetian stranglehold was too strong and in June 1380 they finally had to surrender, handing over nineteen galleys and 4,000 prisoners to the Venetians. The Mercenaries were given three days to leave; Venice had no interest in feeding them.

In Genoa the government managed to get enough money together to fight the rebellions which were still being stirred up by Milan, and to equip a small defensive fleet of thirteen galleys, but the war was lost and they knew it.

Peace negotiations started in Turin and an agreement was signed in August 1381. The fact that both warring nations were exhausted was reflected in the very even-sided agreement. Venice gave Tenedos, the original point of contention, back to Genoa under the condition that the fortifications were torn down and the island would be free to be used by both parties. The Genoese promised not to hinder the Venetian trade in the Black Sea and the Venetians promised not to interfere in Cyprus.

Nothing much had been lost or won, but the cost had been enormous.

In real terms Genoa was nearly destroyed. The cost in men, ships and money had crippled her and the national sport of internal strife did little to improve the situation. Although of course trade was restarted, and nothing in terms of territory had been given away, the state was effectively penniless, and the population could only tolerate so many taxes.

Once again, the situation became ungovernable and, after much discussion, in 1396 the city handed itself over the King Charles VI of France. As before with Milan it did not make much difference, and the French were ousted in 1409.

In 1403 the, probably, last Genoese freebooter fleet set off from Genoa for the East. It consisted of nine galleys and one great galley, an indication of how limited Genoa's capacity had become compared to the tens of galleys raised before the Black Death and the devastating wars with Venice. It made peace with the King of Cyprus, raided Alanya in Anatolia, did likewise in Syria and Beirut, abandoned an attack on Alexandria and then got into a fight with the Venetians on its way home. It was all classic stuff, but times were changing.

In 1420 King Alfonso V of Aragon had designs on Corsica, so Genoa had to send an expeditionary force to the island to protect its interests. Alfonso V then allied himself with Milan, which sent an army towards the city. As there was the usual unrest and mayhem in Genoa, the Doge simply surrendered the city to Milan to rule on the same conditions as the French before them.

This new Milanese rule turned out to work better than any other foreign rule had done before, and the next decade was one of more peace and stability than Genoa had known for a long time, but it turned out to have a flipside.

Milan had several disputes going, one of them with Florence. Florence was allied with Venice and since Genoa was under Milanese rule, Venice and Genoa again ended up at war with each other. Their conflict culminated in a small battle in 1431 in which sixteen Venetian galleys defeated nine Genoese galleys off Portofino south-east of Genoa, but nothing more came off it and peace was restored in 1433. The conflict was, however, one of the reasons the Milanese rule was abandoned again in 1435.

Around this time new development in maritime technology had begun to make Genoa both more effective and at the same time more vulnerable.

The new technology was the great sailing vessels, taking over from more traditional transport of goods by galley and smaller vessels. These new, for the times gigantic, ships were in essence capable of transporting ten times more goods with ten time less crew, something which appealed to the Genoese investors who had from the outset of Genoa's maritime adventures seen trade by sea as a profitable, although risky, way of getting a return on capital.

But where the great sailing vessels were no doubt hugely profitable, they were also vulnerable to pirates, not least so as Genoa was so poor after the endless wars and setbacks that the city could not afford to provide military ships to form armed convoys.

A sailing vessel was, of course, subject to the prevailing winds, so when all went well, they could easily outrun pirates to the nearest safe port. But when the weather went against them, they were like sitting ducks against the galleys of the pirates. However all was not necessarily lost as the battle between three great Genoese vessels and the entire Ottoman galley-fleet outside Constantinople on 20th April 1453 (described in Chapter 4) shows, as due to the sheer height of the great vessels the defenders had a distinct advantage over the low-lying galleys and the ship-mounted cannon, now gradually being introduced, were not powerful enough to make any impression on the stout timbers of the great vessels.

However another disadvantage of these new vessels were that they were far more seagoing than their predecessors, enabling traders from northern Europe to start penetrating into the Mediterranean Sea and, indeed, made it possible for even Genoese merchants to sail from, say, Chios directly to the ports on the Atlantic Coast of Europe, bypassing Genoa itself, generating wealth for Genoese traders, but not for the city. The Genoese business model, favouring the individual over the state, had started to turn on its master.

The next time we see the Genoese emerge in a supporting role is in 1444. As described in Chapter 4, Sultan Murad II, Mehmed II's father, found himself in Anatolia with his army, while a Christian army was progressing south along the coast of the Black Sea. Murad II needed his army ferried across to Europe, sooner rather than later, but found the Dardanelles blocked by Venetian ships.

Murad II marched his army north to the Bosporus and there he found Genoese ships working out of Galata. The Genoese had not signed up for the Christian campaign (a crusade no less), so at a price of one gold ducat a head, they transported the Ottoman army across the strait and enabled Murad II to proceed to Varna and crush the Christian army.

It was suspected, but never proven, that once the Genoese set out on this profitable venture, the Venetians in Constantinople soon followed their example, but whereas the Venetians got off, the Genoese subsequently faced the wrath of the Pope and were excommunicated. Though not for long as soon the Pope would have bigger issues to be concerned about than renegade Genoese captains, namely the emergence of the new Ottoman Sultan, Mehmed II, and his aggressive stance towards Constantinople.

When Mehmed II's intentions on a direct assault on Constantinople became clear during 1452 and 1453, the Byzantine Emperor appealed for help from near and far, but the only ones who provided anything over and above encouraging words were the Pope and the Genoese, by now forgiven for their previous sins.

The Pope paid for 400 archers and the Genoese paid for a small fleet carrying 700 mercenaries, the latter under the command of Giovanni Giustiniani Longo, and once again the Genoese business model was at work. These reinforcements did not, officially, represent the Genoese state, but were a private initiative by Giovanni Giustiniani Longo. This way the Genoese could participate in the defence of Constantinople, but at the same time claim that they had taken no part in it.

This may seem a bit farfetched, but fact of the matter was that Genoa's incapability to control its own citizens in terms of piracy and other independent ventures was such an accepted fact that they long since had established an official Genoese State Department responsible for compensation to anyone who had been attacked by Genoese pirates during times of declared peace. If anyone could get away with this double play it was Genoa.

But the Genoese had to play it carefully. As much as they were on the side of the Byzantines, who by that time they completely controlled, and as much as they had little appetite for the Ottomans controlling the Bosporus and access to the Black Sea, it was after all a business transaction, and there was a solid risk that the Ottomans would win.

Into that equation came the Genoese colony in Galata, surrounded by a wall, but not a wall designed to hold back a determined army with cannon and - if the Genoese was seen as enemies of the Ottomans - sure to fall prey to their attack on Constantinople itself.

So, the Genoese played it down the middle. Giovanni Giustiniani Longo and his mercenaries made up a critical part of the Byzantine defences and at the same time the Genoese in Galata declared themselves neutral in the conflict and happily supplied either side with what goods could be provided amongst the growing shortages caused by the Ottoman blockade of land and sea. Having said that, a large number of Genoese from Galata crossed the Golden Horn to take part in the defence of Constantinople and as long as the Ottoman fleet was outside the Golden Horn, the merchants of Galata kept the city supplied.

The Genoese neutrality worked to such an extent that when Mehmed II's mortars, placed behind Galata, shot at the Byzantine fleet and mistakenly hit Genoese trading vessels and some houses in Galata, the Genoese went to complain to Mehmed II and demand compensation. This at the same time as the Genoese flag was riding on top of the Theodosian Wall and Giovanni Giustiniani Longo was commanding the land defence of Constantinople. Remarkably, the Genoese rouse worked.

The Venetians in Constantinople had done their best to escape the city before the Ottoman siege and had managed to ferry some 700 soldiers as well as a good part of the Venetian contingent away from the city. The remaining Venetians had been forced to stay and fight, but they played a substantially lesser role than the Genoese mercenaries. Despite this the Venetians in Constantinople were treated like all others and the Venetian bailo was executed in the days immediately following the Ottoman conquest.

Contrary to this, the Genoese were left alone. On 29th May, the day of the Conquest of Constantinople, they had presented the keys to their city to Mehmed II, distancing themselves from Constantinople itself. On 2 June, only three days after the conquest, Mehmed II arrived at Galata in person to settle affairs with the Genoese. They were ordered to demolish the defences, apart from the seawalls, but otherwise were left unharmed and their property was guaranteed. Anyone who had left was given three month to return, after which their property would be confiscated. Ottomans were forbidden access to Galata and the Genoese given permission to carry on using their churches as long as did not use the bells and did not build any new churches. The inhabitants in Galata were given a tax exemption even though Genoese traders from outside Galata would have to pay customs.

All in all it looked as if the Genoese had gotten off lightly despite their somewhat ambivalent effort during the siege, but fact is that Mehmed II had more pressing issues than Genoa on his agenda and he would, as we will see, demonstrate that he had a long memory and sooner or later would get around to dealing with the Genoese.

So let us make a quick status check on the Genoese possessions in the Ottoman sphere of interest following the Ottoman Conquest of Constantinople.

On a headline basis, things did not look too bad considering. The Genoese had retained their crucial presence in Galata and although they would have to pay the Ottomans for access to the Black Sea that was a business expense which could be recovered through prizing. On the Black Sea itself the Genoese still had their possession on the Crimea, centred around Caffa, but they also had a colony in Amasra, a Black Sea port on the north coast of Anatolia, which had been under Genoese control since 1261 and the aftermath of the Byzantine Reconquest of Constantinople.

In the Aegean the Genoese had the islands of Lesbos, controlled by the Gattilusio family, Chios, controlled by a private consortium (Maona di Chio e di Focea) and Samos, controlled by the Giustiniani family.

On the Anatolian west coast, the Genoese controlled Phokia and Phokianova (modern day Foça and Yenifoça in Turkey), famed for alum mines, which the Genoese also had controlled since 1261. Another strand of the Gattilusio family controlled the town of Enez on the northern coast of the Aegean Sea along with the islands of Samothrace and Imroz. Finally, the Genoese had control of the town of Famagusta in Cyprus, but not control of the rest of the island.

Although Genoa was only a shadow of its former self, it still had good trading posts in the East and, contrary to the Venetians; they did not pose a military risk to the Ottomans. The fact is, that they could not even afford to protect their own trading vessels, so immediately following the Conquest of Constantinople they were left alone while Mehmed II focused his effort on military matters.

Despite this rosy outlook, the Genoese soon found themselves in conflict with Mehmed II. Without an outright military motive, Mehmed II's motivations were money and piracy, in addition to his long memory regarding the Genoese effort in the defence of Constantinople.

Moneywise Mehmed II simply wanted the profit from the Genoese trade. He needed money to muster armies and whereas for a short time he was willing to just tax the Genoese, his longer-term ambition was to take over.

Piracy had long been a Genoese trademark and the Genoese-held islands in the Aegean were notorious for harbouring pirates, Genoese or otherwise (in particular Catalan), pirates who had no hesitation when it came to attacking Ottoman ships. Where other trading states, including the impotent Byzantines, had satisfied themselves with seeking compensation from the Genoese state, and had been prepared to spend resources to defend their traders, Mehmed II would have none of that.

And so, Mehmed II began a slow, but systematic conquest of the Genoese possession within his field of interest.

The first sign of Mehmed's ambitions came in 1454, only a year after the Conquest of Constantinople. An Ottoman fleet of fifty-six vessels appeared before Caffa in a coordinated effort with the Khan of Crimea who laid siege to the city from the landside. The Khan was bought off with a promise of a yearly tribute, but a similar demand from the Ottomans was initially answered with a request to seek permission from Genoa. The Ottomans did not fall for that, so a tribute was agreed, for which the Genoese were allowed to transport a specific amount of grain through the Bosporus. This time the Genoese managed to pay their way out of trouble, but it would not stay like that.

The following year the Ottomans were back, this time in the Aegean. An attempt on Chios failed, an Ottoman galley was sunk in the process, but in November the Ottomans took Phokianova followed by Phokia before the end of the year. Mehmed II now controlled the lucrative Alum mines, a severe blow to Genoa.

It is worth noticing that contrary to Venice, who as seen in the previous chapter, reacted with determination when Mehmed II threatened their colonies, the Genoese simply did not have resources to fight a war. They watched in anger and despair, but they did nothing of a concerted nature to stop him.

Following up on his successes, Mehmed II was back in early 1456. This time the target was Enez, a campaign led by Mehmed II himself in which the town surrendered without a fight. The Ottoman fleet cleaned up by taking the islands of Imroz and Samothrace, capturing their ruler, Dorino Gattilusio, in the process. Dorino Gattilusio now ceded his, already occupied, possessions to Mehmed II and was in return given a fief in Macedonia.

The Genoese were now left alone for a few years while Mehmed II campaigned elsewhere, but in 1459 the turn had come to Amasra. In hindsight it was only a matter of time before Mehmed II would take this lonely and isolated colony on the north coast of Anatolia. An Ottoman fleet appeared before Amasra in the autumn of 1459, and the town surrendered without a fight. Despite their surrender, two thirds of the population were forcefully moved off to Istanbul as part of Mehmed II's repopulation project.

Back home the Genoese went through the, all too familiar, merry-go-round in turns of government. In 1458 they put themselves under the rule of Charles VII of France, only to negate on French rule again in 1461 leading up to renewed Milanese rule from 1468.

By then the Ottomans had been further chipping away at Genoa's pocket-empire.

In 1462 Mehmed II once again appeared before a Genoese town, this time Mytilene, the capital of Lesbos. The Ottomans laid siege, but the defenders only held for fifteen days before they surrendered. This time one third of the population was allowed to stay, one third was moved to Istanbul and the last third was given to the Ottoman Janissaries as slaves. The ruler of Lesbos, Niccolo Gattilusio, was less fortunate than his kinsman, the former ruler of Enez. He was taken as prisoner to Istanbul where, despite converting to Islam in an attempt to avoid his fate, he was subsequently executed.

The only Genoese possessions in the East now consisted of Caffa, Chios and the town of Famagusta. The latter was lost in 1464, but to a local revolt rather than the Ottomans.

It must have been clear to the Genoese that their remaining colonies would sooner or later be threatened by Mehmed II, but once again a few years of calm followed while Mehmed II was busy elsewhere.

In 1469 Mehmed II was busy building up his fleet, something which was too big an operation to be kept a secret. With the relative ease with which he had taken the Genoese possessions in the Aegean Sea and Anatolia, Mehmed II now decided to see if he could get the Genoese on Chios to surrender. He started a rumour that his new fleet was aimed at Chios, and he sent letters to that extent with a Genoese merchant, Marcantino Perusin, to be smuggled into Chios in order to cause a revolt. The letters and Marcantino Perusin were, however, intercepted before they could be landed in Chios and Marcantino Perusin was hanged while a co-conspirator, Galleazzo Giustiniani, was torn to pieces by a mob.

The following year a messenger arrived from Mehmed II demanding that Chios should send sixty caulkers and all the oared vessels in the region to support Mehmed II's effort, but the Chiots refused, sent their tribute instead and strengthened their fortifications in preparation for an attack. The attack never came though, as Mehmed II's fleet was destined for his conquest of Venetian Negroponte (see the previous chapter) and Mehmed II never went back to Chios again. Indeed, the island stayed in Genoese hands until 1566 when the Ottomans, under Mehmed II's great-grandson, Suleiman I, finally absorbed the island into the empire.

But whereas the island of Chios avoided Ottoman invasion, the Genoese colony at Caffa was less fortunate.

As described earlier, Caffa was located on the south coast of the Crimean peninsula. As a narrow band behind it laid the small Principality of Theodoro (see Chapter 8) but the principal occupants of the peninsula were the Crimean Tatars, descendants of the Mongols.

The Tatars were in principle vassals of the Ottomans, although they were mainly autonomous. Their relationship with the Genoese was at times rather tense, but they had an agreement by which the Tatars had a representation in

Caffa, not unlike the Genoese colony in Constantinople, which was headed by a *tudun*, who was appointed by the Tatar Khan, but only after consultation with the Genoese.

In 1473 the Tudun, Marmak, died and was initially succeeded by his brother Eminek. But Marmak's wife tried to have her son, Sertak, appointed instead. The matter went to the Khan, Mengli Giray, who ended up appointing his own candidate, Kirai Mirza.

The Genoese then put pressure on the Khan to change his mind by threatening to release from their prisons the Khan's brothers, whom had been detained when a war of succession had broken out on the previous Khan's death. In this aspect they had learned well from the Byzantines.

The Khan changed his mind and appointed Sertak, but the Tatar nobles were so much against this that they resorted to appeal to the Tatar's nominal overlord, Mehmed II, asking him to intervene on behalf of Eminek.

To Mehmed II this was the perfect excuse to go deal with Caffa once and for all and take total control of the Black Sea trade.

When Mehmed II took the throne in 1451, there was no Ottoman fleet of note. When the Ottoman fleet, under the command of Gedik Ahmet Pasha, sailed for Caffa in 1475 it consisted of 280 galleys, 3 galleons, 170 freighters and 120 ships loaded with horses. That was an enormous fleet, the biggest fleet one single nation could muster at the time, and it demonstrates how Mehmed II's ambitions to control the seas around his empire had been fulfilled in just twenty-five years.

On 1 June 1475, the Ottomans laid siege to Caffa, On 6 June the town surrendered as most of the citizens supported Eminek anyhow. The Ottoman commander had promised to spare the lives of the inhabitants, and although he proved good on his word, it was not necessarily in the fashion the Genoese had envisaged.

The town was sacked and 3,000 people enslaved. The Italians in the town were forcefully moved to Istanbul. Eminek was reinstated as tudun, but his masters were now Ottoman. The Genoese adventure in the Black Sea had finally come to an end.

By coincidence, the Ottomans had captured the Tatar Khan who was in the area. He was sent to Istanbul, but later released and sent back, his vassalage confirmed.

With Caffa gone, the Genoese colony in Galata, for more than two centuries the centre-point of Genoese trade in the East, had lost its *raison d'être*. It literally was on the road to nowhere. As a consequence, it gradually shrank in size until by the end of the fifteenth century Galata was mainly populated by Ottomans and Greeks.

With the lucrative trade in the East all but destroyed, the Genoese continued their fall from the heights of commercial dominance. Mehmed II did not push them over the edge, they were already in free fall by the time he appeared on the scene, reduced in size and importance by their own internal troubles and the catastrophic wars with Venice in particular.

The internal trouble in Genoa continued. The city put itself under Milanese rule several times, and each time they then tore themselves loose again, attempting one way of self-governing or the other. In the beginning of the sixteenth century, they once again came under French rule, but in 1528 they finally formed a stable republic, initially led by Andrea Doria, and under Spanish suzerainty. This format more or less held until Napoleon first made it a French dependant in 1797 and then annexed Genoa as part of France in 1805.

In the last few centuries of its existence Genoa transformed from the maritime state it once was, to a state that primarily sold its manufactured goods and, even more so, a state that specialized in lending money to other states and rulers, a business which was less dangerous, but not necessarily less profitable, than trading on the high seas.

PART 5

THE BALKANS

12 - THE BULGARIAN EMPIRES
13 - HUNGARY
14 - THE BUFFER STATES
15 - ALBANIA

Part 5 - The Balkans

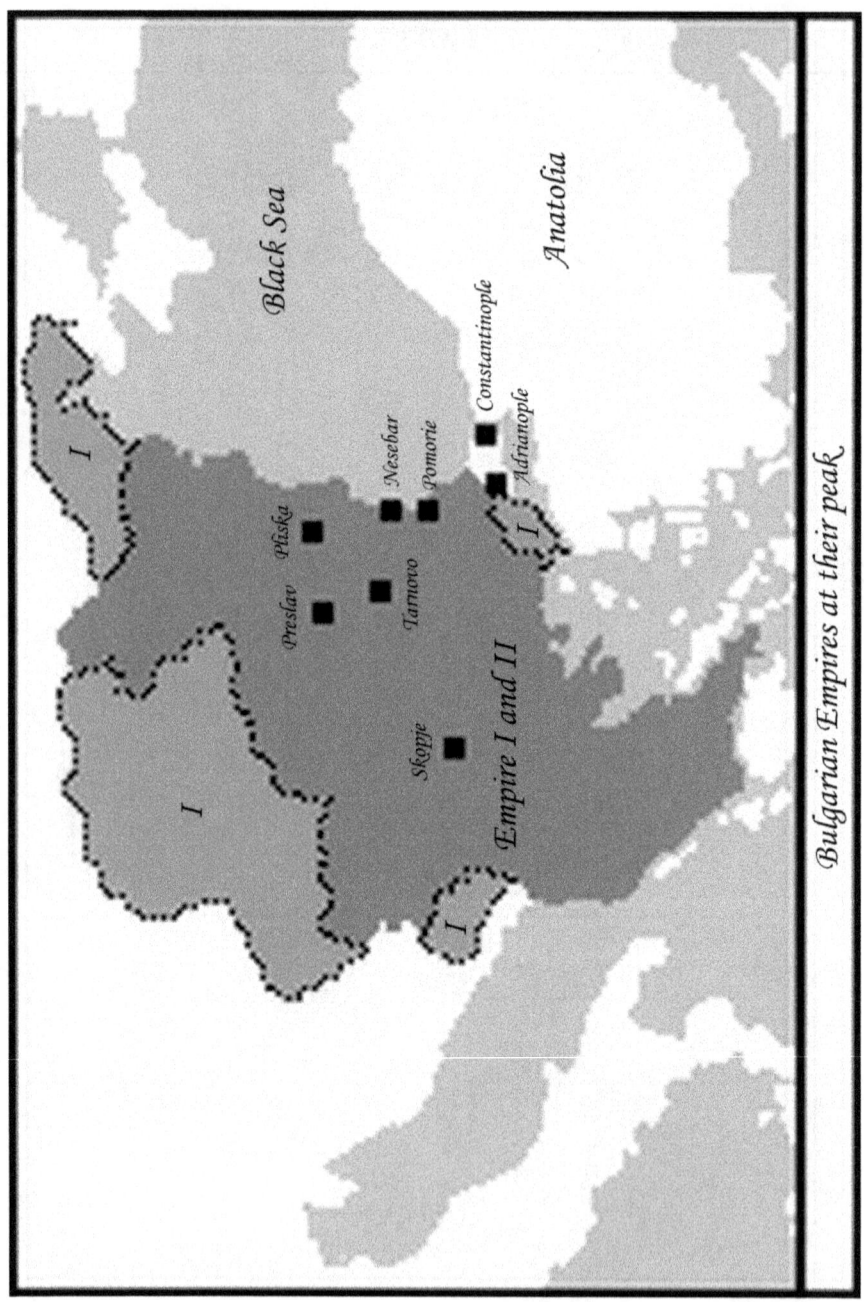

Bulgarian Empires at their peak

12 - THE BULGARIAN EMPIRES

Part 5 - The Balkans

CRITICAL TIMELINE

Year	Event	Involved Parties
Late 600s	'Bulgars' migrate into Byzantine territories south of the Danube River.	Bulgaria Byzantium
680	Battle of Ongal forces Byzantium to recognize Bulgarian state and pay tribute	Bulgaria Byzantium
702	Bulgarians under assist Tervel Justinian II with conquest of Constantinople	Bulgaria Byzantium
708	First Battle of Anchialus	Bulgaria Byzantium
718	Bulgarian army attack Arab besiegers of Constantinople	Bulgaria Byzantium Muslim Empire
719	Bulgarians assist Anastasios II in failed attempt on Constantinople	Bulgaria Byzantium
755	Bulgarian defeat at the Anastasian Wall	Bulgaria Byzantium
756	Byzantine attack on Bulgaria	Bulgaria Byzantium
759	Byzantine attack on Bulgaria ambushed at Rishki Pass	Bulgaria Byzantium
763	Second Battle of Anchialus	Bulgaria Byzantium
774	Byzantine attack on Varna	Bulgaria Byzantium
780	Abandoned Byzantine campaign in Bulgaria	Bulgaria Byzantium
792	Battle at Marcellae. Byzantium agrees to pay tribute	Bulgaria Byzantium
803	Krum becomes Khan of Bulgaria	Bulgaria
805	Bulgarians overrun Avars and take Sofia	Bulgaria Byzantium
809	Byzantine campaign burns Pliska and takes Sofia	Bulgaria Byzantium
811	Byzantine campaign is ambushed and Emperor Nikephoros I is killed	Bulgaria Byzantium
813	Battle at Adrianople. Assassination attempt on Krum	Bulgaria Byzantines
816	Thirty-year peace agreement signed	Bulgaria Byzantium
827	Clashes between Bulgaria and Frankia	Bulgaria Frankia
829	Clashes between Bulgaria and Frankia	Bulgaria Frankia
831	Byzantine attack on Bulgaria	Bulgaria Byzantium
839	War breaks out with new Serbian State	Bulgaria Serbia

12 - The Bulgarian Empires

Year	Event	Involved Parties
852	Boris I becomes Khan of Bulgaria	Bulgaria
854	Bulgaria suffers setbacks in attack on Frankia and Serbia	Bulgaria Frankia
855	Bulgarians suffers setbacks against Croatia and Byzantium	Bulgaria Byzantium Croatia
855	Catholic Missionaries arrive in Bulgaria	Bulgaria The Pope
856	Boris I secures peace with Byzantium	Bulgaria Byzantium
863	Conflict with Byzantium. Orthodox missionaries replace catholic missionaries	Bulgaria Byzantium
864	Boris I is baptized	Bulgaria Byzantium
866	Letters exchanged between Boris I and Pope Nicolas I. Catholic missionaries arrive	Bulgaria The Pope
870	The Patriarch grants the Bulgarian Church status as an autocephalous archbishopric. Bulgaria becomes orthodox	Bulgaria Byzantium
893	Simeon I becomes Khan of Bulgaria	Bulgaria
895	Byzantine and Magyar attack on Bulgaria	Bulgaria Byzantium Magyars
896	Battle of Boulgarophygon. Byzantium pays tribute to Bulgaria. Bulgarians and Pechenegs defeat Magyars	Bulgaria Byzantium Magyars
913	Bulgarian siege of Constantinople	Bulgaria Byzantium
915	Bulgarian siege of Adrianople	Bulgaria Byzantium
917	Third Battle of Anchialus	Bulgaria Byzantium
924	Abandoned Bulgarian attack on Constantinople. Simeon I declared Emperor	Bulgaria Byzantium
926	Unsuccessful Bulgarian campaign in Croatia	Bulgaria Byzantium
965	Byzantium stops paying tribute. Attack by Rus allies of Byzantium	Bulgaria Byzantium Rus
969	Bulgaria invaded by Rus	Bulgaria Byzantium Rus
972	Byzantine attack on Rus in Bulgaria. Bulgaria becomes Byzantine province	Bulgaria Byzantium Rus
976	Boris II is killed. Roman becomes nominal Bulgarian Emperor	Bulgaria Byzantium
986	Byzantine army ambushed at Trajan's Gate	Bulgaria Byzantium

Part 5 - The Balkans

Year	Event	Involved Parties
991	Byzantium starts years-long campaign in Bulgaria	Bulgaria Byzantium
1000	Byzantine campaign restarts with Venice campaigning in Dalmatia	Bulgaria Byzantium Venice
1014	Battle of Kleidion	Bulgaria Byzantium
1018	Final Byzantine defeat of First Bulgarian Empire	Bulgaria Byzantium
1041	Short-lived Bulgarian revolt	Bulgaria Byzantium
1185	Bulgarian revolt. Peter IV appointed Emperor of Bulgaria	Bulgaria Byzantium
1190	Battle of Tryavna	Bulgaria Byzantium
1194	Battle of Arcadiopolis	Bulgaria Byzantium
1202	Hungarian invasion	Bulgaria Hungary
1203	The Pope appoints Kaloyan King of the Bulgarians	Bulgaria The Pope
1204	Fourth Crusade	Byzantium
1205	Baldwin I of Constantinople killed in battle	Bulgaria Constantinople
1207	Boniface of Montferrat killed in battle	Bulgaria Constantinople
1218	Ivan Asen II becomes Emperor of Bulgaria	Bulgaria
1230	Battle of Klokotnitsa	Bulgaria Epirus
1235	Alliance with Empire of Nicaea.	Bulgaria Nicaea
1242	Bulgaria agrees to pay tribute to Golden Horde	Bulgaria Golden Horde
1257	Constantine Tikh becomes Emperor of Bulgaria	Bulgaria
1261	Byzantine reconquest of Constantinople	Byzantium
1264	Bulgarian incursion into Byzantium	Bulgaria Byzantium Golden Horde
1274	Mongol raids into Bulgaria start	Bulgaria Golden Horde
1280	George I becomes Emperor of Bulgaria	Bulgaria
1292	George I abdicates and flee to Constantinople	Bulgaria
1299	Chaka becomes Emperor of Bulgaria	Bulgaria Golden Horde
1300	Chaka is murdered. Theodore Svetoslav becomes Emperor of Bulgaria	Bulgaria Golden Horde
1307	Peace with Byzantium	Bulgaria Byzantium

12 - The Bulgarian Empires

Year	Event	Involved Parties
1324	New peace agreement with Byzantium	Bulgaria, Byzantium
1328	New peace agreement with Byzantium	Bulgaria, Byzantium
1330	Unsuccessful Bulgarian attack on Serbia	Bulgaria, Serbia
1331	Ivan Alexander becomes Emperor of Bulgaria	Bulgaria
1348	Black Death reached Bulgaria	Bulgaria
1350s	Ottoman raids on Bulgaria. Bulgarian Empire starts to disintegrate. Hungary annexes Moldavia	Bulgaria, Ottomans, Hungary
1363	Ottomans annex Adrianople (Edirne)	Bulgaria, Ottomans
1366	Stand-off with Byzantium over Byzantine Emperor's passage through Bulgaria	Bulgaria, Byzantium
1371	Ivan Alexander dies and the Bulgarian state split up	Bulgaria
1373	Bulgarian Emperor accepts vassalage to Ottomans	Bulgaria, Ottomans
1385	Ottomans take Sofia	Bulgaria, Ottomans
1386	Battle of Pločnik.	Ottomans, Serbia
1387	Bulgaria cancels vassalage to Ottomans	Bulgaria, Ottomans
1389	First Battle of Kosovo	Ottomans, Serbia
1393	Ottoman invasion of Bulgaria	Bulgaria, Ottomans
1395	Ottoman mop-up operations in Bulgaria	Bulgaria, Ottomans
1396	Battle of Nicopolis. Bulgarian state becomes an Ottoman province.	Bulgaria, Ottomans

Part 5 - The Balkans

12 - The Bulgarian Empires

Where do you start to tell the story of the melting pot which is the Balkans? There is no good point, or indeed any bad point. As no matter when or where you dwell into the history of this region riddled with faultlines, something interesting happens.

So we could start with the Dacians, the Romans, the Celts, the Huns, the Goths, the Slavs or the Avars, to mention a few of the peoples who came and went, but to reasonably stay within the subject matter we shall start with the First Bulgarian Empire.

In the early part of the seventh century the Turkic state of 'Old Great Bulgaria', located on the northern shores of the Black Sea, disintegrated and its peoples, known as 'Bulgars' started migrating. One of the migration strands went south-west, establishing themselves in the area north of the river Danube.

Here they had powerful neighbours. To the north they had the Avars and to the south, across the river, they had the Byzantine Empire.

Once settled the - semi nomadic - Bulgars started to raid into the neighbouring territories, in term of the Byzantines that meant that the Bulgars crossed the River Danube where they initially raided, but eventually started to settle and mix with the existing population.

Another strand of migrants from Old Great Bulgaria had moved west and then south, arriving in the western parts of the Balkans and northern parts of Greece and soon the two strands of Bulgars started to challenge Byzantine sovereignty in the Balkans. In this context they allied themselves with the seven Slav tribes who had also settled in the Balkans over the preceding centuries.

The problem the Byzantines had at that time was that their main focus was in the East, where the emerging Arab state put their eastern provinces under severe pressure. As we have seen throughout this book, empires are vulnerable to simultaneous pressure on both sides of their territory, so the Byzantines' focus on the Arabs meant that the Bulgars had the opportunity to settle and consolidate with little Byzantine interference.

In 674 the Arab armies laid siege to Constantinople, a siege that would last for more than five years, but finally in 680 the Byzantines drove the Arabs away (see also Chapter 3).

With the Arabs beaten, it was time for the Byzantines to clean up their front-yard and the Emperor, Constantine IV, first sent a fleet on an unsuccessful expedition against the Bulgars and then marched to meet them at the River Danube.

The Bulgars and Slavs had united into a - multi-ethnic - single political entity under Asparukh, who had originally led the south-western migration into the Balkans, and with the Byzantine army on the march they withdrew to the island of Peuce, an island located at the River Danube's confluence with the Black Sea and which has now disappeared due to changes in the rivers flow.

In theory the Byzantines should have mopped up the Bulgarians with relative ease. The Byzantine army consisted of 25,000 battle hardened men-at-arms, against which stood 10,000 nomadic horsemen. The battle is known as the Battle of Ongal and it did not go the Byzantines' way.

The Bulgarians had cleverly located their fortifications in a swampy area, forcing the Byzantines to split the army up in smaller units, depleting their numerical superiority. They tried to storm the Bulgarian palisades several times, but with little success.

The defining moment was, however, caused by the Byzantine Emperor's bad health. He had leg pains and decided to go to the nearby town of Nesebar to seek treatment. A rumour started that he had fled the battlefield and the Byzantine army broke and started a headless retreat, pursued by Bulgarian cavalry who nearly annihilated them.

Though the Byzantines would come back with half-hearted campaigns towards the end of the decade, the Battle of Ongal forced the Byzantines to recognize the Bulgarian Khanate (Empire) and even pay them a tribute to keep the peace while the Byzantines again focused on the Arab threat in the East.

The Bulgarian Khanate at the time went from the river Dnieper in the north-east in a south-western band to the River Danube north of Vidin and south to just north of Sofia, with the capital city at Pliska, but their influence-sphere was spreading through the Balkans and into Greece.

While the Byzantines were busy looking east, the Bulgarians were consolidating and expanding and their Khan, Asparukh, was killed in battle against the Khazars on the Bulgarian north-eastern border around 695.

Asparukh was followed by Tervel, assumed to be his son, and while Tervel consolidated his reign the Byzantines excelled at their favourite sport, that of regicide.

Emperor Constantine IV died in 685 and was succeeded by his son Justinian II. The people had high hopes for Justinian II, but when he failed to deliver and turned out to be exceedingly stubborn and opposed to any criticism he was overthrown by a military coup. His nose was slit, as tradition had it that you could not be emperor without a nose and he was sent off to exile in the Crimea.

Justinian II's successor was the general Leontios. But when he failed to deliver the military success which was expected of him - indeed he lost North Africa to the Arabs - he in turn was overthrown by the army. Leontios had his nose slit too and was put in a convent in Constantinople.

Leontos' successor was a Germanic navy officer called Apsimaros, who quickly changed his name to Tiberios III. Opposite to his predecessor, Tiberios III turned out to be exactly the kind of warlike emperor the Byzantines needed, and he was successful against the Arabs in the East.

Justinian II was, however, not done with. In 704 he managed to escape from the Crimea and sought refuge with the Khazar Khan further north. Here he married one of the Khan's sisters who was renamed Theodora. When the Byzantine Emperor tried to bribe the Khazar Khan to kill Justinian II it was Theodora who warned him and they fled west into the Bulgarian Empire.

Justinian II now convinced Tervel to help him and in 705 he marched on Constantinople ahead of a Bulgarian army. The army laid siege to Constantinople while Justinian II tried, in vain, to convince the population to open the gates.

In a scenario which has a very strong resemblance to the later Reconquest of Constantinople in 1261 (see Chapter 3); some of the soldiers found an unused - and forgotten - passage under the walls and a small expeditionary force was sent into the city. On their arrival the citizens panicked, and the Emperor fled across to Anatolia, where he was soon captured.

Justinian II now had both the former emperors, Leontios and Tiberios III brought in chains to him at the Hippodrome before they were sent off to be beheaded. By this time Justinian II was wearing a nose-prosthesis of solid gold and had proven that an emperor does not need a nose after all.

For the Bulgarian Khan Tervel the situation was good. Like the Genoese would centuries later benefit from their alliance with Michael VIII Palaiologos, Tervel benefitted from his support of Justinian II despite the fact that not a shot had been fired.

Tervel was given land in northern Greece, was declared Caesar, second in the Byzantine Empire only to the Emperor himself, and was promised marriage to the Emperor's daughter (from his first marriage) Anastasia. It is generally believed that this marriage, however, did not actually take place.

One reason could be that Justinian II did not keep the peace with Tervel for long, but rather tried to invade the Bulgarian Empire in 708 but was defeated by Tervel at the (First) Battle of Anchialus near Pomorie on the Bulgarian Black Sea coast.

When, in 711, Justinian II was in trouble, facing internal revolt led by Philippikos Bardanes, he again turned to Tervel for help, but Tervel was somewhat unenthusiastic and sent only 3,000 men in support. When it became clear that Justinian II did not have popular support the Bulgarians turned bystanders and when Justinian II was executed, the new emperor, Philippikos Bardanes, simply sent them home.

Philippikos Bardanes did not last long as emperor himself. He was ousted by a military coup in 713 and followed by Anastasios II, who was also ousted by a military coup from which emerged Theodosios III, who was ousted by a military coup in 717 and followed by Leo III.

The musical-thrones in Byzantium of course gave the Bulgarians a free hand to consolidate themselves. Tervel had - it is believed though the sources are unclear - died in 715 and after a short war of succession he was followed by Kormesiy. Emperor Theodosios III had in 716 made an agreement with the Bulgarians that they would help the Byzantines in the ongoing defence against the Arabs, and it is in this context we see the Bulgarians emerge next.

Not much to anyone's surprise the Arabs came to Constantinople in 717 and laid siege to the city. The Byzantine fleet destroyed the Arab fleet by means of Greek Fire, leaving the Arab army unsupplied over winter, a winter that turned out to be bitterly cold and killed many men and animals. With spring 718 approaching, and further attempts to resupply and reinforce the stranded besiegers failed, the Bulgarians kept to their agreement and swept in from the north, forcing the remaining Arabs to abandon the siege.

It has been speculated by historians that the Bulgarians decided on attacking the Arab besiegers less for their love of Constantinople and more for their own desire to conquer it when the time was right, but it must, on the other hand, also have been a dire prospect to potentially replace as neighbours the impotent Byzantines with the powerful Arabs.

In 719 one of the previous emperors, Anastasios II, attempted to take the throne back. He enlisted the help of the Bulgarians who issued him with both money and troops. No doubt the Bulgarians saw an opportunity here to put their own puppet on the throne, but as it turned out the population of Byzantium had no desire for having Anastasios II back. When this became clear, and with Emperor Leo III writing to Kormesiy reminding him of their alliance, the Bulgarians packed up and went home, leaving Anastasios II to the mercy of his enemies, mercy which he did not find as he was executed by Leo III.

Now a period of peace followed. Leo III turned out to be longer lasting than his immediate predecessors, ruling until 741, and at Kormesiy's death in 721 he in turn was replaced by Sevar, who had no aggressive intentions towards Byzantium, but satisfied himself with the annual tribute they paid.

Sevar died in 737 and was replaced by Kormisosh and when Leo III died and was replaced by his son Constantine V in 741, things started to turn for the worse.

Constantine V was a capable military leader and started out with some success against the Arabs. Indeed, he was so successful recapturing parts of Syria that he could resettle former Byzantine people from Syria to Greece, which he did in 746 and 752. The purpose was not only to get them away from the Arabs, but as much to bring more Byzantine blood into areas that were being populated by Bulgarians.

In addition to this ethnic engineering, Constantine V started to build fortresses on the border to Bulgaria, and the combined effort made

Kormisosh react and demand an increase in the tribute paid by Byzantium. When that was not forthcoming he marched on Constantinople, but was defeated by Constantine V at or around the Anastasian Wall, a 56 km long outer defensive wall stretching from the Sea of Marmara to the Blacks Sea some 60 km west of Istanbul. The wall had at that time fallen into disrepair and had in any case never been an effective deterrent in itself, but on this one occasion it showed its worth.

The defeat cost Kormisosh his throne and he was replaced by Vinekh. Initially it did not go much better for him when Constantine V came in 756, first with a naval attack on the Bulgarian settlements on the Danube Delta and then with the Byzantine army moving into Greece. The armies met at Marcellae and once again the Byzantines were victorious. As part of a peace settlement, Vinekh had to send some of his children as hostages to Constantinople.

It was however Constantine V, rather than Vinekh, who three years later broke the peace again and marched on Bulgaria.

Vinekh was no fool and anticipating the move he had fortified the strategic passes in the mountains that separated the two empires. When the Byzantines reached the Rishki Pass they were ambushed and practically destroyed. Vinekh, possibly due to the reason that his children were being held as hostages, did not follow up on the Bulgarian success with any territorial gains, an act that made him unpopular and he was assassinated in 762 and replaced by Telets.

Telets was warlike and immediately started raiding Byzantine territories, as well as challenging the Byzantine Emperor to a personal test of strength. Constantine V however preferred marching with an army and the two armies met in 763 in the (Second) Battle of Anchialus on the Black Sea coast.

Constantine V had brought both an army and a navy, and Telets had fortified the mountain passes as before. His bravado, however, compelled him to abandon the fortified passes and line up to meet the Byzantines in open combat. The result was catastrophic even though the Byzantines took such heavy losses as well that they could not press their advantage, but nevertheless returned home in triumph.

The defeat cost Telets his life in 765 and he was replaced by Sabin. He, however, preferred diplomacy over warfare so he started negotiations with Constantine V, but when this was discovered he had to flee (to Constantinople) and he was replaced by Umor who lasted a whole forty days before he was replaced by Toktu, who lasted a whole year before he was replaced by Pagan in 767.

Pagan started negotiations with Constantine V and achieved a peace agreement. Constantine V then immediately violated it by taking his army as far as the Bulgarian capital of Pliska itself, after which Pagan was ousted and replaced by Telerig, the seventh Bulgarian Khan in less than a decade.

As playing musical thrones had previously weakened the Byzantines, it was now the Bulgarians who found themselves the weaker party. Telerig started his reign with a few years of peace. It did however not last as in 774 Constantine V attacked Varna.

Even though a peace agreement was made again, Telerig raided into Macedonia and removed the locals to Bulgaria. Constantine V responded by marching an army of 80,000 men into the field to once again beat the Bulgarians in open battle. Now Telerig however showed that he was better at diplomacy than warfare.

He let Constantine V know that his position as khan was threatened and that he was looking to seek refuge in Constantinople, a very plausible scenario given the developments in the Bulgarian Empire in the preceding decade. He then asked Constantine V for a list of people he could trust if he had to flee and he was issued with a list of all the Byzantine agents in Bulgaria. Telerig now had what he wanted and had all the agents murdered.

As Constantine V died in 775 no more came of the affair and Telerig himself had to ultimately do what he had feigned and flee to Constantinople in 777. He was replaced by Kardam, who finally brought some stability to the Bulgarian Empire during his nearly twenty-five years of rule.

Constantine V had been followed by his son Leo IV, called 'the Kazar' as his mother was a Kazar princess. Leo IV's early priorities lay in the East, and it was only in 780 that he found time to once again go on campaign against the Bulgarians. Leo IV however died of a fever at the onset of the campaign and the army returned to Constantinople.

Leo IV was followed by his son Constantine VI, aged nine at the time and under regency of his mother Irene of Athens.

With the instability of a young emperor in Constantinople, Kardam started to raid into Byzantine territory and he was left unchecked until the young emperor, now of age, marched against him in 791. That year's campaign was inconclusive and the armies met again the following year at Marcellae (near modern day Karnobat in Bulgaria) where the Bulgarians won a decisive victory, pursuing the Emperor himself all the way to Constantinople.

Peace negotiations ensued and it was agreed that the Byzantines should once again pay tribute to the Bulgarians.

Constantine VI was ousted by his mother, Irene (of Athens), who was herself ousted in 802 by Nikephoros I. By that time the Bulgarian throne had fallen to Krum, one of the more noticeable rulers of the Bulgarian Empire.

Nikephoros I had issues in the East, where he had refused to pay tribute to the Arabs, so Krum had a relatively free hand in Europe. He used that to unite the Bulgars north and south of the River Danube and then finally overrun the neighbouring Avars, extending Bulgarian influence all the way to modern day Hungary. He then turned his attention on further expansion and consolidation in the south and invaded Sofia.

12 - The Bulgarian Empires

In the meantime, Nikephoros I executed ethnic engineering on a grand scale. Concerned over the number of 'heathen' Slavs in Greece he forcefully removed 'Greeks' from all over his empire and had them moved to Greece, changing the ethnic mix in his favour. Thus, with Krum on the loose in the field and the Byzantine emperor set on ethnic cleansing, war was unavoidable.

Nikephoros I set out to check Krum in 809, marching on the Bulgarian capital of Pliska, he burned the practically undefended city and then continued to Sofia where he rebuilt the Byzantine fortifications before returning to Constantinople in triumph. The Byzantine army had sprung a surprise on Krum, but the two armies were still to meet in the field.

Spurred on by his victories, Nikephoros I took to the field again in 811. Once again, he went to Pliska where the population was massacred despite peace proposals from Krum. Then on the way back to Constantinople disaster struck.

Krum had long since realized that meeting the Byzantine army in open battle was a risky undertaking, so he had mobilized his troops in the mountains, arming women and children to make up the numbers. On 24 July they caught the Byzantine army in an ambush initiated by artificial landslides. The Byzantine army was practically destroyed, Nikephoros I was killed and his son Staurakios taken back to Constantinople with his back broken. Krum had the skull of Nikephoros I mounted in silver and used it for a drinking cup.

As Staurakios was in no position to carry out the job as emperor he was quickly replaced by his brother-in-law Michael I.

Krum now took the opportunity to help himself to Byzantine possessions on the Black Sea coast and in northern Greece. He offered Emperor Michael I peace on the same conditions as in 716, but Michael I did not want to look weak, so he declined. Krum thus continued raiding until finally, in the beginning of 813, the Byzantines took their army into the field and - initially, were successful against the Bulgarians.

The two armies now converged on Adrianople (Edirne) where they eyed each other off for a couple of weeks until finally on 22 June the Byzantines attacked. The Bulgarians won the day and pursued the Byzantines all the way back to Constantinople, which they put under siege.

The direct result was change of emperor, Michael I being forced to retire to a monastery and replaced by Leo V, who took over a rather tense situation.

Leo V tried to resolve it with treachery, inviting Krum to peace negotiations but having him ambushed. Surviving the ordeal Krum withdrew, causing death and destruction in his wake.

Krum died in 814 and was followed by his son Omurtag. Though there was a skirmish early on, Omurtag and Leo V both saw that peace was the better option, so in 816 they concluded a thirty years peace agreement which defined the borders. Contrary to former agreement both parties stuck to this one, the Bulgarians even coming to the assistance of Leo V's successor, Michael II, when there was a rebellion against him in 823.

Omurtag took the opportunity to deal with a new potential enemy, the Frankish Empire (ruled by Louis the Pious), which was emerging on the eastern and north-eastern borders of the Bulgarian Empire. Initially there were inconclusive skirmishes, but diplomacy took over and the Bulgarians and Franks came to an understanding of borders, no doubt aided by the fact that neither of the two empires had any real ambitions in terms of each other's territories.

Omurtag also faced internal rebellion as the Slav tribes were rebelling for increased autonomy, demands that, however, were met by further centralization from Priska.

Showing that he had not slept during the lesson when it came to ethnic cleansing, Omurtag proactively persecuted Christians in his lands, even disinheriting his eldest son, Enravota, because he was favourable to Christianity. Enravota would after his father's death convert to Christianity and as a consequence he was executed by his own brother.

On Omurtag's death in 831, his son Malamir succeeded him. Malamir was very young, which was possibly the reason why the Byzantine Emperor Theophilos decided to renew hostilities by raiding inside the Bulgarian border.

The ensuing skirmishes went the Bulgarians' way, and they proceeded as far as Adrianople (Edirne). Malamir died in 836 and was succeeded by (possibly his nephew) Presian I.

Presian I had a new problem to deal with. In an area not so different from modern day Serbia an ethnic group - loosely defined as 'Serbs' - had formed and in the 830s a strong leader, Vlastimir, had united the Serb tribes as a response to the emerging Bulgarian Empire. The Byzantine emperor Theophilos granted the Serbs independence to win them over as allies and the Bulgarian reacted by invading Serbia.

The ensuing war lasted three years, but by 842 the Bulgarians had been defeated. That same year Emperor Theophilos died, putting an end to the alliance between Serbia and the Byzantines, which also meant an end to hostilities.

Now followed a period of peace, or as much peace as can be had when neighbouring empires grind against each other, until once again the Byzantines stirred things up in the region. Presian I had died in 852 and been replaced by his son Boris I, possibly the most iconic ruler of the First Bulgarian Empire. Since the death of Theophilos his son Michael III had reigned in Byzantium.

Boris I got involved early on in a war against the divided Frankish Empire, supporting the prince of Moravia (modern day eastern Czech Republic), but it did not go well. The Franks defeated the Bulgarian army and at the same time instigated the Croatians to attack the Bulgarians on their north-eastern border. The Byzantines took the opportunity and swept up the Black Sea coast, recapturing former territories, but in the end Boris I managed to make peace with everybody and retain the territories he had lost.

Boris I had not forgotten about the issues with Serbia, opened during his father's reign. He sent an army commanded by his son into Serbia, but they were defeated and he had to make peace with the Serbians.

So far Boris I's rule had been eventful but not entirely successful. His problems were further complicated by the internal strife between the minority - but ruling - Bulgars and the majority Slavs. These internal problems were accelerated by the fact that the Bulgars and Slavs subscribed to different religions, so Boris I came up with the idea to unify his people under a single religion; Christianity.

In this approach of adoption of a communal religion Boris I followed the same model as Muhammad did a couple of centuries earlier when he needed to unite disparate desert-tribes into a single military entity. But whereas Muhammad had the advantage of speaking directly with God Boris I did not, so he got help in the form of missionaries from the Frankish King, the missionaries therefore being Roman Catholic.

The Byzantine Emperor, however, started hostilities against the Bulgarians in 863, at a time where natural disasters had brought famine to the Bulgarian Empire, and when Boris I sued for peace one of the conditions was that the Catholic missionaries were replaced by Orthodox missionaries from Constantinople.

And thus did the Orthodox missionaries arrive, and in 864 they baptized Boris I, the Byzantine Emperor himself acting as his godfather and Boris I taking the additional -considered more Christian - name of Michael. As a by-product the monk, Cyril, chosen to lead this mission, was the first to make an alphabet suitable for the Slavic language in order that the Bible could be translated. The alphabet still carries his name - Cyrillic, to this day.

But Boris I had ambitions over and above changing to Christianity, he wanted a Bulgarian Church, an autocephalous archbishopric with its own bishop and no hierarchical obedience to Constantinople. The Orthodox Patriarch had no such intentions and further refused to even answer a range of question asked by Boris I regarding the compatibility of a range of local customs with Christianity. Not easily rebuffed, Boris I started to play his cards and instead contacted the Pope in Rome with his questions.

The Pope saw the opportunity and started an exchange with Boris I which eventually led to the Orthodox missionaries being replaced by Catholic missionaries including two bishops. The kind of issues in question included such varied subjects as women's right to wear trousers (to which the Pope agreed) and bigamy (to which the Pope disagreed). But when Boris I tried to convince the Pope about his autocephalous archbishopric, the Pope also said no so Boris I returned to Orthodoxy, this time being given what he wanted and an independent Bulgarian Church had been born.

Job done, Boris I decided to retire to a monastery in 889, appointing his son Vladimir as new khan. But that did not go well as Vladimir tried to reverse the Christian movement and return to the old religions. Consequently, Boris I returned from retirement, fought with Vladimir and ultimately had him blinded and sent to a monastery himself. He then appointed his younger son, Simeon I, as khan and retired again. Simeon I would rule for more than three decades and take the First Bulgarian Empire to the heights of its power.

Simeon I had received the best education available at the time, spending years as a student in Constantinople and had been brought up a Christian. That is possibly the reason why he was chosen over his older brother, Gavril, after the initial fiasco of Vladimir.

In Byzantium Emperor Michael II had been replaced by Basil I who in turn had been replaced by Leo VI and on the north-western border of the Bulgarian Empire a new force had started to emerge, namely the Magyars.

Soon after Simeon I came to power there was trouble. Emperor Leo VI forcefully moved the Bulgarian traders from Constantinople to Thessaloniki and subjected them to high taxes. When they complained to Simeon I, he in turn complained to Leo VI who simply ignored the matter.

Simeon I now took matters in his own hands and moved on the Byzantines who had most of their army fighting the Arabs in Anatolia. Emperor Leo VI managed to get an improvised army in the field, but they were easily defeated by the Bulgarians. Leo VI, however, had another trick up his sleeve.

Magyars, originally a splinter group from the Khazars, had penetrated into modern day Ukraine, crossed the Carpathians and entered the Carpathian Basin. Ruled by Árpád they frequently raided into Bulgarian and Frankish territories, and it was here Leo VI found a convenient ally.

At the same time as sending an expeditionary force from Italy, Leo VI convinced the Magyars to attack the Bulgarians from the north, using Byzantine ships to ferry them across the Danube River. Simeon I was forced to turn his army around to face the threat from the Magyars, while still keeping an eye on the Byzantines approaching from Italy. Initially the Magyars were successful, laying waste to the northern parts of the Bulgarian Empire, but Simeon I had learned from Leo VI, so he in turn allied with the Pechenegs, who attacked the Magyars from the east. In the end the Magyars were defeated and had to move their budding principality further west into an area approximately where modern day Hungary is located. We shall meet them again in Chapter 13.

Returning to the issue of Byzantium, Simeon I had deliberately dragged peace discussions on, needing time to deal with the Magyars, but he was now ready to resume hostilities. While Simeon I was busy in the north, the

Byzantines had used the time to gather a considerable army and in the summer of 896 the two armies met for the final showdown in the Battle of Boulgarophygon near the modern Bulgarian-Turkish border.

The Byzantine army was routed, the sorry remains limping back to Constantinople. Leo VI sued for peace and had to agree to cede territories to Simeon I as well as agree to pay an annual tribute. As the Byzantines needed peace with the Bulgarians to focus on their war with the Arabs, the peace actually lasted a good while this time.

On the death of Emperor Leo VI in 912, relations once again changed for the worse. If Leo VI was as clever as his moniker 'the Wise' implies, then his brother and successor, Alexander, was as ignorant.

As was the custom on the change of regent, Simeon I sent an ambassador to reconfirm the annual tribute paid by Byzantium. Alexander, however, hated his brother and everything his brother had done, so refused to live up to the agreement. Simeon I started to prepare for war.

In the meantime, Alexander died (allegedly during a pagan ceremony aiming at retrieving his lost virility) and he was replaced in name by his nephew, Constantine VII, who was only seven years old. Ruling in his place was a regency, which was hardly contested between the Patriarch and Constantine VII's mother, Zoe.

Still without a resolution to the issue of tribute, Simeon I appeared in front of Constantinople with an enormous army and although he probably appreciated that he could not take the city, he could cause severe problems by a blockade.

The Patriarch, an old friend of Simeon I from his days in Constantinople, now negotiated a peace agreement which provided Simeon I with an even better chance of taking Constantinople than by military force. Simeon I was promised, on top of the tribute and more land, that one of his daughters would be married to Constantine VII. Well happy with this new alliance, Simeon I withdrew.

But Simeon I's happiness did not last long. The Patriarch was ousted by a coup and Constantine VII's mother, Zoe, was back. She had absolutely no intentions of her son marrying a 'barbarian' (although of course the Bulgarian princess was Christian) and by 915 Simeon I went into the field again. He besieged Adrianople (Edirne) but was chased off by a determined Byzantine counter-offensive. In 917 he was back, and this time the encounter was more severe.

The Byzantines had now plotted with the Pechenegs - who had previously assisted Simeon I with defeating the Magyars - and sent a fleet up the Danube River to transfer them across. In the meantime, a considerable army set out from Constantinople to catch Simeon I in a pincer movement.

For reasons unknown, but probably due to Simeon I bribing the Byzantine commander, the Pechenegs and the Byzantine fleet immediately started fighting about authority and the Pechenegs eventually turned around and went home.

In the meantime the Byzantine army had progressed up the Black Sea coast and had encamped by a small port-town called Anchialus (modern day Pomorie in Bulgaria). This was the scene of two previous battles between the Bulgarians and the Byzantines and here the Bulgarians caught the Byzantine army and, in the ensuing, (Third) Battle of Anchialus the Byzantine army was annihilated.

But still there were no concrete marriage plans and while the Byzantines fought out a series of small internal civil conflicts, Simeon I kept campaigning. He retook Adrianople, raided on the coast of the Bosporus and created mayhem in the territories outside of Constantinople itself.

Finally, he decided to hire the one thing he was without in order to conquer Constantinople; a fleet. He paid the Caliph of North Africa to supply a suitable fleet, but when in 924 Simeon I once again arrived at Constantinople, there was no fleet besieging Constantinople. The Byzantines had paid more, and the Caliph had stayed home.

Negotiations now began again and a weary Simeon I accepted to withdraw from all occupied areas on the condition that the annual tribute was raised. He realized that his play for Constantinople was at an end and in defiance he declared himself Emperor of the Romans and the Bulgarians as well as promoting the head of the Bulgarian Church from bishop to patriarch.

In his later years, Simeon I re-established Bulgarian suzerainty over Serbia, but a campaign into Croatia was unsuccessful. He died in 927, as far as is known from heart failure.

Simeon I's son, Peter I, succeeded him, initially under regency led by his uncle, and it was Peter I who would benefit from the hard work done by his father.

The Bulgarians once again rattled their sabre, but the Byzantines needed peace so they accepted Peter I's title as emperor (tsar), the Bulgarian Church's independency and furthermore the marriage between Peter I and a granddaughter of the Byzantine Emperor. This time the marriage actually took place, and the peace agreement was signed. It would last for nearly four decades.

But peace with Byzantium did not necessarily mean peace for the Bulgarians. Serbia rose in revolt - aided behind the scenes by Byzantium - and succeeded once again in retaining their independence. In the north Magyars, either as a result of conflict or as a reward for fighting as mercenaries in Serbia, settled in the Bulgarian lands north of the Danube River.

Then in 965, after the Byzantines had paid their annual tribute for thirty-eight consecutive years, trouble resumed. The Byzantine Emperor, Nikephoros II, refused to pay tribute and started skirmishes on the

Byzantine-Bulgarian border. He had, however, no intentions of actually committing the Byzantine army, which was required in the East, so instead he found an ally who would do his bidding for sufficient amounts of gold.

Nikephoros II's ally was the 'barbaric' Rus, a mixture of indigenous Russians and Viking settlers living in the principality of Kiev and ruled by Svyatoslav I. With 15,000 pounds of Byzantine gold in his coffers, Svyatoslav I attacked the Bulgarians from the north, dealing them a devastating blow.

Peter I once again got help from the Pechenegs, who attacked Kiev, forcing Svyatoslav I to turn around, but he was back again in 969.

Peter I had died and his son Boris II had taken the throne, but he had no more defence against the Rus than his father and the Rus simply overran Bulgaria, taking Boris II and his family captive in the process.

The Byzantines now had to reverse their strategy. The Bulgarians may have been an irritant, and the payment of tribute an insult, but for decades there had been peace and in reality Bulgaria had lost its former military power through the peaceful period and Peter I had been a good and peace loving neighbour.

Now, however, the Rus stood on the border of Byzantium, making their presence known by manoeuvring in the border area, clearly preparing for an attack on Constantinople.

The Byzantine emperor, now John I Tzimiskes, had to react and just before Easter 972 he marched ahead of his army to 'set Bulgaria free'. The Byzantine fleet set off to the mouth of the Danube River and the Rus did not have the intimate knowledge of the land that the Bulgarians had, so they had not fortified the critical mountain passes, giving the Byzantine army a direct route to the Bulgarian capital of Preslav.

The Rus had not expected the Byzantines to move out until after Easter and were unprepared when the Byzantines swiftly attacked the Rus army camped outside the city. The battle was fierce, but the Rus army broke and the survivors fled to the city. But the city itself was quickly overrun, and the Bulgarian Tsar Boris II was 'set free'.

Svyatoslav I was not present himself, but had dug down in Dristra (modern day Silistra in north Bulgaria) from where it took the Byzantines three months to smoke him out. Peace was agreed, the Rus withdrew back over the Danube River and the Byzantines returned in triumph to Constantinople.

And some triumph it was! Celebrated according to the old Roman customs, the Emperor should be riding in a gilded chariot pulled by four white horses, but John I Tzimiskes had given the chariot over for an icon of the Blessed Virgin captured in the Bulgarian capital. He himself rode behind it in his gilded armour. At the very end of the procession walked Boris II and his family.

When the procession reached Hagia Sophia, the key trophy which was placed on the altar was, however, not the Icon of the Virgin but the Bulgarian Crown itself.

John I Tzimiskes' intentions were now clear, far from liberating Bulgaria he had taken it back to Byzantium and soon afterward he forced Boris II to formally abdicate, once again making Bulgaria a Byzantine province.

Provinces do not need their own Patriarchs, so as a matter of tying up loose ends John I Tzimiskes also cancelled the Bulgarian Patriarchate. For all intents and purposes, the First Bulgarian Empire had ceased to exist. But the story does not end here.

Tsar Boris II had an uncle, a brother of Peter I, called Roman. John I Tzimiskes had Roman castrated to ensure that the male line of Krum died out, but even without some of his equipment Roman was not done yet.

Although John I Tzimiskes had taken the Bulgarian capital and the Tsar, the western part of the Bulgarian Empire was not under Byzantine control. Instead, it was being run by a local dynasty of nobles, split between four brothers, David, Aron, Moses, and Samuel. David and Moses died in battle and of the two remaining, Samuel eventually had Aron killed.

In 976 Emperor John I Tzimiskes died and the near-obligatory war of succession broke out in Constantinople. During the ensuing confusion that formed Tsar Boris II and his brother Roman escaped from Constantinople and headed for western Bulgaria. Sadly, Boris II was killed by border guards before he was recognized, but Roman made it through and was crowned as Tsar of Bulgaria even though the real power was with Samuel.

While the Byzantines were busy sorting their own succession out, the Bulgarians now once again started to expand and gradually spread out, meeting little resistance.

It was only in 986 that Emperor Basil II finally had enough control of the Byzantine throne to start fighting back. He marched out ahead of his vanguard, aiming for the city of Larissa in eastern Greece, but before reaching his objective he stopped to let the rearguard catch up.

Samuel, now aware of the Emperor's intentions, took the opportunity to prepare the mountain passes, so when the Byzantine army started moving again it was caught in an ambush in a pass known as Trajan's Gate and was as good as annihilated. The Emperor himself escaped and swore revenge over the Bulgarians, a revenge that would be long in coming, but which would eventually come.

Basil II did not go back until 991. He moved his, now highly trained, army around the territories occupied by the Bulgarians for four years. Cities were recaptured, or burned, but little achieved as Samuel satisfied himself with shadowing the Byzantine army, not confronting it in open battle. The Emperor was called away to the Eastern Front in 995 and though an expeditionary force kept up the pressure, it was not until the year 1000 that the Emperor himself would come back in force.

By then Roman had been taken prisoner by the Byzantines and had died in Constantinople. Samuel was now Tsar and had captured Dyrrachium (modern day Durrës) on the Adriatic Sea, extending the Bulgarian Empire from the Adriatic Sea to the Danube River. It was this which moved Basil II to offer the Adriatic Sea to the Venetians, as described in Chapter 10, effectively marking the start of Venice's imperial adventure.

From 1000 and for more than a decade, Basil II gradually took back the eastern part of the Balkans. The Bulgarians were also pressured from Hungary and Croatia and from revolts in Serbia, which they had annexed. Finally in 1014 did the two opposing forces meet in a battle which would show to be decisive.

The battle took place at Kleidion (modern day Klyuch in Bulgaria) on 29 July 1014. Samuel was not in favour of open battle, but his status amongst his own people was waning with the Byzantines gradually carving away at his empire, so he had to make a stand. He chose the specific site because it had a narrow well defended pass and a range of defensive earthworks.

The Byzantines had little choice but to throw themselves at the defences, in which they were mainly unsuccessful. It was only when a wing of the Byzantine army managed to get over the mountains and come down from behind the defending Bulgarians that the battle was won. Samuel himself escaped, first to Prilep and then on to his headquarters in Prespa.

But the war continued with a Byzantine attempt to capture the town of Strumitsa, which they had to abort when one of their commanders, with a good part of the army, was killed in a Bulgarian ambush.

Now Basil II committed an act of atrocity of such proportions that it won him the moniker 'The Bulgar Slayer'. The Byzantines had taken 15,000 Bulgarian prisoners. They were now split into groups of 100. In each group, ninety-nine prisoners were blinded and the last prisoner was blinded in one eye only so he could lead the rest of the group home. The prisoners were then sent on their way back to Prespa where they arrived in October of 1014. Seeing them return Samuel had a fit and died two days later.

Samuel's successors, his son Gavril Radomir was soon murdered by his cousin Ivan Vladislav, but neither had any defence against the Byzantines. The Battle of Kleidion had broken the back of the First Bulgarian Empire and in 1018 it was all over and the Byzantine emperor entered the Bulgarian capital.

Basil II had, true to his word after the defeat at Trajan's Gate more than thirty years prior, annihilated the Bulgarians. Ivan Vladislav had died in battle and his son Presian II had for a short time taken over the throne. On his surrender he was given a position at the court in Constantinople where he got himself involved in so many court intrigues and failed coups that he was blinded and sent away to a monastery in 1030, He was never heard of again.

The First Bulgarian Empire had ceased to exist, and it would of course never come into conflict with Mehmed II in the fifteenth century, but it is relevant in the history of the Balkans because it was the first major power to break the Byzantine-Roman stronghold on the region, forcing the way for other smaller states such as Croatia and Serbia and moulding the political future of the region.

Though the First Bulgarian Empire eventually succumbed to the more mature state of Byzantium, it was only a matter of time before Byzantium would become so exhausted and so involved in infighting that another opportunity would present itself for independence in the Balkans.

The first opportunity presented itself in 1040 where a grandson of Samuel, Peter Deljan, declared himself Tsar of the Bulgarians and started raiding Byzantine territories reaching as far as Dyrrachium on the Adriatic Sea and the Gulf of Lepanto on the Greek south-west Coast.

The Byzantine Emperor at the time was Michael IV, who was severely affected by epilepsy and dropsy. He nevertheless insisted on leading the campaign against the Bulgarians in person, and the army set out in 1041.

Michael IV may have been physically weak, but he was clever in the traditional Byzantine way. Rather than relying entirely on military power, he had also opened a more deceptive way to victory.

Whereas the rebellious Peter Deljan was the son of Gavril Radomir, who had been murdered by his own cousin Ivan Vladislav in the dying days of the First Bulgarian Empire, a son of Ivan Vladislav, Alusian, was living in Constantinople and Michael IV had sent him to the Bulgarian camp to infiltrate the enemy.

Alusian did a splendid job and was received with open arms by his kinsman Peter Deljan, but as there had been bad blood between their fathers, Alusian soon took advantage and while Peter Deljan had passed out drunk, cut his nose off and blinded him with a kitchen knife.

Needing an able-bodied leader, and with Alusian being of royal blood himself, he was quickly elected tsar, but he immediately returned to the Byzantines and the Bulgarian army disintegrated and the revolt fizzled out. It would be nearly 150 years till there would be another independent Bulgaria.

By that time, the Byzantine Empire had undergone dramatic changes. The Seljuks had gained control of most of Anatolia, and there had been challenges in the west from Normans and Hungarians.

What had held Byzantium together through these troubled times was the enduring Komnenos family, producing emperors who in isolation may not have been the greatest emperors ever, but whose dynasty created a level of stability rarely found in Byzantium.

The last Komnenos emperor, Andronikos I Komnenos, was ousted in 1185 (his gruesome death is described in Chapter 8) and the utterly useless Angelid dynasty very quickly destabilized the empire.

During the nearly two centuries of Byzantine rule the Bulgarians had not disappeared as an ethnic entity. The ruling class of landowners still ran the territory on a daily basis and there had been no attempts to 'Hellenize' the population or repeat the attempts of forceful ethnic engineering which both sides had executed during the period of the First Bulgarian Empire.

Small uprisings had taken place over the years, but that was not unusual, and after all, the Bulgarians were Orthodox Christians, so they were treated as a semi-autonomous territory, maintaining their underlying national identity.

The pretext for the next revolt was a raise in taxes, an issue that the Bulgarians first tried to resolve through an appeal to the Emperor, but when the Emperor refused to even discuss the issue the Bulgarians rose in revolt in 1185.

The revolt was led by the brothers Peter and Ivan Asen, who soon started to carve out a new Bulgarian state.

Peter Asen appointed himself Tsar Peter IV and appointed his brother, Ivar Asen I, as co-emperor and military commander.

The Bulgarians affected defeat on the Byzantines in 1190 (Battle of Tryavna) and again in 1194 (Battle of Arcadiopolis) and when the Byzantine Emperor was preparing a new campaign in 1195 - attempting to ally himself with Hungary - he was deposed, blinded and sent to prison by his own brother, Alexios II Angelos.

A strong emperor could have probably still killed off the revolt as others had done before, but Alexios II Angelos was not, but rather a lazy and lavish ruler who soon depleted the Empire of its treasure and allowed the army and navy to fall into disrepair.

This allowed the Bulgarians to expand their budding state and even though Ivar Asen I was murdered in 1196 and Peter IV himself was murdered in 1197, the throne went to their younger brother Kaloyan, who continued the Bulgarian quest for independence and expansion.

Kaloyan played the old card of religion and contacted the Pope to get him to officially recognize his reign and restore the Bulgarian Church as an independent entity. The Pope granted some of Kaloyan's wishes, appointing an archbishop (Catholic of course) and recognizing Kaloyan as 'King of the Bulgarians and Wallachians', Wallachia, modern day southern Romania, here being mentioned as a uniform territory for the first time. We shall cover Wallachia further in Chapter 14.

The weakened Byzantines put up little resistance and instead Kaloyan had to deal with the Hungarians, a growing force to whom we shall return in Chapter 13. The Hungarians invaded and took Belgrade in 1202 and Kaloyan retook it in 1203 at which time the Pope intervened and forced peace between them. Then everything changed.

The reason was the Fourth Crusade. Suddenly there was no Byzantine Empire. Instead there was the Latin Empire of Constantinople, the Kingdom of Thessalonica and the emerging (Greek) Despotate of Epirus in the west.

The new Latin rulers soon decided to re-establish former Byzantine glory, which in the Balkans first and foremost meant suppression of the Bulgarians, but the hastily thrown together Latin states were no match for the by now battle-hardened Bulgarians, who beat the Latins in a range of engagements, killing both the first Latin Emperor, Baldwin of Flanders, and then Boniface of Montferrat, ruler of Thessaloniki, in the years immediately following the Fourth Crusade.

Following up on his success against Boniface of Montferrat, Kaloyan laid siege to Thessaloniki, but here he was murdered by one of his own commanders.

Kaloyan was followed by his nephew Boril, but the choice was not popular. Kaloyan had appointed another nephew, Ivan Asen, as his successor, but he had to flee on Boril's accession and a bitter internal strife broke out, which would last throughout Boril's reign. The weakened state of the Bulgarian Empire meant that part of northern Greece was lost to the Latins and other parts tore themselves away under local leaders. The only party willing to help Boril was the Hungarians, but to gain their support Boril had to cede Belgrade to them.

Boril also created a dynastic tie with the Latin Empire by marrying off one of his daughters to the Latin Emperor, Henry of Flanders, but overall, he was isolated and never managed to gain proper control of the new Bulgarian Empire.

Boril's misery came to an end when Ivan Asen (II) returned from exile in 1218, had Boril blinded and sent off to a monastery after which he mounted the throne originally intended for him.

Ivan Asen II was a competent individual who quickly set out to recover from the disastrous reign of Boril. He started by building relationships with his neighbours through a string of marriages.

Ivan Asen II himself married a daughter, Anna Maria, of the Hungarian King which had the added bonus of Belgrade being part of her dowry and thus being returned to Bulgaria. The generous terms could have something to do with the fact that the Hungarian King at that time was held prisoner by Ivan Asen II who had intercepted him on his way back from crusade.

To secure peace in the south-west, Ivan Asen II entered into a treaty with Theodore Komnenos Doukas, the ruler of Epirus and married away one of his daughters to Theodore Komnenos Doukas' brother, Manuel.

The treaty with Epirus did not last for long though. The reason was that when the Latin emperor, Robert of Courtenay, died in 1228 he left behind a son and successor of only eleven years of age. A regent had to be found and Ivan Asen II became a hot prospect for the job.

Theodore Komnenos Doukas had recently conquered Thessaloniki and Adrianople (Edirne) and had proclaimed himself Emperor of Byzantium, so he had his own designs on Constantinople and little appetite for Ivan Asen II's potential regency. He thus decided on a pre-emptive strike into Bulgaria.

The two armies met 9 March 1230 at Klokotnitsa in southern Bulgaria and the result was a resounding Bulgarian victory. Theodore Komnenos

Doukas was taken prisoner and Ivan Asen II had suddenly gained territories which stretched from the Adriatic Sea to the Black Sea. He divided them to rule (under Bulgarian suzerainty) between his son in law Manual and other family members. He then released all his prisoners of war (minus Theodore), asking them to return home and live in peace.

Ultimately another regent was chosen in Constantinople, Ivan Asen II had become a little bit too strong for that job. This in turn made Ivan Asen II enter into alliance with the Empire of Nicaea, the emerging Greek state in Anatolia.

The alliance between Nicaea and Bulgaria in turn made the Hungarians (supported by the Pope) react and the Hungarians took Belgrade (again) in 1232, and Ivan Asen II took it back in 1233.

This only encouraged Ivan Asen II to further strengthen his ties with Nicaea, and in 1235 he married off his daughter Elena to the son of the Emperor of Nicaea, the later Theodore II Laskaris.

At the same time, he reinstituted the independent Bulgarian Church - once again Orthodox - and Bulgaria was as strong, if not stronger, as it had been at any time during the First Bulgarian Empire centuries earlier.

The alliance with Nicaea became an on-and-off affair, Ivan Asen II wavering in his support. He probably saw the Nicaeans as a useful rebel force, keeping the Latins busy, but did not necessarily want a new Byzantine Empire on his doorstep.

Ivan Asen II died in 1241, but before he died he experienced the Mongol invasion of Hungary (see Chapter 13), although at that time it did not directly threaten Bulgaria.

The throne was inherited by his seven-year-old son Kaliman I, or rather to a council of regents, and the state became weak. It quickly lost its real influence over Serbia and Thessaloniki and worse, it faced invasion by the Golden Horde of Mongols.

Although the Mongols were retreating from the Balkans, they threatened Bulgaria with invasion and devastation and the Bulgarians decided to take the easier option and agree to pay an annual tribute.

Kaliman I died at a young age in 1246 and the reign was passed to his even younger half-brother, Michael Asen I, in reality continuing the regency.

The weakness of the Bulgarian Empire was soon realized by its neighbours and both Hungary, The Empire of Nicaea and the Despotate of Epirus took the opportunity to take back lost territory and in some cases add to it. Furthermore, his father-in-law, Rostislav Mikhailovich, a nobleman of Rus heritage carved out for himself a practically autonomous principality in the Belgrade area.

Although Michael Asen I came of age and tried to recover some of the lost territories, he was unsuccessful and a group of nobles plotted to kill him, which they did in 1256. In the fifteen years since the death of Ivan Asen II, his sons had lost half the empire.

Now a period of confusion followed. The conspirator's choice for tsar was Kaliman Asen II, who forcefully married Michael Asen I's wife, but her father, Rostislav Mikhailovich, appeared before the gates of the capital, the Tsar fled and Rostislav Mikhailovich took his daughter away.

Kaliman Asen II was soon tracked down and killed to be replaced by Mitso Asen, a son-in-law of Ivan Asen II. He in turn lasted a year, as he never gained the acceptance of the nobles and ultimately had to flee to Nicaea. In his place the nobles appointed one of their own, Constantine Tikh, who later adopted the name 'Asen'.

Constantine Tikh married a grand-daughter of Ivan Asen II (who was also a princess of Nicaea). Contrary to his immediate predecessors, Constantine Tikh stayed on the throne for an extended period of time, twenty years to be precise, but despite the stabilizing effect of his long rule, he was not that much more successful.

What had been built over decades was lost in a few years, and soon after Constantine Tikh's accession to the throne the Hungarians tried their luck again with an incursion into Bulgaria. The Hungarians were initially successful, but the Bulgarians soon recaptured the disputed territories on the Danube River, though in effect they were ruled by the local lord with little central control.

Constantine Tikh's wife, Irene, was sister to the lawful Emperor of Nicaea, the under-aged John IV Laskaris, so when he was murdered by Michael VIII Palaiologos following the latter's successful reconquest of Constantinople in 1261, Bulgaria declared against the new Byzantine Empire.

In 1264 Constantine Tikh allied with the Mongols and raided into Byzantine territories, but the gesture was mainly symbolic as the Bulgarians gained nothing in terms of territory.

Relations between Byzantium and Bulgaria however looked poised to improve when the Empress of Bulgaria, Irene, died in 1268 and Constantine Tikh married Maria Palaiologina Kantakouzene, a niece of the Byzantine Emperor. But the Byzantine Emperor was not handing over the Black Sea ports which had been agreed as Maria Palaiologina Kantakouzene's dowry, so Constantine Tikh was soon enough on bad terms with Byzantium again. As a consequence, he started supporting Charles I of Naples who was making overtures in turn of recapturing Constantinople for the Latins.

The Byzantine Emperor in turn entered into an alliance with the Mongols of the Golden Horde, so in 1274 the Mongols came south into Bulgaria, which was a Mongol vassal, raiding and plundering on behalf of the Byzantines.

The Mongol raids were repeated in the following years and finally the Bulgarians had had enough. A rebellion was started, led by a swineherd named Ivaylo, and the rebellion soon became a revolution.

Constantine Tikh went to quell the uprising, but he was killed in the ensuing battle and the situation got really complicated.

Constantine Tikh had a son, Michael Asen, and he was his nominal heir and co-emperor as Michael Asen II. But he was only seven years old, so he ruled through a regency led by his mother; Maria Palaiologina Kantakouzene. Michael Asen II, and his mother, however only had control of the Bulgarian capital, Veliko Tarnovo, while Ivaylo and his rebel army seized control of most of the remaining part of the country.

To add to the confusion, the Byzantine Emperor, Michael VIII Palaiologos, threw in his own candidate, Ivan Asen III, a son of Mitso Asen, and the Byzantines marched north to reassert Byzantine dominance over Bulgaria.

Necessity can make strange bedfellows, so Maria Palaiologina Kantakouzene, realizing that a divided Bulgaria was no match for the Byzantines, offered to marry Ivaylo and make him co-emperor. Although it was a far from happy union, the strategy worked and Ivaylo's army managed to hold back the Byzantine invaders.

But the Byzantines were still in alliance with the Golden Horde of Mongols, who by now routinely raided into Bulgaria and Ivaylo was blockaded by the Mongols inside the town of Silistra. The siege lasted for months and when a rumour was spread that Ivaylo had died, the citizens of Veliko Tarnovo opened the gates to the Byzantines and recognized Ivan Asen III as Tsar.

Michael Asen II and his mother were taken prisoners and moved to Constantinople, but Ivaylo was once again at large and appeared before the gates of Veliko Tarnovo. When he beat off a Byzantine attempt at relieving the city, Ivan Asen III fled to Constantinople leaving the throne for his brother-in-law George I.

Both Ivaylo and Ivan Asen III now tried to gain the support of the Golden Horde, but the Khan, Nogai, had Ivaylo murdered and failed to reinstate Ivan Asen III, leaving Bulgaria with a tsar who would rule for a decade and created some much needed stability, even if that decade would not be one of glory.

George I faced a situation in which Bulgaria was being consistently reduced in size - being pressed further and further north towards the Danube River by the Byzantines - so he tried to form an alliance with Charles I of Naples, who was once again eyeing off Byzantium, but when Charles I of Naples lost Sicily in the aftermath of the Sicilian Vespers, the alliance did not come to anything.

Instead, George I sought an alliance with Serbia, marrying off his daughter Anna to the Serbian King. The alliance was not aimed at conquest but rather to secure that the Serbs did not help themselves further to Bulgarian territories.

Relations with the Byzantines improved after the death of Emperor Michael VIII Palaiologos, but George I's real enemy was the Mongols.

Although the Mongols had not been successful in re-inserting Ivan Asen III, they took that defeat calmly and instead continued their raids into Bulgaria to such an extent that George I had to accept their suzerainty and send his son - and heir - as hostage to the Khan and the Khan's son, Chaka, got one of George I's daughters as a wife.

But finally George I had had enough, and he fled to Byzantium in 1292, leaving the Bulgarian Empire in the hands of Smilets, a Bulgarian nobleman acting as a puppet for the Mongol Khan. But Smilets was not successful in pleasing the Khan, so Mongol raids continued and in 1298 Smilets died, leaving a young son, Ivan II.

Ivan II, and his regent-mother, held on to the throne for only a year as there were bigger movements around them dictating the next phase of the game.

In the north the Mongols had their own internal problems, leading to the murder of Nogai. His son, Chaka, had to flee and led his loyal troops south into Bulgaria and simply took over as tsar.

With Chaka came Theodore Svetoslav, the son of George I who had been sent as a hostage to the Mongols and whose sister was married to Chaka.

Theodore Svetoslav understood that Chaka's rule in Bulgaria could only antagonize the new Mongol Khan, Toqta, so he plotted and had Chaka murdered in 1300, sending his head to Toqta as a peace-offering.

The strategy worked and Theodore Svetoslav was the new Tsar, but more importantly his actions meant that the Mongols shifted their focus away from Bulgaria, having their own issues to deal with further east.

Finally, Bulgaria had a tsar who was capable and who could hold on the throne for long enough to make a positive impact. Compared to the Bulgarian Empire under Ivan Asen II only sixty years prior, Bulgaria had become a pawn caught between more powerful enemies, but Theodore Svetoslav was about to change that.

He started an offensive, retaking lands in the south-east formerly lost to the Byzantines. This of course led to war with Byzantium, but Theodore Svetoslav was mainly successful and even managed to capture a large number of Byzantine officers whom he exchanged for his Father, George I, who was a de-facto Byzantine prisoner.

Official peace was made in 1307, and Theodore Svetoslav married a daughter of the Byzantine Co-Emperor Michael IX Palaiologos. This gave him the opportunity to move across the Danube River and reassert Bulgarian rule in Wallachia.

Bulgaria now entered a period of much needed - relative - peace. Theodore Svetoslav mainly lived in peace with his neighbours, though he did get involved - with Mongol support - in a war between the Byzantine Emperors Andronikos II Palaiologos and Andronikos III Palaiologos in the early 1320s.

12 - The Bulgarian Empires

In 1322 Theodore Svetoslav died and his son, George II, took the throne. George II continued his father's interest in the Byzantine civil-war, taking the opportunity to invade further Byzantine territories in the south-east, moving the border as far as Adrianople (Edirne).

But the Byzantines were able to fight back, recapturing their lost territories and even prepared for an offensive against Bulgaria when George II died, presumably from natural causes, in 1323 after only a year of rule.

George II did not leave an obvious heir, so the Bulgarian throne went to a distant cousin, Michael Shishman, who adopted the name 'Asen' to further his credentials.

The Byzantines now attacked, and initially took Bulgarian territories, but Michael Shishman fought back, resulting in status quo and a peace-agreement signed in 1324.

The Byzantine civil war was still going, and Michael Shishman saw the opportunity to get involved to his own advantage.

First he supported Andronikos III Palaiologos in an alliance against Serbia, then he supported Andronikos III Palaiologos' grand-father, Andronikos II Palaiologos, his real interest being that the conflict kept going, leaving Byzantium weakened.

When Andronikos III Palaiologos finally overcame his grand-father's resistance in 1328, Michael Shishman once more attempted to gain territories, but a Byzantine counterattack set things back as before and finally the Byzantines and the Bulgarians once more made peace in October 1328.

Michael Shishman's new interest in peace with Byzantium was his ambitions to annex Serbia, but his campaigns proved fruitless despite a new alliance with Byzantium and he was killed in battle in Serbia in 1330. He was followed by his son, Ivan Stefan, but he did not have lasting support from the nobles and when a Byzantine incursion went unopposed in 1331 he was deposed and replaced by Ivan Alexander a nephew of Michael Shishman with a weak claim to the throne but support of the nobles.

Ivan Alexander would reign for four decades and his rule would be the countdown to the end of the Second Bulgarian Empire.

The first decade of Ivan Alexander's rule followed the by now almost obligatory pattern of invading and then losing Byzantine territories. In addition, Ivan Alexander had to quell internal unrest, but at least the first decade did not result in any material losses for the Bulgarian Empire.

The second decade of Ivan Alexander's rule started with civil war in Byzantium. The dispute was between John VI Kantakouzenos and John V Palaiologos, the Serbians backing the former and the Bulgarians backing the latter even though the two nations were not, in their own right, hostile to each other. It was during this conflict that John V Palaiologos sought assistance from the Ottomans and enabled their presence in Europe, and it was from the Ottomans the next big threat came.

Before the Ottomans, however, came the Black Death which devastated all of Europe and seriously depopulated Bulgaria as it did everywhere else.

Once the Ottomans had secured their position on the Gallipoli peninsula they started moving fast, really fast. The Byzantines had exhausted themselves through both the Black Death and their seemingly endless civil wars so they were in no position to stop them and very soon the Ottomans became neighbours to the Bulgarians. And they were not the kind of neighbours you would want.

As was the custom of the Ottomans, they immediately started raiding into the neighbouring country; their not too subtle way of softening up an enemy before the final blow.

Ottoman raids through the later part of the 1340s and the early parts of the 1350s saw two of Ivan Alexander's sons killed in battle and an attempted anti-Ottoman union between Bulgaria, Byzantium and Serbia met with little success due to internal suspicion between the unionists.

Ivan Alexander gradually started to lose control over his country, a situation further aggravated by his divorce and subsequent marriage to a converted Jewess. His oldest son and nominal co-emperor, Ivan Sratsimir, effectively set himself up as an independent ruler in the Danube region and the regions north of the Danube, including Wallachia, for all intents and purposes ran their affairs independently from any central Bulgarian authority.

It was not only the Ottomans who saw the increasing weakness of the Bulgarians. The Hungarians annexed the areas north-east of Wallachia and formed the Principality of Moldavia (1352) and subsequently moved in on the Bulgarian territories on the Danube River, taking Ivan Sratsimir prisoner in the process.

Good relations with the Byzantines did not last either, culminating with Ivan Alexander refusing the Byzantine Emperor John V Palaiologos access to Bulgaria when he tried to return home in 1366 (having been travelling to gain support for Byzantium). The conflict forced John V Palaiologos' ally, Amadeus VI of Savoy, to intervene and capture several Bulgarian coastal towns before John V Palaiologos was finally allowed to continue under payment of reparations, which were reinvested in the re-conquest of Vidin on the Danube River and the instatement of Ivan Alexander's son, Ivan Sratsimir, as ruler of the area although under nominal Hungarian suzerainty.

These relative successes were quickly offset by losses in the south-east, where the Ottomans helped themselves to Adrianople (Edirne), Philippopolis (Plovdiv) and Boruj (Stara Zagora) in 1363, Edirne becoming the capital of the Ottoman possessions in Europe.

While preparing for a counter offensive against the Ottomans, Ivan Alexander died in 1371 and now the country fell into a state of complete disorder.

Ivan Alexander had nominated his younger son, Ivan Šišman, as his heir and he was thus crowned tsar in the capital city of Veliko Tarnovo, but the older son, Ivan Sratsimir, established himself as 'Tsar' in Vidin, splitting the already challenged country into two separate domains.

Ivan Šišman, contrary to his brother, was facing the Ottomans directly and although he tried to stay out of direct conflict with them -, refusing to enter into an alliance with Serbia - the Ottomans soon started to move north, peeling off layers of the crumbling Bulgarian country.

In 1373 Ivan Šišman concluded a peace treaty with the Ottomans, a treaty which included his sister, Kera Tamara, being married off to the Ottoman Sultan, Murad II, and Bulgaria becoming an Ottoman vassal state, but even though the treaty led to ten years of nominal peace, the Ottomans continued their raids and eventually started moving again in earnest.

In 1385 the Ottomans conquered Sofia, making their intentions clear, but in 1387 a glimmer of hope emerged. A combined army of Serbians and Bosnians defeated an Ottoman army at Pločnik and although in the bigger picture this was really more of a skirmish than a full-on battle, it was enough to make Ivan Šišman cancel his vassalage to the Ottomans and refuse to assist them with troops.

The Ottoman response was predictable, and they moved with great speed through the remaining Bulgarian territories. Ivan Šišman sued for peace, was granted it on condition of renewed vassalage, but he once again believed that his neighbours would assist him and broke the peace. This time the Ottomans came back even faster, and more furious and new peace terms now included Ottoman troops permanently stationed in key cities.

The Serbians and Bosnians met with the Ottomans again in the (First) Battle of Kosovo in 1389, and this time there was a full battle seeing the Ottomans victorious even though, as covered in Chapter 1, the battle saw Sultan, Murad II, killed in the aftermath of the battle itself.

With their back free, and despite nominal support for Bulgaria from Hungary, the new Ottoman Sultan, Bayezid I, decided to finish the unstable Bulgarians off once and for all, securing Ottoman access to the Danube River.

In 1393 Bayezid I arrived with his army and rolled over Bulgarian resistance, laying the country to waste in his wake. By mid-1395 he mopped up the last remains and killed Ivan Šišman, effectively putting an end to the Second Bulgarian Empire.

There was however still the issue of Ivan Sratsimir reigning from Vidin. He had not done anything to assist his brother, indeed he had taken opportunities to create trouble as and when he could, but as the Ottomans started to dominate the region he could no longer hide behind his brother's territories.

By 1388 Ivan Sratsimir had to submit to Ottoman vassalage, but like his brother he also got lured into a false sense of security by the alliances forming around him.

In 1396 a new alliance between Hungary, Wallachia and various French and German rulers saw a major 'crusade' against the Ottomans and Ivan Sratsimir saw the opportunity to welcome the crusaders, join them and open the gates of the Bulgarian towns, leaving the small Ottoman garrisons virtually defenceless.

The crusade ended with in crushing defeat at Nicopolis in September of 1396 and immediately following his success Sultan Bayezid I moved on Vidin. Ivan Sratsimir was captured and moved to Bursa where he later died, probably murdered.

Although Ivan Sratsimir left a son, who was nominally crowned as Constantine II of Bulgaria, he spent his life in exile and Bayezid I's conquest meant that Bulgaria had ceased to exist as a nation state and its former territories south of the Danube River became an Ottoman province.

There had been a Bulgarian state on and off for seven centuries. It had fought against mighty enemies, first the Byzantines and then the Ottomans and, although it was finally overcome - before the time of the Conqueror - it is important because it in effect enabled other nations to develop behind it, shielded by the Bulgarian state and thus less exposed to the wrath of the mighty empires. It is these other states we shall turn our attention to next.

12 - The Bulgarian Empires

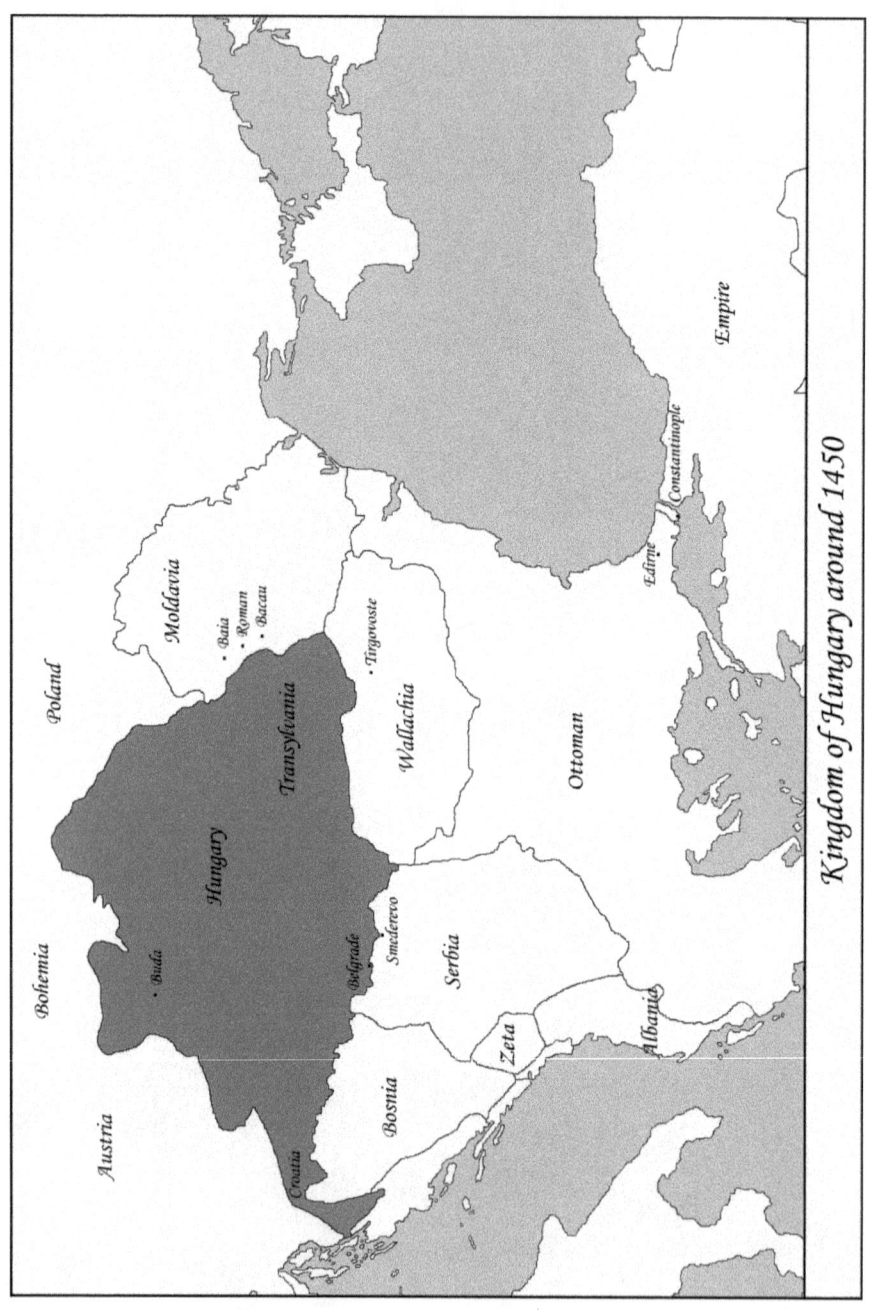

13 - HUNGARY

CRITICAL TIMELINE

Year	Event	Involved Parties
837	First reports of Magyar mercenaries in Bulgarian service	Magyars Bulgaria
895	Byzantine and Magyar attack on Bulgaria	Bulgaria Byzantium Magyars
896	Bulgarians and Pechenegs defeat Magyars. Árpád leads the Magyars across the Carpathian Mountains to Aquincum (Buda) (known as *honfoglalás*).	Magyars
907	Árpád dies. Magyar raiders penetrate into western and eastern Europe.	Magyars Byzantium Bulgaria
955	Battle of Lechfeld ends Magyar raids in western Europe	Magyars Germany
970	Géza becomes Grand Prince of the Hungarians	Hungary
973	German missionaries are allowed into Hungary	Hungary Germany
995	Géza is baptized	Hungary
998	Battle of Veszprém. Stefan I becomes King with papal blessing.	Hungary Germany The Pope
1003	Hungary annexes Transylvania	Hungary
1018	Hungary assists Byzantines in war with Bulgaria	Hungary Byzantium Bulgaria
1041	King Peter Orseolo sent into exile	Hungary
1044	Battle of Ménfő	Hungary Germany
1077	Ladislaus I becomes King of Hungary	Hungary
1091	Hungarian invasion attempt in Croatia	Hungary Byzantium The Pope
1097	First Crusade. Hungarian annexation of Croatia	Hungary Byzantium
1137	Hungary occupies Bosnia	Hungary Bosnia
1162	Byzantine coup sees Ladislaus II as King of Hungary	Hungary Byzantium
1172	Béla III becomes King of Hungary	Hungary
1202	Fourth Crusade conquer Zara	Hungary Venice
1205	András II becomes King of Hungary, Introduces *Novæ institutiones*	Hungary
1211	Teutonic Knights given Burzenland	Hungary Teutonic Knights
1217	Fifth Crusade	Hungary The Pope
1222	Golden Bull	Hungary

13 - Hungary

Year	Event	Involved Parties
1225	Teutonic Knights expelled from Transylvania	Hungary Teutonic Knights
1226	Béla IV becomes Duke of Transylvania	Hungary
1239	Cumans allowed asylum in Hungary	Hungary
1241	Mongol invasion	Hungary Golden Horde
1242	Knights Hospitaller, Cumans and 'Saxons' settlers given land in wake of Mongo invasion	Hungary Knights Hospitaller Cumans
1285	Second Mongol invasion repelled	Hungary Golden Horde
1300	Charles Robert of Anjou lands in Croatia	Hungary House of Anjou
1310	Charles I is crowned as King of Hungary	Hungary House of Anjou
1325	First Florints are minted	Hungary
1330	Battle of Posada. Wallachia becomes independent	Hungary Wallachia
1342	Louis I becomes King of Hungary	Hungary
1347	Hungarian invasion of Naples	Hungary Naples
1350	Second Hungarian invasion of Naples	Hungary Naples
1370	Louis I becomes King of Poland	Hungary Poland
1381	Peace of Turin	Hungary Venice
1382	Mary crowned as King of Hungary	Hungary
1387	Sigismund is crowned as King of Hungary	Hungary
1396	Battle of Nicopolis	Hungary Ottomans Venice France
1403	Ladislaus of Naples land in Dalmatia	Hungary Naples
1408	Hungarian campaigns in Bosnia and Croatia. Sigismund forms the 'Order of the Dragon'	Hungary Bosnia Croatia
1414	Council of Constance	Hungary The Pope
1419	Sigismund becomes King of Bohemia. Hussite Wars	Hungary Bohemia
1428	Hungary and Ottomans agree on new Serbian capital at Smederevo	Hungary Ottomans Serbia
1433	Sigismund becomes Holy Roman Emperor	Hungary The Pope Germany

Year	Event	Involved Parties
1440	Wladyslaw III of Poland becomes King of Hungary	Hungary Poland
1440	Ottoman siege of Belgrade	Hungary Ottomans
1442	Janos Hunyadi expels Ottoman raiders at the Iron Gates	Hungary Ottomans
1443	Long Campaign	Hungary Ottomans
1444	Battle of Varna	Hungary Ottomans Venice
1446	Janos Hunyadi becomes regent	Hungary
1448	Second Battle of Kosovo	Hungary Ottomans
1452	Janos Hunyadi negotiates with Byzantium	Hungary Byzantium
1453	Ottoman conquest of Constantinople	Ottomans Byzantium
1456	Siege of Belgrade	Hungary Ottomans
1458	Matthias I Corvin becomes King of Hungary	Hungary
1458	Hungarian campaign in Bosnia and Serbia	Hungary Ottomans Bosnia Serbia
1463	Ottomans annex Bosnia	Hungary Ottomans Bosnia
1464	Hungarians retake Jajce	Hungary Ottomans Bosnia

13 - Hungary

The presence of the Bulgarian Empire(s) created a front in the north-western part of the Byzantine Empire. For most of the seven centuries in which there was a Bulgarian state the Byzantine Empire was restricted to the lower parts of the Balkans, moving the 'old border' at the Danube River further and further south. This meant that the areas north of the Danube became free of Byzantine quasi-influence and were allowed to develop independently from the mighty empire.

The First Bulgarian Empire had its roots north of the Danube, but gradual expansion - not least the significant expansion under Krum in the beginning of the ninth century - saw the Bulgarian Empire move across the Danube and slide further south towards Rumelia and Constantinople itself.

A century after Krum, the Bulgarian Empire had effectively moved south of the Danube river and only maintained an informal influence north of the river and it was in this hinterland that a new entity arrived in the last decade of the ninth century.

The exact origins of the Magyars is subject to heated discussion between historians and linguists, but the general consensus seems to be that they were nomadic tribes originating from somewhere in central Russia and that they formed part of the Khazars until they broke away and started wandering further south till they reached the Carpathian Basin north of the River Danube.

There are historic records indicating that the Bulgarians hired Magyars as mercenaries as early as 837, but the enterprise was unsuccessful and the Magyars returned back to their territories north of the Danube river.

Next time we encounter the Magyars is in the 890s, where a conflict between Simeon I of Bulgaria and Leo VI of Byzantium sees Leo VI enter into an agreement with the Magyars to attack the Bulgarians from the north (see Chapter 12).

The Magyar attack was successful in its own right, but Simeon I in turn allied himself with the Pechenegs, who attacked the Magyars from the east and eventually the theatre became too hotly contested for the Magyars and they had to move further west.

According to Hungarian history it was in the year 896 that the Magyar tribes, under the command of Árpád, crossed the Carpathian Mountains and entered what is today the core of Hungary, centred around the old Roman settlement of Aquincum on the River Danube. The event defines the birth of the Hungarian nation and is in Hungarian called *honfoglalás*, or 'conquest of the homeland'.

As the history around this (indisputable) event has very strong nationalistic undertones, it can be very difficult to establish the exact details. Where for instance Árpád is the central hero of the Hungarian version, he is mostly ignored, or referred to as the Hungarian's spiritual leader only, by most non-Hungarian sources. Similarly, a tale of how Árpád instructed one of his generals to subdue Transylvania for the Magyars only exists in the Hungarian version and forms the foundation for Hungarian claims on Transylvania even to this day.

Whether Árpád was the political leader or not, the dynasty which followed is known as the Árpád Dynasty, so we will stick with him.

Árpád is reported to have died in 907 and was, according to the Hungarian version, followed by one of his sons, Zoltán, although non-Hungarian historians question this. No matter who followed Árpád one thing is for certain and that is that the emergence of the Hungarians in central Europe started a series of raids into western Europe, spanning as good as all of continental Europe from northern Germany to Spain. In parallel, raids parties were frequently travelling south-east into Bulgarian and Byzantine territories, making the Hungarians the scourge of mainland Europe for the first five decades of the tenth century.

Zoltán is believed to have died around 950, to be succeeded by his nephew Fajsz, another ruler with a very mixed historic background. Under Fajsz the Hungarians continued their raids into western Europe until their hour of destiny came upon them in 955.

Their opponent was Otto 1, King of Germany and later Roman Emperor. Otto I had ruled since 936, but his rule had been marred by rebellions and civil war, leaving the German states weak before the Hungarian raiders. But by 954 the civil war was over and when Otto I heard of yet another Hungarian incursion he decides to solve that problem once and for all.

For the first time in history did a united "German" army take to the field, making a stand on the river Lech outside the town of Augsburg. On 10 August 955 the two forces met in what is now known as the Battle of Lechfeld (or the Battle of Augsburg) and despite numerical superiority on the side of the Magyars, the Germans managed to get close enough to their enemies to prevent them from using their preferred shoot-and-turn tactics, forcing the battle into a close-combat affair in which they were far superior in skill.

The Hungarian army was defeated - although not routed - and limped home while Otto 1 was raised on the shields of his soldiers and declared emperor in the field. The battle stopped any further Hungarian incursions into western Europe, although raids on the Bulgarians and Byzantines continued.

After the Battle of Lechfeld, Fajsz was replaced by Taksony who was a son of Zoltán and who had fought at Lechfeld. Taksony lived in relative peace with his neighbours and is mainly known for the migration of non-

Magyars into the Hungarian state during his rule. On his death in (circa) 970, he was succeeded by his oldest son Géza.

Where Taksony was a rather anonymous ruler, Géza was very different. He first decided to clear the undergrowth of other Árpád family members, more or less eradicating the royal line apart from his own strain. Having done so, he had the Hungarian nobles confirm his son Vajk (later Stefan) as his heir and successor.

Having secured his - and his family's - position inside Hungary, Géza became more active in terms of foreign policies. Seeing a potential anti-Hungarian alliance forming between the Germans and the Byzantines, Géza secured a peace treaty with the Germans, a treaty which included permission for a monk named Bruno to preach and convert inside Hungary.

When Emperor Otto 1 died in 973, Géza saw the opportunity to invade Germany in spite of his agreement to the opposite. Although initially successful, Henry II of Bavaria soon turned the tide and Géza was forced into a new peace treaty which saw him cede lands to the Germans. In addition, the peace treaty secured the marriage of his heir and successor to Giselle, the sister of Henry II.

Towards the end of his life, Géza converted to Christianity, the effort of the monk Bruno showing results. His commitment to Christianity was, however, somewhat shallow although he was baptized and took the name Stefan as his Christian name.

On Géza's death in 997 a war of succession broke out. His proclaimed heir and successor Vajk had also been baptized and had also taken the name Stefan, which we shall call him henceforth.

Stefan's Christian beliefs were, contrary to his father's, genuine and he claimed his right to rule Hungary was a matter of (Christian) divine right. Despite his father having bullied the Hungarian nobles into accepting his right to succession, this was a break with Hungarian tradition according to which the eldest male relative held the right to succession so an uncle, Koppány, one of the few survivors of Géza's family-purge, claimed the right according to tradition.

Stefan was of the (Roman) Catholic faith and Koppány, who had also been baptized, was of the Orthodox faith so the lines were drawn up between tradition and Orthodoxy on one side versus change and Catholicism on the other.

In the end it was neither Christian denomination nor philosophy that won the battle. It was the fact that Stefan had powerful allies through his marriage to Giselle which swung the advantage in his favour. He was sent reinforcements in the form of powerful German knights, and it was those who carried the day when Stefan finally defeated, and executed, Koppány outside Veszprém in 998.

Hungary now had a true Christian (Catholic) ruler and the Pope was not late in recognizing the importance of the 'barbarians' coming into the

Christian fold, not least in the light of the papacy previously having lost the Bulgarians to the Orthodox Church.

According to tradition, Pope Silvestre II sent a jewelled crown to Stefan, accompanied by a cross and a letter of blessing for his appointment as King of Hungary. Also, according to (Hungarian) tradition, this was done with the blessing and agreement of Otto III, the Roman Emperor.

The importance of this is whether Otto III thus in effect recognized Hungary as being independent of the Roman Empire, a claim which has been an issue of contention ever since and, as we shall see later, was to have a direct impact on Hungary's actions during the reign of Mehmed II nearly five centuries later.

With or without Otto III's recognition of Hungary as independent of the Roman Empire, the crowning of Stefan I marked the beginning not only of the Hungarian Kingdom but indeed of the empire that Hungary was to become in the following centuries.

As mentioned above, Stefan I was a man of change. He initially had to fight for his throne against more traditional forces within his newly won kingdom, as well as forces who favoured the Orthodox church, but once he had asserted his authority over the whole kingdom he started a program of forced Christianization and social reforms including the replacement of the traditional runic alphabet with the Latin alphabet and a move towards western feudalism instead of the traditional tribal society.

In his foreign policy Stefan, I continued to expand the Hungarian Kingdom. In 1003 he annexed Transylvania, at that time independently controlled by his uncle Gyula. The annexation of Transylvania would last nine hundred years, and Transylvania is still by many Hungarians considered part of the Hungarian homelands.

He subsequently secured various semi-autonomous regions on the border to Hungary for the Kingdom, partly by inter-marriage and partly by military force.

His wife's brother, Henry II, became Roman Emperor in 1014 and Stefan I supported him in his war against King Boleslaw I of Poland, an alliance which gave Hungary territorial gains when the Polish King was forced to make peace, but no hard feelings existed as Stefan I subsequently supported the Polish King in his wars against the Rus.

In 1018 Stefan I supported the Byzantines in their struggle with the Bulgarians, a campaign which did not see the Hungarians win terrain, but which was used to rob Bulgarian monasteries of holy relics.

When Henry II died in 1024 the new Roman Emperor, Conrad II, rekindled the issue of German supremacy over Hungary and combined with Stefan I's claim of German territories for his son, the result was a short war in which Conrad II tried to invade Hungary but was beaten and finally had to cede border territories to Hungary.

When Stefan I died in 1038, his son and original successor had already died, from a hunting accident, so a period of unrest followed.

Peter Orseolo was Stefan I's nephew through a sister and as his name implies his father was Italian, a Venetian Dodge no less, earning him the nickname 'Peter the Venetian'.

Peter Orseolo was Stefan I's appointed heir and he was crowned on Stefan I's death, but he was not popular. Peter Orseolo was seen as a 'foreigner' who favoured foreign advisors and courtiers over indigenous Hungarians.

Peter Orseolo continued Stefan I's expansion policies, raided into Bavaria and occupied Bohemia, but his confiscation of Queen Dowager Giselle's properties in 1041 resulted in a revolt of the Hungarian nobility, sending Peter Orseolo into exile in Austria and promoting Samuel Aba to the Hungarian throne.

Samuel Aba was of noble origins and either his father or he himself had married another sister of Stefan I, thus connecting him with the royal Hungarian line.

Despite being elected by the Hungarian nobles, Samuel Aba soon became unpopular with his own and with the Church as he seized church property. He unsuccessfully attacked Austria in 1043, followed by a counter attack by the German Emperor, Henry III who supported and housed the deposed Peter Orseolo.

Samuel Aba was defeated at the Battle of Ménfő in 1044 and he was killed immediately after, restoring Peter Orseolo to the throne once again, this time recognizing the suzerainty of the Roman Empire.

Peter Orseolo's second rule was no more popular than his first, this time the issue being his clear submission to the Germans, however it was a popular revolt by pagan peasants which saw him captured, blinded and (possibly) killed in 1046.

The revolting peasants had for a champion one András, a cousin twice removed of Stefan I, and as András I he replaced Peter Orseolo.

The irony of this is that András I was a devout Christian, indeed he earned the moniker 'András the Catholic', so any hopes for a revival of paganism were soon expelled, although as a reward for their support András I did not punish the revolting peasants.

András I invited his brother, Béla, to join him from Poland where he had successfully made a name for himself as a military commander. Béla was appointed military commander of the Hungarian army and given a third of the country to rule.

András I's foreign policy was dominated by war with Germany. Contrary to his successor he had severed links with the Roman Emperor and had refused to accept the Emperor's suzerainty.

Emperor Henry III had no intentions of losing his control over Hungary so he attacked unsuccessfully in 1051 and then again in 1052. Attempts to mediate by the Pope were refused by Henry III, so András I allied himself with the Emperor's rebellious son Conrad II, Duke of Bavaria, which for a time kept the Emperor at bay.

András I had a son, Solomon, who he tried to have appointed as his recognized heir and successor. This was a problem as he had already appointed his brother, Béla, in the same position so the incident led to a break between the brothers, forcing Béla to withdraw to his estates in Poland.

With Béla out of the way, Solomon was appointed heir and András I then proceeded to make peace with the new King of Germany, Henry IV. But the peace was short lived, not because of the Germans, but because of Béla.

With support from the Polish King, Boleslaw II, Béla returned to Hungary with an army and defeated András I's army. András I himself was gravely ill and simply fell off his horse in an attempt to flee to Austria. Béla's followers took him to Zirc where he died, presumably from his illness.

Béla I now became king, but his reign was short and unremarkable. He had spared his nephew, Solomon, and it was he who, with support from Germany, became the next king when Béla I died after ruling for less than three years. His cause of death was injuries sustained when the canopy of his throne collapsed, an incident not necessarily accepted as being coincidental by his contemporaries.

Coincident or otherwise, Solomon I now became king, but his eleven-year rule would be a period of confusion and internal strife. The reason was his three cousins, the sons of Béla: Géza, Ladislaus and Lampert.

Initially the cousins fled to Poland on their father's death, but they returned in 1064 with Polish troops. In an attempt to avoid a devastating civil war, the Hungarian bishops intervened and the parties came to terms. The cousins would accept Solomon I's rule, but they would be granted the right to govern the same one third of the country as had their father before them.

This agreement started a constructive cooperation between Solomon I and his cousins. In the following years they successfully campaigned together in Croatia and Transylvania, but in 1071 it started to go wrong.

An unsuccessful campaign against, Byzantine, Belgrade led to a split between Solomon I and, in particular, Géza and it became clear that sooner or later the parties could not coexist.

Solomon sought support for the forthcoming conflict in Germany, once again accepting German suzerainty, while his cousins relied on Polish and Bohemian family-connections.

The struggle initially went Solomon I's way. He successfully attacked his cousins, who had still not received support from abroad, but when their support did arrive it turned the campaign around and it was Solomon I who was defeated.

Solomon I fled to the western part of Hungary while Géza, was declared King in 1074 as Géza I. Solomon I's German allies attacked once again, but internal conflict in Germany saw them withdraw to deal with matters more close to home.

For the next few years status quo remained, as Géza I could not unseat Solomon I from his possessions in the west and Solomon I did not have the military strength to reclaim the eastern part of the country.

In 1077 Géza I died from disease and his brother Ladislaus was crowned King as Ladislaus I. He was more successful in his campaign against Solomon I and managed to occupy parts of his territories. When he also obtained blessing from the Pope it became clear to Solomon I that the battle was lost, so in 1081 he finally agreed to accept Ladislaus I as king.

Despite this agreement, and the considerable landholdings granted to Solomon I, he was soon plotting against Ladislaus I and was imprisoned.

On the occasion of the canonization of (Saint) Stefan I in August 1083, Solomon I was released and he was soon back in Germany to secure support, The venture was not successful, so instead he turned to the Pechenegs - still living in what would later become Moldavia - and with their support he raided into Hungary. The raids made no impact on the political situation and Solomon I was finally killed during a Pecheneg raid into Byzantine territories.

Ladislaus I had become king less because of who he was and more because of who he was not. As it turned out he, however, became one of the great kings of Hungary and was even made a saint.

The Hungary which Ladislaus I took over had experienced civil war for four decades since the death of Stefan I in 1038 and Ladislaus I realized that before he could pursue an effective foreign policy he needed to get his own house in order.

A string of laws followed, aimed at rooting out lawlessness and 'heresy', introducing mutilation and gruesome executions as punishment for even low-level crimes. He reorganized the Hungarian Church, even accepting the legality of clerical marriage despite the Pope's protests, but by that time (1092) he had in any case severed ties with the Pope over Croatia and was proactively supporting the anti-Pope (Clement III).

With his house in order Ladislaus I started to take an interest in the internal politics of his neighbouring countries, Poland and Germany, lending his support to various factions, but he ultimately withdrew from getting involved in the civil wars raging in Germany, a clever move with gave him room to take an active interest in Croatia instead.

Croatia had gone through its own succession issues, King Stefan II of Croatia dying in 1091 without an heir and as Ladislaus I 's sister, Queen Ilona of Croatia, according to tradition had the right to appoint a new king, she pointed to Ladislaus I who entered Croatia to stake his claim in 1091.

His entry into Croatia was a direct provocation against the supremacy of the Byzantine Emperor, Alexios I, who in a counter-move allied himself with Cuman tribes north-east of Hungary who then attacked Hungary and forced Ladislaus I to withdraw from Croatia to defend his north-eastern borders.

Ladislaus I now turned his attention to the Byzantine possessions around Belgrade, but a new (Byzantine backed) Cuman attack once again took him away to defend the north-eastern borders.

In the meantime the Pope had proposed himself as protector of Croatia, a claim denied by Ladislaus I, which was what had led him to support Antipope Clement III.

The Croatian nobles, having little appetite for neither the Pope nor the Hungarians had in the meantime appointed Petar Svačić, a local nobleman with no dynastic claims, as king and even though Ladislaus I finally marched against him, the Hungarians could only occupy the easternmost parts of Croatia.

Ladislaus I had no male heir and the issue of succession was between his two nephews Coloman and Álmos, the sons of Géza I. Ladislaus preferred Álmos, but Coloman sought support in Poland and in 1095 he entered Hungary with Polish troops to support his claim. His move was perfectly timed as Ladislaus I died at exactly that time, making Coloman's succession a fait accompli.

Coloman was an intellectual, earning himself the moniker 'the booklover' and described by a contemporary Polish chronicler as a king *'who was more educated in literary sciences than any of the kings who was living in his age'*. He was rumoured to have a physical disability, even though it is undocumented in form or impact.

To avoid trouble with his brother, Álmos was in return for accepting Coloman's rule, given a third of the Kingdom to rule as had become the custom in such cases, although with limited success in the past.

And in the case of Coloman and Álmos it did not last either. Álmos never really accepted his brother's rule and sought German support with which he tried, unsuccessfully, to overthrow Coloman in 1098. He then went to join the First Crusade, but on his return in 1108 he again rebelled and finally Coloman had Álmos and his son, Béla, imprisoned and blinded in order to remove any further problems. Álmos then retired to a monastery, but when he later rebelled again against his nephew, Stefan II, he was forced to flee to Byzantium where he died in 1129.

The start of Coloman's rule coincided with the First Crusade and Hungary was on the logical route from western Europe to Byzantium. The result was that rag-tag armies started to make their way through Hungary, leaving chaos and devastating in their wake. Coloman reacted by attempting to bar their access, but he could not maintain the ban with military force so he finally came to an arrangement by which the armies could pass though Hungary under armed escort and only after having delivered hostages to the Hungarian court.

Once the crusader armies had passed, Coloman turned his attention to the unfinished business in Croatia. The Croatian King, Petar Svačić, had pushed the Hungarians east and it was time to get out or take over. Contrary to his uncle, Coloman sought support from the Pope and with his blessing re-entered Croatia which he conquered in 1097, finally gaining control of the coastal towns and islands held by Venice since 1105.

Towards the end of Coloman's reign the Venetians regained control of the towns and islands off the Croatian coast, but when Coloman died in 1116 he had never-the-less secured Croatia for Hungary, making Hungary a true empire just roughly 200 years after Árpád had led his confederation of tribes across the Carpathians with the Bulgarians and Pechenegs snapping at his heels.

Coloman had already secured his son Stefan II as his successor, and with the affirmative action taken against his brother Álmos, the succession was for once smooth.

Stefan II ruled for fifteen years, and his rule was, if not un-eventful, relatively unimportant in the bigger picture. He fought on-and-off with the Venetians over the Dalmatian towns, finally losing control of them. He also fought an on-and-off battle with the Byzantines which did not yield any results on either side.

Stefan II married late, but his wife was caught in adultery and returned to her native Kiev. There she gave birth to a son, Boris, but he was never recognized as royal issue. Stefan II thus did not leave a male heir but rather recalled his (blinded) cousin, Béla, from exile in Byzantium, so when he died from dysentery in 1131 it was the rather unlikely Béla who took the throne as Béla II.

Béla II, strongly supported by his wife, Helena, had to spend most of his reign fighting with Boris, the illegitimate son of Stefan II, who had gained support from the Polish and the Rus; less because of his charming personality and more because both states saw him as an opportunity to gain terrain from the increasingly powerful Hungarians.

The attempts to unseat Béla II were, however, unsuccessful and Béla II entered into dynastic alliances with Bohemia and Austria, two previous enemies of Hungary, both of whom put pressure on the Poles to stop their support of Boris.

Béla II had some military success against Venice in the ongoing battle for control of the Dalmatian coast and he successfully occupied Bosnia, starting decades of Hungarian interference in Bosnian affairs.

When Béla II died in 1141, allegedly from the effects of prolonged alcohol abuse, he left the throne for his oldest son, Géza II.

Géza II, like his father before him, had to fight off an attempt from Boris, this time supported by German and Austrian troops, and when Boris arrived back as part of the French army marching through Hungary as part of the Second Crusade, Géza II asked that French King Louis VII hand Boris over, but the French King refused although he did promise to take him into custody. As a result, Boris was handed over to the Byzantines on the army's arrival at Constantinople.

The Byzantine Emperor subsequently used Boris as a pretext for attacks on Hungary, but Boris was finally killed in battle against the Pechenegs while in Byzantine service.

Géza II mingled in the affairs of his neighbours, supporting allies and kin in their internal struggles, none of which had any lasting impact for Hungary itself. His brothers Stefan and Ladislaus both conspired against him and both ended up in Byzantium, from where we shall see them return later.

Géza II died in 1162, leaving his infant son, Stefan (III) as heir, but Stefan had only just been crowned when he was overthrown by his uncle, Ladislaus (II) who had entered the country with Byzantine support and who was favoured by the Hungarian barons.

Although Ladislaus II was eventually crowned, his reign was not recognized by Lukas, the Archbishop of Esztergom, who excommunicated him. Ladislaus II had Lukas jailed, but he was released on the direct orders of the Pope.

With the problem unsolved and the young King Stefan III ruling in exile while Ladislaus II presided in Buda, Ladislaus II died, possibly from poisoning, after less than a year on the throne.

The Hungarian barons proceeded to give the throne to Ladislaus II's brother, Stefan (IV), so at this time there were two 'King Stefan' of Hungary.

Like his brother before him, Stefan IV was supported by the Byzantine Empire and the Hungarian barons, but when he displayed distinct characteristics as a mere Byzantine puppet, the barons started to defect. In the meantime young King Stefan III had sought the support of Frederick I, the Holy Roman Emperor, and with his military support he entered Hungary and defeated the supporters of Stefan IV. The latter was taken prisoner, but Stefan III released him and Stefan IV retreated once again to Constantinople. From there he launched a couple of half-hearted attacks in order to regain the throne, but he died in 1165, poisoned by his own troops before they surrendered to an opposing Hungarian army. Stefan III now ruled supreme.

Although successful in terms of the battle for the throne, the conflicts with the Byzantine Empire had however proved costly, as the Byzantines had conquered Bosnia, Croatia and the Dalmatian coast. Stefan III tried several times to re-conquer the lost territories, but he was unsuccessful and died suddenly from an undisclosed disease in 1172 at only twenty-five years of age.

Stefan III did not leave an heir, so the throne would pass to one of his brothers, Geza or Béla, the question however was which brother?

Béla had been living at the Byzantine court for many years and was at one point appointed as heir to the Byzantine Emperor, Manual I Komnenos, whose daughter he was also due to marry. Manuel I Komnenos however conceived a son late in life and Béla was rather unceremoniously cast aside for the new blood-heir to the Byzantine throne, his engagement to the Emperor's daughter also cancelled.

Geza had remained in Hungary and although he was the younger of the brothers, he was the favourite of his mother, the Queen Dowager, and Lukas, the Archbishop of Esztergom as well as many of the Hungarian barons.

Béla had however been given a large amount of money by Emperor Manuel I Komnenos, and on his arrival in Hungary he used it to ensure the necessary loyalty from the powerful barons. Once again, the Archbishop of Esztergom refused to crown a king, but the Pope intervened and with his blessing Béla was crowned as Béla III.

To avoid further complication, Béla III attempted to arrest both his mother and his brother, but Geza managed to escape to Austria. The Austrian duke, Leopold V, however had no intentions of getting on the wrong side of Béla III, so he handed his brother back to him.

Geza was not done though. A year later he managed to escape to Bohemia, but his peer in Austria, the Duke, Soběslav II, had no intentions of hiding the refugee, so once again Geza was handed over and returned to jail. Here he lingered until 1189 when he was set free in order to command a small contingent of Hungarians following Frederick I in the Third Crusade. Although he was under orders to return to Hungary he did not, but rather stayed in the Holy Land where he died in 1210.

King Béla III ruled Hungary for twenty-four years, bringing stability and prosperity to the Kingdom. He managed to retake Croatia and Dalmatia from the Byzantines and also supported the city-state of Zara in its rebellion against Venice, the prelude for the Venetian conquest of Zara during the early stages of the Fourth Crusade (see Chapter 3). He also occupied the principality of Halych in modern day western Ukraine although it was lost again when its ruler, Vladimir, escaped from Hungarian imprisonment.

Béla III died in 1196, as far as is known from natural causes. He was at the time of his death probably the wealthiest ruler in Europe, his revenues exceeding those of the French King and double those of the English King.

Following the long and stable rule of Béla III, the ground was well prepared for a smooth transition of power. Béla III had already had his oldest son, Emeric, crowned as co-regent in 1182 and the ceremony was repeated shortly before Béla III's death.

Béla III left specific instructions regarding Emeric's unconditional and undivided right to the throne, and Emeric was duly crowned on his father's death.

Béla III's other son, András, was left with a substantial amount of money, earmarked to finance a crusade which his father had pledged shortly before his death. If he had done that, all would have been good, but he did not.

András had designs on the throne, and used the money left to him to buy support from the Hungarian barons.

András relocated to Austria, where he gained - possibly due to a significant monetary contribution - the support of Duke Leopold VI and with the Duke's support he defeated his brother in battle.

Negotiations were had and it was agreed that whereas Emeric stayed on the throne of Hungary, his brother was given Croatia and Dalmatia with the title of duke. But András was not happy. He once again conspired against his brother, seeking support amongst the nobles in Hungary, including Bishop Boleszlo of Vác. Emeric however had the Pope on his side, eager for András to fulfil his father's pledge for a crusade, and a race for support ensued amongst the brothers, both donating major properties to the Church in order to gain the upper hand.

Emeric finally had enough. He personally went to arrest Bishop Boleszlo of Vác and he stripped other - disloyal - noble families of their properties and privileges. In the summer of 1199, it once again came to battle, this time with Emeric as the winner and a peace was negotiated through which status quo was restored with András in Croatia and Dalmatia.

In the first years of the thirteenth century, Emeric got involved in the succession conflict in Serbia, following the death of its ruler Stefan Nemanja. The sons of Stefan Nemanja, Stefan and Vukan, were fighting each other for supremacy and Emeric interfered on the side of Vukan. The interference initially gave Emeric control of new territories in Serbia, but eventually Vukan's revolt was put down and the Hungarian left without gains.

The city state of Zara had once again confirmed its allegiance to Hungary, so when the Venetians, at the head of the Fourth Crusade, conquered the city, Emeric appealed to the Pope who excommunicated the crusaders. Emeric tried to retake the city by force, but eventually he had to give up and the city was officially separated from Hungary by a treaty.

But Emeric was not well, so he started to worry about succession. Despite further troubles, he reconciled with his brother and had him appointed as regent for his infant son, Ladislaus.

When Emeric died in 1204, the five years old Ladislaus was crowned as Ladislaus III, but his uncle András had no intentions of sharing the power he had finally obtained. Fearing for Ladislaus III's life, his mother, the Dowager Queen Constance, took refuge with her son in Austria. Here Ladislaus III died at the age of six. Finally, András had what he wanted.

Crowned as András II a rule of three decades began, a rule which was not necessarily successful, but was definitely eventful. Before we continue, it is worth noting that around the same time as András II was crowned in Hungary, a small contingent of the Kai tribe of Turkoman nomads, 400 tents strong, arrived as refugees in eastern Anatolia. We shall of course meet them in their later, more powerful, manifestation as the Ottomans.

András II decided to change the internal structure of power in the Kingdom, instituting the '*Novæ institutiones*' or 'new institutions', through which he started giving away the state's property to noble families and various groupings.

Whereas his generosity in general terms benefitted the nobles, it also led to envy, not least since the local nobles believed he favoured the German relatives of his wife, Gertrude of Merania, their suspicions further fuelled when András II gave away Burzenland, the south-eastern part of Transylvania, to the Teutonic Knights.

The idea was to outsource the defence of south-eastern Transylvania and furthermore encourage German settlers, generally referred to as 'Saxons', who were invited to populated the area, acting as support for the stone fortresses built by the Teutonic Knights. As good an idea as that may have seemed, effectively the Teutonic Knights soon set up an autonomous state in the area paying little heed to their Hungarian overlord.

In other areas of the Kingdom already powerful barons started to build estates from former royal domains which made them immensely powerful, in effect undermining the royal authority instead of strengthening it as was the intention behind the '*Novæ institutiones*'.

Externally András II yet again attempted to annex the Halych principality, but despite having successfully occupied it he eventually lost it again. He had better luck in the south, where he managed to take the area around Belgrade away from the Bulgarians.

While András II was away on various campaigns, he left the Kingdom in the hands of his queen, Gertrude. She in turn took the opportunity to bestow even further land, property and privileges on her immediate family and followers until, finally, the Hungarian nobles lost their patience. During a hunt with visiting dignitaries the Queen was assassinated, and her body was torn apart. Although the event forced András II to return from his current campaign in Halych, he decided to only execute the most obvious leaders of the conspiracy and not take direct action against the rest of the conspirators, they were simply too powerful for the King who had given it all away.

The Pope was still eager that András II should go on the crusade he had 'inherited' from his father and finally, in 1217, he went.

The Fifth Crusade, as the expedition would later be called by historians, was not an overall success, but the initial phases in which András II was the commander, met with some success and the Hungarian King II and his substantial army did well for themselves. András II, however, had become sick so at the beginning of 1218 he and the Hungarian army withdrew from the Holy Land and returned home.

On his way home, András II took the opportunity for some hands-on diplomacy and arranged for several marriages of his children into the royal lines of Armenia, Nicaea, Bulgaria and Cilicia, thus expanding the Kingdom's complex network of dynastic ties.

András II probably thought he had done quite well, but if he did, he soon changed his mind when he returned home to a kingdom in utter chaos.

The King's policy of giving away royal property to his loyal supporters had gradually created a new 'middle class' of smaller landowners, and they soon came into conflict with the established noble landowners, who in turn had expanded and consolidated their estates through annexation of royal property.

The regent, Archbishop John of Esztergom, had fled the country and the state's coffers were empty. Chaos ruled and there was discontent at all levels of society.

András II tried to regain some control by issuing new taxes and devaluating the currency, typical financial instruments of the time, and he even 'leased' his future income to Jewish and Muslim moneylenders, adding further discontent to an already explosive situation.

Finally, the nobles had had enough, and they gave András II a clear ultimatum. He would either be forcefully removed, or he would agree to a charter in which the limits of royal power and the privileges of the noble class were clearly specified.

The document, known as 'the Golden Bull', was signed in 1222 and was a unique definition of the Kingdom's power sharing. Possibly inspired by the 'Magna Carta' - signed by the King John of England in 1215 - the document effectively curtailed the royal power and confirmed the substantial privileges enjoyed by the nobles.

The Golden Bull very clearly specified that the Hungarian nobles were exempt from taxes and that they could not be forced to perform military service outside the Kingdom's borders unless they were paid to do so. It also made it clear that property could not be given to foreigners, public offices could not be inherited and that Jews could not be public servants. It furthermore specified that the nobles were not obliged to follow royal commands if they exceed the royal powers given within the document.

András II's son, Béla, had been confirmed as his heir already at infancy, but the relation between father and son would gradually deteriorate.

Béla never forgave his father for not taking decisive action against the conspirators who had his mother murdered and as he became of age the tension grew even worse.

In 1214 Béla was crowned as 'Junior King', or heir apparent, and he was formally engaged to a daughter of the Bulgarian ruler. Nothing ever came of that though and Béla was forced into exile in Austria during his father's participation in the Fifth Crusade.

Béla returned back to Hungary after his father's return and in 1220 he married Maria Laskarina, a daughter of the Emperor of Nicaea as per his father's arrangements.

For reasons unknown András II changed his mind on his son's marriage, and in 1222 forced Béla to divorce his wife. The divorce was, however, not confirmed by the Pope and Béla took his wife with him in exile in Austria.

The parties reconciled and Béla was confirmed as Duke of Croatia, Dalmatia and Slavonia.

Armed with his new powers in the region, and with the blessing of the Pope, Béla gradually started to roll back the mistakes of his father, taking back royal properties which had been given to various parties. The move was not popular, but it was effective in terms of strengthening the royal estate and cleaning up in the undergrowth of local warlords and tyrants.

The behaviour of the Teutonic Knights in south-eastern Transylvania had come to such a point that they operated as a de-facto autonomous state, a point on which the King and the nobles could for once agree, and an army was put together which expelled the Teutonic Knights from the Kingdom in 1225. The knights went back to Prussia and the crown gained important military property in the form of the fortresses they left behind.

To best utilize this newfound power, Béla was appointed Duke of Transylvania in 1226, the first time the 'wild east' territory of Transylvania was confirmed as a single political entity and he continued his efforts to reclaim royal properties and assert central control though the Transylvanian 'Saxons" - the German settlers - were issued with very wide-reaching rights of autonomy as long as they defended the central towns and paid their taxes.

This balance between András II controlling the western part of the Kingdom and Béla controlling the eastern part, continued up until András II's death in 1235.

Béla's younger brother, András, had been killed in battle so this time the succession was smooth and fast. The 'Junior King' became Béla IV.

In the year before his death, András II had further angered his son by marrying Beatrice d'Este who was thirty years his junior. At the death of András II the young queen was pregnant, but Béla IV had her charged with adultery and she had to flee the country. She eventually settled in Italy under the protection of the Pope, but her son, Stefan the Posthumous, was never recognized as legal issue of András II.

Once in control of the whole kingdom, Béla IV continued in his quest of reversing his father's catastrophic undermining of the royal authority. As a symbolic gesture he had the seats of his council burned to force the members to stand in royal presence, but outside the Kingdom a storm was brewing which would, more than anything, come to define Béla IV's rule.

Béla IV sent a Friar Julian of the Dominicans eastwards to *'find the Magyars who remained in the eastern homelands'*. Despite this rather loose definition of his objectives Friar Julian did indeed manage to find the Magyar tribes still living nomadic lives in central Asia. Through them he first heard of the 'Tatars' - or Mongolians - causing havoc in the East and when he later returned to the area, he found that it had been overrun by the Mongolian hordes.

Friar Julian brought this news back to Hungary, and there were other signs of coming troubles. The Cumans had remained an independent entity in the area north of the Black Sea. They had always been a traditional enemy of Hungary, performing raids into Hungarian territory and they were, from Hungarian standards, heathen.

The Cumans were now being pushed westwards by the Mongols and despite the traditional hostility between the two parties, King Béla IV invited the refugees, believed to have been up to 40,000 strong, to enter Hungary and settle as, much needed, subjects loyal to the crown.

The Dominican missionaries had some success in converting part of the Cumans to Christianity, but the local nobles were less than pleased with their new compatriots who maintained a nomadic lifestyle which did not necessarily respect established property boundaries.

But the Cumans provided a capable military force and it was clear to Béla IV that military force would be needed once the Mongols arrived.

Preparations were made to reinforce the fortresses on the Kingdom's borders, but the King's effort was in many places met with resistance from local lords who took the opportunity to try to squeeze out further advantages from the King.

Despite the King's best effort, the Kingdom was thus ill-prepared for the Mongol attack when it came.

On 12th March 1241 the Mongols broke the Hungarian defences on the eastern border and two days later the local Hungarian nobles killed the royal family of the Cumans, who were held under the King's protection. This insane move infuriated the Cumans who simply left without a fight and resettled in Bulgaria.

With a considerable part of his army thus disappearing into thin air, Béla IV still managed to muster an army of around the same size as the invading army, but it suffered an all-out defeat to the battle-hardened Mongols at the Battle of Mohi on 21 April 1241.

With the Hungarian army defeated, the King fled into exile and the Mongolians had a free run of the Kingdom. Buda was sacked and anything that could be carried away was carried away. As many parts of Hungary's military capacity had not been involved in the defining battle, due to the internal problems and infighting, local militias did their best to protect their territory and harass the rear of the Mongolian advance, but the Mongolians reigned supreme when they set up winter-camp on the Hungarian plains.

Then with the coming of spring 1242 the Mongolians packed up their camp and simply withdrew, although they did make sure that their withdrawal included raiding the territories they had previously passed through in their initial push towards Buda. The kingdom of Hungary had been saved, but nobody really knows why.

The dominant theory is that the death of the Mongol Great Khan Ögedei in December 1241 forced the leaders of the Mongol Hordes to return home to take part in the fight for succession. Other theories speculate that the Hungarian plains could not sustain the Mongol army and its horses, that the Mongolian loses from the campaigns in Russia, Poland and Hungary had been so costly that the Mongolians realized that they could not hold Hungary in the long run, or that their strategic objective was not to hold Hungary in the first place but only to soften it up before a bigger campaign into Europe - which did not materialize - at a later day.

It was possibly one of these reasons, or perhaps a combination of reasons, but in any case, the Mongolians left, leaving behind them a kingdom which was alive, but broken both militarily and politically.

Béla IV returned from an unhappy exile in which he had been forced by Duke Frederick II of Austria to hand over his treasure and cede the westernmost counties of Hungary to Austria. He had then sworn to rule under the suzerainty of the Holy Roman Empire should the Emperor, Frederick II, provide him with military assistance, but in the end no assistance came and Béla IV re-entered Hungary without military force.

There were many problems facing Béla IV, but he handled them so effectively that he has gone down in history as 'the second founder' of Hungary.

The Pope absolved Béla IV of the promises made to the Holy Roman Emperor and the counties ceded to Austria were taken back in a short campaign immediately following his return.

Hungary had, despite the devastation of the country, still massive military potential, but the question was how to best utilize it and prevent a new Mongol invasion which was a clear and present danger.

The problem which had surfaced during the Mongol invasion was that the defence of the Kingdom was based nearly entirely on border defences. There were border-castles and fortified passes as well as a certain reliance on natural defences such as the Danube River, but with the right numbers and technology even the strongest castle could be defeated, or isolated, and rivers could freeze. Once an enemy had penetrated the border, there were practically no solid defences to stop them from moving freely around inside the Kingdom.

This problem combined with the lack of central control over the Kingdom's military potential led Béla IV to change his internal policies and revert to promote policies not dissimilar to those of his father, but this time aiming at a specific military purpose.

Once again royal property was given to supporters, but this time it came with a clear obligation to fortify and defend the territory. As his father had given a whole area to the Teutonic Knights, Béla IV gave the territory of Szörény, on the northern side of the Danube, River to the Knights Hospitaller.

The Cumans, potentially representing a significant boost to the Hungarian army were called back from their exile and this time they were given a large area of land between the Danube and Tisza rivers which was simply depopulated in the wake of the Mongolian withdrawal.

'Saxon' settlers were again invited to settle, in particular in Transylvania, under the condition that they fortified and defended their, semi-autonomous, cities. The result was a string of fortified cities which is the reason why Transylvania is called '*Siebenbürgen*' - '*Seven Castles*' - in the German language, even if really there were nine, not seven, fortified cities.

But instead of the Mongolians it was the Austrians who came. They were trying to retake the lost counties and although they were militarily successful, Duke Frederick II of Austria was killed in the ensuing battle, starting a war of succession in Austria. Béla IV utilized this power vacuum to occupy parts of Austria, although he ultimately had to satisfy himself with the Duchy of Styria in order to avoid an all-out war with neighbouring Bohemia. The Duchy was, however, lost again in 1260 after two rebellions.

In the end the Mongols did not come again during Béla IV's lifetime. When they did come in 1285, they were repelled. Although they managed to cross the border and cause some damage, this time they could not occupy the Kingdom due to the many defensive installations in the hinterland. Although he did not live to see it, Béla IV's strategic plan for the defence of the Kingdom worked.

Béla IV's son and heir apparent was Stefan. Like Béla before him, Stefan was crowned as 'Junior King,' in 1246, at the age of five. The title was honourable only, as Béla IV had no intentions of sharing power with his son.

When Stefan came of age, he became increasingly frustrated over his father's lack of willingness to involve him in the affairs of the Kingdom and, in 1458, he took up arms.

It did not come to armed conflict though, as Béla IV agreed to make Stefan Duke of Transylvania, and although father and son campaigned together in Styria and Bulgaria, their relationship was never good. The result was that their various partisans fought mini battles until two powerful clerics intervened. Their intervention led to a formal agreement, in 1263, by which Béla IV ruled in the west and Stefan ruled in the east, once again effectively making Transylvania an autonomous state within the state.

Despite the agreement hostilities continued for another three years, escalating into full civil war, but once again the church-leaders intervened and a final peace, reconfirming the power-sharing model, was agreed in 1266.

The peace lasted until Béla IV died in 1270 and Stefan was crowned as Stefan V.

But the succession was not smooth. Despite Stefan's crowning as 'Junior King' and heir apparent, Béla IV had in his last testament 'entrusted' his followers and Stefan's sister Anna to King Ottokar II of Bohemia. In other words, Béla IV had turned his back on his son and handed over the Kingdom, to the extent he controlled it, to his old enemy.

Stefan V's sister Anna had, with many followers, fled to Prague, so Stefan was crowned without issues, but he would soon spend his time fighting the last testament of his father.

Despite signing a peace treaty, Stefan V and Ottokar II were soon at war and initially luck was with Ottokar II. Stefan V, however, turned the luck around and finally defeated Ottokar II's Bohemians and Austrians. In the ensuing peace Stefan V however had to renounce the Kingdom's claims to the substantial fortune his sister Anna had brought with her from the royal treasury, but at least Ottokar II accepted Stefan V's reign.

With his back free, Stefan V went to Dalmatia where he was due to meet King Charles I of Sicily, whose daughter, Elizabeth, had been married - at the tender age of eight - to Stefan V's son and heir Ladislaus, who was of the same age. On his way there he was, however, informed that Ladislaus had been kidnapped by Joachim Pektar, the Ban of Slavonia.

Stefan V turned around and prepared to meet the Ban of Slavonia with force, but he fell ill and died suddenly, leaving behind a political mess, which was not necessarily of his own making.

Stefan V had been engaged to Elizabeth, a princess of the Cumans, since they were both infants. Their marriage had taken place in 1253 and the kidnapped prince, and heir apparent, was issue from this marriage. Elizabeth had been a heathen before she was baptized in order to enable the royal marriage, and she was not looked upon with favour by the Hungarian nobles.

Although Joachim Pektar brought the kidnapped prince back to Hungary, where he was crowned as Ladislaus IV, it was at a price, namely his inclusion in the regency which ruled during Ladislaus IV's infancy.

The following 5 years were total chaos. Despite Elizabeth's best attempts to protect her son's interests, the country was in the hands of ever-changing factions of barons. She did manage to oust Joachim Pektar, who in return kidnapped Ladislaus IV once again, but this time he was quickly released. Elizabeth's only loyal supporters were the Cumans, her own kin.

Finally, in 1277, Ladislaus IV was of age and a council of barons officially handed power over to him. The Kingdom he inherited was, however, one in which his authority counted for little and, contrary to his predecessors, he had no grand plan.

Having been brought up by Elizabeth, Ladislaus IV soon became known as 'Ladislaus the Cuman.' This was caused not only by his ancestry, but also from his clear preference for the Cumans and their way of life. He would wear traditional Cuman clothes at court, surround himself with Cuman 'advisors' and ignore his noble wife to seek the company of Cuman mistresses.

A papal legate sent to investigate complaints about Ladislaus IV's 'unchristian' behaviour was temporarily held prisoner by his Cuman allies, although in the end it was Ladislaus IV himself who ended up a prisoner of the Voivode of Transylvania.

In short, it was a mess. There was no central authority in the Kingdom, and it was only Transylvania, run by a strong voivode, which was functioning in terms of administration and what little law and order could be found.

The successful defence of the Kingdom against the Mongol attack in 1285 was not due to Ladislaus IV or his royal authority, it was entirely the success of his grandfather, Béla IV's, revision of the defensive system in the aftermath of the first Mongol invasion.

Finally, as a fitting end to a chaotic rule, Ladislaus IV was assassinated in 1290, by Cuman assassins.

Due to his estranged relationship to his wife, Elizabeth of Sicily, he had no heir and with his death a successor of the Árpád dynasty had to be found far away.

We now have to take a step back to András II, Ladislaus IV's great-grandfather. As mentioned earlier he re-married in the year before his death and his new wife had a son, Stefan - the Posthumous - after András II had died. András II's heir, Béla IV, declared Stefan as a bastard and his mother, Queen Consort Beatrice d'Este, had to flee into exile as she was accused of adultery.

Beatrice d'Este found refuge in Italy and her son Stefan grew up in Venice. Stefan in turn married Tomasina Morosini, who came from a prominent Venetian noble family, and they had a son, András, named after his royal grandfather.

After the death of Ladislaus IV, the only living relative of the male-line of the Árpád dynasty, assuming that Stefan the Posthumous was not a bastard after all, was said András - also known as András the Venetian - and it was to this unlikely candidate the Hungarian nobles turned to find a new King of Hungary.

András had been approached even before Ladislaus IV's death. A group of powerful prelates and barons had already realized the need to find a replacement for Ladislaus IV, but András was arrested by another noble faction on his arrival in Hungary, and he was held captive in Austria.

On Ladislaus IV's death, András however escaped and on his arrival in Hungary was crowned as András III.

But the weak royal authority experienced during Ladislaus IV did not suddenly, magically, reverse to a strong centralized government. Indeed the problems surrounding András III's father's birth right was used as an excuse by others to forward their own candidature for the throne of Hungary, and in reality András III only ruled with the support of a small contingent of nobles and prelates in the western part of the Kingdom.

King Rudolph I of Germany considered Hungary to be part of the Holy Roman Empire - following the oaths taken by Béla IV - and he appointed his son, Duke Albert I of Austria, as King of Hungary.

On the assumption that András III's birth right was invalid, Ladislaus IV's sister, Mary, Queen of Naples, threw in her challenge for the throne as first among the female line. She in turn transferred that claim to her son, Charles Martel of Anjou, and on his death (in 1295) to his son Charles Robert (of Anjou).

A pretender, claiming to be András, the younger brother of Ladislaus IV - who had died in 1278 at the age of ten - obtained support in Poland, but he was quickly defeated by András III's supporters when he tried to push the matter through military intervention.

András III now spent most of his time alternating between negotiations and outright conflict with the powerful barons of Hungary, who had grown into semi-autonomous quasi-kings through the decades of weak royal authority, and whose loyalty to the King and the various outside candidates would change with the wind, and the promises given to them by the contenders.

András III's mother, Tomasina Morosini, arrived in Hungary, where she was given the honourable title of Princess of Slavonia, and she turned out to be an asset, acting as the King's ambassador in many negotiations with the rebellious barons and prelates.

Another move which strengthened András III's position was his - second - marriage to Agnes of Austria, the daughter of Duke Albert I of Austria. As András III at that time had no male heir, the privileged status of any male offspring from this marriage satisfied the claims from the Holy Roman Empire and thus eliminated the Austrian claim to the throne.

But the claim from Charles Robert was still alive, and it was very real. Most of the barons in the east of the Kingdom supported Charles Robert, although it was probably more due to his promises of future riches than due to any real concern about András III's birth right, and András III spent considerable time trying to put down rebellions in the east.

In 1300 it became even more serious, Charles Robert landed in Croatia and soon had control of Zagreb.

András III went to meet the invaders, but his mother suddenly died, probably poisoned, so he turned the army around. He himself was also sick, the disease unspecified, and he died in January 1301 without leaving an heir.

András III was thus the last of the long line of the Árpád dynasty which had ruled Hungary from the very birth of the Kingdom 400 years earlier.

The death of András III thus threw Hungary into a de-facto interregnum. Nominally there was a king though.

András III left behind a daughter, Elizabeth, who was betrothed to Wenceslaus, the son of Wenceslaus II, King of Bohemia and Poland, Hungary's powerful neighbours in the north.

Prince Wenceslaus was around eleven and princess Elizabeth around eight years old at the time of András III's death, but their promised union was as good a dynastic claim as any, so King Wenceslaus II 'accepted' the throne of Hungary on behalf of his son, who was then crowned as Ladislaus V.

Ladislaus V, however, had very little support inside Hungary, limited to a few powerful families in the northwest with family-ties in Bohemia and Poland, but he did have possession of both Buda and the crown jewels.

At the other end of the country, Charles Robert enjoyed much broader support, including that of the Pope, and the country was in effect run by the various noble factions.

One of the most powerful families, the Csák family, changed allegiance from Ladislaus V to Charles Robert in 1303, prompting Ladislaus V's father, King Wenceslaus II of Bohemia and Poland to send an occupying force to Buda, but taking a realistic view of the situation the King returned to Bohemia, taking with him his son and the crown regalia of Hungary, leaving in his place a proxy regent, Ivan of Güssing, a member of a noble Hungarian family.

When King Wenceslaus II died in 1305, his son, Ladislaus V, had no desire to keep up the challenge for the Hungarian throne. He renounced it in December of 1305, leaving it to Otto III, Duke of Bavaria, a maternal grandchild of Béla IV, who took the name Béla V and was crowned with the royal regalia of the Kingdom, passed on to him by Ladislaus V.

In terms of sheer dynastic heritage, Béla V's claim to the Hungarian throne was as good as Charles Robert's claim, but support on the ground was swinging between the two contestants, the Pope supporting Charles Robert, but Béla V being in possession of the highly symbolic Holy Crown of Hungary, also known as the Crown of St.Stefan.

Finally, it was the immensely powerful Voivode of Transylvania, Ladislaus Kán, who tipped the balance. In October of 1307 he took Béla V prisoner and took physical possession of the Holy Crown.

With Béla V effectively out of the equation, most of the nobles of Hungary now joined around Charles Robert, who had been crowned as Charles I, but some powerful barons, including Ladislaus Kán, simply ignored the new king, continuing their life as 'mini-kings' inside their substantial estates. Since Charles I had not been crowned with the Holy Crown of Hungary, his kingship was not legitimate, or so the rhetoric went. This issue would re-emerge 150 years later and would at that time directly impact the conflict between Hungary and the Ottoman Empire, but more about that later.

Civil war followed, in which Charles I gradually managed to gain authority over larger and larger parts of Hungary, but it was only through intervention by a papal legate that in 1310 Ladislaus Kán finally handed over the Holy Crown and Charles I could be finally crowned.

But the battle was far from over, indeed for more than a decade following, Charles I would still fight internal battles, although one by one his original opponents died and their heirs could not maintain the power once yielded by the powerful barons emerging from the interregnum.

Once he had restored royal authority over the Kingdom in the early parts of the 1320s, Charles I started to reform the Kingdom's finances, which had fallen into disarray. He re-established the royal prerogative on customs and taxes, which had been run at will by individual barons for decades, and rather than continue the policy of devaluating the currency, Charles I started to mint coins - Florints - with a consistent high content of gold, laying the basis for the Hungarian Florint becoming one of the 'strong currencies' in the centuries to come.

On the external front Charles I was a master of diplomacy, forging alliances with powerful neighbours which enabled him to regain control of border-areas which had been lost during the many years of disarray. One area in which he, however, could not assert his suzerainty was Wallachia, south of the Carpathians, which once and for all claimed its status as a nation state during Charles I's reign after a Hungarian army had been devastated in an ambush (the Battle of Posada) during a campaign in the area, Charles I himself narrowly escaping the incident.

Charles I ruled until his death in 1342, an unbroken reign of more than three decades and exactly the cure that Hungary needed in order to regain its power and unity. Without Charles I, it is doubtful if the Hungarian Kingdom would have been kept as a single nation state, as another weak king would have likely seen the powerful magnates like Ladislaus Kán carve out their own kingdoms and the rest being absorbed by Hungary's powerful neighbours.

By the time of Charles I's death, the small contingent of the Kai tribe, which had fled in front of the Mongols and re-settled in Anatolia at the beginning of the thirteenth century, had developed into a substantial and powerful state, dominating most of Anatolia. A decade later they would cross the sea and settle in Europe.

Charles I's heir was Louis crowned as Louis I on his father's death. Louis I was a 'man's man', although very well educated in classic sciences he was first and foremost a warrior who led from the front and thus commanded near endless respect from his troops.

During his four decades of reign, Hungary would become as influential as it would ever be, but to some extent Louis I became the King of pyrrhic victories, achieving great military success which left the Kingdom exhausted with little political gain to show for the effort. But to his contemporaries he was, however, the archetypical symbol of a warrior king and noble knight.

Louis I was a strong regent. His father's reforms had ensured that the crown once again had substantial income, and Louis I had ambitions on top of wealth.

His first targets were territories lost by his father on the outskirts of the Empire. Quick campaigns saw Macedonia and Kosovo brought back under Hungarian rule and Wallachia and Moldavia bending to the pressure and accepting vassal status.

Next were the coastal cities in Dalmatia, long a source for contention between the Hungarians and the Venetians who ruled supreme in the Adriatic Sea. The first stage of the conflict went to the Venetians, who had paid the Hungarian generals hefty bribes to disclose the Hungarian positions, but finally, assisted by the Bosnian Ban Stjepan II, whose loyalty was also questionable, the sheer numbers of the Hungarian army won the conflict for Hungary. In the kind of outcome which became a trademark for Louis I, Zara, the main city in contention, stayed in Venetian hands, leaving Hungary with the military glory and its opponents with the political victory.

In the meantime, Louis I's brother, András, had been murdered. He had been married to Joanna I of Naples, heiress to the Kingdom of Naples. The complex politics of Italy however caught András in the middle of intrigues also involving the Pope, and as a result he was murdered. His brother, Louis I held Joanna I of Naples responsible - although her guilt was never proven - and in 1347 he moved into Italy with a considerable army.

Once again Louis I was militarily successful, but realized that he had no popular support in Italy, and he finally withdrew, ahead of the Black Death which had reached Italy, with no political results. He went back in 1350, once again succeeding militarily, but once again had to leave, realizing that without papal support he had no real chance of taking the throne of Naples away from Joanna I. Eventually, nearly three decades later, the Pope changed his mind and in 1382 Joanna I was murdered, throwing the Kingdom of Naples into its own war of succession.

In 1357 and 1358 Louis I was back in Dalmatia and this time he was playing for keeps. He deployed the full force of the Hungarian army to the cities on the Dalmatian coast, ultimately winning one of his few political victories, forcing the Venetian and the Dalmatian cities to accept his overlordship and enabling Hungary to start building its own Adriatic fleet.

Hungarian participation in the alliance with Genoa - see Chapter 11 - which forced the Peace of Turin in 1381 established that Venice should pay an annual tribute to Hungary, a state of affairs which only lasted a few years before Venice once again ruled in the Adriatic.

Louis I's uncle was King Casimir III of Poland and Louis I and Casimir III had campaigned together several times against invading Lithuanians, Mongols and Bohemians. Casimir III had no male heir, so he appointed Louis I as his heir, and when Casimir III died in 1370, Louis I became King of Poland as well, uniting Poland and Hungary into a personal union under one king.

During the latter part of his reign Louis I spent a lot of time in the Balkans, more for showing off his power than campaigning per se. He became involved in Bulgaria, Serbia, Bosnia, Moldavia and Wallachia, all states forced to accept vassal-status. He also, with the blessing of the Pope, tried to enforce their conversion - from the Orthodox Church - to Catholicism, which eventually made him, and Hungary, unpopular, once again leaving him with the military upper hand, but a lost political battle.

Another reason for Louis I's attempts to unify the Balkan states was the growing menace from the Ottomans. Last we took status on the Ottomans, at the start of Louis I's rule, they were still in Anatolia. In the meantime, they had migrated across to Europe and established themselves in the ashes of the impotent Byzantine Empire.

From their original base on the Gallipoli peninsula, the Ottomans had in over just a couple of decades, become a serious player. By 1365 they had annexed the city of Adrianople, renamed it to Edirne, and made it capital of the Ottoman territories in Europe. From there they started pushing into northern Greece and Bulgaria, meeting little resistance.

Louis I realized that sooner or later the Ottomans would be knocking on the door of Hungary, and he also realized that unless united, the fragile states of the Balkans stood little chance against the Ottomans. The Byzantine Emperor, John V Palaiologos, had visited Buda in 1366, begging for assistance from the only capable Christian military force in the region, but there was little trust between the - strongly Catholic - King and the - strongly Orthodox - Emperor and nothing of consequence was agreed.

The Ottomans and the Hungarians did, however, not meet in battle during the reign of Louis I. Ottoman raiding parties had started to emerge in the Hungarian sphere of interest, raiding into Bulgaria and Wallachia, but - despite some attempts to rewrite history - no real battles took place between the Hungarian and Ottoman armies in Louis I's lifetime.

Louis I had sent his mother, Elizabeth -herself a Polish princess - to Poland as regent, but she was unpopular and had to flee Poland in 1375, forcing Louis I to both accept his domineering mother back at the court in Buda and also appoint a new regent in Poland, Prince Vladislaus II of Opole, a minor royal who had served Louis I loyally in a range of administrative functions.

When Louis I died, of leprosy, in 1382 his death threw Hungary into a new period of confusion which it did not need. The problem once again was that the King had left no male heir.

He did have daughters though, and the oldest, Mary, had since a very early age been be engaged to Sigismund of Luxembourg - to whom we shall return - and one part of the Hungarian establishment supported his claim to become king - or prince consort - in due time. However, Mary and Sigismund had not been married at the time of Louis I's death, so Mary was appointed as his immediate heir and she was crowned as 'king' - to underline her role as ruler rather than consort - with her mother, Elizabeth of Bosnia, as regent as Mary was only eleven years old.

The Poles did not want to continue the personal union of Louis I, so they instead chose Mary's younger sister, Hedwig, throwing Poland into a war of succession of its own.

Another part of the Hungarian establishment had no tolerance for a female ruler, or for Sigismund of Luxemburg, and they found their own candidate in Charles III of Naples, the closest Angevin male relative of Louis I and former Duke of Dalmatia on behalf of Louis I.

With Charles III of Naples's existing contacts in Dalmatia as the driving force, he ousted Mary in 1385 and was crowned as Charles II of Hungary. His reign was however short, as the ousted regent, Elizabeth of Bosnia, had him murdered in February 1386 to clear the way for her daughter's return to the throne.

In the meantime, and to avoid further issues in regards Mary's gender, she had been married to her fiancée, Sigismund of Luxemburg.

Sigismund was the second son of Charles IV, the Holy Roman Emperor, and his mother was Charles IV's fourth wife, Elizabeth of Pomerania, herself a Polish princess on her mother's side. Sigismund was thus a typical result of his times, a royal with ancestry which was entangled into a whole range of European royal houses, providing him with a mixture of future claims and alliances, He was, however, not related to the Hungarian royal house, but he had been sent to Buda at an early age to learn the language and the culture, as well as Poland to do the same.

Although Sigismund had some claim, through his mother, to the Polish throne, it was the Hungarian throne which he eventually got, but not without complications.

When Mary returned to the throne of Hungary after the murder of Charles II, it was still her mother, Elizabeth of Bosnia, who pulled the strings through her status as regent.

However, the Hungarian barons supporting a male king of the Angevin line were not done. They promoted Charles II's underage son, Ladislaus of Naples, as the rightful heir. Elizabeth of Bosnia believed that the issue could be solved by the sheer presence of her daughter in the rebellious territories, so she and Mary set off with a small escort, but they were ambushed and captured by rebellious barons in support of Ladislaus of Naples.

During their captivity Elizabeth of Bosnia was murdered, but Sigismund finally managed to free Mary, partly by force and partly by diplomacy and the by the summer of 1387 Mary and Sigismund were finally ruling from Buda.

Mary and Sigismund were now co-regents. Mary thus retained her status as regent rather than consort, but in reality, it was Sigismund who now ruled as king.

The confusion around the succession had not been without cost. The weak royal authority had once again been the signal for the Hungarian barons to help themselves to land and privileges and Sigismund had been forced to dish out royal property in return for the support he desperately needed in order to get Mary out of captivity.

The royal authority had thus from its height under Louis I, once again plummeted in only five years since Louis I's death, and it would take Sigismund another decade to fully quell the rebellious barons.

But it was not only the Hungarian barons who had taken the opportunity to help themselves during the period of weak Hungarian authority. The Ottomans had used the opportunity to keep pushing through the Balkans and had by the time Sigismund finally gained control of Hungary, by the early 1390s, rolled over the remains of the Bulgarian Empire and effectively annexed it into the Ottoman Empire. They had also made Serbia a vassal state and started to exert their influence over the other smaller states bordering Hungary, Wallachia and Bosnia.

Effectively the Ottomans stood south of the Danube river with little separating them from Hungary proper. Their progress had been slowed down by setbacks against the Serbs at Dubravnica in 1381 and again at Pločnik, in 1386, but in 1389 the Ottomans had annihilated the Serbian army at the (First) Battle of Kosovo, forcing the Serbs to become vassals of Sultan Bayezid I.

Mary died, from a riding accident, in 1395 and for Sigismund this meant that his claim to the throne once again became weak. He needed a rallying point, but he was not alone in that pursuit, as so did the Pope Boniface IX.

Boniface IX was the Pope in Rome, but he was not the only Pope. There was also a Pope in Avignon, the conflict going back to '*The Western Schism*' which split the Catholic Church in two in 1378 (see Chapter 16).

The Pope in Avignon, Clement VII, had died in 1394 and although a new Pope was appointed in Avignon, Boniface IX felt that it was time to make an impression and try to gather broad support, so he called a crusade against the Ottomans, presumably to help Constantinople which was besieged by Bayezid I. The strategic play was probably a hopeful attempt to pull Byzantium back into a church-union and thus strengthen the position of the Pope in Rome, but regardless of the Pope's motives, he had got the timing right.

As mentioned above, Sigismund needed a rallying cause in Hungary and it just so happened that the (Hundred Years) war between France and England was going through a period of truce, so there was a surplus of warring bands in Europe looking for an opportunity.

In Hungary the Hungarian barons flocked around Sigismund's banner, unifying the Kingdom as was the desired outcome and they were supplemented by French, Germans, Bulgarians, Wallachians, Venetians, Genoese and Knight Hospitallers, making up the first international army to take up arms against the Ottomans in Europe.

But Europe was not the ultimate objective for the crusade. Rather the crusaders managed to talk each other into an ambitious plan similar to the First Crusade.

They would first push the Ottomans back in the Balkans, then relieve Constantinople, then cross to, and march through, Anatolia, continue through Syria and finally re-conquer Jerusalem before returning - triumphantly - by sea.

It was a daring and ambitious plan, and it only missed one thing: a realistic view of the opponent's strength.

Gathering in Buda, the army set out in July and first went to Vidin on the Danube River, the Ottoman commander of which immediately surrendered. This incident further convinced the very confident French that the Ottoman resistance was a mere formality and they raced ahead - through the night - of the main army in order to get first to the next target, the fortified town at Oryahovo further down the Danube, where they managed to secure a strategic bridge, but could make no headway with the town itself.

Once the main army arrived, with Sigismund at its head, the crusaders got as far as up to the walls of the town, and the following morning the town surrendered to Sigismund on his promise of pardon.

The French were furious, convinced that Sigismund was trying to rob them of glory, so they violated the agreement and set the town on fire, murdering its inhabitants - Ottoman and Bulgarian - creating a crisis between the crusaders before they had achieved any of their tactical objectives, let alone had come anywhere close to conquering Jerusalem.

The crusaders now continued to Nicopolis, where two fortified towns built on natural defensive formations made up a very strong fortification.

In their confidence, and to increase their speed, the crusaders had no siege engines, they believed they could quickly starve out the defenders, and they put up camp underneath the fortifications.

This move was based on the underlying theory, strongly advocated by the French in particular, that Bayezid I was afraid of meeting the formidable - French in particular - knights in open battle and would not engage with the crusaders until he was forced to do so before Constantinople or, even, in Anatolia.

So convinced that they were safe, the crusaders started to occupy themselves with eating, drinking and jousting - leaving their camp essentially unguarded.

Locals bringing in supplies, and the few scouts that ventured out, started talking of Ottomans approaching, but the general opinion was that it was merely scouting parties; an opinion further confirmed when a small contingent of French knights managed to successfully ambush a contingent of Ottoman outriders.

In reality what faced the crusaders was the full force of the Ottoman army. Bayezid I had left the siege of Constantinople in the hands of a small occupying force, expecting little capability in terms of the Byzantine defenders, and had force-marched his main army north towards the Danube River in order to face the crusaders.

News reached him of the crusader's set position outside Nicopolis, and he wasted no time but went straight for them.

Gradually it dawned on the crusaders that they were facing real opposition, and they had to quickly come up with a battle plan. Sigismund, based on advice from the Wallachian contingent who had fought the Ottomans before, recommended that an initial attack was done by foot soldiers softening up the Ottoman irregulars in the vanguard, but the French would have no such thing; they were there to fight for glory and they would lead the attack, not cower behind peasants.

The crusader army effectively split into two separate battle-plans and with the Ottomans only hours away, hastily prepared for battle, preparations which included murdering the civilian prisoners they had taken along the way.

It was 25 September 1396 and the first time the Ottoman army had to face the full force of Christianity. The battle would define the political landscape of Europe for centuries to come, and it did not go well for the crusaders.

Although, as always, the numbers are unreliable, modern historians assess that the two armies were probably evenly matched in numbers. The numbers themselves are another issue of dispute, but relying again on modern estimates, either army was probably around 15,000 to 20,000 strong, although contemporary numbers mention hundreds of thousands.

When, at the break of dawn, the two armies approached each other, the Ottoman vanguard starting to trickle down toward Nicopolis from the southern hills, Sigismund once again appealed to the French leader, 24 years old John de Nevers - nicknamed 'John the Fearless' - that the crusader army should wait for the Ottoman irregulars to line up and then execute a concerted attack.

John de Nevers, supported by his equally young cronies, rejected the proposal, fearing that Sigismund was aiming to steal the glory of the certain victory, and the French cavalry instead executed their own charge.

Initially the charge went well. The Ottoman vanguard, which consisted of ill-trained conscripts, gave way to the wall of French steel, but gradually the French attack lost momentum, meeting resistance from mounted Ottoman archers - the Sipahi - and rows of sharpened sticks aimed to stop the horses.

Having created an initial breakthrough, the French quickly conferred as to whether to regroup and wait for the rest of the army, under Sigismund's command to catch up or whether to continue the charge. Once again hot blood won the argument, and the French cavalry continued up the hills and beyond.

But rather than finding the Ottoman army fleeing before them, the French found fresh regiments of Sipahi waiting, and the ensuing battle was a catastrophe for the French, many of whom at this time were not mounted, but fighting on foot. Few managed to flee, but the majority were slain, John of Nevers himself was taken prisoner and only released a year later after his father, Philip the Bold, Duke of Burgundy, had paid an enormous ransom.

With their cavalry screen broken, the remaining Christian army had little with which to counter the Ottoman attack, and it was soon in a state of complete disarray. The Wallachians and Transylvanians, realizing that the day was lost, withdrew in some order and when Bayezid I's Serbian allies, under

Stefan Lazarević, added their numbers to the Ottoman attack, the Christian army fled.

Many drowned in attempts to cross the Danube River. Sigismund himself escaped narrowly, being transported in a fishing-boat to the Venetian ships lying in support in the river.

In the confusion, contact was made between Stefan Lazarević and his brother-in-law Nikola II Gorjanski, who was fighting on the Christian side, and the Christian army formally surrendered.

What followed was wholesale slaughter. Sultan Bayezid I was furious over the severe loses his army had encountered, and his fury boiled over when he found the remains of the civilian prisoners slaughtered by the Christians before the battle.

Having isolated the noblemen for whom a ransom could be expected, the remaining prisoners were bundled in small groups and brought before the sultan. On his orders, they were summarily executed on the spot.

When the bloodlust finally ran out, hundreds, possibly thousands, had been slaughtered, adding to the thousands killed in the battle itself. France had lost the flower of its young nobles, and many of the remaining peers had been taken for random and were only returned to France after years of negotiations.

The Battle of Nicopolis was a catastrophe for the Christian World. Blame ran rampant, especially aimed at the head-strong French at whose door Sigismund had no hesitation to park the responsibility.

Up to this point the Christian rulers had seen the Ottoman's presence in Europe as a nuisance rather than a permanent threat, a fact seen in the ambitious plans for the crusade to march on to Jerusalem itself. From now on the Ottomans were taken seriously, but the Christian states had little to throw at them.

England and France soon started to fight each other again and would continue to do so for decades to come. The Knights Hospitaller, also known as the Knights of Rhodes, retreated to their Island fortress and we shall meet them again in Chapter 17. Venice and Genoa, as covered in Part 3, tried to maintain the precarious balance between politics and trade, and were quite happily to spend their time fighting each other rather than the Ottomans.

After the Battle of Nicopolis, the Second Bulgarian Empire simply crumpled and 'Bulgaria' was annexed into the Ottoman Empire. Around the edges of Hungary, four 'buffer states' survived, Moldovia, Wallachia, Serbia and Bosnia. Their precarious existences in the shadow of the two empires are covered in the following chapters.

Sigismund in the meantime returned to Hungary. The defeat at Nicopolis had not done his royal authority any good, and the Hungarian barons took the opportunity to once again increase their autonomy. Sigismund's initial reaction was to leave Hungary to the barons and instead concentrate on his wider ambitions.

13 - Hungary

As mentioned previously, Sigismund was born with dynastic ties spreading its tentacles deep into the royal houses of Europe, and it was to these ties he now turned. The potential prize was high, as high as it got; namely the crown of the Holy Roman Empire itself.

Sigismund's father, Holy Roman Emperor Charles IV, had died in 1378. His heir was Sigismund's elder (half) brother Wenceslaus IV. Wenceslaus IV had inherited a string of titles, King of Bohemia, King of the Germans and Duke of Luxemburg amongst them.

Wenceslaus IV's primary interests, however, were in Bohemia rather than in Germany, and he never attempted to be crowned as Holy Roman Emperor even if his father had held that title before him.

Wenceslaus IV, despite being married twice, had no children, and it was here that Sigismund saw his opportunity. Temporarily turning his back on Hungary, Sigismund went to his brother, and Wenceslaus IV formally appointed him as his heir.

Wenceslaus IV's absence from Germany brought discord amongst the German barons, and Wenceslaus was ousted in 1400. Although Sigismund was his appointed heir, the Germans instead chose Rupert, a local nobleman, as king and there was little that Sigismund could do about it at the time.

In Bohemia things were not much better for Wenceslaus IV, which can possibly be explained by his nickname - Wenceslaus the Idle - and his reported tendency for excessive drunkenness.

His authority in Bohemia had always been weak, and there had been several episodes of direct revolt. Another such emerged in 1401, this time supported by Sigismund who even took the Bohemian throne as regent for a period of time.

Sigismund however had to put his external ambitions to rest for a while and return to Hungary as things were heating up at home.

With Sigismund's authority weakened, and he himself focusing on the affairs in Germany and Bohemia, renewed support had grown for the next in line of the Anjou dynasty, Ladislaus of Naples, the son of Charles II, the former, short-time, King of Hungary.

Ladislaus of Naples had been a minor when his father was murdered but had now come of age. He had ambitions on the throne of Hungary and sensed that the moment was right. He paid the Venetians by ceding the island of Corfu, and they provided him with passage to Zara on the Dalmatian coast in 1403.

It is unclear what Ladislaus of Naples' further plans were. Perhaps he thought that he would be received by a strong party of Hungarian barons who would carry him in triumph to Buda, but despite widespread support for his cause amongst the Hungarian barons, no such reception awaited him. As a consequence, Ladislaus of Naples arrived, stayed awhile and then proceeded to sell the Hungarian possessions on the Dalmatian coast for 100,000 ducats to the Venetians. Then he went home.

Sigismund now started a long campaign to get Hungary back under control. Rebellious barons were met with violence and a campaign in 1408 in Croatia and Bosnia saw 200 noble families massacred, after which Sigismund could once again claim kingship of Croatia.

In celebration of this victory, Sigismund formed 'the Order of the Dragon', a knightly order based on the principles of the crusader orders and with the specific purpose of fighting the enemies of the (Catholic) Church. The order was by invitation only and thus exclusive to selected European royals and nobles.

In 1410 Rupert, King of the Germans, died and Sigismund simply ignored his brother's original claims and went to Germany to have himself crowned, an important step towards his lifelong ambition to become emperor.

But Sigismund was not going to become emperor unless he did so with papal blessing, and there was a problem with that; namely that there at the time was no less than three popes. The subject is further explored in Chapter 16, but while campaigning against Venice, Sigismund took the initiative to a council of church-leaders to be held in Constance in 1414.

The council lasted three years, and although it was led by Sigismund, he did not preside in person for the whole duration. After much debate, the issue of the papacy was solved and a single pope, Martin V, residing in Rome, was elected by a united church.

The council also condemned the Bohemian priest and church-reformer Jan Huus to death for heresy and had him burned at the stake. This was problematic for Sigismund under whose promise of safe conduct Jan Huus had travelled to Constance, even though it is believed that Huus was killed during Sigismund's absence from the council and not with his consent.

Sigismund proceeded to plot an alliance with England against France, but his brother Wenceslaus IV died in 1419 and Sigismund now turned his attention to Bohemia. He was formally crowned as King of Bohemia, but his assumed role in the killing of Jan Huus now came back to haunt him as the Bohemians rose in revolt against Sigismund's rule. The revolt, known as the Hussite Wars, lasted on and off for fifteen years, in which time Sigismund had no real grip on the power in Bohemia despite his title as king.

The wars in Bohemia became a crusade, in which several European rulers tried to assert the Catholic Church's authority over the heretic Hussites, and militarily it became an expensive and humiliating exercise for Sigismund who just about managed to keep the war from spilling over into Hungary proper.

In 1428 Sigismund agreed with the Ottoman Sultan, Murad II, that Serbia could be a vassal of both the Ottomans and the Hungarians and that a new capital should be located at Smederevo, the old capital of Belgrade having been ceded to Hungary already.

In 1433 Sigismund finally achieved his ambition and was crowned as Holy Roman Emperor. When the Hussite Wars formally ended in 1436 he was also recognized as King of Bohemia, although his actual power in the war-torn country was nominal only.

Sigismund died in December of 1437 after ruling Hungary for five decades. By the time of his death, he had re-established the royal authority in Hungary, but he died without a male heir.

Lacking a direct heir, Sigismund had already appointed as heir his son-in-law, Albert II, Archduke of Austria, married to Sigismund's daughter Elizabeth. Through the web of inter-royal marriages that had gone on for centuries, both had in one way or the other a claim to the Hungarian throne and Albert II's election seems to have been without any significant difficulties. In principle he was also King of Bohemia, but although he was crowned, he had little real power, spending some time fighting rebellious Bohemian barons and their Polish allies.

Somewhat to his surprise he was also elected King of Germany in 1438, but despite his aspirations to eventually follow Sigismund as Holy Roman Emperor, he died suddenly - from dysentery - in 1439.

Albert II and Elizabeth had no male heir, but at the time of Albert II's death Elizabeth was pregnant and after his death she gave birth to a son, Ladislaus, who due to the circumstances was given the moniker 'Ladislaus the Posthumous'.

Immediately following Albert II's death, Elizabeth grabbed the reins and effectively ruled Hungary as regent, even though she was never formally elected or appointed. The birth of her son gave her hope that he would be elected king, and she would remain as regent during his infancy, but the geopolitical situation demanded otherwise.

Since the Battle of Nicopolis the Ottomans had gone from strength to weakness and back to strength. Bayezid I's defeat to Timur in 1402 had thrown the Ottoman Empire into its own interregnum period and there is no doubt that if there was ever a chance to expel the Ottomans from Europe it was during this decade of civil war. However, with the trauma of Nicopolis still strong and with little unity inside the Christian camp, nobody took the initiative to campaign against the Ottomans when they were at their weakest.

Instead the Ottomans sorted themselves out and after Mehmed I had restored order inside the Empire, Murad II saw it as his mission to secure the Empires old borders, which in Ottoman terms also meant raiding across the borders into neighbouring states.

It was thus clear to the Hungarian nobility that the Ottomans after a few decade of relative peace were once again starting to knock at Hungary's door, gaining increasing influence in the areas around Hungary's southern and eastern borders.

Hungary thus needed a strong warlike king, and Elizabeth and her infant son were not the answer to the problem. When the Hungarian nobles finally gathered in January of 1440 to officially elect a successor to Sigismund they therefore decided on Wladyslaw III of Poland.

Wladyslaw III had been King of Poland since 1434, although only as an adult since 1438. When he was elected King of Hungary he was sixteen years of age and the suggestion by the Hungarian nobles that Elizabeth - aged 31 - should marry him to secure the peace did not go down well with her. Instead, she retreated from Buda with her significant retinue of followers.

Elizabeth had powerful supporters, in particular Count Ulrich II of Celje, the richest landowner in the country. With his support she could count on the northern part of the Kingdom, and she managed to have the Holy Crown stolen and brought to her, after which she had Ladislaus the Posthumous crowned as Ladislaus V.

Wladyslaw III was thus crowned without the Holy Crown and the next two years saw Hungary, in desperate need for a strong united front against the Ottoman threat, instead engaging in yet another civil war.

Ultimately Wladyslaw III was successful and Elizabeth died, probably poisoned. Before that she had, however sent her son Ladislaus V to a relative, Frederick V of Austria, whom would later become Holy Roman Emperor as Frederick III. With Ladislaus V came the Holy Crown of Hungary, a story we shall return to a little later.

In the meantime, Murad II had taken the opportunity to assert his domination in the Balkans. He overran Serbia in 1439 (see Chapter 14) and with confusion reigning in Hungary he set his eyes on Belgrade, the gateway to Hungary and western Europe beyond.

In April 1440 he laid siege to Belgrade, putting up an earthen wall on landside and bringing galleys and barges up the Danube River in an attempt to blockade the supply routes to the city.

From behind the earthen walls the Ottoman siege engines threw massive rocks against the walls of Belgrade, while raiding parties penetrated deep into Transylvania and south-eastern Hungary. But the Ottoman siege technology was insufficient against the solid walls, and the naval blockade was also inefficient, so after a few months Murad II had to lift the siege and give up on Belgrade for now. Serbia, however, was his.

One of the strong supporters of Wladyslaw III was a Hungarian 'lesser' noble named Janos Hunyadi. His exact origins are somewhat obscure but generally believed to be 'Romanian' or Cuman rather than indigenous Hungarian.

Janos Hunyadi's father, Woyk, had been ennobled and granted the castle at Hynyad (modern day Hunedoara in Romania).

Janos had been brought up as a warrior and had served King Sigismund in many campaigns, including those of the Hussite Wars, where he had adopted the Hussite use of armoured wagons.

Due to his loyalty and capabilities as a military commander, Janos Hunyadi had been trusted with the defence of the troublesome southern border of Hungary, where Ottoman raiders would cross the border and counter raids would be carried out into Ottoman held areas. He had, in particular, distinguished himself with counter-raids into Ottoman territories following the Siege of Belgrade in 1440 and by repelling a numerically superior Ottoman expeditionary force at the Iron Gates on the Danube River in 1442, proving that the use of armoured 'wagenburgs' could be effective against Ottoman troops.

This combination of the youthful enthusiasm of King Wladyslaw III and the solid military experience of Janos Hunyadi provided Hungary with exactly the level of new military energy which had been the background for Wladyslaw III's election to the throne and the already energetic combination was further set ablaze by the warlike papal legate, Guiliano Cesarini, who preached crusade against the Ottomans.

Once the internal issues had been settled in Hungary - the minor Ladislaus the Posthumous holed up with Frederick III in Austria - it was time to start thinking about the Ottomans.

Whether the opportunity simply presented itself - Sultan Murad II being engaged with the Karamanids in Anatolia - or whether the Karamanid revolt against the sultan was a result of a coordinated effort to squeeze the Ottomans on two fronts is unknown, but in any case the circumstances were ideal for a campaign in Europe.

Compared to the disastrous campaign leading to the Christian defeat at Nicopolis in 1396, the campaign of 1443 was a much more focused affair. As much as the campaign was seen as a crusade, it did not attempt to go to Jerusalem; rather the simple objective was to kick the Ottomans out of Europe by capturing their capital Edirne and push them back across the sea to Anatolia.

That in itself was, however, a major undertaking, as Edirne was far way away from Buda and meant that the army had to cross through mainly hostile territory before it got anywhere close.

On the other hand, Sultan Murad II was away with the main army in Anatolia and the Hungarian army was well prepared in both spirit and manpower.

Troops had been brought in from Bohemia, Germany and Poland and as the army started to move it was further reinforced by substantial contingents from Wallachia and Serbia.

Once the army started moving in July of 1443 it was unstoppable. It marched through Serbia, Bosnia, Albania and Bulgaria, mopping up local Ottoman resistance and even managed to capture Sofia, punching a major hole in Ottoman dominance of the Balkans.

The combination of distance and the onset of winter eventually slowed the army's progress to a halt. Sultan Murad II had in the meantime finished his affairs in Anatolia and returned with his army to Europe. Rather than marching against the crusaders in the middle of winter, he sent groups of skirmishers out to defend every pass, block every road and harass the crusader's substantial supply train from the rear.

Eventually the crusaders simply ran out of steam, their supply lines had become unsustainably long, and the Ottoman resistance had become fiercer and fiercer. By Christmas they simply turned around and started marching back home.

The retreat was harassed by Ottoman raiders, but the crusader's rear-guard fought a series of successful skirmishes, keeping the Ottomans at bay while the army marched on.

As they approached home the crusader army became more and more desperate, gradually leaving behind their spoils of war, anything that was heavy, slow or could not be eaten. This provided a treasure trove for the pursuing Ottomans, who were quite happy to help themselves to the spoils and let the crusader army disappear in the distance.

When the crusaders finally returned to Buda on 25 January 1444 the King himself was on foot, even his horse had been used to feed the troops, but the army's return was celebrated with thanksgiving ceremonies and the campaign, named 'the Long Campaign' became the stuff of legends. But on the ground the situation was somewhat different.

Even though the Long Campaign had for the first time seen some military success against Ottoman dominance in the Balkans, the actual results were few. The Ottomans had simply followed the Christian army home, filling in the vacuum behind them and more or less retaken the control of all the areas which the crusaders had liberated. A single exception was Serbia, where the despot, Đurađ Branković, once again ruled in Smederevo.

A side story, which would become important as time went by, was that an Albanian commander in Ottoman service, George Kastrioti - known as 'Skanderbeg' - deserted from Ottoman service after the crusader army took the fortress at Niš in Bulgaria. Skanderbeg returned to his native Albania where we shall meet him again later.

Sultan Murad II was less than happy with the developments during the Long Campaign. He had issues to deal with in Anatolia and the Christian army's practically unhindered march across his territories showed the dangers of committing his army in one theatre with his back exposed to another.

Murad II therefore suggested a peace agreement, spanning a ten-year period. His concession was primarily that of allowing Đurađ Branković to rule Serbia as an independent territory, albeit as a vassal state. In return he wanted a Hungarian guarantee that they would not cross the Danube river into Ottoman territories.

Đurađ Branković was a strong advocate for the peace agreement and some believe that he bribed Janos Hunyadi with rich estates in return for his support.

In any case Janos Hunyadi did support the agreement, and despite the papal legate's protests, the agreement was signed.

But whereas Murad II though that he now had a safe European theatre, and that he could focus on Anatolia, the Hungarians however had no intentions of sticking to their part of the deal.

Rather than stopping their campaign against the Ottomans, they were already in contact with Ibrahim II of Karaman, urging him to draw the Ottoman army back into Anatolia, a ruse that Murad II fell for.

As soon as Murad II had moved across to Anatolia, a - mainly - Genoese fleet blocked the crossing points at the Dardanelles and the Bosporus while a Venetian fleet moved through to the Black Sea to supply a new Crusader army taking the shorter route towards Edirne.

The papal legate had quickly decided that an oath given to an infidel was invalid, releasing King Wladyslaw III from his commitment to peace, and the trap was set for Murad II, seemingly stuck in Anatolia and with little left to deter the crusaders.

The crusader army was, however, not as strong as before. Hastily put together in the ashes of the Long Campaign, it yet again was a multinational force, but it was smaller than the previous year and it missed one very important element; the Serbians.

Rather than participating in the campaign the newly reinstated Despot of Serbia opted out, well aware that he ruled solely on the grace of the Sultan, and he furthermore sent messages to the Sultan informing him of the Christians' intentions and reducing the element of surprise which was an important part of the Christian campaign.

But the lost element of surprise was not the only thing that went against the crusaders. Their chosen ally, Ibrahim II of Karaman, had no real power to fight sultan Murad II, so as soon as the Ottoman army appeared in Karaman, he not only surrendered, but even supplied the Ottomans with additional troops of his own.

That may per se have been unimportant if the Ottoman army, as was the plan, had been stuck in Anatolia, but the Genoese love of money turned out to be a determining factor.

Once Murad II realized that the crossing to Europe was blocked, he offered a gold ducat for each soldier ferried across to Europe, a substantial price which proved too much of a temptation for the Genoese.

With his army safely ashore in Europe Murad II wasted no more time. This time he was not prepared to fight a defensive battle, the issue had to be solved, and solved it was.

The battle-hardened Ottoman army which resolutely marched up along the Black Sea coast was superior in numbers to the crusader army. Estimates wary, but it is pretty safe to assume that they at least outnumbered the Christians by two to one.

The two armies met outside Varna. The battle was the first major engagement between the full forces of Christianity and the Ottomans since the battle of Nicopolis nearly five decades earlier. The result was the same, and once again youthful enthusiasm played a defining role.

An initial Ottoman attack was repelled by means of a 'wagenburg', but the Ottomans deployed their age-old tactics and turned a feigned retreat into an ambush on the pursuing crusaders.

Janos Hunyadi then lead a Christian counterattack, instructing the young King to remain in reserve, but the youthful spirit of the King made him disobey the order and instead he led his five hundred mounted knights in an attack directly towards the Ottoman centre. The aim was to eliminate the Ottoman Sultan, replaying Alexander the Great's tactics against the Persians nearly 2,000 years before, but the attack failed despite the tremendous power of its initial force.

Wladyslaw III was killed, his body was decapitated and his head was mounted on an Ottoman spear for all to see. The papal legate simply disappeared in the fog of war and was never seen again.

The Christian army fled, although few made it far, even though Janos Hunyadi made it to relative safety with the Voivode of Wallachia, Vlad II Dracul, who took the opportunity to hold Janos Hunyadi prisoner for a time in the aftermath of the battle.

Although the Ottoman loses were heavy, the victory was complete. The military power of Hungary was broken and the death of King Wladyslaw III threw Hungary into a new crisis of succession. The only real force remaining was Janos Hunyadi.

In the aftermath of the failed campaign, and with the King slain on the battlefield, the nobles of Hungary resorted to a temporary government, appointing five 'captains general', one of which was Janos Hunyadi, who was given responsibility for Transylvania and thus the more likely candidate to face further Ottoman aggression.

The temporary government, however, proved to be dysfunctional, so it only lasted for eighteen months after which, in June 1446, Janos Hunyadi was appointed regent on behalf of Ladislaus the Posthumous, now crowned as Ladislaus V. A similar position as regent of Bohemia was given to George of Poděbrady, a local noble and accomplished warlord.

The problem was that over and above Ladislaus V's infancy - he was six years old at the time - he was still held in de-facto imprisonment by Frederick III of Austria, who also held the Holy Crown of Hungary.

Janos Hunyadi tried to resolve the issue by diplomacy, and then by force, none of which worked. When he had to turn his focus back on the Ottoman issue, he agreed a two years truce with Frederick III, an agreement that did not win him many friends amongst the supporters of Ladislaus V, who suspected him of having designs on the throne for himself or his son Laszlo Hunyadi.

With his back free, Janos Hunyadi still subscribed to the idea that a single big win could force the Ottomans out of Europe, in his view a necessary strategy to avoid the Ottoman attack on Hungary proper which was surely looming.

He gathered the Hungarian army, reinforced by - somewhat reluctant - Wallachians and German mercenaries. He initially marched to the Serbian capital of Smederevo, the gathering point for the various parts of the army, but if he had counted on support from Đurađ Branković he was wrong.

Đurađ Branković believed that he was better off being on friendly terms with the Sultan, and he had little confidence in Janos Hunyadi's new expedition, believing it to be to undermanned and under-planned.

As revenge Janos Hunyadi declared Serbia as hostile territory, thus allowing his men to pillage the country as they marched through. As a counter-move Đurađ Branković blocked the progress of Skanderbeg marching from Albania, preventing him from reaching the battlefield until it was too late.

Janos Hunyadi's plan was to provoke the Sultan to meet in an open battle, this time in a place of Janos Hunyadi's choosing. He chose Kosovo Polje, the Field of Blackbirds, close to modern day Pristina.

The field had already been the stage for a battle between the Serbians and the Ottomans in 1389 so the ensuing battle would be known as the Second Battle of Kosovo.

Đurađ Branković had a point in that the Ottoman forces which met the Hungarians were once again superior in number, and the army of Murad II was battle-hardened and ready. Leading its right wing was the heir apparent, Prince Mehmed.

The battle was, however, hard fought. Unusually it lasted two days. The first day saw early Hungarian success, but that was followed by an Ottoman counter which left the Hungarians on their back foot when the battle ebbed to an end at sundown.

Through the night the Ottomans bombarded the Hungarian camp with missiles, drawing cannon fire in response, but when the second day came the Ottomans overran the Hungarians, sheer numbers overwhelming the remaining resistance, the Hungarians hoping till the last that Skanderbeg would emerge with reinforcements.

Many Hungarian nobles were slain in the battle, but Janos Hunyadi got away in the company of the Wallachian Voivode Vladislav II. He did not get far though, before Serbian troops caught him and brought him to Đurađ Branković in Smederevo.

The two men did not much like each other, and Đurađ Branković was now furious that Janos Hunyadi had challenged the precarious peace in the region and old scars, like Janos Hunyadi's role in connection with the broken peace agreement of 1444, were ripped open. In the end Janos Hunyadi was only released after a hefty ransom and having returned the properties he had received - as bribes - from Đurađ Branković in 1444.

Janos Hunyadi already had powerful enemies, in particular Count Ulrich II of Celje, the country's most powerful landowner and a staunch supporter of Ladislaus V's kingship.

When on his return to Hungary Janos Hunyadi once again could not secure the release of King Ladislaus V from Frederick III, Count Ulrich II of Celje openly accused him of conspiring against the King and Janos Hunyadi chose to resign as regent and retreat into relative obscurity for a few years.

Count Ulrich II of Celje was eventually successful in forcing the release of King Ladislaus V - without the Holy Crown - and Janos Hunyadi was reconciled with his enemies and appointed captain general and bestowed with a title of 'perpetual Count of Bistrița'. The year was 1453.

By now Sultan Murad II had died and his son Mehmed II had taken the Ottoman throne. This transition of power has been covered previously as has the lead up to Mehmed II's Conquest of Constantinople in that same year.

It has also been mentioned that Janos Hunyadi did negotiate with the Byzantines in 1452, when it became clear that Mehmed II meant to lay siege to the city, but his demands for assistance included that the Byzantine Emperor handed over the coastal castles of Misivri and Silivri. It is unclear if this was Janos Hunyadi's attempt to put himself or the Hungarian kingdom in possession of the castles, but in any case, by the time the Byzantine Emperor made his mind up on the matter, the castles were already in Ottoman possession.

The Ottoman Conquest of Constantinople put the final nail in the coffin of the theory that the Ottomans could be expelled from Europe as the result of a single battle, the theory which had driven Janos Hunyadi forward this far.

But for Sultan Mehmed II, by now given the moniker 'Fatih' - Conqueror - by his army, being thrown out of Europe was far from his mind. Quite the opposite, he intended to make Europe his.

Having conquered 'New Rome' his next target was 'Old Rome', the spiritual seat of western Europe, but getting an Ottoman army anywhere close to Rome was not so easy.

The Ottomans were the underlings on the seas. Sure, they had managed to launch a significant fleet in support of the siege of Constantinople, but this fleet was made up of galleys, suitable for piracy and some maritime warfare, but not for transport. To get to Italy was thus impossible by sea, even though Mehmed II did have a strategic backup plan to gain control of Albania and launch an attack from there. That, however, was in the future.

The only other way to get to Italy was by land, but that meant passing through Hungary, which spread like a band from the Adriatic in the west to the Black Sea in the east, acting like a lid on top of the Balkan Peninsula and a protective barrier for the Christian World beyond.

Mehmed II really did not have a choice. He needed to crush the Hungarians and the place to do it was Belgrade.

13 - Hungary

Situated at the confluence of two rivers (the Danube and the Sava), Belgrade was the gateway to Europe. Behind it was the waste steppes of Hungary and access directly into the heartland of central Europe, Croatia and Italy.

Belgrade was protected by extensive walls and a massive castle, a setup not that different from Constantinople, so Mehmed II thought he had the formula at hand for a successful siege and conquest.

His plans were known to the Hungarians well ahead of time, the Ottoman Sultan making little effort to hide his intentions, but coming up with a suitable response turned out to be difficult.

Janos Hunyadi took the threat very seriously, but many other Hungarian barons took his warnings as being political, an attempt to once again raise his level of influence, and they did nothing to assist him.

Instead Janos Hunyadi spent his own money on reinforcing the castle at Belgrade and he left it in the hands of his son, Laszlo, and his brother-in-law Mihály Szilágyi while Janos himself went to secure more men.

Luckily Janos Hunyadi found an ally in the papal ambassador Giovanni da Capestrano who had been sent by the Pope to preach crusade after the fall of Constantinople. He and Janos Hunyadi needed each other, so a combined effort saw them recruiting a considerable levy of peasant farmers. They may not have been militarily trained, and they may not have been armed with anything but crude weapons, but contrary to the defenders of Constantinople, they could fill the walls of Belgrade.

Some professional volunteers also arrived from Europe so in the end there were probably around 5,000 professional defenders inside Belgrade and another 5,000 underway together with a peasant army of tens of thousands.

But before the new troops reached Belgrade, Mehmed II struck.

The plan was simple. And adaptation of the successful formula used against Constantinople. First a naval blockade of the rivers, preventing reinforcements and supplies from reaching the fortress. Then a siege blocking the headland on which the city laid, big guns brought in for the purpose of breaking the walls, smaller guns being cast on the spot from raw materials transported by camels.

Mehmed II's fleet, probably around 200 strong, came up the Danube River and was chained together across the river, creating a physical barrier, with other galleys patrolling both rivers.

The army was lined up, the guns were set to work and the strategy was, as with Constantinople, to make breaches in the walls and then send mass infantry attacks into the breaches and overwhelm the defenders with sheer firepower and numbers.

But Janos Hunyadi had also learned from Constantinople and from the previous Ottoman attack on Belgrade in 1440. His main priority was thus to break the naval blockade and ensure that his reinforcements could get to the city and that the city could be resupplied. The Ottoman naval blockade was what strangled Constantinople and Janos Hunyadi had had no intentions of letting that happen at Belgrade.

Janos Hunyadi had therefore managed to get a Hungarian fleet together, matching in size to the Ottoman fleet, but whereas the Hungarian fleet was fully mobile, the Ottoman fleet was chained up and stationary giving great advantage to the attackers. When the Hungarian fleet arrived on the scene, they therefore overwhelmed the Ottoman fleet which was burned, and the Hungarian reinforcements were shipped across to the besieged city.

But Mehmed II was not deterred. The Ottoman attack continued and despite desperate efforts from the defenders to repair the breaches that appeared in the walls, the Ottoman strategy gradually started to work.

On 21 July, after seventeen days of siege, Mehmed ordered an all-out assault on the walls and even though it was ultimately repelled (amongst other means by pouring flammable materials into the moat and setting it on fire), it was clear that the situation was becoming critical and the attackers could only be repelled so many times before they succeeded. Once again, this was a direct copy of the situation at Constantinople, where the Ottomans launched several all-out attacks before the final breakthrough was achieved.

After a quiet day on the 22 July, where the Ottomans were busy recovering their (many) dead from the preceding day's battle and the Hungarians were busy ferrying supplies across the river, something strange happened on 23 July that would change the history of the world, more by chance than by design.

Appreciating the need for every single available hand in the consistent defence and repair of the walls, Janos Hunyadi had issued strict orders that the defenders were not to venture outside the walls and engage the Ottomans. Despite this, a small contingent of the rather undisciplined levy decided to ignore his orders and go outside to harass the Ottomans, now mainly occupied by burying their dead.

The small contingent of defenders started shouting insults at the Ottomans, and some starting shooting arrows at them. When the Ottomans did not respond, more joined, more insults were shouted and more arrows were fired. Once again, the Ottomans did not respond, so more joined in, and the small contingent became a crowd. Spurred on by the passiveness of the Ottomans, the crowd became more aggressive and started to advance on the Ottomans, leading to even more joining in, and ultimately what had started as a bit of a brawl became a full scale attack, finally joined by Janos Hunyadi and the army proper.

The Ottomans never saw it coming, and by the time they realized what was happening they were being overwhelmed. The Christian troops, now in frenzy, went straight through the, thin, Ottoman defences and the Ottoman army - unprepared for battle -did something untypical; they ran.

Mehmed himself was wounded and rendered unconscious and was hastily brought away from harm's way and the Ottoman army went into full flight, harassed by the attacking Christian forces who hacked them down in the thousands.

The Christian did not press their advantage, but returned to behind the walls, not realising that they had won the battle, but rather thinking that they had at best bought themselves some time to repair the walls. An Ottoman comeback, however, never materialised. The remnants of the Ottoman army sneaked off in the night and returned to Edirne, harassed all the way by Serbian troops which took the opportunity to further decimate their numbers.

The Ottomans loses were significant, estimated at up to 75,000 men lost in the battle and the following flight, an enormous number that put a serious dent in Mehmed's ambitions for a while. Mehmed himself was devastated and popular history has it that he had to be forcefully prevented from taking poison in his despair. True or not, he would bounce back later.

But whereas there were many conflicts still to follow in Mehmed II's reign, the Siege of Belgrade was the only battle in which a main Ottoman army met a main Hungarian army, even if that army was mainly a peasant levy. From now on the battle between the two empires would be fought by proxy and in the buffer-states surrounding the southern border of Hungary. We shall cover these states, and conflicts next, but let us first round off the history of Hungary.

Janos Hunyadi, restored to the status of hero, died in Belgrade from plague only three weeks after the successful defence. King Ladislaus V had returned from Bratislava where he had been hiding during the Ottoman threat and came to Belgrade with his influential 'advisor' Count Ulrich II of Celje.

The Count was no friends of the Hunyadis, and he was there to check out the ambitions of Laszlo Hunyadi who, after his father's death, had taken over command in Belgrade. If the Count was looking for answers he found them as Laszlo Hunyadi had him murdered while in Belgrade.

The young and weak King immediately absolved Laszlo Hunyadi from any blame and returned to Buda. From there he invited Laszlo Hunyadi to join him, but when Laszlo arrived, he was imprisoned, accused of plotting against the King and beheaded without trial.

This event made the King so unpopular that he had to flee the country, and he died shortly after in Prague as a result of leukaemia, although popular belief at the time was that he had been poisoned.

King Ladislaus V's death once again threw Hungary into civil war, the followers of Count Ulrich II of Celje fighting the followers of the Hunyadis, led by Janos Hunyadi's son-in-law Mihály Szilágyi. Finally, the Hungarian nobles elected Janos Hunyadi's younger son, Matthias, as king.

The crowning of Janos Hunyadi's son as Matthias I was controversial. Matthias I had no dynastic connections what so ever and both Frederick III of Austria and King Casimir IV of Poland put forward claims to the throne.

His election started a new trend in which the parliament, in Hungary called the Diet, exercised their right to choose freely whom they considered the best choice for king, ignoring bloodlines and dynastic ties.

Needless to say, Matthias I initially had to fight for his position, a position which was made even more precarious by the fact that Frederick III of Austria still had physical possession of the Holy Crown of Hungary, the deeply symbolic crown regalia.

Matthias I navigated his way through the minefield and even managed to raise a mercenary army with which he marched to Serbia and Bosnia in 1458, reinstating nominal suzerainty of these two states. They met only local Ottoman resistance as Mehmed II, not seeing the Hungarian intervention as anything but a propaganda exercise, stayed away.

The following year Mehmed II simply re-annexed Serbia, with no Hungarian army in presence.

In the early 1460s the Hungarians and Ottomans were playing ping-pong over Bosnia and the situation around the Ottoman siege of the fortress of Jajce in 1464 is typical for the lack of willingness on the side of either Mehmed II or Matthias I to meet in full-on battle.

The siege had followed the traditional pattern. The Ottoman cannon having done their job and created significant breaches in the walls, and Mehmed II launching a major assault, but the defenders managed to hold the walls, and the Ottoman losses were horrendous. Mehmed II now had a choice between continuing the siege or leaving it be and for once he decided to withdraw.

Adding to this decision was intelligence that the Hungarian King was on his way with a significant army to relieve the city, and on this basis the Ottoman retreat became close to a complete flight. Five massive cannon were thrown in the river, the baggage train was left behind, and the Ottoman army hastily withdrew to Sofia. The Hungarian army finally arrived a month later, well aware that the Ottoman army had long since withdrawn.

The Hungarians now proceeded to lay siege to nearby fortifications still in Ottoman hands, and though they were successful at Srebrenica, they could not take the fortress at Zvornik, which stubbornly held out into the onset of winter.

The situation leading to the Ottoman withdrawal from Jajce was now entirely reversed. The Hungarians received intelligence that an Ottoman relief army, under the command of Mahmud Pasha, was on its way from Sofia and now it was their turn to panic. They left their artillery - including the Ottoman cannon which had been recovered from the river outside Jajce - and their baggage train and fled in haste. The Ottoman relief army arrived soon enough to hack at the rear-guard, causing injury to insult. Leaving apart the slaughter of the rear-guard of the already fleeing enemy, not a shot had been fired.

King Matthias I took considerable funds from the Pope in order to start a new crusade against the Ottomans, but he used most of the money to buy the Holy Crown from Frederick III, finally getting himself crowned properly in 1464.

The rest was used to maintain an army that would shadow the Ottoman army as it moved in the Balkans but, as the example above, would never in the time of Mehmed II or Matthias I engage in a battle proper.

Historians have tried to fill up this, rather unflattering, vacuum caused by Matthias I's unwillingness to face the enemy head on with minor skirmishes, naming an incident in 1479 the 'Battle of Breadfield' although in fact this incident, in which the Hungarians were victorious, was but a skirmish between Ottoman raiders, reinforced by Wallachians, and a local Hungarian march warden.

Mehmed II's great-grandson, Suleiman I, repeated the attack on Belgrade in 1521, this time successfully and by 1526 had invaded Buda, putting an end to the Hungarian Empire.

The Ottomans were expelled from Hungary in 1718 and a union between Hungary and Austria saw the rebirth of a significant empire which lasted until after the First World War. The Republic of Hungary still lives to this day, consisting of the traditional core of Hungarian lands with Budapest as its capital, but without Bohemia (the Czech Republic), Croatia and Transylvania (now part of Romania).

Part 5 - The Balkans

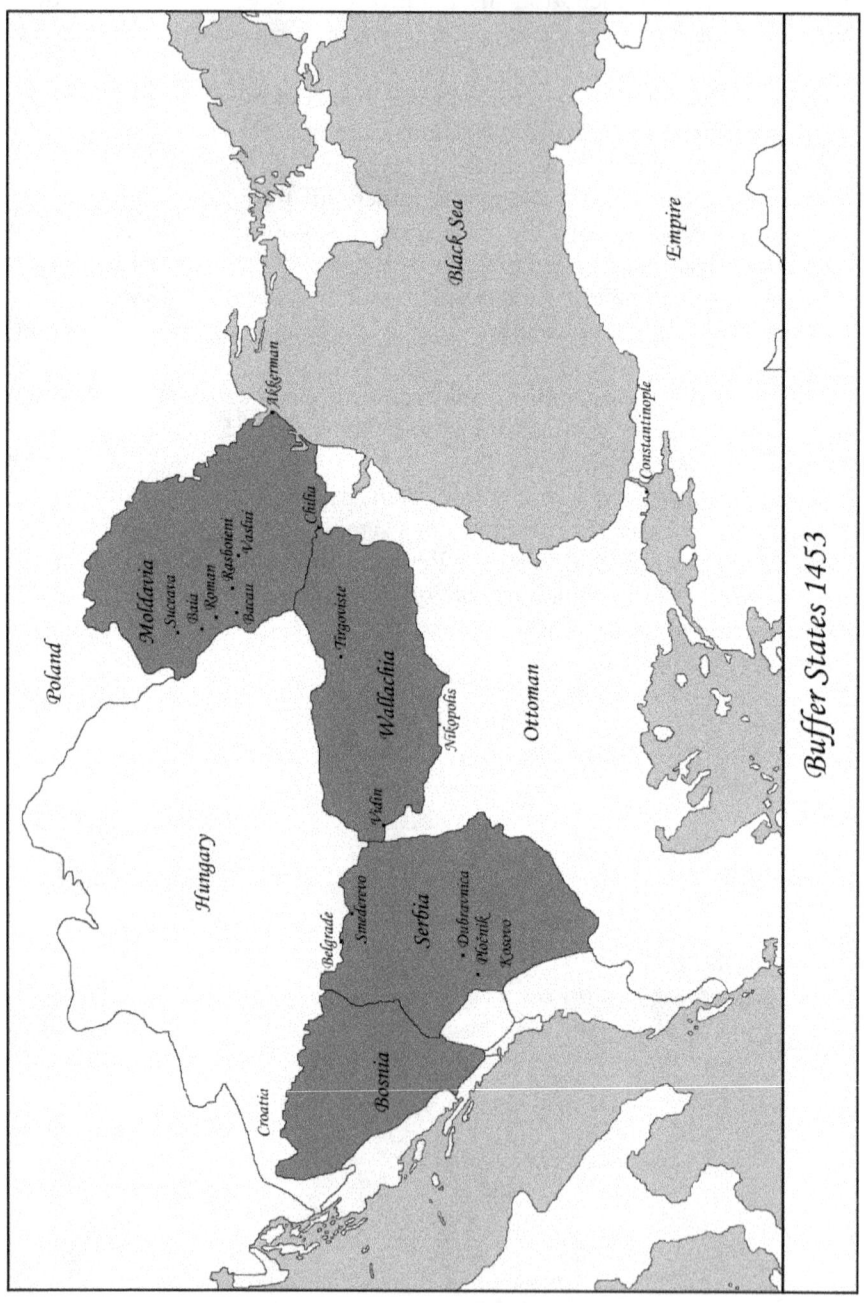

14 - THE BUFFER-STATES

As we have already seen, the Balkans were for centuries the battleground between powerful empires, Romans, Byzantines, Bulgarians, Mongols, Hungarians and Ottomans to name but a few.

As these empires came and went, they created zones of vacuum where gradually independent states, some bigger, some smaller, developed over time. Some disappeared, swallowed up by new emerging empires, some merged into, often uneasy, alliances and by the time of Sultan Mehmed II four states, Bosnia, Serbia, Wallachia and Moldavia, had established themselves in the area between the Ottoman Empire and Hungary.

It was not a coincidence that these particular states had survived the onslaught of time, it was all about location.

Towards the end of the fourteenth century, there was a clear faultline going west to east across the Balkan Peninsula. In the north, Hungary ruled from Croatia on the Adriatic Sea across the top of the peninsula to the eastern Carpathians. In the south, the Ottoman Empire had gradually moved to control the peninsula, annexing most of the former Byzantine and Bulgarian empires into their own emerging empire.

Neither the Hungarians nor the Ottomans were blind to the hostile intentions of their neighbours, but both competing empires had their own problems, internally and externally, and neither were prepared for an all-out conflict.

With this in mind, it was not desirable to have a broad direct border spanning hundreds of kilometres from the Adriatic Sea to the Black Sea, a border which would demand massive amounts of troops to be engaged in border-protection and taking valuable resources away from the empires' other, more pressing, conflicts.

The solution was to have a range of smaller, presumably neutral states squeezed in between the two empires proper. These states would create sufficient buffer to warn either party should the other attack and demand significantly less resources to be permanently stationed on the borders.

But neutrality was an uneasy term. Both empires of course saw it as an advantage that the rulers of these buffer-states were favourable to them, whether as vassal states - under their nominal suzerainty - or in real-political terms.

The rulers of the buffer states thus always walked a narrow line, officially maintaining their neutrality, but at the same time under constant pressure to favour one or the other mighty empire, the two empires, as we have previously seen, going through their own cycles of strength and weakness.

The result was inevitably one of murder, mayhem and upheaval, where opportunists and individuals without scruples would compete with each other for power, influence and financial gains.

The story of the four buffer states is thus similar in many ways, but also different due to their individual characteristics. But one thing they all had in common was that, sooner or later, they would become enemies of Mehmed II the Conqueror and we shall continue with the story of each in turn.

SERBIA

CRITICAL TIMELINE

Year	Event	Involved Parties
500s	Slav migration into western Balkans	Slavs Byzantium
830	Vlastimir mentioned as Knez ('Prince') of Sklaviniai	Serbs Byzantium
840	Bulgarian invasion repelled	Serbia Byzantium Bulgaria
853	Bulgarian invasion repelled	Serbia Byzantium Bulgaria
870s	Serbia recognized as vassal state to Byzantium. Christianity adopted by Serbs.	Serbia Byzantium
897	Serbian state recognized by Bulgaria	Serbia Byzantium
917	Bulgarian invasion	Serbia Bulgaria
921	Bulgarian invasion	Serbia Bulgaria
924	Serbia annexed by Bulgaria	Serbia Bulgaria
933	Serbia reclaimed from Bulgaria. Expands to Adriatic Sea	Serbia Bulgaria Byzantium
960	Časlav Klonimirović dies. Serbia is split up	Serbia Bulgaria Byzantium
1018	First Bulgarian Empire collapses. Serbia becomes Byzantine	Serbia Bulgaria Byzantium
1091	Vukan becomes Grand Prince of Serbia	Serbia Byzantium
1166	Byzantine coup	Serbia Byzantium
1172	Stefan Nemanja in Byzantine imprisonment	Serbia Byzantium
1212	The Pope recognizes Stefan Nemanjić as King of Serbia	Serbia The Pope
1219	Orthodox Patriarch recognizes Serbia. Serbia's first constitution (*Zakonopravilo*) issued	Serbia Byzantium
1242	Retreating Mongols raid Serbia	Serbia Golden Horde
1299	Serbia expands to Macedonia and northern Albania	Serbia Byzantium
1312	Serbia assists Byzantium	Serbia Byzantium
1331	Stefan Uroš IV Dušan becomes King of Serbia	Serbia
1346	Stefan Uroš IV Dušan is crowned as Emperor of Serbia	Serbia

Year	Event	Involved Parties
1355	Stefan Uroš IV Dušan. Serbia is split into smaller autonomous principalities	Serbia
1371	Battle of Maritsa (Ottoman victory)	Serbia Ottomans
1381	Battle of Dubravnica (Serbia victory)	Serbia Ottomans
1386	Battle of Pločnik (Serbian victory)	Serbia Ottomans
1389	First Battle of Kosovo (Ottoman victory)	Serbia Ottomans
1395	Serbia troops serve Ottomans in Wallachia	Serbia Ottomans Wallachia
1396	Battle of Nicopolis. Serbian troops serve Ottomans	Serbia Ottomans Hungary Venice France
1402	Serbia troops serve Ottomans in Battle of Ankara	Serbia Ottomans Timurids
1402	Stefan Lazarević becomes Despot of Serbia	Serbia Byzantium
1427	Đurađ Branković becomes Despot of Serbia	Serbia
1428	Smederevo becomes new Serbia capital. Vassalage is agreed with both Hungary and Ottoman Empire	Serbia Ottomans Byzantium
1435	Mara Hatun marries Ottoman Sultan Murad II	Serbia Ottomans
1438	Serbian troops serve Ottomans in raid on Transylvania	Serbia Ottomans Hungary
1438	Ottoman incursion in Serbia	Serbia Ottomans
1439	Ottomans annex Serbia. Đurađ Branković in exile	Serbia Ottomans
1443	Đurađ Branković supports Hungary during Long Campaign	Serbia Ottomans Hungary
1444	Peace settlement sees Đurađ Branković reinstated as Despot of Serbia	Serbia Ottomans Hungary
1456	Ottoman siege of Belgrade. Serbians harass retreating Ottomans	Serbia Ottomans Hungary
1458	Ottoman invasion of Serbia turns around at Smederevo	Serbia Ottomans
1459	Ottoman invasion of Serbia. Serbia annexed into Ottoman Empire	Serbia Ottomans

Part 5 - The Balkans

14 - The Buffer States - Serbia

We start with Serbia, the first of the buffer states to eventually feel the wrath of Mehmed II.

In the sixth century, a large group of people - generally referred to as 'Slavs' - migrated from eastern Russia and the Baltic states to the Balkan Peninsula. They started to settle in the western part of the peninsula, an area nominally part of the Byzantine Empire, from where they raided further down into Greece.

The Byzantine Empire was not in a position to proactively defend this north-western corner of the Empire, so the Slavs gradually set down roots and created tribal territories. Eventually they converted to (Orthodox) Christianity and accepted Byzantine suzerainty although the imperial authority was mostly at a very low level.

The area, not dissimilar to current day Serbia, and Bosnia, was referred to as Sklaviniai, although it was not a unified political entity.

That began to change in the ninth century when the emerging First Bulgarian Empire started to move west and south, having already consolidated their position on the eastern part of the peninsula against a weakening Byzantine Empire.

Historic evidence is thin, but it seems that the Slavs united under Knez ('Prince') Vlastimir and with Byzantine support tried to stop the Bulgarian expansion which had already annexed parts of Serbia along the southern side of the Danube River.

A Bulgarian invasion attempt was repelled around year 840 and Vlastimir formed an alliance with the ruler of Travunia - approximately similar to modern day Montenegro - which saw Travunia join 'Serbia' even though the cities on the Adriatic coast were still controlled by Byzantium.

Vlastimir's sons - Mutimir, Gojnik and Stojmir - repelled another Bulgarian attack in 853 after which an all too well-known pattern emerged. Mutimir grabbed the power and his brothers, Gojnik and Stojmir, revolted and then took refuge at the Bulgarian court.

This conflict was caused by the local tradition of succession, in which - rather than primogeniture as practiced in the West - heritage was split between the male heirs, in this case three brothers.

Despite constant attempts from his Bulgarian backed - brothers to dethrone him, Mutimir was rather successful, helping the Byzantines in their wars against the Arabs and - with Byzantine help - establishing 'Serbia' as an official Orthodox state with its own bishopric.

When Mutimir died in 890, the situation quickly deteriorated.

Mutimir was succeeded by his son Prvoslav; by he was quickly overthrown by Petar Gojnikovic, the son of Mutimir's brother Gojnik.

The next five years were dominated by - Bulgarian backed - attempts to take the throne back for Prvoslav and his brothers, but in 897 the Bulgarian Khan, Simeon I, accepted Petar Gojnikovic's rule, leading to a twenty year peace agreement and the first real recognition of Serbia as an autonomous nation state.

Petar Gojnikovic used the peace with Bulgaria to expand the Serbian state north and west, but when he got as far as the costal enclave of Zachlumia (overlapping the modern border between Bosnia-Herzegovina and Croatia), he encountered fierce resistance from its ruler Michael.

His overall success however convinced Petar Gojnikovic that he should be more than a de-facto vassal to the Bulgarians, a decision to which he was well helped by the Byzantines, looking for alliances with anyone who could put a dent in the Bulgarian expansion.

The Byzantines therefore financed Petar Gojnikovic in order that he could attack the Bulgarians, but the aforementioned Michael of Zachlumia warned the Bulgarians of Petar Gojnikovic's hostile intentions.

Instead the Bulgarians attacked in 917 and dethroned Petar Gojnikovic - who died a prisoner in Bulgaria, for Pavel Branovic, son of Mutimir's son Bran and a Bulgarian puppet.

Now the Byzantines sent an army into Serbia to promote Zaharije Prvoslaviljevic - another grandson of Mutimir, but Pavel Branovic held fast and Zaharije Prvoslaviljevic fled to Bulgaria.

Pavel Branovic now changed allegiance to Byzantium. The Bulgarians then picked up Zaharije Prvoslaviljevic's cause and successfully invaded Serbia in 921, putting Zaharije Prvoslaviljevic on the throne as their new puppet.

But the new puppet also turned to Byzantium, no doubt lured by gold, and Simeon I of Bulgaria finally decided to settle the issue. He found a new puppet in Časlav Klonimirović, yet another grandson of Mutimir, and ousted Zaharije Prvoslaviljevic in 924. But Simeon I's support of Časlav Klonimirović turned out to be a rouse. When the Serbian nobles were gathered to formally elect him, they were rounded up and sent to Bulgaria along with Časlav Klonimirović. Serbia was annexed as a Bulgarian province and many Serbs fled to the neighbouring countries.

On Simeon I's death the tables turned again. Časlav Klonimirović returned to Serbia, followed by many refugees, and took control of the country once again.

Allying himself with the Byzantines, with whom the Bulgarians were also at peace with at the time, Časlav Klonimirović not only reclaimed Serbia from Bulgaria, but gradually expanded it to cover - what we would now know as - Bosnia, Herzegovina, Montenegro and the previously contested enclave of Zachlumia, giving Serbia access to the Adriatic Sea.

But as we have seen before, and shall see again, too often a strong ruler is followed by chaos. Časlav Klonimirović died in 960 and his death threw Serbia into decades of civil strife, the powerful nobles and royal candidates fighting each other with no clear outcome.

Autonomous principalities emerged and disappeared, some falling to Bulgaria, but when the Byzantines finally broke the First Bulgarian Empire in the early years of the eleventh century, the Balkans simply fell back into Byzantine hands, although many of the local nobles retained a high level of autonomy and would occasionally revolt against their overlords.

A small independent principality named Duklja emerged around what we now know as Montenegro and it even received official recognition from the Pope, but it was soon re-absorbed by the Byzantines and their Venetian allies.

Around 1090 a new Serbian nation state stated to form, known as the Serbian Grand Principality - or Rascia, it consisted of the core Serbian inland territories.

The first recognized ruler was Vucan, styling himself as Grand Prince of Serbia, who through a succession of conflicts with the Byzantines managed to break away from their suzerainty and regularly raided into Byzantine Bulgaria.

Vucan died in 1112 and was succeeded by his nephew Uroš I.

The new ruler initially participated in the battle for the coastal region, contested between the Byzantines and independent princes, but in general spent more than three decades in relative peace, consolidating rather than expanding and marrying his daughter, Helena, to the Hungarian King Béla II, thus forming a new strong alliance against Byzantium.

On the death of Uroš I in 1145, his son Uroš II took the throne.

The family ties with Hungary now came into play. King Béla II of Hungary died, leaving Uroš II's sister, Helena, as regent for her minor son. Furthermore, Uroš II and Helena's brother, Beloš, had long since set himself up at the Hungarian court and between them they effectively ruled Hungary.

The alliance did not sit well with the Byzantines, and Serbia became a pawn in a power-play between Hungary and Byzantium, seeing Uroš II disposed twice by his other brother, Desa Urošević, and finally having to submit to nominal Byzantine Suzerainty.

On his death in 1161, Beloš took over for short time, before the throne finally went to the third brother, Desa Urošević.

A troublesome four year reign followed, in which the Byzantine Emperor Manuel I Komnenos constantly put pressure on Desa Urošević to abandon his Hungarian alliances and submit to Byzantium and finally, in 1166, when Manuel I Komnenos decided that Desa Urošević could not be trusted, he had him replaced by Tihomir, whose exact heritage is unknown although it is known that he was kin to Uroš II.

Tihomir had a younger brother, Stefan Nemanja, who had designs on the throne for himself, and after only a year as ruler, Tihomir was dethroned by his brother.

The Byzantine Emperor recruited a mercenary army for Tihomir, but it was defeated and Tihomir died, leaving Stefan Nemanja in complete control.

Immediately following his accession to the throne, Stefan Nemanja started to work towards independence from Byzantine influence. He joined an anti-Byzantine allegiance with Hungary and Venice, but in 1172 he had to surrender to Emperor Manuel I and was kept in captivity in Constantinople until it was felt he could be trusted again.

He repaid the trust by focusing on internal matters, consolidating his position and suppressing the Bogomils, a heretic sect originating in Bulgaria, and strengthening the Orthodox Church.

When Emperor Manuel I died in 1180, Stefan Nemanja started to act independently of Byzantium and he gradually expanded his territory onto the Dalmatian coast. He also started to expand into the former Bulgarian territories, but the Byzantines defeated him in battle in 1191, forcing him to retreat from Bulgarian lands.

He finally abdicated in 1195, leaving a well consolidated state in the hands of his son Stefan Nemanjić.

But Stefan Nemanjić was the second son of Stefan Nemanja, thus bypassing the older son, Vukan Nemanjić, who had been given a fief on the Dalmatian coast instead.

While Stefan Nemanja lived in retirement, as a monk, status quo remained between his sons, but as soon as he died in 1199, Vukan Nemanjić revolted against his brother.

The times were turbulent, the Hungarian Empire being strong, the Byzantine Empire being weak - only a few years away from the Fourth Crusade, a new Bulgarian Empire was starting to form and Bosnia was developing its own strong identity.

Vukan Nemanjić found support in Hungary, partly because Stefan Nemanjić was married to a Byzantine princess, and with their help he ousted Stefan Nemanjić in 1202.

In order to get the required support, Vukan Nemanjić had promised the Hungarians that he would move Serbia from the Orthodox to the Catholic Church, but he soon got involved with defending his territories against Bulgarian aggression, the Bulgarians successfully annexing Serbian territories along the Danube River including Nis and Belgrade.

The defeats to the Bulgarians combined with his tendency to Catholicism did not please the local barons who in 1204 had Stefan Nemanjić reinstated, leaving Vukan Nemanjić with his original fief.

We are now in the time of the Fourth Crusade, the Byzantine Empire being, temporarily, replaced by the Latin Empire of Constantinople, the Second Bulgarian Empire fighting with the new Latin empire for supremacy of the Balkans, King András II starting to reform the royal authority in Hungary and a small group of nomadic refugees arriving in Anatolia.

In the hinterland behind the bigger conflict between the Bulgarians and the Latins, Stefan Nemanjić involved himself in a range of local conflicts, aimed at getting, keeping or regaining control of, in particular, the coastal cities of the Dalmatian coast, a competition in which the Venetians as well as the Hungarians also took an active role.

In the meantime, Stefan Nemanjić's other brother, Sava, had been busy on his behalf.

Sava - originally named Rastko Nemanjić - had early on chosen a religious career and thus was not a contender for the throne. Quite on the contrary, he served as a diplomat, in particular to the Pope and the Orthodox Patriarch.

In 1212 he brought home a big prize; the Pope's appointment of Stefan Nemanjić as king and his blessing for a Serbian Kingdom.

Stefan Nemanjić became King Stefan II Nemanjić and the Kingdom was subsequently, in 1219, also endorsed by the Orthodox Patriarch, at that time residing in Nicaea, Sava being the first archbishop.

But Sava had not finished yet. Taking a proactive interest in the establishment of a formalized nation state, he wrote a document called 'Zakonopravilo', the first constitution of Serbia, outlining both civil and church law and organizing Serbia into a - for the times - well advanced political entity.

The combination of the brothers Stefan II Nemanjić and Sava had put Serbia on strong footing in a time when the Bulgarians and the Latins in Constantinople mainly focused on each other. Stefan II Nemanjić became ill as he got older and finally abdicated in 1228, withdrawing to a monastery for the remainder of his life. He left the throne to his oldest son Stefan Radoslav.

Stefan Radoslav had acted as governor in Zeta (modern day Montenegro) and had married Anna, daughter of Theodore Komnenos Doukas the ruler of Epirus on the Greek west coast and one of the exile-contenders for the throne of Byzantium.

Anna and her father proved to be dominant, putting Serbia under the quasi suzerainty of Epirus. This was not popular with the locals, so in 1234, after the Bulgarian King Ivar Asen II had defeated Theodore Komnenos Doukas in battle, they disposed of Stefan Radoslav, replacing him with his younger half-brother Stefan Vladislav I.

The country now effectively changed to be influenced by Bulgaria as Stefan Vladislav I was married to Beloslava, a daughter of Ivan Asen II of Bulgaria. The move was not popular with everybody, including the aging Sava, who left for a pilgrimage to Jerusalem and died on his way back.

Ivar Asen II died in 1241, weakening Bulgaria and when the Mongols withdrew from their invasion of Hungary they raided through Bulgaria and Serbia, the Bulgarians ending up agreeing to become vassals of the Mongolians.

This once again tipped the balance and the nobles, now eager to throw off the Bulgarian/Mongol influence dethroned Stefan Vladislav I - who according to some sources was given Zeta to rule - and replaced him with his younger half-brother Stefan Uroš I.

With both Epirus and Bulgaria weakened, there were no imminent threats to Serbia and Stefan Uroš I utilized the situation to strengthen Serbia's economy, inviting Saxon settlers to operate the country's mining industry and strengthening ties with, in particular, Ragusa (Dubrovnik) on the Adriatic Sea, providing Serbia with access to the world markets through Ragusan traders.

The relationship with Ragusa was not always peaceful, indeed two major conflicts broke out, but in the end, they were both resolved peacefully, the pragmatic Ragusans agreeing to pay an annual tribute to Serbia.

There was also conflict with Hungary, Stefan Uroš I attempting to annex Hungarian territories on the Danube, River but in the end that too was settled and Stefan Uroš I's oldest son, Stefan Dragutin, was married to a daughter of the Hungarian heir apparent.

As time went by and Stefan Uroš I had ruled for more than three decades, the issue of his succession emerged. Stefan Uroš I favoured his younger son, Stefan Milutin, but the older brother, Stefan Dragutin, rebelled with support of his family in Hungary and in 1276 forced Stefan Uroš I to abdicate in his favour.

Stefan Dragutin ruled, under strong Hungarian influence until 1282 when he, having suffered a leg injury during a hunt, abdicated in favour of his younger brother Stefan Milutin. He did, however, maintain territories in north-western Serbia - including Belgrade - which he formed into the Kingdom of Syrmia, with himself as king even though in reality he ruled as a vassal to Hungary.

Stefan Milutin, who became Stefan Uroš II Milutin, his father's original choice for the throne, wasted little time.

He attacked the weak Byzantine Empire, occupying Macedonia and northern Albania. The Byzantines had little with which to fight back, so the matter was finally settled in 1299 by Stefan Uroš II Milutin marrying Simonida a daughter of the Byzantine Emperor, Andronikos II Palaiologos, the occupied lands being given to Stefan Uroš II Milutin as Simonida's dowry.

In the meantime, there had been trouble in Syrmia, where Bulgarian renegade warlords raided regularly. Stefan Dragutin, even with Hungarian help, could not control the situation and his brother thus came to his assistance.

Stefan Uroš II Milutin was of the opinion that the newly secured territories should become Serbian, but Stefan Dragutin was of mind to keep them as an independent kingdom, so the two brothers fell out.

On Stefan Dragutin's abdication it had been agreed that his son, Stefan Vladislav, would inherit the Serbian crown, but when the brothers fell out over Syrmia, Stefan Uroš II Milutin instead appointed his own son, Stefan Dečanski, as Prince of Zeta, effectively making him heir apparent.

Serbia had become a dominant force in the Balkans, and in 1312 it lent assistance to the Byzantine Emperor, Michael IX Palaiologos, assisting him in expelling renegade Turcopoles from the Gallipoli peninsula. As a reward, Serbia was given further territories in Albania.

When Stefan Dragutin died in 1314, Stefan Uroš II Milutin settled matters with Syrmia by annexing it, although he later had to cede Belgrade to Hungary.

Also in 1314, Stefan Uroš II Milutin's oldest son, Stefan Dečanski rebelled against his father, but he was defeated, captured, blinded and sent to live in exile at the Byzantine court. Instead, his younger brother, Stefan Constantine, was made heir apparent but Stefan Dečanski and Stefan Uroš II Milutin were reconciled in 1321 and Stefan Dečanski returned to Serbia.

When Stefan Uroš II Milutin died in the same year, a short war of succession broke out, the two brothers fighting for the throne, but Stefan Constantine fell in the ensuing battle and it was Stefan Dečanski who was crowned as Stefan Uroš III Dečanski, with his son, Stefan Dušan, being crowned as 'young king' - or heir apparent - at the same time.

But Stefan Vladislav, the son of Stefan Dragutin, had not forgotten his claim to the throne. He took control of Syrmia and then headed an alliance of Bulgaria, Hungary and Ragusa against Serbia in a bid to take the throne.

The war lasted for years and it was only in 1326 that Stefan Uroš III Dečanski settled the final matters with Ragusa, the contender, Stefan Vladislav, now in exile in Hungary.

Stefan Uroš III Dečanski's sister, Anna, was married to Michael Shishman of Bulgaria, but in a move to seal an anti-Serbian alliance with Byzantium, Michael Shishman divorced Anna and instead married Theodora, daughter of the Byzantine Emperor Andronikos III Palaiologos.

Knowing that a combined attack was forthcoming, Stefan Uroš III Dečanski marched on Bulgaria and defeated Michael Shishman, making the Byzantines rethink and withdraw.

Stefan Uroš III Dečanski now had the opportunity to push further into Byzantine territories, but he decided not to take the opportunity. This was an unpopular move and the Serbian nobles gathered behind his warlike son Stefan Dušan.

The initial revolt was solved by peaceful means, but when it re-emerged in 1331, Stefan Dušan ultimately had his father imprisoned and subsequently strangled.

Stefan Dušan became Stefan Uroš IV Dušan and in more than two decades of rule, Serbia rose to its zenith.

Although Stefan Uroš IV Dušan's primary target was Byzantium, there were more pressing matters. There was unrest in Zeta, its nobles feeling that they had not been sufficiently rewarded for their support to Stefan Uroš IV Dušan, but the problems were stamped out in 1332 and then Stefan Uroš IV Dušan was ready for the Byzantines.

The next twenty-three years saw a succession of Serbian aggression towards the increasingly impotent Byzantine Empire.

Though on occasions Stefan Uroš IV Dušan had to back off in order to defend Serbia against Hungarian incursions, he pushed and pushed. He had secured peace with Bulgaria, even if Serbia and Bulgaria at one point in time supported different sides in the Byzantine civil war, a conflict which also saw Serbian forces facing Ottomans - brought in as mercenaries by the Byzantines - in 1344.

After ten years of continuous war he made his big push, taking control of the western Balkans and penetrating into (Byzantine) Greece.

Not shy in nature, Stefan Uroš IV Dušan had previously added 'Albania and the coast' to his royal titles and he now added 'King of The Romans' as well. In 1346 he finally had himself crowned as 'Emperor' and had the Archbishop of Serbia elevated to Patriarch.

Stefan Uroš IV Dušan's next target was Constantinople itself. But he did not have a fleet, a necessary prerequisite for an effective siege. To get one he started to negotiate with Venice, but it came to nothing as the Venetians had no interest in a strong Serbian Empire but rather were quite happy with their position of dominance in relation to the weak Byzantines.

Instead, he threw his attention on Bosnia, using old territorial claims as his *casus belli*.

The Bosnians did not have the military strength to face the Serbians in open battle, so they withdrew to the mountains, fighting a year-long guerrilla war and refusing to give in to Stefan Uroš IV Dušan's territorial demands.

By the 1350s the Ottomans - once again brought to Europe by the Byzantines - were raiding through northern Greece and Stefan Uroš IV Dušan went to meet them, but he died from illness (possibly poisoning) on the way. With him died the glory of Serbia.

He was succeeded by his son, Stefan Uroš V, who was very unlike his father and would be given the moniker 'the Weak'.

Stefan Uroš V Dušan did not have the personal charisma of his father and was strongly influenced by his mother, Helena, sister to Tsar Ivan Alexander of Bulgaria.

Also the nobles of Serbia had grown rich and powerful in the wake of the country's success, but with Stefan Uroš IV Dušan gone, their loyalty proved to be to themselves rather than to the royal authority.

Serbia simply imploded, segmented into more or less autonomous personal principalities, ruled by the powerful landowners.

The Emperor's own uncle, Simeon Uroš Palaiologos, launched an attempt at the throne, but satisfied himself with taking over Thessaly and Epirus, cutting Stefan Uroš IV Dušan's main conquests off from the central authority.

The north-eastern provinces, controlled by the Rastislalić family broke away and later accepted the suzerainty of Hungary.

The emperor's brothers Stracimir, Djuradj and Balša took control of Zeta.

Moravian Serbia, the north-western territories bordering Hungary, broke lose under the reign of Lazar Hrebeljanović, a minor noble and former civil servant who left the court to seek his own luck.

In the meantime, the Ottomans were helping themselves in Greece and started to push into Serbian territories, to the extent there was such an entity as Serbia left at that time.

Facing the threat from the Ottomans some unity was however found and a united Serbian force went to meet marauding Ottomans at the Maritsa River - in modern day Greece, in 1371. Despite superiority in numbers the Serbians were defeated, and a range of dominant nobles were killed, leaving the state in even more confusion and the Ottomans in control of Greece and Macedonia.

That same year emperor Stefan Uroš V Dušan died, and he was not replaced as emperor, the empire being a thing of the past. Stefan Uroš V Dušan himself did not leave an heir, but his co-ruler Vukašin Mrnjavčević, who had died at the Battle of Maritsa, left a son Marko Mrnjavčević, who became known as 'Prince Marco' and took over western Macedonia which he ruled as an Ottoman Vassal.

The Serbian Empire had in a few decades gone from greatness to destruction, mainly by its own hand and the story continues with Lazar Hrebeljanović who, as mentioned above, had secured Moravian Serbia on the border to Hungary and which we shall now consider to be the only surviving independent Serbian State.

Lazar Hrebeljanović had several buffer territories between himself and the Ottomans, in particular Bulgaria and the 'Principality of Velbazhd', an area in eastern Macedonia ruled by the Serbian noble Constantine Dragaš, but both these areas were Ottoman vassal and soon Ottoman raiders started to emerge in Moravian Serbia.

The raiders were followed by an expeditionary force, possibly led by Sultan Murad I himself, and in 1381 Lazar Hrebeljanović marched to meet them at Dubravnica. The Serbians were successful and stopped the Ottoman expansion, but five years later they were back with a new expeditionary force, this time led by the general Şahin Bey. This time, with Bosnian support, Lazar Hrebeljanović marched to meet them at Pločnik and once again the Serbians managed to turn the Ottomans around.

When they came again three years later, they came with the full force of the Ottoman Empire, led by Sultan Murad I and his heir, Bayezid.

To meet them Lazar Hrebeljanović marched with the Bosnians and his son in law Vuk Branković, who controlled Oblast Brankovića, the areas south-west of (Moravian) Serbia.

The battle, which took place at Kosovo, was a hard-fought affair. The Serbians attacked first, followed by an Ottoman counterattack. Both armies stood their ground and eventually it was a matter of numbers, where the Ottomans had enough of an advantage to gradually annihilate the Serbians until there was no one left to kill.

Lazar Hrebeljanović fell in the battle while Vuk Branković got away. Sultan Murad I survived the battle but was assassinated when he received a Serbian renegade, believed to be named Miloš Obilić, who drew a knife and cut the Sultan down before he himself was slain by the Sultan's guards.

Effectively the Battle of Kosovo (later known as the First Battle of Kosovo) settled Serbia's fate. Although the Ottoman loses were enormous, they could draw on fresh troops from Anatolia and rebuild their army. The Serbians were spent.

Lazar Hrebeljanović's son Stefan Lazarević took the throne in Moravian Serbia as an Ottoman vassal, in which capacity he supplied the Sultan with troops in campaigns including Wallachia (1395), Nicopolis (1396) and Ankara (1402).

Vuk Branković refused Ottoman vassalage and his territories were gradually occupied over the next few years until they were fully annexed by 1396 and Vuk Branković himself died an Ottoman prisoner.

The Ottoman defeat at Ankara in 1402 and the following interregnum provided some relief to Stefan Lazarević. He re-established relations with Byzantium and was appointed 'Despot' of Serbia in 1402 by the Byzantine Emperor. He also took the opportunity to strengthen the internal structure of the country, forming the strongest Serbian state since the sudden demise of the Serbian Empire, a country rich in silver from the mines in Novo Brdo, and, eventually reaching the Adriatic Sea when he inherited the principality of Zeta (Montenegro).

Stefan Lazarević died in 1427 and he left the throne to Đurađ Branković, son of Vuk Branković and Stefan Lazarević's sister Mara.

Đurađ Branković would become an icon of the difficulties that befell a Balkan ruler of the times. The Branković family had rich estates and many family relations in Hungary, relations which were further extended when Đurađ Branković's daughter, Catherine, was married to Hungary's richest landowner Count Ulrich II of Celje.

Đurađ Branković thus instinctively leaned towards Hungary, accepting Hungarian suzerainty, but the Ottomans had reorganized after their interregnum and were once again active in the area.

In 1428 Sultan Murad II and King Sigismund of Hungary agreed that Serbia could, in principle, pay vassalage to both empires and that the Serbians could establish a new castle and capital at Smederevo, the old capital of Belgrade having been ceded to Hungary as the Serbians were not in a position to defend it.

To further strengthen his position in the middle between the two powerful empires, Đurađ Branković had his daughter, Mara engaged to Sultan Murad II in 1431 and they married in 1435 although Mara was but one of several 'political' wives of the sultan (see Chapter 2 for the quote "T*he wife of a very powerful monarch and she, it is generally believed, did not sleep with him*" in which '*she*' is that same - Mara).

The reduced Serbian state had thus been solidly established as a buffer state when the balance turned by the death of King Sigismund in 1437.

The weakening of Hungary following the death of Sigismund was simply too much of a temptation for Sultan Murad II.

First, he organized an expeditionary force to raid into - Hungarian - Transylvania. For this purpose, he requested, and got, support from his vassal in Serbia and his vassal, Vlad Dracul II, in Wallachia.

While the expeditionary force was busy causing havoc in Transylvania during 1438, the Sultan sent another expeditionary force into Serbia, left poorly defended, softening up the border defences in preparation for a second campaign in the following year.

When the Ottomans came in 1439, they came in force. With the border already softened up the year before, they marched straight to the capital Smederevo, which was put under siege. When it became clear that there was no help forthcoming, the castle surrendered in August of 1439.

With the exception of Zeta on the coast and the area around the silver mines at Novo Brdo, Serbia was now Ottoman and there was other bad news for Đurađ Branković.

In the battle for the Hungarian throne after King Albert II's sudden demise, Đurađ Branković had hopes for his son-in-law, Count Ulrich II of Celje's, support for one of Đurađ Branković's sons, but the Count in the end chose to support Wladyslaw III.

The new King immediately seized a range of the Branković estates in Hungary, and Đurađ Branković headed south to take up temporary residence in Ragusa.

While he was there, the Ottomans annexed the silver mines in Novo Brdo, one of the few areas still under Đurađ Branković's control and once again there was more bad news.

During the fall of Smederevo, two of Đurađ Branković's sons, Gregor and Stefan, had been taken prisoners and led off to Edirne, where they were held hostage to ensure their father's compliance. They were now accused of secretly corresponding with their father, who was believed to be plotting against the Ottomans, and they were both blinded with hot irons. That their own sister, Mara, was married to the Sultan did not help them.

Đurađ Branković now returned to Hungary and offered his services to the young king, not because he wanted to, but because he had no other options left.

It was thus with the hope of regaining his lost realm that Đurađ Branković set out in support of 'the Long Campaign' in 1443 and in the end he was the only real beneficiary.

Murad II wanted peace, so he could deal with the Karamanids in Anatolia, and he appreciated the fact that part of the reason for the Hungarian-led campaign had been his annexation of Serbia, previously a mutually comforting buffer zone.

It was therefore a key point in the peace treaty of 1444 that Serbia was restored as an independent state, and Đurađ Branković had his country back.

It therefore did not meet with Đurađ Branković's approval when the Hungarians immediately broke the peace and marched on the Ottomans, leading to their defeat at Varna and even less so when Janos Hunyadi marched through Serbia towards (the Second Battle of) Kosovo in 1448.

Đurađ Branković refused to help the Hungarians and when the Hungarians therefore declared Serbia hostile territory and pillaged their way through the country, Đurađ Branković proactively did what he could to assist the Ottomans, in particular by blocking the route of Skanderbeg, bringing Albanian reinforcements to the Hungarian cause.

Following the Hungarian defeat at Kosovo, Serbian troops rounded up Janos Hunyadi and the Wallachian Voivode Vladislav II and brought them to Đurađ Branković at Smederevo. Here Janos Hunyadi and the Voivode were held for ransom, possibly in the form of Janos Hunyadi signing back property that Đurađ Branković had given him to win his support for the 1444 peace agreement.

Now followed a relatively peaceful period of six years, the last peaceful years of the Serbian Despotate.

After the death of Sultan Murad II and his successor Mehmed II's Conquest of Constantinople, Mehmed II went for Belgrade, as covered in Chapter 13. When the Ottomans were surprisingly defeated and their army fled through Serbia, Đurađ Branković decided that it was time for revenge, so his troops harassed the Ottoman army all the way through Serbia, causing significant damage and possibly killing more Ottomans than had been killed in the siege itself. This action was possibly caused by, false, reports that sultan Mehmed II had been killed at Belgrade.

But Mehmed II was not dead and it was Đurađ Branković who soon after, on Christmas Eve 1456, died aged eighty-one.

Đurađ Branković's oldest sons, Gregor and Stefan had, as previously mentioned, been blinded by the Ottomans and although they had long since returned home, they were considered incapable of ruling. It was therefore Đurađ Branković's younger son Lazar Branković who succeeded him.

But Lazar Branković was not ignorant to the political reality and using his sister, the widow Mara - who had a very close relationship to her step-son Mehmed II - as go-between, he ensured that his accession met with the Sultan's approval, as was custom for a vassal.

The Hungarians were not too keen on Lazar Branković's clear subservience to the Ottomans, and they started raiding into Serbia from Belgrade, for all intents and purposes regarding Serbia an enemy of Hungary.

But it was not the hostile Hungarians who would spell the end for Serbia; they were quite capable of doing damage to themselves.

Đurađ Branković's widow, Irene, died in May 1457 and her calming influence on the family now ended. On the very night of her death, her son Gregor, his sister Mara and Irene's brother fled Smederevo and took refuge with Mehmed II in Edirne, leaving Stefan with his brother Lazar.

The following January saw the death of Lazar Branković, who died of unknown reasons, and now the clock started ticking quickly towards the demise of Serbia.

A regency was declared, consisting of Lazar Branković's brother Stefan, his widow Helena and the Grand Voivode (top official) Thomas Angelović.

Thomas Angelović was brother to the Ottoman Grand Vizier and thus leaned towards the Ottomans, whereas Stefan and Helena leaned towards Hungary.

The weakness and internal strife was soon realized by the Bosnian King Stjepan Tomaš, who took the opportunity to invade. He was only stopped by Ottoman diplomacy and the marriage between his son, Stjepan Tomašević, and Jelena, the daughter of Stefan Branković.

But the real chaos was still to unfold. The Pope now threw his hat into the ring by suggesting that Serbia should be made a papal protectorate, implicit falling under the Catholic Church.

The reaction in Serbia was less than favourable, many declaring that they would rather be under Ottoman rule - with the relative freedom of religion - than under the strongly oppressive Catholic Church.

Alliances formed and a party favouring the Ottoman option formed around Thomas Angelović. He in turn was lured into the castle of Smederevo by Helena, where he was taken capture and handed over to the Hungarians, never to be seen again.

This was enough reason for Mehmed II to get involved. He still had the remaining brother, Gregor, in Edirne and with him as the Ottoman candidate and with the Grand Vizier Mahmud Pasha - the brother of Thomas Angelović - in command, an Ottoman army moved into Serbia in April 1458.

By August most of Serbia had fallen, leaving only Smederevo, but for unknown reasons, possibly not having brought heavy siege equipment, Mahmud Pasha turned his army around and left.

Given another lease of life, the Serbians now turned to Hungary. In January of 1459 it was agreed that the Bosnian Prince Stjepan Tomašević - soon to be married to Stefan Branković's daughter - should rule Serbia under Hungarian suzerainty. Bosnian agreements of vassalage to the Ottomans were cancelled, and the Hungarians appointed protectors of Bosnia as well.

But all the promises and agreements were to come to nothing. The matter may have been settled, but it had not been agreed with Mehmed II, who considered that he held the right to appoint the regent of a vassal state.

Mehmed II may well have turned a blind eye to the situation had it not coincided with the advent of the next phase of his ambitious plan of conquering the world.

The Ottoman defeat at Belgrade had put a dent in his plans, and he was not prepared to risk another outright assault on Hungary, now regaining strength under King Matthias I.

His new plan, devised in the three years since the Siege of Belgrade, was to put a stranglehold on Hungary. With Bosnia, Serbia, Wallachia and Moldavia as buffer-sates between himself and the Hungarians there was little pressure on Hungary, but with the buffer-states gone he could put pressure on Hungary on an ongoing basis, softening them up for a potential future assault.

In this grand new scheme Serbia was first in line. In March 1459 Mehmed II set out from Istanbul, by April he was at Sofia and by June he was in front of Smederevo.

King Matthias I of Hungary was supposed to protect Serbia, but he never lifted a finger and subsequently blamed the Bosnians. Abandoned, the Serbian nobles opened the gates of Smederevo to the Sultan who soon after rounded up any remaining resistance and by the end of the year Serbia had been engulfed into the Ottoman Empire. The Conqueror had unleashed his new strategy for the Balkans.

It was however not Mehmed II who was to carry the strategy to its end. That was left to his great-grandson Suleyman I who launched his successful attack on Belgrade in 1521 from Ottoman Serbia.

Serbia remained part of the Ottoman Empire until 1817, although Ottoman troops controlled the fortress of Belgrade until 1867.

It was Austria's declaration of war against Serbia in 1914 which sparked off WWI, a war in which the Serbians were on the side of the Allies. After WWI the new monarchy of Yugoslavia was formed, encompassing Serbia, Croatia, Slovenia and Montenegro.

After WWII the country was made a communist republic, now also encompassing Bosnia and Herzegovina. This lasted until the fall of the Iron Curtain in 1992.

An inglorious phase followed, where strong nationalist feeling with religious undertones led to a civil war. The eventual result was the splitting up of Yugoslavia into the medieval states of Serbia, Bosnia-Herzegovina, Croatia, Slovenia and Montenegro.

Serbia is, as I write this book, a candidate for membership in the EU and a potential powerhouse in the Balkans in the decades to come.

Part 5 - The Balkans

BOSNIA

Part 5 - The Balkans

CRITICAL TIMELINE

Year	Event	Involved Parties
1136	Hungary forms Banate of Bosnia	Hungary, Byzantium
1167	Banate of Bosnia back under Byzantine control	Hungary, Byzantium
1183	Kulin retakes Bosnia as Hungarian vassal	Bosnia, Hungary, Serbia, Byzantium
1203	John de Casamaris conducts papal inquiry on Krstjani heresy in Bosnia	Bosnia, The Pope
1232	Krstjani revolt	Bosnia
1234	Crusade against Bosnia	Bosnia, The Pope, Hungary, Serbia
1241	Hungarian occupation interrupted by Mongol invasion	Bosnia, Hungary
1242	Retreating Mongols raid Bosnia	Bosnia, Golden Horde
1247	Crusade avoided by diplomacy	Bosnia, The Pope
1250	Hungarian invasion. Persecution of Krstjani	Bosnia, Hungary
1299	Croatian invasion. Renewed persecution of Krstjani	Bosnia, Croatia
1322	Bosnia return to Hungarian suzerainty	Bosnia, Hungary, Croatia
1326	Bosnian attacks on Serbia	Bosnia, Serbia
1340	Catholic missionaries allowed to operate in Bosnia	Bosnia, The Pope
1350	Serbian invasion attempt	Bosnia, Serbia
1363	Hungarian invasion attempts	Bosnia, Hungary
1377	Stjepan Tvrtko I proclaimed King of Bosnia	Bosnia
1388	Battle of Bileća. Ottoman expeditionary force stopped	Bosnia, Ottomans
1389	First Battle of Kosovo	Bosnia, Ottomans, Serbia
1394	Bosnia returns to Hungarian suzerainty	Bosnia, Hungary, Naples
1409	Hungarian invasion	Bosnia, Hungary

364

Year	Event	Involved Parties
1458	Stjepan Tomašević appointed Despot of Serbia under Hungarian suzerainty	Bosnia Hungary Serbia
1459	Serbia lost to Ottomans	Bosnia Ottomans Serbia
1461	Stjepan Tomašević refuses to pay tribute to Ottomans	Bosnia Ottomans
1463	Ottoman invasion. Stjepan Tomašević captured and subsequently executed. Bosnia becomes Ottoman province	Bosnia Ottomans
1464	Hungary and Ottomans skirmish around Jajce	Ottomans Hungary
1482	Herzegovina annexed by Ottomans	Bosnia Serbia

Part 5 - The Balkans

14 - The Buffer States - Bosnia

From Serbia we once again move back in time, this time to the twelfth century, and we move south-west, down towards the coast of the Adriatic Sea.

As already covered in connection with Serbia, the region was populated by Slavs, who had been drifting down since the ninth century and lived in semi-autonomous - tribal - territories in principle under Byzantium, but in reality too far away from the weakening Empire's seat of power for them to easily assert any real central authority.

In 1136 King Béla II of Hungary started taking an interest in the territories to the south-west of Hungary and he suppressed the local tribes and formed the 'Banate of Bosnia' under Hungarian suzerainty. By the 1150 the Ban - taking care of the Hungarian King's interests - was named Borić.

The Byzantines were not too keen on Hungary extending its interest into traditionally Byzantine areas, so they tried to regain dominance over Bosnia several times, succeeding in 1167, annexing the area once again into the Byzantine Empire while Hungary was weak due to succession issues after the death of King Géza II.

The Byzantine Emperor, Manuel I Komnenos, appointed a local nobleman, Kulin, to take care of his interests, but in 1180 the Byzantine Emperor died and it was Byzantium's turn to enter into a period of civil war of succession.

The Hungarians convinced Kulin to change allegiance and in 1183 he together with Hungarian and Serbian troops under Stefan Nemanja pushed into Byzantine Bulgaria, removing Byzantine military presence from the region.

Although Kulin was in principle a Hungarian vassal, he reigned mainly autonomously and he took the opportunity to expand the original Bosnian area, even though at this point in time it did not reach as far as the Adriatic Sea.

His clearly stated urge for independence and a strong rising Bosnian identity started to worry his neighbours in Serbia and Hungary and they tried to undermine his growing ambitions by means of the Pope.

The Bosnians had gradually converted to Christianity; in their case dominated by the Catholics from Hungary, but Bosnia was also the home to a large group of 'Bogomils', a Christian sect - considered heretics by both the Catholic and Orthodox churches - who styled themselves as 'Krstjani'.

Kulin was himself happy to maintain a live-and-let-live policy, but his neighbour, Knez Vukan Nemanjić of Serbia - eager to please the Pope and the Hungarians - accused Kulin, and Bosnia in general, of heresy and the

Hungarians too whispered in the Pope's ear, eager to see Kulin's power cut down to size.

The Pope took the accusations very seriously, and not without cause as the Bogomil movement was very strong in Bosnia, and he even considered a crusade against Bosnia, which would be exactly the casus belli the Hungarians wanted, but Kulin outfoxed them.

He welcomed the papal legate, John de Casamaris, who travelled the country and interrogated prelates, monks, nuns and other good folk about their believes and practices.

John de Casamaris compiled a list of errors he had detected and Kulin called a council of church leaders who signed a document promising to correct their ways and behave as good Catholics. This satisfied the Pope and after John de Casamaris's exit the Bosnians went back to their own ways, the Krstjani becoming even stronger over the next decades to come.

Kulin died in 1204 and his son Stefan Kulinić took his place. Like his father he was a (Roman) Catholic, and whereas he probably inherited his father's tolerance towards the - now quickly growing - Krstjani, he did not have his father's diplomatic capabilities when it came to defy the Pope.

Once again encouraged by the Serbians and Hungarians the Pope first moved the religious authority over Bosnia to Hungary - away from the more tolerant Dalmatian Archbishop - and once again threatened with a crusade, the new Archbishop volunteering himself to lead it.

Eventually Stefan Kulinić caved in to the pressure and started to prosecute his own - heretic - citizens, but he had underestimated the popularity of the Krstjani and in particular the Krstjani's role as a nationalist organization symbolizing Bosnian independence.

The - mainly Krstjani - nobles revolted and in 1232 Stefan Kulinić was ousted.

The nobles appointed one of their own, Matej Ninoslav, a lapsed Catholic, now in support of the Krstjani, but it was not as simple as that.

The Serbians were unhappy as there were family ties between the two ruling houses. The Pope was not happy because of Matej Ninoslav's heresy and the Hungarians were not happy either as Stefan Kulinić had been a strong supporter of Hungary.

So, the Serbians supported the ousted Stefan Kulinić's son, Sibislav, who attempted an invasion. The Pope appointed Johannes Wildeshausen, a German, Bishop of Bosnia and the Hungarian King appointed his own ban of Bosnia, Herzeg Coloman.

The Bosnians did not welcome the new German bishop, let alone the new Hungarian-appointed ban, the Pope eventually called for a crusade against Bosnia.

The crusaders came in 1234 and the campaign lasted five years. The military leader was Herzeg Coloman, who once he had gained control handed over the nominal position as ban to Prijezda, a distant relative to Matej Ninoslav.

But the crusaders met serious resistance. The Bosnians fought guerrilla war every step of the way, mounting attacks and then retreating back into the mountains in the centre of the country.

Johannes Wildeshausen, the bishop, asked to be replaced and the Pope replaced him with a Hungarian Dominican who proceeded to burn as many heretics as he could get his hands on, further fuelling Bosnian resistance.

It was ugly and it was drawn out, but eventually Matej Ninoslav was forced into exile in Ragusa and Prijezda ruled as a Hungarian puppet.

But only two years later the Mongols arrived and the Hungarian army which had been left to support the Bosnian ruler had to return home to defend Hungary, a conflict which saw Herzeg Coloman killed in action.

Rid of the Hungarians, Matej Ninoslav returned and Prijezda fled to Hungary.

Although the Mongols ravaged through Bosnia during their retreat in 1442, the country did not suffer the kind of devastation and depopulation that Hungary did and the following decade was reasonably peaceful.

There was continued tension in relation to the Hungarians, the two states fighting over the city of Split, but Matej Ninoslav managed to use diplomacy to fight off another papal crusade - inspired by Hungary - in 1247.

But when Matej Ninoslav died in 1250, and despite his son's effort to keep Bosnia independent, the Hungarians enforced their will militarily and reinstated Prijezda - now Prijezda I - as ban, ruling under the suzerainty of Hungary.

Prijezda I, despite himself having at one point in time been a Krstjani, now did the bidding of the Catholic Church and proactively persecuted the Krstjani in Bosnia.

As a reward he received lands from the King of Hungary, firmly establishing the borders of Bosnia. He was even at one time granted lands in Serbia, which the Hungarians had conquered, but he had to give them back when the Serbians and Hungarians subsequently signed a peace agreement.

Later on he strengthened the ties between Bosnia and Serbia through the marriage between his younger son Stjepan and Jelisaveta, daughter of Stefan Dragutin of Serbia.

Prijezda I lived to old age, so old that in 1287, aged 76, he was forced to abdicate due to his advanced age. On his abdication Bosnia was split between his two sons, Prijezda (II) and Stjepan (I), in concept as co-rulers but in reality, by a separation of the country. However, this only lasted until 1290 when Prijezda II died and Stjepan I took the role of ban for himself.

Like his father, Stjepan I in principle ruled as a vassal to Hungary, but his marriage to Jelisaveta put him under strong influence from her father, Stefan Dragutin of Serbia.

Through no fault of his own, Stjepan I became involved in the war for succession in Hungary, as did everybody in the area at the time, and when the party of Charles Robert of Anjou (Charles I of Hungary) emerged triumphantly, the new rulers granted land to the party's supporters.

Prominent amongst the supporters of Charles I was Paul Šubić, a powerful Croatian baron who had indeed accepted the title as King of Hungary from the Pope on behalf of - the minor - Charles I.

For his efforts, Paul Šubić was - mainly by himself - granted Bosnia, and he styled himself as Paul I, Lord of Bosnia. Paul I however had many other interests so he quickly appointed his brother Mladen (I) as ban.

With the full support of Hungary, and in particular Croatia in which Paul Šubić ruled practically autonomously, Mladen I quickly took control of the country, even though Stjepan I remained resisting and never gave up his claim.

To please his masters, Mladen I started to persecute the Krstjani, but they too put up resistance, and Mladen I was killed in battle in 1304.

In his stead Paul Šubić's son Mladen (II) was quickly appointed as ban, but the resistance in Bosnia was so severe that Paul Šubić himself had to intervene with Croatian troops and in effect Mladen II was a puppet of his father's military oppression of the Bosnians.

When Paul Šubić' died in 1312 it undermined Mladen II's authority and control and even though Stjepan I did not manage to utilize the situation - he died in 1314 - Mladen II decided to pacify the situation by elevating himself as 'Lord of Bosnia' with Stjepan I's son Stjepan II as ban.

But bigger issues were at play. The Hungarian King, Charles I, had come of age and he was keen to assert his authority over the semi-autonomous barons, not least the Šubić' family in Croatia, and it came to war in which the Šubić' family was defeated in 1322. Mladen II was captured and spent the rest of his life in a prison in Hungary.

Having never formally broken their alliance to the Hungarian crown, Stjepan II's family now became 'the King's men' and Charles I officially reinstated Stjepan II as ban.

But all was not well in Croatia and Stjepan II, partly in an attempt to grab land and partly as ordered by Charles I, became involved in the bloody civil war, eventually - after having changed his allegiance several times - ending up on the winning side, once again endearing him to the Hungarian King.

Stjepan II now turned his attention towards Serbia, where he repeatedly moved against the neighbouring territories. He was so successful that the large amount of Serbian Orthodox people he now included into Bosnia changed the religious demographics so much that the - previously majority - Krstjani became a religious minority.

This shift in the religious balance in Bosnia did not please the Pope and he planned several crusades to beat Bosnia into submission, but internal strife prevented the plans to materialize.

In Croatia there was still civil war between the powerful families, and finally the Hungarian King decided to intervene. Stjepan II took the opportunity to make his own move as well, securing more land for Bosnia.

He then made his peace with the Pope, convincing him of his Catholicism and allowing Catholic missionaries to operate in Bosnia, a move which eventually practically eradicated the Krstjani faith through peaceful conversion rather than violent persecution.

Stjepan II then made a bigger move. The Hungarian King had died and was being replaced by his son Louis I. Stjepan II saw the change of power as an opportunity break his vassalage to Hungary, but the support he sought from Venice and Serbia failed to materialize, so instead he got involved in the widening conflict between Hungary and Venice over the cities on the Adriatic Coast, not least the city of Zara.

Zara had a history of changing allegiance and Stjepan II did the same thing, although by means of stealth and bribery. Officially he was supporting Hungary against Venice, but he first took bribes from Venice in order to withdraw from an early attack on Venetian fortifications and he subsequently took more bribes to reveal the positions of the Hungarian army before the defining battle in 1346. The Hungarian King won the battle but lost most of his army and also his trust in Stjepan II.

And there were unsettled matters between Serbia and Bosnia. Stjepan II's previous incursions into Serbia had not been forgotten and the Serbian King Stefan Uroš IV Dušan had repeatedly demanded the lost territories back. The Venetians brokered a truce, allowing Stefan Uroš IV Dušan to concentrate on his campaign against Byzantium, but Stjepan II – knowing full well that he was the weaker military power of the two - took the opportunity to make a pre-emptive strike into Serbia.

That was enough for Stefan Uroš IV Dušan who decide to invade. In 1350 the superior Serbian forces wiped away all Bosnian resistance in the lower lying areas, but the Bosnians withdrew to the mountains, fighting guerrilla warfare. But the Serbians also knew how to use bribes and gradually fought their way through Bosnia, partly by military might and partly by buying the loyalty of the Bosnian generals.

Stjepan II withdrew further and further into the mountains of central Bosnia, but felt strong enough to refuse a peace-proposal brokered by Venice and Ragusa. Eventually Stjepan II's stubbornness paid off. Stefan Uroš IV Dušan had to leave for Macedonia, leaving a small occupying force and Stjepan II quickly clawed back control of the country without territorial losses. It was a strange conflict in which Stjepan II lost all the battles but won the war.

Stjepan II's daughter Elizabeth was sent to Hungary to marry the - widowed - King of Hungary, but Stjepan II himself was too sick to participate at the wedding, and he died in 1353.

His place was filled by his nephew, Stjepan Tvrtko (I), but as he was only fifteen years old his father, Stjepan II's brother Vladislav Kotromanić, initially ruled in his name. But Vladislav Kotromanić died the year after and Stjepan Tvrtko I's mother Jelena - from the powerful Croatian Šubić family - took over.

That, however, was not popular, both because she was a woman and possibly also because of her family connections to Croatia. Some of the nobles revolted, first amongst them Pavel Kulišić, but Stjepan Tvrtko I took his army to the rebels and suppressed the uprising, showing that he was now of age and in control.

But in reality his control was limited and waning as the strong King Louis I of Hungary consistently increased Hungarian governance over Bosnia, twice in 1363 attempting to actually occupy the country.

But Stjepan Tvrtko I repelled the invaders and as a result started calling himself Ban of All Bosnia *by the mercy of God* instead of *by the mercy of the Hungarian King*.

The reality of the situation was, however, that the wars with Hungary had undermined Stjepan Tvrtko I's royal authority and many of the Bosnian barons operated in open disobedience. The conflict escalated and finally, in 1366, the barons ousted Stjepan Tvrtko I and instead installed his brother Stjepan Vuk.

Stjepan Tvrtko I fled to Hungary, was forgiven for his sins and soon led a Hungarian army into Bosnia where, by 1367, he was back in control. As a matter of courtesy, he reinserted the Hungarian King's name in his title, for the time being.

Over the next few years Stjepan Tvrtko I concentrated on getting his country back under control, suppressing the local barons by a mixture of diplomacy, bribery, and violence.

His brother, Stjepan Vuk, had initially fled to Ragusa, but had later approached the Pope, again telling tales of the Krstjani heresy, which was a dwindling issue, but the Pope decided to promote Stjepan Vuk with a mandate as ban and to raise an army to eliminate the Krstjani once and for all.

Stjepan Vuk got help in Hungary as well, partly because Stjepan Tvrtko I had once again replaced the Hungarian King for God in his title, but the crusade soon fizzled out and ultimately Stjepan Vuk gave up his mission.

An area boxed in between Hungary, Bosnia, Serbia and Zeta (Montenegro) had for a long time been controlled by a rebellious 'prince' called Nikola Altomanović.

Stjepan Tvrtko I had long coveted his lands, and in 1371 he formed an alliance to attack, but the plans were stopped by the Battle of Maritsa where the Serbian nobility - including the heir apparent - was wiped out by the Ottomans. This defeat, followed by the death of Stefan Uroš IV Dušan of

Serbia, led to the end of the Serbian Empire and the area became a free for all.

Stjepan Tvrtko I now allied himself with Lazar Hrebeljanović of Moravian Serbia and they returned to attack Nikola Altomanović, capturing and blinding him after which Stjepan Tvrtko I and Lazar Hrebeljanović split his territories between them.

Stjepan Tvrtko I followed up the success with annexation of western Zeta and with the world's eye focusing on the emerging Ottoman problem, he had himself crowned as king - 'by the grace of Lord God' - in 1377. With Serbia split up into pieces, he also included Serbia in his title, but the real power of Serbia remained with Lazar Hrebeljanović.

The next decade was spent both consolidating Bosnia's new territories and expanding the new kingdom further, utilizing the power vacuum following the death of King Louis I, a vacuum in which Stjepan Tvrtko I acted as protector of Louis I's widow and her daughters. With Hungary weak, Stjepan Tvrtko I annexed areas in Croatia, expanding the Bosnian kingdom to its largest ever.

But the Ottoman soon started to become a problem. Their victory in 1371 at Maritsa had created a range of small 'Serbian' vassal states, but over time they were annexed into the Ottoman Empire proper and the Ottomans became the new neighbours.

Ottoman raids became common and in 1388 Stjepan Tvrtko I ordered his general, Vlatko Vuković, to go and meet a large Ottoman expeditionary force, led by Lala Şâhin Paşa. The two forces met at Bileća and a Bosnian victory secured that the Ottomans were stopped for the time being.

Happy about the outcome of the Battle of Bileća, Stjepan Tvrtko I sent significant support to his ally Lazar Hrebeljanović of Serbia when he took on the Ottomans at Kosovo. The outcome was an Ottoman victory, but with both Lazar Hrebeljanović and Sultan Murad I killed and even the victorious Ottoman army severely reduced, the battle did slow the Ottomans down and was thus a victory for Stjepan Tvrtko I. That, at least, was how he saw it.

The last few years of Stjepan Tvrtko I's life was spent skirmishing with Hungary over border areas on the Danube, River and Stjepan Tvrtko I died in 1391 as the first King of Bosnia.

Replacing him was Stjepan Dabiša, a relative - possibly an illegitimate half-brother - of Stjepan Tvrtko I.

During his reign the Bosnian nobles soon rebelled, mostly supported by Hungary. Initially he managed to quell rebellion on the Dalmatian coast - the area in most dispute - but eventually the nobles, assisted by the King of Naples, rose in open revolt and Stjepan Dabiša had to call on Hungarian support. King Sigismund came to his aid, but Stjepan Dabiša had to once again recognize Hungary as nominal overlord of Bosnia.

Stjepan Dabiša died from disease in 1395. He had recognized King Sigismund as his heir, based on claims held by Sigismund's wife, Mary, but with the excuse that Mary had - recently - died and that Sigismund's claim was thus nullified, the Bosnian nobles instead appointed Stjepan Dabiša's widow, Jelena Gruba, as queen.

The real reason for the Bosnian nobility's choice was that they had no appetite for King Sigismund's authority. Instead, they elected a queen with little authority and the Bosnian nobles started to rule their own areas with little but pro-forma central authority.

The queen was, however, soon replaced with her stepson, Stjepan Tvrtko I's son from his first marriage, Stjepan Ostoja. He in turn became involved in a war against Ragusa, which was a vassal to Hungary, and he was ousted by the Bosnian nobles in 1404, after which he fled to Hungary.

In his place the nobles elected his brother Stjepan Tvrtko II, but the Hungarian King saw his election as yet another attempt by the Bosnian nobles to negate on his suzerainty, so in 1409 King Sigismund sent troops to Bosnia, defeated the nobles and Stjepan Tvrtko II and reinserted Stjepan Ostoja, this time as declared Hungarian vassal.

Stjepan Ostoja did his best to maintain good relations with Hungary, but he died in 1418 and the throne went back to Stjepan Tvrtko II.

Now followed a period of relative peace, but in 1432 the Ottomans, reorganized after their interregnum, started to show an interest in Bosnia again.

This time they came by diplomacy, sponsoring Radivoj, a son of Stjepan Ostoja, who with support from some - but far from all - of the nobles declared himself King of Bosnia.

Radivoj however never gained any real support inside the country, although he was predictably recognized by the Ottomans, and in 1435 he had to give up his claim and flee the country.

Stjepan Tvrtko II died in 1443 without leaving an heir. Instead, his - exactly how is unknown - relative Stjepan Tomaš took the throne.

Stjepan Tomaš soon divorced his wife - considered unsuitable as queen because of her common origins - and instead married the daughter of the most powerful noble in the Herzegovina region, linking Bosnia and Herzegovina in a stronger alliance and ending decades of internal unrest.

Bosnia now lived several decades in relative obscurity whilst the bigger battles between Christianity and the Ottomans took place further away in places like, Varna (1444), Kosovo (1448) and Belgrade (1456), but towards the end of the 1450s they could not hide any more, even if they had long since accepted to pay tribute to the Ottomans in order to be left alone..

Mehmed II's aggressive plan to remove the buffer states and put a stranglehold on Hungary first hit Serbia, and when its long time despot Đurađ Branković died in 1457 and his successors spent their time on internal bickering, Stjepan Tomaš invaded to restore control. His effort was however stopped by Ottoman diplomacy and the agreement that his son and heir,

Stjepan Tomašević should marry the daughter of Stefan Branković, Serbia's latest despot.

The Ottoman diplomacy did not last long however and instead they returned with force in 1458 but turned around without conquering the capital city of Smederevo.

The nobles now came to an agreement, in which Stjepan Tomašević was made despot of Serbia, ruling under suzerainty of the Hungarian King, who took the opportunity to show his presence in both Bosnia and Serbia to make sure that there was no misunderstanding in regards to his authority.

But his suzerainty was in name only. When the Ottomans came back in 1459 and rolled over Serbia once and for all, the Hungarians did not lift a finger, but rather blamed Stjepan Tomaš and Stjepan Tomašević for the fall of Serbia, although it is unclear exactly how they should have defended it against the might of Mehmed II.

Soon after, in 1461, Stjepan Tomaš died and Stjepan Tomašević became King of Bosnia. He had already had the ungrateful honour of being the last despot of Serbia; he would now become the last King of Bosnia.

Stjepan Tomašević had no illusions in regard Mehmed II's intentions, but he needed assistance and King Matthias I of Hungary blamed him for the loss of Serbia and was preoccupied by consolidating his own fragile authority at home.

Instead Stjepan Tomašević turned to the Pope. His letter is best presented by itself (as per translation by Babinger):

'If Mehmed only demanded my kingdom and would go no further, it would be possible to leave my kingdom to its fate and there would be no need for you to disturb the rest of Christendom in my defense. But his insatiable lust for power knows no bounds. After me he will attack Hungary and the Venetian province of Dalmatia. By way of Krain and Istria he will go to Italy, which he wishes to subjugate. He often speaks of Rome and longs to go there. If he conquers my kingdom thanks to the indifference of the Christians, he will find here the right country to fulfill his desires. I shall be the first victim. But after me the Hungarians and the Venetians and other peoples will suffer the same fate. That is what our enemy is thinking, I am informing you of what I have learned lest it be said one day that you were not informed and I can be accused of negligence.'

The Pope listened and urged King Matthias I to patch up his relationship with Stjepan Tomašević, which he did, but only after taking money from him as well as cessation of several Bosnian castles on the border.

But real military help was not forthcoming, not from the Pope, not from Hungary and not from Venice, to whom Stjepan Tomašević had also sent pleas for help.

What came instead was an Ottoman embassy.

The ambassador carried a demand from Mehmed II for the annual tribute, agreed a long time ago and paid also by Stjepan Tomašević's father.

Stjepan Tomašević was well aware of the situation in which he found himself. Many Bosnians noble and peasants alike, had long since decided on the Ottomans, who were promising religious freedom, an issue still important in Bosnia. He was alone militarily and no sum of money would change Mehmed II's plans.

Consequently he took the Ottoman ambassador with him into his strong-room, showed him the money set aside for the Ottoman tribute, but informed him that he had no intentions of paying it and that if Mehmed II decided to attack him as a consequence then at least he had that money to ensure a comfortable life in exile.

The answer no doubt irritated Mehmed II, but he had immediate business to look after in Greece and Wallachia whose voivode, Vlad III Dracula, had led a daring attack into Bulgaria, so it was only in 1463 that time allowed Mehmed II the opportunity to deal with the Bosnian issue.

Stjepan Tomašević had eventually reconsidered, sent the disputed tribute and sought the Sultan's forgiveness, which presumably he granted, but under a cloak of secrecy the Ottomans started a campaign going west and soon swung via Skopje into Bosnia.

The Bosnian underbelly was a soft target. The local nobles were ill-prepared for resistance and many had, as previously mentioned, long since decided that the Ottomans may well provide more freedom than was offered by the country's own Catholic rulers.

Mehmed II thus met little resistance until he stood before the country's strongest castle at Bobovac.

The castle was commanded by the same Radivoj who nearly three decades earlier had tried to make himself King of Bosnia and who had fled to the Ottomans only to once again return to Bosnia.

The Ottomans settled in for a siege, casting cannon on the spot, but Radivoj was as shifty as before so after only three days of siege he accepted an offer of a reward and gave up the fortress.

His reward turned out to be a beheading, as Mehmed II was well aware that he was totally untrustworthy. The population of Bobovac was - as had become Mehmed II's custom - split into three groups. One group was allowed to stay; one group was given to his generals and troops as slaves and the last group was sent to Istanbul to repopulate the city.

The loss of Bobovac was a major blow to Stjepan Tomašević who had expected it to hold out and delay the Ottomans long enough to gather his troops around the capital city of Jajce, potentially even receive some assistance from Hungary or Venice.

Instead Mehmed II now came with full speed towards Jajce and Stjepan Tomašević packed himself and his family and fled towards Croatia.

The Ottoman vanguard, with very specific instructions to apprehend the King, followed hot on his tail and caught up with him holed up in the fortress of Ključ. A short siege followed, but Stjepan Tomašević eventually gave himself up after the commander of the Ottoman vanguard, Grand Vizier Mahmud Pasha, had issued him with a written promise that he would be spared.

The citizens of Jajce, abandoned by their king, had in the meantime surrendered to the Sultan without a fight and Stjepan Tomašević was now used to convince and command the remaining Bosnian fortresses to stand down and allow Ottoman garrisons to establish themselves.

Once he had served his purpose, Stjepan Tomašević was executed. His document had been deemed null and void by Mehmed II's spiritual advisor, Mullah Ali, and either Mehmed II or Mullah Ali is believed to have beheaded Stjepan Tomašević in person.

With the King dead Mehmed II split his army into three parts. Two parts went off to the country's eastern and westernmost parts to ensure that all resistance had been mopped up, while Mehmed II himself took the last part south into Herzegovina.

But the campaign into Herzegovina - presumably to be followed all the way through to Ragusa - was not successful. The mountainous terrain favoured the defenders who, like their counterparts in Albania, defended every pass fiercely while setting up ambushes and attacking the Ottoman supply chain.

The Ottoman army was horse born, and they could not fight their way through the mountains against a determined enemy, so they turned around and left the province alone, to the relief also of the Ragusans.

Mehmed II now went back home, leaving garrisons in the Bosnian fortresses, but doing little to defend the open countryside. Bosnia had fallen, its king had been executed, and a new king had not been appointed. His victory in Bosnia was, however, not left intact. As soon as he had left the theatre King Matthias I moved in, starting the pattern of 'near battle' which he would maintain for decades to come.

The Hungarians laid siege to Jajce where the citizens surrendered to the Hungarians, but the Ottoman garrison held out for three months until they were starved to surrender.

This in turn led to Mehmed II returning in 1464, creating the bizarre scenario described earlier in connection with Hungary and in which both the Ottomans and the Hungarians fled the field without battle on the rumour of each other's approach.

The status quo had now been set. The Hungarians remained in control of Jajce and were thus provided with some protection against Ottoman incursions into Croatia, but the rest of Bosnia was annexed into the Ottoman Empire. The Conqueror had conquered yet another country and had tightened the noose around Hungary's neck.

The province of Herzegovina remained independent until 1482 where it too was annexed. The remaining parts of Bosnia were annexed after Sultan Suleiman I, Mehmed II's great-grandson, overran Hungary in the sixteenth century.

Bosnia and Herzegovina stayed under Ottoman rule until 1878 where it became part of the Austro-Hungarian Empire. After WWI it became part of the Kingdom of Yugoslavia which became the Socialist Federative Republic of Yugoslavia after WWII.

After a bloody civil war, Bosnia and Herzegovina obtained its independence again in 1995, more than 500 years after it was annexed by Mehmed II the Conqueror.

In 1888 a medieval grave known locally as 'the Tomb of the King' was opened and the bones of a beheaded skeleton were disinterred. They are believed - but never proven - to be the remains of Stjepan Tomašević, the last king of Bosnia, and they reside to this day in a glass coffin in the Franciscan church in Jajce.

WALLACHIA

CRITICAL TIMELINE

Year	Event	Involved Parties
1270s	Autonomous barons refuse to pay tribute to Hungary	Wallachia Hungary
1300	Besarab I settles in Campulung as Hungarian vassal	Wallachia Hungary
1325	Wallachia stops payment of vassalage to Hungary	Wallachia Hungary
1330	Battle of Posada. Wallachia becomes independent	Wallachia Hungary
1343	Hungarian invasion	Wallachia Hungary
1345	Hungarian invasion	Wallachia Hungary
1354	Hungarian invasion	Wallachia Hungary
1364	Wallachia becomes Bulgarian vassal, then moves back to Hungary. Amlaş and Făgăraş confirmed as being part of Wallachia.	Wallachia Bulgaria Hungary
1386	Mircea cel Batran becomes Voivode of Wallachia	Wallachia
1388	Wallachia annexation of Dobrogea	Wallachia Bulgaria Ottomans
1393	Ottoman occupation of southern Dobrogea	Wallachia Ottomans
1394	Battle of Rovie. Ottoman invasion	Wallachia Ottomans Serbia
1396	Battle of Nicopolis	Wallachia Hungary Ottomans
1397	Mircea cel Batran back in Wallachia	Wallachia Ottomans
1399	Ottoman annexation of Dobrogea	Wallachia Ottomans
1404	Wallachia retake Dobrogea	Wallachia Ottomans
1415	Wallachia starts paying tribute to Ottomans	Wallachia Ottomans
1420	Ottoman annexation of Dobrogea	Wallachia Ottomans
1431	Vlad II Dracul becomes member of the Order of the Dragon	Wallachia Hungary
1436	Vlad II Dracul becomes Voivode of Wallachia	Wallachia Hungary
1438	Wallachia supports Ottomans during raids in Transylvania	Wallachia Ottomans Hungary

14 - The Buffer States - Wallachia

Year	Event	Involved Parties
1442	Hungary invades Wallachia	Wallachia / Hungary
1443	Ottomans reinstate Vlad II Dracul	Wallachia / Ottomans
1444	Vlad II Dracul imprisons Janos Hunyadi on his return from Battle of Varna	Wallachia / Hungary
1447	Hungarian invasion kills Vlad II Dracul	Wallachia / Hungary
1448	Second Battle of Kosovo. Ottomans install Vlad III Dracula temporarily as voivode	Wallachia / Ottomans
1456	Vlad III Dracula return as Voivode of Wallachia in wake of Siege of Belgrade	Wallachia / Hungary
1461	Vlad III Dracula attacks Ottoman Bulgaria	Wallachia / Ottomans
1462	Ottoman invasion removes Vlad III Dracula	Wallachia / Ottomans
1470	Moldavian invasion	Wallachia / Ottomans / Moldavia
1473	Moldavian invasion	Wallachia / Ottomans / Moldavia
1475	Moldavian invasion	Wallachia / Ottomans / Moldavia
1475	Wallachians assist Ottomans in Moldavia	Wallachia / Ottomans / Moldavia
1476	Wallachians assist Ottomans in Moldavia. Vlad III Dracula returns for short reign	Wallachia / Ottomans / Moldavia
1477	Moldavian invasion	Wallachia / Ottomans / Moldavia
1479	Wallachia again becomes Ottoman vassal	Wallachia / Ottomans
1481	Moldavian invasion	Wallachia / Ottomans / Moldavia

Part 5 - The Balkans

14 - The Buffer States - Wallachia

Moving north across the Danube, river the next buffer-state we meet is Wallachia - modern day southern Romania - located between the Carpathian Mountains in the north and the Danube river in the south.

On the north side of the Carpathians was - Hungarian - Transylvania and south of the Danube River was - Ottoman - Serbia and Bulgaria.

The area was part of the Roman province of Dacia and for centuries after the fall of Rome still under Roman (Byzantine) influence.

People came and people went. Goths, Slavs, Avars, Gepids, Pechenegs and Cumans amongst them, but there was no formation of a nation state. Rather, the area fell under the influence of the First Bulgarian Empire in the seventh century and then under the influence of the Hungarian Empire from the eleventh century forward.

In the thirteenth century the Mongols came and went, after which the area, became strategically important.

It was in the interest of Hungary to create a buffer zone, or an extended defensive perimeter, and sometime around 1300 a minor noble already controlling the small principalities of Făgăraș and Amlaș in southern Transylvania crossed the Carpathians and settled himself as voivode - or prince - of Wallachia with his capital in Campulung.

His name was - according to folklore - Radu Negru, but the most likely historic candidate is Basarab I, although there had been rebellious barons in the area since the 1270s, refusing to pay tribute to - the much weakened - Hungarians.

Basarab I set up in Campulung as a Hungarian vassal, and he initially occupied himself with securing his authority, but once he was established he (probably around 1325) negated on his vassalage to Hungary, declaring Wallachia independent and even annexing royal land.

King Charles I of Hungary was well unpleased and in 1330 he led an army into Wallachia to bring things back under control. But the Wallachians first avoided battle with the superior Hungarian army and then ambushed it at Posada. The Hungarian King narrowly escaped and was forced to accept the Wallachians' independence - for now.

As much as Wallachia was henceforth in principle free and independent; in reality it was never really either. Its position as a buffer zone, between powerful empires simply meant that its neighbours never gave up trying to assert their influence.

Basarab I continued to assert his authority in the region, reaching from the Black Sea in the east to Vidin in the west, but the area was controlled by individual landowners (boyars) with a high level of autonomy and central authority was weak.

Basarab I allied himself - through marriage - with the Bulgarians and assisted them in their ongoing conflicts with the Byzantines, but in 1343 and again in 1345, the new warlike King of Hungary, Louis I, once again campaigned in the area and reasserted Hungarian suzerainty.

The population of Wallachia was, as was the case in Transylvania and Moldavia, mainly 'Romanian'. The Romanians were the indigenous population of the region and stood apart from the Hungarians by means of their own Romanian language - a Latin-based language dating back to the Roman occupation - and the fact that they were Orthodox rather than Catholic. Indeed, many Romanians had for centuries drifted across the mountains from Transylvania to avoid the oppression of their Hungarian overlords who treated the Romanians as, mainly, landless peasant labourers with no rights.

Something else the Romanian population had brought with them was their own traditional succession rules. Where the Hungarians, in principle at least, subscribed to 'western' primogeniture, the right of the first born male to succeed his father, and the Slavs subscribed to a model in which lands were inherited by being split up between the surviving sons, the Romanians subscribed to a model in which a ruler was elected by the boyars - the landowners - and all males of the royal bloodline were eligible for election, the royal bloodline being defined purely from the father without regard to the mother's legitimate status.

Over time, time created a multitude of eligible candidates for the throne of Wallachia and an environment in which the loyalty of the boyars could be bought and sold.

Across the Carpathians, in southern Transylvania, there were several 'Saxon' cities - first amongst them Brasov and Sibiu, run as semi-autonomous city-states populated by Saxon settlers. The Saxons were master craftsman and produced manufactured goods which stood in high value in, mainly agricultural, Wallachia.

As an independent state the ruler - and the ruling class of boyars, could collect taxes and customs revenues from the Saxon traders, but with Hungarian suzerainty the Saxon traders were allowed to trade in Wallachia free of taxes and custom.

The question of being independent or being Hungarian vassals was thus not just a political - or religious - question but also had some very practical financial consequences. As we shall see, this created further complications when it came to determining the loyalty of the Wallachian rulers.

Basarab I had cleverly circumvented any potential issues of succession by making his oldest son, Nicolae Alexandru, co-ruler so when he died in 1352 the succession went smoothly.

Nicolae Alexandru initially abandoned the suzerainty of Hungary and he founded the first Wallachian Metropolitan seat, Wallachia's own Orthodox bishopry.

But King Louis I asserted his rights again in 1354 and Nicolae Alexandru had to accept both the Saxon trader's right to trade tax-free and the establishment of Catholic missions in Wallachia. Despite these enforced ties to Hungary, Nicolae Alexandru further strengthened Wallachia's ties to Bulgaria by marrying his daughter, Anna, to the Tsar of Bulgaria; Ivan Sratsimir.

On Nicolae Alexandru's death in 1364 his son, Vladislav I, took over and he immediately allied himself with Bulgaria, making Wallachia a Bulgarian vassal. The Hungarians were not happy, so they once again tried to assert their suzerainty, leading to an agreement in which Wallachia once again became a Hungarian vassal, but the traditional principalities of Amlaș and Făgăraș - located in Transylvania, and the region of Severin were confirmed as being part of Wallachia.

Vladislav I died in 1377 and the throne went to his brother, Radu I, who continued the ongoing battle with the Hungarians for dominance.

The Hungarians tried to enlist the support of the Saxons in Brasov by promising them tax-free trade in Wallachia and Radu I tried to endear his subjects by building several churches and monasteries.

Radu I's rule was short, he died in 1383, and the throne went to his son Dan I. He also ruled for only a few years as he got involved in the civil war in Bulgaria between Ivan Šišman and Ivan Sratsimir and was killed in battle against Ivan Šišman in 1386.

Dan I was followed by his brother Mircea I, later given the moniker 'cel batran' (the Elder) as he would rule Wallachia for nearly three decades, a period which would see Wallachia expand to its most powerful position both geographically and politically.

Mircea did not rule as a Hungarian vassal, but he made sure that he entertained a close relationship with the Hungarian King Sigismund I, himself a long-time ruler. Their interests were similar, namely, to resist the newcomers in the area, the Ottomans.

Around the time Mircea I ascended the throne of Wallachia, the Bulgarian Tsar, Ivan Sratsimir, submitted to Ottoman suzerainty, effectively making the Danube River the borderline between Christian and Ottoman interests, but on the far eastern side of Wallachia, was the area of Dobrogea, nested between the Danube and he Black Sea and providing critical access to the sea.

Dobrogea had formed a semi-autonomous existence, first dominated by the Tatars, the successors of the Mongol Golden Horde, and then forming part of Bulgaria. Long a sought-after prize, Mircea I took the opportunity of the weakened Bulgarians to annex the area in 1388, fighting off the Ottoman vanguard.

Mircea had no illusions as to the aggression of the Ottomans though, so he enforced a strong central authority on the boyars of Wallachia and created a 'great army' of peasants to supplement the troops which could be assembled by the boyars.

With the Danube River as the natural border, Mircea I renovated and reinforced the fortresses on the Danube and he entered into trade agreements with both the Saxon merchants in Brasov and the merchants of Poland and Lithuania, securing a sound economic base for the country.

Mircea I's assumptions regarding the Ottomans proved to be correct. Sultan Bayezid I was not happy about the Wallachian annexation of Dobrogea and in 1393 he occupied the southern parts.

Bayezid I's next move was against Wallachia itself, which he entered with an Ottoman army in 1394. Despite his 'grand army', Mircea I had no illusion when it came to his capability to defend against the Ottoman army at full strength, so he fell back, avoided an open battle and instead conducted guerrilla warfare, striking at smaller units of the Ottoman army and attacking their supply lines.

Finally, Mircea I chose a forested and swampy terrain near the Arges River as his choice of battleground, the terrain preventing the Ottomans from utilizing their numerical superiority to the full.

The Battle of Rovine - as it would later be labelled, was a scrappy affair. The professional army of Bayezid I, reinforced by Serbian troops under Stefan Lazarević, was decimated by Wallachian archers protected by the difficult terrain, but even though the battle has become an important heroic milestone in Romanian folklore, it was eventually the Ottomans who prevailed, albeit with heavy casualties.

Mircea I had to flee to Hungary and the Ottomans installed Vlad I - called 'Uzurpatorul' (the Usurper) on the throne as their puppet before they withdrew. Vlad I's exact origins are disputed, but it is assumed that he was probably a half-brother of Mircea I.

From his exile, Mircea I participated in the ill-fated crusade which culminated in the Battle of Nicopolis in 1396, where the combined Hungarian and French army was soundly defeated by Bayezid I, but Mircea I survived to lead a Hungarian-backed army into Wallachia the year after, retaking the throne from Vlad I.

The Ottomans sent expeditionary forces into Wallachia twice in the following three years, but they were defeated by Mircea I on both occasions although they did take the remaining parts of Dobrogea, cutting Wallachia off from the Balck Sea coast and establishing the Danube River as the de-facto border.

Bayezid I's defeat to Timur in 1402 created new opportunities and Mircea I retook Dobrogea in 1404, after which he shortly involved himself in the civil war during the Ottoman interregnum, supporting Musa when he crossed the Black Sea to attack his brother, Suleyman, from the rear.

The Ottomans came back though - once consolidated under Mehmed I - and finally Mircea I pragmatically agreed to pay them an annual tribute of 3,000 gold pieces on the condition that they stayed out of Wallachia.

When Mircea I died in 1418, he had both expanded and consolidated Wallachia, forming a strong and independent nation state, now solidly planted between the ambitious empires of Hungary and the Ottomans. With Mircea I died also Wallachia's golden age.

Mircea I had long before secured succession by making his oldest son, Mihai I, his co-ruler, so the succession was eventless, but Mihai I faced trouble from the outset.

Sultan Mehmed I was eager to consolidate the former borders of the Ottoman Empire and immediately following Mircea I's death he came for Dobrogea. Mihai I went out to meet him, and following several battles he died protecting his lands in 1420, leaving Dobrogea in Ottoman hands for good.

A fight for control in Wallachia now followed which, as good as anything, highlights the precarious situation of a buffer-state stuck between competing empires.

The Hungarians, who worried about potential Ottoman dominance on their southern border, moved quickly to install Dan II as voivode.

Dan II was a son of Dan I and thus of the 'House of Dăneşti' one of the two competing royal lines which were developing in Wallachia. He was a capable warrior and statesman, but his rule was to be marred by Ottoman ambitions.

Sultan Murad II, who took the Ottoman throne in 1421, had his own interests in the control of Wallachia, which provided access to Transylvania, the soft underbelly of Hungary, so he appointed as his champion, and puppet, Radu II - called 'the Simple Minded', a son of Mircea I and a representative of what would later be called the House of Drăculeşti.

Wallachia, which had in the latter decades of Mircea I's rule known peace and prosperity, was now thrown into a state of chaos and upheaval that would last for decades.

Supported by the Ottomans, Radu II invaded and took the throne in 1421. Dan II, with Hungarian support, took the throne back later that same year. Two years later Radu II went back, but Dan II took the throne again in the same year. The following year Radu II took the throne for a two-year period, but Dan II went back in 1426. Radu II attacked again in 1427 and then, finally, that same year Dan II retaliated and Radu II was killed in the battle.

After repelling a further Ottoman attempt at invasion in 1428, Dan II made peace with the Ottomans, but in 1432 they were back, this time supporting another of Mircea I' sons, Alexandru I Aldea who, after Dan II had been killed, managed to hold on to the throne as an Ottoman vassal for nearly five years before he died from natural causes, a treat which was quickly becoming rare for a ruler of Wallachia.

Many years before, probably sometime in the 1390s, Mircea I had sent another of his son, Vlad, off to the Hungarian court of King Sigismund I. Here Vlad was brought up in the style of a western prince, receiving training in both warfare and diplomacy, something which was abundant in the lively court of King Sigismund I.

Vlad is known to have acted as ambassador for the Hungarian court in both Poland and Constantinople and it is likely, although not documented, that he would have fought in one or more of Sigismund I's armed conflicts.

One way or another Vlad distinguished himself in the eyes King Sigismund I, as he was selected for investiture into the prestigious Order of the Dragon in 1431, an occasion which prompted Vlad to take the surname 'Dracul' which, at the time, meant 'the Dragon' in Romanian.

At the same time King Sigismund I appointed Vlad Dracul governor of Transylvania, in which capacity he moved to Sighisoara in southern Transylvania. Here he was biding his time.

When his (half) brother Alexandru I Aldea died in 1436, King Sigismund I asked Vlad Dracul to, with all possible haste, gather an expeditionary force and move on Wallachia, where he reached the - by then, capital of Târgoviște without a fight. The Wallachian boyars were not of a mind to resist the Hungarian King's wishes, so they elected Vlad (II) Dracul as voivode.

But Vlad II Dracul's powerbase quickly disappeared when King Sigismund I died in December 1437 and he did what he could under the circumstances.

First, he appointed his oldest son, Mircea II Dracula, as co-ruler to secure the succession, the surname 'Dracula' meaning 'son of the Dragon'.

Next, he approached Sultan Murad II, promising to continue to pay the tribute agreed with Mircea I, but the Sultan had little faith in the - Hungarian raised - Voivode. To test his loyalty, the Sultan commanded that the Voivode participate in an Ottoman raid into Transylvania in 1438, a matter in which Vlad II Dracul had little choice.

Vlad II Dracul then ruled in peace for a few years, but his alliance with the Ottomans did not please Janos Hunyadi, the new strong man of Hungary, and in 1442 he invaded Wallachia.

Vlad II Dracul fled to the Ottomans, leaving his son Mircea II Dracula in charge, but Janos Hunyadi forced the issue and Mircea II Dracula also had to flee, leaving Basarab II, a son of Dan II, as voivode.

At the Ottoman court Vlad II Dracul now stuck a new deal with the Sultan. Over and above the annual tribute, he agreed to also supply 500 boys for Devşirme, training as Ottoman Janissaries or civil servants, and with that agreement in place the Sultan equipped Vlad II Dracul with an expeditionary force with which he went back to Wallachia and retook his throne in 1443.

But the Sultan did not necessarily - and with some cause, trust the shifty Voivode, so he forced him to leave behind as hostages his two sons Vlad and Radu.

Vlad II Dracul continued to show his shiftiness, or clever statesmanship, in the following years. When the Christian armies marched on Varna in 1444 he met them and tried to persuade them to turn around, but when he could not convince them, and they demanded his participation in the ill-fated campaign, he left Mircea II Dracula with a contingent of Wallachians, thus both participating and not participating.

When Janos Hunyadi returned from the lost battle of Varna, Vlad II Dracul took him prisoner and they are known to have entered into heated debates about the campaign and its ramifications before the Voivode let Janos Hunyadi continue on his way.

The Hungarian was however far from satisfied by the Wallachian Voivode's position and when he had regained his power, he led a fresh Hungarian army into Wallachia in 1447. The Wallachian boyars supported the Hungarian intervention and killed Mircea II Dracula, presumably first blinding him and then burying him alive. Vlad II Dracul fled towards the Ottomans, but he was caught and killed, presumably beheaded, somewhere in the vicinity of Bucharest.

Janos Hunyadi now placed himself as regent, until he found a suitable candidate of the blood, this time Vladislav II, another son of Dan II, who forthwith ruled as Janos Hunyadi's personal puppet.

Vladislav II went with Janos Hunyadi to the (Second) Battle of Kosovo in 1448 and was with him when they were both intercepted and held for ransom by Đurađ Branković, the Despot of Serbia, on their way back from the lost battle.

Their fate unknown, for a time presumed killed in the battle, left a vacuum in Wallachia that the Ottomans were quick to fill.

On the death of their father the previous year, Vlad II Dracul's two sons, Vlad and Radu Dracula, who had been left as hostages with the Sultan, were now free. They both, however, chose to stay, but for very different reasons.

Radu Dracula had become a favorite of the heir apparent, Mehmed, the Conqueror to be. Mehmed is well known to have been, if not outright homosexual then, distinctly bi-sexual and Ottoman chronicles specifically mention that Radu, who would later be known as "Cel Frumos" (the Beautiful) for his good looks, caught young Mehmed's eye and, after initial resistance, showed himself amendable to Mehmed's advances.

Vlad Dracula, on the other hand, had no such reason to stay, but with his father and brother having been killed by Janos Hunyadi and a new voivode of the competing House of Dăneşti residing in Târgovişte, his prospect of surviving long in Wallachia were severely limited.

But with both Janos Hunyadi and Vladislav II missing in action, Vlad Dracula suddenly became a valuable pawn.

Sultan Murad II quickly sent an expeditionary force into Wallachia and in the summer of 1448 they installed seventeen year old Vlad III Dracula on the throne.

Vlad III Dracula's first rule was shaky from the outset. Presumably, he had as much right as any other prince of the blood to take the vacant throne, but was it really vacant?

The Saxons in Brasov did not think so. In an exchange of letters with Vlad III Dracula, holed up in Târgovişte with his Ottoman troops, they point out that until the fate of Janos Hunyadi was known, he, Vlad III Dracula, should come to them and wait. It is worth noting that in their letter they completely ignore the fate of Vladislav II, clearly regarding Janos Hunyadi as the de-facto power behind Wallachia at the time.

Vlad III Dracula decided to stay put, telling the Saxons in Brasov that if Janos Hunyadi should emerge then `we will meet him and we will make peace with him`, but when Janos Hunyadi and Voivode Vladislav II did re-emerge in December of that same year, Vlad III Dracula did the smart thing, he ran back to the Ottomans.

Vladislav II was back on the throne, but Janos Hunyadi's power was once again waning. He abdicated as regent of Hungary and disappeared into relative obscurity for a few years.

Without his protector and with Hungary's minor King being held for ransom in Austria, Vladislav II now took a pragmatic stance and approached the Ottomans. The tribute was paid once again and a trade agreement made between Janos Hunyadi and the Saxons in Brasov was cancelled.

In response Janos Hunyadi occupied the principalities of Făgăraş and Amlaş, located inside Transylvania, but the region was relatively quiet as the Ottomans were busy elsewhere.

Sultan Murad II had died in 1451 and his son, Mehmed II, was on the loose. Two years later he was master of Constantinople. Three years further on, in 1456, he was in front of Belgrade.

Mehmed II's defeat at Belgrade created a short power vacuum and Janos Hunyadi, in one of his last acts before he died of plague in Belgrade was to once again unleash Vlad III Dracula in Wallachia.

Since Vlad III Dracula had fled from the returning Janos Hunyadi in 1448, he had lived a life in exile, partly in Moldavia, and his cousin Stefan - later to be Stefan III of Moldavia - had brokered peace between Vlad III Dracula and Janos Hunyadi.

Vlad III Dracula had been presented at the court in Buda and had been assigned a position as protector of Transylvania with quarters in Sibiu. Now he was activated.

With his Transylvanian troops he swept into Wallachia where Vladislav II was killed in the ensuing battle. According to folklore it was Vlad III Dracula who killed him himself, but that is unsubstantiated.

For the next six years Wallachia went through a transformation, still to this day celebrated in Romania as a new golden age.

Since the death of Vlad III Dracula's grandfather, Mircea I, less than four decades earlier, the throne of Wallachia had changed hands no less than sixteen times between eight rulers, one of whom had died from natural causes. Vlad III Dracula was determined to make a difference.

The country was impoverished, the local boyars made themselves rich by changing allegiances. They were paid well by both the neighbouring empires to cast their vote for one candidate or another and the Saxons in Transylvania were not shy to bribe them for the right trade agreements either.

Vlad III Dracula took stock of the situation and started to do something about the threats he faced.

First, he had to secure his internal position, which meant dealing with the untrustworthy Wallachian boyars. He called them to a feast in Târgoviște and here he arrested those he considered to be particular untrustworthy and those he considered to be responsible for his father and brother's deaths.

The captured boyars were impaled in the courtyard, and their families were led in chains to the castle at Poienari where they were used as slave labourers during Vlad III Dracula's renovation of the castle.

Next on Vlad III Dracula's list was Hungary. The problem here was that the Hunyadi clan was in open civil war with the King, and with Janos Hunyadi's support for Vlad III Dracula he could easily be seen as 'Hunyadi's man' even after Janos Hunyadi himself had died. Vlad III Dracula thus stood most to win by supporting the party going against the King, so he assisted Mihai Szilágyi, Janos Hunyadi's son-in-law, when his subjects in Bistrița rose in revolt. As it turned out he had chosen the right party, as soon thereafter Janos Hunyadi's son, Matthias I, became King of Hungary.

But Vlad III Dracula was not done yet. His centralization of power in Wallachia, and his growing independence was not good business for the Saxon traders in Brasov and Sibiu. They were used to benefitting from lucrative trade agreement, facilitated by pliant voivodes and boyars, many of whom Vlad III Dracula had now replaced by his own trusted men.

The Saxons thus kept under their protection another couple of candidates for the Wallachian thrones, one being Vlad III Dracula's own half-brother Vlad Călugărul and one being another Dan, a brother of Vladislav II and of the competing House of Dănești.

Vlad III Dracula first tried with diplomacy by writing to the elders of Sibiu and Brasov and asking them to hand over the pretenders, but when they did nothing of the kind he simply crossed the border into Transylvania and attacked both cities, leaving fire and destruction in his wake.

Vlad Călugărul managed to get away, but Dan was killed and the Saxon city-states were pacified for a while. As a biproduct of these campaigns, the Saxons had propaganda pamphlets printed, using the latest technology of the times, vilifying Vlad III Dracula in an attempt to make the Hungarian King move against him. This in turn made Vlad III Dracula famous and his name survives across oceans of time till our days.

While Vlad III Dracula was busy consolidating his reign, and securing peace and prosperity in Wallachia, King Matthias I was busy in Hungary trying to secure his own kingship, desperately short of the strongly symbolic Holy Crown of Hungary.

At the same time Mehmed II was busy further south, annexing Serbia into the Ottoman Empire in 1459, clearly signalling his new strategy of absorbing the buffer-states and getting closer to Hungary. This meant danger to Wallachia, a danger clearly seen by Vlad III Dracula.

As little as his grandfather had been able to defend the country against a full-scale invasion by the Ottomans, as little could Vlad III Dracula expect to do the same, he needed help, but luckily that help was seemingly close at hand.

King Matthias I of Hungary was the Pope's appointed champion and had received considerable funds from the Pope to equip an army to fight the Ottomans. He had also received funds from the Diet, the Hungarian parliament, specifically for that purpose, and his interest in keeping Wallachia as a buffer between Hungary and the Ottomans were obvious.

Vlad III Dracula therefore bet on Hungary and stopped paying tribute to the Sultan. Mehmed II decided to deal with Vlad III Dracula, whom he probably knew personally from Vlad III Dracula's time as hostage, and in the autumn of 1461 he sent an embassy to Wallachia with the above-table purpose of addressing the missing tribute but with a below-table agenda of apprehending Vlad III Dracula and taking him to the Sultan.

The scheme was, however, detected and it was Vlad III Dracula who apprehended the ambassadors who were impaled for their effort.

And now Vlad III Dracula let loose a vicious attack on - Ottoman - Bulgaria. It was winter and with a large retinue of riders he crossed the frozen Danube River and started causing chaos along the south side of the Danube. Anyone who got in his way was killed, anything that stood in his way was burned and anything which could be carried away was taken.

He proudly wrote King Matthias I that *'So that you know Your Highness, that I broke peace with them [the Ottomans] not for any use of ours, but to honour you, Your Highness, and for the sake of the Sacred Crown of Yours, and for keeping Christianity as a whole, and unifying the Catholic law'*.

From this it is clear that Vlad III Dracula expected Hungarian assistance when - in his own words - *'As soon as the weather gets better, that is, in spring, they are going to come back as enemies, with all their strength'*.

And Mehmed II did come back, and he came in force. This was a provocation of unheard severity from a vassal ruler of a minor state. The Sultan intended to make an example of Vlad III Dracula, but the question was where the Hungarians stood?

Matthias I had used some of the money he had received from the Pope to build up the promised army, but most of the money had been used to buy the Holy Crown of Hungary from Frederick III. Matthias I still had to actually obtain the crown and get properly crowned, so he had no appetite for a risky and expensive battle with the Ottomans at that time, Indeed he never did through three decades as king.

Vlad III Dracula was thus alone when the full Ottoman army, led by the Sultan himself, came across the Danube River in the summer of 1462. With the Sultan rode Radu Dracula, Vlad III Dracula's brother, clearly signalling the Sultan's purpose.

The Wallachians never stood a chance, but that did not mean that they gave up without a fight, quite on the contrary. The Ottomans and the Wallachians probably both expected Hungarian reinforcements to arrive, so the Wallachians did their best to slow the Ottomans down.

The first obstacle faced by the Ottoman army was crossing the Danube River. In a strategic move during his winter raids, Vlad III Dracula had destroyed most of the crossing-points, but he had left Vidin intact and it was predictably here the Ottoman army first tried to cross the river.

The details are sparse, but an eye-witness account exists, even though it is not exactly reliable in its details. From this we learn that Vlad III Dracula's first line of defence was the river itself and that he initially managed to repel the Ottoman crossing. The Ottoman army, however, spread out, and crossed the river by boat to build a small bridgehead further down the river. When Vlad III Dracula became aware of this he attacked, but the Ottoman bridgehead had become too strong, and after a bloody skirmish the Ottomans prevailed and the Wallachians withdrew. What was to follow was classic guerrilla warfare, assisted by an unpredictable ally, the weather.

The summer of 1462 was unusually warm. Indeed, it was so warm that the eyewitness account says you could cook kebabs on the soldier's mail-shirts. This was in favour of Vlad III Dracula's plan as the first element of his strategy was to keep the Ottoman army without supplies, in particular food and water. To do so he burned the ground behind him.

The large Ottoman army relied on food and water found on the way, and scouts constantly rode ahead of the main army to find fresh supplies. But wherever they looked the found the same picture, burned fields, villages devoid of man or beast and water sources poisoned or filled in with dead animals.

Mehmed II was less than impressed with this situation and he alternately blamed the scouts and his commanders for lack of planning. This indicates that the Ottoman army initially had made no plans for supplies to be brought up from the rear, but was entirely relying on finding local supplies, which it did not.

While the Ottoman army slowly made its way north through Wallachia, worse for wear after each day of marching, Vlad III Dracula deployed classic guerrilla principles of raiding. The Wallachian cavalry would appear out from the forest, attack, and withdraw. Typically, they would attack smaller and weaker elements of the Ottoman troops, constantly snapping at Mehmed II's heels and forcing the Ottoman army to keep alert at all times.

Vlad III Dracula could never hope to beat the Ottoman army in open battle, not even if he deployed the same choice of terrain for a battle that his grand-father had successfully done, and which in turn was a strategy inherited from Alexander the Great and the Battle of Issus.

But there was one more strategic move that Alexander had deployed at Issus, and whether Vlad III Dracula knew this or not, deliberately or by chance, he too decided on that very strategy.

Alexander had realized that the Persian army had one weak point, its command structure completely dependent on the King's presence and initiative. Without the King, the army would simply not be able to move, so if the King could be removed, the army would be defeated. Alexander himself led a suicidal cavalry attack straight through the Persian centre and got so close to King Darius III that his spear killed the King's chariot-driver. Even if it did not kill the King, it was enough to make him flee, and as predicted the Persian army fell apart once he was gone.

Vlad III Dracula had similarly realized that he could paralyze, and most probably make the Ottoman army turn, if he could kill Mehmed II, perhaps even if he could just wound or scare him.

He had good reason to think so, as the command structure in the Ottoman army was not dissimilar to that of the Persian army. Furthermore, he would have known that the Ottoman army's flight from Belgrade was partly caused by the fact that Mehmed II had been wounded, rendered unconscious and unable to restore order when the army broke.

So, Vlad III Dracula planned to do like Alexander and personally lead an attack aimed directly at the person of the Sultan. Contrary to Alexander, Vlad III Dracula did not have an open battle to use as a launch-pad for the attack, and an attack on the main Ottoman army during the day would be ritual suicide, so Vlad III Dracula came up with a different idea; a night attack.

The Ottoman camp was a large affair with the Sultan's tent in the middle, unmistakable, but heavily protected by janissaries and possibly even a 'wagenburg' of wagons mounted with firearms.

That the attack was daring is an understatement, but fortune favours the bold, and Vlad III Dracula was closer to changing world-history than anybody else who ever took on Mehmed II.

And although one thing is certain, namely that Vlad III Dracula's attack did not manage to kill or wound the sultan; there are two very different versions as to the success of the raid.

The Wallachian version says that the raid was so fast and furious that the Wallachians withdrew (albeit without their main purpose achieved) without the loss of a single man. It furthermore says that Mehmed was so scared that he fled and had to be convinced, practically forced, to return.

The Ottoman version describes the attack as a complete and utter fiasco, with the Wallachians aiming towards the centre of the camp because they thought it was the way out and Vlad III Dracula's raiders being cut down, even by ten years old boys.

Neither version is, of course, true. The likely truth lies somewhere in the middle, most probably that Vlad III Dracula's raiders, disguised in Ottoman uniforms, were discovered when they came closer to the well protected middle and a fierce battle broke out between the raiders and the Janissaries in the immediate vicinity of Mehmed II's tent. Both sides would have taken loses, but the Sultan was unhurt.

Vlad III Dracula's desperate attempts at getting the Ottoman army to turn around, which now seems to have been his main military objective, had failed, but he had one more idea to undermine the Ottoman morale and make them realize the futility of their undertaking.

Slowly, and looking over their shoulders day and night, the Ottoman army marched on towards Târgoviște, which they expected to be defended. Once they reached the city they, however, found that it was abandoned and undefended.

No doubt wondering what Vlad III Dracula's next move was, or even silently hoping that he had perhaps just given up and fled, they continued past the city, and there they discovered what exactly he had prepared for them.

What lay in front of the Ottoman army was 'a forest' of impaled bodies. The number of impalements is unknown, as the contemporary sources cannot be trusted when it comes to numbers, but there must have been plenty to make a strong statement, possibly hundreds.

Vlad III Dracula had basically executed all the prisoners he had collected in Târgoviște, some from the winter's raids into Bulgaria, some from the current campaign.

The sight must have been terrifying, the stench unbearable and the sheer brutality unbelievable. The moniker "Tepes"' (The Impaler) was born here and was to become the common name for Vlad III Dracula amongst the Ottomans forthwith.

Finally, Mehmed II had had enough. He had basically achieved his objectives. There was no armed resistance of note left, Târgoviște was his and Vlad III Dracula had obviously fled. He saw to it that Radu (III) Dracula was elected voivode, left a contingent of troops and turned around to go back to Istanbul (to which he had recently moved the Ottoman court). He was totally exhausted and utterly disgusted.

What had started as a power-demonstration in submission had turned into a messy brawl, nearly cost him his life, and shown his army as being vulnerable if opposed by a determined enemy, even if that enemy had a significant numerical disadvantage?

But Vlad III Dracula had not fled Wallachia. Indeed, he had holed up in his newly modernised castle in Poienari. This castle was the only Wallachian castle actually placed high above the surrounding terrain, on a lonely rock formation overlooking the road between Wallachia and Făgăraș.

Radu III Dracula sent troops north to get rid of his brother whom he did not need lurking around in the background as a potential rallying point for dissidents. As had now become custom they set up cannon and tried to shoot the castle walls down. But the castle had recently been modernised with walls designed to withstand cannon, and the locals, loyal to Vlad III Dracula, made sure that the castle was supplied with food via mountain and forest tracks known to them, but not to the besiegers.

Probably still hoping that King Matthias I would come to his rescue, Vlad III Dracula stayed in Poienari for a few weeks, but finally sneaked out overnight and rode north into Transylvania, where he continued to the town of Brasov. Here he waited for Matthias I, who had eventually put an army in the field and slowly marched it down through Transylvania.

However, Matthias I had no appetite for a fight, even if it only was to oust the remaining Ottoman contingent from Wallachia. Instead, he had Vlad III Dracula arrested on trumped up charges of treason and put him in house-arrest in Buda. He then marched his army westwards but stayed in Transylvania, shadowing the Ottoman army on its retreat.

Peace now reigned in Wallachia for nearly a decade. Radu III Dracula was ruling as 'pasha' on the behalf of the Sultan, effectively making Wallachia an Ottoman protectorate.

Matthias I was busy elsewhere, and not particularly interested in Wallachia, but in the 1470s King Stefan III of Moldavia started to sense that it was his turn next. Moldavia was the last remaining buffer state and an Ottoman attack was most likely to come through Wallachia.

Stefan III decided to make a proactive move, so he, unsuccessfully, attacked Wallachia in 1470 and in 1473 he went back, this time beating Radu III Dracula in battle.

Stefan III's candidate was Basarab (III) Laiotă, a son of Dan II, and in a twist of fate he was to repeat his father's achievement of ruling Wallachia on five separate occasions, four times replacing the same competitor.

The Ottomans sent an expeditionary force back into Wallachia at the end of the year, restoring Radu III Dracula. Stefan III returned the following year putting Basarab III Laiotă back, but before the expected Ottoman counterattack came, Basarab III Laiotă changed sides and accepted Ottoman vassalage.

Stefan III's original purpose had thus not been achieved, so he returned in support of Radu III Dracula. The Ottomans then put Basarab III Laiotă back, after which Stefan III put Radu III Dracula back and it was only when

Radu III Dracula died, from natural causes, in 1475, that the merry go round stopped. After five years of conflict the Ottomans still controlled Wallachia.

Mehmed II now decided to deal with Moldavia and in two campaigns in 1475 and 1476 he unsuccessfully attacked Stefan III. On both occasions the Ottomans were assisted by Wallachian troops under Basarab III Laiotă.

During the second campaign the Hungarians started a counter-campaign in Bosnia to divert Mehmed II's attention and after having achieved little of importance, apart from killing and burning, the Hungarian expeditionary force turned back north and assisted Stefan III in harassing the retreating Ottoman army. Commanding the Hungarian troops was Vlad III Dracula.

After fourteen years of house-arrest Vlad III Dracula had been unleashed. After the Ottoman aggression towards Moldavia it was clear that the status quo was not going to remain and King Matthias I now needed a warlike champion.

As the Ottomans retreated through Wallachia, the Hungarian expeditionary force and the Moldavians under Stefan III pursued, with Basarab III Laiotă following the Ottomans the scene was set for Vlad III Dracula's return as voivode.

The situation was far from clear though and Basarab III Laiotă came back later in the year with fresh Ottoman troops. It came to battle and Vlad III Dracula was killed, putting Basarab III Laiotă back once more.

This time Basarab III Laiotă's rule lasted less than a year as in 1477 Stefan III came back with a new champion, Basarab (IV), a son of Basarab II and Basarab III Laiotă fled to Hungary, once again changing sides.

Basarab IV in turn quickly realized that he too was likely to last longer if on good terms with the Sultan, so he accepted Ottoman vassalage and in 1479 the Ottomans called on his help, forcing him to participate in a larger than usual raid into Transylvania.

The raiders swept into Transylvania, but they were intercepted by the local Hungarian Voivode of Transylvania, also assisted by Basarab III Laiotă, and a skirmish - known as the Battle of Breadfield - ensued, in which the Ottoman raiders were beaten back, losing their loot.

Stefan III of Moldavia now intervened again, this time bringing forth Vlad IV Dracula, called Vlad IV Călugărul (the Monk) who ousted Basarab IV in 1481.

In the by now all too familiar story, the Ottomans reinserted Basarab IV that same year, with Stefan III reinserting Vlad IV Călugărul again later in the year only to be replaced again by Basarab IV before the end of the year.

The following year Vlad IV Călugărul was back and this time he stayed until 1495. By now Mehmed II had died, his son Bayezid II had his focus on Anatolia and we have exceeded the scope of this story.

Although Wallachia continued to be a turbulent buffer state between the Ottomans and the Christian World, contrary to Serbia and Bosnia - and often under strong Ottoman influence - it maintained its status as an independent principality throughout the history of the Ottoman Empire.

In 1859 Wallachia united with Moldavia and in 1866 the union became the Principality of Romania, which in 1881 - again including Dobrogea - became a kingdom. The Kingdom was expanded by Transylvania after WW I, forming the country which - after decades of communist rule following WW II - is now the Republic of Romania, a member of both NATO and the EU.

MOLDAVIA

Part 5 - The Balkans

CRITICAL TIMELINE

Year	Event	Involved Parties
1353	Dragoş is sent to Moldavia to create a buffer against Tatars	Moldavia Hungary
1360	Bogdan I established himself as independent Voivode of Moldavia	Moldavia Hungary
1371	Laţcu obtains papal acceptance of title as voivode and independent Moldavian bishopry	Moldavia The Pope
1387	Moldavia becomes Polish vassal	Moldavia Poland
1400	Alexandru I becomes Voivode of Moldavia	Moldavia
1410	Moldavia assist Poland	Moldavia Poland
1420	Moldavia repels Ottoman attack on Akkerman	Moldavia Ottomans
1422	Moldavia assists Poland	Moldavia Poland
1430	Moldavian attack on Poland	Moldavia Poland
1457	Stefan III becomes Voivode of Moldavia	Moldavia Wallachia
1462	Moldavian attack on Chilia	Moldavia Ottomans Hungary Wallachia
1465	Moldavian conquest of Chilia	Moldavia Hungary
1467	Battle of Baia	Moldavia Hungary
1470	Moldavian attack on Wallachia	Moldavia Wallachia
1471	Wallachian counter-attack on Moldavia	Moldavia Wallachia
1472	Tatar attack on Moldavia	Moldavia Genoa Golden Horde
1473	Moldavian attack on Wallachia	Moldavia Wallachia
1474	Moldavian attack on Wallachia	Moldavia Wallachia
1475	Moldavian attack on Wallachia	Moldavia Wallachia
1475	Battle of Vaslui	Moldavia Ottomans
1476	Battle of Rasboieni. Stefan III puts Vlad III Dracula back on the throne of Wallachia	Moldavia Ottomans Wallachia
1503	Moldavia agrees to pay tribute to Ottoman Empire	Moldavia Ottomans

14 - The Buffer States - Moldavia

Moldavia has already been mentioned a few times and in this section, we now go back and look at its own story. It started a few decades later than that of Wallachia, but very much for the same reasons.

After its incursions into the Balkans in the thirteenth century, the Mongol Golden Horde established itself on the northern coast of the Black Sea, spreading southwest as far as the Danube River and counted Bulgaria beyond it as a vassal state.

But as the decades went by the Mongol's focus shifted away from the Balkans and when the Black Death hit them hard in the middle of the fourteenth century they abandoned their ambitions in the Balkans altogether.

The Hungarians had, in the century since the initial Mongol invasion gradually expanded their security zone, Wallachia forming a buffer in the south, and with waning Mongol influence the opportunity arose to also create a buffer-zone in the east, between the Carpathians and the Black Sea.

There had been plenty of ongoing skirmishes in the area, but it was Charles I of Hungary who in the 1320s first sent organized expeditions into the region. He was militarily unsuccessful, but people - mainly of Romanian decent - started to drift across the mountains as had also been the case further southwest in Wallachia.

Charles I's son, Louis I, rekindled the Hungarian interest with several campaigns in the area in the 1340's which, in combination with the Black Death, led to the withdrawal of the remaining Mongol - now known as Tatar - troops.

To claim the area for Hungary, and the Catholic Church, King Louis now appointed a nobleman from the Maramureş area in Transylvania named Dragoş as his representative and voivode of the new territory of Moldavia.

Dragoş began to organize the new territories as a protective barrier against the Tatars and he was - presumably on his death - a couple of years later, replaced by his son Sas who continued his work. He in turn was possibly - the sources are unclear on the issue - replaced by his son Balc.

But whether it was Sas or Balc who ruled on behalf of the Hungarian King at the time, the important newcomer was another nobleman from Maramureş; Bogdan.

Bogdan was a rebellious noble who at some point before he went to Moldavia was describes as *'an inveterate faithless subject'* by Hungarian sources. He was in dispute with King Louis I and sometime around 1360 he decided to move, with his retinue, to Moldavia and take over.

Balc opposed him, but he was beaten back and Bogdan appointed himself voivode of Moldavia and negated on Hungarian suzerainty.

Bogdan - now Bogdan I - inspired even more Romanians to move across from Maramureș, creating a quickly growing anti-Hungarian, Orthodox, population in the new buffer-state.

King Louis I was not happy with Bogdan I's coup and sent troops across the Carpathians to retake the area, but his forces were unsuccessful and Bogdan I fought them off, enjoying wide popular support.

When he died in 1367 Bogdan I was replaced by his grandson Petru I - son of Bogdan I's oldest son - but he was quickly ousted by his uncle, Bogdan I's younger son Lațcu.

Lațcu was raised in the Orthodox faith, but he used religion in an ingenious way to consolidate Moldavia's independence from Hungary.

Lațcu approached the Catholic bishop in Poland, an emerging empire creeping up behind Hungary in a line from the Baltic Sea toward the Black Sea. With his help Lațcu personally converted to Catholicism - though his family remained Orthodox - and sent a mission to the Pope to apply for an independent Moldavian Bishopric, under the supervision of the Polish, rather than Hungarian, church.

Lațcu's gamble was successful and the Pope granted Moldavia a separate diocese under the Polish bishop, but soon thereafter King Louis I of Hungary also became King of Poland, so the immediate effect was limited. The diocese however also came with the Pope's official blessing of Moldavia as a nation state with Lațcu as its ruler.

Otherwise Lațcu attempted to keep a peaceful relationship with King Louis I, although the question of suzerainty is somewhat weakly answered in historic sources.

On Lațcu's death in 1375 - where it is worth mentioning that he was buried in the Orthodox cathedral - his nephew, Petru II, took the throne of Moldavia.

Petru II continued the diplomacy started by his father, keeping good relations with his mighty neighbours, and also expanding the Orthodox faith in Moldavia despite being at loggerheads with the Patriarch in Constantinople when it came to appointment of bishops.

When King Louis I died in 1382, Petru II once again leaned towards Poland as an antidote to Hungary, accepting vassalage to Poland in 1387 and facilitating diplomatic ties between Poland and Wallachia.

The southern parts of Moldavia (squeezed in between northern Moldavia and Wallachia) had initially still been populated by Tatars, but over the decades they were integrated into Moldavia, and under Petru II a single state finally formed bordering Wallachia to the south.

On Petru II's death in 1391 his brother, Roman I, became voivode. Roman I consolidated the state's borders, now reaching from the Carpathians to the Black Sea and initially upheld Moldavia's vassalage to Poland.

For unknown reasons he decided, however, to support a local Polish noble's revolt against the King and when the King won the contest, Roman I was in a compromised situation.

The Moldavian nobles, seeing Poland as the only antidote to Hungary did not wish to be on the wrong side of the King, so in 1394 they forced Roman I to abdicate, placing instead his son Stefan I on the throne.

Stefan I was in 1399 - presumably on his death - replaced by his brother Iuga who in turn was replaced by another brother, Alexandru I, at the turn of the century.

Where Stefan I and Iuga had been unspectacular and had satisfied themselves with maintaining status quo, Alexandru I would reign for more than three decades and become one of the great voivodes of Moldavia.

Alexandru I was an organizer and he re-organised the administrative structure of the country, clarifying roles and responsibilities, creating a fiscal code and adding a Chancellery to the government offices.

He also secured the trading routes leading through the country from Poland to the Black Sea ports and concluded trade agreements with the merchants in Krakow and Lviv.

But Alexandru I's hobby horse was the capability to defend Moldavia against a superior invader, with several potential invaders around.

He entered into a defensive alliance with Mircea I of Wallachia and with Poland, mainly aimed at protecting the parties against Hungary, but with the Ottomans now also lurking in the area.

Moldavia proactively assisted Poland in 1410 when they defeated the Teutonic Knights in the Battle of Grunwald and again in the Gollub War in 1422.

But the Polish failed to come to Moldavia's assistance when the Ottomans attacked them for the first time, trying to occupy the coastal city of Akkerman (modern day Bilhorod-Dnistrovskyi). Alexandru I beat the Ottomans back, but he was not happy about the lack of Polish support.

In a twist of statesmanship, which was symptomatic of the times, Alexandru I supported two Ottoman puppets on the throne of Wallachia; Radu II and Alexandru I Aldea. Not that Alexandru I had anything positive to say about the Ottomans per se, but the second Moldavian - heavily fortified - city on the Black Sea coast, Chilia, was on the border between Moldavia and Wallachia and the Hungarians had designs on controlling the strategically located castle. The best way to keep them out was to support an Ottoman backed voivode in Wallachia, so that is what Alexandru I did.

When Polish succession ended up with civil war in 1430, Alexandru I took the opportunity to solve long-disputed territorial issues with an attack on Poland, but the issues were finally solved by treaty in 1431. The year after, Alexandru I died.

The three decades of stability and prosperity under Alexandru I were now followed by years of internal strife.

Alexandru I's designated heir was his oldest son Iliaş I. He succeeded his father as planned and maintained his father's close relationship with Poland.

However, a group of local boyars, possibly with Wallachian assistance, ousted him the following year in favour of his brother, Stefan II. The rebels bought off the Poles by means of territorial concessions in the border area, and the Poles arrested Iliaş I, who had fled to them in exile.

But the year after Iliaş I was free again and with Polish support entered Moldavia. Here he fought a number of indecisive battles with his brother and finally the Polish King facilitated a peace agreement by which Iliaş I was to nominally rule the country, but with Stefan II as semi-autonomous lord of the south. Both were to have their seat in the capital city of Suceava, and the Poles took more land concessions as payment for their services.

The arrangement was of course just a time bomb, so when the Poles lost interest in Moldavia the hostilities flared up again. Stefan II rebelled in 1443 and caught Iliaş I whom he blinded.

Free again the blind voivode fled to Poland with his wife and son. Iliaş I died sometime later, but his - Polish born - wife was received well in Poland where she was given the fief of Pokuttya on the border to Moldavia - the same area which had been given to the Poles in order to accept Stefan II's first rebellion - and when her son became of age he took over the area, styling himself as voivode of Moldavia.

In the meantime, Stefan II took another of his brothers, Petru III, as co-regent. The brothers tried to retake Pokuttya but with no success.

Iliaş I's son Roman had now become old enough to be considered a contender, so with Polish support he entered Moldavia in 1447, where his uncle, Stefan II was killed in the ensuing battle.

As Roman II he ruled either alone or with his uncle, Petru III, but in any case, he was ousted in 1448 after only a year on the throne. He fled to Poland where he died shortly after aged only twenty-two.

Petru III now ruled alone, but in the following year he was replaced by Ciubăr, apparently a boyar without royal lineage, who was replaced in turn by Alexandru II, another son of Iliaş I, in the same year.

Alexandru II's first reign only lasted until later that same year when he was replaced by a son of Alexandru I, Bogdan II. His rule was in itself not very significant, but as it turned out would become influential because it launched the claim of his son, Stefan, who would end the civil strife in Moldavia a few years later.

Bogdan II's competitor for the throne was his brother Petru III who allied himself with some of the boyars and had Bogdan II assassinated while attending the wedding of one of the conspiring boyars. Bogdan II's son, Stefan, was also present but got away as did his cousin, Vlad III Dracula, who lived in exile at the Moldavian court during that time. Elsewhere Mehmed II had just taken the throne of the Ottoman Empire.

14 - The Buffer States - Moldavia

Moldavia was once again thrown into a quick exchange of competing voivodes. Petru III was pro-Polish and even agreed to pay tribute to the Ottomans to prevent them from attacking.

Pitched against him was Alexandru II, now with Hungarian backing. Petru III ruled for two years then Alexandru II ruled for two years then Petru III rule for one year then Alexandru II ruled for less than a year and then Petru III ruled for two years. Elsewhere Constantinople had fallen and the Ottomans stood before Belgrade.

Bogdan II's son Stefan had, as mentioned, fled Moldavia on his father's assassination and he had spent the following years in exile in Transylvania. With him was his cousin, Vlad III Dracula, and the two had stayed together through the years.

When Vlad III Dracula took the throne in Wallachia in 1456, Stefan was at his side and as soon as Vlad III Dracula was secure on his throne it was his turn to help his cousin.

Vlad III Dracula supplied Stefan with 6,000 Wallachian cavalry-men and with this Stefan returned to Moldavia and ousted Petru III who fled first to Poland and later to Transylvania.

Stefan became Stefan III, and he would over time earn the moniker 'the Great'.

With Stefan III ended twenty-five years of chaos in Moldavia. Since the death of Alexandru I there had been eight voivodes ruling a total of fifteen times between them, statistics not so different from those facing his cousin Vlad III Dracula in neighbouring Wallachia, but contrary to his cousin, Stefan III would come to rule for an uninterrupted period of forty-seven years.

The year was 1457 and it was only Moldavia's relatively isolated location which had protected it from being annexed into one of surrounding empires while its royals and nobles were playing musical thrones.

But now the times had changed; Moldavia needed to stand up for itself and Stefan III was the man to do it. Although he was distinctly anti-Hungarian, his first action was an incursion into Poland in order to chase down Petru III. He was met with armed resistance from the Poles, but an agreement was reached in which Stefan III accepted vassalage to Poland and the Poles agreed to not support Petru III and not allow him to return to Moldavia.

Stefan III had plenty to do at home in the following years, consolidating royal authority after nearly three decades of anarchy, but in 1462 a new opportunity presented itself, which was too good to miss out on.

As covered in connection with Wallachia, in the summer of 1462 Sultan Mehmed II came with the full Ottoman army in Wallachia as a response to Vlad III Dracula's raids in Bulgaria the previous winter. Stefan III had no appetite for facing the Ottomans, not even to help his cousin, but the conflict opened up the opportunity to capture the strategic fortress at Chilia.

Chilia was on the border with between Wallachia and Moldavia and - importantly - it was on the mouth of the Danube River, where the river spills into the Black Sea.

This very important strategic position made Chilia attractive to all the political parties in the region, and in particular the Hungarians and the Ottomans. The Hungarians had thus with dismay seen how the thrones of Wallachia and Moldavia had changed hands repeatedly, making the political landscape muddy at the best of times, so they had long since moved in and taken physical possession of the fortress at Chilia, maintaining a Hungarian garrison.

The Hungarian possession at Chilia did not please Stefan III and with the Ottomans in Wallachia and the Hungarians seemingly doing their best not to get involved, this was a good time to take what Stefan III considered rightfully his.

So while the Ottomans were slowly moving through Wallachia with Vlad III Dracula harassing them every step of the way, Stefan III personally led an attempt to take Chilia.

The attack turned out badly. The Hungarians fought off the Moldavians, Stefan III injuring his leg, and when Wallachian and Ottoman troops were sent to the spot as well, the Ottomans routed the Wallachians; further reducing Vlad III Dracula's fighting capability.

But Stefan III was not done. Three years later, in 1465, he was back and this time he successfully took the fortress and replaced the Hungarian garrison with his own men.

Stefan III's attacks at Chilia, combined with his clear pro-Polish and anti-Hungarian views finally became too much for King Matthias I of Hungary. The Moldavian voivode was out of control, and he needed to be called to heel.

King Matthias I, who was supposed to be fighting the Ottomans on behalf of Christianity, now recruited for a campaign against Moldavia, but Stefan III slowed him down by supporting a popular revolt in Transylvania which kept the Hungarian King busy for a while.

When King Matthias I had dealt with the rebellious Transylvanians he marched on Moldavia. With him he had Petru III, making his intentions clear. But it did not go his way, not at all.

Due to the uprising in Transylvania the Hungarian army - superior in numbers to the Moldavian army - only entered Moldavia at the beginning of November 1467, finding all passes and access roads blocked by rocks and felled trees. They proceeded through Bacau and Roman, both cities being set on fire and their populations slain, before they reached the city of Baia in the second week of December.

So far, the Hungarians had met little organised Moldavian resistance apart from a few skirmishes between scouting parties. At Baia, however, the

Hungarians became aware that Stefan III had his army lying ready and that he intended to attack.

King Matthias I ordered his troops to take up positions inside the town and make fortifications and barriers at its edges. But the Moldavians were well prepared and commenced their attack by setting fires at several places inside the town. While the Hungarians were fighting fires, the Moldavians attacked by foot, gradually edging their way inside the town where the heavily armed Hungarian knights could not easily be deployed.

The Hungarian King himself was wounded by three arrows - all in his back - and he was *'carried from the battlefield on a stretcher, to avoid him falling into the hands of the enemy.'*

Eventually the Hungarians retreated, having taken severe casualties, and they withdrew into Transylvania despite Moldavian attempts to stop their flight.

Stefan III pursued the Hungarians into Transylvania until he found what he wanted, Petru III. Seventeen years after the assassination of his father, Stefan III had his murderer executed after which he withdrew back to Moldavia.

For the Hungarians this was effectively the end of their claims on Moldavia. Stefan III and Matthias I made an uneasy peace, and as we shall see even cooperated on later occasions.

With the Hungarian issue solved, Stefan III now started to worry about Mehmed II.

While the Moldavians and the Hungarians had spent their time and resources fighting each other, Mehmed II had annexed Serbia, done the same to most of Bosnia and installed his own puppet, Radu III Dracula, in Wallachia.

It did not take too much political sense to realize that sooner or later Mehmed II would come for Moldavia, and that when the attack came it would come through Wallachia.

So, Stefan III decided to create his own buffer zone. If King Matthias I did not want to protect his interests in Wallachia, Stefan II would do so himself.

He attacked in 1470 but only got as far as Braila, which was routinely burned. The next year Radu III Dracula returned the favour by an incursion into Moldavia, which in turn was repelled.

The following year Stefan III had to defend Moldavia from a Tatar attack from the north, probably inspired by the Genoese, nervous about Stefan III's rising power and his potential ambitions in the Black Sea.

But in 1473 Stefan III again had a free hand, and he marched on Wallachia where in November he won the deciding battle at Rimnicu Sarat. Radu III Dracula fled across the Danube River and Stefan III's candidate, Basarab III Laiotă, took the throne in Wallachia. A month later the Ottomans put Radu III Dracula back.

The following year Stefan III once again forced the issue and put Basarab III Laiotă back, but before the Ottomans could counter, the new voivode changed sides and declared as an Ottoman vassal.

Stefan III had thus achieved nothing despite three campaigns, but he did not give up. He now made Radu III Dracula his champion and he managed to put him on the throne of Wallachia twice before Radu III Dracula died in 1475.

Up to this point the Ottoman forces participating in the battle for control of Wallachia had been local garrisons and small expeditionary forces as Mehmed II was away with the main army in Anatolia. But towards the end of 1474 he was back in Europe, and he decided to deal with Stefan III once and for all.

Although the Sultan did not personally lead the attack on Moldavia, the Ottomans came at full strength under the command of Hadân Suleiman Pasha reinforced by Wallachian troops under Basarab III Laiotă.

Stefan III was well aware that he could not possibly match the numbers of the Ottomans, but he was on his own terrain, and he had the weather with him.

Contrary to the very hot summer of 1462 when the Ottomans marched on Wallachia, the winter of 1474/1475 was extremely cold. The Ottoman troops were already exhausted from campaigning in Albania during summer and now Stefan III scorched the earth behind him as he gradually withdrew in front of the Ottoman invaders, constantly attacking their supply and communication lines.

Stefan III had carefully picked his battleground. He had chosen a location close to Vaslui, where a narrow valley with marshy ground was bordered by wooded hillsides. In addition to the ground, making it difficult to use the Ottoman superiority in numbers, the weather was misty, so when the Moldavians sprang their trap and ambushed the Ottomans, it was impossible to see from where the attack was coming.

The Moldavian archers pelted the Ottomans with arrows from the woods, practically invisible in the mist and aiming at a large mass of packed Ottomans. Cannon fire supplemented the archers and the Ottomans turned and fled, pursued by Moldavian cavalry emerging from the woods.

When told of the Ottoman defeat at Vaslui, Mehmed II was furious. He refused to see anyone for days and put everything else aside. He wanted revenge on Stefan III, not only for his insolence, but also to make an example of what happened when you opposed the Sultan.

Although Mehmed II did not campaign in the summer of 1475 due to severe gout, the following year saw him leading his troops in person and once again the target was Moldavia. Basarab III Laiotă was with him again with a fresh contingent of Wallachians and they had new allies.

Mehmed II had asked his allies, the Crimean Tatars, to attack Moldavia from the north, spreading Stefan III's forces on two fronts. But the Tatar attack came before Mehmed II's main attack from the south and was repelled with relative ease by Stefan III.

Stefan III now dispersed his troops into smaller bands which could harass the Ottomans during their march, which, once again, was slowed down by the scorched earth that met them.

But Mehmed II had taken note of Stefan III's strategy, so he had deployed a small Ottoman fleet in the Black Sea which could keep the army supplied from the seaside, cutting down the length and vulnerability of the Ottoman supply lines.

He had also predicted Stefan III's battle plan, so when they met at Rasboieni and Stefan III tried to drag Mehmed II into an ambush similar to what he had done to Hadân Suleiman Pasha at Vaslui, Mehmed II did not fall for it, but rather managed to send the Moldavians fleeing before him.

Mehmed II then proceeded to the Moldavian capital of Suceava, but he had not brought siege engines with him and could not take the city. He thus turned around and started the journey home.

But behind him Stefan III still had most of his army intact, only a small part of it having been deployed at Rasboieni and as the Ottoman slowly retreated, their supply fleet was hit by a severe storm and had to retreat leaving them with limited supplies.

Then the Hungarian expeditionary force commanded by Vlad III Dracula arrived and with Stefan III's remaining troops they pursued the Ottomans all the way to the Danube River. Twenty years after they initially rode on Wallachia, the two cousins Stefan III and Vlad III Dracula once again rode together, and again they secured the Wallachian throne for Vlad III Dracula.

Stefan III left a bodyguard of 200 Moldavians with Vlad III Dracula, but it was not enough to prevent him from being killed in battle with Basarab III Laiotă later that same year.

In Istanbul Mehmed II sat unsatisfied. He had won the major battle but not exactly won the war. Stefan III too had little to cheer about. He had, at great cost, defended Moldavia, but Wallachia was once again ruled by an Ottoman puppet and nothing had really been solved.

After the death of Mehmed II, Stefan III managed to forcefully insert a voivode of Wallachia four more times, the last attempt putting Vlad IV Călugărul on the throne in 1482.

Stefan III's problems with the Ottomans were, however, not over with the death of Mehmed II. In 1484 the Ottomans annexed Akkerman and Chilia, the Moldavian seaports and strategic fortresses, and they twice raided into Moldavia in the following years.

Stefan III also had trouble with Poland in his later years, and in 1503 he settled matters with the Ottomans by accepting to pay the annual tribute which he had deliberately stopped paying three decades earlier in a -successful- attempt to wind up Mehmed II.

Stefan III died in 1504. He had managed to keep Moldavia free, if not completely independent, and as one of the few enemies of the Conqueror he had survived the experience.

Moldavia remained an Ottoman vassal until the nineteenth century, but in 1792 the north-eastern part, the Transnistre, was ceded to Russia. It is today the country of Moldavia.

The remaining part broke loose from the crumpling Ottoman Empire in the nineteenth century and united with Wallachia to become Romania, joined also by Transylvania after WW I.

14 - The Buffer States - Moldavia

Part 5 -The Balkans

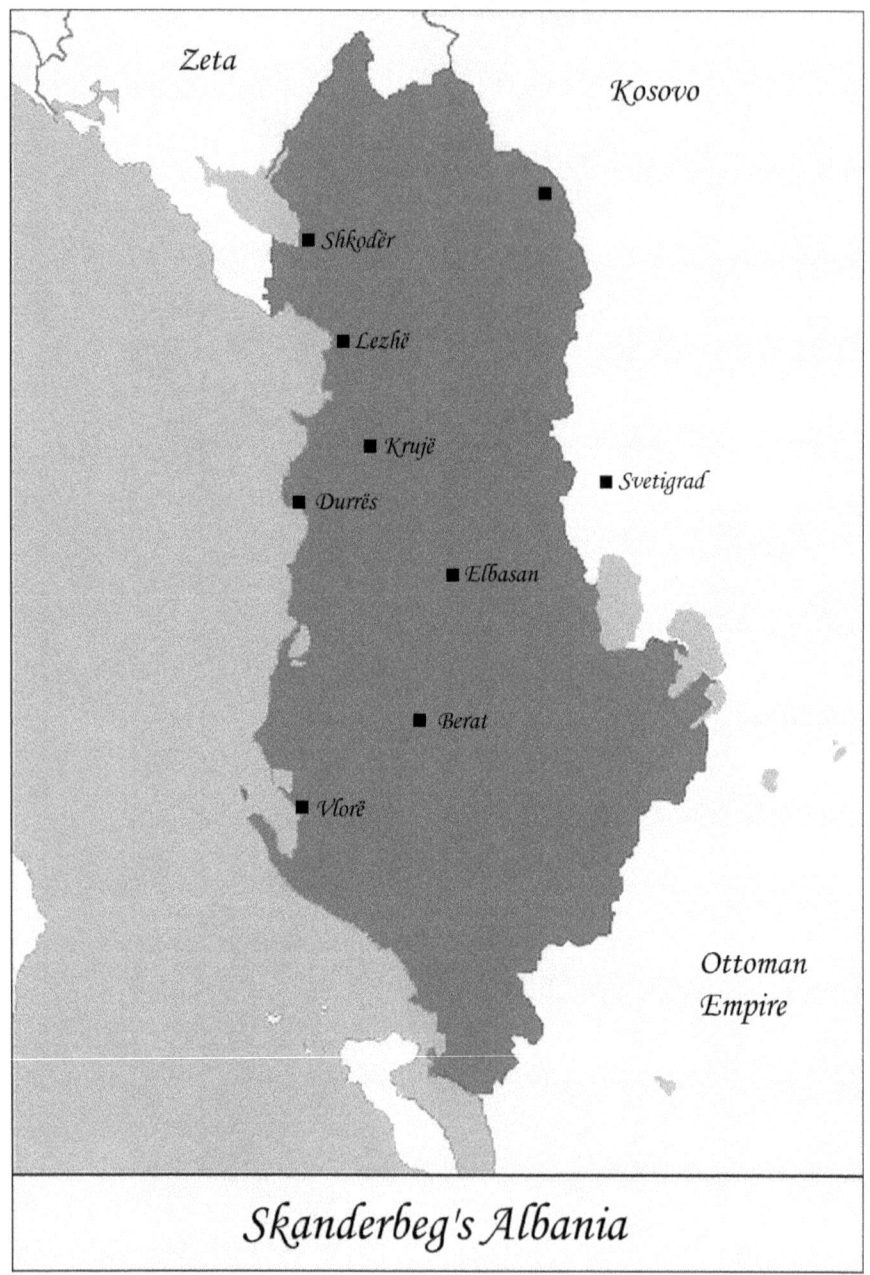

Skanderbeg's Albania

15 - ALBANIA

CRITICAL TIMELINE

Year	Event	Involved Parties
1000s	'Albanoi' people mentioned in historic sources	Byzantium
1190	Principality of Arbanon forms around Krujë	Arbanon
1204	Durrës becomes Venetian	Venice
1208	Arbanon is allied with Serbia	Arbanon / Serbia
1213	Arbanon suppressed by Epirus	Arbanon / Epirus
1257	Arbanon invaded by Naples	Arbanon / Naples
1259	Nicaea invades Arbanon	Arbanon / Naples / Nicaea
1261	Naples retakes Arbanon	Arbanon / Naples
1266	Independence from Naples	Albania / Naples
1272	Albania becomes part of Naples by agreement	Albania / Naples
1274	Byzantine attack on Albania	Albania / Byzantium / Naples
1282	Sicilian Vespers. Full Byzantine control of Albania	Albania / Byzantium / Naples
1296	Serbian attack	Albania / Serbia
1304	Revolt against Serbians	Albania / Serbia
1342	Serbian Invasion	Albania / Serbia
1371	Battle of Maritsa. Serbian Empire disintegrates	Albania / Serbia
1368	Karl Topia conquers Durrës	Albania / Naples
1383	Durrës falls to Zeta	Albania / Zeta
1385	Karl Topia retake Durrës with Ottoman help	Albania / Zeta / Ottomans
1389	First Battle of Kosovo. Serbian Empire disintegrates	Ottomans / Serbia
1392	Durrës ceded to Venice. Rest of Albania becomes Ottoman province.	Albania / Venice / Ottomans
1436	Albanian rebellion	Albania / Ottomans
1443	The Long Campaign. Battle of Niš. George Kastrioti - Skanderbeg - returns to Albania	Albania / Ottomans

Year	Event	Involved Parties
1444	League of Lezhë	Albania
1444	Ottomans defeated at Torvioll	Albania, Ottomans
1445	Ottomans defeated at Mount Mokra	Albania, Ottomans
1446	Ottoman defeat at Otonetë	Albania, Ottomans
1447	Albanian attack on Venetian Albania	Albania, Venice
1448	Second Battle of Kosovo. Ottoman defeat at Svetigrad	Albania, Ottomans
1450	Ottoman siege of Krujë	Albania, Ottomans
1451	Treaty of Gaeta	Albania, Naples
1452	Ottoman invasion repelled	Albania, Ottomans
1454	Albanian defeat at Berat	Albania, Ottomans
1456	Ottoman defeat at Svetigrad	Albania, Ottomans
1457	Ottoman defeat at Ujebardha	Albania, Ottomans
1461	Albanian assistance to Ferdinand I of Naples	Albania, Naples
1464	Albanian victory at Ohrid. Abandoned crusade	Albania, Ottomans, Venice, The Pope
1466	Ottoman siege of Krujë, Ottomans build castle at Elbasan	Albania, Ottomans
1467	Ottoman campaign at Krujë and Durrës. Skanderbeg dies	Albania, Ottomans, Venice
1468	Krujë and Shkodër ceded to Venice	Albania, Venice
1478	Ottomans conquer Krujë	Ottomans, Venice
1480	Albania used to launch Ottoman attack on Italy	Ottomans, Venice
1481	Ottomans conquer Shkodër	Ottomans, Venice

15 - Albania

Rounding off the story of the Conqueror's enemies in the Balkans we turn to Albania.

The territory we today associate with Albania was in antiquity populated by a tribe of Illyrians, a Greek people who were included into the Roman Empire in the second century BC.

At that time the area was part of the province of Illyricum, which later became Dalmatia.

Roman suzerainty continued for centuries and when the Roman Empire was split between the Western and Eastern Empire in the fourth century, Dalmatia became part of the Eastern Empire, or Byzantium, even though religiously it was still attached to Rome rather than Constantinople.

The original Greek population was gradually supplemented by Slavs during the seventh century, as was the case with all of western Balkans and eventually, in the eight century, internal strife in the Catholic Church led to the area falling under the See of Constantinople rather than Rome.

The First Bulgarian Empire (see Chapter 12) also included Albania and after the fall of the First Bulgarian Empire the area returned to Byzantine suzerainty.

A distinct Albanian identity was first recorded in the eleventh century when the Byzantine historian Michael Attaliates specifically mentioned the 'Albanoi' as having participated in a revolt against Byzantium.

The weakened state of Byzantium towards the end of the twelfth century created opportunities in the outlying provinces and while the Second Bulgarian Empire started to form inland, a small principality, named Arbanon, formed around the town and fortress of Krujë.

The details are sketchy, but the formation of the principality is normally credited to one Progon, an official who held the fortress in Krujë on behalf of Byzantium. Progon was still a vassal of Byzantium when the principality was formed in c.1190, but after the Byzantine Empire was dissolved following the Fourth Crusade in 1204, the area, as well as western Greece, was given to Venice when the Byzantine Empire was distributed between the victors.

The Venetian's intentions were unclear, but soon turned out to only cover the coastal cities, which in the case of Arbanon meant the port of Durrës - Durazzo in Italian - while the hinterland remained as was.

By then the throne had passed to Progon's son Gjin Progoni who in turn was succeeded by his brother Dimitri Progoni in 1208.

With Byzantium gone for the time being, and the Venetians having taken what they wanted, the Principality in principle became autonomous, but it seems to have bound itself to the Despotate of Epirus, which had formed on the Greek west Coast.

Dimitri Progoni is the first of the rulers of Arbanon of which we have any details. He married Komnena Nemanjić, daughter of Stefan II Nemanjić of Serbia, allying Arbanon and Serbia.

As a safeguard towards further Latin ambitions Dimitri Progoni at a point in time approached the Pope to convert the Principality back to Catholicism, but nothing came of it in the end.

On Dimitri Progoni's death the power was temporarily left with his wife, Komnena Nemanjić, who soon remarried to Gregory Kamonas, a local - Orthodox - noble.

Komnena Nemanjić's influence on the rule of Arbanon ensured that the Principality was tightly allied with Serbia, despite a Serbian attempt to take the town of Shkodër, and the principality became a vassal of Serbia rather than Epirus.

Gregory Kamonas and Komnena Nemanjić had no male offspring, but their daughter had married a local noble, named Golem, who took the throne on Gregory Kamonas' death in 1253.

At that time Arbanon's neighbour in the south, the Despotate of Epirus was fighting a bitter war with the Empire of Nicaea as to who should be the dominant Greek successor state to Byzantium.

Golem was drawn into the conflict and first supported Michael II Komnenos Doukas of Epirus. The Albanians blocked the Nicaeans at Kostur, but John III Doukas Vatatzes of Nicaea convinced Golem to change sides on promises of continued autonomy.

When the two warring Greek empires soon after signed a peace treaty in which Epirus accepted Nicaean suzerainty, the Albanian fortress in Krujë was handed over to Nicaean troops.

But soon the hostilities broke out again when the Nicaeans took Durrës, which had been taken from the Venetians by Epirus in 1213, and then continued to Krujë, ignoring the promised autonomy of the Albanians and putting an effective end to the Principality of Arbanon.

The Albanians once again sided with Epirus, but others had designs on the area.

Manfred, the King of Sicily, had his own designs on western Greece and in 1457 he invaded Arbanon.

Michael II Komnenos Doukas could not fight on two fronts, so he arranged the marriage of his daughter, Helena, to Manfred, giving Manfred's territories in Arbanon as her dowry, thus confirming Manfred's rule.

Manfred and Michael II Komnenos Doukas now became allies against the Nicaeans, but lost a key battle in 1259, after which the Nicaeans recaptured most of Arbanon, but a counter offensive in 1261 - while Michael VIII Palaiologos was occupied by the Reconquest of Constantinople - restored Manfred to power.

From the outset Manfred respected the semi-autonomy of the state, appointing local nobles in key posts and also using Albanian troops in his campaigns on mainland Italy.

But in 1266 Manfred was killed in the Battle of Benevento and his domains - by right of conquest - were now in the possession of Charles I of Naples, who had even bigger ambitions, namely the conquest of Constantinople itself.

However, the local Albanian nobles saw an opportunity for renewed independence. Michael II Komnenos Doukas first tried to move on Albania, filling the power vacuum, but the nobles opposed him and refused to hand over the local strongholds. Next came emissaries from Charles I of Naples, but they too were repelled.

For a few years the locals ruled themselves, but in the early 1270s Charles I of Naples sent negotiators to Albania, promising that the area would retain its autonomy under his nominal rule, and in 1272 an agreement was signed.

Charles I became King of Albania in 1272, but his rule soon turned out to give the locals anything but autonomy. The most important official offices were given to Charles I of Naples's entourage and local land was confiscated and reallocated to Italian lords.

The Albanian nobles now approached Emperor Michael VIII Palaiologos in Constantinople, who had a vested interest in stopping Charles I of Naples attempts to gain a foothold in the Balkans.

In 1274 the Byzantines attacked and conquered most of Albania, leaving Charles I of Naples with only a few isolated inland pockets under his control.

But Charles I of Naples had no intention of giving up, despite a papal edict not to attack Byzantium. He found a new ally in Nikephoros I Komnenos Doukas, the new despot of Epirus, and together they invaded Albania, laying siege to the stronghold of Berat.

The Byzantine Emperor now counterattacked, and his attack forced the troops of Charles I of Naples and Nikephoros I Komnenos Doukas to abandon the siege of Berat and once again retreat into the few remaining strongholds under their control.

This failed attempt at taking Albania convinced Charles I of Naples that Constantinople could not be taken by land. Instead, he entered into a grand-alliance with Venice which - now with papal blessing as a crusade - would assemble a great fleet and attack Constantinople by sea.

But despite a massive build-up of ships and troops his plans came to nothing. The fleet was assembled in Sicily and during the Sicilian Vespers in 1282 it was partly destroyed, putting a permanent stop to Charles I's ambitions towards Byzantium.

Although the Italians continued to control the isolated enclaves in Albania for some time, the Byzantines gradually took control of the country and by the 1280s all of Albania was back as a Byzantine province with some level of autonomy.

In 1296 the Serbians captured Durrës, but they were thrown out by a local revolt in 1304. But the pressure from the emerging Serbian state was growing and in the 1340s Albania, with the exception of Durrës, was annexed into the Serbian Empire.

But the Serbian Empire was soon in decline, following the Serbian defeat at the Battle of Maritsa in 1371.

Like the rest of the Serbian Empire, Albania became a patchwork of local lords. Prominent amongst them was Karl Topia who had already carved out his own territory in the Durrës area in the years leading up to the fall of the Serbian Empire.

Karl Topia controlled the countryside but not the town of Durrës itself, which was still in the control of the successors of Charles I of Naples.

Over the years Karl Topia tried to capture Durrës several times and he finally succeeded in 1368. But his neighbours in Zeta also had designs on the port city, so they made several attempts to capture it, finally succeeding in 1383.

Karl Topia now turned to the Ottomans and received help from Sultan Murad I, with whose help he regained control of Durrës in 1385. But with the area in turmoil his small principality was in great danger of being overrun, so he allied himself with Venice and shortly after his death, his son, Gjergj, handed Durrës over to Venice for good, now to be known as 'Venetian Albania'.

The rest of Albania was run by local lords ruling without central authority and after the (First) Battle of Kosovo the Ottomans simply annexed it and turned it into a 'sanjak', a fully integrated province of the Empire. The only parts that stayed outside of Ottoman control were the small Venetian enclaves on the coast as Sultan Bayezid I was not in a position to wage war on Venice at that time.

If Albania had stayed like that, it would not have made it into the story of the Conqueror's Enemies. But one man changed that, his name was George Kastrioti, mostly known by his nome de guerre 'Skanderbeg'.

Even though Albania had become an Ottoman province, the local population still maintained their Albanian identity and on occasions there were local revolts against the Ottoman regime. One such revolt took place in the 1420s, when the local lords revolted against the Ottomans immediately following the succession of Murad II to the Ottoman throne.

Murad II put the revolt down, but as was common he asked for hostages to be sent to the Ottoman court to keep the local lords honest. One of the hostages was George Kastrioti, son of Gjon Kastrioti, an Albanian lord and one of the instigators of the revolt.

Life of a hostage at the Ottoman court was not unpleasant. Hostages were treated like visiting nobles and their education was continued while in the Ottoman's care. Apart from not being capable of leaving, they were like welcomed guests and even when they were allowed to leave, some decided to stay.

Exactly what happened with George Kastrioti is unknown. He was around eighteen years of age when he arrived in Edirne in 1423 and in 1428 his father had to officially apologize to the Venetian Senate due to his son fighting on the side of the Ottomans. Somewhere in those five years George Kastrioti must have made a deliberate decision to seek a career in the Ottoman army, as he would not have been forced to fight for the Ottomans.

One possible explanation is that he had little to come home to. He was the youngest son of nine children and had three older brothers, so his prospects at home were probably limited to a life as a landless knight, one amongst many.

As it turned out, George Kastrioti had a talent for warfare. He quickly worked his way through the ranks in the Ottoman army and became a Sipahi, which means that he was a professional cavalry soldier, paid either by a salary or a fief. He was also, as a Sipahi, treated on even terms as a free-born Muslim despite his origins.

His father rebelled against the Ottomans several times, and since George Kastrioti was not punished over this, the Ottomans must have stopped looking at him as a hostage.

When his father rebelled in 1436, he called his son home to participate in the uprising, but George Kastrioti remained loyal to the Sultan and stayed in the Ottoman army. Here he fought in several campaigns for Murad II and he distinguished himself to such an extent that he was compared to the legendary Alexander the Great and given the nickname 'Lord Alexander', 'Iskender Bey' in Turkish which, with the mix-up of languages in the area at the time, became 'Skanderbeg' (Skënderbej in Albanian). We shall know him as such hence forth.

In 1438 Skanderbeg had risen to the title of Wāli - Governor - and for a short period of time even acted as governor in parts of Albania which included his father's domains.

By 1440 Skanderbeg was a Sanjak-bey - district commander - and had responsibility for the Sanjak of Dibra which included Krujë and other parts of north-western Albania. Through this period, he maintained close contact with his only surviving brother, Stanisha, as well as maintaining civil relations with many of the Albanian nobles in the area, and it is perhaps here we shall seek the explanation for what happened next.

During the 'Long Campaign' in the winter of 1443, where the Hungarian army marched through Ottoman Balkans, there was a major skirmish at Niš in Bulgaria. Skanderbeg was fighting on the Ottoman side and after the Ottoman troops were forced to retreat, he simply upped and left the Ottoman army, taking with him his nephew and protégé Hamza Kastrioti and 300 Albanian-born cavalrymen.

Forging a letter from the Sultan he tricked his way into the fortress at Krujë and soon after he forced several smaller fortifications in the area into submission.

Skanderbeg now truly changed his colours. He abjured Islam - indicating that he had at least nominally converted - and declared himself the avenger of Albania.

Sultan Murad II was busy elsewhere, including negotiating the ill-fated peace with Hungary of 1444, so Skanderbeg had some time on his hands.

He assembled the Albanian lords in the town of Lezhë in March of 1444 and here they formed an alliance - later dubbed the League of Lezhë - between the various Albanian lords, agreeing to resist Ottoman suzerainty and fight together as a single army under Skanderbeg's command. All the lords, however, maintained their autonomous rights and there was no central political state or authority over and above the military alliance.

Skanderbeg expected a reaction from Murad II and it was not late in coming once the Sultan had signed the peace agreement with Hungary.

In June of 1444 an expeditionary force under the command of Ali Pasha (the Sultan was in Anatolia with the main army) entered Albania to put the rebellion down.

The Ottoman force was 25,000 strong against which Skanderbeg had an army of perhaps 15,000.

Conventional wisdom would have it that Skanderbeg should have fought a guerrilla war against the numerically superior enemy, utilizing his troop's intimate knowledge of the terrain which is heavily wooded and mountainous in large parts of Albania. But contrary to this, Skanderbeg lined his army up in a defensive position at the plain of Torvioll and to make matters worse; despite having his choice of battlefield, he chose to take position at the bottom of a hill instead of taking the advantageous high ground.

Ali Pasha quickly assessed that a single big assault, led by a cavalry charge and followed by infantry, would route the Albanians, so he attacked head on.

The Albanians gave way and moved to pre-set positions from which they could push the Ottoman wings inwards, creating a crescent shape with the Ottomans in the middle. Then Skanderbeg sprang his trap.

Hidden in the woods behind the Ottomans were 3,000 Albanian cavalry and once they unleashed an attack on the Ottoman rear and flanks, the Ottoman army dispersed and fled, Ali Pasha narrowly escaping the battle himself and the Ottomans taking heavy casualties compared to limited Albanian loses.

Skanderbeg had stated his intent, and his victory, with little else to cheer about, was praised in the Christian World. Skanderbeg's - in light of bigger events - small revolt had become a powerful symbol of resistance against the Ottomans, a symbol which only increased in value when Murad II annihilated the Hungarians at Varna later that same year.

15 - Albania

In light of his victory at Varna, Murad II decided to talk sense to Skanderbeg, He sent him a letter, reminding him of how he had been taken in by the Sultan, and also reminding him of the mighty force which stood against him. But Skanderbeg responded back that he was with Jesus Christ and thus was fighting with the mightier force. Skanderbeg assumed that the response would be violent, and he was not wrong.

Murad II created a new expeditionary force, 9,000 strong and led by Firuz Pasha. Their immediate task was to block Skanderbeg from marching on Macedonia and expanding his territory, but Firuz Pasha became bold. He was told that the Albanian army had been disbanded for the winter, which was partially true, and decided to surprise Skanderbeg with a quick attack on Krujë.

Skanderbeg had indeed disbanded part of the army, but his personal retinue, 3,500 men strong, had stayed with him and they were not surprised at all.

Rather, they were well prepared for the Ottoman incursion and had prepared an ambush in a valley near Mount Mokra in the Prizren area of Kosovo.

The valley was narrow and with few main routes, all of which had been blocked by the Albanians. The Ottomans proceeded further and further into the valley and when they were practically immobile due to the blocked roads, the Albanians attacked from the surrounding woodlands causing the Ottomans to panic and flee. Firuz Pasha was killed in action as were many of the Ottoman troops, once again offset with very limited casualties on the Albanian side.

Once again Skanderbeg was the darling of the Christian World. The Pope pronounced him 'Defender of Christendom' but of real value were ambassadors from Alfonso V of Aragon, one of the most powerful regents of the times and an ally of the kind that would eventually prove useful to Skanderbeg.

Now Murad II changed his tactics. A small mobile army like Skanderbeg's depends heavily on local support for shelter and supplies, so the Sultan decided to fight a war of attrition, laying Albania bare and terrorize the population.

A fresh expeditionary force of 15,000 cavalry under Mustafa Bey entered Albania in the summer of 1446. Mustafa Bey split the army in two; one part was sent out to accomplish the main mission of burning and pillaging and the other half took up a fortified position as a reserve and foraging point. They camped at Otonetë on the (modern day) border between Albania and Macedonia.

Instead of pursuing the raiders, Skanderbeg instead led his army of 5,000 to Otonetë. Here the Ottoman camp was not expecting any trouble and was on low alert. Skanderbeg's troops tore through the camp and turned it into a slaughterhouse. 5,000 Ottoman soldiers lost their lives, and all the expeditionary force's supplies were lost to the Albanians.

Without a secure point of re-supply, the Ottoman raiders left the country and took up patrol duty on the border instead.

Skanderbeg had now defeated the Ottomans three times in three years, but while most in the Christian World sung his praise, the Venetians were becoming anxious.

Initially they had supported Skanderbeg's revolt. It was good business to have him between their positions on the Dalmatian coast and the Ottomans, but as his power increased and he became the dominant force in the area, they started to suspect his ambitions in terms of their possessions, in particular Venetian Albania and the profitable harbour city of Durrës.

The pretext for war was trivial given the stakes, but in essence, an Albanian noble, Lekë Zaharia, had been murdered by another noble who had designs on his properties. Lekë Zaharia's mother had inherited his estate which included several castles on the border to Venetian Albania, first amongst them the castle at Dagnum.

After various intrigues, in which members of the Albanian alliance fought each other - including at the wedding of Skanderbeg's sister - Lekë Zaharia's mother donated the property and the castles to Venice, who were quick to take possession.

Skanderbeg asked Venice to return the castles, which he considered to be of significant strategic importance, but the Venetians refused and offered to buy them off him. With support from Alfonso V of Aragon and in alliance with Đurađ Branković of Serbia and Stefan I Crnojević of Zeta - who had their own issues with Venice over Zeta (Montenegro) - Skanderbeg decided to attack.

In December of 1447 he laid siege to the castle at Dagnum and blocked the inland access routes to and from Durrës, forcing Venice to supply it from the sea.

The Venetians were probably not expecting this level of aggression and as a reaction they put a prize on Skanderbeg's head promising a monthly pension of 100 gold ducats to anyone who could kill him.

The situation was bizarre. The only fighting force in the Balkans seemingly capable to cause injury to the Ottomans was now fighting the only force capable of checking the Ottomans at sea. The Sultan must have thought he was dreaming.

Sensing that Skanderbeg was at his weakest, Murad II launched a major assault on the fortress at Svetigrad, which barred his preferred marching route into Albania. Skanderbeg had left a small detachment of his army to keep an eye on the Ottomans but could not relieve the garrison, which held on for a considerable time against the full force of the Sultan's besieging army.

15 - Albania

In the meantime, Skanderbeg maintained pressure on the Venetians. He crossed the river Drin and approached Shkodër, forcing the Venetians to come out and meet him.

As was the norm by now, Skanderbeg was outnumbered, but he was facing a mercenary army - partly Albanian - whereas his battle-hardened army was fighting for their cause.

The two armies came together in a mighty clash, Skanderbeg deployed the better tactics but the Venetians had superior in numbers. The battle raged for hours, but then the Venetians broke ranks, a move not uncommon with mercenaries if a battle became to drawn out or the outcome too unpredictable.

Taking heavy casualties, the Venetians were now stretched to defend their strongholds, however they had an ace up their sleeve.

On the basis that my enemy's enemy is my friend, the Venetians had, earlier in the conflict, made contact with the Ottomans, urging them to attack Skanderbeg from the rear. The only thing holding the Ottomans back was the fortress at Svetigrad, but that had finally surrendered on the very same day, 23rd of July, that the Albanians had defeated the Venetian in front of Shkodër.

Sultan Murad II was by now aware that Janos Hunyadi was moving south towards Serbia, so he took the main army and swung away towards Kosovo, eventually meeting the Hungarians at the Second Battle of Kosovo in October of that same year.

Svetigrad was now manned by an Ottoman contingent and an expeditionary force of 15,000 headed for Albania commanded by Mustafa Pasha.

Skanderbeg had earlier left a small force of 5,000 to shadow the Ottomans and this force now joined up with the Albanian main force arriving from Shkodër.

The Albanians were still outnumbered, but they engaged the Ottoman expeditionary force on the border to Macedonia. According to tradition two selected champions first fought man-to-man, with the Albanian winning, after which the army came together.

Once again, the superior discipline and motivation of the Albanians won the day, sending the Ottomans fleeing, twelve high ranking officers including Mustafa Pasha were captured and later ransomed.

That was enough to send the Venetians to the negotiation table. An uneasy peace agreement was signed in early October, leaving Dagnum with Venice, but prescribing a range of compensations in the form of money and supplies. It is worth noticing that Skanderbeg only represented some of the Albanian lords at the peace conference, another group was represented by Gjergj Arianiti, Skanderbeg's own father-in-law who, like others, had broken out of the Albanian Alliance.

With peace in hand, and even though skirmishes continued for some time, Skanderbeg now had his back free to join the Hungarians at Kosovo, but Đurađ Branković of Serbia had no appetite for the campaign and barred Skanderbeg access through Serbia. The Albanians never reached the battle, which became a resounding Ottoman victory and the last grand single battle attempt at pushing the Ottomans out of Europe.

Two years later, in 1450, the Ottomans were back in Albania. Despite Albanian attempts to retake the fortress at Svetigrad, it was still held by the Ottomans providing them with easy access into Albania.

This time the Sultan came himself, accompanied by his heir apparent, Mehmed, and an army of some 100,000 men with a full siege train, including cannon.

The target was Krujë, the key mountain stronghold of Skanderbeg.

With only around 12,000 troops left, Skanderbeg could do little to stop the Ottomans, so he maximized his power by leaving 4,000 troops inside the fort (enough to man its walls) while he set off with the rest to consistently harass the Ottoman supply and communications lines.

The Venetians in Durrës kept Skanderbeg supplied, while the Venetians in Shkodër did likewise for the Ottomans, so at least someone gained something from the whole affair.

The Ottomans arrived in May, and it was to be a long summer for all involved. Murad II had powerful mortars founded on the spot, hurling 400-pound stone balls against the fortress walls. But the fortress was solidly built, and furthermore, was sitting on the top of a rock and practically impossible to undermine as well as difficult to storm.

And Skanderbeg was not idle either. Before the Ottomans arrived the Albanian morale had been low, but luckily - so the priests reported - people had seen cherubs and angels flying over Albania and Skanderbeg himself claimed that he had received a vision of St.George handing him a flaming sword with which to *'destroy the enemies of true religion.'*

Skanderbeg - as far as is known, without a flaming sword in hand, started to harass the Ottoman camp. Although Murad II had sent scouts out to keep an eye on him, he managed to make a daring dusk raid into the Ottoman camp, barely escaping with his life intact. Murad II now ordered a general attack on the fortress, but the attackers were repelled.

Having now learned Skanderbeg's intentions, the Ottomans sent a sizeable contingent - commanded by Prince Mehmed - out to block Skanderbeg's access road to the Ottoman camp. Skanderbeg sent a small decoy force against it while he himself led the main force around the Ottoman camp and attacked it from the other side.

An Ottoman attempt to break down the main gate of the fortress had also been a failure and in order to avert further attacks from Skanderbeg, some of the cannon had now been turned outwards from the Ottoman camp, easing pressure on the fortress itself.

But Skanderbeg was not done yet. He once more approached the Ottoman camp, but this time a force of no less than 8,000 Ottoman cavalry waited for him and chased him off. What they did not know was that Skanderbeg had divided his forces into three groups and while he retreated in front of the Ottomans, the other two groups once again attacked the Ottoman camp from other directions.

Murad II now turned to bribery. He offered Vrana Konti - commander of the fortress - a considerable fortune to surrender the fortress and emissaries were sent to Skanderbeg himself to offer him an annual stipend should he surrender Albania to Murad II. Both men refused.

After a final failed assault Murad II gave up. His camp was in disarray after the Albanian attacks, morale was low, disease rampant and winter was coming. At the end of October, the Ottomans left. Shortly after his return to Edirne, Sultan Murad II died.

The Ottomans may have been exhausted, but Skanderbeg was effectively out of resources. He went begging for help and received some assistance from Ragusa, the Pope and Venice, but he needed more so he approached Alfonso V of Aragon.

In 1451, the first year of Mehmed II's reign as sultan, Skanderbeg and Alfonso V of Aragon signed the 'Treaty of Gaeta'. In this treaty Skanderbeg accepted the overall suzerainty of Naples, but with a promise of autonomy and self-rule. If any of the cities in Albania were to be attacked and needed military assistance, then such cities would be handed over to Naples. In addition, Skanderbeg promised to only buy salt from Naples, but at the same price as was offered by the Ottomans, giving us a rare insight into the fact that the warring parties quite happily continued trading with each other.

In addition to Skanderbeg, nine other Albanian lords signed similar agreements with Alfonso V of Aragon, again demonstrating that the League of Lezhë effectively had been disbanded after only six years despite the distinct success in its stated purpose of fighting the Ottomans.

Sultan Mehmed II's focus on Constantinople and other larger issues gave Skanderbeg a bit of time. Although a small expeditionary force was repelled in 1452 the Albanians did not see much of the Ottomans and instead started to receive contingents of troops from Naples. Skanderbeg himself became the father of a male heir, Gjon Kastrioti II in 1454.

In that same year he decided to improve his situation further by capturing the fortress of Berat, which the Ottomans had captured in 1450.

The Albanians laid siege, utilizing a specialized unit of artillerists arrived from Naples, and the situation soon became difficult for the Ottoman commander. Negotiations were had, and the Ottoman commander promised to surrender the castle unless Ottoman reinforcements arrived within a month.

Matters seemingly settled, Skanderbeg left half his army - including the artillery - under the command of Muzaka Thopia to keep an eye on the castle and withdrew with the rest of the army.

In the meantime, messengers had reached the Ottoman army campaigning in Serbia and a detachment of 25,000 were sent in relief of Berat under the command of Ishak Bey Evrenoz.

When the Ottoman relief forces arrived, they caught the Albanians napping. Nobody had expected reinforcements to arrive, so the Albanians were resting and passing time when the Ottomans came upon them. Wholesale slaughter ensued in which most of the besieging force was wiped out, including its commander Muzaka Thopia and most of the artillerists.

Skanderbeg received alarmed messages and turned around, but by the time he reached the scene it was all over and the Ottoman relief-forces had retreated. All he could do was treat the wounded, bury the dead and give up the siege. For once he had been outsmarted.

The few remains of loyalty and alliance in Albania now disappeared. The alliance was history; several of the Albanian lords decided to support the Ottomans and one of them, Moisi Arianit Golemi, actually fled to the Ottomans to return later.

It was to be two years before the Ottomans returned, this time led by Moisi Arianit Golemi and a contingent of 15,000 troops, partly Albanian.

Skanderbeg knew Moisi Arianit Golemi well, and was aware that the opposite was also true, so he did not try his usual tricks, but rather shadowed the advancing Ottoman force until they reached Oranik and chose to fight in the same place he had defeated Mustafa Pasha in 1448.

The numbers were even, possibly slightly in favour of the Ottomans, but Skanderbeg had the advantage in cavalry and the Albanian's powerful opening cavalry charge showed to be the determining factor.

Beaten, Moisi Arianit Golemi led the remains of his army away from the battle and returned to Edirne. Here he was not particularly welcome, so he repented and returned to Albania where Skanderbeg forgave him and once again enrolled him in his army.

Later that same year Mehmed II was defeated before Belgrade, but rather than providing some well needed respite in Albania, Mehmed II's long term strategy now became a top priority to him, and that strategy very much included Albania.

We shall return to the subject in the next chapter, but in essence Mehmed II had his eyes on Rome and with access overland seemingly out of reach after his defeat before Belgrade and without naval superiority outside the easternmost part of the Mediterranean Sea, Mehmed II's strategic plan was to launch an invasion by crossing to the Italian mainland across the narrowest possible point of the Adriatic Sea, and well away from Venice. The perfect spot for that was Albania.

It was thus not by coincidence that Mehmed II's first military campaign after the defeat at Belgrade was to send a considerable force into Albania to pave the way for his strategy.

The year before Skanderbeg's own nephew and protégé Hamza Kastrioti - who had been with him since they both deserted the Ottoman army in 1443 - deserted back to the Ottomans and Mehmed II was not late in utilizing his intimate knowledge of Albania and Skanderbeg. Also in command was Isak Bey Evrenoz who had led the Ottoman relief of Berat in 1454, and behind them they had perhaps up to 50,000 (contemporary sources being inherently unreliable on the subject) Ottoman troops.

Up against two veteran commanders (one of whom knew his tactical thinking as well as anyone) and seriously outnumbered Skanderbeg had to come up with something new.

First, he shadowed the Ottoman army's progress, as he had done with the expeditionary force sent the year prior, and then he disappeared.

The Ottoman scouts found no trace of Skanderbeg or his army which seemed to have vanished into thin air. They marched on in the direction of Krujë but decided to put up camp in a naturally well protected mountain area instead of proceeding to besiege the fortress.

From their camp the Ottomans sent scouts in all directions and penetrated more deeply into Venetian territory to find Skanderbeg. But they found nothing. The Pope received a message from Skanderbeg that Albania had been lost, news which soon reached the Ottomans as well and finally they concluded that Skanderbeg had fled and his army had dispersed. On that basis they stood down and prepared to move on.

But whereas Skanderbeg's army had indeed dispersed, it was not because he had fled and neither was it in anything but very good order.

Skanderbeg had split his army up into several small groups, each of which had put enough distance between themselves and the Ottoman to remain invisible. On a pre-agreed signal, they would reconvene and once Skanderbeg had ensured that the Ottomans had taken the bait, he sent the signal and his army reformed close to the Ottoman camp, now only lightly guarded.

The Albanians split into three attack groups and without warning they attacked the Ottoman camp. Totally unprepared the Ottoman troops were overwhelmed. They were forced towards the centre of the camp, seemingly surrounded by an enemy which was supposed to be non-existent.

Half the Ottoman army were killed, and an enormous number of prisoners were taken, In addition the Albanians gained all the Ottoman's supplies and treasure making the battle the most successful of all fought by Skanderbeg.

Isak Bey Evrenoz was among the few who got away, but Hamza Kastrioti was among the prisoners, and he was sent to Naples to be kept under arrest. It was only his kinship with Skanderbeg that kept him alive.

But Skanderbeg's victory was not easily won, He was basically out of funds and what he received from Alfonso V of Aragon did not cover his costs, The Pope tried to help him, but he was not at the time in a particularly good financial situation himself and the Venetians withheld the funds they had promised, even under threat from the Pope.

A good development was that ambassadors exchanged with Mehmed II obtained a peace agreement valid for three years. This allowed Skanderbeg to lend support to his Nepalese overlords when Alfonso V of Aragon died and left his realms to his son Ferdinand I. A civil war followed and Skanderbeg played a critical role in securing the throne of Naples for Ferdinand I.

But as grateful as Ferdinand I was, he was not his father and whereas Alfonso V of Aragon had long harboured an idea of a big crusade against the Ottomans, with Skanderbeg and Albania playing a critical role, Ferdinand I had no such ambitions leaving Skanderbeg with the tactical advantage but without a strategic objective.

Whereas Ferdinand I may have been lacking initiative, the Pope had plenty. Pius II had for a long time wanted to start a new crusade against the Ottomans, but he could not get the critically important Venetians to buy in. That changed when the Venetians declared war on the Ottoman Empire in 1463.

The Venetians now agreed to support the crusade. They sent troops to Skanderbeg and promised to supply a grand fleet to ferry 20,000 troops from Ancona to Albania, from where the crusade would start.

Skanderbeg received the Venetian troops and now commanded an army of 20,000, the biggest army he had ever had and whilst the other half of the crusading army assembled in Ancona, he started things off by softening up the borders Ottoman-style.

The Albanian/Venetian raiders penetrated deep into Macedonia where they successfully skirmished with the Ottoman forces sent to meet them and they obtained a symbolic victory at Ohrid. But apart from irritating the Sultan, the incursions into Macedonia did not achieve anything material and then they received bad news.

On 12 August 1464, the Venetian fleet finally arrived at Ancona, but on 15 August the Pope died and on 18 August the Venetians left for home, where the crusader fleet was disarmed and put in storage.

Skanderbeg was once again alone and without an overall strategy.

The same could not be said for Mehmed II. He knew exactly where he was going and the war with Venice was his ticket to attack not only Skanderbeg's inland fortresses but also the Venetian possessions on the Albanian coast.

Mehmed II maintained a sabbatical year in 1465, but in February 1466 he was on the march again. The destination was Albania and the immediate target was Krujë.

But Krujë was a tactical objective only. Mehmed II had a strategic objective in mind. He was quite happy to wear Albania and Venice down and the way to do it was to leave the mountains to Skanderbeg but take permanent control of the lowlands and build a strong castle to defend the Ottoman possessions.

The Ottomans, however, first laid siege to Krujë. The fortress as per usual held out, but Skanderbeg was so pressed for funds that he personally went to Italy to convince the Pope to help him out. Apart from promises nothing came of it, but the Venetians did send reinforcements to Krujë.

Having established the siege of Krujë, Mehmed II left the siege in charge of Ballaban Badera - an Albanian - while he himself went to Elbasan, his chosen site for the new castle.

Elbasan is located on the Shkumbi River, which provides access directly into the Adriatic Sea and the site was only 48km from the Venetian port of Durrës.

On his way to Elbasan, Mehmed II's troops looted the countryside, burned the crops and killed the livestock, deliberately putting pressure on the civilian population who they - not without reason - suspected of supporting Skanderbeg's rebels.

Not unlike his previous fortress-projects Mehmed II had the new fortress built in a month, completing it in July. He then set up the administrative infrastructure and the military establishment necessary to maintain the Ottoman supremacy and then he left.

The Ottomans maintained the siege of Krujë, but with winter approaching and Mehmed II having left the theatre, Skanderbeg - with Venetian help - attacked the Ottoman camp and annihilated the Ottoman besiegers including their commander Ballaban Badera.

On Venetian insistence Skanderbeg then proceeded to the new Ottoman fortress at Elbasan, but the fortress was solidly built and the Albanians lacked heavy siege weapons so the siege was eventually abandoned.

The 1466 campaign had been a mixed bag. The Ottoman siege of Krujë had been unsuccessful, and they had taken serious losses when Skanderbeg attacked, but they had achieved their strategic objective of bringing large parts of the Albanian countryside under control and built a strong fortress deep inside Albanian territory and within striking distance of the Venetian ports on the Adriatic coast. That winter Mehmed II probably slept better than Skanderbeg.

However, Mehmed II had not forgotten about Albania, quite on the contrary. The following spring he was back at the head of his army. He was once again heading for Krujë, but as per the previous year he had secondary objectives.

The Ottoman devastation of the Albanian countryside the year before had left the civilian population in dire straits, physically and emotionally. To give them a chance to head to the mountains ahead of the advancing

Ottoman army, Skanderbeg launched a series of skirmishes and raids which, however, had little military effect.

The 1467 expedition was not really about besieging Krujë, it was more of a power demonstration and really meant for the Venetians rather than the Albanians.

Although the Ottomans did lay siege to Krujë, it was really only to keep the Albanians in place while Mehmed II continued to the Venetian city of Durrës. Here he bombarded the city without any sincere designs to try to capture it and he then pillaged the countryside outside both Durrës and Shkodër before he picked up the forces besieging Krujë and marched on.

The point made by Mehmed II was that with control of the Albanian countryside and with his new fortress at Elbasan, he could reach anything he wanted in Albania. He was 48 km from the Adriatic Sea, 140 kilometres from Brindisi in Italy and to further illustrate the issue he sent raiders from Albania along the coast and deep into Croatia.

With the Ottomans gone Skanderbeg tried to regain control of the interior, but in the winter of 1467, he fell ill with a fever and on 17 January 1468 he died.

There was no suitable successor to Skanderbeg. His son Gjon Kastrioti II did not command the authority and respect offered to his father and he had to leave Albania and live in exile in Italy after his father's death.

The fact of the matter was that the League of Lezhë had long since been dysfunctional and it was only the loyalty to Skanderbeg as a person which made concerted Albanian resistance against the Ottomans possible.

The Venetians were as aware of this as any, so they convinced Skanderbeg's widow - the only remaining authority - to hand over both Krujë and the other remaining Albanian fortresses under Skanderbeg's control to Venice, the only real power in the area capable of defending them.

After twenty-five years of powerful leadership and - relative - freedom, Albania had effectively ceased to exist as a political entity. The interior was controlled by the Ottomans and the coastal areas by the Venetians leaving little room for autonomy.

Mehmed II conquered Krujë and Shkodër from the Venetians in 1478 and 1481 respectively. Durrës was taken by the Ottomans in 1501, thirty years after the death of Mehmed II, making all of Albania an Ottoman province.

The Ottoman suzerainty over Albania lasted until the war of independence broke out in 1912 and Albania became independent in 1914, but a combination of internal strife - not uncommon when a country regains its freedom after a long period of suppression - and WW I threw the country into chaos in which several invaders came and went and finally Albania ended up first Italian and then split up between different states.

But the Albanians revolted, they insisted on their own state, and with American help - and after several successive governments - they succeeded in forming a republic in 1924, followed by a kingdom in 1928.

Once again, a World War tore Albania apart. First Italy invaded, Mussolini considering Albania part of the Roman Empire, and after the Italian capitulation in 1943 the Germans moved in.

A significant resistance movement was now in operation spearheaded by the Communist Party and when the Germans were expelled in 1944 the communist leader, Enver Hoxha, emerged as the strong man of Albania, forming a totalitarian communist state.

Albania became the most isolated and estranged nation state in Europe. Any internal dissent was gruesomely repressed and interaction with the outside world was limited and strictly controlled.

It was only in 1992 Albania, as the last of the countries behind the Iron Curtain, re-entered society. Since then, Albania has been a democratic republic, making quantum leaps towards full integration into twenty-first century Europe.

PART 6

THE POPE AND THE CRUSADER KNIGHTS

16 - THE POPE
17 - THE CRUSADER KNIGHTS
18 - THE OTTOMAN EMPIRE AFTER MEHMED II

Part 6 - The Pope and the Crusader Knights

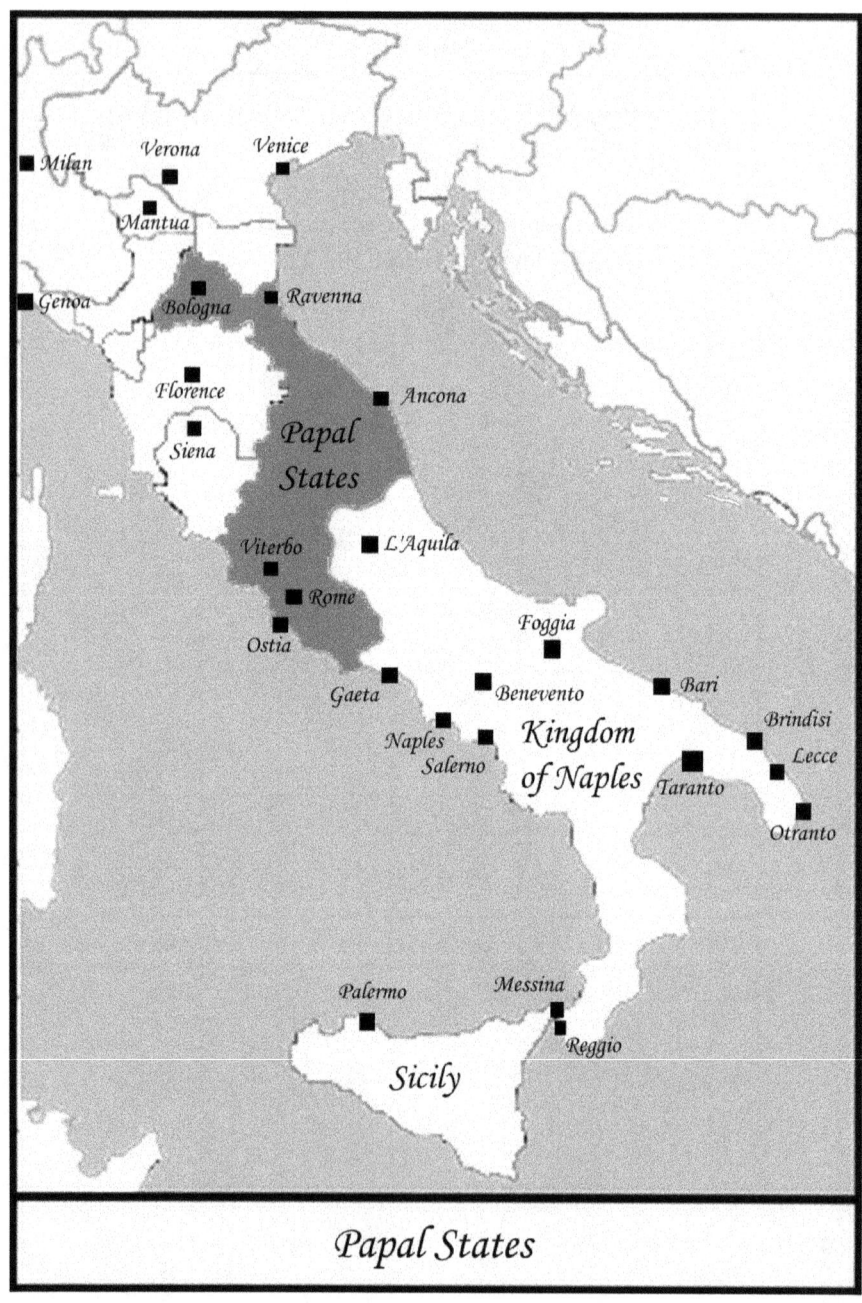

Papal States

16 - THE POPE

CRITICAL TIMELINE

Year	Event	Involved Parties
64	Persecution of Christians in Rome	Roman Empire
301	Christianity becomes State Religion in Armenia	Armenia
311	Emperor Constantine allows Christianity in Roman Empire. Miltiades is first official Bishop of Rome	Roman Empire
314	Sylvester I is first officially elected Bishop of Rome	Roman Empire
324	Foundation of Constantinople as a Christian city. San Giovanni in Laterano becomes the official Arch Basilica and the Lateran Palace the seat of the Bishop of Rome.	Roman Empire
325	Council of Nicaea	Roman Empire
380	Christianity becomes only official religion of Roman Empire	Roman Empire
381	First Council of Constantinople. Constantinople becomes a see	Roman Empire
395	Roman Empire split into Eastern (Byzantine) and Western (Roman) part	Rome Byzantium
410	Rome is sacked by Visigoths under Alaric, Western Emperor moves to Ravenna	Rome Visigoths
439	Vandals establish kingdom in northern Africa with Carthage as capital	Rome Vandals
440	Leo I becomes pope	Rome
451	Battle of Catalaunum	Rome Visigoths Huns
452	Pope Leo I meets Attila at Mantua	Rome Huns
455	Vandal sack of Rome	Rome Vandals
476	Odoacer becomes King of Italy	Rome
493	Theodoric becomes Ostrogoth King of Italy	Rome Ostrogoths
494	Pope Gelasius I issues *Duo Sunt* letter and start questioning Monophysitism in Constantinople	Rome Byzantium
519	Reunification of Western and Eastern churches	Rome Byzantium
526	Felix IV becomes first politically appointed pope	Rome
536	John II is first pope to change his name	Rome
536	Byzantine invasion of Rome	Rome Byzantium
545	Pope Vigilius is forcefully brought to Constantinople	Rome Byzantium
550	Ostrogoth sack of Rome	Rome Ostrogoths
553	Second Council of Constantinople. Compromise agreed on Monothelitism	Rome Byzantium
568	Lombards first appear in Italy	Rome Lombards
638	*Ecthesis* is issued as an Imperial Edict	Byzantium

16 - The Pope

Year	Event	Involved Parties
648	*Type of Constans* is issued	Rome / Byzantium
649	Lateran Council condemns *Type of Constans*	Rome / Byzantium
653	Pope Martin I is brought as prisoner to Constantinople	Rome / Byzantium
655	Battle of the Masts	Byzantium / Muslim Empire
663	Emperor Constans II enters Rome	Rome / Byzantium
674	Muslim siege of Constantinople	Byzantium / Muslim Empire
680	Third Council of Constantinople	Rome / Byzantium
692	Quinisext Council	Byzantium
710	Pope Constantine goes to Constantinople	Rome / Byzantium
726	*Iconoclasm* in Constantinople	Byzantium
728	The Donation of Sutri	Rome / Lombards
754	The Donation of Pepin	Rome / Frankia
787	Second Council of Nicaea	Rome / Byzantium
800	Charlemagne becomes Emperor of the Romans	Rome / Roman Empire
812	*Pax Nicephorus*	Roman Empire / Byzantium
818	Lothair I crowned as King of Italy	Rome / Roman Empire
824	*Constitutio Romana* is issued	Rome / Roman Empire
846	Saracens raid St. Peter's Cathedral	Rome / Saracens
849	Battle of Ostia. Foundation of the Leonine City	Rome / Saracens
858	Nicholas I becomes pope. Emperor Louis II submits to the Pope's authority	Rome / Roman Empire
866	The Pope writes *Responsa Nicolai ad consulta Bulgarorum* to Boris I of Bulgaria	Rome / Bulgaria
891	Formosus becomes pope	Rome
897	Cadaver Synod	Rome
904	Pope Sergius II gets elected as pope. Start of the *Saeculum obscurum*	Rome
911	Rollo is baptized	Rome / Normandy
928	Marozia takes Rome. Pope John X is imprisoned	Rome
955	John XII becomes pope	Rome

Part 6 - The Pope and the Crusader Knights

Year	Event	Involved Parties
962	Otto I is crowned as Roman Emperor. *Diploma Otonianum* is issued	Rome, Roman Empire
1032	Benedict IX becomes pope	Rome
1049	Leo IX becomes pope	Rome
1053	Battle of Civitate. The Pope recognizes Norman lords in southern Italy	Rome, Normans
1054	*East-Western Schism*. Break between the Eastern and Western churches	Rome, Byzantium
1066	Guillaume II conquers England under a papal banner	Rome, Normandy, England
1076	The *Walk to Canossa*	Rome, Roman Empire
1084	Norman sack of Rome	Rome, Normans
1095	Council of Clermont. Pope Urban II calls for a crusade to relieve Constantinople	Rome, Byzantium
1099	The First Crusade conquers Jerusalem	Jerusalem
1113	Pope Paschal II confirms the Knights Hospitallers as a religious order	Rome, Jerusalem
1122	Concordat of Worms	Rome, Roman Empire
1128	Agreement hat Kingdom of Sicily is papal fief	Rome, Sicily
1129	The Knights Templar are confirmed as a religious order	Rome, Jerusalem
1137	Roger II unifies Sicily and Naples into Kingdom of Sicily	Sicily
1139	Pope Innocent II recognizes Kingdom of Sicily	Rome, Sicily
1144	Commune of Rome removes the Pope's temporal powers	Rome
1145	Pope Lucius II is killed during street battle in Rome	Rome
1145	Pope Eugene III calls for Second Crusade	Rome, Jerusalem
1155	Frederick I becomes Holy Roman Emperor	Rome, Roman Empire
1156	Treaty of Benevento	Rome, Sicily
1167	Battle of Monte Porzio	Rome, Roman Empire
1176	Battle of Legnano	Rome, Roman Empire
1187	The papal bull *Audita tremendi* starts the Third Crusade	Jerusalem, Roman Empire, France, England

16 - The Pope

Year	Event	Involved Parties
1194	Emperor Henry VI conquers Kingdom of Sicily	Roman Empire Sicily
1198	Teutonic Knights confirmed as a religious order	Rome Jerusalem
1198	Pope Innocent III calls for the Fourth Crusade	Rome Jerusalem
1204	Fourth Crusade conquers Constantinople	Rome Constantinople Venice
1214	Battle of Bouvines	Roman Empire
1218	Fifth Crusade	Rome Roman Empire Jerusalem
1228	Sixth Crusade	Jerusalem Roman Empire
1254	Battle of Foggia	Rome Sicily
1266	Battle of Benevento	Rome House of Anjou Sicily
1274	Council of Lyon	Rome Byzantium
1282	Sicilian Vespers	Sicily Aragon Naples
1291	Fall of Acre	Jerusalem
1300	Jubilee Year in Rome	Rome
1302	Treaty of Caltabellotta	Sicily Naples
1303	Pope Boniface VIII is arrested	Rome France
1305	Pope Clement V is consecrated at Lyon	Rome France
1307	Knights Templars arrested in France	Rome France Knights Templar
1309	Curia is moved to Avignon	Rome France
1310	Henry VII enters Italy	Rome Roman Empire
1312	Knights Templar dissolved	Rome Knights Templar
1328	Louis IV is crowned as Holy Roman Emperor in Rome	Rome Roman Empire
1347	Hungarian invasion of Naples	Naples Hungary
1353	Papal campaign starts in Italy	Rome
1355	Charles IV is crowned as Holy Roman Emperor in Rome	Rome Roman Empire

Part 6 - The Pope and the Crusader Knights

Year	Event	Involved Parties
1366	Savoyard crusade	Rome Ottomans Savoy Bulgaria Byzantium Egypt Venice Knights Hospitaller
1367	Urban V enters Rome	Rome
1378	Pope Urban VI moves the Curia back to Rome	Rome
1396	Battle of Nicopolis	Rome Hungary France Ottomans
1399	Ladislaus of Naples consolidates the Kingdom of Naples	Naples
1408	Conclave at Pisa elects third pope	Rome
1414	Council of Constance	Rome Hungary France Roman Empire
1417	Pope Martin V becomes only pope	Rome
1431	Council of Basel	Rome
1433	Sigismund of Hungary is crowned as Holy Roman Emperor	Rome Roman Empire
1439	Council of Florence	Rome Byzantium
1443	The Long Campaign	Rome Hungary Poland Ottomans
1444	Battle of Varna	Rome Hungary Poland Ottomans
1452	Papal support to Constantinople	Rome Byzantium
1453	Ottoman conquest of Constantinople	Byzantium Ottomans
1456	Pope Callixtus III calls for crusade in support of Belgrade	Rome Hungary Ottomans
1459	Council of Mantua	Rome
1461	Vlad III Dracula raids Ottoman Bulgaria	Wallachia Ottomans
1463	Crusader alliance is formed	Rome Venice Albania Hungary
1464	Pope Pius II dies. Crusade abandoned	Rome

16 - The Pope

Year	Event	Involved Parties
1472	Small papal fleet participate in raid on Smyrna	Rome, Venice
1479	Venice signs peace agreement with Ottoman Empire	Venice, Ottomans
1480	Ottoman army lands at Otranto	Rome, Naples, Ottomans
1481	Sultan Mehmed II dies. Ottoman invasion is abandoned	Rome, Naples, Ottomans

Part 6 - The Pope and the Crusader Knights

16 - The Pope

In the twenty-first century when we look at the Pope, some see an influential spiritual leader, others see an anachronism. The more politically interested may see the leader of a nation state - albeit only spanning a few city blocks in Rome, but we all see a powerful icon, known to practically everybody regardless of their religious belonging.

But in the fifteenth century - in the Conqueror's World - the Pope was much more than that.

The Pope was the ruler of a powerful and significant European state straddling the Italian mainland. He was a landowner in his own right, a politician, a warlord - sometimes in person - and occasionally he was not even the only Pope as there was more than one Pope at various times.

Indeed, at the beginning of the papal institution there was more than one Pope by design, but let us go back to the origins of Christianity and build up the story of the Pope and how he became the enemy of Mehmed II the Conqueror.

The Pope is a bishop, a leader of Christianity, and although we now see that position as something very powerful, even glamorous, it was far from either at the advent of Christianity in the first century AD.

Christianity was not a religion which at its birth was popular with neither the political nor the religious regime. Having its roots solidly inside the Roman Empire, the new religion challenged the establishment, not only at a local level in Palestine, but very much so in the wider perspective of the Empire as a whole.

Jesus of Nazareth challenged the doctrine of the established (Jewish) Church - his cleansing of the Temple in Jerusalem being perhaps the most famous example - and his messages such as 'the meek shall inherit the Earth' did not go down to well with the ruling and political classes.

But his movement obtained a critical mass of followers; enough for them to start spreading out from Palestine and convert new followers, in particular in the bigger cities of the Roman Empire where Jesus' messages sat well with the poor multitudes.

The twelve apostles themselves are attributed with creating several centres of Christianity called 'Sees' or 'Patriarchates', each headed by a leader referred to as Patriarch or Bishop. These centres - called apostolic sees - include cities such as Jerusalem, Rome, Milan, Alexandria, Antioch Athens, Ephesus, Seleucia-Ctesiphon (Bagdad) and Thessaloniki.

The apostle Simon Peter (St. Peter) had taken upon himself the task of bringing Christianity to the capital of the Empire, Rome, and was successful enough to attract the attention of the Emperor, Nero.

In the year 64 the Christian community in Rome was violently suppressed when Nero accused the Christians of having caused the Great Fire of Rome (not unlike the way Hitler used the fire in the Reichstag in 1933 as a pretext for persecuting the Communists). Simon Peter himself was executed; according to tradition by being crucified upside down.

But Christianity was catching on, over time it snaked its way into powerful Roman families. The Kingdom of Armenia, on the outskirts of the Roman Empire, declared Christianity as the state religion in 301 and approximately ten years later Constantine the Great removed all bans on Christianity in the Roman Empire although he himself seems to have lingered between the old and the new religion.

Despite his own position, Constantine the Great decreed that his new imperial capital, Constantinople, should be built as a Christian city with churches rather than temples, and he called the Council of Nicaea in 325.

At the Council of Nicaea the Christian bishops from around the world (which was mainly the Roman Empire) met for the first time to discuss and settle a range of issues, some canonical and some practical.

With its newfound popularity and official recognition, the loosely organised Church needed some formal organization and the most important issue in that regard was to establish the roles and responsibilities of the various sees.

After much debate an official list was made of the four dominant sees; Rome, Alexandria, Antioch and Jerusalem (the latter being more honourable than practical). Each of these sees had a bishop who was responsible for an allocated area, including a range of minor sees. As far as the conclusions of the Council of Nicaea can be interpreted, the bishops of the four sees were equals.

With officialdom also came the (re-) writing of history and as far as the Bishop of Rome was concerned a list of bishops leading back to Simon Peter (now St. Peter) was created. The Bishop of Constantinople - emerging as the key competitor to Rome - did not recognize that St. Peter was the first Bishop of Rome or that he had been ordained in that capacity by Christ himself, but never the less the list contains thirty Bishops of Rome since St. Peter and leading up to the first official bishop, Miltiades. The historical accuracy is questionable, but all of them were saints.

Since the early days of Christianity in Rome there had been internal problems. Fighting over various issues of religious dogma the Church had at times been split and the authority of the Bishop challenged. We now call the alternative leaders 'anti-popes,' although in their own time they would not have been given such a label. The first known anti-pope emerges as early as the beginning of the third century where a priest named Natalius is believed to have been heading a splinter-group in Rome, although he later was reconciled with the official bishop of Rome, Zephyrinus.

Other early anti-popes followed, perhaps the best-known being Hippolytus who in the early part of the third century challenged the authority of no less than three popes, although he was finally reconciled with Pope Pontian. They were both made saints, but they have to share the same feast day.

The first official pope, Miltiades, was followed by Sylvester I, the first Bishop of Rome appointed openly in the now officially recognized religion. He was not a person of particular influence - choosing to participate in the Council of Nicaea by delegates - even though he did supervise the building of the first Christian cathedrals in Rome.

One of the new cathedrals, San Giovanni in Laterano consecrated in 324, became the official Arch Basilica of the Bishop of Rome, a status it maintains to this day. Next to the cathedral is the Lateran Palace, originally a seat for the imperial administration, which was given to Miltiades or Sylvester I by Constantine the Great as the administrative headquarter of the Church and residence of the Bishop of Rome. It maintained that status until the early fourteenth century.

Sylvester I would, however, become famous mainly for something he did not actually do, but we shall return to that later. He was, however, a saint.

Now followed a few Bishops of Rome, leaving no lasting impression although they all, with a single exception, were saints. The odd one out is Liberius (352 - 366) who fell out with the Emperor, Constantius II, and had to live in exile in Greece for two years. The Emperor appointed an anti-pope, Felix II, and although it was the intention that the two bishops should rule together after Liberius had been reconciled with the Emperor, the congregation expelled Felix II and Liberius once again ruled supreme.

Liberius was followed by Damasus I who reign as Bishop of Rome coincided with the reign of Emperor Theodosius I. The Emperor made Christianity the only religion in the Roman Empire, once and for all stamping out any remaining paganism, and he called a new church council in 381, this time to take place in Constantinople, which in the meantime had become the imperial capital. Theodosius I was a strong leader and he was of a mind to consolidate the political and religious power in one single place; Constantinople, under one undisputed leader; himself.

At the Council of Constantinople the list of sees was thus expanded to also include Constantinople and a few other adjustments were made such as granting independence to the See of Cyprus.

Another result of the Council of Constantinople which would have profound implications was that the council adopted a somewhat ambiguous decree which, according to some (the Catholic Church in particular), expresses the opinion that the Bishop of Rome is ranked higher than the other bishops and therefore, by implication, is the head of the Christian Church. According to others (in particular the Orthodox Church) the stipulations only appoint the Bishop of Rome as first among equals. This duality should later form the academic reasons for the schism between the Western (Catholic) and Eastern (Orthodox) churches.

Theodosius I was the last emperor to rule over a united Roman Empire. After his death his sons Honorius and Arcadius became emperors in Rome and Constantinople respectively, effectively splitting the Roman Empire into a western and eastern empire.

If the struggle for religious supremacy between Rome and Constantinople had already been brewing inside the united Roman Empire, the political split only served to further polarize the two sees.

And the political split was not the only issue. Without going too far into the multiple, dogmatic issues that marred early Christianity, there were cultural differences which separated the two factions. First and foremost was that of language.

In Rome, and the Western Roman Empire, people spoke Latin, whereas in Constantinople and the Eastern Empire people spoke Greek. The Bishop of Rome thus believed that Latin should be the unified language of the Church, but the Bishop of Constantinople believed that the Church should speak Greek.

When (Saint) Damasus I died in 384, his succession was a disputed affair which saw an anti-pope (Ursicinus) emerge alongside the official Bishop of Rome; Siricius. According to some sources Siricius was the first Bishop of Rome to be titled 'Pope' (Papa -Father). This is however disputed, but we shall stick to the term from now on. What is undisputed is that he was a saint.

Siricius issued a decree in 385 which stated that priests should live in celibacy, even if they were already married (which was common practice up until that time).

Siricius was followed by Anastasius I, who only reigned for two years before he died. He too is a saint. He in turn was followed by Innocent I who, according to one contemporary source, was indeed the son of Anastasius I. Whether he was or not, he was a saint, and he also lived through a difficult time for Rome, namely the sack of Rome by the Visigoths under Alaric in 410 (see Chapter 9).

Some saw the sacking of Rome as punishment for having abandoned the old gods and making Christianity the only allowed religion, but the Visigoths moved on and although Innocent I had to temporarily tolerate paganism in Rome it soon fizzled out and by his death in 417, order had been restored.

Innocent I was followed by Zosimus, a saint, who only lived as pope for a couple of years. His most important legacy is a decree in which he forbids clerics to frequent public drinking houses.

On Zosimus' death a dispute broke out. On the very same day he was buried, a new pope, Eulalius, was elected, but the clergy was split and another pope, Boniface I was elected subsequently.

The clergy could not decide on the matter and the supporters of both popes turned violent. The matter was thus referred to the Emperor, Honorius, who since the Visigoth invasion had reigned from Ravenna. The Emperor initially pointed to Eulalius, who he argued had been appointed first, but as more violence broke out in Rome he ordered both contenders out of the city and referred the decision to a council to be held at a later date.

Eulalius however considered himself so much in front that he broke the ban and entered Rome, causing the Emperor to cancel the planned council and declare Boniface I the true and only pope. Eulalius thus goes into the history books as an anti-pope.

Boniface I would prove that he was a worthy pope by the fact that he managed to convince the Byzantine Emperor, Theodosius II, to return Illyricum (western Balkans and Greece) to the sovereignty of the see in Rome, thus vastly expanding the influence of Rome, although only temporarily as the area was back under Byzantine control by 437. Needless to say, Boniface I was a saint.

On Boniface I's death in 422 he was followed by Celestine I, a devout dogmatic who sent the first mission to Ireland, a mission first headed by one Palladius and later successfully continued by (Saint) Patrick.

Celestine I was on his, saintly, death in 432 followed by Sixtus III, whose contribution to history is mainly in the form of a range of Church projects in Rome.

He died, saintly, in 440 and was replaced by one of the more significant popes of the era; Leo I, who happened to be pope at the same time as the emergence in Italy of two notorious warlords, Attila of the Huns and Genseric of the Vandals.

Since the sack of Rome by Alaric in 410 the Western Empire had been little but an anachronism with a weak central authority. 'Barbarians' - by definition anyone not a Christian - were pushing on the Empire's borders and one such group were the Vandals. They originated in or around modern-day Poland, but had been pushed first south into the Balkans and then west, by the Huns to whom we shall return later.

In the early parts of the fifth century the Vandals wandered into (Roman) Gaul where they fought several battles with the 'Franks' (Romanized locals) before they proceeded south into the Iberian Peninsula. Here they were eventually granted land by the Romans, but to some it was not enough.

A new strong king, Genseric, had emerged as King of the Vandals and he wanted more. Well aware that the Western Roman Empire was as good as without a central authority in 429 he set sail for northern Africa and the Roman provinces of Numidia and Mauretania (modern day Algeria, Tunisia and Morocco).

The Vandals met some uncoordinated resistance and had to lay siege to some of the bigger towns, but within a decade they had full control of Roman North Africa including the prize city of Carthage, which was made

Part 6 - The Pope and the Crusader Knights

the capital of the Vandal Kingdom. The latter was a major blow to Rome, as Carthage was the primary food-source of the city.

From here the Vandals, in possession of a strong fleet, kept attacking the Western Empire, over the following years taking possession of Sicily, Sardinia, Corsica and the Balearic Islands as well as consistently raiding the coastal areas of both the Roman empires.

In the meantime, back in Europe, the Western Empire faced a new and even more dangerous enemy, the Huns.

The Huns had been terrorizing the Eastern Empire for decades, raiding into the Balkans, pushing other peoples, such as the Goths and the Alans, in front of them. In 434 they had a new strong king, Attila, who had ambitions in the West.

The Huns had already raided into the Western Empire on several occasions, and they had even acted as mercenaries when civil war broke out between the Western Emperor Valentian III and the usurper Joannes in 424. But Attila did not come as hired help, he came to conquer.

Initially Attila concentrated his efforts in the East, fighting over Armenia with the Sassanids, He had a peace agreement with the Eastern Empire, according to which Constantinople paid him a considerable tribute to stay north of the Danube, River but after an unsuccessful campaign in Armenia around 440, Attila again started to raid across the Danube River.

At that same time the Western Empire decided to do something about the Vandals, in particular their possession of Carthage, so they practically emptied the Balkans of troops, which were sent to Sicily to build up for a campaign in North Africa.

Attila was not late to take the opportunity and he crossed the Danube River and raided across the - practically defenceless - Balkans.

The Roman troops were sent back to the Balkans and although Attila proposed peace-terms they were rejected, He thus returned in 443, laying waste to the Balkans and he finally defeated an Eastern Roman army outside Constantinople.

However the city itself was too much of a challenge, so a new peace agreement was made, Attila once again withdrew across the Danube River loaded with Byzantine gold.

This time the peace only lasted till 447, when Attila once again raided through the Balkans and into Northern Greece, but his primary interest was now the West.

Although Attila hardly needed a casus belli - as he had previously been quite happy to raid as and when it suited him - he was given one in any case.

The Western Roman Emperor, Valentian III, had a sister called Honoria. She was to be married to a Roman Senator, but not of her choice. In desperation she appealed to Attila for help, as he generally had a good relationship to the Emperor and, in particular, to the powerful consul and general Flavius Aetius.

16 - The Pope

Her appeal, in the form of a letter, was accompanied by her engagement ring. This caused Attila to assume that her appeal was indeed a marriage proposal, which he accepted on the condition that her dowry was (the northern) half of the Western Empire.

Emperor Valentian III had no intentions of agreeing to neither the marriage nor the dowry, and he sent Honoria into exile. Attila however now had a claim, and he made it clear that if he was not given that which was 'rightfully' his, then he would come and get it himself.

With the moral high ground ensured, Attila burst into Gaul in 451. He had a range of allied tribes with him, and they went straight west until they reached Belgica (Belgium). He came to conquer and had he been successful he would have extended his realm to reach the Atlantic coast.

But Gaul was held by the Visigoths, who previously fled in front of the Huns, so resistance was strong. The Romans too watched Attila's progress with great concern, an alliance was made between the Romans and the Visigoths and an army was raised under the command of Flavius Aetius and the Visigoth king Theodoric I.

The two armies first engaged outside Orleans, causing Attila to abandon an attempt to take the city, and the Allied army then shadowed the Huns until they forced them into battle outside Catalaunum (modern Châlons-en-Champagne in north-eastern France).

The Battle of Catalaunum, as it should later be known, was indecisive, and possibly not by accident. The allied Roman and Visigoth army had the advantage, but the Visigoth King Theodoric I was killed in the battle and the Roman general Flavius Aetius failed to press his advantage and rout the Huns. The most likely explanation is that the Romans were not too keen on an outright Visigoth victory, as that would strengthen the Visigoths, but rather were content with reversing Attila's army, which went back to their heartlands in (modern day) Hungary.

However, Attila was back the following year. Realizing that the Western Empire was weak he went straight for Italy itself.

Tradition has it that Attila's attack on Italy was the reason for the early Venetians to flee to the sandbanks in the lagoon and start building their new city on the inaccessible islands. The fact is that Attila laid waste to northern Italy.

The Empire had little with which to fight back. General Flavius Aetius could do little but to fight a guerrilla war, slowing down but not stopping the marauding Huns.

They razed the city of Aquileia and continued to Mantua, but there they halted.

The reasons why they halted are unclear, but it is highly likely that Attila found difficulties with feeding his army, not least the many horses on which the Huns depended. There had been hunger in northern Italy already before

Part 6 - The Pope and the Crusader Knights

Attila and the Huns arrived, and it is also generally believed that there was plague going around.

In any case, the Emperor sent an embassy to Attila, and one of the three ambassadors was Pope Leo I.

Popular history has it that Leo I convinced Attila to turn around and leave Italy, and whereas it is true that Attila did exactly that, it is less likely that it was due to anything Leo I said to him.

It is more likely that the general situation regarding supplies and disease had already made Attila see the futility of any further campaigning, and it also added to the equation that he would have received messages that an Eastern Roman army had crossed the Danube River and was pushing the troops he had left to defend his homelands. On his return Attila started to plan a new attack on the Eastern Empire, but he died suddenly in 453 and his empire collapsed on his death.

Whether one reason or the other for the Huns' withdrawal, Pope Leo I was a hero and it was not the last time he would be seen to save Rome, although not necessarily the Empire.

Even though Attila and the Huns went home, the Western Empire was still under threat from the Vandals in North Africa.

Peace between Rome and Carthage had however been agreed and part of the peace agreement was that the son of King Genseric, named Huneric, would marry the daughter of Emperor Valentian III, named Eudocia.

With the threat from the Huns gone it was time to cement the peaceful relationship with the Vandals, but before it got to that the Emperor was overthrown.

Shortly following the Huns' departure Emperor Valentian III had eliminated the strong and popular General Flavius Aetius, by many seen as the saviour of Rome after his successful defence against the Huns at Catalaunum.

Flavius Aetius had been engaged to the Emperor's other daughter, Placidia, but both Valentian III and his closest advisors suspected that Flavius Aetius had ambitions on the throne, possibly for his son. They thus decided to eliminate him and he was murdered, possibly by the Emperor himself in 454.

The key advisor to the Emperor was the senator Petronius Maximus, who had been instrumental in orchestrating the fall from grace of - his competitor - Flavius Aetius. On Aetius' death Petronius Maximus assumed that he would be given some of the valuable offices formerly held by Aetius, but the appointments did not come forth as expected.

There is a popular story about how the Emperor lusted for Petronius Maximus' wife and used deception to make her bend to his will, but in reality Petronius Maximus was probably driven by political ambition when, in March 455 he had the Emperor murdered and himself appointed Emperor.

16 - The Pope

To establish his links with the imperial dynasty Petronius Maximus himself married the murdered Emperor's widow, Licinia Eudoxia, and arranged for his own son, Palladius, to marry the late Emperor's daughter, Eudocia.

But Eudocia had already been promised to the Vandal king's son, so Petronius Maximus made himself an enemy of Genseric.

Armed with a casus belli that strongly resemble the casus belli of Attila a few years before - both claiming an unfulfilled promise of marriage into the imperial dynasty of Rome - Genseric mustered his army and set sail for Italy.

With Flavius Aetius gone there was little coherent resistance and the Vandals marched straight for Rome.

With the news of Genseric's approach the Emperor had attempted to leave the city, where he had been meeting with the Senate. He was attacked by an angry mob and killed outside the city gates. His reign had lasted seventy-eight days. His son, Palladius, was also killed although probably in a separate incident.

Left without central authority, Pope Leo I was the popular choice for leader of Rome and it fell upon him to, once again, negotiate with an invading warlord.

Contrary to Leo I's negotiations with Attila, the negotiations with Genseric were not as to whether Genseric should attack Rome; that was a given. Rather Leo I's role was to negotiate the best possible terms, and he managed to agree with Genseric that if Rome surrendered and opened its gates to the Vandals, the city and its inhabitants would be spared.

So, the Vandals moved in without a fight and now the contemporary accounts become somewhat contra dictionary. According to some sources - glorifying Leo I - the Vandals did not plunder the city or its inhabitants. According to other - possibly less biased - sources the Vandals did plunder the city and some of its inhabitants were led away as slaves. Indeed, the term 'vandalism' echoes down through history as a term of meaningless destruction, but it is clear that even though the Vandals probably did plunder the city, it was mainly plundered of its portable valuables, and the buildings and infrastructure were mainly left intact rather than razed.

Contrary to Attila, Genseric achieved his target and his son Huneric indeed married Eudocia the following year.

Before the invasion by the Vandals, the Emperor had sent a long serving senator and civil servant, Eparchius Avitus, on an embassy to Gaul.

Eparchius Avitus was of Gaul origins and he had, through decades of civil service, as Governor of Gaul amongst other tittles, built up a good relationship with the Visigoths, and it had been Eparchius Avitus who convinced the Visigoth king Theodoric I to ally with Rome against Attila before the Battle of Catalaunum.

Emperor Valentian III had sent Eparchius Avitus back to Gaul to negotiate a new alliance between Rome and the Visigoths, now ruled by Theodoric I's son, Theodoric II.

But before anything practical could come from Eparchius Avitus' embassy, news reached Gaul of Genseric's sack of Rome and the death of the Emperor.

Theodoric II saw the opportunity - the Visigoth presenting the only military force available to Rome - and proclaimed Eparchius Avitus as Emperor of Rome, with the Visigoths as the his puppeteers.

Avitus first remained in Gaul and then marched with his Visigoths to Italy. Securing Ravenna on the way he entered Rome towards the end of September 455.

By now the Vandals had retreated. They had come to claim Huneric's bride and whatever plunder presented itself, but they soon again caused trouble in southern Italy and Avitus managed to assemble enough military power - partly using Germanic mercenaries - to defeat them both at land and at sea, temporarily keeping them at bay.

Avitus was probably an able emperor and he tried hard to unite the fragmented remains of the Empire, but he was not popular with the locals in Rome. His Gaul roots and his reliance on the Visigoths as his power base caused resentment.

He responded by dismissing his Visigoth guards, melting down precious pieces of art to have the necessary means to pay them. This led to even further resentment and in the background a shadowy kingmaker started to appear, the Roman general Ricimer.

It was Ricimer, himself of Gaul origins, who had led the army and navy which had successfully engaged the Vandals and although Ricimer realized that he himself was as unacceptable a choice for emperor as was Avitus, he started to campaign against him, instead promoting the much more Roman general Majorian.

The Roman Senate took on Ricimer's cause, and in 456 authorized him to commence military action against Emperor Avitus, who was in Ravenna.

A short campaign followed in which Avitus was defeated, and although he was allowed to live, he died only a couple of years later in disputed circumstances.

With Avitus out if the way, the road was clear for Majorian, who was proclaimed emperor by the Senate.

Majorian was an able emperor and managed to bring some of the crumbling empire's border regions back under central control, but he also had ambitions in terms of administrative reforms, reforms that would curb the power and influence of the aristocracy for the benefit of the people.

The reforms were not welcomed by the Senate, consisting of exactly the aristocrats that would be hit by them, so they once again turned to Ricimer who intercepted and beheaded the Emperor who was on his way to Rome.

16 - The Pope

A few months later a new puppet emperor was appointed, this time Libius Severus, an aristocrat entirely depending on Ricimer's support. The appointment was in direct opposition to claims made by the Emperor in Byzantium and Genseric of the Vandals, both putting forward their own candidates.

At around the same time - November 461 - Pope Leo I died in Rome.

Leo I had witnessed a range of major conflicts, several emperors and first and foremost the near destruction of the Western Empire. In this context Leo I is important because he is the first Pope who - as seen in his taking on the leadership of Rome at the arrivals of the Vandals - emerges as a political leader over and above a spiritual one. Leo I had, as far as is known, no political ambitions, but he was the only authority left in a world of chaos, a situation that would not become unknown to several of his successors.

By the end of 461 there was both a new emperor - albeit a puppet - and a new pope in Rome. The new pope was named Hilarius, and as most of his predecessors he too would become a saint.

Hilarius was a strict disciplinarian who concerned himself with maintaining the central authority of Rome, but in 467 he too became involved in politics.

The problem was that Emperor Libius Severus had died and in his place Procopius Anthemius had become emperor.

Anthemius was the choice of the Byzantine Emperor as he was born to a noble Byzantine family and had a successful military career behind him. He was thus probably a good choice, but he had introduced a number of 'foreign' advisors and favourites into the civil administration and not all of them were good Catholics.

To cater for them Emperor Anthemius introduced a law, which changed the state's policy from that of allowing only a single religion - Catholic Christianity - to one of tolerance of other religions and denominations.

Pope Hilarius did not find it funny. He voiced his opinion loud and clear, berating the Emperor in public during mass in St.Peter's Cathedral, but Pope Hilarius died the following year with the issue unresolved.

His replacement was Simplicius, another stout church disciplinarian and his reign as Bishop of Rome would see the final nail put in the coffin of the Western Empire.

Emperor Anthemius fought unsuccessful campaigns against the Visigoths in the north and the Vandals in the south, but both campaigns were generally unsuccessful. As before, it was really Ricimer who called the shots and when public opinion turned against the Emperor - due to unsuccessful military campaigns - Ricimer once again turned on his own puppet.

A new candidate, Olybrius, emerged. He was a Roman noble who also happened to be the son-in-law of the former emperor Valentinian III. He was on friendly terms with the Visigoth leader Genseric and had been elected as mediator by the Eastern Emperor in the strife between by Ricimer and Emperor Anthemius.

Ricimer used Germanic mercenaries, led by one Odoacer, and after a siege of Rome in 472 ousted Emperor Anthemius, who was killed when he tried to flee disguised as a beggar.

Olybrius was then appointed emperor, but he died the same year, from dropsy, as did his puppet-master Ricimer who had been the de-facto power behind four emperors, three of whom he himself subsequently ousted.

With Ricimer gone, the last remains of central authority effectively disappeared. The army, with Ricimer's nephew Gundobad as the strong-man, appointed a military man, Glycerius, as emperor.

But Glycerius was not recognized by the Eastern Emperor, who instead favoured Julius Nepos, the governor of Dalmatia. After a short delay, Julius Nepos crossed the Adriatic Sea and marched on Ravenna. Emperor Glycerius had fled to Rome bur soon capitulated without a fight. As a reward he was allowed to live and became Bishop of Salona in Dalmatia.

Julius Nepos thus began a short rule as emperor. He normalized relations to the Visigoths in Gaul, but could do little to stop the Vandals raids in the south. As his military commander he chose the Germanic general Orestes, who turned out to be a bad choice, as Orestes soon turned against him and forced him to flee Italy and go back to Dalmatia.

Orestes was not a Roman citizen, but his twelve years old son Romulus Augustus was, so Orestes had him appointed emperor, even though Julius Nepos maintained the title in exile in Dalmatia.

Now an internal fight between the Germanic generals who had long since dominated the 'Roman' army ensured. The powerful Odoacer, who had amongst other things fought as a mercenary leader for Ricimer, demanded land from the young emperor - and his father - and when the request was denied Odoacer moved on Ravenna. Orestes was killed in the battle and Romulus Augustus was taken prisoner. With his father gone he posed little threat and was allowed to live in exile.

Odoacer now ruled in Italy, and he was as clever as he was powerful. He approached the Eastern Emperor and asked to rule as Viceroy in Italy. Nominally he was subject to Julius Nepos and under the suzerainty of the Eastern Emperor. This lip-service to servitude secured Odoacer peace with the Eastern Emperor, and although he in all matters acted completely autonomous, in concept, the Western and Eastern Empires had been reunited.

To most historians Odoacer's rule marks the end of the Western Roman Empire and witnessing the debacle from Rome was Pope Simplicius. He had kept a low profile, not wanting to get involved, and the reality of the situation was that for him as well as for the general population the nominal re-unification of the two empires and the emergence of a Germanic leadership made little difference.

16 - The Pope

Central authority was limited, but the spiritual leadership was as strong as ever, as the re-unification did not diminish the role of the Bishop of Rome.

Pope Simplicius died in 483 and was replaced by Felix III (sometimes called Felix II, depending on whether the previous Felix II is counted as a Pope or an Anti-Pope).

Felix III is also a saint, and his reign would see yet another major transformation of the former empire.

The Ostrogoth tribes had for a couple of decades caused trouble in the Eastern Empire. They presented a problem to the Byzantine Emperor, Zeno, and so did Odoacer.

In the Emperor's opinion Odoacer was becoming too autonomous and too powerful, so he came up with a brilliant piece of political manoeuvring worthy of a Byzantine Emperor.

Zeno simply offered Italy to the Ostrogoth leader Theodoric (the Great) on two conditions; one that he could take it from Odoacer and two; that he would rule as Viceroy under Zeno's suzerainty.

Theodoric took the bait and Zeno had rid himself of two potential threats without lifting a finger himself.

With the Emperor's blessing, in 488 Theodoric led his tribe across the Balkans and into Italy where a string of battles ensued. Odoacer did not give up without a fight, but the Ostrogoths soon became the dominant party. Within a year they ruled in the north and after another four years of war they took Ravenna. A peace-treaty was signed, according to which Odoacer and Theodoric would share the power, but at the celebratory banquet, Theodoric himself killed Odoacer.

As it happened, Theodoric turned out to be a good choice for Italy. He did his best to ensure that the ruling 'Germans' and the indigenous 'Romans' were treated equally and much needed peace fell upon the land for a few decades.

With political stability the road was clear for a resumption of religious warfare between the East and the West.

Pope Felix III started to show some teeth and claim the sovereignty he believed belonged to the Bishop of Rome. When a Bishop of Antioch was elected without approval from the Pope, Felix III excommunicated the newly elected bishop. The same was repeated when a new Bishop of Alexandria was elected and this time it came to a serious dispute between the Pope and the Bishop of Constantinople. The dispute went further than the simple question of the election of bishops, but it is outside the scope of this book to examine in detail the complex theological issues involved.

When Felix III died in 493 the throne of St. Peter went to one of his trusted administrators, Gelasius I, who continued the fight with the Eastern Church.

Gelasius I was particularly concerned over the Eastern Church's acceptance of so called Monophysitism, the view that Christ has only one -

divine - nature, which stood in stark contrast to Gelasius I's Dyophysite view, according to which Christ has two - Divine and Human - natures. It was Gelasius I's view that a break between the two churches was inevitable as the Eastern Church promoted heresy.

And Gelasius I did not leave it a Church politics. He wrote a letter - called *Duo sunt*, which outlines the separate roles played by the religious ("*holy authority of bishops*") and secular rulers ("*royal power*"), a split of authority which has ever since dominated the political structure of Europe and which we today would associate with "secular" - non-religious - government.

Gelasius I also picked up the challenge first started by Pope Hilarius, urging the lawmakers to forbid heathen festivals and return to the one faith once again.

As dynamic as Gelasius I's reign as pope was; it was however short. He died in 496 after only four years as pope, but he had done enough to become a saint.

He was replaced by Anastasius II who contrary to most of his predecessors was not a saint, and there was a reason for that. Anastasius II wanted peace inside the Church, and he approached the Eastern Emperor in an attempt to re-unite the quickly unravelling Christian Church. In attempting to do so Anastasius II was willing to make compromises, including accepting into the Church those who had been baptized using the Monophysitic rite. Whereas this may well have been necessary it was not popular with more conservative Catholics and some saw it as divine justice when Anastasius II suddenly died in 498.

But Anastasius II's attempts to reconcile the Church also had supporters, so two factions now emerged. One was against Anastasius II's compromising policies and they elected Symmachus as pope, and one was for Anastasius II's policies and decided on Laurentius. The two popes were ordained on the same day.

The conflict now spread outside the upper echelons of the Church. Groups of supporters started to fight each other in the streets of Rome, where it was always easy to rouse a mob.

The church-leaders now referred the matter to Theodoric, who resided in Ravenna. They may have realized, but chose to ignore, the fact that the issue of who should be pope was now being referred to a king who was an 'Arian' Christian and thus a heretic in the eyes of the Church.

Theodoric declared that the true pope should be the one who was ordained first and who had the most (clerical) supporters. He then reviewed the evidence presented and concluded that Symmachus was the rightful pope.

Peace restored, Symmachus returned to Rome and called a synod (meeting of church-leaders). During this synod his competitor Laurentius was given a position as Bishop in Campania in south-eastern Italy, a noble gesture although it is believed that Laurentius never actually took up the position.

It should probably have ended there, but Laurentius' supporters - spearheaded by the influential senator Rufius Postumius Festus - were not done yet.

Having lost the first round, they quickly regrouped and forwarded accusations against Pope Symmachus. He was - according to his accusers - guilty of unchastity, misuse of Church funds and celebrating Easter on the wrong day. Initially only the last of these charges was made public and Pope Symmachus went to Rimini to answer to that charge in front of Theodoric.

On arrival Pope Symmachus was made aware of the additional charges and he panicked and fled. To many this was as good as admitting his guilt.

Laurentius' supporters brought him back to Rome, now with broad backing from the clergy, but Theodoric - although sympathetic to Laurentius' cause - intervened and called a synod to take place after Easter. It was a church matter and should be sorted by the Church.

When the Synod met it turned into a farce.

First Symmachus went on the offensive. He took exception to the fact that Theodoric had asked a visiting bishop, Peter of Altinum, to conduct Easter Mass and take temporary charge of Church administration. Symmachus argued that leaving matters - religious and practical - with a visiting bishop was as good as declaring the Bishop's (of Rome) seat vacant, thus demonstrating that he - Symmachus - had already been declared guilty before the trial had even begun.

The church-leaders pondered the argument, agreed to disagree, and referred the matter back to Theodoric (the heretic). But Theodoric had no intentions of removing Peter of Altinum from his caretaker position.

The Synod was thus gridlocked, and the mob once again turned to violence, both between supporters of the two parties and towards the clergy in general. Several bishops fled the city in terror, and a petition was sent to Theodoric asking for the synod to be moved to Ravenna. But again Theodoric stood his ground; it was a church matter and should be resolved in Rome.

On Theodoric's insistence, the synod resumed in September. This time it was the accusers who attacked. They presented a document which stated that the King (Theodoric) was already aware of Symmachus' guilt and that the synod should thus just listen to the evidence and then pass the 'guilty' sentence (which kind of proves Symmachus' original point).

Subsequently Symmachus and his retinue were attacked by a mob and two priests were killed. Symmachus now holed up in St. Peter's Cathedral and refused to come out.

Once again, the synod referred matters to Theodoric - who must have been well tired of the whole thing by now - asking that the synod could be dissolved. But Theodoric wrote the synod back, asking that they please conclude their business.

So, the synod reluctantly resumed. This time they agreed that since the Bishop of Rome was the successor of St. Peter, he could not be judged by mortals - not even bishops. They urged all parties to reconcile their differences and then they all went home.

With no real resolution, possession became the law and it was Laurentius who was best positioned, so he, for all intents and purposes, continued as pope.

But the struggle continued, with Theodoric as the target for petitions and pleas. What finally settled the issue was a set of forgeries, presented to Theodoric by the supporters of Symmachus. These forgeries - later known as 'the Symmachean forgeries' - pretended to go back in history and back up Symmachus' claim.

Most prominent amongst them, and likely to have swung the verdict, was a forged report on a fictitious synod held by Pope Sylvester I (you may remember that I made the point previously that Sylvester I - despite being a saint - would be most famous for something he had not actually done). In this synod - it was claimed in the document – that it had been agreed that no clergy could be accused by anyone of a lower grade, with the Pope being above accusation at all.

The forgeries worked. Theodoric now finally settled the matter, ordered that Rome be turned over to Symmachus and that the arguments and violence should come to a halt.

History thus knows Symmachus as both a pope and a saint, whereas Laurentius is noted down through history as an anti-pope. He retired to one of Festus' estates and disappeared from the public eye.

Although Symmachus did not take a proactive aggressive stand towards Constantinople, he did nothing to engage in further conversation neither. That changed when he died in 514 and the position of pope fell to Hormisdas.

Contrary to Symmachus, Hormisdas was keen to resolve the conflict with Constantinople, though he did insist that the resolution was on his, and Rome's terms. He had little success until he was helped by chance. In Constantinople a civil war brought a self-made general to power as Emperor Justin I. He was an unlikely candidate for a range of reasons. He was illiterate - coming from peasant stock, he was nearly seventy years of age and he was a Catholic.

Suddenly Hormisdas' efforts bore fruit, and the two churches were reunited with pomp and ceremony on 28 March 519.

However, although peace had now been found - for the time being, between the two factions of the Church, religion was becoming an issue in Italy itself.

16 - The Pope

Theodoric was growing old and somewhat irritated. Although in spite of his own Arian beliefs he had granted - even insisted on - a high level of autonomy for the Catholic Church, there was increased hostility towards the Arians, tension not least coming from Constantinople, where Arians were considered heretics, and proactively persecuted.

Pope Hormisdas died in 523 and was replaced by the ailing Pope John I. For reference John I was the fifty-third Bishop of Rome counting from St. Peter and like fifty of his successors he would turn out to be a saint. But before it came to that there was work to do.

Theodoric sent for Pope John I and told him in no uncertain terms that he had come to the end of his patience when it came to the Church's position on Arians. John I was told to go to Constantinople and sort the issue out, and should he fail then Theodoric would counter by a proactive persecution of Catholics in his Italian kingdom.

Reluctantly John I went to Constantinople where he met with Emperor Justin I, which illustrates that this mission was not a clerical issue, but rather a political embassy at the highest level.

Emperor Justin I agreed to all Theodoric's terms, with the exception of a smaller issue of whether converted Arians should be allowed to re-convert, and John I returned to Theodoric in Ravenna with his mission accomplished.

But for some reason Theodoric did not believe that John I was being honest, so he had him imprisoned, accused of secretly co-operating with Emperor Justin I. As mentioned, John I was a frail man already at his appointment as pope and he did not last long in jail. He died in May of 526.

Now the election of a pope, for the first time, became political, a practice which would be repeated many time in the centuries to come.

Theodoric was not going to take any chances in regard to a hostile pope. He put pressure on the papal electorate who, after a two-month vacuum, elected the pope Theodoric wanted, Felix IV.

Felix IV was not a particularly spectacular pope, but he was friendly to the Goths and liberal in his views of Arianism. He would also become a saint.

Job done, Theodoric died towards the end of 526, before he could start a planned campaign against the Vandals, who were still raiding southern Italy.

With Theodoric gone both the strong central authority and the precarious balance between the ruling Goths and the local 'Romans' very quickly disintegrated.

Theodoric left as his heir apparent his ten year old grandson Athalaric, but due to his age he was nominally ruling under the regency of his mother, Theodoric's daughter, Amalasuntha.

Amalasuntha believed that her son should be brought up as a 'Roman', which put her in opposition to the ruling Gothic nobles. Relations became strained and Amalasuntha even considered moving herself, her son, and the entire Italian treasury to Constantinople. But before it came to that her son, Athalaric, died.

Amalasuntha now became queen, but she was aware that her position was not stable. To stabilize matters she thus appointed her cousin, Theodahad, as co-regent, but he had his own ambitions and had her arrested shortly after and sent into imprisonment on a small island in Lake Bolsena in Tuscany. Here she was murdered in her bath a few months later.

On the papal side Pope Felix IV died in 530 and his death started a succession drama of its own. Apparently, he had expressed the opinion that his successor should be one Boniface II, who was Visigoth of birth and religiously liberal. But the clergy in general did not agree, and with Theodoric gone they took matters in their own hands and appointed their own candidate, Dioscorus.

Both new popes were ordained on the same day, but just as the battle was heating up, the mob in Rome was mobilized again, Dioscorus died after only three weeks as pope. Boniface II was now the undisputed Pope and Dioscorus goes down in history as an anti-pope. A lasting consequence was that it was forthwith, and to this day, made illegal to discuss or nominate a successor to a pope during his lifetime.

Boniface II died in 536, he was not a saint. He was followed by John II, the first pope to change his name, as his given name was Mercury, the same as a Roman god.

John II was another politically appointed liberal but stood in surprisingly good stead with the Byzantine emperor despite his tolerance towards Arians. But he too did not last long as he died in 535. He was not a saint.

His successor was Agapetus I, who spent most of his short time as pope in Constantinople, where he was ambassador for the new Gothic ruler, Theodahad, in an attempt to get the Byzantine Emperor's blessing for Theodahad's rule and possibly prevent a looming Byzantine invasion of Italy. He was not successful in either and died in Constantinople in 536. He was a saint.

He was followed by Silverius, a lowly member of the clergy appointed on the specific instructions of Theodahad and, of course, another pope with a tolerant view. He was, curiously, son of the former Pope Hormisdas, who had been married before he became pope.

That Theodahad had taken matters in his own hands was a small piece in a bigger picture as the political situation in Italy had taken a dramatic turn.

The Byzantine Emperor Justinian I had followed his uncle Justin I and he would turn out to be one of the great emperors of Byzantium.

Justinian I was determined to raise the Roman Empire to its former glory and that included reuniting the two separate empires into one.

Justinian I first dealt with the Vandals in North Africa, long the bane of both empires. He successfully campaigned in North Africa in 533 and 534, by which time he had conquered Carthage and effectively retaken the former

Roman territories in North Africa. It was now time to bring Italy back into the fold.

Justinian I's general, Belisarius, crossed from North Africa to Sicily in the summer of 535, while his counterpart, Mundus, attacked in Dalmatia.

By the end of 535 Sicily had been taken and the Byzantines controlled the capital-city of Salona in Dalmatia.

The year after the Goths came back and reconquered Salona, General Mundus was killed in battle, and the Byzantines withdrew from Dalmatia.

But while the Goths were busy in Dalmatia, Belisarius crossed from Sicily to main-land Italy where he secured the coastal city of Reggio (modern day Reggio Calabria) and then continued to Naples, which he had secured by the autumn, In the meantime the Byzantines under general Constantianus had re-conquered Dalmatia. The Goths were in disarray.

Theodahad's incapability to defeat the Byzantines lead to his deposition and over the next nineteen years there was six Gothic Kings of Italy, mainly as the result of internal strife in lieu of the Byzantine advance.

By December 536 Belisarius stood before Rome.

As had been the case when the Vandals under Genseric stood before Rome eighty years prior, the town surrendered to the invaders. Naples had fallen after a costly siege and had been thoroughly sacked. If that had been a message, it had been clearly received.

Once again it was the Pope, Silverius, who stood before the conquerors as spokesman for the city, but it did him no good.

The new Goth King of Italy, Vitiges, laid siege to Rome for several months, causing hunger and hardship. During the siege, General Belisarius accused Pope Silverius of betrayal and he was formally deposed and subsequently exiled to a remote Greek island where he died a few months later. He was a saint.

It was now the turn of the Byzantines to appoint the next pope, and their choice was Vigilius.

Pope Vigilius was a clearly political choice and he had an interesting history. He was originally appointed as successor by Pope Boniface II, but with the controversy surrounding the appointment by a pope of his own successor, the decree was subsequently nullified and burned.

Instead Vigilius was appointed as Papal Legate to Constantinople. Here he became close to Emperor Justinian I's formidable Empress, Theodora.

Theodora was a former prostitute and exotic dancer, who despite the norms of Byzantine society had been elevated to Empress. She was very religious and although some had forgotten about the theological dispute over Monophysitism, which had previously split the Church, she had not.

She promised Vigilius the position as pope, and a large amount of money, if he would accept Monophysitism, Vigilius apparently accepted the offer and it was on this basis that the Empress Theodora pushed him forward as pope.

She probably also orchestrated the deposal of Silverius to make the position available.

But the agreement between Empress Theodora and Vigilius did not hold. Once installed in Rome, Pope Vigilius did not support Monophysitism, but rather maintained the Western Church's view of Dyophysitism.

The Empress was not happy, and an exchange of opinions developed between Pope Vigilius and Constantinople, Emperor Justinian I himself becoming involved in the dispute.

Finally Pope Vigilius was ordered to appear in Constantinople and when he did not rush to answer the call, the Byzantines apprehended him and took him to a ship bound for Constantinople in December of 545.

At that time Rome was again under siege by the Goths, now under the last of their capable rulers, Totila, who the following year managed to force the city to surrender. The city was sacked, but Totila had to withdraw when it was relieved by Belisarius.

In the meantime, Pope Vigilius had arrived in Constantinople. Here he stood his ground for eight years, until he finally conceded to a tolerant compromise brought forward by Emperor Justinian I and agreed to at the Second Council of Constantinople (which was dominated by Eastern representatives).

The compromise introduced a third view, called Monothelitism which prescribes that Christ has two natures but only one will, thus combining the views of Dyophysitism and Monophysitism.

Free to return, Pope Vigilius set sails for Rome, but he died on the way. His was not a saint.

During Pope Vigilius' absence the war in Italy effectively ended. The Goths had been defeated and the Byzantines had control of Italy. But the victory had come at great cost and the Empire was exhausted. Northern Italy, where fighting had been going on for nearly twenty years, was depopulated and fell into a steep decline.

While Pope Vigilius had been in Constantinople, his office had been maintained by Pelagius, himself a former apocrisiarius (papal ambassador) to Constantinople.

It thus fell on Pelagius to seek mercy from the Goth King Totila when he sacked Rome and although he was not very successful in this context, he was chosen by Totila to act as a peace emissary. He was sent to Constantinople to seek peace with Justinian I on behalf of Totila, but by the time he reached Constantinople the situation had turned in Italy and he was sent back with a message that no peace was forthcoming as the Byzantines were already in control.

On the death of Vigilius, Pelagius was the obvious choice and he was duly elected. Before his election was secured he had to ensure the Byzantine Emperor of his support for the Emperor's compromises in the Church's affairs, an act which secured him the papacy but alienated him from many in

- particular northern - Italy and the rest of western Europe who did not agree on the Emperor's clear interference in clerical matters.

Pope Pelagius I ruled for five years and died in 561. He did not attempt, or succeed, in doing anything spectacular, and he was not a saint.

His replacement, John III, would see significant changes to the political situation in the thirteen years he acted as pope.

In 565 Justinian I died, and with him died absolute Byzantine domination in Italy.

Justinian I was replaced by his nephew Justin II. What he took over was the greatest unified empire since the birth of Constantinople, a policy of paying off hostile tribes in the Balkans and a completely empty treasury. That Justinian I had achieved great things was undeniable, but it had cost the Empire everything it owned.

Justin II thus reversed the policy of paying off hostile tribes, in particular the Lombards, Avars and Gepids. The result was that these tribes once again started raiding into the Balkans, shifting the Empire's focus well away from Italy.

The Avars and Lombards had united to destroy the Gepids and they then turned on each other. The Avars came out as the stronger and the Lombards started drifting out of (modern day) Austria and into Italy.

In northern Italy they found the perfect environment for re-settlement. Contrary to the invasions by Ostrogoths, Visigoths and Vandals, the Lombards did not arrive as a single unit of people. Rather, the migration of the Lombards was spearheaded by an armed vanguard, in the wake of which people simply trickled in over a period of time, filling in the vacuum left behind from two decades of war between the Goths and the Byzantines.

Byzantine authority did not expand far outside the city gates of Ravenna. The Empire was exhausted and broke, and it had problems with Avars and Persians. The Exarch (imperial representative) in Ravenna had but a small garrison available, enough to keep the peace but not enough to repel a determined invader.

The Lombards vanguard, led by Alboin, first started to appear in 568, three years after the death of Emperor Justinian I, and by the end of the following year they had conquered Vicenza, Verona, Brescia and Milan.

The Byzantine Exarch could only effectively defend his coastal possessions, which could be resupplied by sea, the Lombards having no naval capability and by 572 the Lombards had taken Pavia, which they turned into the capital of what had in a few years become a de-facto Lombard state.

The Lombards now continued south, conquering Tuscany and then crossed to the west coast of Italy continuing into the regions of Spoleto and Benevento.

This left Italy split into a very messy political makeup. The Byzantines held onto the coastal areas in the north-west, the areas around Ravenna in the north-east (separated by the Lombards), the area around Rome, reaching north-west towards Ravenna and south-east towards Naples, the area around Naples and the south-westernmost and south-easternmost areas of the peninsula.

The Lombards were very close to Rome and once again the lack of central authority made the Pope the de-facto leader on the ground.

Pope John III was not happy with the apparent inactivity of the Byzantine Exarch, Longinus, who sat in Ravenna as nothing more than a spectator. He had more confidence in the former Exarch, Narses, who had recently been replaced due to his reputation as a pocket-dictator and who was, at the time, preparing in Naples for his return to Constantinople.

The Pope went to Naples and managed to convince Narses to go with him to Rome and command its defences. But Narses' reputation was so bad with the general populace that his return was less than welcome and the anger at Narses soon spilled over onto the Pope himself, who had to flee the city and take up residence in the old Christian catacombs on the Via Appia outside of Rome itself.

But the most immediate threat from the Lombards to Rome disappeared due to internal problems amongst the Lombards themselves.

The Byzantines had reverted to their well-known tactic of political intrigue. They secretly supported Alboin's wife, Rosemund, who apparently had been forced into marriage after Alboin had murdered her father. She thus hated him, and with Byzantine support ensured she recruited Alboin's foster brother Helmichis. Together they had Alboin murdered in June 572 and then they quickly married to secure Helmichis as the new king.

Whereas that suited the Byzantines, it did not please the Lombard lords. They did not recognise Helmichis and Rosemund's reign and instead elected Cleph, one of their own as king.

Rosemund and Helmichis fled to Ravenna, taking with them Alboin's daughter Albsuinda and the treasure of the Lombard kingdom. In Ravenna they later fell out and had each other murdered, after which the treasure and Albsuinda were shipped off to Constantinople – no, I am not making it up!.

The new Lombard leader, Cleph, continued where Alboin left off, further securing the Lombard positions in the south, but then he in turn was murdered by a slave, probably paid by the Byzantines.

The Lombard dukes, now solidly placed across Italy, decided to not appoint a new king, but to rule together, entering into a period of consolidation which took some pressure off the remaining Byzantine territories in Italy.

However, the Lombard invasion had not only changed the political pattern of Italy, it had also changed the religious situation.

Arianism had finally been eradicated with the Byzantine defeat of the Goths, but the Lombards re-introduced it along with elements of paganism. Against it stood the Catholic Church and the Pope.

16 - The Pope

Pope John III died in 574, around the same time as Cleph. He was not a saint.

His replacement was Benedict I, but it took nearly fifteen months after the death of John III to find a new pope appointed, communication lines with Constantinople being hampered by the Lombards.

For that very same reason, and Rome's effective isolation, there is not much to say about Benedict I. He is not recorded as having done much, as there was little he could do. He died in 579 and he was not a saint.

Neither was his replacement, Pelagius II, although he was significantly more active. He appealed to the Emperor in Constantinople to assist his subjects in Italy, but when no help arrived, he devised another scheme, now proactively playing the Statesman rather than the religious leader.

The Lombards had moved north from Italy, entering Provence (in modern day Southern France). This had enraged the Franks - whom can be loosely defined as Germanic tribes living in modern day France - and it was to them that Pope Pelagius II offered financial support should they in turn attack the Lombards from the north. The Frankish intervention caused a quick reaction from the Lombards. First, they paid the Franks more than the Pope in order to stay away and then decided that it was time for the election of a new king, a more suitable structure of government for when the Kingdom - of Italy - was under direct attack. Their choice was Authari, the son of Cleph.

The Franks returned and Authari spent his six-year reign in constant battle on the northern front of his kingdom.

This gave Pope Pelagius time to deal with church-matters, which included getting on unfriendly terms with the Bishop of Constantinople, who had started to use the title of Ecumenical Patriarch, thus indicating that he was superior to the Bishop of Rome.

In 590 both Pope Pelagius II and the Lombard King Authari died. The latter probably died from poisoning and his wife, Theodelinda, soon remarried the new king, Agilulf.

The new Pope was Gregory I, who would not only become a saint, but also achieve the moniker 'the Great', somewhat uncommon for a religious leader and not at all in the spirit of the man himself.

Pope Gregory I was an energetic individual. He was a monk but had been appointed to represent the Roman Church in Constantinople. On his return to Rome he preferred a return to a quiet life in a monastery, where he could continue his substantial writing on religious matters, but he instead hesitantly accepted the position as pope.

Even as pope he continued his writings, managing to reel the outer lying parts of the Church back in under Rome's authority. He was also responsible for sending the first - successful - missionaries to Anglo-Saxon England, but his coup de grâce was the conversion of the Lombard King.

Part 6 - The Pope and the Crusader Knights

Queen Theodelinda was a Christian and a Catholic Christian as was - on her insistence, the new king. Agilulf was baptized before he could ascend the throne, but whereas that made him a Christian, he was first and foremost an Arian Christian and many heathen Lombards followed him into the Arian faith.

That was better than nothing, but the aim of Theodelinda was to make the Lombard's Catholics and to that end she had the full support of the Pope. The two exchanged letters, and the Pope sent Theodelinda gifts, including a piece of the True Cross.

In return Theodelinda delivered King Agilulf who, in 603, finally converted to Catholicism and subsequently eased the pressure on the lands around Rome, although he aggressively expanded into other Byzantine areas in Italy and the Balkans.

Indeed such was the success of King Agilulf that the Byzantine Emperor Phocas ended up agreeing to pay a tribute so he could focus on more pressing matters in Greece and Persia.

Pope Gregory I died in 606, leaving behind a legacy of letters and other writings as well as 'Gregorian chanting', named after him.

His replacement was the rather anonymous Sabinian, another former Papal delegate to Constantinople and a political appointee selected by the Byzantine Emperor. Pope Sabinian was only pope for two years, in which he is best known for having sold grain (from Papal lands) expensively during a period of famine in Rome. He was not a saint.

Neither was his successor, Boniface III, but that is probably due to his very short tenure as pope (less than a year), as Pope Boniface III actually left something useful behind for posterity.

Boniface III was, as had become the norm, the Papal Ambassador to Constantinople at the time of his election. But rather than accepting a political election, Boniface III insisted that proper procedure for a clerical election should be upheld, and it took a year before he was officially elected and returned to Rome.

On his return he immediately put his thoughts on papal election down as a decree, making the discussion of a papal successor a crime worth excommunication and establishing the rule that no practical steps relating to the election of a new pope can start until at the earliest three days after the former Pope's death.

Additionally Pope Boniface III, who had a very good relationship to Emperor Phocas in Constantinople, achieved a major victory in the ongoing fight for dominance between the Bishops of Rome and Constantinople. The Emperor decreed that 'the See of Blessed Peter the Apostle should be the head of all the Churches', thus settling the discussion of who is the true Ecumenical Patriarch (for the time being).

Having achieved all this in less than a year, Pope Boniface III died at the end of 607.

His successor, Boniface IV, became a saint. With permission from the Emperor in Constantinople he performed the first conversion of a heathen temple in Rome into a Christian church by converting the Pantheon, a temple dedicated to all the Roman gods, built during Emperor Augustus and latest renovated in 126 AD. The Pantheon has, to this day, the largest dome made of unreinforced concrete in the world.

Boniface IV was challenged, on the behest of the Lombard King Agilulf, over the Church's acceptance of the Second Council of Constantinople, which was really a challenge of the Pope's connections with the Emperor in Constantinople, but he avoided a confrontation and subsequently died quietly in 615.

He was followed by Adeodatus I, who ruled as pope for less than two years, but nevertheless was a saint.

He in turn was followed by Boniface V, a mild-mannered man who officially established churches as a place of refuge for criminals.

During Boniface V's reign there was trouble in Italy. The Byzantine Exarch, Eleutherius, revolted in 619, declaring himself emperor and marching on Rome, which he intended to make his new capital. This would have left Boniface V with a major dilemma, but luckily Eleutherius' own soldiers started a counter-revolt, killed their leader and sent his head to Emperor Heraclius in Constantinople.

Another event during Boniface V's reigns would have far longer lasting effects, although at the time it was not an event which was noticed in Rome as it took place in far-away Arabia.

There, a merchant in Mecca named Abū al-Qāsim Muḥammad ibn ʿAbd Allāh ibn ʿAbd al-Muṭṭalib ibn Hāshim - usually referred to as Muhammad - had received revelations from God and started to preach. His mission met with resistance and in 622 he relocated with a small group of followers, to the city of Medina. The event is known as Hijra in Islam.

Pope Boniface V died in 625 and he was not a saint. Neither was his successor Honorius I, indeed he would later be declared a heretic.

Honorius I was a supporter of Monothelitism and the old battle inside the Church flared up again. A synod was called in Cyprus in 634 and Honorius I, with the support of the Byzantine Emperor Heraclius, maintained his position, much to the regret of the representatives of the Archbishop of Jerusalem.

By the time Honorius I died in 638, the Prophet Muhammad had made a significant impact in Arabia. His followers had been transformed into an army, unified under the new religion of Islam. In 629 they had fought the first - unsuccessful - battle against the Byzantine Empire at the Battle of Mu'tah in modern day Jordan. By 630 Muhammad was back in Mecca and by the time he died in 632 he was in control of the whole Arabian Peninsula. From here his followers would unleash holy war for centuries to come.

It would take nearly two years to confirm a successor to Honorius I. Not because a candidate was not at hand, on the contrary, Pope Severinus was appointed after the prescribed three days after the burial of Honorius I, but because the issue of Monothelitism was far from solved.

An embassy was quickly sent to the Emperor in Constantinople, seeking his confirmation of Severinus as pope, but it was ambushed by the Patriarch of Constantinople, Sergius I.

He had convinced the Emperor, the aging Heraclius, to force the new Pope to sign a document - named the Ecthesis - which clearly states that Christ has two natures, but only one will (thus supporting Monothelitism).

The papal ambassadors would not sign on behalf of the Pope and Sergius I convinced the Emperor to make the document an imperial edict. This in turn activated the Exarch in Ravenna, Isaac, who decided to force the Pope's hand.

He in turn left matters to his Chartoularios - Highest Fiscal Official - Maurice to press the issue in Rome, and confiscate the Pope's treasure in the Lateran Palace in the process.

It took Maurice two attempts to get into the Lateran Palace, the Pope himself convinced a mob against the plan on the first attempt, but finally Maurice forced his way in and spent a week plundering the palace. The plunder was distributed up and down the line of command, some even reaching the Emperor in Constantinople.

The Emperor was, however, dying and he finally accepted the Papal Embassy's pleas and confirmed Severinus as pope in 640. The new Pope only officially ruled for a few months before he died of old age. He was not a saint.

His successor John IV was not a saint either. He was from Dalmatia and his short reign was focused on this region where pagan Slavs had started to appear. He sent missionaries to the Slavs and did his best to support the local faithful, although devastation of the local churches meant that he had to relocate many sacred relics to Rome.

Now let us for a moment return to the big issue which still faced the unity of the Church.

A discussion had long raged as to the nature of Christ. It was accepted that Christ was indeed the Son of God, but the discussion was about how that was possible in terms of Christ's nature.

The two main lines of thinking were that either Christ had a single nature, which was a synthesis of his divine and human natures. This school of thought was called *Monophysitism*. The opposite line of thought was that Christ had two natures, namely a human and a divine nature. This school of thought was called *Dyophysitism*.

On the initiative of the Patriarch of Constantinople, Sergius I, a compromise solution had been found. It stated that Christ had two natures (divine and human), but only one will. It was known as *Monothelitism* and had

16 - The Pope

- as mentioned above - been confirmed in a document called the Ecthesis issued by the Byzantine Emperor Heraclius in 638.

The Pope at the time, Honorius I, had agreed in concept to the principle of Monothelitism, but on a personal basis rather than at a matter as dogma. The Emperor, the Patriarch of Constantinople and the Pope all thought they had done quite well by defusing the age-long strife inside the Church by accepting a reasonable compromise, but their successors thought differently.

Pope Severinus, as described previously, would not agree to Monothelitism and his successor, John IV, even less so.

John IV wrote to the Emperor, convincing him to extract the offending Ecthesis document on his deathbed, and also explained how Pope Honorius I had never given his actual support to Monothelitism, but had only supported the notion that the two wills of Christ were, indeed, not conflicting.

The reign of John IV only lasted short of two years, and when he died in 642 he was replaced by Theodore I, who continued the fight against Monothelitism.

Theodore I, a Greek born in Jerusalem, continued to argue the Western Church's points with the new Byzantine Emperor, Constans II, and the Patriarch of Constantinople, Paul II.

Not seeing eye-to-eye, the Pope excommunicated the Patriarch of Constantinople, who in turn destroyed the Roman altar in the royal palace and imprisoned the Papal Ambassadors in Constantinople.

The young Emperor Constans II however, realized that the situation was not viable, so he issued the *Type of Constans*, an imperial decree which declared that any further discussion of the nature of Christ was forbidden within the Empire and that '*the situation which existed before the strife arose shall be maintained, as it would have been if no such disputation had arisen.*'

It was probably meant as an attempt to make peace, but it had the exact opposite effect. As far as Pope Theodore I was concerned, the *Type of Constans* made a mockery of an extremely important issue, so he called a Lateran council, but he died before it could be conducted. He was not a saint.

His successor, Martin I, however was a saint, and even a martyr. He was elected without approval from Constantinople and immediately proceeded with the Lateran Council as planned by Theodore I.

The Lateran Council of 649 issued twenty canons - decrees - condemning Monothelitism, anyone who had to do with it or promoted it and specifically condemned both the Ecthesis and the Type of Constans as being heretic.

The Emperor did not take this lightly. The appointment of Martin I without his approval was in itself an insult, the condemnation of the *Type of Constans* even more so. He instructed his representative in Italy, the Exarch of Ravenna, to apprehend Pope Marin I.

The execution of this order tuned out to be difficult, but finally in June 653, the Exarch managed to capture Pope Martin I who was taken as a prisoner to Constantinople where he was tortured and interrogated before he was sent in exile in the Crimea, where he died shortly after in 655.

In the meantime, a new pope, Eugene I, had already been appointed in 654, when it became clear that Martin I would not be returning.

Eugene I immediately sent letters, seeking the Emperor's approval of his appointment, to Constantinople. His embassy returned with a letter from the Emperor instructing him to listen to the Patriarch of Constantinople, and a letter from the latter setting forth his demands in terms of doctrine.

The letter from the Patriarch of Constantinople was, in light of the situation, rather uncommitted, but the clergy in Rome completely refused it, instructing the Pope to, not under any circumstances, accept it.

The new Pope was now in the same predicament as his predecessor, opposing the Emperor's will. The Byzantine ambassadors threatened Eugene I with the same fate as that which had met Martin I, but he was saved by the most unlikely of candidates, the emerging Muslim Empire.

Since the death of Muhammad in 632, his movement, riding on a combination of religion, politics and military force, had continued its expansion from the Arabian Peninsula into Egypt and they were now spilling up into Anatolia by land and attacking Byzantine islands in the Aegean Sea.

Emperor Constans II had set out to meet them, most forcefully so in the Battle of the Masts outside Phoenix (modern day Finike in Turkey) in 655, where the Muslim fleet annihilated the Byzantine fleet and the Emperor himself barely survived.

The Muslims now prepared for a siege on Constantinople, but as has been the fate of empires before and after, their ambitions - and favourable position – were ruined by the outbreak of civil war.

This gave Constans II the opportunity to re-group and also re-take his possessions in northern Africa which had been swept up by the Muslims. He continued on to Sicily and eventually landed on the mainland, where he unsuccessfully attempted to oust the Lombard lords in southern Italy. Finally, in 663, he ended up in Rome, the first Byzantine Emperor to enter the City for two centuries.

In Rome Pope Eugene I had died, quietly, but saintly, and his successor was Vitalian, who would also turn out to be a saint.

The first issue on the agenda for Pope Vitalian was to seek some kind of peace with the Emperor in Constantinople. Like his predecessors he sent letters to the Emperor, asking for his approval of his appointment, and this time the Emperor, with plenty problems of his own, gave his permission unconditionally and even sent gifts for the Church of St. Peter.

Communications were also had between the Pope and the Patriarch of Constantinople, an exchange of letters which did not touch on the issue of Monothelitism, but rather confirmed a peaceful status quo.

16 - The Pope

It was thus Pope Vitalian who welcomed the Emperor on his twelve day visit to Rome, a visit which saw the Emperor attending mass at St. Peter's Cathedral several times, as well as having dinner with the Pope. However, the Emperor was short of resources, so on leaving the City he confiscated several bronze artworks and the bronze roof tiles of the Pantheon. The Emperor then proceeded to Sicily, where he was assassinated in 668.

On the death of the Emperor his son, Constantine IV, became emperor, and during his reign things started to change for the better - seen from the perspective of Rome.

Pope Vitalian had continuously tried to consolidate his supremacy over the Church at large, fighting with both the Archbishop of Ravenna and the Patriarch in Constantinople. The situation was unclear, as was the issue of Monothelitism.

The new Emperor in Constantinople was made from more solid stuff than his immediate predecessors. He had been co-emperor (along with his brothers) since 654, and when his father was assassinated in 668, he became senior emperor.

Emperor Constantine IV was well aware of the problems that faced him. Although the Muslims were still engaged in in-fighting, it would only be a matter of time before they re-united and continued their invasion of the Byzantine Empire.

He quickly, and with the assistance of Pope Vitalian, subdued the revolt in Sicily that had let to his father's murder. He then prepared for the inevitable Muslim attempt on Constantinople.

The Muslims had started to gradually expand westwards across Anatolia, capturing several coastal towns from where they were preparing their attack. Finally in 674 they were ready. But so was Emperor Constantine IV, who had done his best to reinforce the city and make sure it was well supplied.

The siege was an extended affair which lasted five years. Each spring the Muslim army landed outside the walls of Constantinople and each winter they left a small holding force and withdrew with the main army to winter-quarters in the town of Cyzicus on the Anatolian side of the Sea of Marmara (close to modern day Erdek in Turkey).

Another part of Constantine IV's preparation was the construction of warships with nozzles that could spray highly flammable 'Greek fire', a compound that up to this point had only been used on land.

Still suffering from the defeat at the Battle of the Masts, Constantine IV had realized that he could not beat the Muslim navy on numbers, so he had gone the route of superior technology and finally, in 679, he managed to deploy his fire-ships in a decisive victory over the Muslim fleet outside their winter quarters.

The remaining Muslim fleet was further destroyed by a violent storm and their land army was attacked and severely damaged by Byzantine troops while marching back through Anatolia. The Muslims sued for peace and an agreement was made by which the Muslims, for the time being, paid an annual tribute to the Emperor of Byzantium.

While this was going on, the emerging First Bulgarian Empire helped themselves to Byzantine possessions in the Balkans and Constantine IV's attempts at getting rid of them did not go well. In 680, at the Battle of Ongal, the Byzantines were defeated and the Emperor had to recognize the new Bulgarian state.

Military matters settled for the time being, Constantine IV now turned his attention to the Church. It was not in his interest, with both Muslims and Bulgarians on the loose in the Empire, to have unrest in the Church, so he called a council known as the Third Council of Constantinople.

In Rome, Pope Vitalian died, saintly, in 672. While the Empire was in peril, two popes - Adeodatus II and Donus - had quietly come and gone leaving little trace in history. Neither was a saint.

It was thus their successor, Pope Agatho, who received the invitation to the Third Council of Constantinople and who arranged for synods to take place at local level throughout the Western Church in order to elect the members representing the Pope in Constantinople.

The Counsel started in November 680 and lasted until September of 681. The Emperor himself preceded over the initial and final sittings, although he did not offer a theological argument.

That same cannot be said about Pope Agatho, who had prepared a letter to be read out which clearly and categorically declared that Christ had two natures and two wills.

Since the invasion by the armies of Islam, most of the believers in Monothelitism were now under Muslim rule, so it was a relatively easy matter to get the Pope's views approved. Monothelitism was abandoned and declared heretic as was its known supporters including Pope Honorius I.

One final argument on the side of Monothelitism was made by a priest who claimed he could raise the dead. A dead body was put at his disposal, but as he failed to revive it, the claim did nothing to support Monothelitism.

The final findings of the Council were approved by the Emperor and then sent to Rome to be ratified by the Pope. There Pope Agatho had died a saintly death and been replaced by Leo II.

In actual fact, it took more than a year from the death of Agatho until Pope Leo II was finally consecrated. The reason was the finalization of an agreement between Pope Agatho and the Emperor in which the Emperor abolished the taxes previously paid by the Holy See upon the consecration of a new pope.

Once in an official capacity to do so, Pope Leo II eagerly wrote all the bishops in the Western Church, informing them of the outcome of the Council of Constantinople and urging them to live accordingly. He also settled matters with the Archbishop in Ravenna who once again submitted to the Pope's authority after the Pope abandoned the taxes he would normally put on his approval of a new bishop.

Pope Leo II died, saintly, after just short of a year as pope and he was replaced by another short-time appointee, Benedict II. As was the case before him, Benedict II's confirmation lasted nearly a year and he managed to convince the Emperor that the election of a pope should be a clerical matter and if secular approval was necessary, such could be obtained from the Exarch in Ravenna rather than from the Emperor himself. Having ruled as pope for only 317 days, Pope Benedict II died, saintly, on 8 May 686.

With their new powers to appoint a pope, John V, was appointed within a few weeks of the old Pope's death. As a token of the reconciliation inside the Church, John V was from the East, born in Antioch, although he had been a papal legate at the Third Council of Constantinople.

To further cement the improved relationship, the Emperor abandoned a further range of taxes, allowing John V to generously spend money which was distributed among the clergy. There are no historic records of money being spent on the poor, which may be why John V is not a saint.

John V also lasted a very short time on the Throne of St. Peter and on his death in 686 the new electoral powers given to 'the people of Rome' turned out to be a double-edged sword.

Unfortunately, they could not agree on a new pope, a situation that would not come to stand alone as time went by. The clergy favoured one Petros while the Army favoured one Theodoros. The two factions placed themselves in two different churches and from there 'ambassadors' ran to and from without much success. Finally, the clergy offered an acceptable compromise. They suggested Conon, and elderly priest from a military family.

Pope Conon was clearly a compromise, also due to his advanced age, and he only lasted 335 days as pope. He was not a saint, and on his death the hostilities between the factions in Rome broke out again.

This time the fight was not between the clergy and the military, but between more mixed groupings. One group favoured the Archdean Paschal, who had conveniently also bribed the Exarch of Ravenna, but an even larger group supported the Archpriest Theodore.

The two groups started a violent clash, in which both candidates ended up possessing part of the Lateran Palace. But sense resumed as a group of clergy, military officers and citizens met separately, to agree on a compromise candidate, Sergius I.

They forced the issue by marching on the Lateran Palace. Both anti-popes submitted to Sergius I, but the Exarch of Ravenna - bribed by Paschal - arrived in the City with a military force shortly after. He, however, read the situation correctly, plundered the Lateran Palace and left the City without getting involved in its intricate politics.

Part 6 - The Pope and the Crusader Knights

After a string of short-lived popes, Sergius I now ruled for fourteen years, long enough to become a saint and to take the Church into the eighth century.

In Constantinople Emperor Constantine IV died in 685. In concept he had ruled with his brothers, Heraclius and Tiberius, as co-emperors, but he had them both mutilated in 681 to pave the way for his son, who on his father's death took the Byzantine throne as Justinian II.

We have met Justinian II before - in Chapter 12 - and you may remember that he was ousted and had his nose slit, only to regain power wearing a nose-prosthesis of solid gold. In any case, the reason for his ousting, and ultimately for his execution, was that he was stubborn and completely unwilling to listening to criticism of any kind.

As far as the Church was concerned he had little time for niceties towards the Pope, but rather, he condoned a new council in 692, this time exclusively consisting of clergy from the East, who met in Constantinople and agreed on a range of issues regarding doctrine.

Although this council, known as the Quinisext Council, did not reopen the matter of Monothelitism, it did decree a range of changes to doctrine, mainly aimed at Rome to make changes in alignment with Constantinople.

Many of the issues concerned had roots in (Western) Christian adaptation of heathen traditions and were an integral part of Western Christianity. Pope Sergius I thus had no inclination to agree with the decrees of the council in which he had not even participated.

Emperor Justinian II ordered Pope Sergius I arrested, as had been the case with Pope Martin I four decades earlier. But the Emperor had not properly assessed the mood in Italy. The militias in Ravenna and Rome revolted and protected the Pope. Instead, it was the Emperor who, in 695, was ousted and exiled to the Crimea.

Ten years later, Emperor Justinian II was back, assisted by Tervel of the First Bulgarian Empire and he had not forgotten old scores to settle. Pope Sergius I had died a saint in 701 and had been followed by the non-descript Pope John VI who, in turn died in 705. He was not a saint.

Next in line was John VII and it was he who first had to face-off against the reinstated emperor. If Justinian II had been despotic before; during his second reign he was both despotic and vindictive. Although his campaigns against the external enemies of the Empire - the Bulgarians and Muslims - were unsuccessful, he had more success with suppressing his internal enemies.

He ordered Pope John VII to accept the decrees from the Quinisext Council, but John VII declined and held his ground until his death in 707. He was not a saint.

His successor, Sisinnius, was so sick that he only lasted three weeks before he died. He was quickly succeeded by Constantine, who through seven years as pope would see some up and downs, but would eventually triumph even though he was not a saint.

Emperor Justinian II demanded the Pope's presence in Constantinople and Constantine did not hesitate, but rather hastened to Constantinople to meet the Emperor

Pope Constantine was a real politician, as was Justinian II, and the two met and agreed on a compromise. Pope Constantine agreed to some, but not all, of the decrees from the Quinisext Council, effectively agreeing to minor issues only, but it was enough for the Emperor who claimed a victory for himself. Business done, Pope Constantine returned to Rome in 711. It would be 1,256 years before a pope again entered Constantinople (Pope Paul VI's visit to Istanbul in 1967).

In Constantinople the situation soon changed again. Emperor Justinian II was ousted once more and this time he was executed. The new emperor was Philippikos Bardanes and to complicate things he was a Monotheist and had relied on other Monotheists in his uprising against Justinian II.

The new emperor now wrote the Pope and demanded that he recognize Monothelitism and renege on the decrees of the Third Council of Constantinople.

The Pope refused and the Emperor threatened him with military intervention, but before it came to that the Emperor was ousted by his secretary who became Anastasios II.

Emperor Anastasios II soon confirmed to the Pope that the imperial Court was once more behind the Third Council of Constantinople and that it had no appetite for Monothelitism.

Pope Constantine thus died the victor in 715, but it was his successor, Gregory II, who would become a saint.

Emperor Anastasios II only ruled for two years and was followed by the similar short reign Theodosios III. Now followed the long reign of Emperor Leo III, which would see a new conflict arise between the churches in the East and the West and between the Emperor and the Pope.

Taking power in 717, Emperor Leo III immediately faced an Arab siege of Constantinople, the second of the kind, which he successfully expelled, helped by Bulgarian reinforcements.

He now threw himself at a series of re-organization projects, revising all aspects of Byzantine civil and military administration, but it was his religious reforms that would cause trouble within the Church.

The Emperor decided that for the better of public morale, the worship of icons should be forbidden. The concept is known as *iconoclasm*, literally translated as 'icon breaking'.

The range of Imperial decrees issued between 726 and 729 sent shockwaves through the Empire. Apart from some local nobles and a small part of the clergy, nobody wanted *iconoclasm* which broke with centuries of tradition.

Part 6 - The Pope and the Crusader Knights

The Patriarch of Constantinople resigned and was replaced by a puppet, but the Pope in Rome had no intentions of resigning, he intended to fight.

As it was, Pope Gregory II had already been in conflict with the Emperor before. Needing money, Leo III had attempted to tax the Pope on Church land - or papal patrimony - and the Pope had refused. The Emperor's new iconoclast edicts were thus just further sparks to set off a waiting powder keg.

And off it went! The Imperial garrisons in Ravenna and in the Duchy of the Pentapolis revolted against the Emperor and killed all officers loyal to Constantinople. The Byzantine troops in Italy even considered marching on Constantinople, and it was Pope Gregory II who convinced them differently.

The Pope now convened a synod which met in Rome in 727 and quickly condemned *iconoclasm* as heresy. The Emperor responded by putting his possessions in Southern Italy under the authority of Constantinople, but they too refused to follow the Emperor's orders.

A failed attempt to militarily subdue the garrison in Ravenna and two failed attempts on the Pope's life finally ended the Emperor's attempts to regain control in Italy and, in effect, the Empire had once again lost control of the Italian peninsula.

Pope Gregory II died in 731 and was replaced by Gregory III, who would reign in parallel to Emperor Leo III for the next decade to come.

Like his predecessor and namesake, Gregory III had his hands full and would become a saint.

Iconoclasm had created a great divide inside the Byzantine Empire. Although the Exarch of Ravenna still wielded some military power on the ground, ties had been cut to Byzantium. The relationship between the Byzantines, their Roman subjects and the neighbouring Lombards had never been good. Whereas there was mostly not war, there was not really peace either. Both parties would regularly raid into the other's territories and castles and towns would change hands.

With central Byzantine authority broken, the Lombards sensed that this was the time to strike. The Byzantines had plenty to do with both internal strife and growing threats from both Bulgarians and Arabs, so Italy lay open.

The papacy had maintained good, if not overly warm, relationships with the Lombards. Politics aside, they were spiritual subjects of the Pope.

The Lombards had already attacked the Byzantine provinces during the reign of Pope Gregory II and although they had not taken Ravenna itself, many cities fell under their rule and their king, Liutprand, marched on Rome itself in 728. But Pope Gregory II had gone to meet him outside the City and had convinced him of his wrongdoing as a good Catholic. Indeed, Liutprand had so repented that he granted considerable amounts of land to the Church. The donation is known as 'the Donation of Sutri' (Sutri being the main town contained within the territories) and was the first land possessions of the Church outside the Province of Rome.

16 - The Pope

Pope Gregory III was in little doubt that sooner or later the problems with the Lombards would resurface so he immediately started works to reinforce the walls of Rome and various fortifications in its immediate surrounds.

Like his predecessor he vehemently detested *iconoclasm* and as a countermove spent considerable amounts of money on lavishly decorating the churches of Rome with icons and works of religious art.

In the meantime Liutprand had allied himself with Charles Martel, the increasingly powerful King of the Franks, as it was in their common interest to stop the Muslim Moors' advances from Spain into southern France.

But in 738 the Lombard Duke of Spoleto revolted against Liutprand and when he was defeated he sought refuge with the Pope in Rome.

Liutprand demanded that the rebellious duke be handed over, but Pope Gregory II refused on the reasons of sanctuary.

The Lombards now returned to Rome, capturing the outlying province and laying siege to the City itself. The Pope sent ambassadors to Charles Martel, trying to convince him to come to Rome's rescue, but Charles Martel did not want to get involved and instead tried to mediate.

While negotiations took place in 741 both Gregory III and Charles Martel died, as did Emperor Leo III in Constantinople.

Gregory III was replaced by Pope Zachary who was a charismatic diplomat. He soon convinced Liutprand of the futility of his quest and had him return all the lands he had occupied during his disagreement with Pope Gregory III.

The death of Charles Martel had sent the Frankish Kingdom into a succession crisis. The nominal king was Childeric III, but the real power was wielded by Charles Mantel's son Pepin the Short.

Pepin the Short was ambitious and decided to turn to the Pope for an ally. He corresponded with the Pope on the question as to whether the title of king should reside with the person of royal lineage (Childeric III) or the person who held the real power (himself).

After the unsuccessful overture made to Charles Martel, Pope Zachary was not late to realize the potential of an alliance with the Franks. He thus did not hesitate but supported Pepin the Short, declaring him the rightful king of the Franks. Childeric II was tonsured and sent off to a monastery and Pepin was crowned with papal blessings.

In Constantinople, the death of Emperor Leo III had elevated his son, Constantine V to the throne. He was an even stronger advocate of *iconoclasm* than his father, so the divide inside the Church was at its highest when Pope Zachary died, saintly, in 752.

Zachary's replacement was quickly appointed, but he died before he could be consecrated, and a new appointment was made in Pope Stephen II. His saintly reign would see a new culmination of papal power.

Pope Stephen II immediately continued the alliance with the Franks. He crossed the Alps and entered into the Frankish kingdom. Here he met with Pepin the Short and anointed him as king. It is uncertain whether the Pope made this unusual move to speed things up or whether he, as claimed by some, effectively fled Italy, but the outcome was the same.

It was now Pepin the Short's turn to pay back the favour given to him by the Pope. He entered Italy and forced the Lombard king, now Aistulf, to give up the possessions the Lombards had conquered from the Byzantines.

The former Exarch of Ravenna was now re-established as a political entity and then it was given to the Pope as his own country. The transaction is known as 'the Donation of Pepin' and established the Pope as a temporal, as well as spiritual, ruler.

From Emperor Constantine the Great and forward it had been common practice that rulers donated land to the Church. Successive popes had further bought land and many wealthy faithful had, over the centuries, further donated land to the Church for their spiritual salvation. The Church was thus already a substantial landowner.

Furthermore, as we have seen, the Pope gradually filled a power-vacuum and became the de-facto power in Rome itself, but never before had the Pope been an official political entity, and even a sovereign - as he was now.

But even though the Lombards had been forced to give up the Exarch of Ravenna, they still maintained their own former possessions in Italy. King Aistulf died in 756 and his successor Desiderius rekindled the internal unrest on the peninsula.

Indeed, the borders in Italy were not clear. There were Lombards living inside the (new) Papal States, there were still Lombard occupation in other parts and there was also Frankish occupation in parts of traditional Lombard possessions.

When Pope Stephen II died in 757, becoming the first papal sovereign but nevertheless not a saint, his brother became pope as Paul I. His appointment met with some opposition, but the key reason for Paul I's appointment was a desire for him to continue the foreign policies of his brother.

Pope Paul I was a careful diplomat. To maintain as good relations with the Byzantine Emperor as possible under the circumstances, he even submitted his own papal appointment for approval by the Exarch of Ravenna, despite now being the formal sovereign of Ravenna himself.

The diplomatic tasks were stacked up before him. The Lombard King Desiderius was a constant threat to the new Papal States and Pope Paul I attempted to pacify him by acting as go-between. Pope Paul I wrote a letter to Pepin the Short in which he asked him to consider the Lombard claims for restoration of lands held by the Franks, while at the same time he wrote a second letter to Pepin informing him of a Lombard alliance with Byzantium and asked for his military intervention on behalf of the Papal States.

Pepin the Short decided not to intervene but rather enter into negotiations with the Lombards. Gradually the Lombards returned the areas of the Papal States which they had occupied and both Pope Paul I and Pepin the Short managed to maintain enough of a peaceful relationship with the Lombards to avoid the creation of an armed alliance between them and the Byzantines.

Pope Paul I died in 767 - contrary to his brother he was a saint - and Pepin the Short died in 768, leaving the playing field open to a new set of players.

Pepin the Short was followed by an uneasy co-rule between his sons Charles I - known as Charlemagne (Charles the Great) - and Carloman I.

Pope Paul I's succession was even more troublesome. The Pope had been ailing for a good while and a powerful landowner, Toto of Nepi, had prepared for the Pope's death.

With the Pope now the sovereign of a considerable nation state, the stakes were high so Toto had assembled a considerable number of troops and when it was clear that the Pope was dying, he marched on Rome.

In the Lateran Palace the nearest bishop at hand was forced at swordpoint to quickly ordain Toto's brother Constantine, as a priest and then immediately elevate him to bishop. The brothers then proceeded to take armed control of the election process and have Constantine elected as Pope Constantine II.

The new Pope immediately wrote to the Frankish rulers to get them to verify his appointment, but they ignored him. In the meantime, members of the clergy had gone to the Lombard King Desiderius and asked for his help.

Desiderius sensed an opportunity to assert his own influence on the infant state, so he agreed to help. Lombard troops arrived in Rome and a fight broke out in which Toto of Nepi was killed. His brother, the Pope, hid in a church but was captured and thrown in jail.

The Lombards now played the same game and quickly appointed a new pope, Philip (whom they had dragged out of a monastery against his will), but at the same time the clergy had elected their own candidate, Stephen III, and Philip's appointment was annulled.

Anti-pope Constantine II was later convicted by a clerical court, was beaten, had his tongue ripped out and was sent off to live the rest of his life in a monastery.

The new Pope was not directly involved in these proceedings, which were mainly organised by Christophorus, the Lateran Court's shadowy Primicerius (top administrative officer) and his son Sergius who was the Treasurer.

Once secured as pope, Stephen III had his work cut out. The tumultuous election process had clearly shown that with the papal position now political as well as spiritual, it was a potential scene for murder and mayhem. To avoid such in the future, Stephen III set about to further regulate the election process to ensure that it could no longer be hijacked by ambitious nobles. It could be argued whether he was successful or not.

The new Papal States were fragile, not only politically, but also militarily. It had been created by force, Frankish force as it was, but had little force of its own with which to defend itself or even back up the claims it had on various territories still held by the Lombards.

The Lombards, still under King Desiderius had also shown their interest in the papal crown by their attempt to appoint their own pope and they could not be trusted to hand over the disputed territories or refrain from seeking further concession by force.

Pope Stephen III thus appealed to the Frankish rulers to assist him in consolidating the new state.

But the Frankish Kingdom had trouble of its own. The relationship between the co-ruling brothers was uneasy to say the least. Charlemagne was the more proactive and Carloman had on one occasion sulkily withdrawn his military support to Charlemagne while he was putting down a revolt in Aquitaine.

The only thing that prevented a direct civil war was the mother of the two rulers, Pepin the Short's widow, Bertrada of Laon.

It has been claimed by some historians that Bertrada favoured Charlemagne, her first-born, but whether she did or did not, she was the only person who managed to prevent the animosity between brothers breaking into violence. She furthermore turned out to be a skilled diplomat.

The trouble that the Franks had was the Lombards, a potential enemy they shared with the Pope. As a neighbour they threatened both the Frankish kingdom directly and of course were a constant threat to the Papal States, nominally under Frankish protection.

Bertrada took the bull by the horns and went on an embassy to the Lombard King Desiderius. Here she negotiated a marriage between *'one of her sons'* - which would later turn out to be Charlemagne - and King Desiderius' daughter, Desiderata.

Pope Stephen III was less than happy about that. Not only did he see it as a bad idea for the Franks to ally themselves with the Lombards, who he considered the common enemy, but both Bertrada's sons were already married.

Bertrada had foreseen the Pope's displeasure, so she had also negotiated the Lombard surrender of the territories claimed by the Pope, which however did little to calm the Pope down.

Nevertheless, the marriage went ahead towards the end of 770, and for a short time served its purpose by securing peace in the region. But the peace did not last long.

The following year Carloman I died, according to history from natural causes, although it was very convenient as it secured Charlemagne a free reign.

16 - The Pope

Charlemagne did not hesitate for long before he took full advantage. Desiderata had fulfilled her purpose. The marriage was annulled and she was sent back to her father.

But it was not only in the Frankish Kingdom that politics ran high. The elevation to capital had with all possible haste made the Lateran Court a nest of intrigues, at the time controlled by Christophorus and his son Sergius, the masters behind the appointment of Stephen III.

Christophorus and Sergius were vehemently anti-Lombard, and with some right, given the Lombard King's attempt to put his own puppet on the papal throne. They were also a direct threat to the papal authority as they effectively controlled the court and could, to a large extent, pick and choose what the Pope did and did not know about.

King Desiderius of the Lombards now planned to get rid of the two powerful enemies inside the Lateran Court. He found a willing ally in the Papal Chamberlain, Paulus Afiarta, who had a personal interest in removing his rival from power. Whispers about Christophorus and Sergius started to circulate inside the court, designed to reach the Pope's ears, but when it did not yield the desired result King Desiderius forced the matter.

Escorted by a military contingent he arrived at the gates of Rome. He claimed to be on a pilgrimage, but on the orders of Christophorus and Sergius the gates were closed, the walls were manned and the Lombard King was kept waiting. He now demanded to speak to the Pope in person.

Pope Stephen III was not afraid of Desiderius, or if he was, he decided to conceal it, so he left the security of the City to meet the Lombard king in St. Peter's Cathedral, which was outside the City Walls.

While the Pope was out the Chamberlain, Paulus Afiarta stirred up a mob in an attempt to overthrow Christophorus and Sergius. A fight broke out and it was Paulus Afiarta who had to flee to the Lateran Palace in the end.

On the Pope's return, he was met by a riot in progress, and he just about managed to make the warring mobs disperse. He was forced to swear that he would not turn Christophorus and Sergius over to the Lombards, and it was clear that the situation was far from under control.

The following day the Pope once again left the city, this time to seek the protection of King Desiderius. The King was clear in his demands; he wanted Christophorus and Sergius. The Pope sent two envoys back to the City and the King sent a message to the people of Rome, ensuring them of his protection on the condition that Christophorus and Sergius were handed over to him.

Eventually Christophorus and Sergius left the City to join the Pope in St. Peter's Cathedral. It is unknown if they did so entirely of their own free will (relying on the oath they had forced from the Pope) or whether they were proactively assisted.

In any case the Pope could now return to the City and the following day Paulus Afiarta and his partisans joined King Desiderius to discuss the fate of Christophorus and Sergius.

It was decided to torture and blind them. Christophorus died from his injuries three days later and Sergius was thrown in a cell at the Lateran Palace.

To ensure that the proceedings in Rome would not stir up trouble with Charlemagne, Desiderius' last act was to force the Pope to write a letter to the Frankish king, explaining that Christophorus and Sergius had plotted with his brother, Carloman I, to have the Pope murdered.

Furthermore, the Lombard king once again refused to hand over papal territories under his control - despite many agreements to do so - berating the Pope not to push his luck. The Lombard King had removed the people who effectively controlled him, and the Pope should be content with that.

Paulus Afiarta was now the new strong-man at the Lateran Court but exerted his power with enough stealth to avoid the Pope's displeasure. Indeed, he waited until the Pope fell mortally ill until he tied up the loose ends. While the Pope was drawing his last breaths, Paulus Afiarta had the last supporters of Christophorus and Sergius expelled from the City and had Sergius dragged from his cell and strangled.

When Pope Stephen III died in January of 772, the last remnants of the power struggle was thus gone, and Paulus Afiarta was in full control. Pope Stephen III was not a saint.

Neither was his successor Adrian I even though he came to be one of the few popes to rule for more than twenty years.

At the start of Adrian I's rule matters may well have been settled internally in Rome, but the issued with the Lombards was still alive and well.

King Desiderius had not taken well to the return of his daughter after the annulment of her marriage to Charlemagne. He therefore welcomed Gerberga, the widow of Carloman I, and her sons when they sought refuge with him in 772.

Gerberga claimed that her sons were entitled to their father's half of the Frankish Kingdom, which Charlemagne had absorbed on his brother's death. King Desiderius was happy to back that up and he once again occupied papal lands in an attempt to force the Pope to recognize the claim of Carloman I's sons.

But the Pope had no such intentions, and he appealed for help from Charlemagne. He in turn was prepared to settle matters with Desiderius once and for all, so in the summer of 773 he crossed the Alps and entered Italy as his father had done before him.

The last time the Franks invaded they had satisfied themselves with restoring the former Byzantine possessions, this time they went for annihilation of the Lombard reign in Italy altogether.

16 - The Pope

The war lasted until 774 when Desiderius surrendered himself and his family to Charlemagne to avoid further bloodshed. The Lombard King and his family were forced to enter monasteries. Gerberga and her sons were brought before Charlemagne and disappeared from history. It is assumed they too were forced into monasteries, away from public life.

In concept the Lombard Kingdom - now under Frankish control - covered both northern and southern Italy, geographically separated by the Papal States, but in real terms only the northern parts were under Frankish control.

The Lombards in the southern part of Italy submitted nominally to Charlemagne, but in reality developed into smaller Lombard dukedoms with de-facto autonomy which would only be sporadically challenged in the following centuries by both Franks and Byzantines, the latter also maintaining small isolated enclaves in the extreme south.

Finally, there was peace in Italy and it was time for the Pope to deal with Church matters and in particular the issue of *iconoclasm*.

In Constantinople Emperor Constantine V - a devout supporter of *iconoclasm* - had died in 775. He was succeeded by his son Leo IV (the Kazar). He was brought up as an iconoclast, but his wife Irene (of Athens) was as *iconodule* (in support of icons). Leo IV thus sought to reconcile the clergy in Constantinople, continuing the iconoclastic rules but allowing its opponents back into the City. This, however, did not impress the Pope.

When Emperor Leo IV died in 780 the situation changed again. His son and heir apparent, Constantine VI, was only nine years old and his mother, Irene, ruled as his regent.

Irene seized the opportunity and decided to deal with the matter once and for all. She invited the Pope for a Council in which the issue would be discussed by the Church at large, as so far various councils held on the matter had been either exclusively Eastern (pro-iconoclastic) or Western (anti-iconoclastic).

Pope Adrian I happily received the invitation and the Council met in Constantinople in 786. But it turned out to be trickier than expected. Byzantine army-units in support of *iconoclasm* entered the Church of the Holy Apostles where the council took place and proceedings had to be abandoned.

The iconoclastic army units were subsequently ordered on a campaign in Anatolia, but it was a rouse and once away from Constantinople they were disarmed and disbanded.

But Constantinople was still not considered safe, so the council was recalled in Nicaea in September of 787 and this time the proceedings were allowed to proceed. The council is thus known as the Second Council of Nicaea and it irrevocably abandoned *iconoclasm*, once again uniting the Church to the extent it was ever really united.

Curiously, it was Charlemagne who took some exception to the Council's decrees. He had his own theologians look at the Council's transcript and issued no less than two proposed alterations. The Pope did not agree, and a (purely Western) council held in Frankfurt in 794 did not resolve the issue.

Good relations were however maintained between the Pope and the King of the Franks, and Pope Adrian I left his realm in a good state when he died in 795.

The Romans took no chances in terms of political interference but immediately (on the very day Pope Adrian I was buried) elected a new pope who was consecrated the following day. Their choice was Leo III, a churchman through and through who at the time of his appointment was Cardinal-Priest of St. Susanna.

The new Pope immediately wrote Charlemagne, informing him of the election and Charlemagne in turn wrote back to congratulate Leo III to whom he also granted a considerable gift in cash, newly won in Charlemagne's campaign against the Avars.

Pope Leo III thus started out in a position of both power and wealth, but all was not well. For reasons that are unknown, relatives of the deceased Pope Adrian I had a deep hatred of Leo III. It can only be speculated that the motive possibly was a desire to turn the papacy - and thus the de-facto kingship of the Papal States - into a dynasty but, no matter the reason, they conspired against the Pope and on 25 April 799 they struck.

The Pope was in a religious procession when he was attacked by armed men. He was pushed to the ground, rendered unconscious and an attempt was made to tear out his tongue and eyes. He was rescued before the assailants could complete the job, but he was left deeply shaken and sought refuge with the Duke of Spoleto before he proceeded to Charlemagne's camp in Paderborn.

The King received the Pope with great honours. It was the second time in fifty years that a pope had left Italy to seek help and protection from a Frankish king and like Pepin the Short before him, Charlemagne readily offered his protection.

After a few months in Paderborn, Pope Leo III was escorted back to Rome and shortly thereafter Charlemagne himself arrived.

A synod was now called, but it declared that it could not judge a pope; in line with the decree of the synod held 300 years before when Pope Symmachus stood accused in front of King Theodoric. The Pope, however, volunteered to swear an oath on his innocence (he was officially accused of adultery and perjury) and then intervened on behalf of his attackers, having their death sentences reverted to exile.

As was the case when Pepin the Short had intervened on behalf of the Pope five decades earlier, there now came a political follow up.

It is unclear how much had been arranged beforehand, perhaps even in Paderborn, or whether the Pope acted on his own initiative, but in any case, the event which followed would have an enormous impact on the political landscape in Europe for centuries to come.

On Christmas Day 800, at mass celebrated in St. Peter's Cathedral, when the King knelt at the altar, Pope Leo III crowned him as *Imperator Romanorum* ("Emperor of the Romans"), effectively restoring the Western Roman Empire which had not been an active political entity for centuries.

As mentioned, Charlemagne appeared to be surprised by the Pope's actions and is even (according to his own historian) quoted to have said that if had known what was about to happen, then he would not have entered the church, but both his contemporaries and modern historians doubt that, if for no other reason, then due to the massive crown which was waiting for him on the altar.

In any case this revival of the Roman Empire was a clear and direct insult to the imperial authority of Constantinople, and would trigger hostilities for a decade to come.

If he was indeed surprised, Charlemagne overcame the initial shock quickly and added *serenissimus Augustus a Deo coronatus magnus pacificus imperator Romanum gubernans imperium* ("most serene Augustus crowned by God, the great, peaceful emperor ruling the Roman Empire") to his title.

Charlemagne was now by far the most powerful magnate in Europe, ruling not only by force, but as Emperor with the blessing of God's own representative on earth.

The Pope had now cemented the relationship between the Papal States and the Carolingian Empire, as Charlemagne's realm would be known, ensuring military protection of the new papal state.

Apart from its enclaves in the southern part of Italy, Byzantium also held Venice, the last part of the Exarch of Ravenna still under its control, as well as the Dalmatian coast. Attempts were made between the Franks and Byzantines to define the exact borders between the two empires, a process made complicated by Byzantium's refusal to acknowledge Charlemagne's title.

Violence broke out when Venice revolted and submitted to Frankish suzerainty and the Byzantine territories on the Dalmatian coast to some degree did the same.

Successive attempts were made to restore peace and finally an agreement, known as *Pax Nicephori'*, was reached around 812, confirming Venice and the Dalmatian islands and coastal cities (but not the hinterlands) as being subjects of Byzantium. Although the agreement, in principle, accepted the new empire, the Byzantines did reserve the right to the title *Emperor of the Romans* for themselves. In practical terms the new Western Empire eventually became known as the *Holy Roman Empire*, although Voltaire famously expressed the opinion that it was *'neither holy, nor Roman, nor an empire'*.

With the security of the Papal States ensured, Pope Leo III now started to organize the administration of the new state, transforming the Lateran Court into an organization suitable for a nation state. He died in 816 and despite his efforts he was not a saint.

Part 6 - The Pope and the Crusader Knights

Within a few days a new pope was elected and anointed. The choice was Stephen IV and it is seen by some that the quick election was a statement by the Church that they were entitled to appoint the Pope without seeking approval from the Roman Emperor.

That same Emperor was now Louis the Pious, the son of Charlemagne who had inherited the crown on his father's death in 814. Indeed, he had not only inherited the crown, he had indeed crowned himself in Aachen shortly after his father's death.

As a consequence, and to assert his rights as giver of the crown, the Pope travelled to Rheims to meet the Emperor.

It is reported that the Emperor prostrated himself three times in front of the Pope, who then proceeded to crown him properly. Formalities settled, the Pope returned to Rome where he died after a reign of 226 days, He was not a saint.

His successor, Paschal I, turned out to be one of the more controversial popes of the times.

Paschal I was also elected and consecrated very quickly after the death of his predecessor and a letter was sent to the Emperor, apologizing in principle, but stating that the quick election was necessary in order to avoid infighting between factions inside the Church.

The Emperor's response is unknown as a letter expressing his consent and indeed giving his permission to proceed with papal elections without his approval, is probably a forgery.

In the meantime, Constantinople had been going through a period of unrest, seeing the Empress Irene come and go. Power was now in the hands of Leo V who was locked in battle with the Bulgarians under Krum. Contrary to his immediate predecessors he ultimately had some success - after Krum had died - and he decided that prior Byzantine misfortune was caused by the abandonment of *iconoclasm*. He thus reinstated *iconoclasm* and took the opportunity to confiscate Church property and purge the clerical ranks. The latter indicates that his motives may have been less religious and more temporal.

The purge in Constantinople created a stream of refugee monks and clerics. With nowhere else to go they made their way to Rome and Pope Paschal I offered them shelter.

The controversy began when Pope Paschal I anointed the son of Louis the Pious, Lothair I, as King of Italy. The title had been won by the Franks in conquest (of the Lombards) and was used as a holding title for the heir apparent for the Imperial Crown.

Lothair I was crowned in Rome, which set a precedent for the Pope crowning the King and for the procedure to be conducted in Rome. This was politically important for the Pope at a phase were the Pope appointed the Emperor, and the Emperor appointed the Pope and the exact balance of power between the two was precarious.

16 - The Pope

Lothair I's title was thus really supposed to be nominal, but Lothair I had other ideas. He started to take an active interest in affairs in northern Italy and supported a claim against the Curia (the Lateran Court) by the Farfa Abbey located north of Rome.

The issue was one of misappropriation of property and, with royal support, the Abbey won the claim. This was possibly a small matter, but it outraged the local nobility and clergy, so much so that a revolt erupted in northern Italy, led by the Pope's own (former) legate Theodore, and his son Leone.

The revolt was suppressed; Theodore and Leone were taken to Rome to testify. But before they could state their case they were arrested at the Lateran Palace, blinded and executed.

Popular opinion was that the two defendants were executed because they had proof of the Pope's personal involvement in the issue with Farfa Abbey. The Pope swore his innocence and the matter eventually died and so did Pope Paschal I.

The Pope suffered the post-mortem shame of not being buried in St. Peter's Cathedral with the other popes. It was considered that he had brought shame on the Curia and he was put to rest in Santa Prassede, a church which Paschal I had elaborately redecorated, amongst other things with a mosaic of his mother known as 'Episcopa Theodora' and a mosaic of himself. His shame was however reverted when he later was recognized as a saint after all.

After the death of the controversial Pope Paschal I, a new fight broke out. The clergy wanted one candidate, Eugene, as pope and the people wanted another, Zinzinnus. Eventually Lothair I got involved and arrived in Rome.

Lothair I was already at this stage of his long reign a smooth politician, so he used the opportunity to lay down the law, literally. He issued, in agreement with the papal candidate Eugene, a constitution, known as *Constitutio Romana*, which regulated not only the election process of the pope (who was to be consecrated only after the Emperor's approval), but also established a range of legal parameters for the rule of Italy, including the appointment of two commissioners - one appointed by the Pope and one by the Emperor - who could intervene in temporal matters in case the Pope failed to do so. Furthermore, the *Constitutio Romana* specified that if in doubt, the temporal power of the Emperor outranks that of the Pope.

After the issue of the *Constitutio Romana*, Lothair I put his power behind Eugene, who became Pope Eugene II and immediately ratified the constitution.

Pope Eugene II only lasted three years. He spent them focused on Church-matters, issuing a range of disciplinary decrees, many regarding education which was a subject close to his heart, and some regarding the *iconoclasm* which was still in force in Constantinople. He died in 827. He was not a saint.

One of the decrees of the new *Constitutio Romana* specified that the election of a pope had to involve both the clergy and the nobility of Rome. This was a break from the doctrine previously set by Pope Stephen III by which it was a clerical matter only.

On the death of Pope Eugene II the nobles immediately took advantage of their newfound inclusion and elected their own favourite, Valentine, as the new pope. Although noble by birth, Valentine was also an Archdeacon, but not a priest, thus technically not eligible for the papacy. Furthermore, he was rumoured to be either the (illegitimate) son, or even the (more illegitimate) lover of Pope Eugene II, but in any case, he was quickly elected and consecrated.

The plan was to apologize to the Emperor in a letter subsequent to the new Pope's consecration, but Pope Valentine died after only five weeks as pope and the letter was never sent.

The nobles of Rome now proceeded to appoint another candidate. This time it was Gregory IV who, at that time, was Cardinal priest of the Basilica of St Mark in Rome. Gregory was reluctant, but he was dragged to the Lateran Palace where he was appointed as pope-elect. This time letters did go to the Emperor, and it was only after his approval that the new pope was consecrated.

Pope Gregory IV got himself severely mixed up in imperial politics. The underlying reason was a looming civil war between Louis the Pious and his sons, spearheaded by Lothair I.

Without going into the intricate details of the conflict itself, in 833 Lothair I asked the Pope to act as a mediator and convinced him to join him in France. The Frankish bishops were on the side of Louis the Pious and the Pope's apparent siding with Lothair I caused a revolt. The bishops declared that they would not submit to the papal authority on this matter - even though Pope Gregory IV apparently never asked them to do so in the first place - and the parties were threatening excommunication of each other, the bishops arguing that the combined power of all the bishops outranked the power of the Pope.

In any case Gregory IV's mediation was unsuccessful. Louis the Pious was forced to abdicate - to the benefit of Lothair I - although he was restored the following year (834).

Pope Gregory IV left for Rome. His attempts at intervening in imperial politics had done nothing but damage.

After his restoration to power, Emperor Louis the Pious sent ambassadors to Rome to investigate the Pope's role in the previous years' debacle. The Pope managed to convince them of his good intentions at all times and the Emperor accepted his explanation.

16 - The Pope

The Pope had learned his lesson and now focused entirely on Church matters, which included a range of building activities, both religious and temporal. He did try to mediate, this time by proxy, when civil war broke out in Frankia again, this time caused by Louis the Pious' death and leading to the Empire being split between his sons with Lothair I as the new Emperor.

The Pope died in 844. He was not a saint. On his death a new battle broke out between the clerical and noble factions. The clerical side appointed one John VIII whereas the nobles elected Sergius II. The nobles brought the clerics in line by means of violence, and Sergius II had to step in personally to save the life of Anti-Pope John.

The new Pope was consecrated in haste and without the approval of Emperor Lothair I. A letter was sent to inform (rather than apply to) the Emperor, but Lothair I was not as forgiving as his predecessors. He was the architect behind the *Constitutio Romana,* and he expected it to be adhered to. He therefore sent an armed response to the letter, which arrived at the gates of Rome under the command of his son Louis (II).

The Pope, and the nobles of Rome, submitted to the Emperor's authority - albeit a little late - and the Pope crowned Louis II as King of Italy.

Pope Sergius II now started a range of building projects in Rome. To finance them he made Simony (the sale of Church offices) commonplace, but the Church would soon suffer a blow which was both financial and emotional.

Saracens had slowly but surely spread from Arabia into the Mediterranean. By the eight century they had control of south-eastern Spain (The Caliphate of Cordoba) and in the ninth century there was an ongoing battle for control of Corsica and Sicily.

Saracens were also used as mercenaries by the various - and often at war with each other - lords in southern Italy. One such mercenary band of Saracens was fighting in Campania in south-western Italy when in 846 they raided up the coast and landed at the Roman harbours of Ostia and Portus.

The Saracens who - according to contemporary sources - were very well aware of where they were going and what they were looking for marched directly on Rome. The Roman militia closed the gates and manned the walls, but the target was not Rome itself.

Instead the targets were the cathedrals outside the walls; prime amongst them St. Peter's Cathedral and the - aptly named - Basilica of Saint Paul Outside the Walls. The cathedrals, filled with treasure, were thoroughly sacked and the Saracens withdrew loaded with plunder.

The blow was devastating. Priceless treasure was lost, but the mere thought that Muslim raiders could, with relative ease, plunder the centre of (Western) Christianity was mind-blowing. Pope Sergius II ordered the defences of Rome improved, but he died soon after. He was not a saint.

It fell on his predecessor, Pope Leo IV to complete the defences of Rome and fight against the Saracens when they returned for more.

Part 6 - The Pope and the Crusader Knights

The appointment of Leo IV held no controversy and he set to work quickly. His first concern was the potential of another Saracen attack. There were Saracens with a powerful fleet off Sardinia and although the Pope continued the strengthening of the walls that Pope Sergius II had started, it did not solve the problem of the outlying churches and districts of the city.

The Pope thus realized that the key to discourage the Saracens was to beat them at sea before they got the opportunity to land in the harbours of Rome. The Papal States had limited naval capability, and to beat the Saracens they needed help.

The Pope now formed an alliance with the naval cities of Naples, Amalfi and Gaeta. The united fleet was assembled off Ostia, which had also been reinforced after the Saracen attack and there it was waiting for the enemy. The Pope went to Ostia in person and led the troops in prayer before the enemy approached.

The battle was raging when a storm broke out. The Christian ships managed to get back to the harbour, but the Saracen fleet was scattered, and they were easy pickings for the Christians who rounded up the stragglers once the storm had subsided.

Whereas the battle - as battles are concerned - was not exactly a big affair, it was made immortal by Raphael some 650 years later, when he painted the *Battaglia di Ostia* in the Apostolic Palace. In the painting we can see Pope Leo IV giving thanks to God for the storm, but the features of the Pope are actually those of Pope Leo X who ordered the painting.

With the Saracen fleet defeated, it was time to sort the issue of defences. As mentioned, two main cathedrals, many smaller churches, and the neighbourhood of Borgo was actually outside the ancient city-walls. Pope Leo IV now had new walls built which reached across to the right bank of the Tiber River and encapsulated the endangered churches and neighbourhoods. The newly walled area is to this day known as the Leonine City.

With the defences improved, Pope Leo IV now started a refurbishing programme in the looted churches. Large sums were spent on replacing the gold and precious stones which had been removed by the looting Saracens, the gold used for the altar in St. Peter's Cathedral alone weighing in at nearly 100 Kg.

After eight hectic years as Pope, Leo IV died in 855. He was a saint. His successor was chosen with some difficulties.

The first choice was one Hadrian, but he refused the position. The clergy then decided one Benedict III, but a group of nobles close to the Emperor had in the meantime decided on one Anastasius (sometimes, but not positively identified as Anastasius Bibliothecarius, the Chief Archivist of the Church).

The nobles forced the election of Benedict III to be annulled and installed Anastasius, but public pressure forced them to change their mind and Benedict III was consecrated on the condition that he did not pursue matters with Anastasius or his supporters.

That same year Emperor Lothair I had died and his sons started a civil war even though Louis II had been anointed as the new Emperor. As his predecessor had done, Pope Benedict III attempted to mediate in the imperial battle, but he had more success with religious matters, playing host to King Æthelwulf of Wessex and his son, the future King Alfred the Great.

After just short of three years as pope, Benedict III died in 858. He was not a saint.

As it happened, Emperor Louis II was in the vicinity of Rome when the Pope died. He took the opportunity to visit the city and personally participate in the election process.

The choice fell on Nicholas I a stout disciplinarian known for his piety. The Franks had problems with Saracens in the south and Norsemen (Vikings) in the north so the election of an upstanding and iconic pope was not entirely a coincidence.

The Emperor stayed for the consecration ceremony and the new Pope visited the Emperor in his camp outside the gates of Rome before the Emperor moved on. On this occasion the Emperor, famously, dismounted his horse and led the Pope's horse by the bridle, by many contemporaries seen as a token of the Emperor's submission to the Pope's supremacy.

If Pope Nicholas I was elected to be a symbol of Catholicism he did not disappoint, but that did not necessarily make him popular. The problem was that his first task of a principal character was the annulment of the marriage of the Emperor's brother, Lothair II.

Lothair II had inherited part of Emperor Lothair I's empire. Whereas his brother, Louis II had got the title as Emperor, Lothair II ruled as king and his territories were named after him as Lotharingia (later changed to Lorraine).

As was common during the time he had been married off at an early age to a bride chosen by his father for political reasons. The bride was Teutberga whose father was Count of Turin and Valois.

As most readers will appreciate, the role of the marriage itself was to secure a political union and the role of Teutberga was to produce an heir. But Teutberga was incapable of bearing children. That, however, was not a problem for King Lothair II's mistress, Waldrada, so Lothair II wanted the marriage to Teutberga annulled and to make Waldrada - herself of noble lineage - his new queen.

Lothair II sought, with mixed success, the support for his mission from his brother, the Emperor, and his two powerful uncles, Charles the Bald and Louis the German.

Political manoeuvring followed, the two uncles, in particular, were not blind to the opportunities offered if Lothair II could not produce an heir, and generally it was only Louis the German who supported Lothair II in his request.

In 857 Lothair II took matters in his own hands. In an accusation - which would be copied by King Henry VIII some 700 years later when he wanted his marriage to Anne Boleyn annulled - Lothair II accused Teutberga of incest committed with her brother Hucbert, who happened to be the lay abbot of St. Maurice's Abbey (in modern Switzerland).

Then Lothair II initiated a synod of all the bishops inside his realm. It was presided over by the archbishops Günter and Thietgaud, who both happened to be relatives of Lothair II's mistress Waldrada. Not surprisingly the synod found Teutberga guilty, but her brother, Hucbert, was less than amused and took up arms.

Teutberga however resolved the situation without violence - relatively speaking - by submitting to ordeal by boiling water. Basically, this ordeal, which was still used by the Catholic Church in the twelfth century, meant that the suspect would place his or her hand in boiling water. If after three days God had not healed the wounds (which in practice meant that they were healing rather than festering), the suspect was guilty of the crime. Teutberga passed the ordeal and Lothair II had to take her back.

But the issue was still unsolved, so Lothair II continued his quest to win allies and, by cession of lands, won the support of his brother, Emperor Louis II. He also bribed the local clergy to, once more, at a synod held in Aachen, agree on the annulment and to his marriage to Waldrada, which he celebrated in 862. To make matters even more valid, a new synod of Frankish bishops in Metz confirmed the local clergy's decision the following year.

Teutberga was sent to a monastery, but she escaped and made her way to the court of Lothair II's uncle, Charles the Bald, who had been opposed to the annulment. From here she appealed to Pope Nicholas I.

As mentioned, Pope Nicholas I was a stout church disciplinarian and he took the sacred oath of marriage very seriously. He was also a vehement enemy of corruption and mismanagement -as we shall see again later - so he took immediate action on the issue of Lothair II and Teutberga.

The Pope summoned the two archbishops, Günter of Cologne and Thietgaud of Trier, and a Lateran Synod was called in Rome in October of 863.

The two archbishops were excommunicated and deposed (as were others, which we shall see later). The findings of the two previous synods were declared void, as was Lothair II's marriage to Waldrada. Lothair II was under threat of excommunication, ordered to take Teutberga back.

Now Lothair II's support by his brother, Emperor Louis II, came into play. The Emperor declared his support of the two deposed archbishops and Lothair II took up arms and laid siege to Rome.

But Nicholas I was not moved. After two days of siege, and under new threats of excommunication, Lothair II gave up. The two deposed archbishops were ordered to go home and Lothair II once again took Teutberga back.

To finish the story, a few years later Teutberga finally agreed on an annulment of her marriage. Lothair II went to Rome to get the consent of the Pope, at that time Nicholas I's successor Pope Adrian II. He died while on the trip and Teutberga withdrew to a monastery until she died in 875. Lothair II thus had no legal heir, and his land was split between his uncles. His illegitimate son, Hugo, was made Duke of Alsace.

Coming back to Pope Nicholas I, he also had to make a decision in another high-profile case, this one also involving Charles the Bald. His daughter, Judith, had married Baldwin I of Flanders without her father's consent. The Frankish bishops had excommunicated Judith, but Pope Adrian I urged leniency in order to protect the freedom of marriage and convinced Charles the Bald to accept the marriage. As a twist in the tale of this story, the couple had sought refuge from Charles the Bald's anger with no other than Lothair II.

But the intrigues of political marriages were not the only issues which occupied Pope Nicholas I. Archbishop John of Ravenna, in charge of the Church's affairs in and around the town of Ravenna, was a despotic individual who extracted money from the both Church and the inhabitants by means of violence towards lay-people, bishops and priests alike.

Thrice the Pope called Archbishop John of Ravenna to Rome to explain himself, but he did not go so the Pope excommunicated him. The deposed archbishop now went to the Emperor, who sent two delegates with him to Rome. The Pope was unimpressed and cited John of Ravenna before a synod called in 860. The disgraced archbishop consequently fled Rome.

The Pope now went in person to Ravenna where he cleared up the mess left by John and instituted the regulations necessary to run things properly.

But John of Ravenna was not done yet. He appealed to the Emperor once more, but the Emperor told him to repair the relationship with the Pope. John thus returned to Rome where he submitted to the Pope in front of a synod held in 861.

He was later accused of cooperation with the two archbishops Günter of Cologne and Thietgaud of Trier and was excommunicated with them at the synod in Rome in 863 (the same synod which annulled Lothair II's marriage to Waldrada). He later submitted to the Pope once more but disappears from history.

Further unrest in the Church saw the Pope in conflict with Archbishop Hincmar of Reims. The Archbishop had presided over a local synod which had excommunicated a bishop. The bishop had appealed to the Pope, but Archbishop Hincmar questioned the Pope's authority to intervene in local matters.

Hincmar had chosen the wrong pope to stand up to. Pope Nicholas I made it very clear to Hincmar that the Pope had every right to intervene and pass independent judgment in important legal matters, Hincmar accepted the Pope's decision even though he did try to undermine the Pope's authority once more, in connection with the appointment of a bishop, but once more he was called to heel and had to accept the Pope's ultimate authority.

I 843 *iconoclasm* had once more been suppressed in Constantinople by Empress Theodora, so that particular issue of tension between the Eastern and Western Churches had disappeared, but there were other things they could disagree on.

A couple of years before the election of Pope Nicholas I, Emperor Michael III had come of age and removed his regent-mother from power. A purge followed, and one of the victims was the Patriarch of Constantinople, Ignatius, who was replaced by a politically appointed patriarch, Photios, who was a lay-man when appointed.

The clergy in Constantinople were less than happy by this and they appealed to Pope Nicholas I to intervene. Reluctantly the Pope did intervene, declaring the Patriarch of Constantinople elected against ecclesiastical law and eventually he had both the Emperor Michael III and Patriarch Photios excommunicated in 863.

The reaction from Constantinople was the excommunication of the Pope followed by a lecture on the Pope's place as one of several bishops rather than the supreme head of the Church. However, the Eastern bishops, in need of support, accepted the Pope's supremacy, at least for now.

But the battle was really not about position of ecclesiastical law; it was a battle for souls, Bulgarian souls. As also covered in Chapter 12, the Bulgarian ruler, Boris I, had decided to unify his people - consisting of Slavs and Bulgars - under a single religion. He had made contact with King Louis the German who sent - Catholic - missionaries to the Bulgarians.

But in 863 the Bulgarians suffered a crushing defeat at the hand of the Byzantines and one of the peace conditions imposed on them was that the Catholic missionaries were sent away and replaced by Orthodox missionaries from Constantinople.

Boris I himself was baptized with the Byzantine Emperor as his godfather and it looked as if the battle of the Bulgarian souls had been lost for Rome.

Boris I, however, wanted more. He wanted a full Bulgarian Church with its own patriarch and no ties to Constantinople. His request fell on deaf ears when it came to Patriarch Photios. Furthermore, Photios refused to answer a letter that Boris I had written, asking for the Church's opinion on a range of issues (see Chapter 12). Boris I then decided to try the Pope in Rome to see if he was more interested, so he sent the same letter to Pope Nicholas I.

For Nicholas I this was both an opportunity to make a principal stance on a range of ecclesiastical issues and an opportunity to win back the Bulgarian souls lost to Constantinople.

There were 106 questions and the Pope's answer is known as *Responsa Nicolai ad consulta Bulgarorum*. In this, Pope Nicholas I provided the Church's stance on a wide range of issues relating to Bulgarian customs and traditions from women's right to wear trousers (to which the Pope agreed) to bigamy (to which the Pope disagreed).

The Pope's answer was delivered by two bishops (which both would later become popes) and Boris I as a consequence returned the Greek missionaries to Constantinople and once again allowed Catholic missionaries to move amongst the Bulgarians.

But Pope Adrian I's coup did not last. Boris I soon asked the Pope for autonomy of the Bulgarian Church, which Nicholas I refused. Boris I asked again, this time to Nicholas I's successor, and once again he was refused. As a consequence, he once again replaced the Catholic missionaries with missionaries from Constantinople and so finally the Patriarch granted him his wishes for an independent Bulgarian Church. The Bulgarians souls were lost to Constantinople for good, but not from lack of trying by Pope Nicholas I.

The Pope died in November of 867. He was a saint, but even in his manifestation as a mere mortal he was truly formidable pope who would be known by the moniker 'Nicholas the Great'. He was elected to counter the challenges faced by Saracens and heathen Norsemen and he did just that, taking a firm stand on matters of morality and law.

The new Pope was Adrian II, who came from a noble Roman family. Adrian II had more history than most of his predecessors in that he had married in his younger years and had a daughter. Although it can be presumed that he had technically annulled the marriage on his entry into the Church, he nevertheless moved his wife Stephania and their daughter into the Lateran Palace after his appointment.

Whereas Adrian II did continue some of the activities of his illustrious predecessor, such as getting involved with the inheritance after Lothair II and participating (by proxy) in the Fourth Council of Constantinople, it is the fate of his wife and daughter that really defines his legacy.

As previously mentioned, Anastasius Bibliothecarius, who by some has been identified as the Anastasius who was shortly in the role of anti-pope before the consecration of Benedict III. Anastasius was the Chief Archivist of the Church and was also used on diplomatic missions. He, for instance, was one of the representatives of the Pope at the Fourth Council of Constantinople. He was also involved with the Imperial Court of Louis II, his uncle Arsenius being Bishop of Orte and confidential adviser to the Emperor.

Indeed, it is reported that Anastasius was one of the imperial collaborators inside the Curia who aimed to ensure that the Pope acted according to the Emperor's wishes.

Anastasius had a brother named Eleutherius. Little is known about him except for one incident, namely that in 868 he abducted the Pope's wife and daughter, both of whom were subsequently killed.

Eleutherius was caught and executed. An assumption was made that Anastasius was behind the murders - possibly on orders from the Imperial Court - and he was excommunicated and expelled from Rome. He took up residence at the Imperial Court from where he returned to Rome and his previous job, after the death of Adrian II.

Adrian II died on 14 December 872 after exactly five years on the throne of St. Peter. He was not a saint, possibly due to his refusal to abandon his family.

The next pope was John VIII, one of the more well-known popes despite the fact that he too was not a saint. He faced a range of problems, which he tackled in a hands-on manner that is the basis of his fame.

Basically, there were two main problems, which intertwined. The first was the fact that the rulers of Frankia were getting old and dying. The other was that Saracens had gradually established themselves in coastal mini-states in southern Italy from where they raided along the coast and, much to the regret of the Church, practiced their religion of Islam.

Southern Italy, although nominally under the rule of Emperor Louis II, was in effect a patchwork of small autonomous dukedoms, the remnants of the Lombard Kingdom mixed with small Byzantine enclaves and now also small coastal Saracen enclaves.

These were the Papal States' neighbours to the south and they were not stable or trustworthy so Pope John VIII set out to do something about it, in particular about the problems with the Saracens.

The Pope had little in terms of a regular army, so he needed military assistance and the obvious place to get that was from the Emperor, the nominal overlord of Italy.

But Louis II had little real control of southern Italy. He had previously campaigned against the Saracens with some success on land but little success at sea since he had no navy of notice. He had allied himself with the Emperor in Constantinople, Basil I, and although they had some success together, they soon started fighting over who was the real emperor.

After having driven the Saracens out of Bari, Louis II was captured by one of the local Lombard dukes, Adelchis of Benevento, who kept him in captivity until the Saracens were back and Louis II was needed once more.

On his release in 871 the Emperor went to Rome, where he received confirmation from Pope Adrian II on his title as Emperor and was relieved from an oath he had given to Adelchis of Benevento not to attack him.

Armed with this he once again expelled the Saracens from Capua and then went on to revenge his former humiliation at the hands of the Duke of Benevento. That enterprise was not successful, and the Emperor returned to northern Italy where he was camped when Pope John VIII called upon him.

16 - The Pope

But Louis II was not in good health, and he died in 875 before he could provide any proactive assistance to the Pope.

Pope John VIII now went on a campaign among the southern dukes. He tried to form an alliance with the rulers of Salerno, Capua, Naples, Gaeta and Amalfi, an alliance that basically consisted of the Pope giving money to the rulers to first and foremost prevent them from proactively cooperating with the Saracens and secondly assist him in taking the conflict to the Saracens.

After the death of Emperor Louis II the Pope also needed a new strong emperor and his choice fell on Louis II's uncle Charles the Bald. He received the new Emperor in Rome and crowned him accordingly, but where the Pope had hoped for a new military champion, it soon became clear that between the Vikings raiding in northern France and the Emperor's brother, Louis the German, and his sons starting a war of succession, Charles the Bald had little with which to assist the Pope and he died shortly after his appointment while on his way from Italy to France.

His brother, Louis the German, had also died and the Frankish Empire was now split between the son of Charles the Bald, Louis the Stammerer , and the two sons of Louis the German, Carloman and Charles the Fat.

Carloman was King of Italy, which he had conquered from Charles the Bald, but Pope John VIII was less interested in titles and more interested in military capabilities. He thus first leaned towards Louis the Stammerer, but when he refused to help, the Pope turned to Carloman. He did however become increasingly ill and eventually died in 880.

The throne of Italy now went to his brother Charles the Fat, who emerged as the de-facto heir to the Empire. His cousin, Louis the Stammerer, had died young and left his part of the empire with his two sons. They, however, also died young and eventually Charles the Fat inherited from them as well.

However, that was a few years in the future, so Pope Paul VIII saw Charles the Bald as the emerging star, and it was to him he eventually turned for military assistance.

In the meantime, the Pope's problems had compounded. The new Duke of Spoleto, Guy II, was young and ambitious and he invaded part of the Papal States in order to expand his own realm.

The Pope was now desperate for help so he crowned Charles the Fat emperor, in an attempt to link him to the protection of the Papal States that came with the title. But Charles the Fat did not act in a military way. Instead, he called a council and eventually brokered peace between the Pope and the Duke of Spoleto. The peace was uneasy, and it was only when Guy II died a couple of years later that the occupied lands were returned to the Pope.

As for the Saracens, Pope John VIII had, with some success, raised a fleet and fought off Saracen attacks. He had also fortified more outlying areas of Rome, but in the end realized that he could not muster reliable military assistance to fight the Saracen raiders, so instead he agreed to pay an annual tribute to the Emir of Sicily in order to avoid further attacks.

In December of 882 the Pope died after 10 years on the throne. Despite the various threats facing the Papal States and the confusion of the succession to the Frankish Empire, he had managed to keep the state intact and Rome safe. In the process he had crowned no less than three emperors, none of whom had been particularly effective in their role as protector.

The new pope was Marinus I, a lifetime cleric who had acted as papal ambassador in Constantinople on several occasions. He had also been one of the bishops sent to Bulgaria. He ruled for less than two years and did not do anything of great importance. He was not a saint.

His successor was Adrian III, who ruled for only a year. By the time he became pope the problems with the Saracens and the issues of succession in the Frankish Empire had reached such heights that Emperor Charles the Fat called a meeting at Worms in Germany to discuss the matters. The Pope died on his way there. He was a saint.

The new pope, Stephen V, was also a Roman from a noble family. He was quickly appointed by an unusually agreeable electorate. Although the Emperor should, in concept, agree to the appointment, he made no fuss due to the electorate's unity and the fact that he needed the Pope to agree on the appointment of his illegitimate son as heir.

However, the new Pope did not give his support to the Emperor's plans. He cancelled his attendance at the next planned meeting on the subject and instead decided to become closer to the new Duke of Spoleto, Guy III.

Emperor Charles the Fat was eventually deposed and his realm was dissolved into fragments. He held six different titles; each of these was taken over by a different contender.

Two of his titles; that of King of Italy and Emperor of the Romans were technically the Pope's to decide. The title as King of Italy was heavily disputed, but eventually Pope Stephen V adopted Guy III of Spoleto as 'his only son' and bestowed the crown on him. In 891 he subsequently, made Guy III emperor as well, focusing his attention on securing peace in Italy rather than getting further involved in the political intrigues following in the wake of Charles the Fat's deposition.

Pope Stephen V died later that year. He was not a saint. Neither was his successor, Formosus, indeed he was one of the most unlikely candidates for the papacy and would become one of the most controversial popes ever.

The controversy was not only due to his actual papacy, to which we shall return, but as much about what happened before and, not least, after.

Formosus was one of the bishops who had been sent to Bulgaria by Pope Nicholas I. At that time, he was the Bishop of Porto. As has been covered previously, Boris I of Bulgaria really wanted an independent Bulgarian Church and applied to the Pope to have one of the bishops sent to him appointed Archbishop of Bulgaria. The Pope refused, using the argument that according to Church law a bishop could not change from one see to another. Boris I later tried the same request with the other bishop, and later pope, Marinus, with the same result.

It should probably have ended there. Surely Marinus I had not had any problems with his election as pope, but for Formosus it was a different story.

Formosus was a candidate for the election of pope in 872 and the eventually successful candidate, Pope John VIII, did not like Formosus at all. Indeed, he believed, or at least declared, that Formosus had deliberately encouraged the Bulgarians to apply for his appointment and that he thus had been proactively involved in the events that eventually led to the loss of the Bulgarians to Constantinople.

True or false, the accusations were dangerous and Formosus decided to flee Rome before the Pope could take formal action against him.

Pope John VIII then called a synod and ordered Formosus, under threat of excommunication, to appear before it. Formosus did not go and was excommunicated and condemned for a range of crimes against the Holy See ranging from the Bulgarian issue to conspiring against the Church and despoiling cloisters in Rome.

This would have been the end of most, but Formosus managed to wiggle his way back. In 878, still under the pontificate of John VIII, his excommunication was lifted under the conditions that he would never return to Rome and never again act as a priest.

That may have saved Formosus' soul, but his real stroke of luck was the fact that his old comrade in arms from Bulgaria, Marinus, was elected pope after the death of John VIII.

Marinus I reversed the condemnation of Formosus and reinstated him as Bishop of Porto. Marinus I only ruled for a short time as did his successor (Saint) Adrian III. He was in turn followed by the relatively short and uneventful reign of Stephen V, by the time of whose death Formosus was the front-runner and was elected unanimously. In less than twenty years Formosus had been a papal candidate, excommunicated, barred from Rome, reinstated and finally elected pope.

His reign would last five years, but as it had begun with controversy, so it would continue.

Pope Formosus had no trust in the Emperor, Guy III. His dislike was so obvious that the Emperor forced him to crown his son, Lambert (II), as co-emperor in 892 in order to confirm both his own position and to secure a dynastic succession. But even that did not deter the feisty pope.

Looking around for military assistance his choice fell on Arnulf of Carinthia, a grandson of Louis the German. Arnulf had inherited East Frankia and had enough ambition to accept the Pope's overtures.

Arnulf first sent his son Zwentibold with an army into Italy, and although they were militarily successful against Guy III, they left with little done, partly because Guy III paid them off and partly because fever had broken out in the army.

In 894 Arnulf returned to Italy, this time in person. Once again, the Frankish army was successful, and it got as far as the River Po when Guy III died leaving Lambert II as sole ruler. But Lambert II was only fourteen years old, so he ruled through a regency led by his mother Ageltrude.

Ageltrude was politically astute and she quickly moved on Rome to get Pope Formosus to reconfirm her son as both King of Italy and Emperor of the Romans. But the Pope had no such intentions, relying on Arnulf to sort out Ageltrude and her son. He was locked up in Castel Sant'Angelo to rethink, but soon the army of Arnulf arrived and drove Ageltrude and Lambert II from the city.

Pope Formosus now crowned Arnulf as emperor and King of Italy, despite both titles belonging to Lambert II. Accordingly, Arnulf continued his campaign against Spoleto, but on his way there from Rome he suffered a stroke. The campaign was discontinued and the army returned to Bavaria.

Although militarily successful, Arnulf's campaign did not leave any lasting results in Italy. The territories he had conquered soon reverted to the control of Lambert II and the Pope had achieved nothing of real value.

Whilst facing a possible new invasion by Lambert II and his mother, the Pope died in 896. His attempts at playing politics at the highest level had been a failure and he left the Papal States weakened.

Once again, under normal circumstances this would be the end of the tale, but somehow things around Pope Formosus do not seem to be 'normal'.

On the death of Pope Formosus, Ageltrude once again moved quickly on Rome. Her purpose was to ensure that the next pope would ensure her son's crowning, but the electorate was aware of her intentions and quickly elected a new pope, Boniface VI, a local cleric with a somewhat unimpressive record. He lasted fifteen days.

It is unclear whether he died from gout or whether he was conveniently removed, but in any case his sudden death cleared the space for Ageltrude to impose her will and have her own candidate, Stephen VI elected.

What now followed was grotesque. Pope Stephen VI demanded that the rotting corpse of Pope Formosus was exhumed and put on trial before a synod. The episode is known as the '*Cadaver Synod*' and took place in the Arch basilica of St John Lateran in January of 897.

Pope Formosus' body was put on a throne and a deacon appointed to answer on its behalf. The accusations were dire; from perjury to having illegally ascended to the papacy and the appointed deacon must have done a bad job for Pope Formosus was found guilty on all charges.

The corpse was stripped of its papal vestments and the three fingers used for blessings were cut off. The corpse was buried in a cemetery for foreigners and then once again exhumed and thrown into the Tiber River.

This treatment of the Pope's body was bad enough, but furthermore the synod decided to make all decisions and appointments made by Pope Formosus null and void. This created a wave of chaos in the church, where appointees made by Formosus had in their own context appointed others and so on.

Popular history goes that the people of Rome now rose, apparently after the corpse of Pope Formosus had washed up from the river and started to perform miracles. A more pragmatic approach is that the judgment of the synod simply was not practical. In any case Pope Stephen VI was imprisoned and later strangled in his cell.

His death cleared the way for Romanus, a non-descript cleric who ruled for only four months. On his death, Theodore II was elected and the one thing he did was to annul the result of the *Cadaver Synod*, which meant that Pope Formosus could be reburied and, possibly more importantly, the chaos in the Church could come to an end. He then died after twenty days as pope.

Pope Formosus was finally laid to rest in St. Peter's Cathedral, and the faction from Spoleto once again had their preferred candidate, John IX, appointed.

But the new pope was not the rebel rouser that Stephen VI had been. Quite on the contrary, he sought to bring peace and unity. He confirmed the findings of Theodore II, restoring Pope Formosus. He ordered the acts of the *Cadaver Synod* burned and issues an edict against future trials of dead people.

The Pope then proceeded to prepare for the crowning of Lambert II as emperor, but Lambert II died suddenly from a riding accident, and he was soon followed by the Pope who ruled for only two years.

The ninth century had seen twenty popes, only four of whom were saints. The next century would see twenty-three popes and not as single saint among them.

The first pope of the tenth century, consecrated in February of 900, was Benedict IV. With Lambert II gone, his primary task was to look for a new protector of the Papal States; someone who could, and would, be emperor.

His choice for emperor was Louis the Blind, a grandson of Emperor Louis II and also the adopted son of Charles the Fat. In the constantly developing cabal of rule over the Frankish realm, he had entered Italy in early 900 and made himself King of Italy by defeating the incumbent king, Berengar I.

Louis the Blind continued to Rome where the Pope crowned him as emperor in 901. But Louis the Blind turned out to be a poor choice of champion for the Pope as he turned out to be incapable of ruling northern Italy and could do nothing to stop Magyar (early Hungarian) incursions into Dalmatia.

Part 6 - The Pope and the Crusader Knights

The following year he was beaten by Berengar I, who crowned himself as King of Italy once more. The Emperor had to flee to his native Provence and take an oath never to return to Italy.

But in 905 he did return and once again attacked Berengar I. After some initial success he found himself in Verona with only a small contingent of troops and Berengar I, sneaking into the city at night, captured him. The Emperor now earned his name as he was blinded as punishment for having broken his oath. He was also forced to abdicate as emperor before he was sent off to Provence.

By then Pope Benedict IV had died and his death had sparked off a new crisis of succession in the Papal States. Even the official list of popes from the Vatican has over time changed its view on who was the legitimate successor of Benedict IV, however I will stay with the current official view.

According to this, the next pope was Leo V. He was elected immediately after the death of Benedict IV in July 903. The problem was that he was not a cardinal, but an ordinary priest, so his election was strongly disputed and after only four months as pope he was imprisoned. The main instigator was Christopher, the cardinal-priest of San Lorenzo in Damaso, who was subsequently elected pope.

Into the fray now enters an influential Roman noble, Theophylact I, Count of Tusculum, and his family known as the Theophylacti.

With the defeat and abdication of Louis the Blind, the position of the Emperor as the protector of Rome had effectively failed. Rome was thus left to be dominated by powerful nobles and, at the time, Theophylact I was the most powerful amongst them.

Seeing an opportunity to obtain de-facto rule of the Papal States, Theophylact I, assisted by his influential wife Theodora, stepped into the fragile situation surrounding the papacy and used his influence - and it can be assumed a considerable amount of money - to have Pope Christopher replaced.

The new pope was Sergius III, himself belonging to a noble Roman family, possibly even directly related to Theophylact I.

The election of Sergius III once and for all settled the issue of who was pope. Although it was never proven to be the work of Sergius III - and implicit Theophylact I, Pope Leo V was strangled in his prison and (anti) Pope Christopher was either also killed or sent into exile in a monastery.

Although the Roman nobles had previously been proactively involved in the papal decision process, this was the first time a single noble family exerted its influence to effectively grab power. The following six decades have by historians been named *Saeculum obscurum* (the Dark Age) although, admittedly, this behaviour would become rather commonplace later in history.

16 - The Pope

Sergius III had an interesting background. He was against the appointment of Pope Formosus who then appointed him Bishop of Caere in Tuscany, an appointment aimed at getting Sergius away from Rome.

In the confusion following Formosus' death he was a member of the *Cadaver Synod* and a papal candidate already in 898 where he was actually at one point elected, although his election was overturned. Pope John IX thus had as little interest in having Sergius in Rome as had been the case with Formosus, and he was forced into exile in Caere where he formed strong ties with the local nobles including the Theophylacti. Indeed, his relations to the family were so strong that it is generally believed he was the lover of Theophylact I's daughter, known as Marozia.

Once pope, Sergius III's hatred for Formosus once again came to the surface. He once again declared the appointments made by Pope Formosus as null and void, but for practicality he allowed the incumbent holders to keep their positions if they submitted to a re-appointment by him. Although not recorded, it can be safely assumed that such re-appointment would be subject to a modest fee.

Furthermore, he had a laudatory epitaph added to the tomb of Pope Stephen VI, the otherwise vilified instigator of the *Cadaver Synod*.

Technically Louis the Blind was still emperor when Sergius III rose to power, but soon after he was blinded and exiled by Berengar I. He in turn wanted to become emperor, but politics in northern Italy was confused due to the lack of central authority.

Pope Sergius III - who was guided' in all matters by 'Theophylact I and Theodora - reluctantly agreed to appoint Berengar I as emperor in 906, but Berengar I was physically prevented from going to Rome by other local factions so the Pope reversed his decision. For now, the position as emperor was vacant.

As reward for their services, the Theophylacti received a range of valuable papal appointments and titles. Theodora was given the title '*senatrix*' (senatoress) and Theophylact I was given titles such as *sacri palatii vestararius*, *magister militum*, *senator*, *glorissimus dux*, and *dominus urbis*. Leaving little doubt as to who really ruled in Rome.

Pope Sergius III then made himself an enemy of the Patriarch of Constantinople, Nicholas Mystikos. Although there were constant theological disputes between the two sees and a unified church was effectively a distant dream, the matter at hand was of a rather more practical nature.

The issue was with the Byzantine Emperor Leo VI. He had been married three times but had not yet produced a male heir. That said, he had recently produced a son with his mistress, Zoe Karbonopsina, and to make his heir legitimate he wanted to marry her.

But canonical law as practiced in the Eastern Church prevented more than three marriages, even if the Emperor was a widower. The Emperor and the Patriarch fell out over the issue, and they both separately referred the matter to Pope Sergius III.

The Western Church had no such canonical law so Pope Sergius III gave his permission which greatly satisfied the Emperor and equally greatly not so the Patriarch. The Emperor married Zoe, their son later became Emperor Constantine VII and the Patriarch was sacked (although he was reinstated later).

Pope Sergius III died in 911. His replacement - chosen by Theophylact I - was Anastasius III. He only ruled for two years and accomplished little apart from one small, but as history would show, never the less important deed - christening of Rollo, the founder of Normandy.

Rollo was a Viking chief of either Danish or Norwegian origins. He had participated in raids in France since the 880s. When the Vikings were bought off after an attack on Paris in 885, he stayed behind and started to dominate areas in northern France. When Rollo himself laid siege to Paris and Chartres in 911 he was beaten back, but as part of the peace negotiations he was given large territories - nominally under the suzerainty of the French king - and it was agreed that he should be christened.

The conversion to Christianity of Rollo and his followers was important as it enabled them to start integrating as well as inter-marry with the local, Catholic, population in their domains. In turn their territories became known as 'Normandy' (from 'Norsemen') and the mixed population became a warlike tribe known as the Normans, who would seriously influence the known world in centuries to follow.

On Pope Anastasius III's death in 913 he was replaced according to Theophylact I's wishes by Lando, who died after only six months as pope. He in turn was replaced by John X.

It is believed by some that Pope John X was the favourite of Senatrix Theodora. Some even claim that the two were lovers. Regardless, he was already an archbishop and thus technically not able to a change of sees (as had been the case with Formosus in Bulgaria), but with Theophylact I and Theodora in charge nobody felt like making that an issue at the time.

John X was probably chosen as yet another puppet-pope, but he turned out to be a far more independent and powerful pope than could have been imagined from the outset of his fourteen-year papacy.

John X had, in his capacity as archbishop, been involved in the - later annulled - decision to appoint Berengar I emperor under Pope Sergius III. The reason for his support of Berengar I was a strong belief in a united Italy, a union he saw as necessary to fight off the increasingly aggressive Saracen raiders.

There was a Saracen stronghold at the mouth of the river Garigliano, located on the southern border of the Papal States. From here the Saracens launched repeated raids into both the Pope's own domains and southern

16 - The Pope

Italy. Pope John X was determined to solve that problem and he was not afraid of leading from the front.

It is unclear how much Pope John X acted on his own and how much he acted according to the wishes of the Theophylacti, but once installed in the Lateran palace, John X moved fast.

As mentioned, he believed that only a unified Italy could efficiently take up the Saracen challenge, so he started a hectic burst of diplomacy in an attempt to create a Christian union.

He managed to secure support from a range of dukes and princes in southern Italy and from the Byzantines who still maintained a colony in Bari, but his prize ally was Berengar I who sent troops from his northern Italian domains.

In its capacity as the first comprehensive Christian alliance against a Muslim foe, the alliance was in effect the precursor for future crusades. It was commanded by Duke Alberic I of Spoleto and Pope John X himself.

600 years after Constantine the Great had removed the ban on Christianity in the Roman Empire; its bishop in Rome had developed from underground-leader through officialdom to temporal ruler and, now, warlord.

The campaign was a success, and the Saracens were driven from the Italian mainland for now. Honours were distributed between the participating princes, but the biggest prize was given to Berengar I. After many years in waiting, he entered Rome in 915 to be crowned Emperor of the Romans.

Again, it is unclear if Berengar I was really the choice of the Theophylacti or whether he simply - with the Pope's blessing - seized the moment. In any case the Theophylacti came out to meet him when he approached Rome (with his army, which may give a clue to the answer) and all was good, on the surface at least.

Pope John now threw his weight into a range of clerical issues, something mainly ignored by several of his immediate predecessors. He re-confirmed an earlier papal decision that mass had to be said in Latin, unless there was a shortage of Latin-speaking priests. He made up with the Patriarch in Constantinople and even urged the Tsar in Bulgaria to do the same when he approached the Pope for a possible change to the Western Church.

But in Rome the Pope's time was running out. Emperor Berengar I was deposed and murdered in 924 as the culmination of the never-ending feudal wars in Italy. Soon thereafter Theophylact I also died as did the third of Pope John X's powerful backers, Alberic I of Spoleto, his former co-commander in the campaign against the Saracens.

The power-balance in Italy now became very fragile. Pope John X quickly picked a new King of Italy, Hugh of Provence, presumably on the condition that he would act as protector, but Hugh of Provence had competition for the throne and was never in a position to do anything of a practical nature to honour his obligations.

Although Theophylact I had died, his family was still active. His daughter, Marozia, was no friend of the Pope. It has been speculated that she may have been angry over his suggested relationship with her mother, but there were plenty of real-political reasons for her enmity.

Pope John X ,had to a large extent, shown that he was his own man and that he took the papacy serious. He had effectively managed to break the dependencies to his political masters and that was not in Marozia's taste.

Previously rumoured to be the lover of former Pope Sergius III, she had married Guy, Margrave of Tuscany. And they had no appetite for the Pope's independence or his unilateral choice of King of Italy.

Pope John X managed to keep the couple out of Rome through the use of Magyar mercenaries commanded by his brother, Peter, but eventually, in 928, the troops of Guy of Tuscany and Marozia entered Rome. Peter was slain in the Lateran Palace and the Pope was thrown in jail. Here he died the following year. Some say that he was strangled by Guy of Tuscany himself, others that he simply succumbed to his incarceration.

As far as the papacy was concerned, Marozia had a very clear plan. She had a son, Johannes, who was generally accepted to be the lovechild of Pope Sergius III. He had been raised in the service of the Church from a young age and Marozia was determined that he should be pope.

But Johannes was very young, only eighteen or nineteen by the time Pope John X died, so Marozia needed a bit of time. She therefore appointed first Leo VI - who only lasted eight months - and then Stephen VII who lasted two years. Neither added anything of great value to the papacy.

When Pope Stephen VII died in 931 Marozia's son had turned twenty-one and as far as Marioza was concerned that was old enough.

Johannes thus became Pope John XI and, if the rumours about his parentage were true, then he was the only illegitimate son of a Pope to have become Pope himself.

No matter who his father was, it was his mother who held his reins. Guy of Tuscany had died in 929 and Marozia had her eyes on his brother Hugh of Arles for her next husband. He had been appointed King of Italy, but he was inconveniently married already.

But when you own the Pope that is not such a big issue, so Hugh of Arles' marriage was annulled and he was engaged to Marozia. The union did, however, not suit Marozia's other son, Alberic II, who first quarrelled with Hugh of Arles at the wedding and then raised a mob and performed a coup d'état.

Hugh of Arles escaped, but Marozia was imprisoned by her son. She died, still a prisoner, five years later. Over and above Pope John XI, a grandson, two great grandson, and one great-great grandson of hers would become popes.

16 - The Pope

Alberic II now called the shots in Rome, and was the controller of his half-brother, the Pope. He married Alda, a daughter of his stepfather Hugh of Arles, the King of Italy, with whom he had a son, Octavianus.

By then his half-brother, Pope John XI, had died. Alberic II now proceeded to appoint tame popes. Leo VII, Stephen VIII, Marinus II and Agapetus II all came and went. They were allowed to deal with clerical matters but were not allowed to intervene in politics unless Alberic II needed the threat of excommunication to convince others to see things his way.

In the last year of the 'rule' of Agapetus II, Alberic II died. Before he did so he made sure that it was understood who the next pope should be so, when Agapetus died in 955 his successor was John XII, born Octavianus, the son of Alberic II.

Like his uncle, John XI, Pope John XII was young, probably around twenty, when he was elected pope. He had been groomed from an early age to become both a secular and religious leader, but his interest was in all matters leaning towards the life of a secular prince rather than a religious example to others.

In the words of one historian *'ecclesiastical affairs did not seem to have had much attraction for John XII'* and the way he saw himself as both prince and pope was clear from the fact that the secular orders he issued were issued in his birth name Octavianus and only clerical orders were issued under his papal name as John XII.

The nine years of John XII's papacy would thus not surprisingly be known for its very ungodly character. John XII, or perhaps rather Octavianus, was living a life of wine and women, in some contemporaries' opinion turning the Lateran Palace into a brothel.

It is therefore not surprising that little happened in terms of Church matters and that John XII rather threw himself at politics and war making.

The local dukes surrounding the Papal States never ceased to push the Pope in terms of their bordering territories, a situation only made worse by the weak papacy. Pope John XII decided to go on the offensive.

Allying himself with one group of local dukes, he went to war with another group, leading from the front as military commander. All in all the campaign managed to do little but swap territories around, but it also alerted the King of Italy, Berengar II, to the fact that Pope John XII was a loose cannon on the deck.

In 960 Berengar II moved on the Papal States and the Pope found himself in dire straits. The local Roman nobility were hard to control, Pope John XII simply was not his father, and Berengar II presented a clear and present military danger.

The Pope fell back on the remedy which had been used repeatedly by his predecessors, namely the hunt for a suitable protector. The choice fell on the strong King of German, Otto I.

Part 6 - The Pope and the Crusader Knights

The Carolingian dynasty of Charlemagne had long since disintegrated. Originally it had been split into Western, Middle and Eastern Frankia, which over time had developed into a 'French' part and a 'German' part. Otto I ruled over a vast territory covering (roughly) modern day Germany, Holland, Belgium, Austria and Switzerland and he was the obvious choice for protector of Rome and the coveted title of Emperor which had been vacant since Berengar I's death in 924.

Otto I had previously campaigned in Italy, but problems in the north had forced him to take the majority of his troops out of Italy and leave the title as King of Italy to Berengar II, albeit with Otto I as nominal, but absent, overlord.

Berengar II's aggression was as good a casus belli as was required, so Otto I re-entered Italy in August of 961 and by Christmas he had possession of Pavia where he had himself crowned as King of Italy.

At the start of 962 he marched on Rome, and there Pope John XII anointed him as Emperor of the Romans on 3 February 962. Immediately, the Pope and the Emperor in unison called a synod.

The synod resulted in the *Diploma Ottonianum*, a document reconfirming the Donation of Pepin and further expanding the Papal States to formally include the duchies of Spoleto and Benevento. The Pope was reconfirmed as the spiritual head of the Church and temporal head of the Papal States. The Emperor in turn was recognized as the temporal overlord and protector of the Church. As before, the Pope appointed the Emperor, and the Emperor had to approve the Pope.

Formalities completed the new Emperor expressed the opinion that the Pope should reform himself and the way the Curia was currently operating, before he set out to perform his duties and expel Berengar II and his son and co-ruler Adalbert from the Papal States and bring northern Italy firmly under control.

Despite Pope John XII's distinct lack of morality and capability as a pope, as a prince he had been rather more successful. The Papal States were bigger than ever and protected by the most powerful lord in Europe. But for John XII that simply was not enough.

While Emperor Otto I campaigned in Italy, Pope John started to conspire against him. Now that the Emperor had saved Rome, the Pope decided to cut his influence down.

Messengers went out to the Hungarians, the Byzantines and even Adalbert, who shortly before - with his father Berengar II - had threatened the Papal States. The Pope was proposing a great alliance against the Emperor. At the same time ambassadors went to the Emperor, telling tales of the Pope's ongoing work to reform the Curia as per the Emperor's request.

But the Pope's messages were intercepted, and their content became known to the Emperor. He had in the meantime more or less finished his

16 - The Pope

business, capturing Berengar II who was sent to prison in Germany where he died a couple of years later.

Adalbert was however still free and when it became known to Otto I that he had been allowed entry to Rome in order to negotiate with the Pope; the Emperor had enough of his shifty ally.

Otto I marched on Rome, which he reached in the summer of 963. In Rome he found that chaos reigned. Supporters of the Emperor had barricaded themselves in one part of the city with supporters of the Pope barricaded in the other part.

The Pope and his supporters initially decided to fight, but when it became clear that they could not resist Otto I, the Pope and Adalbert fled the city and took refuge in Tivoli some thirty kilometres out of Rome. To ensure that he would not suffer during his exile, the Pope took the papal treasure with him.

Otto I now called a synod and ordered the Pope to appear before it to defend himself. The Pope however declared the synod illegal and threatened excommunication on anyone taking part in it.

The synod went ahead regardless, and a contemporary historian provides the following summary of the charges against the Pope:

'Then, rising up, the cardinal priest Peter testified that he himself had seen John XII celebrate Mass without taking communion. John, bishop of Narni, and John, a cardinal deacon, professed that they themselves saw that a deacon had been ordained in a horse stable, but were unsure of the time. Benedict, cardinal deacon, with other co-deacons and priests, said they knew that he had been paid for ordaining bishops, specifically that he had ordained a ten-year-old bishop in the city of Todi. They testified about his adultery, which they did not see with their own eyes, but nonetheless knew with certainty: he had fornicated with the widow of Rainier, with Stephana his father's concubine, with the widow Anna, and with his own niece, and he made the sacred palace into a whorehouse. They said that he had gone hunting publicly; that he had blinded his confessor Benedict, and thereafter Benedict had died; that he had killed John, cardinal subdeacon, after castrating him; and that he had set fires, girded on a sword, and put on a helmet and cuirass. All, clerics as well as laymen, declared that he had toasted to the devil with wine. They said when playing at dice, he invoked Jupiter, Venus and other demons. They even said he did not celebrate Matins at the canonical hours nor did he make the sign of the cross'

With the Pope missing from the proceedings, it did not take the synod long to decide in his guilt. Pope John XII was deposed and, on the Emperor's instructions, Leo VIII was elected as Pope, even though as a layman he had to be ordained through the ranks of the Church before he could be consecrated.

Technically both the synod and the election of Leo VII were uncanonical and John XII still had many supporters in Rome. A combination of hostility against the Emperor and bribes arriving from John XII caused an uprising, aiming to kill both the Emperor and the new Pope, but the uprising was soon killed by the Emperor's troops and Otto I took hostages from several noble Roman families.

But Pope Leo VIII realized that the Emperor could not protect him in person for ever, so in an attempt to win over the noble families he had the Emperor release the hostages. Shortly after, in February of 964, Emperor Otto I left Rome.

As soon as the Emperor was out of sight, John XII returned with his retinue of supporters. Leo VIII fled to the Emperor and Rome was once again in the control of the nobility.

John XII now called a new synod which declared the Emperor's synod and the election of Leo VIII uncanonical. He then sent an ambassador to the Emperor to seek some kind of solution to the crisis.

It is unlikely that the Emperor would have been interested in any kind of reconciliation, but the problem sorted itself out as John XII died in May of 965. It is said that he did so befittingly during an adulterous sexual encounter.

The death of John XII threw Rome in a short but bloody civil war. Factions for and against the Emperor clashed in the streets but finally the militia prevailed and their choice of pope was Benedict V a learned cleric who had participated in both the recent synods, one of which elected Leo VIII and one which rejected him.

The nobles swore to protect the new Pope from the Emperor, and Otto I's response was not long coming. He once again marched on Rome which he besieged in June of 964.

Inside the City there was soon a shortage of food and prices shot up to astronomical levels. Pope Benedict V himself urged the population on from the walls of the city, but soon reality kicked in.

The gates were opened for the Emperor and Pope Benedict V and his most staunch supporters were handed over by the same nobles who had sworn to protect him.

A short trial followed. Benedict V asked for forgiveness and his life was spared. He was even allowed to stay in the Church, maintaining a position as deacon, but to avoid further trouble Otto I had him moved to Germany where he died shortly after.

Order had been restored and Leo VIII now finally ruled supreme as pope. It had taken Otto I three trips to Rome to settle matters and by June of 964 he left once more.

Normality now settled on the papacy for short while and Pope Leo VIII took care of Church business until his death in 965.

On Leo VIII's death the nobles in Rome asked the Emperor to have Benedict V back. But even though Benedict V was still alive at that time, the Emperor was not of mind to let him return to Rome. Instead, he suggested as an alternative a well-respected cleric who came from a noble Roman family, Bishop John Crescentius, who met with general approval and was elected as John XIII.

As far as the nobles in Rome were concerned, John XIII was one of their own; someone who would make sure that the power over Rome remained in Rome. But they had misjudged John XIII.

The Pope had no intentions of being a puppet of the Roman nobles, so he appointed his own supporters into important positions and generally sought closer ties with the Emperor.

That was not what the nobles had expected, and they rose in a revolt spearheaded by the Prefect of Rome. At the same time Adalbert re-appeared in Italy with an army of his own and the Pope was taken prisoner in Castel Sant'Angelo. He was, however, shortly after moved to a castle in Campagna in order to not be a rallying point for a counter-revolt.

Amazingly Emperor Otto I now had to return to Rome once more. In the meantime, the Pope had managed to escape from Campagna and had sought refuge with a local duke loyal to the Emperor. From here he rallied his supporters and initiated an uprising in Rome which saw the leaders of the coup against him captured.

Thus, by the time Emperor Otto I made his entry into Rome towards the end of 966, John XIII had already been restored. What remained was to clean up. The Pope advocated for leniency to keep the nobles on side, but the Emperor was not having it. On his command the leaders of the coup were publicly and gruesomely executed.

Having on three previous occasions left Rome after restoring order, this time the Emperor stayed. The Empress Adelaide and the eleven year old crown prince, Otto II, had arrived with him from Germany and he now left them in the care of the Pope while he went to campaign in southern Italy which had never been under his control and where the Byzantine Empire had started to show some aggression.

Otto I's campaign in the south was short and the Byzantines sued for peace. He returned to Rome towards the end of 967 as there was business to attend to.

His heir apparent, Otto II, was crowned as co-emperor by the Pope, securing a dynastic succession in the Empire. Then the Pope and the Emperor started a successful partnership where they, both residing in Rome, started to get their houses back in order.

The Pope caught up with a massive backlog of Church issues, including appointments of clergy throughout the Empire. The Church had been left to fend for itself for decades and Pope John XIII was exactly the medicine it needed.

On the Imperial front the Emperor was keen to ensure a union with the Emperor in Constantinople, Nikephoros II Phokas. With the Pope as middle-man he proposed that Otto II should marry a daughter of the Byzantine Emperor.

But the effort went wrong from the start. The Pope wrote to the Byzantine Emperor as 'Emperor of the Greeks' to which he took offense as he still considered himself the Emperor of the Romans. The Byzantine Emperor henceforth refused to correspond directly with the Pope. Otto I proposed that as dowry, the Byzantine Emperor should give the Byzantine duchies of Longobardia and Calabria, which would in effect end Byzantine presence on the Italian peninsula. The Byzantine Emperor proposed instead that it was Otto I who should give him the - former Byzantine - Exarch of Ravenna, which was now part of the Papal States.

The proposal went no further until Emperor Nikephoros II Phokas died in 969 and his successor, Emperor John I Tzimiskes agreed to give his niece to Otto II and it was Pope John XIII himself who performed the marriage of Otto II and Theophanu in April of 972.

Immediately after the wedding the Emperor finally returned to Germany. In September Pope John XIII died and the Emperor followed him in May of 973. Together they had restored the Roman Empire, Rome and the papacy.

Rome was still split into pro- and anti-imperial factions (at this time not yet known as *Ghibellines* and *Guelphs* as they would be later). The anti-imperial faction preferred a papal candidate named Franco Ferrucci, but it was the pro-imperial faction that had its will and elected Benedict VI, a Roman of German descent. It took a while to get the Emperor's approval, so Benedict VI was finally consecrated in January of 973.

With Emperor Otto I dying and trouble in Germany in connection with the succession of Otto II, now sole Emperor of the Romans, the new Pope could concentrate on Church matters. But despite the Pope not getting involved in politics, the Roman nobles still considered him a representative of the Emperor, so when the Emperor's power took a dip, the nobles struck at the Pope once more.

Spearheaded by a powerful noble known as Crescentius the Elder and the aforementioned former papal candidate Franco Ferrucci, the Pope was arrested and placed in Castel Sant'Angelo. Not surprisingly Franco Ferrucci was elected pope as Boniface VII.

News of the affairs in Rome eventually reached Otto II. He sent an ambassador to Rome, demanding the instant release and re-instatement of Pope Benedict VI. As a response Pope Benedict VI was strangled in his cell, it is generally believed on the orders of Boniface VI.

The Imperial ambassador, Count Sicco, soon regained control of Rome and Boniface VII fled. First, he went to Castel Sant'Angelo from where he removed the papal treasure and then, with the treasure, continued to - Byzantine - southern Italy.

Count Sicco and the nobles loyal to the Emperor elected Benedict VII as pope. He too had noble Roman connections linking him to both the Theophylacti and the Crescenti and he was as good a compromise as could be found.

16 - The Pope

Peace was restored in Rome and Pope Benedict VII went about clerical affairs and stayed out of politics. But politics did not stay out of Rome just because the Pope was not interested.

Although the Pope had held a synod which had excommunicated Anti-pope Boniface VII, the strong anti-imperial party of nobles may have been subdued, but they had not disappeared. Their next attempt at gaining power came in 980 when Pope Benedict VII left Rome for business outside the city.

While the one pope was out, another pope arrived and a coup in Rome saw Boniface VII reinstated to power, at least in Rome itself.

Pope Benedict VII appealed to the Emperor, and Otto II appeared in person with his army and once again subdued the ambitious nobles of Rome. Anti-pope Boniface VII once again fled the city, this time all the way to Constantinople.

Towards the end of 983 Pope Benedict VII died. The Emperor - who had been campaigning in southern Italy - took no chances and appeared in Rome in person to ensure that the election of the new pope was according to his wishes. The Emperor's choice was Pietro Canepanova, Bishop of Pavia and Imperial Chancellor, who was consecrated as John XIV.

Pope John XIV was not a popular choice. He was clearly a puppet of the Emperor, but nobody was in a position to do much about it. That situation changed dramatically very shortly after the papal election.

Emperor Otto II died suddenly in Rome, probably from Malaria. He was only twenty-eight years-old and his heir apparent, Otto III, was only three years-old. A regency was formed under Otto II's - Byzantine - wife Theophanu and despite some attempts at overthrowing the young King of Germany, the Empire generally held together until Otto III came of age.

In Rome the initial power-vacuum was obvious, so the nationalist faction of nobles took the opportunity to get rid of the unpopular Pope John XIV. He was imprisoned in Castel Sant'Angelo and Anti-pope Boniface VII reappeared in Rome, backed by Byzantine troops and Saracen mercenaries.

By April 984 Anti-pope Boniface VII was pope for the third time and Pope John XIV lingered in jail where he died four months later. Whether he was proactively murdered or just died from the hardship of the ordeal is unknown.

Boniface VII's final reign only lasted eleven months, He quickly became unpopular, possibly because of Byzantine - rather than nationalistic - sympathies, but he died in July of 985 from unknown causes, leaving the Throne of St. Peter empty once more.

The new strong-man in Rome was Crescentius II, who had himself appointed *Patricius Romanorum*, de-facto political ruler of Rome. It can therefore be assumed that he must have agreed to the election of the next pope, although the relationship between them would become troubled.

The choice for pope was John XV, a Roman who would soon be known for widespread nepotism and bribery. His political views are unknown, but he was not content with a role as puppet to Crescentius II, although he had to endure it for a while.

That changed when the Empress Regent Theophanu decided to rule from Rome in 989. Her presence curbed the ambitions and influence of Crescentius II and gave the Pope an opportunity to break his ties. Not that he used it for much other than getting into a fight with the King of France over the election of bishops.

The Empress left again in 991, but in 996 her son, Otto III had come of age and it was time for him to become emperor. Pope John XV had maintained good relations to the Imperial Court and he was ready to crown Otto III on his arrival, but before Otto III could get to Rome the Pope died.

With the Emperor-elect waiting in Ravenna, Crescentius II realized that this was not the time to push the issue of the papacy so instead he referred the matter to Otto III.

The choice was Otto III's cousin and chaplain, Bruno of Carinthia, who at the age of only twenty-four became Pope Gregory V.

The new pope was different not only due to his young age, but also because he was German and obviously closely tied to the Emperor rather than the Roman nobility.

Once in place the new Pope's first act was to crown his cousin Emperor of the Romans and the new power-structure in Rome was complete. But it was fragile, depending entirely on the Emperor's capability to exercise control.

To ensure the imperial power the new Pope and the new Emperor held a synod in Rome where the Roman nobles, Crescentius II amongst them, were called to account for their various acts of rebellion. The nobles were declared guilty as charged and exiled.

But Pope Gregory V did not want to start out on unfriendly terms with the nobles, so he had the exiles annulled. Crescentius II was stripped of his titles but was allowed to remain in Rome to live out his life in peace.

With his house presumably in order, the young Emperor left the young Pope in Rome and set out to return to Germany. The uneasy peace in Rome did not last long.

Crescentius II was far from done. He found a co-conspirator in John Philagathos, Archbishop of Piacenza and a former papal ambassador and even at some point chaplain and advisor to Empress Theophanu. Also finding willing support from the Byzantine Emperor, Basil I, Crescentius II staged a coup in April of 997.

The Pope was deposed but managed to flee to Pavia. John Philagathos was consecrated as Pope John XVI and Crescentius II was back in power in Rome.

Pope Gregory V excommunicated Pope John XVI from his exile, but the real question was whether the Emperor had the capability to regain control on the ground in Rome.

16 - The Pope

The Emperor realized the seriousness of the situation and - campaigning in Saxony - turned his army south and into Italy. Despite the alleged support of the Byzantines, the Roman nobles had little with which to defend the city, so they allowed Otto III to enter the city unopposed in February of 998.

Anti-pope John XVI fled, but he was soon captured and brought back to the city. His ears and nose were cut off, his tongue was cut out, his was blinded and his fingers were broken. After appeals by a saintly monk called Nilus the Younger his life was spared, and he was moved to a monastery in Germany to live out his life. He died there in 1001.

Crescentius II had holed up in his family's stronghold of Castel Sant'Angelo and he was not coming out. The imperial army laid siege to the castle and eventually managed to break through. Crescentius II was executed and his body was hung from a gibbet.

Pope Gregory V, and the imperial party, were now back in power, but in February 999 the Pope died, at not thirty years of age. The reason for his death is unknown, but foul play has been neither proven nor ruled out.

With the Roman nobility neutralized for now the Emperor was once again free to choose his own pope. His choice was, wisely, Gerbert of Aurillac, who became Pope Sylvester II.

The new pope was French born and a life-time cleric. He was also a scholar, having studied in many countries and even amongst the Arabs. He had been a tutor to both Otto II and the young Emperor himself.

Pope Sylvester II started a reform of the Church. Simony and concubinage amongst the clergy were condemned and science was promoted, introducing such things as Arabic numbers and the abacus into Europe.

The Emperor too had settled in Rome and peace reigned for a short while. But then the citizens of Tivoli, close to Rome, revolted against the imperial authority. Otto III went to besiege and invade the city. In an act of clemency, he decided to leave the city intact and forgive the citizens for their transgressions.

Otto III's clemency in turn angered the Romans, who had no warm feelings for the competing city of Tivoli. They rose in revolt and Emperor and Pope both had to flee from Rome to Ravenna.

Peace emissaries were sent from Rome, where Count Gregory I of Tusculum - a Theophylacti - was the emerging power. Although a peaceful resolution to the conflict was agreed, the Emperor and his advisors did not trust the shifty Roman nobles, so the Emperor decided to wait for military reinforcements before he proceeded towards Rome.

Late in 1001 Otto III was ready and he marched on Rome. On 24 January 1002 he succumbed to fever and died still 65 kilometres out of the city.

Despite the uncertain political situation, Pope Sylvester II returned to Rome. His rule was not challenged by the rebellious nobles, and he reigned until his death the following year.

Part 6 - The Pope and the Crusader Knights

The death of Otto III threw the Empire into chaos. Otto III was due to marry Princess Zoe, second daughter of the Byzantine Emperor Constantine VIII, but she had only just disembarked in Puglia and was on her way to meet him when he died. Otto III thus died without an heir.

In Rome a power struggle ensued. The Theophylacti had risen to power after the execution of Crescentius II, Gregory I of Tusculum gaining the title of "Head of the Republic", but the Crescentii family - who held Castel Sant'Angelo - returned after the death of the Emperor and Gregory I had to abandon his title.

At the turn of both the century and the millennium, it may be worth casting a glance at the power-structure in the immediate area.

Venice had started to exercise its position as a maritime power and had taken de-facto control of the Adriatic Sea and Dalmatia (although nominally under Byzantine suzerainty).

The Byzantine Empire was pushed between the Seljuk Turks in the East and the remains of the First Bulgarian Empire in the West, with civil war and unrest dominating the domestic political scene.

France - formerly the western part of Charlemagne's Roman Empire - had recently changed dynasty with the Capetian dynasty of Hugh Capet replacing the Carolingian dynasty of Charlemagne.

Germany - formerly the eastern part of Charlemagne's Roman Empire - was in a crisis of succession after the premature death of Emperor Otto III.

Italy itself was still effectively split between the northern states, nominally part of the roman Empire and the southern states which were either autonomous or under Byzantine influence. The Saracens, based in Sicily, still raided mainly unchecked due to the lack of central authority.

The new strongman in Rome was John Crescentius, the son of the executed Crescentius II, and it was he who held the reins when a new pope was to be elected.

First, he had Pope John XVII consecrated. He was a puppet who lasted less than a year. He was followed by John XVIII who was a life-time cleric with no political ambitions.

Others, however, had political ambitions. In the power vacuum in northern Italy, Arduin, Margrave of Ivrea and a nephew of Berengar II, had himself crowned as King of Italy in 1002.

In Germany Henry II - a second cousin of Otto III - had emerged as the new King of Germany. He was also crowned as King of Italy albeit in Germany and thus with little effect on the ground.

Henry II sent an expeditionary force to Italy, but it was defeated by Arduin who had support from some, but not all, the nobles in northern Italy.

In 1004 Henry II appeared in person and this time he beat Arduin and took the control that came with the title of King of Italy.

The local nobles were still split in pro- and anti-imperial factions and the citizens of Pavia rose in revolt against the new king shortly after his crowning. Henry II initiated a massacre and he then returned to Germany rather than proceed to Rome for crowning as Emperor.

The reason for Henry II's return to Germany was probably twofold. One was that his position was far from secure, and would remain so for another few years, and two, was that the Pope supposedly did not approve of him. The latter should probably be seen as the opinion of John Crescentius and the Roman nobles, who were notoriously anti-imperial, rather than necessarily as a political opinion of the pontiff himself.

Instead, the Pope concentrated on clerical matters and he was for all intents and purposes a capable, if inglorious, administrator.

In 1009 Pope John XVIII decided to abdicate. His reasons are unknown, but as he died shortly after at the monastery to which he had retired, ill health may well have been the reason.

He was replaced by Sergius IV. He was a shoemaker's son called Pietro Martino who had entered the Church at an early age. He was as non-political as his master could have wished for.

Pope Sergius IV was not someone who left many traces of his papacy although he may have left a papal bull calling for Muslims to be driven from the Holy Land after the Church of the Holy Sepulchre was destroyed in 1009. The authenticity of the bull is, however, disputed.

John Crescentius died in May of 1012. Either by coincidence or design, Pope Sergius IV died a week later.

The power-structure in Rome was now a green field, as John Crescentius did not leave a male heir. One faction appointed '*a certain Gregory*' as Pope Gregory VI while another party, supported by the Theophylacti, appointed Benedict VIII, himself a Theophylacti and son of Gregory I of Tusculum.

The Theophylacti did not hold the advantage on the ground, so Pope Benedict VIII fled the city and made his way to Henry II. The King of Germany promised to reinstate Benedict VIII, but there was an associated cost; the King wanted to become emperor.

The imperial army arrived in Rome early in 1014 and on 14 February Henry II was crowned Emperor by Pope Benedict VIII. Antipope Gregory VI disappeared from history.

Henry II still had issues at home, so he soon left Rome. Pope Benedict VIII seems to have had a reasonable amount of autonomy, not being under the direct influence of the local nobles.

Like his immediate predecessors he focused on matters clerical, but events in southern Italy forced him to get involved in politics.

The Byzantines had never ceased to claim suzerainty in Italy, not least in the parts south of the Papal States.

Melus of Bari, one of the few surviving Lombard lords, rose in revolt against the Byzantines in 1017. He hired Norman mercenaries, something which in itself would have major consequences in the decades that followed. After some initial success Melus was beaten and fled to the Papal States.

Part 6 - The Pope and the Crusader Knights

The Pope was worried about the Byzantine success in the south, where the Pope and the Byzantines constantly fought for spiritual overlordship.

In 1020 the Pope set out on a trip to Germany where he met the Emperor at Bamberg sometime in the spring. The subject of discussion was the Byzantines in southern Italy and the Emperor agreed to address the issue with force.

The Emperor marched on southern Italy in 1022. He had some limited military success, and appointed Melus as Duke of Apulia although that was a title with no actual power.

When the Emperor returned to Germany he had achieved little than showing his hand as he left no working power-structure behind. The only lasting effect of the unrest was that Norman mercenaries made it home to Normandy with tales about a territory void of central authority. This in turn led to an influx of Norman adventurers who, as the century moved on, took control of southern Italy, eradicating the last remains of Lombard and Byzantine control in the area.

Both Pope Benedict VIII and Emperor Henry II died in 1024. Contrary to what could be expected, the transition of power was relatively peaceful despite the fact that Henry II died without an heir.

In Germany the nobles quickly settled on Conrad II, a relatively lowly noble, who turned out to be a very good choice.

In Rome the choice fell on John XIX, the brother of Benedict VIII and thus an indicator that the Theophylacti were still the most powerful faction in the city. Pope John XIX was the second great-grandson of Marozia's to sit on the papal throne.

Pope John XIX was possibly not the best choice as he was a layman and had to be quickly accelerated through the clerical hierarchy before he could be consecrated. His lack of understanding in clerical matters was probably the reason for the way he handled the relationship to the Patriarch of Constantinople, escalating into a conflict which would develop further and lead to an outright break within the Church three decades later.

The issue at hand was an attempt by the Patriarch Eustathius to solve issues over sovereignty inside the Church. Although the compromise he suggested was partly aimed at settling the disputes in southern Italy, it had far reaching consequences in terms of the papacy's position as the primary see.

In short what Eustathius proposed was that the Patriarch of Constantinople was given ecumenical - that is to say superiority over all religions - in its own sphere (mainly in the East) while the Pope was given similar powers inside his sphere, although the latter was expressed with a bit pomp and circumstance as '*in universo*' (globally) with the implicit exception of the Byzantine sphere.

As far as the - clerically naive - Pope was concerned that was a fair enough deal, in effect formalizing what was already the situation on the ground. He was allegedly also helped to this decision by a substantial bribe.

16 - The Pope

But the Pope's decision on the matter was so against the tradition of the western Church that he - facing an outright revolt - quickly had to reverse his decision and reject Eustathius' proposal.

John XIX however saved some face by agreeing that the Byzantine rite could be used in southern Italy on the condition that the Roman rite could be used by Catholics in Constantinople.

Politically the Pope, it can be assumed through the opinion of the Theophylacti, supported the election of Conrad II whom he crowned as Emperor at Rome in 1027. When he died in 1032, he thus left a somewhat bruised Church and a stable political situation to his successor.

The next pope was, despite the existence of an Emperor, also an appointee and member of the Theophylacti. Born Theophylactus of Tusculum and being as young as twenty (some say even younger) he had no clerical experience, but he nevertheless became Pope Benedict IX. He would rule as pope no less than three times, a feat not outdone by anyone before or after.

A nephew of his two most recent predecessors, he would also bring a whole new level of depravity to the papacy, despite the attempts made by some of his predecessors.

Pope Benedict IV did not leave a legacy in terms of clerical matters, something which did not seem to be of any real interest to him. Instead, he left a legacy of depravity that one would not expect from a pope.

Historians have left him with legacies such as *'feasting on immorality'*, *'It seemed as if a demon from hell, in the disguise of a priest, occupied the chair of Peter and profaned the sacred mysteries of religion by his insolent courses'*, *'a disgrace to the Chair of Peter'* and *'his rapes, murders and other unspeakable acts. His life as a pope was so vile, so foul, so execrable, that I shudder to think of it.'*

The fact that Benedict IX was outright homosexual did nothing to improve his reputation.

Four years into his papacy he was chased from the city by an angry mob, but the Emperor put his support behind him, and he was able to return.

Eight years later, in 1044, Benedict IX was chased from the city once again. The electorate appointed Giovanni dei Crescenzi–Ottaviani, Bishop of Sabina, as Pope Sylvester III. As indicated by his name, the Crescentii seems to have been back in some position of power in Rome.

But the Theophylacti were still powerful and they supported Benedict IX with troops and marched on Rome. By 1045 Benedict IX was back in control. Sylvester II was forced to give up the papacy but was allowed to keep his original bishopry.

This time Benedict IV's papacy lasted only from April to November of 1045. His godfather, John Gratian, Archpriest of St. John by the Latin Gate, who was a lifetime cleric, was shocked by his behaviour and the damage it had done to both the papacy and the family. He decided to incentivize Benedict IX with the only thing he seemed to really care about, money.

John Gratian simply bought the papacy from Benedict IX who abdicated and handed the papacy to John Gratian, now Pope Gregory VI.

But Benedict IX soon decided that life outside the Lateran Palace was not as good as inside, so he returned to Rome and withdrew his abdication. At the same time the former pope, Sylvester III, also returned and reclaimed his title, so now there were three popes in Rome.

Opposing factions dug down in the city, each controlling specific neighbourhoods and the situation was violent, volatile and completely out of control.

If Rome ever needed an outside authority, this was the time, but the Emperor, Conrad II, had died in 1039 so there was no official protector of the Church and the Papal States.

Shortly before his death, Emperor Conrad II had been campaigning in southern Italy where the usual unruly dukes had now been supplemented by an influx of Norman adventurers.

In Germany, Conrad II had had his son, Henry III, crowned as King of Germany immediately after his own crowning as emperor, securing the succession well before his death.

Henry III had initially concentrated on the easternmost part of his realm, but in 1046 he was on his way to Italy to secure control of the North. He was met by a group of clerics pleading for his intervention in the crisis in Rome.

It is unclear if the clerics had come on their own initiative or the initiative of the Pope - and in that case which pope - but in any case, Henry III seized the opportunity.

He set up court at Sutri towards the end of December 1045. Here he heard the cases of all three popes. Henry III came to a pragmatic solution to the problem; he in effect dismissed all three claimant popes.

Sylvester III was dismissed on the reason that he had been elected while there was already a pope. He was sent to a monastery, but historic records show that he continued as Bishop of Sabina for more than a decade after his conviction.

Benedict IV was dismissed on the reason that he had abdicated and had no right to re-appoint himself. He had decided to not appear in front of Henry III and made himself scarce.

Gregory VI was not directly dismissed, he was the latest appointed pope, but Henry III urged him to abdicate on the grounds that he had obtained the papacy by means of simony. With a potential synod discussing that issue in more detail hanging over his head, Gregory VI decided to follow Henry III's advice on the matter. Henry III attached Gregory VI to his court and he died a few years later in Germany.

With Henry III as the de-facto power, he was free to make his own decision on a new pope. He had no intentions of leaving the papacy with another Italian, so he appointed one of his own prelates, Suidger von Morsleben, Bishop of Bamberg, as Pope Clement II.

16 - The Pope

The court moved to on to Rome where the new pope was officially 'elected'. He was consecrated on Christmas day and then, on the same day, proceeded to crown Henry III as emperor.

Clement II immediately, and with the Emperor remaining in the city, called a synod which decided on a range of disciplinary and administrative matters which had been left unattended during the chaos of the preceding years. The synod in particular banned simony.

The Pope and the Emperor now continued the campaign already started by Henry III before he was forced to intervene in matters in Rome. They paid a visit to the Theophylacti in their capital of Frascati and seized the strongholds of the Crescentii, demonstrating the Emperor's clear design to break their stranglehold on Rome.

The Imperial entourage then proceeded to southern Italy where Henry III brokered an uneasy peace between the Lombard and Norman lords, for the first time recognizing the Norman conquests in the region.

Matters settled in Italy, both Emperor and Pope returned to Germany. The Pope set out to return to Rome in October 1047 but died on his way there. Contemporary rumours claimed that he had been poisoned by lead sugar, a theory which was subsequently proven true by a scientific examination of his remains in the twentieth century. Lead sugar was however also used as medicine, so it is unclear whether his poisoning was premeditated or accidental.

The twice former pope, Benedict IV was not slow to take advantage of the death of the absent pope. He once more marched on Rome and installed himself in the Lateran Palace. His family, more specifically Boniface III, Margrave of Tuscany, provided him with the necessary troops and Benedict IX still had plenty of gold to spread around to secure his position.

However, emissaries from Rome had reached the Emperor, whose prerogative it was to appoint the Pope. The emissaries had a proposal from the Romans; Halinard, Archbishop of Lyon, who was not an Italian but spoke the language to perfection.

The Emperor however did not want to rush things. Rather he asked a scholar, Wazo of Liège, to tell him who was the best, rather than most popular, choice for pope.

Wazo of Liège contemplated the issue for some time and then suggested that the most suited person was the former Pope Gregory VI, who was still in the imperial retinue.

That was not the answer the Emperor had been looking for, so he made his own choice and appointed the ageing and scholarly Poppo, Bishop of Brixen, as pope-elect.

The Emperor now set out for Italy in person, but trouble elsewhere meant that he had to turn around. He left Poppo in the care of the Margrave of Tuscany, Boniface III, the very same relative of Benedict IX who had recently helped re-install him in the Lateran Palace.

Part 6 - The Pope and the Crusader Knights

Boniface III was not too happy about the situation, and distinctly anti-imperial in his political views, so after the Emperor had turned around he made excuses to Poppo, telling him that since Benedict IX was now in Rome, and since he was an old man himself, he could not - as ordered by the Emperor - escort him to Rome after all. Stranded, Poppo returned to Germany and the Emperor. Pope Benedict XI still resided in the Lateran Palace.

The Emperor was furious with Boniface III. He sent Poppo back to Tuscany, this time carrying a letter to Boniface III. The letter best speaks for itself:

'Learn, you who have restored a Pope who was canonically deposed, and who have been led by love of money to despise my commands, learn that, if you do not amend your ways, I will soon come and make you.'

Out of options and excuses Boniface III now escorted Poppo to Rome. With his former ally now turning his arms against him, Benedict XI vacated the Lateran Palace. He then disappeared from history. He died in 1056.

Poppo finally entered Rome under much pomp and circumstance; He was consecrated on 17 July 1048 as Pope Damasus II. His troubles had caused him severe exhaustion, so he immediately withdrew from the city to recover at Palestrina. On 9 August he died there, having ruled as pope for twenty-three days.

This time there was no immediate candidate so the Emperor could take his time. He called a conference at Worms in December of 1048 and the imperial and Roman parties both agreed on Bruno of Egisheim-Dagsburg, Bishop of Toul.

Bruno was a noble with a distinguished clerical and scholarly record. Although he accepted the election, he insisted that it be done properly, so he proceeded to Rome as a pilgrim. He was received well and on 12 February 1049 he became Pope Leo IX. The Emperor had wanted a strong pope, and he had finally found one.

Pope Leo IX immediately called a synod to be held at Easter. At the synod the issue of simony was once more condemned, and celibacy of the clergy was re-enforced. That these two issues were at the forefront of the Pope's mind is no surprise giving the state of the Church over the preceding decades.

The Pope then did something highly unusual. Realizing that the weak central authority had undermined the papal authority outside of Italy he went on a European tour. He went to Germany and France where he had meetings with the local clergy. Local issues were discussed and settled and the Pope messages about celibacy and simony were delivered in person.

16 - The Pope

He was back in Rome for another synod by Easter 1050 after which he did another tour, this time round Italy before he went to Germany, to where he also returned in 1052.

Back in Italy by 1053 the Pope must now have decided that the Church's affairs had been put in order, as he now threw himself into a far more temporal project.

Norman lords had continued to expand their influence in southern Italy and were now effectively threatening the remaining Byzantine possessions on the peninsula. With little capability to support their colonies in Italy, the Byzantines turned to the Pope.

Not only was the Pope himself a stakeholder in Italy, now bordering Norman-held territories, but the Normans were also Catholic, their Viking forefathers having been christened in 911, during the pontificate of Anastasius III.

It was therefore both as a temporal lord and the spiritual lord of the Norman invaders that the Byzantine Emperor implored the Pope *'to liberate Italy that now lacks its freedom and to force that wicked people, who are pressing Apulia under their yoke, to leave.'*

The Pope assembled an army of Italians and Swabian mercenaries and set south in the spring of 1053. The Pope was leading from the front as commander-in-chief.

When the two opposing forces met in June, the papal army was however led by Gerard, Duke of Lorraine, and Rudolf, Prince of Benevento while the Pope himself retreated to the town of Civitate close to the battlefield.

The battle went the way of the Normans. The Italian levy fled on the first encounter with the enemy, and it was only the personal bravery of the Swabian mercenaries which left the papal forces with a minimum of dignity.

After the battle, the Pope came out of Civitate, Some say that he came out by his own free will to avoid further bloodshed and others say the citizens of Civitate forced him out to avoid a siege. In any case, he was received well by the victorious Normans, under the overall command of Humphrey of Hauteville, the Count of Apulia.

Pope Leo IX now suffered nine months of imprisonment, although suffering perhaps is a somewhat misleading term. He was treated as a guest, with all comforts provided, but also 'encouraged' to sign a number of documents which, in effect, recognized the Norman rulers of southern Italy.

He was possibly stalling for time, hoping for relief from either a Byzantine army coming from the south or an imperial army coming from the north, but the Byzantine army had re-embarked from Bari and returned home after the defeat of the papal army and the Emperor had no appetite for a fight with the Normans.

The Pope finally returned to Rome in early 1054 and entered into his last, and by far most far-reaching, project.

For reasons unknown the Pope decided to have it out with the Patriarch in Constantinople and the Easter Church.

Although the two sides of the Christian Church had been at loggerhead with each other since the fourth century, there had mainly been peace for a good while. The last controversy being Pope John XIX's clumsy handling of the compromise proposed by the Patriarch in Constantinople a few decades earlier, but even that had been sorted out diplomatically in the end.

One possible reason was that the Pope felt let down by the Byzantines who had abandoned their mission in southern Italy during his imprisonment. No matter the reason, the Pope wrote a letter to the Patriarch of Constantinople, Michael I Cerularius, possibly during his captivity in 1953.

The letter was in turn a response to accusations between Greek and Roman clerical scholars, covering such material matters as the use of unleavened bread a matter which had eventually reached the Pope himself.

In the letter the Pope refers to a document called *the Donation of Constantine*. This document has later been shown to be an eight-century forgery, but at that time the Pope believed that it was genuine.

The Donation of Constantine was supposedly a decree issued by Constantine the Great in the early part of the fourth century. In the decree the Emperor specifically expresses the opinion that the Bishop in Rome is superior to the other bishops and is in effect the head of the Church globally.

Pope Leo IX pointed this out very clearly to the Patriarch, attempting to assert his dominance of the Church as a whole. Over time the sees in Alexandria, Antioch and Jerusalem had been lost to the Muslims, so this matter was really a head-to-head showdown between Rome and Constantinople.

The Patriarch outright rejected the opinion, and in his letter back to the Pope addressed him as 'brother' rather than 'father'. The Pope then sent a delegation to Constantinople to further discuss the issue with the Patriarch and the Emperor.

The delegation was led by Humbert, the Cardinal-bishop of Silva Candida and papal secretary who had originally brought the issue to the Pope's attention and was probably the main instigator of the conflict.

Humbert was received well by the Emperor, Constantine IX Monomachos, but it was really the Patriarch he had come to see and the Patriarch refused to see him.

But Humbert came well prepared for that situation so once he had waited a few months for the Patriarch to grant him an audience, he took matters in his own hands. With him he had decrees of excommunication of the Patriarch and if the Patriarch did not want to see him, he would go to see the Patriarch.

On 16 July 1054, the papal representative burst into Hagia Sophia where the Patriarch was conducting mass. Humbert slammed the decree of excommunication onto the high altar and left the stunned assembly.

16 - The Pope

Technically there was a problem. Back in Rome Pope Leo IX had died in April and the excommunication was thus really invalid at the time it was served, but nobody really cared about such details.

The Patriarch immediately responded to the provocation by excommunicating both Humbert and the Pope. He subsequently closed the Catholic churches in Constantinople, a provocation which was met with the closure of the Orthodox churches in Rome.

This conflict was not of benefit to the Emperor of Byzantium, who was still aiming for a military alliance with the Pope against the Normans, but he died soon after and his effort of reconciliation was in vain.

This conflict, known as the *East-West Schism*, was the final break between the two parts of the Church. From this point on they ran as independent entities even if repeated attempts were made over time to re-unite them. Although, as a matter of good will, the mutual excommunications between the Pope and the Patriarch were rescinded by Pope Paul VI and Patriarch Athenagoras in 1965, the Catholic and Orthodox Churches remain separated to this day.

Back in Rome, as mentioned, Pope Leo IX had died in April 1054. He was a saint and the first such since Pope Adrian III with forty un-saintly popes in between them.

A delegation was duly sent to the Emperor, led by a monk called Hildebrand, who had been a favourite of Leo IX and who we shall meet again later as pope.

The Emperor appointed Gebhard, Count of Calw, Tollenstein, and Hirschberg. He was a Bishop of Eichstätt and a trusted advisor and kinsman of the Emperor. With no opposition he went to Rome and was consecrated on 13 April 1055 as Pope Victor II.

The new Pope and the Emperor met again in Florence, where a synod confirmed Leo IX's stern views on celibacy and simony and the Pope now followed the Emperor back to Germany where the Emperor died on 5 October.

The Emperor left his son Henry IV as his heir, but he was only six years of age. A regency was formed with his mother, Agnes, as regent and Pope Victor II as his guardian.

This was the most power a pope had exercise of ever, ruling undisputed over the papacy and being in the innermost circle of the Imperial Court.

Pope Victor II made no big waves but used his power to maintain peace and order in both the Empire and the Church. He returned to Rome in the summer of 1057 and died shortly after. He was not a saint.

The death of Victor II left a brief power-vacuum. The Empire was weak and with Victor II gone its strong links to the papacy were also gone.

In Rome the electorate decided on Frederick of Lorraine as the new Pope. He was a cardinal and the younger brother of Godfrey III, who amongst other titles was the current Margrave of Tuscany as he had married the widow of Boniface III.

Once consecrated as Pope Stephen IX, the new Pope prepared to elevate his brother to emperor. Godfrey III had been at loggerheads with the Emperor for more than a decade and his elevation to emperor would have been a complete break of the ties between the German court and the papacy. But before it came to that, Pope Stephen IX fell sick and died after only eight months on the throne. He was not a saint, but his death started yet another succession crisis on Rome.

Before his death Pope Stephen IX had decreed that his successor should not be appointed until after the return of Hildebrand, who had been sent to the Empress-regent Agnes to obtain her confirmation of Stephen IX's own appointment.

But the Theophylacti once again showed their position of power in Rome. Not waiting for the return of Hildebrand they forced - by means of threats and bribes - the election of Giovanni, Cardinal Bishop of Velletri and a brother of the notorious Pope Leo IX.

Giovanni became Pope Benedict X and the cardinals and others who protested against his election were driven from Rome.

Hildebrand heard about the election of Benedict X while on his return journey to Rome and he went to Florence where he obtained the support of Godfrey III. He proposed Gérard de Bourgogne, Bishop of Florence, and agreement was obtained from Empress-regent Agnes.

The new party now proceeded to Sienna where they met up with the cardinals who had fled Rome. Here the cardinals elected Gérard de Bourgogne as Pope Nicholas II and excommunicated Benedict X. Once again there were two popes, and soon they were both in Rome.

It soon became clear the party of Pope Nicholas II was the stronger and Pope Benedict X fled the city under the protection of one of the noble families supporting him.

Pope Nicholas II now put the final nail in the coffin of Byzantine presence in Italy. He allied himself with the Normans - a few years earlier the papacy's enemies, confirming their rights by conquest in southern Italy, thus paving their way for getting rid of the last Lombard and Byzantine influence, a task they completed by 1075 at which time they had also expelled the Saracens from Sicily.

After the Pope's recognition, the Normans lent military support to the Papal States and very soon the last rebellion had been suppressed. Pope Benedict X, now considered an anti-pope, was not punished, but allowed to settle in Rome. That changed in 1060 where he was finally prosecuted for his role in the revolt and exiled.

Pope Nicholas II now called a synod which made one very important decision. In effect the papacy had been a tug-of-war between the Roman nobles and the Emperor, the winner determined by the strength of the

Empire at the time. Now the synod agreed that henceforth the Pope would be elected by the College of Cardinals with no secular participation and that the election would take place in Rome. At a point in time where neither the nobles nor the Empire was particularly strong, the Church had made its own declaration of independence.

With Pope Nicholas II's reform in place, you would have thought that the election of the next pope would be easy, but as it turned out it became one of the more prolonged battles for the papacy.

For as much as the Church had declared itself independent, the declaration was unilateral and the Empire, represented by Empress-regent Agnes, had no intentions of handing over the right to appoint the Pope.

When Nicholas II died (unsaintly) in 1061, the cardinals, as per the new rules, met and elected their new pope. The choice was Anselmo da Baggio, Bishop of Lucca, who was consecrated as Pope Alexander II.

But when news of the new pope's election reached Germany, the Empress-regent, supported by German and Lombard bishops, held her own council in Basel where they elected Pietro Cadalus, Bishop of Parma, as their pope under the name of Honorius II.

Once again chaos reigned and it did not ease up any when Honorius II, supported by German troops, marched on Rome. Once there they fought it out with the supporters of Alexander II and as had been the case before, the city ended up being divided between the two warring parties.

This time it was Godfrey III who came to the city's rescue. He convinced both competing popes to withdraw to their sees while he sorted the politics out and he then went into dialogue with the German court to seek a resolution.

The outcome would have probably been a given, Pope Honorius II already an imperial appointee, but as it happened the Empress-regent Agnes was ousted by a coup and the new regent was Anno, Archbishop of Cologne. He in turn did not like Honorius II, but to look fair he appointed his nephew, Burchard II, Bishop of Halberstadt, to go to Rome and investigate whether the election of Alexander II was as per regulations (as there were rumours of simony).

The legate found that there was nothing wrong with the election of Alexander II, so the Empire changed sides and declared for Alexander II, leaving their own candidate, Honorius II, without a champion.

But Honorius II still had some local support and managed to re-enter Rome and set up in Castel Sant'Angelo. He eventually had to flee the city and was excommunicated, and although he played no further role, he maintained his right to the papacy until he died. According to the official records he was an anti-pope, but it was close call.

The most important thing that happened in the papacy of Pope Alexander II was when he received an embassy from Guillaume II, Duke of Normandy, in 1066. The young duke believed he had a claim to the throne of

England and he wanted the Pope's blessing on his claim and the campaign he was planning.

Relations with the Normans now a key issue for the Papal States, the Pope blessed the duke's claim and his campaign. It was thus under a papal banner and with a letter from the Pope to the English Church that Guillaume II, later to be known as William the Conqueror, invaded England in 1066.

When Pope Alexander II died (unsaintly) in 1073 the tension between the Pope and the Emperor was to become even tenser than before.

We already seen the name Hildebrand appearing a couple of times. Born Hildebrand Bonizi he was originally a monk who was 'discovered' by Pope Benedict VI and attached to the Curia. Since then, he had played a number of roles as diplomat and was the mind behind the reforms carried out by Pope Nicholas II.

On the death of Alexander II, Hildebrand was of the right age and, according to contemporary sources, there arose a loud outcry from both clergy and people: "*Let Hildebrand be pope!*" and '*Blessed Peter has chosen Hildebrand the Archdeacon!*'

The public demonstration of support for Hildebrand was probably well orchestrated, but in any case, he was brought to the Lateran Palace, elected by the Cardinals and consecrated as Pope Gregory VII.

Hildebrand's elevation to Gregory VII did not initially lead to a new confrontation with the Empire. Hildebrand was a well-known and respected Church reformer and the King of Germany, Henry IV, who had now come of age, had other issues to deal with closer to home where his reign was constantly challenged by rebellious dukes, counts and princes.

Gregory VII's first challenge was thus the Norman adventurer and strongman in southern Italy, Robert Guiscard, Duke of Apulia and one of the Norman lords whose rule had been recognized by Pope Nicholas II.

By the time Gregory VII became pope in 1073 Robert Guiscard had pushed the Byzantines out of Italy and was well on his way in getting rid of the last Lombards. But he was not entirely trustworthy, so he attacked Benevento, one of the Papal States.

Pope Gregory tried to arrange a meeting with Robert Guiscard, but it was not possible and eventually the Pope reverted to excommunicating him.

However bigger issues were at play in the world. In 1071 the Byzantines had been beaten by the Seljuks at the Battle of Manzikert and they were constantly pushed back in Anatolia. The new Pope was not a great friend of the Byzantines, but he realized the danger of the Muslim onslaught on the Christian communities in the East.

Pope Gregory VII thus called on the lords of Christianity to unite and go to free the Church of the Holy Sepulchre in Jerusalem but, contrary to a similar call from his successor Pope Urban II some twenty years later nothing came of it.

16 - The Pope

Apart from these and other isolated issues, the big issue during the reign of Gregory VII, and the issue which would eventually see him disposed, was the dispute he started with the kings of western Europe, Henry IV in particular.

Basically, Gregory VII, as he had done in his guise as the monk Hildebrand, believed absolutely that the Church was the supreme power on earth. While temporal structures were necessary, they should be subject to the Church in matters of real importance. He had already been the pen behind Nicholas II's election reform and now he wanted to take it further.

The Church had, over the centuries, built up a substantial landownership based on donations from private individuals, nobles and even kings. The revenues from such lands were collected by the local bishops, or sees, and represented a substantial income.

It had long since become custom that kings appointed their own bishops, who often were also holders of public office and the land presided over by the bishop thus became de-facto crownland from which the crown took considerable revenues in terms of both taxes, fraud and simony.

Pope Gregory VII had already - like his immediate predecessors - issued decrees about simony and he now issued a decree specifying the Pope's absolute right to appoint bishops.

For Henry IV this was a step too far. Not only would he lose the political value of such appointments, but the revenues from the bishop's lands would now go to the Church.

The King, for he was not yet emperor, protested and rejected the Pope's decree. The Pope then excommunicated a number of his council members as a warning shot.

But there was trouble in the King's realm, in Saxony in particular, so the King did not have the time or resources to fight with the Pope. He made penance, at Nurnberg, in 1074 and promised to support the Pope in his endeavours for reform.

The King's penance lasted only until the following year. He had now ended the revolt in Saxony and was once again in a mood to do battle with the Pope.

Angry letters were exchanged, and on Christmas night 1075 the Pope was apprehended and kidnapped while performing mass at Santa Maria Maggiore. His captor was one Cencio I Frangipane, a Roman noble of some standing. He released the Pope the following day, due to public pressure, and survived the encounter - as he reappears in history later.

The Pope had no doubt that Henry IV was behind the attack and in January of 1076 the King further progressed his attack by holding a synod in which the German bishops declared the Pope deposed. It was quickly followed by a similar synod held by Lombard bishops. To counter the Pope now held his own synod which excommunicated and dethroned the King.

Both combatants had played their cards, and it was now up to the people to decide who had the best hand. It turned out to be the Pope.

Simply put, the King had more enemies than the Pope and they took the opportunity to revolt. Revolt broke out in Saxony again and the King found it difficult to even gather his nobles now that an excuse to disobey was at hand.

Finally, the Princes of Germany held an assembly to find a replacement for Henry IV. They could not agree and instead decided to inform Henry IV that if he was still excommunicated on the anniversary of his excommunication, they would consider the throne of Germany empty and select a successor. They also invited the Pope to Germany to consult on the matter.

King Henry IV now had to accept the unavoidable and headed for Italy to seek the Pope's forgiveness. The Pope refused to see his emissaries and set out for Germany.

The two travelling parties met in northern Italy. The Pope, fearing violence, retreated to the Castle of Canossa, held by Matilda of Tuscany, a strong supporter of Gregory VII and no friend of the King of Germany.

But Henry IV appreciated the fact that violence was not the means to the end. Instead, he appeared in person, dressed as a pilgrim, in front of the castle in January of 1076. It was bitterly cold, but the King remained without food and water for three days before the gates of the castle before the Pope allowed him in.

The King did penance and promised his support for the Pope. The Pope in turn cancelled the excommunication which the King interpreted also as a reinstatement of his kingship although it was, deliberately, not actually mentioned by the Pope.

Returning to Germany it became clear that even if the King had sorted things out with the Pope, the local princes had only used the conflict with the Pope as a catalyst for revolt. Civil war followed and the Pope stayed neutral until Henry IV was, apparently, finally beaten in January of 1080 at which time the Pope declared for his competitor Rudolf of Swabia and shortly thereafter excommunicated Henry IV once more.

However, Rudolf of Swabia died shortly after and despite more competition it was Henry IV who eventually emerged, like a phoenix from the flames, as King of Germany once more.

This time there were no rebellious princes left and popular opinion was for the King. Like before the King now held his own synod, in which he excommunicated and deposed the Pope or, in his own words *'the false monk'*.

Further, the synod also appointed a new pope. Guibert, Bishop of Ravenna, was elevated as Pope Clement III although he was yet to be consecrated.

Henry IV now marched on Italy. He deposed Matilda of Tuscany, who had supported Gregory VII on Henry IV's last expedition to Italy and proceeded to Rome, He laid siege to the town, but eventually retreated to Tuscany.

While there he received a much-needed donation of 360,000 gold Ducats from the Byzantine Emperor Alexios I Komnenos. The reason for the Byzantine support was that Robert Guiscard - having secured absolute control of southern Italy and Sicily - had crossed the Adriatic Sea and was marching on Constantinople, so the Byzantine Emperor could only benefit from military conflict in Italy to distract Robert Guiscard.

With fresh resources Henry IV marched on Rome again. His attack was unsuccessful and so instead he ravaged Tuscany. Finally in 1082 he returned to Rome for a third time and this time he broke through.

Henry IV occupied the Leonine City and Pope Gregory VII holed up in Castel Sant'Angelo. Negotiations were had and the Pope was absolutely insistent that the King had to once more do penance and submit to his authority.

The Roman nobles now agreed with Henry IV that the issue should be settled by a synod. The Pope was not part of the agreement and the synod turned into a farce as Henry IV prevented the pro-papal bishops from attending.

Matters unsettled, the King left Rome and went south to create a second front in the Norman realms as per his agreement with the Byzantine Emperor.

His campaign yielded little result and he returned to Rome in 1084. This time the Roman nobles opened the city to him and Pope Clements III was consecrated. He immediately went on to crown Henry IV as Emperor of the Romans.

However, Henry IV's campaigns in southern Italy had not gone unnoticed. The Pope had reconciled his differences with Robert Guiscard and the Norman duke left his brother in command of the troops in Greece and returned to Italy where he marched on Rome to help the Pope - still in Castel'Sant Angelo - and to get rid of Henry IV.

Henry IV was not equipped to fight the battle hardened Normans so he left the city, taking Clements III with him and the Normans entered Rome and released the Pope.

But the Normans did not come in peace. Whether they simply could not be controlled, or whether their right to the city was part of the agreement with the Pope is unknown, but the Normans sacked the old town for three days. A popular uprising followed and in the end the Normans set fire to the city and left with Pope Gregory VII who, as far as the Romans were concerned, was to blame for the Norman's behaviour.

There were now two popes, neither of whom resided in Rome. Pope Gregory VII finally settled in Salerno where died he embittered in 1085. His papacy had seen an absolute low in terms of the relationship between the Church and the Empire. He was, however, rewarded in afterlife as he was recognized a saint, one of only two in his century. There was to be 35 popes, and more than 200 years was to go by, before a new saintly pope would emerge.

The election of the next pope became a prolonged and confused affair. The top candidate, according to the wishes of Gregory VII and supported by the Normans, was Desiderius, the Great Abbot of Monte Cassino.

Desiderius was of Lombard origins, but on good terms with the Norman rulers in southern Italy. He was pro-reform but more moderate than Gregory VII, so he was the perfect candidate. But there was a problem; Desiderius did not want to become pope and he specifically did not want to become pope unless properly elected by the Cardinals in Rome rather than by force.

He went to Rome to consult with the Cardinals, but when he found they were determined to elect him without competition he retreated to Monte Cassino.

He returned to Rome once more in the autumn of 1085 and the same scenario played out. In the spring of 1086, the College of Cardinals once more called him to Rome. Twice they offered him the papacy and twice he refused.

Finally, a competing candidate was found in Odo, Cardinal-Bishop of Ostia, so when Desiderius won the vote again, he finally accepted. In May of 1086, a year after the death of Gregory VII, Desiderius was elected as Pope Victor III.

But the new Pope did not stay long in Rome. Four days after his election and still not consecrated, the Imperial Prefect attacked the Lateran Palace and the pope-elect and cardinals fled the city. Once they were away the new Pope laid down his papal insignia and returned to Monte Cassino.

It took another year before the imperial troops were finally expelled from Rome, mainly due to an effort by Matilda of Tuscany. Pope Victor III was finally consecrated on 9 May 1087 and he again left Rome for Monte Cassino from where he performed his papal duties. He did not achieve much though, as he died in September.

Throughout the reign of Victor III the Anti-pope Clement III still upheld his claim to the throne. On the death of Victor III, he returned to Rome, once again in the hands of the pro-imperial party.

A meeting of cardinals at Terracina in March of 1088 elected the former candidate, Odo, Cardinal-Bishop of Ostia, as the new pope under the name of Urban II. Although the conditions of his election were not perfect, his papacy would become one of the most significant in history.

It took Urban II five years to claim his place in Rome and oust Anti-pope Clement III. He did so by gradually forming a very strong anti-imperial alliance. Matilda of Tuscany was one of the foundation blocks of the alliance which gradually grew to include the Normans in the south, the remaining Lombard lords in the north and finally, as the coup de grâce, Emperor Henry

16 - The Pope

VI's own son, Conrad II, who was crowned King of Italy in 1093 after his father had been defeated in northern Italy.

Once Urban II was secure in Rome he picked a fight with the King of France, Philip I, who the Pope excommunicated due to his self-instituted divorce of Queen Bertha - who he claimed was too fat - and his subsequent marriage to Bertrade de Montfort, herself already married.

But it was an appeal for help from the Byzantine Emperor, Alexios I Komnenos - who, a decade earlier, had paid for Henry IV's campaign against Gregory VII - that accelerated Urban II's papacy into history.

I have already covered this issue in Chapter 3, and we shall also return to it in the next chapter, but in summary the Byzantine Empire was in dire straits. Following the Byzantine defeat at Manzikert in 1071, Seljuks had gradually flowed into western Anatolia, establishing their own beyliks and reduced Byzantine possessions to a few coastal enclaves.

Desperate for help, the Byzantine Emperor asked for help from the Pope. His call was to help save Christianity from the assault of Islam and his call was received well by the Pope for a range of reasons.

Western Europe was torn apart by wars large and small. When nation states did not fight each other, local conflict broke out between counts and dukes. A new class of 'knights' emerged, landless nobles trained for war who, with their own retinues or men at arms caused chaos and upheaval.

A popular movement inside the Church had called for *'Pax Deiu'* - the Peace of God - trying to define rules of war such as defining peasants, women and children as non-combatants and avoiding battle on Sundays, but it was only loosely adhered to when circumstances were favourable for such considerations.

At home the Pope had the powerful and warlike Normans bordering his realms in the south, and although they were technically allies, it was only a matter of time before they would once again start to expand their territories into the Papal States.

The Byzantine Emperor had probably hoped to get papal support in the form of mercenaries, paid by the Pope, but the Pope had no money to spare so instead he decided to re-try a previously unsuccessful concept of 'pilgrimage' which historians have later labelled 'crusading' (which we shall call it for convenience).

Where previous calls for crusade had been limited - and highly political - affairs mainly aimed at kings, this time the Pope went public and the effects were unpredicted, unsurpassed and would last for 200 years.

The Pope was in Piacenza when he received the Emperor's ambassador and a council was called to take place in Clermont in November the same year, to discuss the Emperor's petition.

The Council of Clermont was so big that it was held outdoors, and Urban II was well prepared. He had prepared a sermon in which he urged all and sundry to go to the aid of the Christians against the Muslims, retake "The

Holy Land" and as a further incentive he promised absolution for all participants.

If the Pope had hoped to perhaps motivate some of the idle knights of Europe to go to Constantinople and help the Emperor out at their own expense he got his will. But he got far more than that.

The 'crusade' became a public phenomenon once it was preached from the pulpits of Europe's churches. People simply started to march to Constantinople where they arrived en mass before a city not prepared to receive them. The masses were transported to Anatolia where they, in due cause, were massacred by the Seljuks.

But in their wake professional armies followed. In particular Norman lords had responded to the Pope's call and once they had been via Constantinople, once again facing closed gates, they marched through Anatolia and against all odds managed to take Jerusalem, forming the Latin states of the Kingdom of Jerusalem, the County of Tripoli, the Principality of Antioch and the County of Edessa. All of these states were Catholic, so the Pope had suddenly expanded his sphere into the Middle East, leaving the Patriarch of Constantinople stranded in the middle.

The Crusaders conquered Jerusalem on 15 July 1099. Exactly two weeks later Pope Urban II died. He had not yet been informed of the final Christian victory which he had initiated.

On the death of Urban II, and despite the insistent claims of Clement III in Germany, the cardinals elected the monk Ranierius as Pope Paschal II.

Pope Paschal II would come to rule for nineteen years the first ten of which were relatively peaceful as most of the warlike European lords were involved in the consolidation of the new Latin states in the Holy Land.

His first involvement in politics came in 1104. Emperor Henry IV had round the same time as Paschal II became pope finally defeated his rebellious son Conrad II of Italy. In his place, as King of Italy, he had put his other son and heir, Henry V, under the specific conditions that Henry V would not interfere with politics in Germany until Henry IV had died.

Five years later the young heir apparent lost patience with his father's, increasingly unpopular, rule. He went to the Pope and asked to be released from his oath to his father. The Pope was a stout supporter of Gregory VII's reforms, which he had already reconfirmed in a synod, but which were duly ignored by Emperor Henry IV.

It was therefore in the Pope's interest to support the young King of Italy and he was released from his oath. Henry V proceeded to Germany where he managed to oust his father in 1106 taking the title as King of Germany.

But the new King was not as loyal to the Pope as he may have pretended. He was absolutely against the Church reforms and maintained his right to appoint bishops. He invited the Pope to come to Germany and discuss the issue, but the Pope had no intentions of putting himself at the mercy of the

King of Germany, so he simply renewed the Church's position on the matter.

Finally in 1110 the King decided to solve the matter by force. He entered Italy and forced the Pope to meet him at Sutri. Once there the King effectively arrested the Pope. They entered into an 'agreement' by which the King agreed to recognize the Church's authority in terms of appointments, but on the condition that the Church returned all lands added to its possessions inside the Empire since Charlemagne, and that the King became emperor.

The agreement was destined to be rejected by the Church in general, and when it was read out in Rome a public uprising followed. The King was wounded in the mêlée and withdrew from Rome with the Pope and sixteen cardinals under armed guard.

The King held the Pope prisoner for two months before he finally agreed to leave the rights to appoint bishops with the King and crown him emperor.

Duly crowned in April of 1111 the new Emperor left for Germany. Once he was across the Alps a synod nullified the Emperor's rights to appoint bishops - as it had been made by use of force - and the Emperor was excommunicated by the Archbishop of Vienne, although the Pope decided not to personally ratify the decree.

In terms of church matters, easily forgotten in the potent political environment, The Byzantine Emperor tried to see if he could obtain a re-union of the eastern and western Church, The Pope was however absolute in his demand for status as head of the Church, so the negotiations came to naught.

In the new states in the Holy Land things started to become organised. A hospital called the Hospital of St. John of Jerusalem had for a long time served pilgrims in Jerusalem. It now sought, and obtained, status as a separate religious order which was under the sole authority of the Pope. Under the Pope's protection they could stay out of the already heated political environment in the Holy Land as well as avoid local taxes.

As a curiosum, the Pope also appointed one Erik Gnupsson as Bishop of Greenland and Vinland, The latter was the Viking settlement in Newfoundland and Erik Gnupsson was thus the first Christian bishop on the American continent.

The uneasy peace with the Emperor broke in 1115 when Matilda of Tuscany died. She left her estate to the Church, but the Emperor also claimed it as she was an imperial fief.

Henry V arrived back in Rome and the Pope fled south. Once in Rome Henry V forced the remaining clergy into re-crowning him as emperor to avoid any doubt. The bishop who crowned him was Maurice Bourdin, the Archbishop of Braga. At the same time the Archbishop of Milan excommunicated the Emperor again and all was chaos while the Emperor campaigned in northern Italy to put his new possessions in order.

Part 6 - The Pope and the Crusader Knights

Finally, Pope Paschal II gathered support from the Normans in southern Italy and they moved on Rome. The Emperor withdrew and the Pope was back in Rome by January 1118 and there he died a few weeks later.

The Cardinals quickly elected the Chancellor, Giovanni Caetani, as the new pope but before he could become consecrated, the Emperor had turned around and returned to Rome. The Pope-elect fled and the Emperor installed the tame Archbishop of Braga (the same person who had crowned him) as pope under the name of Gregory VIII.

In the meantime, the new Pope-elect was consecrated at Gaeta as Gelasius II. From there he immediately excommunicated both the Emperor and his puppet pope.

Once again with Norman assistance the Pope finally made it to Rome in July, but the city was still split between imperial and anti-imperial factions and the Pope was driven from the city again. He decided to do a (in isolation successful) tour of France where he died in January of 1119. Little had been achieved.

Still in France, the Cardinals appointed Cardinal Guy de Burgundy as the new pope under the name of Callixtus II.

From the outset the new Pope looked to have the lesser hand, but he had one major advantage. Guy de Burgundy was of noble decent and he was, through the intricate patterns of noble alliances and marriages, connected to pretty much every major noble house in Europe.

It was probably through pressure from these connections that the Emperor agreed to meet the Pope at a council at Rheims in order to see if the problems between them could be reconciled.

The Pope arrived with a retinue of European nobles, including the King of France, and four hundred bishops and abbots. The Emperor arrived in the vicinity with 30,000 men at arms but never actually participated in the Council. As a result, it was resolved to excommunicate him, and Gregory VIII.

With solid backing from his relatives the Pope now marched on Rome. On his arrival Gregory VIII fled to Sutri. The pro-papal troops laid siege in April of 1121 and after eight days the citizens of Sutri handed over Gregory VIII. He was subsequently moved around between various monasteries until he died in 1137.

There was once again only one Pope and he resided in Rome. But the issue with the Emperor had still not been settled. The Emperor had experienced a backlash in popularity since his latest encounter with the Pope at Rheims and finally it was agreed to meet at Worms.

By September of 1122, the parties had reached an accord. Appointment of bishops would from now on be a dual process. The Emperor could appoint bishops in their secular capacity - which included their obligation as landowners to provide troops to the Emperor's army - whereas the Pope had to appoint them in their religious capacity.

16 -The Pope

Each wished the other peace and the parties departed. The Pope then called a synod in Rome which ratified the agreement in March of 1123. By the end of 1124, the Pope was dead and a few months later, so was the Emperor.

Whereas the Emperor's position had retained some of the powers he desired, it was still without practical power to appoint the new pope. Although in principle this power now sat with the Cardinals, the real power in Rome was now again split between factions of noble families.

The two most powerful factions were those of the Frangipani and Pierleoni families. If the Cardinals had to appoint a Pope, then the powerful families were determined to have their own family-members and partisans appointed as cardinals, a development which would continue for centuries in Rome.

The College of Cardinals was split between 'foreign' - mainly French - cardinals appointed by Callixtus II and Italian cardinals appointed during the reigns of Urban II and Paschal II. The foreign group had the support of the Frangipani family and the Italian cardinals had the support of the Pierleoni family.

Inside Rome the Frangipani had control of the area around the Coliseum, which they had fortified, and the Pierleoni had control of the Tiber Island and the fortified Theatre of Marcellus. The battle lines were drawn up.

The main contenders were Teobaldo Boccapecci, supported by the Pierleoni family, Saxo de Anagni, who was the popular choice of the people and Lamberto Scannabecchi supported by the Frangipani family. All were cardinals and all were thus eligible for election.

Pope Callixtus II had died on 13 December 1124. Three days later, and in accordance with canon law the College of Cardinals met. Intense diplomacy had already been carried out, each party wooing the cardinals with lavish promises and bribes. As it turned out the Pierleoni family had done the best job. Their candidate Teobaldo Boccapecci was elected unanimously.

But the Frangipani family were not unprepared. As soon as the new Pope had been elected and chosen the name Celestine II, an armed party of Frangipani partisans broke into the proceedings. A scuffle ensued and the Pope-elect was wounded in the mêlée. Confusion reigned and before the College of Cardinals dispersed in chaos, Lamberto Scannabecchi had been elected as Honorius II (a name already previously used by an Anti-pope appointed in 1061).

The wounded Pope-elect, Celestine II, submitted to the election of Honorius II but his backers, the Pierleoni did not. A few days of fighting in the streets of Rome broke out. Parallel to the fighting, the Frangipani were actively trying to bribe the supporters of Celestine II, and their tactics worked.

Gradually the support for Celestine II fell away and the parties agreed on Honorius II. He, however, was not content with the way he had been 'elected', so when the Cardinals met again on 21 December he resigned. A new vote was called, and he was formally re-elected unanimously. He was consecrated on the same day. The Pierleoni family had lost the battle, but they were ready to fight another day.

Although the rule of Pope Honorius II would only last five years, the last of which he was partly incapacitated by disease, he was an active pope who conducted his business with some success.

His first lucky break came in the year of his consecration. Emperor Henry V, with whom the Pope had a short fight over the lands in Tuscany left by Matilda of Tuscany, died in May 1125. He did not leave an heir and the throne of Germany was up for grabs.

Like in Rome, Germany was dominated by powerful noble families. The Hohenstaufen was the most powerful, but the smaller noble families, supported by most of the clergy, feared the establishment of a new dynasty. They therefore elected another major landowner, Lothair of Supplinburg, and he was, with the support of the Chancellor and Archbishop of Mainz, crowned as Lothair II, King of Germany.

As far as the nobles were concerned, Lothair II was the perfect candidate as he was fifty years of age and did not have an heir, thus leaving the future kingship in the control of the nobles.

But the Hohenstaufen did not agree, and civil war broke out in Germany. To gather support, Lothair II did something unusual; he asked the Pope to approve his kingship.

The kingship of Germany was not traditionally the Pope's to give, but in lieu of the preceding decade's battle for authority between the papacy and the Empire, the request was a gift horse which Honorius II did not look in the mouth for long.

The Pope gave his blessing to Lothair II and also promised him the title of emperor. The King confirmed the Concordad of Worms and paid homage to the Pope, but the situation in Germany prevented him from appearing in Rome for his crowning as emperor.

As the struggle in Germany went on, the Pope eventually excommunicated Lothair II's opponent, Conrad Hohenstaufen, as well as the Archbishop of Milan who had crowned Conrad Hohenstaufen as anti-king. However, the Pope never got to crown Lothair II as emperor.

With his back free from the battle with the Empire which had dominated the reign of his immediate predecessors, Pope Honorius II had the opportunity to deal with things closer to home, both within and outside the Church itself.

Over time two particularly powerful monastic centres had developed. One was at Monte Cassino in southern Italy and one was at Cluny in France. Both monasteries were run by the Benedictine order, which during the period of weak papal authority, had developed into semi-autonomous states-within-the-state.

16 - The Pope

The Abbot of Monte Cassino, Oderisio di Sangro, was no friend of the Pope. They had previously been at loggerheads when the Pope was Cardinal-Bishop of Istia and the Abbot had refused to assist the new Pope financially after his ascension to the throne. There were also rumours that the, noble born, Abbot was making fun of the Pope's humble background, so it was time to reel him in.

Reports reached the Pope that the Abbot had been misusing Church funds, so the Pope - labelling him a *'soldier and a thief, not a monk'* requested the Abbot appear before the Pope in Rome. No less than three times did the Abbot refuse until, during Lent of 1126, the Pope deposed him. But the Abbot ignored the Pope's decree and continued as before, fortifying the monastery just in case the Pope should decide to enforce his will by means of arms.

In the end it was the people of Cassino who took matters in their own hands. The Abbot was - no doubt due to his fraudulent behaviour - unpopular with the people and with the Papal Decree behind them they forced their way into the monastery and forced the Abbot to resign.

The monks now elected one Niccolo as the new Abbot, but the Pope had no intentions of leaving matters in their hands. He appointed his own Abbot, Seniorectus, the provost of the monastery at Capua which led to violent skirmishes between the supporters of the two Abbots. Eventually the monks had to accept defeat and the Pope's Abbot was duly appointed. For good measure the Pope excommunicated Niccolo and forced an oath of obedience from the monks.

In Cluny, Abbot Pons of Melgueil had lived a worldly and unholy life and had been expelled by his own monks in 1122. He went to the Holy Land and in 1126 he returned to Cluny. This time he had an armed band with him and they took possession of the monastery and reinstated the Abbot. His followers then proceeded to terrorize the surrounding towns and news reached the Pope.

The Pope sent a legate to investigate and under threat of excommunication the Abbot finally presented himself before the Pope in Rome. Here he was officially deposed and sent to prison where he died.

Over and above internal church matters, the Pope got involved in several issues. He had a short but intensive fight with the French King over the right of investiture, but the matter was solved in a quicker and less chaotic manner than a similar issue with the King of Germany.

One concern of the Pope's was the southern Papal States. First there were problems in Campania, where the local lords were terrorizing the local population by means of roaming armed bands. The Pope assembled an army and subdued the wayward lords, also re-taking papal fortresses left with autonomous castellans.

But the Pope's greater concern was his Norman neighbours. The Normans had consolidated their possessions into the Kingdom of Sicily.

That was good from the perspective of keeping the Saracens away, but it was bad because the Kingdom of Sicily represented a single powerful neighbour to the Papal States.

King Roger II of Sicily was keen to further expand his rising kingdom, so when the Duke of Apulia died in 1127 and did not leave an heir, Roger II moved on Apulia and Calabria. The Pope, however, was of the opinion that the Duke had left his possessions to the Church, so he moved with an army to occupy the territories before Roger II could get to them.

Gradually the Pope won allies from the local nobles, who were also afraid of Roger II's increasing power, and a bigger coalition army managed to hold Roger II off. Eventually the coalition started to break apart, and ultimately the Pope and Roger II agreed that Roger II should hold the territories as papal fiefs, a solution similar to that which had been achieved in northern Italy.

In or around 1119 a new religious order had been formed in Jerusalem. It was unusual because it was an order of knights, aiming to protect the pilgrims coming to Jerusalem from marauders, but at the same time they saw themselves as monks. They had obtained status as a noble order from the King of Jerusalem, but they now approached the Pope for his blessing as a religious order.

The combination of fighting monks was new and unusual, but the situation in the Holy Land was in itself unusual so the Pope gave his blessing to the new Order and asked the opinionated abbot, Bernard of Clairvaux, to draw up suitable rules which included the traditional wows of poverty, chastity and obedience.

The Pope further decreed that the Order was under his direct authority which, as was the case of the Hospital of St. John of Jerusalem, meant that the new order could operate independently of the shifting tides of politics in Jerusalem. The King of Jerusalem had given the Order quarters on the Temple Mount in Jerusalem and from that they drew their name; 'the Poor Fellow-Soldiers of Christ and of the Temple of Solomon,' which in common use was shortened to the Knights Templar.

The active Pope started to suffer from sickness in 1129. When it was clear that he was mortally ill he was moved to the San Gregorio Magno al Celio monastery in Rome and now a dance-macabre started to unfold around the dying pontiff.

With the Emperor-elect not yet crowned, the selection of a new pope was an entirely local affair in Rome. Although the competition between the two leading families had been limited to isolated outbreaks of violence during the reign of Honorius II, his expected death quickly mobilized the Roman factions.

As it happened the monastery to which the ailing Pope was brought was in a neighbourhood controlled by the Frangipani, giving them an advantage as they could control the news relating to the Pope's condition.

16 - The Pope

A rumour surfaced that the Pope had died and supporters of the Pierleoni stormed the monastery. They were however, met by the still living Pope, kitted out in full regalia - and so had to leave.

The intentions of the Pierleoni were now clear, so the Frangipani made their plans and when the Pope actually died on 13th February 1130, they barred the gates to the monastery. Inside they quickly buried the dead Pope, and a selection of partisan cardinals elected the Frangipani candidate, Gregorio Papareschi, who took the name Innocent II.

Outside the monastery the remaining cardinals, supported by the Pierleoni, now elected their own candidate Pietro Pierleoni, who took the name Anacletus II.

Once again there were two popes in Rome. But the party behind Anacletus II was the strongest, made up of a coalition of everybody who were against the Frangipani, and soon Pope Innocent II had to flee Rome, leaving Anacletus II in control.

There was much dispute as to whom had been elected pope the right way, and the truth probably was that it was neither, but once Innocent II had left Rome he made his way to Genoa and then France. Here he gathered support for his cause. He got the influential Bernard of Clairvaux on his side, and eventually also got the support of the King of Germany, the King of France and the King of England.

In Rome Pope Anacletus II had also managed to garner some outside support. He was supported by William X, Duke of Aquitaine and Roger II of Sicily whom he had quickly confirmed as King of Sicily after his election as pope.

Neither pope did much in terms of clerical affairs, their focus was on the claim for the papacy itself. On the promise of being made emperor, Lothair II finally marched on Rome, with Pope Innocent II, in 1133.

Lothair II had brought only an expeditionary force, as his main army was still required in Germany and with that, he managed to occupy only parts of Rome.

Pope Anacletus II - and the Pierleoni - controlled St.Peter's Cathedral, but Pope Innocent II - with the Frangipani and the imperial troops - controlled the Lateran Palace and the Arch basilica of St. John Lateran so it was there, on 4 June 1003 that Pope Innocent II crowned Lothair II as emperor. The imperial troops then withdrew, taking Innocent II with them, once again leaving Rome in control of Pope Anacletus II.

Three years later the Emperor was back in Italy. He had finally secured peace at home, and his target was the Kingdom of Sicily and King Roger II. The King had actively supported Anacletus II with a small contingent of troops in Rome so the Emperor had the full support and encouragement of Innocent II. He was also supported by John II Komnenos, the Emperor of Byzantium who feared further Norman aggression once Roger II had consolidated all of southern Italy.

At a local level, Roger II's brother-in-law, Ranulf II Count of Alife, had rebelled a few years earlier and managed to defeat Roger II in battle. He was present at the Emperor's crowning in Rome and had expected the Emperor to continue south in his support, but after the Emperor left Rome for Germany he lost most of the territories he had conquered in a counter-offensive by Roger II.

However, this time the Emperor went straight to the south. His campaign was successful, Roger II sat tight at Sicily and left the sporadic fighting to his local representatives. Soon the Emperor had conquered Capua and Apulia and Ranulf II was appointed as Duke of Capua.

The imperial army left a small contingent in support of the new Duke and headed back towards Germany. On 4 December, while the army was crossing the Alps, the Emperor died.

In southern Italy it took Roger II two years and one more lost battle to recover the lost ground and also integrate the city-state of Naples into his unified Kingdom of Sicily.

Shortly after the death of the Emperor, Pope Anacletus II died in Rome. He was officially registered as an anti-pope. His supporters quickly elected Gregorio Conti as Pope Victor IV, but this time support for Innocent II was overwhelming and, after the mediation of Bernard of Clairvaux, Victor IV submitted to Innocent II only two months after his election. Finally, there was only one pope and he returned to Rome.

The Pope now restarted an old battle between the papacy and the King of France over the appointment of bishops. The Pope went as far as placing the entire country under interdict, but it still took until 1145 before King Louis VII finally gave in and went on a crusade for his sins.

Closer to Rome the Pope was still worried about King Roger II of Sicily. On the Pope's return to Rome, Roger II had asked him for his blessing of his kingship. In return the Pope wanted the Principality of Capua as a neutral buffer between Roger's kingdom and the Papal States. Roger II disagreed so the Pope decided to take military action.

In 1139 the Pope set south in person, leading an army with the purpose of obtaining by arms what he could not obtain through diplomacy. With him he had Robert II of Capua who had been deposed by Roger II of Sicily.

Before they could achieve anything, the papal army was ambushed by a small force led by Roger II's son, Roger III, Duke of Apulia. The Pope and his retinue were taken prisoners and two days later, at Mignano, the Pope was forced to accept Roger II as King of Sicily. The Pope later, in 1143, reneged on the treaty, but when Roger II marched on the Papal States it was re-confirmed.

After an eventful, but not particularly successful, reign of thirteen years, Pope Innocent II died in September of 1143.

In an unusually peaceful election, indeed the first in more than eight decades, the Cardinals elected Guido di Castello, a life-time scholar, and

Cardinal-Priest of San Marco. He took the name Celestine II (a name also used by the Pope-elect who was overthrown by Honorius II in 1124).

Celestine II was an opinionated individual and although he had supported Innocent II, he did not necessarily agree with him on a range of matters.

He disagreed with Innocent II's concessions to Roger II of Sicily and his choice of side in the raging civil war in England, but his short papacy meant that he did not manage to pursue his policies in a material way. He accepted the penance of King Louis VII of France, lifted the interdict and then organised a collection in favour of the Knights Templar as he was a strong supporter of the military orders of the Holy Land. He then died after only 164 days as pope. The College of Cardinals elected Cardinal-Priest Gherardo Caccianemici dal Orso, who took the name Lucius II.

Apart from various clerical matters, Lucius II threw his effort into renegotiating the relationship with Roger II of Sicily. The two were actually well acquainted, the Pope being godfather to one of Roger II's sons, but when they met at Ceprano in June 1144 the relationship soon turned sour.

The subject was Capua which Roger II held as a Papal fief. The Pope wanted it returned and Roger II wanted more papal land. The Pope insisted and Roger II ordered one of his generals to attack Campania. The Pope had nothing with which to counter the attack, so he had to ultimately agree to Roger II's demands.

During the last part of Innocent II's rule a new political movement had started to gain momentum in Rome. Actually, it was not new at all, but rather the revival of an age-old institution, the Roman Senate, which had last been in session at the beginning of the seventh century. Dissatisfaction - in particular, within the ranks of merchants and artisans - with the way Rome was governed when it came to temporal issues gave growth to a popular movement which split Rome into fifty-six constituencies, each of which elected a Senator.

The new Senate chose as its leader Giordano Pierleoni with the title of Patrician. Both Pope Innocent II and his brief successor had had skirmishes with the new Senate, but Lucius II had initially managed to avoid confrontation and even managed to convince some of the Senators to give up their quest.

But when the Pope returned from his ill-fated campaign against Roger II in September 1144, the Senate, as representatives of the people, had had enough of failed papal adventures.

The Senate resolved to demand all temporal power in Rome, declaring Rome a Commune. The Pope would be reduced to head of the Church and would retain only such incomes as were directly related to the Church.

The Pope obviously did not agree, and he first sought help from Roger II of Sicily. But the King had no appetite for a fight with the Romans or for helping the Pope. Next the Pope appealed to the new King of Germany, Conrad III, but his answer was long in coming.

Part 6 - The Pope and the Crusader Knights

Instead, the Pope played the old fractures of Rome and got the support of the Frangipani family. They set up their base at Circus Maximus and were probably not too difficult to convince in the first place as the leader of the commune was a Pierleoni.

The Forum in Rome then became the battleground and with a band of armed men the Pope himself attacked enemy positions on the Capitol in February of 1145. During the attack the Pope was hit on the head by a stone thrown by a defender, and he died from his injuries a day later.

Rome was now effectively in the hands of the Commune and although the College of Cardinals met in Rome to elect a new pope, the actual consecration had to be held outside the city and the new Pope spent the majority of his reign in exile.

And it was not so easy to find anyone who really wanted to be pope under the prevailing circumstances. The job had proven to be both difficult and dangerous and with the Commune ruling Rome did not seem to be any less so. The candidate who was finally elected was thus not one of the Cardinals but the Abbot of the monastery of S. Anastasio alle Tre Fontane called Bernardo da Pisa.

Bernardo was a Cistercian monk of humble origins and a strong follower of the teachings of Bernard of Clairvaux, indeed some historians have claimed the since Bernardo was, in the words of Bernard of Clairvaux himself, *'innocent and simple'*, the influential Abbot of Clairvaux was indeed the puppet master behind Bernardo's papacy.

In any case, Bernardo was consecrated at the monastery of Farfa in February of 1145, and he took the name Eugene III. He immediately appealed for help and a range of cities, hostile to Rome even though they also were governed as Communes, pledged their loyalty to the Pope. Also assisted by Roger II of Sicily he managed to force the Senate to allow him to reside in Rome and it was here that he received bad news from the Holy Land.

The County of Edessa, the northernmost of the Crusader States in the Holy Land had fallen to the Muslims. Really the decline of Edessa had been a gradual affair that had started the moment the unsustainable state was formed during the First Crusade, but now it had finally fallen to Zengi, the Seljuk Atabeg of Mosul.

The Pope, driven by the religious zeal of Bernard of Clairvaux and his own need for a unifying cause, declared that it was time for the Princes of Christianity to fight back. In terms of history, we now know this as the Second Crusade.

The Pope's call for crusade went out in early December of 1145, but the response was so limited that he had to repeat it in March 1146. By that time he had moved from Rome to Viterbo as the return of the cleric and political agitator Arnold of Brescia had seen an upswing of hostility towards the Pope in Rome.

16 - The Pope

The Pope now authorized his spiritual master Bernard of Clairvaux to preach crusade on his behalf. If the Pope himself could not raise much enthusiasm, Bernard was just the man for the job. At Speyer in 1146 he preached crusade to Europe's kings and princes. The French King, Louis VII, had already agreed to go and the King of Germany, Conrad III, fired up by Bernard, also pledged his support.

Compared to the First Crusade, which was really a conglomerate of privateers and fortune seekers, the Second Crusade was thus a much better organised affair with participation of nation states and a broad range of nobles from many parts of Europe. Nevertheless, the campaign was a military disaster.

The Crusader Army snaked its way through Europe (see Chapter 13) and made its way to Constantinople. The Byzantine Emperor had it ferried across to Anatolia as quickly as possible, as before.

The Germans and the French travelled separately, and once in Anatolia both armies encountered severe Seljuk resistance, effectively having to fight their way through and experiencing several defeats along the way. It has been speculated that the Seljuks were indeed encouraged and paid by the Byzantine Emperor, but the truth of that is an open historic question.

Finally, the army arrived in Jerusalem where it was reinforced by a French contingent which had arrived by sea. But instead of trying to retake Edessa, it was agreed that they would make an attempt on Damascus, which was a more relevant target for the King of Jerusalem and the resident Knights Templars.

The combined army now marched on Damascus, but the planned siege lasted only four days until the enormity and futility of the operation became apparent and the Crusader Army retreated to Jerusalem. The Germans went home and the French followed the following year. Nothing much was achieved apart from in-fighting.

The Pope's call for a crusade had also been responded to in northern Europe where campaigns were aimed at the heathen Baltic States, although in honesty the campaigns, disguised as holy war, had more to do with local politics and looting.

A third leg of the crusade took place on the Iberian Peninsula. King Alfonso VII led a contingent of Catalan and French crusaders against the Moors and it was reinforced by enrolling an English contingent on its way to the Holy Land. The campaign saw the Moors expelled from Lisbon - which was really the only tangible result of the Second Crusade - and most in the English contingent settled in Portugal and never continued to the Holy Land.

While this was going on the Pope had had to leave Rome again in 1146. He had refused to participate in a war on the town of Tivoli and the environment became so hostile that he moved to Viterbo. He then moved to Siena and then on to France where he held synods in Paris, Rheims and Trier.

Part 6 - The Pope and the Crusader Knights

By 1149 the Pope was back in Italy, albeit at Viterbo rather than Rome and here he met with King Louis VII of France on his return from the Holy Land. With support from Roger II of Sicily he once again entered Rome in 1150, but only to leave again shortly after as the Commune had no appetite for the Pope becoming involved in the city's temporal matters.

The King of Germany, Conrad III, died in 1152 and was replaced by his nephew, Frederick I, also known as 'Barbarossa' which refers to his red beard. The new king of Germany had imperial ambitions and thus promised to help the Pope regain control of Rome, but Pope Eugene III died at Tivoli in 1153 before any of the plans came into action.

Pope Eugene III had not spent much time in Rome, but the Romans nevertheless respected him for his role as spiritual head of the Church, so he was allowed a burial in St.Peter's Cathedral with full honours. But his successor had to be elected outside of Rome and never entered it during his - short - papacy.

The College of Cardinals chose its own aging dean, Corrado Demetri della Suburra, who took the name Anastasius IV. The new Pope was clearly a place-holder, residing outside of Rome and focusing on solving a couple of age-old disputes regarding the appointment of bishops in Germany and England. He was probably more than eighty years-old when he became pope, and he lasted only until the end of the following year when he died from old age.

By the time Anastasius IV died, the English-born Bishop of Albano, Nicholas Breakspear, had returned from a successful papal mission in Scandinavia. It is possible that the College of Cardinals had appointed Anastasius IV for the sole purpose of holding the papacy until Nicholas Breakspear could return, as he was immediately elected pope on Anastasius IV's death.

Taking the name Adrian IV, the new Pope was relatively young - in his early fifties - and very dynamic. His first priority was to regain control of Rome. To achieve this purpose, he devised a double strategy.

The first part of his strategy was a powerful political and military alliance. King Roger II of Sicily had also died in 1154, so the obvious choice was King Frederick I of Germany who had clear ambitions on Italy and the title as emperor. He had previously promised to help Pope Eugene III, so he was easy to convince. This alliance would secure external pressure on the Roman Senate.

The second part of the Pope's strategy was to create internal pressure in Rome. The city depended on income from pilgrims, not least over the Easter season, so to hit the population where it hurt them the most, in their pockets, the Pope put an interdict on Rome before Easter of 1155.

At the same time King Frederick I moved through northern Italy, where he had himself crowned King of Italy, and he then marched on Rome. Inside Rome there was upheaval as the Pope's interdict had meant that the expected pilgrims had not come, so by the time the King and the Pope arrived, the citizens had decided to exile the leader of the Commune, Arnold of Brescia, who fled the city only to be captured by the German army.

The Pope's double strategy had worked beautifully, and he took full advantage of his regained position in the city. Objectively, he to a large extent owed his newfound position to Frederick I, but Pope Adrian IV was determined to demonstrate his elevated position in a very public way, also when it came to the Emperor-elect.

You may remember that some 300 years back, when Emperor Louis II arrived in Rome to participate in the consecration of Pope Nicholas I, the Emperor had symbolically dismounted his horse and led the Pope's horse by the bridle, something which was seen as a sign of submission to the Pope's superiority. Now, Adrian IV expected the same from King Frederick I.

The Pope rode out to meet the King in his camp. The King received him in his tent, and kissed his feet as was the custom, but he had not come to meet him, and he had not led the Pope's horse to the tent. Adrian IV was not content, so he left the King's camp and returned the next day where the King now came to meet him and led his horse to the tent. As far as the Pope was concerned, that was the required gesture of submission to his supremacy so on 18 June 1155, the Pope crowned Frederick I as Emperor of Rome or - as had now became the customary title - Holy Roman Emperor.

The exiled, and captured, leader of the Commune, Arnold of Brescia, was executed and his body was burned before it was thrown into the Tiber River. This created some unrest in Rome which the new Emperor put down hard-headedly, leaving more than 1,000 Romans dead in the streets. To give the people an opportunity to calm down, the Emperor and the Pope then withdrew from the city itself.

Frederick I had taken the opportunity to help the Pope, but his real purpose in Italy was to assert his own authority. He had successfully done so in the north, and his ambition was to also subdue the Kingdom of Sicily, now in the hands of Roger II's son, William I, called 'the Wicked'.

The Emperor however had both health problems and problems with rebellion at home, so he left Italy to return to Germany without confronting the Kingdom of Sicily.

There were, however, others who also had an interest in the southern kingdom, perceived to be in a weakened state after the death of Roger II. The Byzantines had never forgotten their claim on southern Italy and Emperor Manual I Komnenos decided that this was the time to take back what was rightfully his.

The Byzantine Emperor found an ally in Pope Adrian IV, who preferred to have the Byzantines as neighbours and also saw an opportunity to use the Byzantine Emperor's ambitions to forward his own aims; a re-unification of the Church, still split after the schism a century earlier.

While negotiations between the Emperor and the Pope were started on the subject of unification, the Pope raised a mercenary army from Campania, which met up with an invading Byzantine army. They successfully took some of the coastal cities on the eastern and southern coast of Italy, but then their campaign came to a halt due to internal strife between the commanders. Soon the Normans launched a counter-offensive and the mercenaries - having been refused a substantial increase in pay - drifted away, as did the local allies, who started to see which way the campaign was going.

The Normans gradually re-took the cities they had lost, ending with Brindisi, and by 1158 the Byzantines had once again left Italy. The Pope was now alone facing the Normans, and finally negotiated a lasting peace known as the Treaty of Benevento, in which the two states recognized each other's right to existence.

That was just as well because the negotiations between the Pope and the Byzantine Empire had also collapsed. The Pope insisted that a re-unification should once and for all recognize him as the supreme head of the Church - a demand which was totally unacceptable to the Byzantines - and the Emperor demanded that he should be recognized as the secular over-lord - a demand totally unacceptable to the Pope - so by the time the military campaign came to a halt, so did the talks of re-unification.

Pope Adrian IV decided instead to clarify the papacy's role in relation to the Holy Roman Emperor - who had campaigned in northern Italy in 1158 and brought the area under strong imperial influence - an effort through which he managed to alienate the Emperor to such an extent that there was talk of a possible excommunication. It did not come to that though as Adrian IV died in 1159, reportedly by swallowing a fly with his soup, although Peritonsillar Abscess is a more likely reason.

The conflict with the Holy Roman Emperor was, however, far from over. Indeed, it would cause the election of two popes and a dual papacy that would last more than two decades.

The anti-imperial party - now known as *Guelphs* - in Rome elected Roland of Siena, the papal chancellor and a Roman noble by birth, who took the name Alexander III. He is to this day the officially recognized pope.

At the same time the imperial-party - now known as *Ghibellines* - with the support of the Holy Roman Emperor, elected Ottaviano dei Crescenti, Cardinal priest of Santa Cecilia, who took the (previously briefly used) name of Victor IV.

Pope Alexander III thus started with problems on two fronts. His relationship with the Roman Senate was precarious and would indeed lead to him being exiled from Rome twice during his papacy. The relationship with the Holy Roman Emperor was even worse.

A political cabal now enfolded, with the European rulers taking sides in the papal battle along purely political lines. The Pope was the Head of the Church, but religion had taken a very secondary position.

16 - The Pope

Indeed, there is little left of the early part of Alexander III's papacy which relate to Church matters. Politically he was initially supported only by the kings of Portugal, Sicily and Spain, but eventually the French King Louis VII, the Hungarian King Géza II and King Henry II of England came to his side, mainly because they did not like Frederick I.

In Rome the Pope was arrested by the Senate in 1162. He was released on the insistence of Oddone Frangipane - one of the most influential *Guelphs* in Rome - and went into exile in France.

Emperor Frederick I was still busy in Italy. He once again subdued the notoriously independent city-state of Milan - at great cost to the city - and generally ensured that the northern Italian territories remained under his control, whereas his ambitions in southern Italy was ruined by a strong anti-imperial alliance which included Pope Alexander III.

He was therefore in the area when Anti-pope Victor IV died in 1164 and he made a personal appearance in Rome to ensure the election of his successor, Guido of Crema, who took the name Paschal III However the new Anti-pope was driven from Rome in 1165, leading to the return of Alexander III.

Frederick I was back in northern Italy by 1167, amongst other things laying siege to Ancona, which had put itself under the protection of the Byzantine Emperor. The Roman Senate now decided, against the advice of Alexander III, to attack Frederick I, but the Romans were defeated in the Battle of Monte Porzio and Frederick I moved on to Rome, forcing Alexander III into exile once again.

Anti-pope Paschal III was with the Emperor, and he now re-crowned Frederick I, as well as crowning his wife, Beatrice of Burgundy, as empress.

The road to southern Italy was now clear, but an outbreak of either malaria or plague forced the Emperor to once again cancel his plans for a southern campaign. He withdrew to Germany so Rome was Alexander III's again.

The next few years were relatively peaceful. Frederick I spent it trying to resolve diplomatic issues with the kings of France and England and even the Emperor in Constantinople.

The English King got himself into trouble with Pope Alexander III over the death of Thomas Becket, resulting in a treaty in which the English King amongst other things promised to go on a crusade, although he never did.

Back in Italy the anti-imperial *Guelphs* had the upper hand, and there was rising tension in the northern cities. The Pope was quick to utilize this to his advantage, and he was the driver behind the Lombard League, which was formed as an alliance against Frederick I's dominance in northern Italy.

The Lombard League led to the northern Italian cities, including Milan in 1169, breaking away from the Emperor, for all intents and purposes seeing the birth of the (quasi) independent Italian city-states which would survive for centuries to come.

Part 6 - The Pope and the Crusader Knights

In 1174 the Emperor had had enough, so he once again marched on Italy. But the new alliance was too strong for him. He was defeated first at Alessandria in 1175 and then at the Battle of Legnano in 1176, where the Emperor was wounded and for a period of time feared dead.

Peace was brokered in Venice in 1177 and finally the Pope and the Emperor were reconciled, the Emperor recognizing the victorious Pope and his right to temporal power in the Papal States. The conflict did, however, continue until 1183, where the Italian cities finally got their own freedom though the Peace of Constance.

In the meantime, Anti-pope Paschal III died - in 1168 - and a new anti-pope, Callixtus III, was elected. He finally submitted to Alexander III in 1178 and was given a position as Rector of Benevento.

The Pope now held a council in Rome, where it was agreed that from now on a pope could only be elected with the votes of at least two-thirds of the Cardinals. This rule still applies.

The Pope experienced a backlash of popular opinion in Rome and was once again exiled. In his place the Roman Senate engineered the election of Lanzo of Sezza as Anti-pope under the name Innocent III. The political mood in Rome swung again however, and Innocent III was captured and sent to the monastery of La Cava.

Pope Alexander III, however, did not return to Rome, he died at Civita Castellana in August of 1181. The College of Cardinals now elected its own dean, Ubaldo Allucingoli, as new pope under the name Lucius III. He was a determined member of the anti-imperial party and he immediately started a new conflict with the Emperor, this time rekindling the old conflict of ownership of the lands in Tuscany left by Matilda of Tuscany on her death in 1115.

The issue had never been fully settled and the Emperor now proposed that the Church renounce its claim, receiving in exchange two-tenths of the imperial income from Italy, one-tenth for the Pope and the other tenth for the Cardinals. But the Pope did not agree and not even a meeting between the Pope and the Emperor in 1184 could settle the issue.

The Pope now deliberately tried to chicane the Emperor, bringing into doubt the appointment of the Bishop of Treves and refusing to crown the Emperor's son, Henry VI, as his heir apparent. Finally, the Emperor started campaigning in northern Italy in 1184, but soon bigger events took centre stage.

The new Sultan of Egypt and Syria, Ṣalāḥ ad-Dīn Yūsuf ibn Ayyūb, known in the West as Saladin, had started a major offensive in the Holy Land. He had taken Aleppo and was now threatening to take Jerusalem itself. Weakened by infighting, the Kingdom of Jerusalem appealed for help from the Pope, and Pope Lucius III had started an appeal for a new crusade, when he died in 1185.

16 - The Pope

As new pope the Cardinals elected Uberto Crivelli, Archbishop of Milan, who took the name Urban III. Contrary to tradition he maintained his position as Archbishop, and he soon found himself in conflict with the Emperor.

Frederick I had made an alliance with the Kingdom of Sicily in which his son and successor, Henry V, married the daughter and heir of the King of Sicily, for the first time uniting the two parts of Italy on either side of the Papal States. The marriage was to take place in Milan, a highly symbolic gesture given the city's history, but the Pope refused to conduct the ceremony.

Bolted up in Verona and later in Ferrara, with Frederick I blocking his way out of Italy, the Pope became increasingly isolated and was threatening to excommunicate the Emperor when he died in 1187. It was reported that he died from the shock of hearing of Saladin's Reconquest of Jerusalem, but that is unlikely as Jerusalem capitulated on 2 October and the Pope died on 20 October which is probably not enough time for the news to have reached Italy.

A new pope was quickly elected and the choice was Alberto di Morra, Chancellor of the Holy Roman Church, who took the name Gregory VIII, which had already been used by one of the (supported by the Emperor) anti-popes.

Gregory VIII only ruled as pope for 57 days, but he left a strong legacy namely the Third Crusade. As mentioned above, Jerusalem had fallen to Saladin and the Christian world was in uproar. The new Pope was determined to do something, so he issued a papal bull called *Audita tremendi* in which he urges - in particular - the kings and princes of Europe to go to the Hole Land and free Jerusalem from the infidels.

But urging the European monarchs on was not enough. Logistically the new crusade would greatly benefit from travel by sea, so the Pope set out for Pisa to broker a peace between them and Genoa to ensure that local bickering did not prevent the crusade from getting underway. Having succeeded in his quest, he died in Pisa.

Once again, a new pope was quickly elected, in December of 1187. The choice was Paolo Scolari, Cardinal Bishop of Palestrina, who took the name Clement III, which strangely enough had also been used previously by an anti-pope.

Like his predecessor, Pope Clement III's top priority was the crusade, and he continued to make peace in order to ensure that all internal strife was settled. His own issue was the continuing duel between the papacy and the Roman Commune, and he immediately settled it by reaching a compromise with the Senate. Henceforth the Pope would once again rule the Papal States, but the Senate had the right to decide on matters which involved war and peace. Practically, the Senate could appoint magistrates, but the Pope could appoint the Prefect. In reality, the new solution soon meant that the Senate lost its power and within a few years the Pope was back as absolute ruler of Rome.

The Pope also made peace with Emperor Frederick I, and with that done, all was set for a new crusade. Indeed, it was Emperor Frederick I who in May of 1189 set out first, leading a massive German army (probably around 100,000 strong) through Europe, where it also picked up reinforcements from the Hungarian King Béla III. It arrived in Constantinople and was quickly transferred to Anatolia. Here the German army met resistance from the local Seljuks - some say paid by the Byzantine Emperor - and their march towards the Holy Land was both slow and bloody.

However, before they got to the Holy Land a catastrophe befell the Germans. On 10 June 1190, at the River Salep, the Emperor decided to cross the river on his horse as the bridge was full of moving troops. During the crossing he fell from his horse, hit his head on some rocks and drowned. With the Emperor dead the German contingent lost its will to continue, and the vast majority left for Germany, with the upcoming election of a new king in mind. A meagre 5,000 remained and had been further reduced by fever by the time they arrived at Acre.

The crusade was now left with King Philip II of France and King Richard I (Lionheart) of England. Their combined armies met at Sicily where a Genoese fleet was waiting. Philip II went directly on to the Holy Land, while Richard I made a detour to Cyprus (which he took by force and subsequently sold to the Knights Templar). The two contingents finally met up in June 1191.

The campaign was partly successful. Although they never actually reached Jerusalem, they managed to free Acre and Jaffa, pushing Saladin back and ensuring important Christian harbours on the Palestinian coast. A treaty with Saladin secured the coastal possessions and also provided pilgrims with access to Jerusalem and other holy cities in Palestine. Fans of *Ivanhoe* will be aware of Richard I's troublesome return to England following the campaign, a subject we shall return to a little later.

By that time the Pope had died, but not without drama. On the death of Emperor Frederick, I his son, Henry VI, was crowned King of Germany. He had the usual issues with securing the throne, but an even bigger issue with Sicily. Henry VI had - much to the regret of Pope Lucius III - married Constance of Sicily, a union aimed at uniting the Kingdoms of Sicily and Germany under one rule. Constance's nephew, King William II of Sicily, had also recently died (in 1189) and as he had no heir Constance was next in line.

On William II's death the throne of Sicily had been taken by Tancred I, Constance's younger nephew, who had the backing of the Norman nobles in southern Italy. Furthermore Tancred I had obtained an uneasy agreement with Philip II of France and Richard I of England and, much to Henry VI's irritation, also the blessing of Pope Clement III who had little appetite for German rule of southern Italy.

16 - The Pope

The relationship between the Pope and the Emperor was once again heating up, but Pope Clement III died in March of 1191 and the new Pope initially made it a priority to normalize relations.

The new Pope was Giacinto Bobone, once again a noble-born Roman, who took the name Celestine III. He was a *Ghibelline* - pro-imperial - and received Henry VI in Rome immediately following his consecration as pope. Here he proceeded to crown Henry VI as Holy Roman Emperor, and supported Constance's claim to the throne of Sicily.

The new Emperor continued to Naples, which he put under siege with naval support from Pisa and Genoa. But the local nobles were strongly anti-imperial and fought back hard. Ultimately, Henry VI had to abandon the siege and retreat. His wife remained at Salerno, where she was captured by Tancred I.

The Pope now intervened and managed to negotiate her release, but only on the condition that the Pope, again, recognized Tancred I as the lawful King of Sicily. The Emperor was both grateful and angry with the Pope, but soon the relationship turned very sour.

On his way back from the Holy Land, King Richard I was seized by Duke Leopold V of Austria, who handed him over to the Emperor who in turn demanded the enormous sum of 150,000 silver marks for Richard I's release. His reasoning was that Richard I had given his support to Tancred I, and some of Henry VI internal competitors for the German throne, thus making himself an enemy of the Holy Roman Empire.

The Pope was livid. Richard I was a crusader returning from the Holy Land and to capture and hold him at ransom was unheard of. The Pope now started a series of excommunications, which would come to define his papacy. The Emperor was amongst those excommunicated but duly ignored the issue and proceeded with securing Richard I's ransom.

By 1194 Richard I's was free again and the Emperor immediately put the ransom money to good use. He once again moved on the Kingdom of Sicily and as Tancred I had recently died, this time he succeeded. He was crowned King of Sicily on 25 December 1194.

In the meantime, the Pope had found others to confront. He first put an interdict on Pisa. He then condemned and subsequently excommunicated King Alfonso IX of León after which he put an interdict on all of León.

But the Pope also had some brighter moments, and it was he, who, as his last act as pope, confirmed the statutes of the Teutonic Knights, the newest of the knightly crusader orders.

In January of 1198 the Pope died. His successor was only thirty-seven-year-old Lotario dei Conti di Segni, another Roman noble, who took the name Innocent III (which had also previously been used by an anti-pope).

The new Pope had an interesting opportunity at hand. Emperor Henry VI had died in September 1197 leaving as his heir his four-year-old son Frederick II. To the Pope this created an opportunity to break the unified

German rule over northern and southern Italy, which put the Papal States in a constant predicament, squeezed in between as they were.

Henry VI's widow, Constance of Sicily, had a very realistic view of the situation and rather than attempt to rule Germany on behalf of her infant son, she instead focused on Sicily, where she died the year after her husband, having left Frederick II in the care of the Pope who thus effectively controlled the Kingdom of Sicily.

Constance's reading of the situation in Germany turned out to be correct. The nobles had no intentions of waiting for Frederick II to come of age or be ruled by either a woman or the Pope, so they appointed their own candidates. There was a party loyal to the Hohenstaufen dynasty and they elected Philip of Swabia, Henry VI's brother, as King of Germany. But they were opposed by a party hostile to the Hohenstaufen dynasty who elected Otto IV, Duke of Brunswick, as king. To add to the confusion, Philip was supported by King Philip II of France and Otto IV was supported by his uncle; King Richard I of England.

Pope Innocent II played the situation beautifully. He offered his support to Otto IV, which served his own interest best, but to secure the Pope's support Otto IV had to make concessions in Italy. The Pope then proceeded to encourage a northern Italian league hostile to the German king. He also ensured that the agreement with Otto IV secured the papacy the rights to appoint bishops and all in all established himself as a powerful "kingmaker".

The conflict in Germany continued for a decade until Philip of Swabia was assassinated by a nobleman blaming the King for his lack of success in securing a good marriage.

With his competitor out of the way, Otto IV once again ensured the Pope of his privileges in Italy and was crowned as Holy Roman Emperor in Rome on October of 1209.

But as soon as Otto IV became emperor, his tone towards Pope Innocent III changed. Whereas before he had needed the Pope's blessing - and the Pope's excommunication of all who stood against him - he was now free to operate and he had no intentions of splitting the Empire, by losing the Kingdom of Sicily, ruled by the Pope's ward; Frederick II.

The Pope now changed his support away from Otto IV and instead had the Hohenstaufen party in Germany elect Frederick II as King of Germany. Ultimately it came to a deciding battle at Bouvines in 1214, in which King Otto IV and King John of England were defeated by Frederick II and King Philip II Augustus of France.

For the Pope this was the best achievable result. Top prize would have been a separation between Germany and Sicily, but second prize was that at least the rule was now united under his own ward.

Parallel to this, the Pope, who was a strict disciplinarian and absolutely hated heresy, had called for a new crusade. His papal bull *Post Miserabile* had already been issued in 1198 and had urged the monarchs of Europe to once again attack Jerusalem, this time through a landing in Egypt.

But the European monarchs were too busy fighting each other, so it was instead a group of nobles, spearheaded by Theobald III, Count of Champagne, who organised the campaign, Theobald however died and his place was taken by Boniface of Montferrat, Marquess of Montferrat.

I have gone through the details of the disastrous Fourth Crusade earlier in this book (in particular in Chapter 3), so I will not expand on the campaign itself any further here. From the Pope's perspective though, the campaign was not a complete disaster.

During the campaign the Pope had twice excommunicated the crusaders, once when they attacked Zara and once again when they attacked Constantinople, but when the returning crusaders brought back substantial amounts of gold conquered in Constantinople and donated it to the Pope, he nevertheless received it. He also accepted the fact that the Fourth Crusade had brought about the submission of Constantinople to Rome, although not necessarily by agreement. The crusaders were thus forgiven for their trespass, and the Pope lent his support to the new Latin Empire of Constantinople.

A sub-clause on the Pope's eagerness to root out heresy was his strong condemnation of the Cathars in southern France. With his blessing the French king conducted a gruesome 'crusade' in the Languedoc region, known as the Albigensian Crusade, in which 20,000 civilian 'heretics' were slaughtered.

Pope Innocent III died in 1216. He had been one of the most influential Popes for a long time, restoring much of the land and power which had previously been ceded to the Emperor and, of course, he left Rome in control of Constantinople.

But the situation was fragile, the new Emperor being an unknown entity and conflict rife in Europe. The College of Cardinals therefore decided on a compromise candidate, Cencio Savelli, who technically was a cardinal-priest, but who on a practical level had been the tutor of Frederick II during his youth as a ward of the Pope. He took the name Honorius III.

The new Pope was a scholar and disciplinarian, and he continued with the policies of his predecessor, concentrating on eradicating heresy and the re-conquest of Jerusalem.

In the aftermath of the disastrous - from the perspective of recapturing Jerusalem - Fourth Crusade, Pope Innocent II had already started planning for a new crusade during the Fourth Council of the Lateran held at Rome in late 1215. From here the call went out for a new campaign and it was established that it should start in 1216. To ensure that critical resources were kept at hand and at the disposal of the crusaders, a ban on trade with Muslims was also called.

Part 6 - The Pope and the Crusader Knights

The death of Pope Innocent III meant that Pope Honorius III inherited the project which was much to his own liking anyhow. But apart from the Pope, few backed the campaign.

The idea of the campaign was, like it had been for the Fourth Crusade, to invade Egypt and then move north to Jerusalem. To assist in this, aim the Pope managed to ally with the Seljuks in Anatolia, who would launch an attack in the north to split the Egyptian forces on two fronts. The plan was probably sane, but the implementation was not.

Having had the bad experience of the Fourth Crusade turning into a private Venetian enterprise, the Pope insisted that he (although not in person) should lead the campaign. The practical implementation was left to his legate Pelagio Galvani.

The campaign has been described in some detail in Chapter 11, but in essence it was another military disaster. First a small Hungarian contingent achieved some success in Palestine, but left when the King of Hungary fell ill. Then a larger contingent went to Egypt where they besieged Damietta and forced the Egyptians to offer them Jerusalem if they were to abandon the siege. Here the Papal Legate made a fundamental blunder. He expected Frederic II to bring reinforcements, so he refused the offer.

When the crusaders did manage to secure Damietta anyhow, they started an in-fight about who should control it, which eventually led to parts of the army leaving the campaign. Once the army was, partly, re-established it marched on Cairo only to be caught between flooding rivers and the Egyptian army which had by then fought off the Seljuks in the north. The crusaders had to surrender and leave with nothing achieved. Frederick II never arrived.

Not that Frederic II had not committed to go on the crusade, indeed he had, but he consistently came up with excuses for not going at that particular time. The Pope had tried to motivate him by crowning his as Holy Roman Emperor in 1220, but all that achieved was a small German contingent participating in the failed campaign in Egypt.

Many, including the Pope, blamed Frederic II for the failure of the crusade and the increasingly autonomous city-states in northern Italy once again developed an anti-imperial stance. Frederick II called an Imperial Diet in northern Italy in order to reassert his authority, but as a direct countermove the Lombard League, led by Milan, was re-established to unite against imperial influence.

To gain support from the Pope, Frederick II now agreed to go on a crusade no later than 1227, to personally lead the campaign and to accept excommunication should he fail to do so. To further commit the Emperor to the agreement, the Pope brokered his marriage to Isabella II of Jerusalem, the ruling titular Queen, which in effect made Frederick II King of Jerusalem and thus prevented any future in-fighting should the mission succeed. This time Frederick II was left without excuse, so he set off on what history would call the Sixth Crusade in August of 1227.

By that time Pope Honorius III had died without seeing his ambitions accomplished. The College of Cardinals elected Ugolino di Conti, Cardinal Bishop of Ostia, who took the name Gregory IX. Like his predecessors he was a strong believer in papal supremacy, and it did not take long before he got his first opportunity to show his power over the temporal rulers and not any ruler, but the Emperor himself.

The new Pope had only just been consecrated when Frederick II turned his ships around and returned to Italy. An epidemic had broken out, and the Emperor had decided to return to terra firma. Despite the assurances of the Master of the Teutonic Knights that indeed Frederic II was sick and had to return, the Pope was not buying it, as was the case with many contemporary chroniclers.

As far as the Pope was concerned, Frederick II was once again trying to delay or cancel the crusade he had promised and so when Frederick II did not show signs of getting the crusade back on track, the Pope excommunicated him toward the end of September of 1227.

Technically once the Emperor was excommunicated, he could no longer go on a crusade, so when he actually eventually set out again in June of 1228 that also angered the Pope, who excommunicated the Emperor once more.

The crusade itself was a strange placid, but successful, affair in which Frederick II negotiated Jerusalem itself back from the Muslim rulers and then proceeded to crown himself as King of Jerusalem despite the fact that Isabella II in the meantime had died and left their son, Conrad IV as her heir. Frederick II was immensely unpopular in the Holy Land and in 1229 he returned to Italy. Jerusalem was lost again in 1244.

While the Emperor was away his regent in the Kingdom of Sicily, Rainald of Spoleto, attacked the Papal States. The Pope had responded in kind and invaded, and occupied, large parts of southern Italy so when the Emperor arrived back at Brindisi in June of 1229 chaos ruled.

The Emperor quickly asserted his authority, and the rebellious barons were punished. A peace agreement was made with the Pope, which also cancelled the Emperor's excommunication. And soon the Pope and the Emperor needed each other again.

The Pope had a revolt on his hands in Rome and had to leave the city for Anagni south of Rome. The Emperor on the other hand had trouble with the lords in northern Italy, so they once more allied and tried to bring about control in northern Italy in 1232. The campaign was not very successful and although the Pope was soon back in Rome, the Emperor had to leave for Germany where the local princes were also in revolt.

A few years later the Emperor had sorted things in Germany and once more returned to Italy. The Lombard League was still in place, although the Pope's participation was shifting with the winds of fortune.

Part 6 - The Pope and the Crusader Knights

The city states of northern Italy, even those supposedly part of the Lombard League, were still torn between the anti-imperial *Guelphs* and the imperial *Ghibellines* factions and over the next few years northern Italy descended into total chaos.

Cities changed allegiance depending on what advantages they could obtain from the Emperor on one side and (most of the time) the Pope and Milan on the other side. Frederick II swept through Italy on a violent rampage, which saw some cities destroyed and some blossom.

The Pope tried several times to obtain peace through diplomacy, but at the same time he was such a determined *Guelph* that nothing came of it. The Emperor was mainly militarily successful but also suffered setbacks when armies consisting of various cities and the Papal States counter attacked.

In 1241 Pope Gregory IX died. The Emperor's personal animosity towards the Pope was such that his death led the Emperor to give back some of the territories he had conquered from the Church and free a number of (but not all) prelates who had been arrested during the conflict. This he did to signal that his problem was with the Pope as a person, not with the Church as such.

Frederick II had been excommunicated again, but with the Pope's death there seemed to be light at the end of the tunnel.

However, the hope for peace did not last long. The College of Cardinals first elected Goffredo da Castiglione as new pope, and he took the name Celestine IV.

The election was held under duress as the Emperor had 'demanded' his own candidate be elected, as had Matteo Rosso Orsini, the Senator of Rome who was a stern *Guelph* and had been appointed by Pope Gregory IX to secure that Rome stayed loyal to the anti-imperial cause. His sole-rule as Senator over Rome was the sad remains of the Roman Commune.

Placed in a run-down palace in Rome, with rain seeping through the roof, the Cardinals finally agreed on Celestine IV as a compromise solution, but Celestine IV was not young and not in particularly good health so he died only seventeen days after his election, before being formally consecrated. The only thing he achieved was to excommunicate Matteo Rosso Orsini for his rough handling of the Cardinals (one of whom died during the election process).

It took a year and a half to elect a new pope. The political factions were so far apart that a majority could not be secured for anyone until an agreement finally, in June 1243, was reached to elect Sinibaldo Fieschi, Vice-chancellor of the Holy Roman Church, who took the name Innocent IV.

The new Pope was a *Guelph*, but he was also a personal friend of the Emperor and had maintained good relations with him even after the Emperor's excommunication and the on-going conflict with the papacy.

However Innocent IV had no intention of letting his personal friendship with the Emperor get in the way of his political ambitions. He demanded,

16 - The Pope

like his predecessors, that the Emperor return all occupied territories in the Papal States and that all prelates, including two cardinals held for ransom, should be freed.

The Emperor had no intentions in that regard, so if peace had been the purpose of Innocent IV's election, then it did not work. With tension rising in Rome and the Emperor camped at nearby Tivoli, the Pope realized that in order to be effective he needed to leave Rome so he left under disguise and eventually turned up in Lyon after an extended stay in his native Genoa (see Chapter 11).

At Lyon Innocent IV called a council. Bishops came from France and Spain and even from The Latin Empire of Constantinople. The bishops from the Holy German Empire generally stayed away and representatives from the Balkans were prevented from going due to the Mongol invasions.

Although the Emperor had sent his own ambassador, Taddeo da Suessa, who vigorously defended the Emperor's cause, the Council decided to not only confirm the excommunication of Frederick II, but also to formally depose him as emperor and king and release all his subjects from their oaths of loyalty to him. If there had been any doubt as to where the Pope stood on the subject of who should be calling the shots, there were none left now.

To underline its decision, the Council elected Henry Raspe, Landgrave of Thuringia, as King of Germany, creating an anti-king the same way previous emperors had appointed anti-popes. When Henry Raspe died the following year, he was replaced by William II of Holland.

The Emperor's reaction was that of more violence in Italy. He pursued his military campaign with even more force and held a Council in Turin in which he effectively replaced all the important Church positions in Italy with his own relatives. Cities alternatively revolted and submitted to the Emperor, but when he seemed to finally have the upper hand an attack of his camp outside of Parma in February of 1248 (while the Emperor himself was out hunting) saw him lose the imperial treasure, which presented a major setback in his ability to campaign.

Frederick II finally died in 1250. He had been ill for some time and had already withdrawn from personal participation in the on-going campaigns. His will specified his son (with Isabella II of Jerusalem) Conrad IV as his heir in Germany and Italy and also stipulated that the disputed lands and prisoners should be returned to the Church.

The Emperor's death allowed the Pope to return to Italy, although he had to initially stay at Perugia until Rome was considered safe again in 1253.

Even though Conrad IV had been appointed King of Germany as his father's heir, he had to continue the armed struggle with the anti-king William II of Holland. When the anti-king was successful in 1251, Conrad IV decided instead to go to Italy. Supported by Venice, he managed to subdue Apulia and Naples, but he never managed to gain full control of the Kingdom of Sicily and he died from malaria in 1254.

Immediately before the death of Conrad IV, the Pope had decided to give Sicily - which technically was not his to give - to Edmund Plantagenet (later called 'Crouchback'), the younger son of Henry III of England. This move was aimed at preventing the throne of Sicily to fall to Conrad IV's brother, Manfred, or his infant heir Conradin. The Pope's ambition was to once and for all take control of the Kingdom of Sicily, initially through a puppet and eventually by inclusion into the Papal States.

The stakes were high and with Conrad IV dead his brother Manfred of Sicily, as expected, made a move. The Emperor's will surprisingly trusted his infant heir Conradin to the care of the Pope - which put a temporary end to the Pope's use of Edmund Plantagenet - but Manfred took control in Sicily as self-appointed regent for his nephew. In Germany William II of Holland remained the anti-king, although his real grip on power was limited.

The Pope had no intention of giving up on his ambitions for the Kingdom of Sicily which were now so close to fruition, so he sent a papal army against - the excommunicated - Manfred, but it was defeated outside Foggia towards the end of 1254. The news of the defeat allegedly was the final nail in the already ailing Pope's coffin and he died in December of 1254.

As a curiosum, Pope Innocent IV introduced the concept of a 'legal entity' into law. This was done to be able to treat entities such as monasteries as a single entity, separate from the individuals within it. It was of course the birth of corporate law.

The College of Cardinals quickly elected its own dean, Rinaldo di Jenne, as the new pope, and he took the name Alexander IV. He was elected to continue the anti-imperial line of his immediate predecessors and that is exactly what he did.

Although the Pope was in charge of the young Conradin, and promised to look after his interests, he did exactly the opposite. With Manfred sitting on the throne in Sicily, the Pope now re-kindled the alliance with King Henry III of England and the plan to give Sicily to his young son, Edmund Plantagenet.

However, this time there were conditions. The Pope wanted an annual tribute of 2,000 ounces of gold, the service of 300 knights as and when required and, not least, the sum of 130,000 Marks to cover his expenses thus far.

130,000 Marks was nearly the same as the enormous ransom which had been paid for the release of Richard I and which had crippled the English economy just six decades earlier, but King Henry III thought it was a good deal and he agreed to the Pope's terms.

The problem Henry III had however was that his kingship was weak. Following the rule of King John - Richard I's younger brother - the King of England was subject to a range of controls (as defined in the Magna Carta) and King Henry III had to ask Parliament for the money to pay the Pope.

Parliament refused and Henry III could not raise the money, or the required army.

By 1258 the Pope lost his patience and sent emissaries to England threatening the King with excommunication if he did not meet his obligations. In response the King raised new taxes, mainly on the Jews and the Church. But it was all in vain as the English barons rose in revolt and the King had to once again accept an increased level of control by his government. The English army and the payments to the Pope never arrived, though Henry III was successful in having his brother, Richard, 1st Earl of Cornwall, elected (anti) King of Germany after the death of William II of Holland, although another faction in Germany elected Alfonso X of Castile as (anti) king instead.

In Sicily a rumour had been circulated that Conradin had died, and his uncle Manfred thus had himself crowned as King of Sicily. When it became clear that the rumour was false, Manfred refused to step down, citing the need for a strong and present king in Sicily.

All in all, it was not going the Pope's way. Manfred further consolidated his power through alliance with some of the northern Italian city-states, in particular Florence, and his only ace, Conradin, was still underage and under the direct control of his uncle, Louis II, Duke of Upper Bavaria, at whose court he had spent his childhood.

In Rome there was increasing support for the imperial party, the *Ghibellines*, so much so that the Pope felt unsafe and moved the Curia to Viterbo where he died in 1261. He had achieved little, but not for lack of trying.

As new Pope the cardinals elected Jacques Pantaléon a Frenchman of modest origins who took the name Urban IV. Over and above the problems he inherited in relation to Germany and Sicily he had another problem at hand. Immediately before his election the Latin Empire of Constantinople was re-captured by the Byzantines under Michael VIII Palaiologos.

Although the papacy had originally been against the conquest of Constantinople during the Fourth Crusade, it had resolved the problems of interference in both Church and temporal matters from Constantinople. The Pope was thus determined to re-establish the Latin Empire indeed he saw the issue as worthy of a crusade.

However, the Pope's appeals had little impact. Nobody had an appetite for a crusade against Constantinople to re-establish a nominal empire which in effect was a glorified Venetian trading-station, albeit a Catholic one.

The Pope instead had to satisfy himself with sorting out the situation in Italy where political factions were fighting each other, both inside individual cities and on a city-to-city basis. In the middle of the melée sat Manfred of Sicily.

The Pope approached Manfred with an offer. If Manfred would help the Pope with a campaign against the resurrected Byzantines, then he would recognize Manfred's rule in Sicily. Manfred did not feel particularly threatened by the Pope, so he refused.

In anticipation of Manfred's refusal the Pope had, in parallel, started a whole new line of approach. He had found a new champion, Charles of Anjou, the younger brother of King Louis IX of France, and a deal was struck in which Charles would get Sicily and in return pay the Pope an annual tribute of 10,000 ounces of gold as well as promise not to get involved in northern Italy or the Papal States. Contrary to King Henry III, who could not raise the funds to campaign in Sicily, Charles was immensely rich and could fund the campaign with only spiritual assistance from the Pope. As the last part of the deal, the Pope promised to block Conradin's election as King of Germany in order to not give him a powerbase from which to pursue what was rightfully his inheritance. By the time the deal was done Pope Urban IV died and it was up to his successor to carry the deal through.

It took four months to elect a new pope. Discussions were concentrated on whether to continue the deal with Charles of Anjou or abandon the anti-imperial policies. Eventually it was decided to continue the deal with Charles of Anjou and the Cardinals elected Gui Foucois, Cardinal of Sabina, who took the name Clement IV.

Clement IV had been married and had two daughters and had only joined the Church after his wife had died. He was French and a former advisor to the French king. He was therefore the perfect candidate for executing the deal with Charles of Anjou.

The tension in Italy was so high that the new Pope had to enter Italy in disguise and take up residence at Viterbo as Rome was unsafe. Only when Charles of Anjou arrived in April of 1265, he went to Rome to be proclaimed King of Sicily, even if it had to be done by the resident cardinals, as the Pope's safety could not be guaranteed. Of course the Crown of Sicily was not necessarily the Pope's to give in the first place, but Charles of Anjou, now also called Charles of Naples, was a popular figure, even in Rome, and his considerable wealth gave him the advantage over Manfred of Sicily.

While he was waiting for his army to arrive Charles of Anjou started diplomatic efforts - no doubt backed by considerable sums of money - to secure his support in northern Italy where there were pockets of support for Manfred. He was mainly successful and Manfred's support in the North dwindled while he himself was hunting in Apulia. When Charles of Anjou's army arrived, as well as his wife Beatrice, he was finally crowned as King of Sicily in January of 1266.

The campaign which followed was short and decisive. Once Charles of Anjou started moving south from Rome, Manfred took a more proactive interest. He shadowed the French army and decided on an early blow, attempting to cut the French supply lines by attacking while the army was crossing a river. The two armies were evenly matched; Manfred using both

16 - The Pope

German and Saracen mercenaries, and initially his attack seemed to be successful.

The German mercenaries were in coats of steel plate and looked to be impossible to stop until the French realized that their plate armour did not cover their armpits, leaving them exposed when they lifted the arm to strike. Once the Germans had been stopped the situation became difficult for Manfred, as the battlefield, outside Benevento, only had a single bridge leading over the river from Manfred's position to Charles of Anjou's position. Fleeing troops trying to cross the bridge in one direction collided with reserves trying to cross in the other direction and the French soon had the advantage. Manfred changed his surcoat with that of an ordinary solder and threw himself into the battle where he was killed.

This single battle, and the death of Manfred, settled the issue and Charles of Anjou took control in the Kingdom of Sicily, which he ruled from Naples.

Despite Charles of Anjou's promises not to take an interest in northern Italy, he had in already started to do so even before his campaign in the South. Charles of Anjou was therefore in effect in the same position as the Emperor before him, squeezing the Papal States in the middle between his Italian possessions.

But Charles of Anjou was not unchallenged. Conradin was coming of age and he had not forgotten his claim on the throne of Sicily. Despite Charles of Anjou's relative popularity there were still many *Ghibellines* left in both northern and southern Italy. They now sent emissaries to Conradin in Bavaria, promising him their support. Prime amongst them was Rome itself.

Encouraged by the Italian emissaries, Conradin marched on Italy with support of Spain, Pisa and Rome and also a contingent of German mercenaries. He later joined up with Saracen mercenaries who had long been in the employ of Sicily in southern Italy.

Revolts were stirred up in both the north and south, and a Spanish fleet assisted by knights from Pisa landed in Sicily where only the cities of Palermo and Messina could resist the invaders.

Despite the fury of the Pope, Conradin was given a hero's welcome in Rome in the summer of 1268. The Pope proceeded to excommunicate him, but he took that in his stride and continued south to face Charles of Anjou.

The two opposing forces met Tagliacozzo on 23 August 1268. Initially the battle went Conradin's way. His first two attacks were successful and broke up the lines of Charles of Anjou. The attackers thus proceeded to pillage the French camp, but what they did not know was that Charles of Anjou had kept a third of his army hidden in reserve. Once the discipline of the invading army had broken and turned into pillage, the reserves attacked and routed the invaders.

Conradin managed to flee to Rome, but was quickly advised to leave the city where he was not safe. He thus proceeded towards Genoa but was

Part 6 - The Pope and the Crusader Knights

arrested by members of the Frangipani family and handed over to Charles of Anjou.

With Conradin was his childhood friend, Frederick of Baden, and both youth (Conradin was sixteen and Frederick was nineteen) were imprisoned in Castel dell'Ovo in Naples under harsh conditions. They were then tried and convicted for treason and on 29 October 1268 they were both beheaded. With Conradin the Hohenstaufen line died out and it was the end of a dynasty which had dominated Europe since 1138.

A month after the execution of Conradin, the Pope died. What followed was the longest election process in the history of the papacy. The College of Cardinals met at Viterbo (Rome still being unstable) and as before the big issue was the political situation on Italy. One faction wanted an Italian pope, who could protect the Papal State's interests against Charles of Anjou and another faction wanted a French pope who would be better suited to deal with Charles of Anjou on diplomatic terms.

Pope Clement IV had died at the end of November 1268. Nearly two years later the citizens of Viterbo removed the roof of the building in which the Cardinals met and bricked it up in attempt to force a decision. From that point on the Cardinals were only fed bread and water, but it still took them until September of 1271 to come to a decision.

Finally, the choice fell on Teobaldo Visconti who was a good compromise as he was Italian but had spent his entire career north of the Alps, primarily in the Low Countries. He was thus not as deeply inserted into Italian politics as most of his compatriots.

However, the new Pope was neither in Italy, nor in the Low Countries. He was in Acre, where he was on (the Ninth) crusade with Charles of Anjou. Surprised he left Acre for Rome where he was consecrated 19 March 1272, nearly three and a half years after the death of his predecessor. He took the name Gregory X.

The new Pope prioritized the situation in the Holy Land, where the crusader states were in dire straits, and the situation in Constantinople. He had inherited an agreement between his predecessor and Charles of Anjou to launch a crusade against Constantinople, but nothing had come of it yet as Charles of Anjou had gone on Crusade in the Holy Land instead.

To forestall a revocation of the idea of a crusade against Constantinople, the Byzantine Emperor, Michael VIII Palaiologos, who did not have the resources to fight a combined French and Papal crusade, decided to solve the issue by means of diplomacy. His ace in the sleeve was a re-unification of the Eastern and Western Churches, separated since the schism that culminated in 1054.

The Emperor approached Pope Gregory X on the subject, which was enough to keep the Pope away from any proactive crusading, and to solve this issue and promote further action in the Holy Land the Pope called a Council to be held in Lyon in 1274.

16 - The Pope

The (Second) Council of Lyon was a grand affair which attracted no less than 300 bishops, 60 abbots and more than 1000 prelates. Indeed, so many people turned up that the Pope had to ask those who had not been specifically invited to leave with his - and God's - blessings. The Council eventually issued thirty-one constitutions, but the three key issues were the re-unification, crusades, and recognition of a new German king.

In terms of crusades, a new taxation system was agreed to support further campaigns, and the movement also found a new champion. It just so happened, that Rudolf I of Swabia, and a member of the Habsburger family, had been elected a King of Germany after several years of interregnum. He had both internal competition and the competition of the Anti-king Alphonso X of Castile, so it was instrumental to him that he could obtain the blessing of the Pope.

The Pope struck a hard bargain. Rudolf I had to officially give up any claims in Sicily, Rome and the Papal States, but on the other hand the Pope ensured that Alphonso X gave up his claim in the throne. The Council thus agreed to recognize Rudolf I as King of Germany. He was, however, not made emperor, but he did promise to personally lead a crusade. As it turned out this promise was in vain as the new King had to spend his life consolidating his power at home.

Also, in vain were the promises made by Emperor Michael VIII Palaiologos regarding the re-unification of the Church. The Emperor agreed to a full reconciliation under papal control, but it turned out to be impossible to actually implement in Constantinople. Even the Emperor's use of violence to enforce the agreement turned to nothing and the agreement was cancelled in 1282 when his son, Andronikos II Palaiologos, succeeded him.

What the Byzantine Emperor did achieve, however, was recognition of his rule over the former Latin territories as well as a stop to any further papal support of Charles of Anjou. As mentioned elsewhere, the Emperor followed this up by his active participation in the Sicilian Vespers, which gave Charles of Anjou other things to deal with other than a reconquest of Constantinople.

Matters settled, the Pope set off back to Rome, but he died on the way in January of 1276. The College of Cardinals quickly elected Pierre de Tarentaise, the Dominican Cardinal-bishop of Ostia, as pope. He took the name Innocent V.

The new Pope only lasted six months before he died, a reign in which he proactively chased Michael VIII Palaiologos for a final implementation of the unified Church.

On the death of Innocent V the College of Cardinals elected Ottobuono de' Fieschi, Cardinal Deacon of San Adriano, who took the name Adrian V. He was an experienced diplomat, and his election was strongly supported by Charles of Anjou. But the new Pope died thirty-eight days after his election, before he could even be properly consecrated.

Part 6 - The Pope and the Crusader Knights

Once again faced with the task of electing a new pontiff, the College of Cardinals now turned to Pedro Julião, Portuguese by birth and Cardinal-Bishop of Frascati. The new Pope wanted to use the name 'John', but there was some confusion in the archives, which led to the (faulty) belief that an earlier 'Pope John' had not been counted. The last 'Pope John' was XIX, so the new Pope decided to correct the error and thus became John XXI.

The new Pope was a scholar and also a physician. He immediately followed the line of his predecessors, chasing the actions which should have followed the Second Council of Lyon, but he also found time to further study medicine. To ensure that he had the necessary peace and quiet to do so, he had a new apartment built at the papal residence at Viterbo. Here he could retreat to work in solitude and that was exactly what he was doing when the roof collapsed and killed him on 20 May 1277.

For the fourth time in eighteen months the College of Cardinals had to elect a new pope. This time they returned to tradition and elected Giovanni Gaetano Orsini, a Roman noble, who took the name Nicholas III.

Where his immediate predecessors had spent their, short, reigns on pursuing the decision of the Second Council of Lyon, Nicholas III was a much more pragmatic politician. He became the raw model for the 'Renaissance Pope', even if the Renaissance was still a few decades in the future.

Politically the Pope negotiated with King Rudolf I, who guaranteed the integrity of the Papal States. Furthermore, it was discussed to split the Empire into four kingdoms with Rudolf I as Emperor, but the plan was not implemented.

At home the Pope instituted a much-debated law that prevented foreigners from holding public office in Rome, but what really made him iconic was his blatant practice of simony and nepotism. He appointed three of his relatives as Cardinals and sold, or gave away to his family, other important Church offices. Indeed, he became so famous for this that Dante in his Divine Comedy reserves him a place in the Third Circle of Hell.

Adding to his Renaissance Pope image, he spent enormous sums of money on renovation of the Lateran Palace and a brand new country-residence at Viterbo. Pope Nicholas III did not last long though. He died from a heart attack or stroke in August of 1280 after less than three years on the throne of St. Peter.

This time Charles of Anjou took no chances when it came to the election of a pliant pope. His candidate was the Frenchman Simon de Brion, but his candidate could not get the necessary majority, so Charles of Anjou had two cardinals arrested on the accusation of having manipulated the elections. Without these two cardinals Simon de Brion got the necessary majority. He took the name Martin IV (the popes Marinus I and II also counting as Martin II and III).

16 - The Pope

The new Pope was elected in January of 1281. That same year, in far-away Anatolia, the ruler of a small tribal beylik around the town of Söğüt named Ertugrul Bey died and left his tribe in the hands of his son Osman. The tribe would soon become known as the *House of Osman*, or *Ottomans*.

After a decade of reasonably successful independence of, and even supremacy over, the Emperor, the Pope was once again a puppet, even if Charles of Anjou was not actually emperor.

Charles of Anjou still had issues with Constantinople. He was not happy with the outcome of the Second Council of Lyon, which had effectively removed papal support for his ambitions to re-establish the former Latin Empire of Constantinople. It was not difficult to convince the new Pope that the promised reunification of the Church was not going to happen, so the Pope excommunicated Emperor Michael VIII Palaiologos.

The Romans were not at all happy with the French puppet-pope, so the Pope could only take residence in Rome once he had appointed Charles of Anjou as Roman Senator, but soon Charles of Anjou had his own issues to deal with when Peter III of Aragon overthrew him following the Sicilian Vespers. The Pope of course excommunicated Peter III of Aragon, but he could not muster any outside support for his master.

When Charles of Anjou died in 1284, Rome once more became unsafe for the Pope and he had to withdraw to Perugia where he died in March 1285. Dante places him in Purgatory for his love of food and wine.

In a quick election, the College of Cardinals now elected Giacomo Savelli, a native Roman, as pope. He took the name Honorius IV. He was not physically well, indeed he could neither walk nor stand, but he managed to remain alive for another two years and 1 day.

The Romans received the new Pope well and welcomed him back in Rome, contrary to his unpopular, French, predecessor. Despite his physical disabilities the new Pope quickly took action in regard to Sicily, the most potent problem of the day.

Honorius IV was a vastly experienced diplomat, but in the Sicilian issue he inherited a very messy situation. Shortly before both Pope Martin IV and Charles of Anjou died, a counter-attack on Sicily had failed and Charles of Anjou's son and heir, Charles of Salerno, had been captured by Peter III of Aragon (now also known as Peter I of Sicily). In response, Pope Martin IV had - over and above the excommunication - deprived Peter III of the Kingdom of Aragon, which he instead gave to Charles of Valois, son of King Philip III of France.

Neither the excommunication nor the deprivation of Aragon had any real effect as the population of Sicily strongly supported Peter III of Aragon, having suffered great hardship under the rule of Charles of Anjou. Similarly, nobody in Aragon took the issue of the Pope's intervention too seriously.

The Pope continued his support for the House of Anjou although he did issue laws for the protection of the Sicilian population, laws clearly aimed at the brutal rule of Charles of Anjou. Although the situation was far from good, it did not get any better when Peter III of Aragon died in November of 1285.

Peter III's realm was divided between his sons. His eldest son, Alfonso III, got Aragon and his younger son, James II, got Sicily. Neither was of course recognized by the Pope, who considered both realms forfeited by Peter III. The Pope excommunicated James II and he in return sent a fleet to raid the coast outside of Rome and burn the town of Astura.

With Charles of Salerno still in captivity in Sicily, there was little the Pope or anyone else could do but wait, but finally the situation broke in February of 1287. The instigator was King Edward I of England.

King Edward I had no direct interest in the conflict per se, but he was keen on participating in a new pan-European crusade and he was well aware that with the houses of Aragon and Anjou at war with each other, Europe could not unite. He therefore made it his mission to broker a deal and facilitated talks in Paris during 1286.

The outcome was that Charles of Salerno was released on a set of conditions. He had to relinquish his claim on Sicily, although he was allowed to keep Naples. He was to convince his cousin, Charles of Valois, to renounce his claim on Aragon, for which he would receive 20,000 pounds of silver. Lastly, he was to leave three of his sons and sixty nobles as hostages and promise to return a prisoner and pay a fine of 30,000 marks in case he could not complete the deal within three years.

With an apparent solution to the problem, Charles of Salerno was released and immediately went to Rome where the Pope absolved him of any promises he had made in order to secure his release. Then the Pope died. Before he died he had also tried to make a deal with Rudolf I of Germany, which would see Rudolf appointed as Holy Roman Emperor, but that deal came to naught as well as there was strong resistance towards it inside Germany.

The College of Cardinals was deeply divided over the handling of the Sicilian issue, and it took ten months to elect a new pope. Finally, the choice fell on Girolamo Masci, Cardinal Bishop of Palestrina, who was seen as a suitable compromise. He took the name Nicholas IV.

The new Pope was deeply devoted to the Church and was a far more peace loving individual than his immediate predecessors. But he was no fool, and he took full advantage of the situation, forcing Charles of Salerno to accept the Pope as his overlord before he crowned him King of Sicily in 1289.

Of course, the title was only nominal as James II still ruled on the ground in Sicily. The same could be said about Charles of Valoise who had never been able to actually take power in Aragon, but who had finally decided to make a - French backed - military move towards Alfonso III of Aragon. The campaign was seen as a crusade and this new threat made Alfonso II more pliable and finally an agreement was struck.

The Treaty of Tarascon was made between Pope Nicholas IV, Alfonso III of Aragon, Charles of Salerno and King Philip IV of France. In the treaty it was agreed that Alfonso III would recognize the Pope as his overlord and pay him tribute. Furthermore, he would personally go to Rome to get his excommunication overturned and he would withdraw all troops from Sicily. Finally, he would go on crusade. In return the Pope annulled his predecessor's appointment of Charles of Valois as King of Aragon.

The Treaty seemed to at least solve one of the problems and was a diplomatic triumph for Pope Nicholas IV. Sadly, Alfonso III of Aragon died a few months after its conclusion and it all came to nothing. Instead, James II quickly took over in Aragon, once again uniting the crowns of Sicily and Aragon as had his father before him. Despite years of diplomatic effort involving popes and kings, the issue was still not resolved.

About the same time as Alfonso III's death, the Pope received news of the fall of Acre. This was the last crusader city left in Palestine and it was conquered and devastated in May of 1291, effectively putting an end to the Latin adventure in Palestine which had begun nearly 200 years earlier with the First Crusade. The Pope reacted by calling for a new crusade, something which was difficult for a number of reasons, not least the fact that the Sicilian issue was still unsolved. Thus, nothing came of the Pope's calls, and he died in February of 1292.

What now followed is one of the strangest and saddest stories of a pope. The College of Cardinals was once again split in factions. Some supported the papacy's support of the House of Anjou, others supported a break with the French. All in all, the Cardinals could not agree on a new pope.

The conclave was gridlocked for more than two years between April 1292 and July 1294. Then a letter arrived. The letter was from one Pietro di Morrone, an eccentric monk who had lived most of his life in a cave and had founded his own ascetic order (which would later be named the Celestines. but at the time was a fringe-branch of the Benedictines).

Pietro di Morrone wrote to the College of Cardinals to urge them to get on with their duties and elect a new pope or divine vengeance would fall upon them. When the letter was read out, the Dean of the College of Cardinals, Latino Malabranca, cried out *'In the name of the Father, the Son, and the Holy Ghost, I elect Brother Pietro di Morrone.'* As mad an idea as it was, the Cardinals quickly agreed and a deputation was sent to inform the monk of his election.

Pietro di Morrone had no intentions of becoming pope. He tried to flee the delegation, but he was finally convinced to come with them to the city of L'Aquila, where he was consecrated on 29 August 1294. He took the name Celestine V.

Part 6 - The Pope and the Crusader Knights

The new Pope was 79 years old, he was totally politically naive, and he did not want to be pope. He therefore accepted an offer of assistance from Charles of Salerno (now Charles II of Naples) who offered him accommodation in Naples, away from the politically loaded atmosphere of Rome. In effect Charles II of Naples now had himself a pliant pope and soon a string of appointments followed, favouring the family and partisans of Charles II of Naples.

When he wanted to fast during advent and appointed three cardinals to rule in his place, he was refused, and Celestine V soon realized that he was as unsuitable as he was reluctant to be pope. Taking advice on the matter, the Pope now did the only smart thing during the whole affair. He used his powers to issue a decree which established a Pope's right to abdicate, and then he did just that on 13 December of 1294 after 161 days as pope.

The voluntary abdication of a pope is a rare event; indeed, it is so rare that the next instance was in 2013 when Benedict XVI (Joseph Aloisius Ratzinger) abdicated due to bad health. But the College of Cardinals accepted the abdication - realizing that Celestine V's election was a bad idea in the first place - and quickly elected a new pope.

The choice fell on Benedetto Caetani, a Roman noble and Cardinal-Bishop of Ostia, who took the name Boniface VIII. This choice was a return to the traditional election of a highly political Italian as pope, and Boniface VIII did not disappoint.

One of the first things Boniface VIII had to deal with was his predecessor. All Celestine V (now again Pietro di Morrone) wanted to do was to go back to his simple life at the Monastery of Sulmona, but he had become a dangerous political pawn. The French party, mainly King Philip IV and Charles II of Naples, did not accept the legality of the Pope's resignation - which meant they lost their puppet - and there was real danger that they might try a coup or the installation of Celestine V as anti-pope.

Pietro di Morrone was therefore arrested (having twice tried to flee) and detained in the castle of Fumone where he died ten months later. The new Pope was accused of having caused his death and the King of France initiated Celestine V's elevation to saint in 1313. He was the first saintly pope since Gregory VII more than two centuries earlier and the last saintly pope we shall meet in this tale.

Pope Boniface VIII did thus not start off on the best possible standing with the French and his personality and beliefs did nothing to rectify the situation. Boniface VIII was a strong believer of the tradition that the Pope was the supreme authority on all religious and secular matters. As far as he was concerned a pope outranked a king any day, and it soon brought him into conflict with the crowned heads of Europe.

One of the first issues in which the Pope got involved in was the still unsolved issue of Sicily. James II of Sicily now ruled in both Sicily and Aragon, but he was looking for a peaceful solution. He therefore met with representatives of the Pope, Charles II of Naples, Philip IV of France and his uncle James II of Mallorca (whose island had been conquered by Alfonso III and annexed into Aragon).

A treaty was agreed at Anagni in central Italy, which aimed to finally settle the on-going issues. According to the treaty, James II of Sicily and Aragon agreed to hand Sicily over to the Pope, who in turn would hand it over to Charles II of Naples and to also give the Balearic Islands back to James II of Mallorca. In return the Pope recognized the rule of James II in Aragon and cancelled the claim of Charles of Valois. James II was to have his excommunication lifted and marry Blanche, a daughter of Charles II of Naples.

But there was a problem. When James II left Sicily for Aragon, he had left his younger brother Frederick as regent. It was understood that Frederick, who had broad popular backing in Sicily, would not just up and leave, so the treaty also stipulated that James II would lend military support to Charles II of Naples in order to install him in Sicily.

If it was expected that Frederick would cause problems - he did not disappoint. He declared himself King of Sicily as Frederick II and the local bishops happily crowned him as such. The Pope excommunicated Frederick II and put an interdict on Sicily, but both were ignored and Frederick II enjoyed more popular support than any other Sicilian ruler of the times.

But the issue of Sicily soon became a secondary issue, although we shall return to it later. The Pope had problems with King Philip IV of France which hurt him in two places: his pride and his pocket. Philip IV was keen to consolidate France into a strong central power, a proper nation state rather than the union of semi-autonomous principalities that made up most European kingdoms at that time.

A central authority needs money, derived through taxes, and as the Church was the by far wealthiest entity in the country, Philip IV started to tax the Church in France. This was completely unheard of. Not only did it deprive the Pope of revenue which he considered to be his, it also went in the exact opposite direction of the Pope's beliefs in his own supremacy.

A papal bull issued in February 1296 specifically disallowed taxation of the Church without prior approval of the Pope. The bull specified excommunication on those who transgressed, but King Philip IV reacted by stopping the transfer of money from France to Rome. Now the Pope got really angry. He needed the substantial revenues from France, so he informed King Philip IV that *'God has set popes over kings and kingdoms.'* Philip IV's reaction was to further stop export of gold, silver, precious stones and food to Rome. Further the King expelled the papal agents who were still collecting money for a future crusade.

The Pope now had to cave in. He issued a new bull in September of 1296 in which he specified that the Church could give volunteer donations to a state in situation where it is needed for the defence of the state and allows that it is the Kings who defines such needs. King Philip IV now removed the ban on exports and the King and the Pope were reconciled, for now.

In southern Italy the situation went from bad to worse. Frederick II had landed in Italy and captured several towns. He instigated a revolt in Naples and eagerly engaged in alliances with anyone who was against the Pope, including the powerful Colonna family in Rome, which also became engaged in a family in-fight which in turn led to the destruction of the family's strongholds.

Charles II of Naples now struck back, helped by the defections of some of the Sicilian nobles. Frederick II was now on the defensive, but when the sons of Charles II of Naples, Robert and Philip, landed in Sicily, it was Frederick II who was successful and even captured Philip (who in the meantime had married Frederick II and James II of Aragon's sister Yolanda).

The war raged on with both sides taking the initiative in turn, but finally, in 1302, Charles of Valois, fighting on behalf of the Pope, had to sue for peace when his army was struck by plague. The peace agreement, known as the Treaty of Caltabellotta was finalized in August of 1302.

Effectively it confirmed the status quo and formally split the former Kingdom of Sicily into the island of Sicily itself, ruled by Frederick II, and called the Kingdom of Trinacriat, and the mainland ruled by Charles II of Naples as the Kingdom of Naples (although it was actually still referred to as the Kingdom of Sicily at the time). Furthermore, it was agreed that on Frederick II's death, the island of Sicily would once again fall under the House of Anjou. To seal the deal Frederick II married Eleanor, the daughter of Charles II of Naples, who went on to give him no less than nine children. For now, the Sicilian issue had finally been solved. The only major player who did not get anything from the deal was Charles of Valois, who had to contend himself with having been appointed a cardinal back in 1285.

In the meantime, the Pope decided to introduce a Jubilee year, a year in which pilgrims went to Rome and obtained forgiveness for their sins. The year 1300 was selected and the event was hugely profitable for the city. The idea was to repeat it each hundred years, but as it turned out it would be celebrated more frequently than that and we shall come back to it again.

The Pope also involved himself with internal strife in Florence. Fighting had been going on for years between the (imperial) *Ghibellines* and (anti-imperial) *Guelphs*. A battle in 1289 had seen a *Guelph* victory and the *Ghibellines* had been banned from the city. But now an internal split took place which saw the *Guelphs* divide into two factions called the White and the Black Guelphs. Basically, it was a power struggle, centred on the amount of papal influence the city should endure.

The White Guelphs believed in minimal papal influence whereas the Black Guelphs believed in increased papal influence. The two factions fought each other and the Black Guelphs were expelled from the city. The Pope reacted by engaging once more with his loyal soldier, Charles of Valois, who

16 - The Pope

was sent to make peace, but the Florentines did not trust his, or the Pope's, intentions.

A delegation therefore went to the Pope to plead their case. It was led by the poet Dante Alighieri, who I have also mentioned previously. Nothing much came of the delegations pleads and with the exception of Dante it was sent home. When Charles of Valois arrived in Florence, accompanied by the Black Guelphs, he razed the city and confiscated the property of the White Guelphs. Dante was exiled and never returned to Florence. His somewhat strained relationship to the papacy has remained part of his legacy.

Even though Pope Boniface VIII and King Philip IV of France had made peace after the French embargo on Rome in 1296, King Philip IV had continued to go his own way. He still taxed the Church and when he got into a dispute with the Papal Legate, Bernard Saisset, King Philip IV had him tried before a Royal Court.

This latest act of defiance set the Pope off again and he wrote to Philip IV to submit to the Pope's supremacy, stop taxing the Church and stop trying clerics before a common court. The King had the letter publically burned in front of a crowd in Paris. An exchange of letters followed, one particularly insulting from the Pope possibly a forgery, and finally King Philip IV was excommunicated.

The King's response was to send an expeditionary force to Italy where it surprised the Pope at his country retreat at Anagni. The Pope was arrested, possibly beaten, but released again after three days to be in the care of three cardinals of the Orsini family who had arrived from Rome. On his return to Rome the Pope fell ill and died in October of 1303. Rumours were spread that he had gone mad and gnawed his own hands off and smashed his skull against the wall. This was proven wrong when his remains were investigated in the seventeenth century.

Pope Boniface VIII was a hard act to follow and as it turned out the last had not been heard about him yet. But in the meantime, the College of Cardinals elected Nicola Boccasini, Bishop of Ostia, who took the name Benedict XI.

The new Pope was a mild-mannered person and although the idea was that he should continue the confrontational line with the King of France, Benedict XI was not the fighter that his predecessor had been.

Rather than put more pressure on King Philip IV, the new Pope lifted his excommunication although he did excommunicate his councillor, Guillaume de Nogaret, who he held personally responsible for the capture and rough handling of Boniface VIII. When the Pope died suddenly in July of 1304, after only 259 days on the job, it was widely speculated that he had been poisoned by Guillaume de Nogaret, but the theory was never proven.

The death of Benedict XI led to an interregnum of nearly a year. The College of Cardinals was split down the middle between Italian and French cardinals, and it was impossible to agree on a policy towards the King of

France and a suitable candidate to carry out that policy. Finally, in June of 1305, a compromise was found in Raymond Bertrand de Got, Archbishop of Bordeaux, who took the name Clement V.

It was probably the idea that Clement V, untainted by the politics of Rome, could easily be controlled by the Cardinals, it would turn out to be very wrong indeed.

Messengers found Clement V at Bordeaux and asked him to go to Rome for his consecration. Instead, he went to Lyon. Here his crowning was celebrated with pomp and circumstance in November of 1305. Among the guests was King Philip IV of France and the new Pope proceeded to immediately appoint nine new French cardinals. Then he moved to Poitiers where he set up his court (*curia*).

The new Pope then withdrew Boniface VIII's bull called *Unam Sanctam*, in which Boniface VIII had clearly specified that the Pope held both religious and temporal supremacy over the secular rulers. That the move was initiated by King Philip IV is unquestionable and that was not the only task in which Clement V showed to be a willing tool of the French King.

The episode that I am particularly referring to is the suppression of the Knights Templar, an episode that more than anything defined Clement V's legacy. I shall come back in more detail about this episode in the following chapter, but in essence King Philip IV decided to confiscate the Knight Templar's possessions and their alleged treasure, one of the last items to be carried aboard when they left Acre in 1291.

But there was a problem with getting at the Knights Templar, namely that they were under the direct jurisdiction of the Pope, having deliberately been put so by Pope Honorius II in 1129 in order to keep them out of the rampant politics of the Crusader States in the Holy Land.

King Philip IV had already filed charges against the Templars in 1306, but the Pope had stalled for time, aiming instead at seeking a merger between the Knights Templar and the Knights Hospitaller, both of whom were without a reason d'être after the collapse of the Crusader States. But the French King had no intention of waiting, he needed money, he needed it soon and he had the Templars in his sights.

When the Pope formally asked for the King's help in the investigation of the charges, the King immediately seized the opportunity. On 13 October 1307, an unusually well-coordinated exercise saw the Templars in France arrested at the same time and thrown in prison. The Pope allowed this to happen, even when it eventually led to the public burning of a number of prominent Templars in Paris and he furthermore obliged to the King's demands by issuing a bull in November 1307 which commanded that all the European Kings should arrest the Templars and confiscate their assets.

The reaction to the papal bull was mixed, but gradually most kings complied. Most Templars tried outside of France were acquitted, but the

16 - The Pope

Order was finally dissolved by the Pope in 1312 and its assets were transferred to the Hospitallers.

While this was going on the Pope once again moved the Curia. Not to Rome, as would have been expected, but to Avignon where it was to stay for more than six decades.

Rome was in a state of chaos, mainly caused by violent clashes between the two dominant families, the Colonna and the Orsini. Furthermore, the Basilica di San Giovanni in Laterano had been damaged by a fire, and these were the official reasons for the Pope's choice of Avignon. In reality of course the real reason was to keep close to his French master, but the choice of Avignon was clever in that whereas it placed the Pope well outside the dangers of Rome and well within the protection of the King of France, it was not actually a part of the French Kingdom, but rather an imperial fief held by the King of Naples (who of course was related to the King of France). It could thus not be said that the Pope favoured France over Italy.

But the Pope's actions spoke more than clever technicalities. King Philip IV pressed the Pope to commence a post-mortem trial against Pope Boniface VIII. The trail began in 1309 - this time without the body of the dead Pope being present - with the charges being a mix of heresy and the generic charge of sodomy. The purpose was really to find a reason to lift the excommunication of the King's minister, Guillaume de Nogaret, and other participants in the seizure of Boniface VIII. The Pope ended up finding a compromise in which the trial was postponed to a later council, but the Pope in the meantime lifted all the excommunications. The latter trial was a short-lived affair with none of the charges being upheld as the purpose of the exercise had been obtained anyhow.

Although the Pope had taken up residence in Avignon, he was still the head of the Papal States, so he appointed three cardinals to rule on his behalf. But the on-going battle between the (*Guelph*) Orsini and the (*Ghibelline*) Colonna families made the city impossible to govern. The solution came from a somewhat unexpected source, namely from the King of Germany.

In Germany the death of Rudolf I in 1291 had seen the rise of another count, Adolf, to the throne. Rudolf I had never achieved his ambition to become Holy Roman Emperor and neither did Adolf, who was never officially sanctioned by the Pope. Rudolf I's son, Albert I, contested Adolf's kingship and Adolf was killed in 1298 in a battle between the two parties.

Albert I was now King of Germany and although he, like his father before him, negotiated with Pope to be crowned emperor, nothing came of it due to Boniface VIII's death. Albert I had disinherited his nephew, Duke John of Swabia, and as a consequence the Duke murdered the King in 1308.

Two candidates now emerged for the throne of Germany. One was Duke Rudolf I of Bavaria and the other was the ever-present Charles of Valois who was supported by King Philip IV and, possibly, by Pope Clement V. The

Part 6 - The Pope and the Crusader Knights

German princes were not too keen on either, so they ended up electing an independent compromise candidate, Henry VII, Count of Luxembourg, who was both a capable ruler and free of any dynastic connections.

The new King immediately sought the blessing of the Pope. Despite the French King's own candidate being rejected in favour of Henry VII, Pope Clement V agreed to confirm the new King of Germany, which as per tradition also meant that he would be crowned Holy Roman Emperor. Before that was agreed, the Pope took the opportunity to negotiate - or possibly dictate - the terms, according to which the Emperor Elect promised to protect the Holy Church, to respect the integrity of the Papal States and to go on a crusade.

Matters thus settled, Henry VII had first to attend to problems in Germany and Bohemia so it was not until late 1310 that he was ready to go to Rome. He had tried to arrange a marriage between his daughter and the son of Robert of Anjou, who was now King of Naples after the death in 1309 of his father, Charles II of Naples. It was an attempt to create a bond between the *Guelphs* (who saw Naples as the anti-dote to the Empire) and the *Ghibellines*, but in the end nothing came of it as Henry VII would not meet the monetary demands of Robert of Anjou.

To say that Henry VII's expedition to Italy was chaotic would be a gross understatement. With no central authority to (nominally or directly) control northern Italy, the city states had developed into strong autonomous entities. Some of them were *Guelphs* (anti-imperial) and others were *Ghibellines* (pro-imperial), but a common trait was that whichever party was currently in control in the city expelled the members of the other party.

A motley crew of expelled or otherwise hard done by exiles thus started to gather around the King when he entered Italy in October of 1310. Each had a story to tell and after initially drawing in the exiled *Ghibellines*, *Guelphs* - including Dante - they also started to come to Henry VII for justice.

Henry VII had a simple, possibly naive, plan; the city-states would surrender to him and he would appoint or re-appoint the local government, local laws would be replaced by imperial law, all exiles would be allowed to return and everybody would live happily ever after. However, none of the elements of his plan turned out to be workable.

Although the *Ghibelline* towns welcomed the Emperor Elect, they mainly ignored his call to take back their exiles and the *Guelph* towns put up resistance. When some, like Cremona, submitted and then were punished by the razing of its walls, it only stiffened the resistance of the others, with Florence, Lucca, Siena and Bologna as the main opponents to imperial power and Robert of Anjou. King of Naples, as the rallying point.

The Pope, now under pressure from the French King, also started to withdraw his support for Henry VII and the traditional battle-lines between the *Guelphs* and *Ghibellines* only hardened further despite the Emperor Elect's plan for the opposite.

16 - The Pope

Henry VII finally made his way to Rome in the spring of 1312, but Rome itself was in a state of turmoil and the Pope decided to not make his way there. The new Emperor was thus crowned on 29 June at the Lateran by three *Ghibelline* cardinals who had joined him during his march through northern Italy.

The *Guelph* party soon managed to oust the Emperor from Rome and he retreated to Pisa where he prepared for war against Robert of Anjou. His first target was Florence, the dominant *Guelph* city-state and the city was put under siege in September of 1312. Although the Emperor was too strong for the Florentines to take on in open battle, they defended their city valiantly during six weeks of siege which saw the city only effectively closed off from the side where the Emperor's army was camped and, in the meantime, keeping trade and supplies flowing through the gates that faced away from the Emperor.

When the Emperor abandoned the ineffective siege of Florence he went on a more successful campaign to subdue Tuscany, now having learned from his earlier mistakes and showing leniency towards his former enemies. He then returned to Pisa where he waited for reinforcements from Germany and in the meantime extracted every penny he could from the city and its inhabitants.

By the beginning of August 1313, the Emperor was ready to resume his campaign, and he first moved to besiege Siena. Within a week the Emperor fell ill from malaria and on 22 August he died. Although Dante provides him with the legacy as "*he who came to reform Italy before she was ready for it*", nothing came of the Emperor's efforts and his empire fell into civil war on his death, leaving Italy once again free of imperial supremacy.

Back in Avignon, the Pope gradually washed his hands of Henry VII and had instead taken up the quest for a new crusade, an adventure which the French King signed up to, but both the Pope and the King of France died in 1314 putting an end to that initiative.

On the death of Clement V in April 1314 a new interregnum emerged, with the cardinals split over the question of the papacy's location and political affiliation. It was only in August of 1316 that a conclave of cardinals met (preceded over by the Regent of France) in Lyon and elected Jacques Duèze, Cardinal-Bishop of Porto, as the new pope. He took the name John XXII.

The new Pope was French; he resided in Avignon and he was in all matters aligned to the French crown. On the death of Philip IV his eldest son, Louis X, had taken the throne of France, but he died a couple of month before the new Pope was elected. He had no living male heir, but his wife was pregnant, so a regency was set up under his brother, Philip. When the Queen of France gave birth to a male in November 1316, the infant boy was made king, under the name of John I, but he only lived for five days. His

Part 6 - The Pope and the Crusader Knights

uncle was then elevated from regent to king as Philip V (also called 'the Tall").

In Germany a civil war raged between Louis IV ("the Bavarian") and his cousin Frederick the Fair, both elected King of the Germans by separate factions. The Pope stayed neutral until Louis IV captured his rival in 1322.

The Pope excommunicated Louis IV, who as a reaction agreed to release his rival under the condition that the later convinced his brother, Leopold, to put down arms and submit to Louis IV. Frederick the Fair was unsuccessful in this task and he thus honoured his promise to Louis IV and returned to captivity.

Impressed by the honesty of his rival, now openly supported by the Pope, Louis IV agreed to co-rule the Empire with his former enemy. Frederick the Fair would remain King of Germany while Louis IV would take on the title of Holy Roman Emperor and rule in Italy.

This agreement was made without the Pope's blessing, and he had no intention of making Louis IV emperor. But the Emperor Elect took matters into his own hands. He set out to Italy and was first crowned King of Italy in Milan in 1327. He then entered Rome in January of 1328 and had himself crowned as emperor by the *Captain of the Roman People,* Sciarra Colonna.

The new Emperor's legitimacy was of course questionable as the Pope - backed by the King of France and Robert of Anjou - did not agree to it, but if Philip V of France could have his own pope, so could Louis IV!

The Emperor had a Franciscan preacher, Pietro Rainalducci, appointed pope as Nicholas V, residing in Rome as a pope should. The appointment was a double insult to the Pope, as John XXII had specifically condemned the Franciscans whom he thought were excessive in their claims that the clergy should emulate the poverty of Christ (something that did not match the princely lifestyle of the Pope himself).

The new Anti-pope initially stayed in Rome with the Emperor but then withdrew to Viterbo as the mood in Rome became increasingly anti-imperial. Under pressure from the anti-imperial authorities in Rome, he then moved on to the imperial stronghold of Pisa. Here he - encouraged by the Emperor - started a process against John XXII, who was represented by a suitably attired straw dummy. The Pope was convicted of heresy, and the straw dummy was handed over to the authorities for execution. It is, needless to say, that Pope John XXII excommunicated Nicholas V.

But without the Emperor to protect him the Anti-pope could not hold out and he finally submitted the John XXII personally at Avignon in 1330. He was forgiven but held in comfortable house arrest until his death in 1333.

In Germany, Frederick the Fair decided to distance himself from the controversy and withdrew to Austria. He died in 1330 leaving Louis IV as the sole ruler. The Emperor now returned to Germany where he focused his attention on internal matters.

16 - The Pope

Pope John XXII died in December of 1334 and a conclave was quickly called to find a successor. It was custom that in the first round of the ballot, the Cardinals would vote for a candidate who had no chance of winning the final vote. This was done to assess the direction of the electorate before the more important voting began. But on this occasion the process backfired. By coincidence all the Cardinals, with one exception, voted for Jacques Fournier, who was a rather non-descript cardinal, mainly known for his suppression of Cathar heretics in southern France. But it was done and the accidentally elected Pope took the name Benedict XII.

Contrary to his predecessors, the new Pope had no intentions of being a puppet of the French King. Indeed, their relationship is known to have been cold at best. He also aimed for peace with Louis IV and took a more lenient approach to the Franciscans and their view on poverty. He even tried to introduce some level of modesty amongst the clergy, which however did not prevent him from building the imposing Palais des Papes in Avignon, a papal stronghold and palace which still stands on the rock of Doms overlooking Avignon.

But the negotiations with Louis IV did not go well and instead the Emperor called the German electorate together in Rhens in 1338, where they not only confirmed Louis IV's election and legitimacy but also issued a declaration that henceforth allowed the election of the King of Germany without papal consent.

The Pope died in 1342 with matters between the papacy and the Emperor unresolved. In his place the conclave - and this time not by mistake - elected Pierre Roger, cardinal-priest of Santi Nereo e Achilleo (born a French noble) as Pope Clement VI.

Contrary to his predecessor, the new Pope was strongly loyal to the King of France, now Philip VI, and had no desire for poverty. He is quoted for saying that he *'lived as a sinner among sinners'*, surrounding himself with great luxury and artists, in particular musicians.

Politically the Pope had two main issues to deal with. First there was the issue of the Holy Roman Emperor, Louis IV. Like his predecessors the new Pope tried to come to an understanding with the Emperor, but when that failed he instead proactively backed the appointment of an anti-emperor, Charles IV, who promised not to interfere in Italy, obey the Pope and also agreed to hand a considerable amount of money over to the Pope for his efforts.

The appointment of Charles IV was only supported by some German princes, but the issue solved itself when Louis IV died in 1347, leaving Charles IV alone as King of Germany. A few years later he went to Rome without an army - fulfilling his promises to the Pope - was crowned as Emperor by a suitable cardinal and returned to Germany.

In the Kingdom of Naples the long-time ruler, Robert of Anjou, died in 1343. He left no direct male heir, and the throne was given to his granddaughter, Joanna I of Naples. She in turn married András, the brother of the Hungarian King Louis I, but the local nobility was far from happy with the Hungarian influence and wanted András crowned only as consort. The Pope initially supported this, but after a considerable bribe - paid by András' mother - he changed his mind and supported András' coronation as king.

A conspiracy of nobles now had András murdered and the Hungarian King blamed the murder on Joanna I of Naples. King Louis I invaded Naples but had to withdraw as he had no popular support. To settle matters the Pope instigated a trial of Joanna I of Naples in Avignon in 1352, a trial in which she was acquitted of any involvement in the murder of her husband. In a transaction that was hardly coincidental, the Pope at the same time bought the rights to Avignon from Joanna I of Naples - who held the title to the city - for 80,000 crowns, thus making Avignon his own.

But as important as these political issues were, the defining event of Clement VI's papacy was the arrival of the Black Death. The plague hit Europe around 1347 and decimated the population, killing between one and two thirds. Death was everywhere and the Pope had a council of experts put together to explain the phenomenon. They concluded that the plague was a result of the conjunction of Saturn, Jupiter, and Mars in 1341. Satisfied with this explanation the Pope proactively did what he could to prevent persecution of Jews, by many blamed for the misfortune.

The catastrophe was of such dimensions that all normality ceased to exist. There simply was not enough consecrated land to bury the death, and the Pope therefore consecrated the Rhone River in its entirety so corpses could be thrown into the river and still be considered properly buried.

Despite warnings to leave the city, the Pope stayed put and he never contracted the disease himself. Rather, he died from natural causes at the end of 1352, by which time the plague had mainly burned itself out.

The College of Cardinals quickly elected Etienne Aubert, Cardinal-bishop of Ostia and Velletri, as new pope and he took the name Innocent VI.

The new Pope inherited an estate that was nearly ruined from the excesses of his predecessors, and he immediately tried to gain better financial control by selling, rather than buying, pieces of art, however his papacy would be known for its precarious financial situation.

One of the consequences of the Pope's poverty was that he turned down an offer from John Kantakouzenos, a contender in a civil war raging in Byzantium, by which the Pope was offered a reunification of the Churches if he would support John Kantakouzenos. But the Pope had no spare resources, so he declined the offer and John Kantakouzenos instead hired Ottoman mercenaries, who were garrisoned on the Gallipoli peninsula. The Ottomans never left Europe but rather fortified their positions and started hacking away at the crumbling Byzantine Empire in Europe.

What money the Pope did have was spent on expeditions into Italy. The Pope intended to restore his supremacy in northern Italy now that any

16 - The Pope

immediate threat from the Holy Roman Emperor had been eliminated. He sent two expeditions, under the command of Cardinal Gil Álvarez Carrillo de Albornoz and although the expeditions successfully retook control of all the major cities in northern Italy, including Milan and Pisa, the area was impossible to control and a by-product of the campaigns left companies of - now master less - mercenaries roaming freely and helping themselves to anything they could get their hands on.

The Pope had more success with brokering peace between England and France. What would be known as 'the Hundred Year's War' had raged for decades, but with the Pope as broker a peace settlement was made in 1360, known as the Treaty of Brétigny. The peace did not last, but it did stand for nine years before hostilities broke out again.

Innocent VI died in September of 1362. Little of his efforts had any long-term consequences, but his failure to support John Kantakouzenos did. The Ottomans had, up to this point, been an entirely Byzantine problem, but now they were rapidly becoming a very clear and present danger in Europe.

There is some confusion as to exactly what happened next, but it is clear that the College of Cardinals initially elected a new pope who refused the appointment. The most likely candidate was that of Cardinal Gil Álvarez Carrillo de Albornoz, the commander of the papal army in Italy, but the issue is somewhat unclear.

In any case, the College of Cardinals could not agree on a new candidate amongst their own ranks, so they turned to the respected scholar, William de Grimoard, Abbot of the Abbey of St.Victor, who at that time was on a mission as Papal Legate to Naples.

Fearing for William de Grimoard's safety on his passage through Italy should his election be known to the ever shifty Romans, the Legate was called home to Avignon 'to consult with the Conclave' and his election as pope was only made known to him and the world on his safe arrival. He took the name Urban V.

Although Urban V was a scholar, he also had in him a, somewhat anachronistic, quest for crusades. He was well aware of the threat now posed by the Ottomans in Europe and he had a desire for a new crusade to the Holy Land.

Crusading vows were taken by the King of France, the King of Cyprus and (later) Amadeus VI Count of Savoy, and a plan was made for an invasion of Alexandria. The plan was executed by Peter I of Cyprus in cooperation with Venice and the Knight of Rhodes. Peter I of Cyprus was the titular King of Jerusalem and with a considerable fleet he attacked Alexandria in October of 1365. The crusaders took 5,000 prisoners, to be sold as slaves, burned and looted extensively, and then left again after four days. A plan to continue to Cairo was abandoned as it was clear that the crusader army could not hope to hold any territories they would conquer.

Part 6 - The Pope and the Crusader Knights

The following year the Byzantine Emperor, John V Palaiologos, found himself unable to enter Bulgaria on his way back from a meeting in Hungary. His cousin, Amadeus VI of Savoy, with significant financial backing from the Pope set out to rescue him and to throw the Ottomans out of Gallipoli. The expedition, which first went to Bulgaria, was successful. The Bulgarians were forced to give the Byzantine Emperor free passage home and then the Ottomans were expelled from the Gallipoli peninsula.

The effect was, however, limited. The Ottoman had by now established themselves, with Edirne as their European capital, and within a few years they were given the Gallipoli peninsula back by John V Palaiologos' son, Andronikos IV Palaiologos, as reward for their military assistance in a civil war against his father.

More lasting effect had the Pope's attempts to reconcile the papacy with Rome. Urban V had inherited the last stages of the campaign in Italy from his predecessor. Although the papal army was, per se, militarily successful, it was proving impossible to consolidate any central authority in Rome - and northern Italy in general - without the Pope residing in Rome. The city states were fiercely autonomous and opportunistic princes and fortune-seekers consistently kicked up a conflict.

Urban V made a decision to appear in Rome in person. He entered on 16 October 1367, more than six decades since the last pope had set foot in Rome. The populace greeted him enthusiastically and he played host to no less than the Emperor himself and other dignities such as Peter I of Cyprus and Joanna I of Naples.

But there was still much unrest in the Papal States and the Pope was ailing. He finally left Italy by ship in September of 1370 and after arriving in Avignon was taken to the house of his brother (who had been made a cardinal). Here he died on 19 December.

Despite Pope Urban V's attempts to re-establish the papacy in Rome, the College of Cardinals elected another Frenchman, Pierre Roger De Beaufort, who took the name Gregory XI.

The new Pope initially concentrated on the eradication of heretics, most specifically the Lollards, and went into correspondence with both the Lollard John Wycliffe and Johannes Klenkoka, but he had not forgotten the initiatives regarding Rome taken by his predecessor.

It was clear that the populace wanted the Pope back in Rome, but the papacy had conditions. In essence, they demanded the submission of the city states to papal authority and some, in particular Florence and Milan, started an armed revolt in opposition to the Pope's demands.

Like his predecessor, Gregory XI decided that a personal visit to Rome was required and he entered on 17 January 1377. The visit was supposed to be exactly that; a visit, but before the Pope and his court could extract themselves the Pope died in March 1378.

16 - The Pope

The College of Cardinals now met in Rome for the first time since the election of Benedict XI in 1303 and the Roman population were not taking any chances. A mob broke into the voting chamber, and they forced the Cardinals to elect an Italian pope.

The elected pope was Bartolomeo Prignano, Archbishop of Bari, who took the name Urban VI. He was not a cardinal, and neither was he Roman, but rather from Naples. But at least he was not French and that pacified the mob long enough for French the Cardinals to flee Rome and return to Avignon.

But the Pope stayed. For the first time in more than seven decades the Pope resided in Rome and soon he started to make his opinions known.

At the time he was elected he was considered a rather non-descript individual, whose primary qualification - as mentioned - was that he was not French, The College of Cardinals expected that he could easily be controlled, but it turned out very differently.

Hardly had the French Cardinals returned to Avignon before the Pope started asserting his new-found authority. He spoke out against gratitudes and gifts given to the Curia and he forbade them to receive annuities from laypeople, royal or otherwise. Finally, he condemned the luxurious lives of the Cardinals and declared that he intended to stay in Rome.

The sudden change in character of Urban VI led some to believe that he had lost his mind, possibly by the power going to his head, and the Cardinals immediately started to plot his downfall.

But Urban VI was not so easy to get rid of. As the first Italian Pope for more than seven decades and with his decision to reside in Rome he was immensely popular with the common people. He also had powerful allies, in particular Joanna I of Naples.

So, the Cardinals in Avignon decided to appoint their own pope. They condemned and excommunicated Urban VI and elected Robert of Geneva, a cardinal best known for authorizing a massacre of thousands of civilians at Cesena during the ongoing conflict in northern Italy. He was thus nicknamed 'the Butcher of Cesena', but he himself chose the name of Clement VII.

The new Anti-pope quickly settled in Avignon where his main concern was to raise enough money to run the papal administration.

As it happened, the French Cardinals cold have left Urban VI to hang himself. The Pope had an unusual ability to alienate the people around him. After his initial alienation of the French Cardinals, he quickly made an enemy of his ally Joanna I of Naples who switched her allegiance to the Pope in Avignon.

Joanna I of Naples had no heir, her only son, Charles Martel, had died as an infant as had her two daughters. The succession in Naples was therefore a key political issue of the times. When Joanna I of Naples switched allegiance, she appointed Louis I, Duke of Anjou and the younger brother of King John II of France, as heir to Naples. In a countermove Pope Urban VI declared her a heretic, dethroned her and made Naples a papal fief which he bestowed upon Charles of Durazzo, the husband of Joanna I's niece, who would later become Charles II of Hungary as well as Charles III of Naples.

Both contestants were ready to move militarily to secure their heritage, but the death of King Charles V of France in 1380 forced his brother, Louis I of Anjou, to stay in France where he acted as regent for his infant nephew, Charles VI.

Instead, it was Charles of Durazzo who, with a Hungarian army, moved on Naples in the summer of 1381. The resistance they met, under the command of Joanna I's husband Otto, was weak and they quickly secured Naples itself where Joanna I was holed up in Castel dell'Ovo. Her husband came to her rescue but was captured, leading to Joanna I's surrender and she was imprisoned in the fortress of San Fele.

King Charles III of Naples was thus crowned with the consent of Pope Urban VI. But Louis I of Anjou had not forgotten his claim. Pope Clement VI in Avignon crowned Louis I as King of Naples and with the support of the King of France (his nephew), Bernabò Visconti (Lord of Milan) and Amadeus VI of Savoy he launched a considerable army (said to be 40,000 men strong) on Naples in 1382.

Hearing news of the French expedition, Charles III of Naples had Joanna I murdered so that she could not act as a rallying point. He had to rely on a smaller army of mercenaries, and with that, he managed to spread out the French army and avoid of siege a Naples itself.

Reinforcements from France enabled Louis I to capture the city of Arezzo, but then the campaign started to crumble. Amadeus VI of Savoy fell ill and died in March 1383 and when Louis I of Anjou also died in September of 1384, the campaign stopped. Arezzo was sold to Florence and the remaining French army withdrew.

Charles II of Naples had now secured his kingdom, but his relationship with Pope Urban VI soon turned sour. One again Urban VI managed to alienate a former ally, this time under accusations of conspiracy against the papacy, and things turned violent.

The Pope ended up under siege in the castle at Nocera, from where he was only rescued by two Neapolitan barons who had turned against Charles III. He fled to Genoa, where he holed up for the next few years.

In the meantime Charles III of Naples had moved on to Hungary where King Louis I had died. He had himself crowned as King Charles II of Hungary, but he was assassinated in 1386 by partisans of Elizabeth of Bosnia.

A war of succession now started in Naples and Pope Urban VI was quick to utilize the situation. He left Genoa and quickly re-asserted his authority in northern Italy. In the summer of 1388, in front of a considerable army, he was ready to move back to Rome, but he fell from his mule during the march on the city and died at Rome in October of 1389. Some say he died from his injuries, some that he was poisoned.

Within three weeks the College of Cardinals in Rome had elected Piero Tomacelli as the new Pope. He took the name Boniface IX.

One of the preoccupations of the new Pope became the succession in Naples. Only the day before his consecration had the (anti) Pope in Avignon, Clement VII, declared Louis II (the son of Louis I of Anjou) as King of Naples. Boniface IX therefore sided with Ladislaus, the son of Charles III of Naples.

Ladislaus was, however, holed up in the fortress of Gaeta with his regent-mother. They had been exiled from Naples itself and had little local support. Nevertheless Boniface IX had Ladislaus crowned as King of Naples as a counter-move to Louis II and Pope Clement VI in Avignon.

The situation on the ground was however not in favour of Ladislaus of Naples. When Louis II invaded he managed to take Naples itself and the surrounding area, while Ladislaus held onto the outer lying parts of the country. Their war for control would last nine years.

Despite having survived an attempt of poisoning which left him stuttering, Ladislaus gradually, with consistent support from Pope Boniface IX, managed to gain control of the Kingdom. In 1399 he managed to take Naples itself and Louis II gave up and returned to France.

On the death of (anti) Pope Clement VI in 1394, the French Cardinals elected Pedro Martínez de Luna y Pérez de Gotor, a Spaniard, as the new Pope in Avignon. He took the name Benedict XIII.

Support for Boniface IX was dwindling, but over and above the successes in Naples he had another ace up his sleeve. In Hungary Queen Mary had died in 1395, leaving her husband, Sigismund, with only a weak claim to the throne. Both the Pope in Rome and the King of Hungary needed a cause to boost their support and they found each other in a call for a crusade against the Ottomans - at that time laying siege to Constantinople.

The campaign is described in further details in Chapter 13, but in essence it was an ambitious attempt to chase the Ottomans out of Europe and then march on to Jerusalem. The army consisted of Hungarians French, Germans, Bulgarians, Wallachians, Venetians, Genoese and Knight Hospitallers, making up the first international army to take up arms against the Ottomans in Europe.

After some early success the campaign ended in a disastrous defeat to the Ottomans at Nikopolis in September of 1396, but despite the actual outcome of the campaign, the Pope's involvement with the crusading movement started to swing support in his favour.

In 1398 the French King, Charles VI, withdrew his support to the Pope in Avignon, leaving Benedict XIII with recognition only from Scotland, Sicily, Aragon, and Castile. Avignon came under siege by Jean Le Maingre, the Marshal of France, and in 1403 the (anti) Pope was forced to flee his bolt hole and live under the protection of Louis II who had by now abandoned his claim on Naples and had returned to Anjou. The Pope in Avignon thus no longer resided in Avignon, like the Pope in Rome had for long periods not resided in Rome.

During these same early years of the fifteenth century, a civil war in Germany had ended with the election of Rupert as King of Germany, an appointment which met the approval of Pope Boniface IX in 1403. With matters in Europe thus solved, the Pope died in April of 1404.

As it happened, there were representatives of (anti) Pope Benedict XIII in Rome at the time Pope Boniface IX died. The College of Cardinals now tried to solve the schism between the two papacies by extending an offer to Benedict XIII. If he would abdicate, then the College of Cardinals in Rome would not hold an election in isolation but rather invite the French Cardinals to participate in one single election of a new pope.

But Benedict XIII made it very clear that he would never resign, so the College of Cardinals proceeded with their own election and decided on Cosimo de' Migliorati, cardinal-priest of S. Croce in Gerusalemme, who took the name Innocent VII.

The election of the new Pope was however done in the shadow of an agreement between the Italian Cardinals that they would continue to pursue an end to the schism and, if necessary, the Pope would resign as part of an agreement.

If this worried Pope Innocent VII then it was in vain as an agreement was not reached during his reign. Indeed, he proactively took actions which for all intents and purposes ensured that an agreement could not be had.

A new public revolt inspired by the *Ghibelline* parties in Rome erupted following the election of the new Pope. To restore order, Ladislaus of Naples intervened militarily and as a reward for his services the Pope promised him that he would not enter into any agreement with the Pope in Avignon which included a change in sovereignty in Naples. With (anti) Pope Benedict XIII currently living under the protection of Ladislaus of Naples' only contender, Louis II, this effectively blocked any further negotiations which probably suited Innocent VII just fine.

But Pope Innocent VII showed to be a poor picker of allies. In an act of blatant nepotism, he elevated his relative Ludovico Migliorati - a renowned mercenary - to cardinal. The new cardinal soon showed his warlike character by capturing eleven members of the rebellious Roman *Ghibelline* faction and had them very publicly executed and their bodies thrown in the streets. This aroused the Roman mobs, and the Pope had to flee to Viterbo pursued by an angry mob which killed thirty members of his retinue.

In the meantime, his ally Ladislaus of Naples had occupied part of Rome, including Castel Sant'Angelo. Officially he was protecting the Pope's interests, but in reality, he used the occasion to conduct raids both inside Rome and in the surrounding area. When calls by the Pope to stop this activity fell on deaf ears, the Pope went as far as excommunicating Ladislaus of Naples. This did the trick and it was Ladislaus who once again restored order in Rome, enabling the Pope to return in the beginning of 1406.

While all this was happening Pope Innocent VII had at surface level tried to establish a meeting to sort out the schism. He was strongly encouraged to do so by most of the dominant rulers in Europe, but in reality he postponed more than he organised and as Benedict XIII also had no real desire to negotiate, the two Pope's basically accused each other for the lack of progress neither party had any interest in actively pursuing. If you feel that sounds familiar, then you have probably been watching the News recently.

In November 1406 Pope Innocent VII died in Rome. His papacy had been short but eventful. The College of Cardinals in Rome now elected Angelo Correr, cardinal-priest of San Marco, who took the name Gregory XII.

Like his predecessor the new Pope was elected on the condition that he would vacate his seat if a compromise agreement could be reached for a unified papacy, as well as a promise to not appoint any new cardinals.

Also like his predecessor Pope Gregory XII had no real intentions about reconciliation with Avignon, but pressure was building.

The rulers of Europe as well as the cardinals on both sides had had enough and they pressed the Pope for a resolution to the schism. Instead, the Pope withdrew from Rome and set up base at Lucca, where he, despite his promises of the opposite, proceeded to appoint four new cardinals, all relatives belonging to the Correr clan. He then ordered his cardinals not to leave the city.

But seven cardinals managed to get out and they formed the core of a group of cardinals who in cooperation with French renegade cardinals - and with support of Charles VI of France - set up a conclave at Pisa in 1408 to which they invited both the competing popes.

Neither Pope came, and the conclave thus proceeded to depose them both. They then elected Petros Philargos de Candia as new pope under the name of Alexander V.

Needless to say, that the respective Popes now excommunicated each other, but as it was, the situation of having two popes had now escalated into having three popes, none of whom could claim any real supremacy.

Interestingly, this very first decade of the fifteenth century was the time where the Ottomans were at their weakest, going through their own interregnum following Bayezid I's defeat to Timur in 1400 and the following war of succession. But as the Pope, or rather Popes, were busy fighting each other, there was no room for an initiative which could very possibly have seen the Ottomans expelled from Europe.

As it was fairly clear that the Church could not solve the matter by its own means, a new initiative was taken in 1414. The primary driver was

Part 6 - The Pope and the Crusader Knights

Sigismund of Hungary, and the council which took place at Constance in Germany had the support of all the European rulers.

At the Council of Constance there were no more compromises. It was made clear that an Ecumenical Council held the absolute power of the Church, even if it was in disagreement with the Pope (a view dubbed *Conciliarism*). As a consequence, all three popes were officially asked to resign, however, only Gregory XII did.

Benedict XIII did not appear and did not resign. He eventually fled to Aragon where he maintained his claim to the papacy until his death in 1423.

John XXIII - who had replaced Alexander V on his death in 1410 - fled from the Council, but he was captured and brought back. Having been deposed he was evicted of a range of wrong doings after which he was imprisoned. He was eventually freed and given the title of Cardinal Bishop of Frascati which he held for a short time before his death in 1419.

As a reward for his compliance, (former) Pope Gregory XII was now made Cardinal Bishop of Porto and Santa Ruffina, the second most senior position in the Church and as no new pope was actually elected, he thus maintained de-facto control over the Church even after his abdication, Furthermore the cardinals appointed by him were re-confirmed.

When he died in 1417, the Council - which was still in session - elected Otto Colonna, Cardinal-Deacon of San Giorgio al Velabro and a Roman noble, who took the name Martin V. With his election the schism finally ended and there was only one Pope, who resided in Rome. There were short-lived after-shocks following the death of the former Benedict XIII in 1423, where no less than two anti-popes named Benedict XIV and one named Clement VIII tried to claim his inheritance. These initiatives were however local manifestations (in Aragon) without any general recognition or consequences.

Pope Martin V was in a precarious situation. His papacy depended on the support of both the Cardinals and the dominant rulers of Europe and both parties wanted reform; that is to say concessions, from the Pope.

But Martin V was a sly diplomat and rather than agreeing to general concessions he negotiated individual deals with the dominant kings and never formally agreed to the view that the Ecumenical Council held the absolute power over the Church.

Martin V finally agreed to exterminate the Hussites, which gave Sigismund of Hungary the necessary pretext to intervene in Bohemia, and after six months of intense negotiations he finally left the Council in May of 1418.

The Italy that Martin V returned to was in a state of utter confusion and upheaval. If there was any papal authority left it was only in Rome itself. The rest of northern Italy and the Papal States were held by the powerful city-states, various petty princes and opportunistic fortune-seekers like the renowned mercenary Braccio da Montone who fought for whomever paid him and, in the process, managed to build a principality for himself.

The Pope first went to Florence where he started a range of negotiations in order to secure the integrity of the Papal States. In Naples, King Ladislaus had died all the way back in 1414 and his sister, Joanna II of Naples, had been involved in a series of conflicts to hold on to her title. Pope Martin V gave his blessing to Joanna II's crowning and thus secured peace with his most powerful potential enemy. Peace was made with Braccio da Montone and other petty lords and finally in September of 1420, could the Pope proceed to Rome with a reasonable amount of temporal control of his domains.

But even though the Queen of Naples had sought the support of the Pope, she had no intention of helping him financially, so Pope Martin V therefore changed his stance on Naples. Once again, he lent his support to the French contender for the throne of Naples, declaring Louis III of Anjou the rightful king.

With papal support, Louis III entered Naples and sent Joanna II into exile. But the Pope had no intention of just letting matters be in Naples, he wanted something for his effort, so he invited both warring parties to negotiations in Rome. Smelling a rat, Joanna II declared Alfonso V of Aragon (the protector of the deposed Pope Benedict XIII) as her heir and the Spaniards then moved on Naples where they expelled the French.

After a short while the relations between Joanna II and Alfonso V soured (when he had her lover murdered) and she now agreed to appoint Louis III as her heir. Alfonso V had to return to Aragon, leaving the stage to Joanna II and her new heir settled in Calabria. However, he died before Joanna II and never became king.

Part of the terms which had been set by the Council of Constance was that a new Ecumenical Council was to be held every five years. Although he had no desire of such, Pope Martin V did call for a council to be held at Pavia in 1423. It was then moved to Sienna due to an outbreak of plague. The Council was held with little enthusiasm from either the Pope or the participating clergy and the bigger issue of *Conciliarism* was left untouched.

A new Council was agreed, to be held in Basel, but it took the Pope seven years before he finally called it in February of 1431. Compared to the Pope who had left the Council of Constance in 1418, Martin V was in a much stronger position. He had reasonable control of the Papal States and there was peace in Naples. He may well have felt that this was a good time to take on the confrontation in regards the supremacy inside the Church, but shortly after he had opened the Council he died.

Even though the Council in principle continued, the College of Cardinals proceeded to elect a new pope. Their choice fell on Gabriele Condulmer, Cardinal Priest of the Basilica di Santa Maria in Trastevere and with dynastic links to both Roman and Venetian nobility. He took the name Eugene IV.

The new Pope, through a delegate, re-opened the Council of Basel in June 1431, but it was, by this time, ill attended and by December 1431 the Pope dissolved the Council, with the promise to call a new council at Bologna eighteen months later.

This move may have seemed reasonable given the false start of the Council of Basel, but it also indicated a papal prerogative which did not sit well with supporters of *Conciliarism*. As a consequence, the Council opposed its own dissolution and rather confirmed the Council's rights over the Pope.

Looking for allies, the Pope now agreed to the crowning of Sigismund of Hungary as Holy Roman Emperor and he was crowned in Rome in May of 1433. The new Emperor now brokered a deal by which the Council of Basel was re-started and the Pope promised to appoint a new chairman.

However, in Rome the Pope's situation turned bad. He had, from the start of his papacy, made a concerted effort to oust members of the Colonna family from important church-positions given to them by their kinsman Pope Martin V and a war between Florence and Milan now spilled over into Rome. The Pope had to flee, disguised as a monk.

He eventually took up residence in Bologna and the warring parties agreed to a truce. By means of a mercenary army the Pope regained control of the Papal States, although he still could not securely return to Rome, and by January 1438 he was ready to once again commence battle with the Council which still was in session in Basel.

Rather than attend the Council, the Pope instead called an alternative council in Ferrara, which was later moved to Florence due to an outbreak of plague. At this council the Pope excommunicated the participants of the Council of Basel. In return the Council of Basel excommunicated and deposed Eugene IV and elected an alternative pope, Amadeus VIII, Duke of Savoy, who took the name Felix V.

Although the Council of Basel probably counted on the support of the dominant kings of Europe, their support turned out to be weak, eventually completely lacking. As much as they supported the principles of *Conciliarism* - which gave them significant advantages in regard to income from Church property - they had little appetite for a new schism in the Western Church.

The Pope now started a flurry of diplomatic activities to secure his position. In Constantinople John VIII Palaiologos was desperately seeking military support in his struggle against the Ottomans and when he had nowhere else to turn he looked for help from the Pope. What he offered in return was nothing less than a reunification of the Eastern and Western Church, an achievement which would significantly boost Pope Eugene IV's standings.

The Council of Florence approved the reunification in 1439 and although it never became effective due to resistance from the Byzantine population, it marked a turning point in the Pope's fortunes.

16 - The Pope

Frederick III, King of Germany, openly declared his support for Eugene IV in 1440, and eventually others followed.

His success in terms of Constantinople was followed up by a call for a crusade against the Ottomans, but his call only reverberated in eastern Europe. Lead by his own legate (the warlike Cardinal Guiliano Cesarini) and Wladyslaw III of Hungary and Poland, a multinational force set out to give battle to the Ottomans in the summer of 1443. The final result (as covered in Chapter 13) was a crushing defeat at Varna, but as far as the Pope was concerned it was just another piece in the puzzle which aimed to put him back in control.

In Naples Joanna II had died in 1435. After the premature death of her declared heir, Louis III of Anjou, his brother Rene of Anjou, had been appointed heir, but he was impoverished and could put up little resistance when Alfonso V of Aragon invaded the Kingdom in 1441. Pope Eugene IV now moved to approve Alfonso V's title as King of Naples, ensuring support from yet another powerful ruler.

After a short war with Milan, which concluded in a peace-settlement, the Pope was finally able to re-enter Rome in September of 1443. His last diplomatic success led to Frederick III declaring the Council of Basel dissolved in 1447. Eugene IV then died in February of that same year.

With papal supremacy once again re-established, the College of Cardinals proceeded to elect Tommaso Parentucelli, Cardinal-Priest of Santa Susanna, who took the name Nicholas V, a name also used by a previous anti-pope.

The Council of Basel had, after its dissolution, re-convened at Lausanne, but it soon became clear that it had lost its support. As a consequence, it decided to dissolve itself in 1449 and (anti) Pope Felix V resigned. He was made a Cardinal for his efforts and lived until 1451.

His seat secure, Pope Nicholas V concentrated his efforts on Rome itself. The city had gradually fallen into decay, and he started a range of projects for its renewal. The Ancient aqueducts of Agrippa were restored and emptied into a massive basin which would eventually become the Trevi Fountain. He then started a complete rebuild of the Vatican and St. Peter's Cathedral as well as a range of other public works.

However the defining moment of Nicholas V's papacy would not happen in Rome, rather it would happen in Constantinople, the age-old competitor for supremacy.

In 1451 Sultan Murad II died and his son, Mehmed II, took the throne of the Ottoman Empire. By 1453 he had done the unthinkable; conquered Constantinople.

As much as Constantinople had been a constant thorn in the side of Rome, it nevertheless represented one of the oldest centres of Christianity, not less so when surrounded by the Muslim forces of the Ottomans.

The Emperor, Constantine XI Palaiologos, was well aware of the imminent danger from Mehmed II and he had sent pledges for help to all and sundry. One of the few who reacted was Pope Nichols V, who saw a chance of once again reunifying the two Christian churches.

In May 1452 he sent Cardinal Isidore of Kiev and 200 archers to Constantinople. The archers were there to defend the city; the Cardinal was there to negotiate the unification.

The Emperor had no choice but to accept the supremacy of Rome, but his population at large refused to accept the union. They boycotted the church of Hagia Sofia, which was consecrated as a Catholic church, and the whole affair did little to unite a population in desperate need of a union which was much more practical than theological.

Furthermore, the Pope paid for three (Genoese) ships loaded with provisions and men. They left for Constantinople, but did not arrive before the siege began. Along the way they had met up with a fourth ship, this one from Constantinople, crewed by Italians, and full of corn purchased in Sicily.

After a much famed sea-battle on 20 April 1453 (covered in Chapter 4) the ships managed to break the Ottoman blockade and land in Constantinople, but their effect was that of too little too late and Constantinople fell to the Ottomans on 29 May 1453.

Perhaps a more war-like pope could have united the European kings to come to the rescue of Constantinople, but it is unlikely. In any case Pope Nicholas V was not a warrior but rather a lover of arts. In many ways he laid the foundation for the Renaissance which would flourish after his death on the arrival of scholars and artists from Greece in the wake of the Ottoman conquests.

The last years of Pope Nicholas V's reign were dominated by his attempts to pacify the ever-rivalling powers in Italy and vague attempts at raising interest in a renewed crusade against the Ottomans. But his efforts were in vain and he died in March of 1455, by all accounts a bitter man.

The College of Cardinals struggled to elect a new pope, but finally they agreed on a compromise, Alfons de Borja (pronounced 'Borgia' in Italian), a Spaniard who had been instrumental in the negotiations between Alfonso V of Aragon and Popes Martin V and Eugene IV. He took the name Callixtus III.

If Nicholas V had been a founder of the Renaissance in terms of his interest in arts, Pope Callixtus III became a founding father in terms of the nepotism that would be a trademark of the papacy for years to come.

He appointed two of his nephews as cardinals, most prominently amongst them Rodrigo de Borja, who outside the scope of this book would become one of the most famous, or infamous, popes under the name of Alexander VI.

Like his predecessor he tried to rekindle the crusading spirit, but also like his predecessor his appeals fell on deaf ears amongst the monarchs of Europe.

16 - The Pope

A defining moment of his papacy was the Ottoman Siege of Belgrade in 1456. Once again, the Pope preached crusade and once again it was ignored. To boost his call he decreed the ringing of church bells at noon in support of Belgrade, but the only effect his efforts had was a small number of independent volunteers, many of them peasants, who gathered around Janos Hunyadi and eventually secured the Christian victory in front of Belgrade. He died in August of 1458 after just over three years as pope.

In his place the College of Cardinals elected Enea Silvio Bartolomeo Piccolomini, Bishop of Siena and a much-experienced diplomat. He took the name Pius II. His reign would also be short, but very eventful.

Sultan Mehmed II - not called 'Fatih' ('the Conqueror') - had turned out to be far from the dim-witted boy-sultan that the world had initially perceived him to be.

Despite his defeat outside Belgrade in 1456 he did not give up or slow down. In 1459 he annexed Serbia. In 1460 he cleaned up in Greece and annexed the Morea. In 1461 he annexed the pocket-empire of Trebizond and in 1462 he invaded Wallachia following Vlad III Dracula's raid into Bulgaria the winter before.

The Ottomans were now a clear and present danger and Pope Pius II did not sit idle. Rather, he tried to once and for all unify the rulers of Europe and initiate a crusade.

He quickly threw his support behind Ferdinand I of Aragon who was involved in yet another fight for the throne of Naples. Aragon was important in the Pope's plans as they had pro-actively supported Skanderbeg in Albania and had ambitions to establish themselves in the Balkans.

Next the Pope called for a council to be held at Mantua where he wished to discuss a crusade with representatives from the Kingdoms of western Europe.

The Council started in May of 1459 and lasted until January 1460. Very few of the participants had any appetite for a crusade, but nevertheless a crusade was called, and it was to last for three years. While the Council was in session, Mehmed II annexed Serbia.

The only countries that showed any proactive interest at the time were Hungary and Wallachia. King Matthias I of Hungary needed both papal support for his weak kingship and money to buy the Crown of St. Stephen from Frederick III. He got both, although the promised crusade never happened. Voivode Vlad III Dracula in Wallachia started his own crusade when he raided into Bulgaria in the winter of 1461. The year after he was chased out of Wallachia by Mehmed II and put under house arrest by King Matthias I. He got much praise from the Pope but lost his crown.

The real key to a new crusade was Venice. She had simply refused to participate in any meaningful aggression against the Ottomans as her primary interest was the continuous flow of trade. But when war broke out between

Venice and the Ottomans in 1463, the Venetians were suddenly willing to listen to the Pope.

An alliance was now formed and a grand plan agreed. Venice, Hungary, Albania and Philip the Good, Duke of Burgundy were the participants, under overall control of the Pope.

The campaign would come out of Albania. Skanderbeg would muster an army of 20,000 men, including a Venetian contingent, and another 20,000 men, mainly paid for by the Pope, would be assembled at Ancona and sailed across to Albania on Venetian ships. Furthermore, embassies were sent to Uzun Hasan, the Karamanids and the Tatars of the Crimea to try to orchestrate a combined attack from the East and the West.

The Venetians held their end of the bargain and delivered troops to Skanderbeg. He in turn started attacking the Ottomans in Macedonia while he waited for the second half of the crusaders to arrive.

They started to trickle into Ancona during the spring and summer of 1464, but they were a motley crew of mercenaries and fortune-seekers. When no pay was immediately forthcoming, they started to dwindle away, some selling their weapons to pay for their trip home.

The Pope arrived at Ancona in June. He was sick with fever but insisted on going anyway, ready to take personal command of the expedition. This demand was probably one of the reasons why the Venetian Doge was less than keen to get going and it was not until 12 August that the Venetian fleet arrived in Ancona. Three days later the Pope died, having been able to do nothing but watch proceedings from a window. Three days later the Venetians left for home, where the crusader fleet was disarmed and put in storage. The crusade came to nothing and Skanderbeg was left to fight the Ottomans on his own. By then Mehmed II had annexed most of Bosnia, and was gradually pulling the Venetians apart.

The College of Cardinals now elected Pietro Barbo, Archpriest of the Vatican Basilica, who took the name Paul II.

The new Pope was a Venetian, which was probably not a coincidence as it was in the Church's interest to keep the Venetians engaged in the battle against the Ottomans. He was also enormously wealthy and promised to buy a villa in the country for each of the cardinals if he became pope. The election of Paul II was subject to a range of terms. The Pope was not to appoint more than one 'cardinal-nephew' (a term used for clearly nepotistic appointments), the number of cardinals was to be kept at twenty-four, a Council was to be held every three years and the Pope could not leave Rome without consent from the College of Cardinals.

If the Cardinals thought that they had secured a pliant pope who would continue the war against the Ottomans, they were wrong.

Pope Paul II soon turned into a recluse. It was nearly impossible to get an appointment with him and when someone did it was often at night. He ignored the conditions to which he had agreed and appointed a range of new cardinals as he saw fit, often in secret, their appointments only disclosed at a later date (some even only by his testament).

Treasure was being collected throughout the Christian World in order to support the war against the Ottomans, but the Pope horded the treasure instead of using it for the purpose it was intended for. The good thing about it was that on his death, Pope Paul II left a vast treasury. The bad thing was that no progress was made in the war.

It was not that the Pope could not spend money. He collected art and antiquities and built the impressive Palazzo Venezia in Rome for his personal use, but apart from continued financial support for King Matthias I of Hungary - who spent some of the money to buy his crown and some to campaign in northern Bosnia - little was spent to fight to the Ottomans.

Pope Paul II died in 1471 from a heart-attack. Some say he had the attack due to excessive eating, others that he died while sodomizing a page-boy. The truth is unknown.

In the seven years of Paul II's reign, Mehmed II had taken the opportunity to neutralize the Karamanids, consolidate his conquest of most of Bosnia and constantly press on in Albania where Skanderbeg had died in 1468. He had also continued the war with Venice, which was not going the way of the Venetians.

On Pope Paul II's death the College of Cardinals elected Francesco della Rovere, Cardinal-priest of Basilica of San Pietro in Vincoli, who took the name Sixtus IV.

The new Pope was a true Italian Renaissance Pope, in all the ways we can stereotype such. He was a patron of artists and artisans, commissioning amongst other things the Sistine Chapel. He made a range of nepotistic appointments, which made his family one of the wealthiest in Rome, and he lived a life of indulgence, some say involving a passion for beautiful young men.

But apart from a brief involvement in a mainly Venetian initiative, which saw a small fleet paid for by the Pope participate in a campaign in 1472 which achieved little but a pirate-style attack on Smyrna, he did little to take the fight to the Ottomans. As it happens, in the end it was the Ottomans who came to him.

Another stereotypical papal trait was the involvement in Italian politics and an attempt to expand the Papal States. One such involvement was the attempt to murder the ruler of Florence, Lorenzo de'Medici, and his brother Giuliano in 1478. Although the Pope was not directly involved, he provided his carefully worded blessing to the undertaking and, subsequent to the failed coup (which saw Giuliano dead and the coup-makers gruesomely executed), put Florence under interdict for two years.

King Ferdinand I of Naples initially sided with the Pope against the de'Medici and a combined Papal and Neapolitan army laid siege to Florence. But when Lorenzo de'Medici - at great personal risk - made a personal appearance in Naples, he managed to change the allegiance of King Ferdinand I. The Pope was furious and henceforth considered Naples an enemy.

Venice had fought a long and disastrous war against the Ottomans since 1463 and finally, in 1479, had to sue for peace. The war had all but ruined the Republic and the terms of the peace seriously reduced the merchant-city's influence in the eastern Mediterranean Sea. Italy was thus both split and weakened when Mehmed II decided to make his move.

The Sultan's appetite for Italy was not a surprise. If we go all the way back to the beginning of this book, and the beginning of Mehmed II's rule, you may remember the words from the Venetian Giacomo de Languschi, who says of the young Mehmed II:

'He speaks three languages, Turkish, Greek and Slavic. He is of great pains to learn the geography of Italy and to inform himself of the places where Anchises and Aeneas and Antenor landed, where the seat of the Pope is and that of the emperor and how many kingdoms there are in Europe. He possesses a map of Europe with the countries and provinces. He learns of nothing with greater interest and enthusiasm than the geography of the world and military affairs; he burns with desire to dominate; he is a shrewd investigator of conditions. It is with such a man that we Christians have to deal.' ... 'Today, he says, the times have changed, and declare that he will advance from East to West as in former times the Westerners advanced into the Orient. There must, he says, be only one empire, one faith and one sovereignty in the world.'

Although seemingly spreading his conquests far and wide, Mehmed II had never forgotten his ambition to spread his empire into Europe, and - with Constantinople already in his hands - to first and foremost take possession of the remaining throne of Christianity; that of the Pope. It was surely also in Mehmed II's mind that whereas little love was lost between the rulers of Europe, the Pope was the only entity who could potentially unify them against the Ottomans, even if previous attempts to do so had been less than successful.

Mehmed II's early attempt to break through at Belgrade in 1456 had not been successful and he had therefore worked according to a longer strategic plan. He had effectively eliminated the Ottoman weakness of being vulnerable to a combined attack from the East and the West by getting rid of the Karamanids and the White Sheep as well as any remnants of the Byzantine Empire. He had subdued the Balkans and he had grown an inferior Ottoman navy into a power that could take on even the superior Venetians and Genoese.

But the road to Italy was still difficult. Even with superiority in the Balkans he would still have to fight his way through northern Bosnia and (Hungarian) Croatia before even reaching Venice should he go the land-route. Sending raiding parties along this route, as he had done during the war

16 - The Pope

with Venice, was one thing, but moving a full army was another venture which he was not ready to risk. The only road to Italy was thus by sea and in that context his long fight for Albania was crucial, as was the war with Venice.

The Albanian port of Vlorë - which was under Ottoman control - was only 130 kilometres from the Italian port of Bari and it had been a key strategic objective of the costly campaigns in Albania. But even with control of Vlorë the Venetians were still a force to be reckoned with in the Adriatic Sea.

It was therefore of the utmost importance that Venice was somehow neutralized, or an Ottoman fleet was unlikely to ever complete the trip from Vlorë to Italy.

After sixteen years of war with the Ottomans the Venetians were unwilling to renew the war, and the general situation in Italy further encouraged them to even lend passive support to the Sultan's ambitions.

The Venetians feared the influence of King Ferdinand I of Naples, who had rather open ambitions for an expansion of his domains into northern Italy, and their bailo in Istanbul whispered into the Sultan's ears that as far as the Republic was concerned, Brindisi, Taranto and Otranto were old Byzantine possessions and thus rightfully belonged to the ruler of Constantinople.

That was enough of a guarantee of neutrality for Mehmed II to finally initiate the execution of his long-standing plans for a move on Italy and the Pope in Rome.

In the summer of 1480, an Ottoman fleet assembled in Vlorë. It consisted of 140 vessels and carried around 20,000 troops. The invaders were under the command of Gedik Ahmed Pasha and their original destination was Brindisi. Intelligence obtained from a captured merchant had however revealed that whereas Brindisi was heavily fortified, the port-city of Otranto further south was not, so Gedik Ahmed Pasha changed his plans and on 28 July the fleet left Vlorë.

A Venetian fleet was at that time stationed just off Corfu and was able to follow the progress of the Ottoman fleet. It gave chase and shadowed the Ottomans, but when it became clear that they were going west - and thus not towards Venice - the Venetians broke off the chase and returned to their station at Corfu.

First a small contingent of cavalry was offloaded at the castle of Roca and while they made their way towards Otranto, the main army was offloaded. The initial campaign was masterfully executed. The Ottomans quickly rounded up all the people and cattle they could, the latter to complement their relatively light provisions. A sortie from Otranto managed to free many of the captives, but soon the Ottomans stood under the walls of the city.

As per tradition the city was given the option to surrender, but when that was refused the Ottomans let loose with all they had. Cannon had been brought over from Albania and a violent bombardment of the city began. Only lightly defended, and without cannon to counter the Ottoman artillery, the city fell on 11 August. The aftermath was bloody.

When the Ottomans entered the city, it was not just sacked, but the entire male population over the age of fifteen was slaughtered. The Archbishop of Otranto, Stefano Pendinelli, with many of his clergy, was murdered in front of the altar of the Cathedral. 800 selected captives were marched to a nearby hill and asked to convert to Islam, when they refused, they were beheaded.

Of the city's population of 22,000, 12,000 were killed and another 5,000 marched off to be sold as slaves. 813 of the victims were made martyrs as late as May 2013 and their remains are buried in the Cathedral of Otranto.

Having put down a marker and sent a clear signal to the other cities as to his intentions, Gedik Ahmed Pasha now ravaged the countryside and made raids on Lecce and Brindisi further north and Taranto further to the west.

The population fled in front of the marauders. Anyone who could get out of the area did so, and this started to present a problem to the Ottomans. They had brought only light provisions with them and had expected to live off the land. But with the peasants gone - and in many cases their livestock with them - there was soon a shortage of food.

The Ottoman invasion had of course not gone unnoticed by the Italian lords either. King Ferdinand I of Naples had managed to muster an army and sent it off to camp in the vicinity of Otranto. It did not have the strength to attack, but it at least kept the Ottomans pinned on the coast. He also sent a fleet round the southern tip of Italy, but it arrived too late to interfere with a partial Ottoman withdrawal to Vlorë. The remaining Ottomans, around 6,500 strong, entrenched themselves in Otranto and waited for supplies and reinforcements as winter set in.

Gedik Ahmed Pasha had followed the troops which were returned to Vlorë and he made it hastily overland to Istanbul to consult with the Sultan. He needed provisions and men and the Sultan provided both.

Supplies to last for three years as well as fresh troops were ferried across to Otranto, partly by Venetian vessels, and furthermore a message from the Sultan was given to the commander in Otranto, Heyreddin Bey.

When the Neapolitans demanded his surrender - and reparations amounting to 800,000 gold ducats - he blatantly refused and furthermore relayed the Sultan's message to the Italians; in the coming spring the Sultan would personally appear with an army of 200,000 men with which he intended to invade all of Italy!

It did not take long for the message to reach Rome. Indeed, by the time it got there it had been marginally improved to say that the Sultan was already at Vlorë with the main Ottoman army.

Initiatives had already been taken to form some kind of unified response to the Ottoman invasion but now panic hit. The Pope was considering fleeing Rome, but the King of Naples tried to instil some kind of control over the situation, He flatly declared that unless he got help, he would concede to the Ottomans demands and hand over the regions of Brindisi, Otranto and Taranto to the Sultan.

With the danger now looming clear, the factions finally came together. The Pope, much to his regret, declared his support for the King of Naples and sent him as much money as he could. New taxes were approved for the purpose and an official alliance was made between Naples, The Pope, Florence, Genoa, Hungary and Milan. The Venetians refused to participate; they argued that they had singlehanded felt the sharp end of war with the Ottomans without any help from the others and that they had no intentions of breaking their peace with Mehmed II.

Fleets were prepared to lay siege to Otranto and the Hungarians sent a contingent of ground-troops to Naples, but in the end it was not the hastily prepared and uneasy alliance which defeated the Ottomans, it was the Ottomans themselves.

As believable as the Sultan's message was, given his track record, it was a bluff. Gedik Ahmed Pasha had on his visit to Istanbul found the Sultan seriously ill and in May 1481, rather than appear in Italy ahead of his army, Mehmed II died. He had long been suffering from gout and a hard life split between military campaigns and excessive living had put an end to the Conqueror at the age of forty-nine.

The death of Mehmed II was the prelude to a civil war of succession in the Ottoman Empire, and in the meantime the troops in Otranto were left to their own devices. Their situation soon became unsustainable and in September an agreement was reached by which the remaining Ottomans were allowed free passage back to Albania.

As he had intended to do, Sultan Mehmed II had come for the Pope, but he had left it too late. Had he lived just a few more years, and had he been physically capable of fulfilling his promise to bring the main Ottoman army to Italy, then the world we live in would possibly look very different than the way it looks today.

The Papal States of the middle-ages have gone. The nation state belonging to the Church maintained its existence - apart from a few years during Napoleon - until the unification of Italy in 1861, although formally it was only dissolved in 1870. After nearly six decades without an independent state, the Church was given its own nation state back by Benito Mussolini in 1929, albeit that state is the smallest in the world and consists only of a few city-blocks around St. Peter's Cathedral in Rome.

The Pope still reigns in the Catholic Church. As I write this - in August 2015 - the Pope is Francis (born Jorge Mario Bergoglio), the same pope who canonized the Martyrs of Otranto more than 500 years after their gruesome death at the hands of the Ottomans.

Part 6 - The Pope and the Crusader Knights

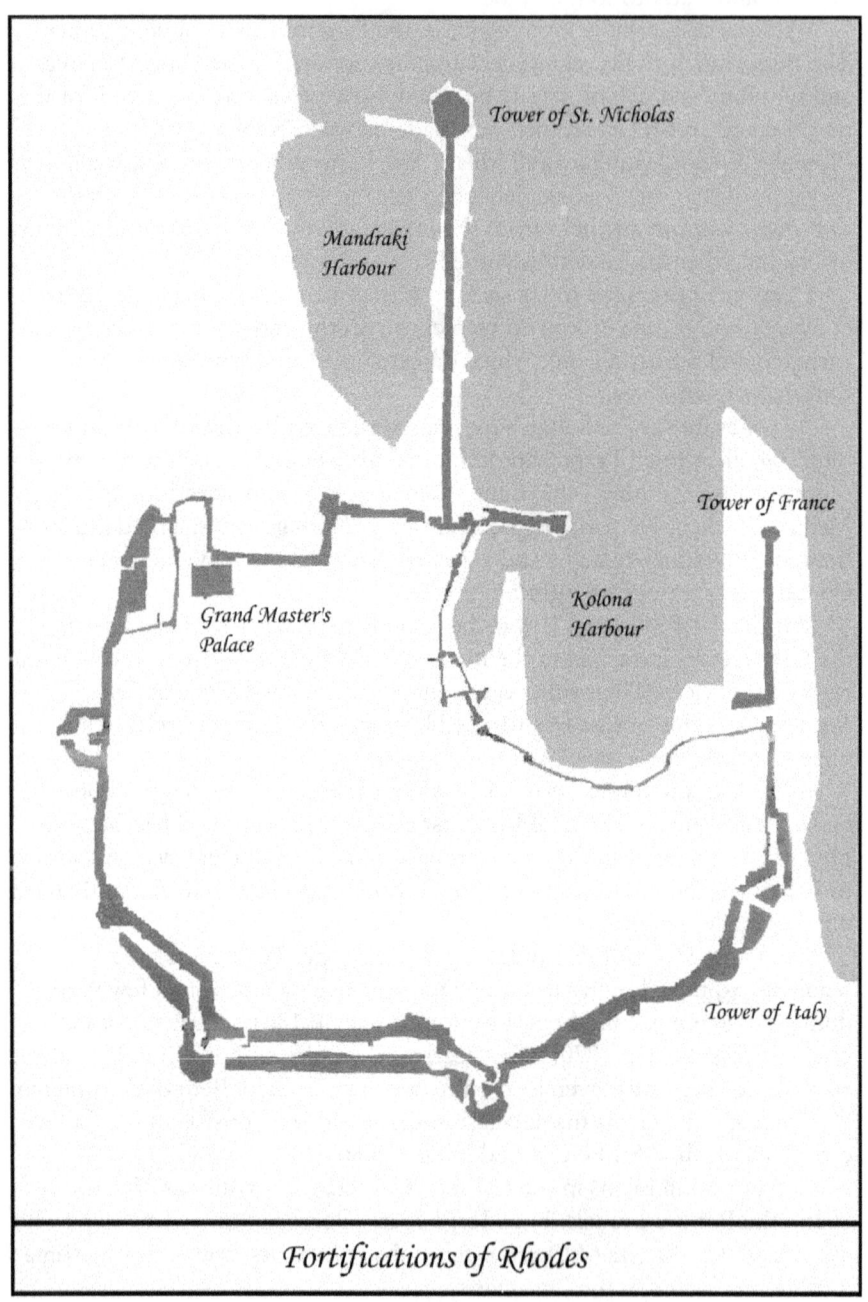

Fortifications of Rhodes

17 - THE CRUSADER KNIGHTS

Part 6 - The Pope and the Crusader Knights

CRITICAL TIMELINE

Year	Event	Involved Parties
1060s	Hospital of St. John established in Jerusalem	Amalfi Egypt
1099	First Crusade conquers Jerusalem	Jerusalem
1113	Gerard Thom obtains papal blessing for the Religious Order of St. John	Hospitallers The Pope
1129	Knights Templar becomes religious order	Knights Templar The Pope
1140s	Knights Hospitaller build Krak de Chevalier castle	Knights Hospitaller
1186	Knights Hospitaller buys Marqab castle	Knights Hospitaller
1198	Teutonic Knights get papal blessing as religious order	Teutonic Knights
1271	Krak de Chevalier is lost	Knights Hospitaller Egypt
1285	Marqab is lost	Knights Hospitaller Egypt
1291	Fall of Acre	Knights Hospitaller Egypt
1307	Knights Templars are arrested in France	Knights Templar France
1309	Knights Hospitaller conquer Rhodes	Knights Hospitaller
1312	Knights Templar are dissolved and their assets given to the Knights Hospitaller	Knights Hospitaller Knights Templar The Pope
1315	The Knights Hospitaller buys Kos from Venice	Knights Hospitaller Venice
1402	Castle at Smyrna is lost to Timurids	Knights Hospitaller Timurids
1404	New castle is founded at Halicarnassus	Knights Hospitaller Ottomans
1440	Mamluk attack on Rhodes	Knights Hospitaller Egypt
1480	Ottoman attack on Rhodes	Knights Hospitaller Ottomans
1523	Knights Hospitaller expelled from Rhodes	Knights Hospitaller Ottomans
1565	Ottoman siege of Malta	Knights Hospitaller Ottomans

17 - The Crusader Knights

While Gedik Ahmed Pasha led the invasion of Italy in 1480, Sultan Mehmed II had a second military venture running in parallel; that of expelling the last crusader knights from their island fortress of Rhodes.

The notion of crusader knights was something of an anachronism at the end of the fifteenth century. The crusader states of the Holy Land had finally collapsed in 1291, but the Knights Hospitaller - at that time also known as the Knights of Rhodes - had outlived the crusades and were still an enemy to be taken serious.

There had been a hospital in Jerusalem, caring for sick pilgrims from before the crusades started. The first hospital possibly dates back as far as the seventh century, but the hospital that stood when the First Crusade brought about the Latin Conquest of Jerusalem in 1099 was from the 1060s. It was run by Benedictine monks and financed by the merchant-city of Amalfi.

Shortly after the Conquest of Jerusalem an individual named Gerard Thom, who, according to some sources, was himself from Amalfi, arrived in Jerusalem. Here he became the Guardian of the hospital.

The exact reasons why Gerard Thom decided to form a separate religious order based on the hospital is unknown, but a couple of possible reasons should be mentioned.

The First Crusade may have had a loosely defined plan for winning the war, but it had no plan for winning the peace. The moment the - mainly Norman - knights were in control of the Holy Land, the area became thick with politics and intrigue. It is very possible that this prevented any effective running of the hospital and that Gerard sought to officially put the operation directly under papal control.

It is also possible that Gerard realized that the only way to raise the necessary funds to run the hospital, and indeed expand it in line with growing demand, was to have direct control of the income rather than have to go through Amalfi and/or the Benedictines.

No matter his motivation, Gerard applied to the Pope for his sanction of a new and separate religious order called the Religious Order of St. John. In 1113 Pope Paschal II granted his approval of the new order, headed by Gerard Thom who would also be known as 'the Blessed Gerard'.

The new Order soon became very popular and donations poured in, many donations taking the form of property throughout Europe from which the hospital could maintain a steady income.

The Order's purpose was to care for and protect Christian pilgrims in the Holy Land, but at that time that care and protection was purely humanitarian rather than military.

Part 6 - The Pope and the Crusader Knights

That particular gap, the military protection of pilgrims, was noticed by a small group of Norman knights who had arrived in Jerusalem shortly after the conquest. The group was led by Hugues de Payens and consisted of him and eight other knights all believed to be his relatives.

They probably also found themselves in the situation of wanting 'to do something', but got caught up in politics and so to get out of this situation they took a page from Gerard Thom's book and improved it further.

First, they approached King Baldwin II of Jerusalem. They asked for his permission to form an order of knights with the specific purpose of providing armed escort to pilgrims. The situation in the Kingdom of Jerusalem was such that even though Jerusalem itself was safe, the surrounding areas were not, and it was common that pilgrims on their way to Jerusalem were attacked, robbed and sometimes killed by roaming bandits.

King Baldwin II liked the idea and granted the knights rights as a noble order in 1120. As a favour he provided them with quarters in the royal palace on the Temple Mount in the captured and converted Al-Aqsa Mosque. From this they eventually got to be known as the Knights Templar.

But the Knights Templar still had the problem of being subject to the King of Jerusalem and thus subject to local politics. To avoid this, they developed the idea of 'fighting monks', i.e. an order which was both knights and monks at the same time.

The idea was unique, but very applicable to the fluid situation in the Holy Land and it caught the attention, and strong support, of Bernard of Clairvaux, the influential Abbot of Clairvaux. He in turn produced a set of rules for the new order and was a strong advocate for its adaptation by the Church.

Bernard's letter *'In Praise of the New Knighthood'* became a much discussed and admired work and in 1129, at the Council of Troyes, the new order obtained status as a religious order.

Like the Religious Order of St. John, the new 'Templar' order became very popular in Europe and soon received substantial financial backing, enabling it to start opening chapters - known as 'Temples' - throughout Europe and maintain substantial revenues.

But the problem of political independence still remained until Pope Innocent II in 1139 declared the Order independent of local law, answering only to the Pope, just as was the case with the Religious Order of St. John.

The two new orders obviously competed for funding and a deep hatred developed between them. To some extent the Templars had the stronger message, being novel in their combination of religion and warfare and at some time towards the middle of the twelfth century the Religious Order of St. John also adopted a military arm. They henceforth became popularly known as the Knights Hospitaller, or 'Hospitallers'.

When Jerusalem was lost in 1187, and Acre was under siege, merchants from Lübeck and Bremen decided to found a hospital specifically for

Germans and it soon became modelled on the Hospitallers and Templar, receiving papal recognition by Pope Celestine III in 1198 as religious fighting order under the name of The Order of Brothers of the German House of Saint Mary in Jerusalem, popularly known as the 'Teutonic Knights', due to their distinct German character.

The Holy Land was a unique mix of Latin residents, pilgrims, fortune-seekers and, occasionally, crusaders, surrounded by a hostile Muslim population. Many people came and went. Some were seeking peace and religious contemplation; some were seeking war. Depending on when they arrived, they might find one or both.

Although we, in the hindsight of history, see the history of the Holy Land as a series of crusades, the reality on the ground was very different. The 'crusades', i.e. organised armies arriving under the command of a capable leader, were rare and short-lived events and in daily life it was extremely difficult to rely on these external resources which may, or may not, happen to be around when military force was required.

The King of Jerusalem only had limited means to maintain an army so the knightly orders, first the Templars and Hospitallers and later the Teutonic Knights, became the de-facto standing army of the Holy Land, maintaining their political independence and thus being capable of picking their battles independently of local politics.

Following the Norman model for conquest (as also applied in newly conquered England) the Orders gradually built castles throughout the Holy Land, bases from which they could dominate the surrounding lands and maintain military presence.

The most famous castles built by the Hospitallers are Marqab and Krak des Chevaliers, both in modern day Syria. The castles were built to extreme specification and still stand today after nearly a thousand years despite having been neglected and subject to adverse weather conditions.

As the fortune of Latin rule in the Holy Land waned during the thirteenth century, the position of the knightly orders became more and more difficult. They were still immensely rich, possessing significant amounts of property, but their cause, their raison d'être, gradually fizzled out. In 1271 the Mamluk Sultan Baibars captured Krak des Chevaliers, supposedly by way of a forged letter from the Hospitallers' Grand Master that caused the Knights to surrender. In May of 1285, the castle at Marqab was also given up after a siege by the Mamluk Sultan Qalawun which saw the castle undermined by sappers and parts of the walls collapsing.

Like the Knights Templars and the Teutonic Knights, the Hospitallers were gradually driven back to Acre; the last stronghold of the Latin kingdom in the Holy Land and when that fell in 1291 the knightly orders underwent the following transition in very different ways.

The Teutonic Knights had already effectively started their migration from the Holy Land in the beginning of the thirteenth century. In 1211 they were offered a substantial area in south-eastern Transylvania by King András II of Hungary (whose wife was German). The idea was that the Teutonic Knights should strengthen the border of Hungary and help attract German ('Saxon') settlers to the area. But they soon started to act as an autonomous entity, paying little heed to their Hungarian overlord.

When King András II returned from the Fifth Crusade he was forced to sign the 'the Golden Bull', which limited his central authority and one of the issues he had to deal with to pacify his angry nobles was the Teutonic Knights. Now acting completely outside any central authority, they were expelled in 1225.

After their exit from Hungary the Teutonic Knights went on to conquer (what would become known as) Prussia, where they formed their own independent state called the *Deutschordensstaat* (State of the Teutonic Order), which was gradually extended, for example by the purchase of Estonia from Denmark in 1346.

The state gradually lost its importance as the areas around it all became Christian and had little use of a crusader state in their midst. By the fifteenth century it gradually dissolved and by the sixteenth century it ceased to exist as a religious state altogether. Prussia lived on as a secular state until the unification of Germany in 1871.

Unlike the Teutonic Order, the Templars and Hospitallers did not have a distinct national belonging. The Templars were fundamentally Norman French and the Hospitallers were originally probably Italian, but over the years the Orders had attracted so many people and so much property that they were truly international.

The Templars bought the island of Cyprus from Richard I of England following the Third Crusade, but they soon sold it on after a bloody revolt on the island had convinced them that overlordship of a nation-state island was not for them. They should have probably held on to it, for with the fall of Acre they had nowhere to go.

Initially they set up on the small island of Arwad just off the Syrian coast - with temporary headquarters in Limassol, Cyprus - but that was conquered in 1302. The Templars now spread out to various Temples in Europe, but they were particularly present in southern France, not least so in the area of Languedoc. Being very wealthy they also acted as bankers, and they lent significant amounts of money to King Philip IV of France.

Looking at the Teutonic Knights and also the growing ambitions of the Hospitallers, it is very likely that the Templars had designs on their own nation state. It has been speculated that they were looking to offer Philip IV an exchange; Languedoc for his debts, but Philip IV had found his own solution.

In a move that both removed the threat of the Templar's presence and eliminated his debts, he had the Templars arrested on 13 October 1307. With papal consent the European rulers were urged to do likewise, which some did and others did not. A show-trial followed and the Order was officially disbanded by Pope Clement V in 1312 and its (remaining) property given to the Hospitallers, adding significantly to their fortunes. In 1314 the Order's Grandmaster was burned at the stake in Paris.

In the meantime, the Hospitallers had sought refuge in Cyprus. Here they found themselves at odds with the local ruler and soon started to look for their own state. They decided on the island of Rhodes, held by the Genoese adventurer Andrea Morisco, and in 1307 (the same year the Templars were persecuted) the Hospitallers moved on Rhodes.

The invasion of Rhodes lasted two years, but eventually the Hospitallers were successful. They captured Rhodes, some of the surrounding islands, the island of Kastellorizo (Megisti) and enclaves on the Anatolian coast such as Halicarnassus (Bodrum), Smyrna (Izmir) and Telmessos (Fethiye). In 1315 they bought the island of Kos from the Venetians.

True to their Norman roots they immediately started to build castles in their new possessions. Some of the smaller islands were gradually lost - Kastellorizo for instance was lost in 1440 to the Egyptians - and the coastal town of Telmessos, with its natural harbour, was lost somewhere along the way, although nobody knows exactly when (as a side-comment, I can see the ruins of the crusader castle behind Telmessos from my window as I write this).

The castle and port at Smyrna were conquered by Tamerlane following his victory over the Ottomans in 1402. The Hospitallers lent their assistance to Sultan Mehmed I during his fight for control of the Ottomans throne and as a reward they were given permission to fortify Halicarnassus in lieu of the castle they had lost at Smyrna. In 1404 they started building a substantial castle across from their existing castle on the island of Kos. The way the Hospitallers were organised - reflecting their international character - was by division into *Langue*, or 'Tongues', consisting of knights from various countries. Each Langue was responsible for building, maintaining and manning a stretch of wall and at least one bastion. The different parts of their fortifications were therefore known by the Langue, e.g. 'the English Tower' or 'the Tower of Italy'.

The castle at Halicarnassus was a massive affair. It sat on a promontory with access from the mainland only by a drawbridge. The Hospitallers helped themselves to rock from the tomb of Mausolos - a fourth century BC ruler - and a papal decree from 1409 granting a guaranteed place in heaven for the construction workers helped things along. It still took more than three decades to complete the castle, but the work paid off when an Ottoman attack in 1453, shortly after the fall of Constantinople, was repelled.

Whereas the castle at Halicarnassus was primarily exactly that, a castle, the fortifications on Rhodes were more extensive, effectively surrounding the whole town of Rhodes on the northern tip of the island.

The town already had extensive Byzantine fortifications, but they were demolished, extended or improved until the new walls covered an area of no less than 42 hectares.

Work continued on Rhodes for more than a century, constantly expanding and improving the fortifications and building an impressive infrastructure to cater for the Hospitaller's administrative headquarters, including the Palace of the Grand Master which was a fortification in its own right inside the fortification. The fortifications also wrapped around the inner Kalona Harbour, protecting both the Hospitallers own fleet and visiting traders. The outer Mandraki Harbour was situated just north of the main fortifications and separated from the inner harbour by a long-fortified mole which ended at the Tower of St. Nicholas, protecting the entry to both harbours.

The Hospitaller fleet became an increasingly important weapon in their arsenal. Of course the Hospitallers were not originally sea-faring, being founded in Jerusalem, but their capability to adapt, in particular after the loss of the Holy Land, was what allowed them to survive.

With their own state consisting of spread-out islands and coastal enclaves, they quickly became master sailors, building and maintaining an extensive fleet of both war ships and trading vessels which enabled them to dominate the surrounding seas. And that dominance of the sea was a problem for the Ottomans.

I have previously explained how sea travel in the fifteenth century was normally not a sea-crossing voyage but rather a string of short trips between ports placed either on the mainland or on suitable islands. Whoever controlled these ports and/or islands would not only benefit in terms of taxes and trade but also be in a position to dominate the immediate area militarily.

A quick look at a map of the eastern Mediterranean Sea will reveal that possession of Rhodes, the close-by islands such as Kos and the mainland port of Halicarnassus enabled the Hospitallers to more or less control the ship-lanes off south-western Anatolia.

The Mamluks of Egypt tried to solve this problem in 1440 by an attack on the Hospitallers and although they did manage to take possession of the small island of Kastellorizo, a 40 day siege of Rhodes was unsuccessful. It was however a warning-shot to the Hospitallers, and the walls were further reinforced following the Egyptian attack.

When Mehmed II took over as sultan in 1451 the Ottomans were not a strong naval power, indeed they were not seen as a naval power at all, one of their key-problems was their lack of consistent and predictable free passage between Europe and Asia.

Three decades later the picture was very different indeed. A combination of fortifications and an extensive programme to build, equip and maintain an Ottoman fleet had been executed under Mehmed II. The Black Sea and the

Sea of Marmara had been turned into Ottoman lakes and the Ottoman fleet had proven strong enough to take on the mighty Venetians in a prolonged war between 1464 and 1479.

Once that war was over, with the Venetians suffering significant setbacks, Mehmed II was ready to complete his dominance in the Aegean Sea and the key to that was Rhodes.

The Venetians still had possession of Crete and the smaller island of Karpathos (between Crete and Rhodes), but with the Venetians maintaining a strictly neutral policy towards the Ottomans, it was only the Hospitallers who still held out against Ottoman dominance and without Rhodes the route in and out of the Aegean Sea was not secure.

Once the war with Venice was out of the way an attack was clearly imminent, and it was not long in the coming.

In the spring of 1480, while one contingent of Ottomans were preparing their invasion of Italy, another contingent was preparing for an invasion of Rhodes. The Pope in Rome and his last remaining crusaders were to be put under siege at the same time.

It is reasonable to assume that the invasion in Italy was primarily a pre-emptive strike to secure a bridgehead for a bigger invasion to follow and that the invasion of Rhodes was the main campaign of that year.

100 Ottoman vessels under the command of Mesih Pasha - a nephew of the last Byzantine emperor, Constantine XI Palaiologos, who had been raised at the Ottoman court after the fall of Constantinople - left their home ports and headed for the coast of Anatolia where the main Ottoman army had been wintering in preparation for the attack.

On 23 May 1480, two months before the landing in Italy, the Ottoman fleet landed on Rhodes. The garrison, which only held a few hundred knights reinforced by local militia, defended as well as they could against the invaders, but the Ottomans managed to land west of the town and proceed to take the western side of the Mandraki Harbour.

The plan was as per usual. Large cannon, allegedly sixteen of them, had been brought along under the control of German cannoneers. The contingent of foot-soldiers were said to be 100,000, but that is probably exaggerated and it was probably no more than half of that.

The cannon were set to work from the west of the city-fortress and soon started to make their presence felt. The main target was the Tower of St. Nicholas, the fall of which would both allow the Ottoman fleet to enter the Mandraki Harbour and provide access to the fortress-complex itself.

The Tower was heavily bombarded, receiving no less than 300 hits from gigantic cannonballs over the first six days of engagement, but a workforce of 1,000 men managed to consistently repair the breaches with a combination of earth- and woodwork, so when the Ottomans attacked the stricken tower, they were repelled. A second attack was also unsuccessful.

A new approach was attempted. The Ottomans build a pontoon-bridge, as they had done at both Constantinople and a decade earlier at Negroponte. The idea was to draw the pontoon-bridge across the entry of the Mandraki Harbour, allowing access directly from the opposite shore where the Ottoman infantry was at the ready.

The first attempt at getting the pontoon-bridge in position was by securing an anchor at the bottom of the tower and run a cable through it. But an English sailor, who mastered the art of swimming, managed to detach the cable during a nightly sortie.

A second attempt at positioning the pontoon-bridge by means of boats was more successful, and on 19 June the Ottomans attacked across the bridge. They brought everything they had, from infantry to siege-machines and cannon, indeed they brought so much so fast that the pontoon-bridge collapsed. As many as 2,500 Ottoman soldiers were lost in the sea as were many pieces of heavy equipment.

The three failed attacks on the Tower of St. Nicholas put an end to Ottoman activity in that particular area. Instead, they focused on the walls around the Jewish Quarter, on the south-eastern side of the city. Here the walls were thinner than other places and the Ottoman cannon were placed to put the walls under constant attack, the main target being the Tower of Italy.

The defenders did their best to deter the attackers. They had a massive catapult which they used to pelt the Ottomans with giant rocks, ironically called 'tribute' by the locals.

A German master cannoneer, Meister Georg, had originally accompanied the Ottomans, but he had defected to the Hospitallers soon after the landing. He was now asked to set up a second catapult, but when it started firing it hit the walls from the inside and Meister Georg admitted, under torture, that he had indeed been sent by the Ottomans to sabotage the defences. He was hanged for his efforts.

But the Ottoman bombardment of the walls went on. Gradually the walls started to fall apart and the attempts to repair them became more and more desperate.

It was clear that the defenders were living on borrowed time and Mesih Pasha decided to try for a negotiated solution. His reasoning was that if he could take the city by means of surrender, then its riches would fall to the Sultan after Mesih Pasha had secured himself a not unreasonable share. He therefore sent a Greek emissary to the Grand Master, Pierre d'Aubusson. The Grand Master was offered free passage for his knights in exchange for surrender and conversion to Islam. He had no intentions of such.

As we shall soon see, the idea of securing the riches of Rhodes for himself and the Sultan was a driving force behind Mesih Pasha, but as the Grand Master did not want to bend to the inevitable, Mesih Pasha ordered an all-out attack through the stricken wall. The date was 28 July 1480, the very same day the second Ottoman fleet left Vlorë for its attack on Italy.

17 - The Crusader Knights

The outcome of the attack seemed predestined. The walls were ruined in places and no attempt at repairing them could keep the attackers out. The attackers outnumbered the defenders many fold, with around 40,000 Ottoman infantry and the Ottoman troops were well prepared. They too were fighting for personal riches, with the city at their mercy and they had equipped themselves with sacks in which to carry loot, ropes with which to tie captured slaves and stakes with which to impale the Knights Hospitaller.

When the Ottomans attacked, they progressed as expected. Although the defenders, local militia and knights alike, put up as much resistance as they could, with hand-to-hand battle facing the Ottomans as they came through the wall and made their way up the narrow streets, the situation inside the city became more and more desperate. Then something very, very strange happened!

The Ottoman commander, Mesih Pasha, had not given up on securing the riches of the city for himself and the Sultan. When it was clear that the attackers were about to rout the last of the organised defence, Mesih Pasha had criers mount the walls, where they declared that looting was forbidden and that all treasure belonged to the Sultan.

This shocking message, out of line with tradition and definitely not what the Ottoman troops had expected, turned the tide. The Ottoman infantry simply lost the incentive to fight, and they turned around and left, with the equally surprised Hospitallers hacking at them from behind.

Ottoman loses were estimated at 9,000 killed and 15,000 wounded and although the defenders had nearly fought to the last man, there was no more fight in Mesih Pasha or rather in his unhappy troops. He ordered the siege equipment burned and the troops back on board the fleet.

The last of the encounters was a small sea-battle. Two ships with reinforcements from King Ferdinand I had arrived. Their approach into the harbour was blocked by the Ottomans, more as a matter of principle than because it had any real practical implications, but one by one they managed to enter the harbour, adding insult to injury.

The core of Ottoman infantry was offloaded at Marmaris and would make their way home by land. Mesih Pasha and the fleet continued to Halicarnassus where he made a vain attempt at an attack on the Hospitaller castle. The attack was unsuccessful and probably only an attempt to better Mesih Pasha's reputation before he arrived back in Istanbul.

His worries were not without reason. The Sultan had a fit of rage when he received news of the aborted campaign and the underlying reasons. Mesih Pasha was stripped of his rank and sent off to Gelibolu to serve as a lowly provincial governor.

The death of Sultan Mehmed II in January 1481 put an end to Ottoman attempts against the Hospitallers for four decades. By 1520 Mehmed II's great-grandson, Sultan Suleiman I, took over an empire that now included Palestine and Egypt, further isolating the Knights of Rhodes as the last

Christian outpost in the eastern Mediterranean Sea. Suleiman I had ambitions at sea as well as on land and he decided to finish the job started by his illustrious great-grandfather.

After the siege of 1480, the Hospitallers had further extended and improved the walls on Rhodes. The ruined Tower of Italy had been replaced with an imposing bastion called Chemin de Ronde and all the walls had been rebuilt to be able to withstand cannon-fire.

But when the Ottomans went back to Rhodes in 1522 they arrived in force. With a ground-contingent approaching 200,000 soldiers and headquarters set up in Marmaris the Ottomans had all intentions of finishing the job. The siege started on 24 June and on 28 July, exactly forty-two years after the last disastrous Ottoman attempt at storming the fortress, the Sultan himself arrived at Rhodes.

In the forty odd years since the last confrontation between the Knights of Rhodes and the Ottoman Empire the Hospitallers had engaged the best brains in the world when it came to defensive construction. Their fortress was now state-of-the-art, with angled walls designed to deflect cannon-fire and itself bristling with cannon to counter the enemy artillery.

The Ottomans, on the other hand, had further developed their siege techniques and had engaged the best brains when it came to offensive warfare. The meeting on Rhodes was thus a meeting of the best defenders versus the best attackers.

But the playing field was not even. The Ottomans had put an iron-ring around the small island, and it was next to impossible to get reinforcements and supplies into the besieged fortress. The Ottomans themselves were, however, well supplied from their headquarters in Marmaris and other ports on the Anatolian coast.

Gradually the Ottoman cannon showed to be more powerful than the defences, but despite several all-out attacks they could not gain the final advantage.

As winter followed fall, most commanders would have packed up and left, but the Sultan had no such intention, he had come to settle business and that was exactly what he intended to do.

By December, the situation was so desperate inside the walls of Rhodes that negotiations were started. Finally, and much to the regret of the Grand Master, Philippe de Villiers de L'Isle-Adam, a deal was struck.

The Hospitallers had to abandon Rhodes, Kos and their fortress at Halicarnassus. They were free to leave and the population that was left behind was free to remain Christians and their churches were not to be converted to mosques.

On New Year's Day 1523 the Hospitallers left Rhodes. There were 180 knights left alive and they took the Order's treasure and insignia with them onto four ships. Once again, the Order was homeless.

17 - The Crusader Knights

But even without a home, the Order was still wealthy. After a few years of uncertainty, the Order established themselves on Malta, granted by the King of Sicily against the annual payment of one Maltese Falcon.

On Malta the Hospitallers re-organised and re-fortified. But the world had moved on and just over four decades after the final battle for Rhodes, Sultan Suleyman I was once again at their door.

The Ottoman Empire had by now expanded into northern Africa and from their island the Hospitallers were once again a thorn in the side of Ottoman supremacy and command of the sea.

In 1565 the Ottomans attacked Malta, but this time fortune was with the knights. Although it was close affair, the Ottomans finally withdrew from Malta after a bloody siege which has gone into history as one of the greatest sieges ever.

The Hospitallers, now known as the Knights of Malta, gradually lost most of their possessions in Europe following the Reformation. But they still ruled in Malta until Napoleon put an end to their rule in 1798.

Withdrawing to Rome, the order once again transformed, this time into a mainly charitable, but still chivalry, order, known as the Sovereign Military Order of Malta. Although the Order does not hold any sovereign land, its unique status as a de-facto state is seen by the fact that it has observer status at the United Nations and diplomatic relations with (as per July 2014) 104 countries and the European Union.

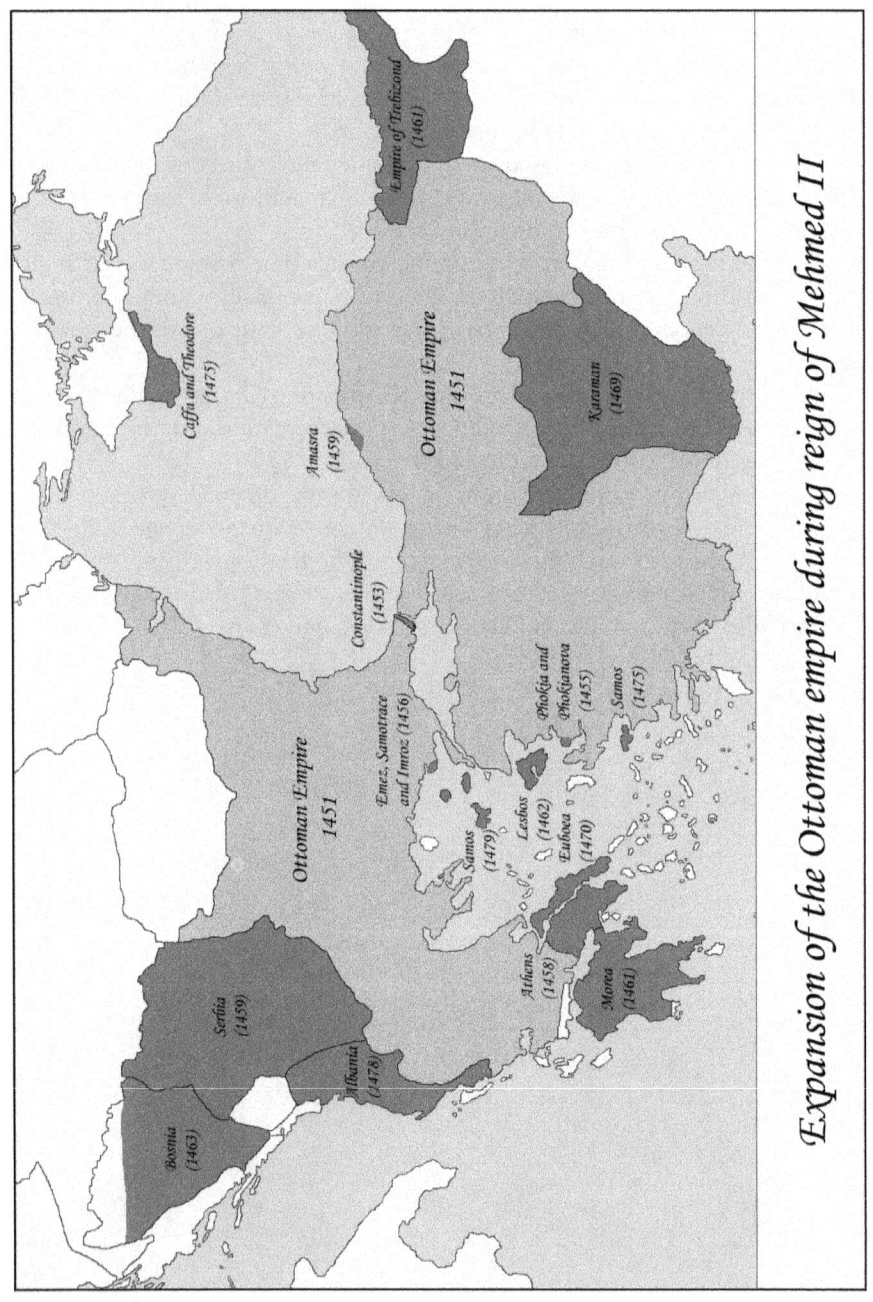

Expansion of the Ottoman empire during reign of Mehmed II

18 - THE OTTOMAN EMPIRE AFTER MEHMED II

In the preceding parts and chapters of this book I have tried to outline the fate of each of the Conqueror's enemies as it unfolded after their confrontation with the Ottomans under Mehmed II. It is only fair that I do the same for the Ottomans, even if the immediate scope of this book ends with the death of Fatih Sultan Mehmed II in May of 1481.

The Conqueror Sultan was buried in a türbe outside the Fatih Mosque, built in his name in Istanbul. There he still resides and if you happen to be passing by, do go and pay your respects. It is a place of great reverence to this day.

His own words of wisdom *'Whichever of my sons inherits the sultan's throne, it behoves him to kill his brothers in the interest of world order'* were ignored and his sons Bayezid II and Cem soon entered into a civil war of succession.

Bayezid II was the eldest son and the appointed heir apparent, but exactly as Mehmed II had predicted the presence of more than one son opened up the stage for conflict. Mehmed II's younger son, Cem, went into alliance with the Mamluks in Egypt - who would not have minded their own puppet on the Ottoman throne - and civil war followed.

Eventually Bayezid II was victorious and Cem had to seek refuge with the Knights of Rhodes at their castle in Halicarnassus. From there he eventually made his way to the protection of Pope Innocent VIII (and later his successor Alexander VI). The Pope regularly threatened the Ottoman Sultan with the release of his brother, as well as seeing him as a potential pliant ruler in Europe should a forthcoming crusade be successful.

But as the Sultan paid the Pope 120,000 crowns, plus an annual fee of another 45,000 ducats to keep his brother where he was, Cem never became more than a pawn. He died in 1495 while participating in a military expedition against Naples.

Sultan Bayezid II cleaned up the Morea of the last remaining Venetian outposts, but he was not as aggressive as his father. His sons, Ahmet and Selim, however, were ambitious and Ahmet showed his hand by staging a revolt in Anatolia, soon marching on Istanbul.

To counter the challenge of his brother, Selim staged a revolt in Greece, but he was defeated by his father and had to flee to Crimea. Ahmet had by now reached Istanbul and his father realized that he was aiming for nothing less than the throne.

Selim was welcomed back by the Janissaries and Bayezid II was forced to abdicate in favour of his son, who became Selim I. The armies of the two brothers now met in battle and Selim I was victorious. Lesson learned his brother Ahmet was executed.

Part 6 - The Pope and the Crusader Knights

Compared to his father, Selim I was more of the warlike conqueror his grandfather had been. In his short reign of eight years he conquered Persia, Syria, Palestine, Egypt and the Arab Peninsula, tripling the size of the Ottoman Empire. He officially became Khalif, head of Islam, combining secular and religious power into one person and one empire. He had his eyes on Hungary when he died from disease in 1520.

His son, Suleyman I took over from where his father had left the continuous expansion of the Ottoman Empire. We have already met him in the previous chapter, ousting the Hospitallers from Rhodes, and he managed to do what his great-grandfather, Mehmed II, had not been able to do; the conquest of Hungary. He also expanded into northern Africa, which is what brought him into renewed conflict with the Hospitallers, at that time located at Malta.

Furthermore, Suleyman I was a great patron of art as well as a vivid lawgiver, earning him the moniker 'Kanuni' (the Lawgiver'), even though in the West he was called 'the Magnificent'.

The rule of Suleiman I was the zenith of Ottoman power and expansions and is now referred to as the '*Golden Age*'. From the death of Suleiman I in 1566 the Ottoman Empire entered into a period of gradual stagnation that lasted 350 years.

Not that the Empire was not militarily active though. The longest period of peace was an uninterrupted period of twelve years between 1718 and 1730 - during the reign of Sultan Ahmed III - which due to its unusual calm and an upsurge in cultural development is known as the '*Tulip Period*'.

By then the concept of a warrior-sultan had long gone. The Sultan had become a distant, unapproachable figurehead and the state was run by powerful ministers and ambitious courtiers, often eunuchs serving in the Harem (the Sultan's household).

Towards the end of the nineteenth century the Sultan had all but been put aside by a government of former army officers and after the Ottoman Empire's disastrous participation in the First World War, the Empire was officially dissolved on 1 November 1922.

The Ottoman Empire was split into a number of autonomous nation-states, distributed between the dominant western empires of the time. After a short war of independence the secular Turkish Republic - consisting of Anatolia and Rumelia - was formed under the leadership of Mustafa Kemal Atatürk. The Republic exists to this day.

NOTES AND INDEX

Notes and Index

NOTES

I have consistently used the term "Ottomans" instead of "Turks." That is on purpose as the Ottoman Empire contained millions of people who were not Turks, and many Turks lived outside the Ottoman Empire.

In Chapter 16 I have repeatedly noted that a pope was, or was not, a 'saint'. I have noted this in connection with the death of a pope, which is technically wrong.

A person, pope or not, is only considered for sainthood after their death, indeed normally well after. They are thus rather 'recognised as being a saint' at a later date, rather than 'being a saint' upon their death. I hope the readers will excuse this deliberate error, which is done for the reason of readability.

It is also worth noting that I have only noted sainthood for those popes who are recognised as true saints, and not those who are only 'blessed,' a lesser (post-mortem) recognition of a person's holiness.

This book is not an academic work. It is deliberately not so, as I have prioritised readability over academia.

Notes and Index

INDEX

Aachen, 488, 494
Acre, 160, 188, 190, 229, 230, 231, 236, 237, 554, 566, 571, 576, 606, 607, 608
Adalbert, 5, 510, 511, 513
Adeodatus I, 469
Adeodatus II, 474
Adrian I, 5, 484, 485, 486, 495, 497
Adrian II, 5, 495, 497, 498
Adrian III, 5, 500, 527
Adrian IV, 5, 548, 549, 550
Adrian V, 567
Adrianople. See Edirne
Adriatic Sea, 56, 93, 167, 168, 169, 170, 179, 180, 181, 182, 183, 185, 187, 197, 202, 203, 210, 219, 237, 245, 246, 276, 278, 280, 317, 341, 348, 352, 356, 367, 428, 431, 432, 456, 518, 533, 599
Aegean Sea, 66, 149, 187, 195, 200, 201, 204, 240, 250, 252, 472, 611
Afghanistan, 34, 86
Africa, 44, 52, 169, 171, 179, 219, 220, 222, 223, 234, 237, 264, 274, 449, 450, 452, 462, 463, 472, 615, 618
Agapetus I, 462
Agapetus II, 508, 509
Agatho, 474
Ageltrude, 5, 502
Agilulf, 5, 467, 468, 469
Ahlat, 29
Aistulf, 5, 480
Akkerman, 403, 409
Aksaray, 138
Akşehir, 138

Alaattin Ali, 5, 132, 133, 134, 135
Alans, 450
Alanya, 138, 247
Alaric, 5, 168, 448, 449
Albania, 32, 45, 84, 88, 91, 93, 94, 95, 96, 150, 167, 183, 195, 197, 198, 199, 202, 203, 209, 210, 329, 330, 333, 334, 352, 353, 354, 377, 408, 417, 419, 420, 421, 422, 423, 424, 425, 426, 427, 428, 429, 430, 431, 432, 433, 595, 596, 597, 599, 600, 601
Alberic II, 508, 509
Albert II, 5, 327, 357
Alboin, 5, 465, 466
Alexander II, 5, 529, 530
Alexander III, 5, 550, 551, 552
Alexander IV, 562
Alexander the Great, 332, 394, 421
Alexander V, 589, 590
Alexandria, 53, 221, 247, 445, 446, 457, 526, 583
Alexandru I Aldea, 5, 387, 388, 403
Alexandru I of Moldavia, 5, 403, 404
Alexandru II, 5, 404, 405
Alexios I Komnenos, 5, 50, 54, 157, 183, 184, 185, 225, 533, 535
Alexios I of Trebizond, 5, 159
Alexios II Komnenos, 6, 186, 225
Alexios III Angelos, 6, 57, 59, 60, 64, 65, 67, 158
Alexios Strategopoulos, 69
Alexios V Doukas, 62
Alexius Angelus, 6, 57, 58, 60, 61, 62, 63, 64, 227

Alfonso V of Aragon, 6, 247, 423, 424, 427, 430, 591, 593, 594
Alfonso VII of Castile, 6, 222, 547
Ali Pasha, 422
Al-Kamil, 6, 228, 229
Almeria, 222, 223
Alp Arslan, 6, 53, 122, 123
Alusian of Bulgaria, 278
Amadeus VI, 6, 244, 286, 583, 584, 586
Amalasuntha, 6, 461, 462
Amalfi, 170, 492, 499, 605
Amasra, 250, 251
Amasya, 34, 135, 150, 162
Amlaş, 380, 383, 385, 390
Anacletus II, 6, 543, 544
Anadoluhisarı, 33, 35, 84, 98, 193
Anagni, 539, 559, 573, 575
Anastasian Wall, 267
Anastasios II, 6, 265, 266, 477
Anastasius Bibliothecarius, 6, 492, 497
Anastasius I, 448
Anastasius II, 458
Anastasius III, 6, 506, 525
Anastasius IV, 548
Anatolia, 29, 30, 34, 35, 36, 42, 44, 52, 53, 54, 55, 65, 66, 67, 68, 71, 79, 80, 81, 82, 84, 86, 87, 88, 90, 91, 92, 93, 97, 104, 106, 113, 115, 121, 122, 123, 124, 131, 132, 133, 134, 135, 136, 137, 138, 145, 146, 147, 149, 150, 157, 159, 160, 171, 179, 184, 190, 193, 194, 195, 208, 220, 223, 228, 231, 237, 238, 241, 242, 244, 247, 248, 250, 251, 252, 265, 272, 278, 281, 306, 317, 318, 321, 322, 329, 330, 331, 351, 356, 358, 397, 408, 422, 472, 473, 485, 530, 535, 536, 547, 554, 558, 569, 610, 611, 617, 618
Anchialus, 274

Ancona, 170, 179, 201, 430, 551, 596
András I of Hungary, 6, 299, 300
András II of Hungary, 6, 306, 307, 308, 309, 314, 351, 608
András III of Hungary, 6, 314, 315
Andronikos I Komnenos, 6, 158, 225, 278
Andronikos II Palaiologos, 6, 72, 79, 80, 237, 238, 284, 285, 352, 567
Andronikos III Palaiologos, 6, 80, 81, 192, 284, 285, 353
Andronikos IV Palaiologos, 6, 244, 584
Andros, 186
Anjou, 314, 325, 569, 570, 571, 574, 578, 585, 588, 591, 593
Ankara, 29, 34, 133, 134, 149, 356
Antalya, 123, 132, 134, 135, 149
Antioch, 53, 55, 185, 220, 221, 225, 445, 446, 457, 475, 526, 536
Anzio, 245
Apulia, 183, 246, 520, 525, 530, 542, 544, 561, 564
Aquileia, 244, 451
Aquincum, 292, 295
Aragon, 71, 235, 241, 247, 423, 424, 427, 430, 569, 570, 571, 572, 573, 574, 587, 590, 591, 593, 594, 595
Aral Sea, 121
Arbanon, 417, 418
Arduin, 518
Arezzo, 586
Arges River, 386
Argos, 198, 199, 200
Arian, 458, 461, 468
Armenia, 122, 145, 307, 446, 450
Arno River, 235
Arnulf of Carinthia, 6, 501, 502
Árpád, 7, 272, 292, 295, 296, 297, 303, 314, 315
Arsuf, 221

Asparukh of Bulgaria, 264
Astura, 570
Athalaric, 461, 462
Athens, 66, 93, 185, 191, 197, 198, 203, 238, 445, 485
Attila, 7, 168, 449, 450, 451, 452, 453
Augsburg, 296
Austria, 167, 169, 209, 211, 228, 244, 299, 300, 303, 305, 306, 308, 311, 312, 314, 315, 327, 328, 329, 332, 337, 338, 339, 360, 390, 465, 509, 555, 580
Authari, 467
Avars, 263, 268, 383, 465, 486
Avignon, 321, 577, 579, 580, 581, 582, 583, 584, 585, 586, 587, 588, 589
Avitus, 7, 453, 454
Babinger, 1, 375
Bacau, 406
Baghdad, 122, 145, 146, 160
Baia, 406
Baibars, 7, 131, 607
Baldwin I of Constantinople, 66, 67, 221, 495
Baldwin II of Jerusalem, 7, 69, 70, 232, 233, 606
Baldwin of Flanders, 7, 56, 66, 280
Balearic Islands, 450, 573
Balkans, 53, 67, 89, 103, 168, 170, 180, 193, 209, 263, 264, 277, 278, 279, 281, 295, 318, 319, 320, 321, 328, 329, 330, 339, 341, 349, 351, 353, 354, 360, 361, 401, 417, 419, 421, 424, 449, 450, 457, 465, 468, 474, 561, 595, 598
Bari, 183, 498, 507, 525, 585, 599
Basarab I, 7, 383, 384
Basarab II, 7, 388, 397
Basarab III Laiotă, 7, 396, 397, 407, 408, 409
Basel, 529, 591, 592, 593

Basil II, 7, 180, 276, 277
Basilica of Saint Paul Outside the Walls, 491
Battle of Anchialus
 First, 265, 652
 Second, 267, 652
 Third, 274, 652
Battle of Arcadiopolis, 279
Battle of Benevento, 419, 655
Battle of Bileća, 373
Battle of Boulgarophygon, 273, 652
Battle of Breadfield, 339, 397
Battle of Catalaunum, 451, 651
Battle of Chioggia, 193, 655
Battle of Dubravnica, 32, 321, 355
Battle of Gallipoli, 35, 656
Battle of Grunwald, 403
Battle of Issus, 394
Battle of Kleidion, 277, 653
Battle of Kosovo
 First, 32, 33, 287, 321, 356, 420, 656
 Second, 43, 333, 389, 425, 657
Battle of Lechfeld, 296, 652
Battle of Legnano, 552, 654
Battle of Manzikert, 53, 122, 530, 653
Battle of Maritsa, 355, 372, 420, 655
Battle of Meloria, 236, 655
Battle of Ménfő, 299, 653
Battle of Mohi, 28, 310, 654
Battle of Monte Porzio, 551, 653
Battle of Mu'tah, 469, 651
Battle of Nicopolis, 33, 324, 327, 386, 656
Battle of Ongal, 264, 474, 651
Battle of Otlukbeli, 151, 658
Battle of Pelekanon, 30, 80
Battle of Pločnik, 32, 133
Battle of Rovine, 386
Battle of the Masts, 472, 473, 651

Battle of Tryavna, 260, 279
Battle of Varna, 194, 657
Bavaria, 297, 299, 300, 502, 563, 565, 577
Bayezid I, 7, 33, 34, 76, 84, 85, 86, 87, 93, 97, 98, 133, 134, 193, 287, 288, 321, 322, 323, 324, 327, 386, 420, 589
Bayezid II, 7, 397, 617
Beirut, 190, 236, 247
Béla I, 300
Béla II, 7, 303, 349, 367
Béla III, 7, 305, 554
Béla IV, 7, 309, 310, 311, 312, 314, 316
Béla V, 316
Belgica, 451
Belgrade, 162, 202, 206, 279, 280, 281, 300, 302, 307, 326, 328, 334, 335, 337, 339, 350, 352, 353, 357, 358, 359, 360, 374, 390, 394, 405, 428, 429, 595, 598
Belisarius, 7, 463, 464
Benedict I, 7, 467
Benedict II, 475
Benedict III, 7, 492, 493, 497
Benedict IV, 7, 503, 504, 521, 522, 523
Benedict IX, 8, 521, 522, 523, 524
Benedict V, 512
Benedict VI, 7, 514, 530
Benedict VII, 514, 515
Benedict VIII, 7, 519, 520
Benedict X, 528
Benedict XI, 8, 524, 575, 585
Benedict XII, 581
Benedict XIII, 8, 587, 588, 589, 590, 591
Benevento, 465, 498, 510, 525, 530, 550, 552, 565
Berat, 419, 427, 428, 429

Berengar I, 8, 503, 504, 505, 506, 507, 510
Berengar II, 8, 509, 510, 518
Bernard of Clairvaux, 8, 542, 543, 544, 546, 547, 606
Bertrada of Laon, 482
Beylik of Aydin, 81
Beyşehir, 133, 135, 138, 149
Bileća, 373
Bistriţa, 334, 391
Blachernae, 59, 62
Black Death, 82, 191, 192, 240, 245, 247, 285, 318, 401, 582
Black Sea, 34, 42, 44, 51, 52, 62, 66, 67, 69, 91, 92, 97, 98, 99, 103, 104, 123, 145, 147, 157, 158, 160, 161, 167, 171, 182, 185, 188, 189, 190, 191, 195, 196, 199, 204, 205, 209, 226, 232, 234, 238, 239, 240, 241, 242, 246, 248, 249, 250, 253, 263, 264, 265, 267, 269, 271, 274, 280, 282, 309, 331, 334, 341, 383, 385, 386, 401, 402, 403, 406, 407, 409, 610
Black Sheep, 145, 146, 147, 160, 161
Bobovac, 376
Bodrum. See Halicarnassus
Boğaz Kesen, 99
Bogdan I, 402
Bogdan II, 8, 404, 405
Bogomils, 350, 367, 368, 369, 370, 371, 372
Bohemia, 88, 204, 299, 303, 305, 312, 315, 316, 325, 326, 327, 329, 332, 339, 578, 590
Bologna, 578, 592
Bone, 220
Boniface I, 8, 66, 67, 68, 448, 449
Boniface II, 8, 462, 463
Boniface III, 8, 468, 523, 524, 528
Boniface IV, 8, 469
Boniface IX, 8, 321, 587, 588

Boniface of Montferrat, 8, 56, 65, 66, 187, 227, 280, 557
Boniface V, 469
Boniface VI, 8, 502, 514
Boniface VII, 8, 514, 515
Boniface VIII, 8, 572, 575, 576, 577
Borgo, 492
Borić, 367
Boril of Bulgaria, 280
Boris I of Bulgaria, 8, 270, 271, 272, 496, 497, 500, 501
Boruj, 286
Bosnia, 45, 138, 197, 199, 200, 201, 202, 203, 210, 303, 304, 318, 321, 324, 326, 329, 338, 341, 347, 348, 350, 354, 360, 361, 367, 368, 369, 370, 371, 372, 373, 374, 375, 376, 377, 378, 397, 407, 596, 597, 598
Bosporus, 30, 33, 35, 51, 84, 92, 97, 98, 99, 101, 104, 106, 109, 150, 161, 191, 193, 194, 195, 198, 204, 232, 237, 241, 248, 249, 251, 274, 331
Bougie, 222
Braila, 407
Brasov, 384, 385, 386, 390, 391, 396
Bratislava, 337
Brescia, 465, 546, 549
Brindisi, 203, 237, 432, 550, 559, 599, 600, 601
Buda, 304, 310, 315, 316, 319, 320, 322, 325, 328, 329, 330, 337, 339, 390, 396

Bulgaria, 31, 33, 42, 44, 68, 71, 80, 83, 84, 85, 91, 124, 132, 133, 150, 194, 199, 203, 263, 266, 267, 268, 274, 275, 276, 277, 278, 280, 281, 282, 283, 284, 285, 286, 287, 288, 295, 307, 310, 312, 318, 319, 324, 329, 330, 348, 349, 350, 351, 352, 353, 354, 355, 367, 376, 383, 385, 392, 395, 401, 405, 421, 500, 501, 506, 507, 584, 595
Burgundy, 149, 199, 323, 538, 551, 596
Bursa, 30, 34, 36, 80, 88, 134, 288
Cadaver Synod, 502, 503, 504, 505
Caere, 504, 505
Caesarea, 221
Caffa, 163, 190, 191, 234, 238, 239, 240, 250, 251, 252, 253
   Conquest of, 253, 658
Cairo, 134, 221, 229, 558, 583
Calabria, 463, 514, 542, 591
Caliphate of Cordoba, 491
Callixtus II, 8, 538, 539
Callixtus III
   Anti-Pope, 552
   Pope, 594
Campagna, 513
Campania, 458, 491, 541, 545, 550
Campulung, 383
Çandarlı Halil Pasha, 8, 42, 43, 93, 97, 108
Canossa, 532
Cape Chaunar, 237
Cappadocia, 147
Capua, 498, 499, 541, 544, 545
Carloman I, 8, 481, 482, 484
Carpathians, 272, 303, 317, 341, 383, 384, 401, 402
Carthage, 449, 450, 452, 462
Casimir III of Poland, 318
Časlav Klonimirović, 348
Caspian Sea, 121

Castel Sant'Angelo, 502, 513, 514, 515, 517, 518, 529, 533, 588
Castile, 222, 563, 567, 587
Catalan, 30, 45, 80, 96, 191, 237, 238, 239, 251, 547
Catalaunum, 452, 453
Cathars, 557, 581
Celestine I, 8, 449
Celestine II
   Anti-Pope, 539
   Pope, 545
Celestine III, 8, 555, 607
Celestine IV, 560
Celestine V, 8, 571, 572
Cem, 9, 617
Cephalonia, 186
Ceprano, 545
Cesena, 585
Chaka of Bulgaria, 284
Charlemagne, 9, 169, 481, 482, 483, 484, 485, 486, 487, 488, 509, 518, 537
Charles I of Hungary, 9, 370, 383, 401
Charles I of Naples, 9, 70, 71, 233, 234, 235, 282, 283, 419, 420, 564, 565, 566, 567, 568, 569, 570
Charles II of Hungary, 9, 319, 320, 586, 587
Charles II of Naples, 9, 569, 570, 571, 572, 573, 574, 578, 586
Charles Martel, 479
Charles of Valois, 9, 569, 570, 571, 573, 574, 575, 577
Charles the Bald, 9, 493, 494, 495, 499
Charles the Fat, 9, 499, 500, 503
Charles V of France, 586
Childeric III, 479
Chilia, 403, 405, 406, 409
Chioggia, 245, 246
Chios, 46, 186, 236, 239, 240, 248, 250, 251, 252

Christopher, 504
Christopher Columbus, 44, 180, 237
Cilicia, 136, 307
Çimpe, 30, 31, 82, 83
Circus Maximus, 546
Ciubăr, 404
Civitavecchia, 230
Clement II, 522, 523
Clement III
   Anti-Pope, 9, 301, 302, 532, 534, 536
   Pope, 9, 553, 554, 555
Clement IV, 9, 564, 566
Clement V, 9, 576, 577, 578, 579, 609
Clement VI, 9, 581, 582, 586, 587
Cleph, 9, 466, 467
Clermont, 54, 535
Cluny, 540, 541
Coliseum, 52, 539
Coloman, 9, 302, 303, 368, 369
Conon, 475
Conrad II, 9, 298, 520, 521, 522
Conrad II of Bavaria, 300
Conrad II of Italy, 536
Conrad III, 9, 545, 547, 548
Conrad IV, 9, 559, 561, 562
Conradin, 9, 233, 562, 563, 564, 565, 566
Constance of Sicily, 9, 554, 556
Constans II, 10, 471, 472
Constantine (Pope), 9, 476, 477
Constantine II, 10, 288, 481
Constantine IV, 10, 263, 264, 473, 474, 476
Constantine IX Monomachos, 526
Constantine Lascaris, 65, 67
Constantine the Great, 10, 51, 446, 447, 480, 507, 526
Constantine Tikh, 10, 282
Constantine V, 10, 266, 267, 268, 479, 485

Constantine VII, 10, 273, 506
Constantine XI Palaiologos, 10, 78, 96, 97, 99, 102, 103, 104, 109, 110, 111, 114, 115, 593, 611
Constantinople, 31, 33, 34, 36, 43, 44, 46, 51, 52, 53, 54, 57, 58, 59, 61, 63, 64, 65, 66, 67, 68, 69, 70, 79, 80, 82, 83, 84, 85, 86, 87, 88, 89, 90, 92, 93, 96, 97, 98, 99, 101, 102, 103, 104, 105, 107, 114, 115, 116, 123, 124, 137, 157, 158, 159, 160, 161, 168, 169, 180, 182, 183, 184, 185, 186, 187, 188, 189, 190, 191, 192, 194, 196, 199, 204, 206, 220, 223, 224, 225, 226, 227, 228, 231, 232, 233, 234, 235, 241, 242, 243, 244, 247, 248, 249, 250, 253, 263, 264, 265, 266, 267, 268, 269, 271, 272, 273, 274, 275, 276, 277, 278, 279, 280, 281, 282, 283, 295, 303, 304, 321, 322, 334, 335, 336, 350, 351, 354, 388, 390, 402, 405, 417, 419, 427, 446, 447, 448, 450, 457, 460, 461, 462, 463, 464, 465, 466, 467, 468, 469, 470, 471, 472, 473, 474, 475, 476, 477, 478, 479, 485, 487, 488, 489, 496, 497, 498, 500, 501, 505, 507, 513, 515, 520, 521, 526, 527, 533, 536, 547, 551, 554, 557, 561, 563, 566, 567, 569, 587, 592, 593, 594, 598, 599, 609, 611, 612
  Conquest of, 1, 115, 116, 162, 195, 196, 249, 250, 251, 334, 358, 657
  Reconquest of, 71, 189, 250, 265, 282, 418, 654
Constantius II, 447
Copernicus, 44
Corfu, 57, 183, 184, 185, 186, 187, 193, 211, 233, 234, 325, 599
Corinth, 86, 93, 199

Coron, 66, 88, 185, 187, 198, 200, 211
Corsica, 219, 222, 235, 236, 247, 450, 491
Cremona, 578
Crescentius II, 10, 515, 516, 517, 518
Crete, 66, 187, 189, 204, 205, 207, 211, 226, 232, 611
Crimea, 157, 158, 163, 199, 234, 238, 250, 251, 252, 264, 265, 408, 472, 476, 596, 617
Croatia, 167, 180, 203, 209, 274, 277, 278, 300, 301, 302, 303, 304, 305, 306, 309, 315, 326, 335, 339, 341, 360, 361, 370, 371, 372, 373, 376, 377, 432, 598
Crusade
  Albigensian, 557
  Fifth, 307, 308, 608
  First, 55, 123, 157, 185, 190, 220, 222, 236, 302, 321, 546, 547, 571, 605, 653
  Fourth, 28, 55, 56, 60, 66, 68, 70, 79, 88, 98, 102, 114, 115, 123, 158, 162, 186, 187, 201, 223, 226, 227, 228, 231, 233, 234, 279, 280, 305, 306, 350, 417, 557, 558, 563, 654
  Second, 303, 546, 547
  Sixth, 559
  Third, 55, 123, 305, 553, 608
Cuman, 301, 302, 309, 310, 311, 313, 314, 328, 383
Curia, 222, 489, 497, 510, 530, 563, 577, 585
Curzola, 237
Cyclades, 187, 198, 204
Cyprus, 149, 151, 208, 209, 211, 243, 244, 246, 247, 250, 447, 469, 554, 583, 608, 609
Cyzicus, 473
Dagnum, 424, 425

Dalmatia, 181, 305, 306, 309, 313, 317, 318, 319, 320, 375, 417, 456, 463, 470, 503, 518
Damasus I, 10, 447, 448
Damasus II, 524
Damietta, 228, 229, 558
Dan I, 10, 385, 387
Dan II, 10, 387, 388, 389, 396
Danishmends, 123
Dante Alighieri, 10, 568, 569, 575, 578, 579
Danube River, 85, 90, 92, 167, 168, 263, 264, 267, 268, 272, 273, 274, 275, 277, 282, 283, 284, 286, 287, 288, 292, 295, 311, 321, 322, 324, 328, 329, 330, 335, 347, 350, 352, 373, 383, 385, 386, 392, 393, 401, 406, 407, 409, 450, 452
Dardanelles, 30, 92, 97, 104, 107, 192, 193, 194, 198, 201, 204, 207, 208, 243, 248, 331
David Komnenos, 10, 67, 159
David Megas Komnenos, 10, 147, 162, 163
Denmark, 86, 608
Desa Urošević, 349
Desiderata, 482, 483
Desiderius, 10, 480, 481, 482, 483, 484, 485, 534
Devşirme, 32, 388
Dimitri Progoni, 10, 417, 418
Dioscorus, 462
Dobrogea, 385, 386, 387, 398
Don River, 190, 240
Donation of Pepin, 480, 510
Donus, 474
Double Columns, 104, 107, 108
Dragoş, 401
Dristra, 275
Dubrovnik. See Ragusa
Duklja, 349
Dulkadir, 134
Đurađ Branković, 10, 41, 90, 91, 95, 96, 330, 333, 356, 357, 358, 359, 374, 389, 424, 426, 657
Durazzo. See Durrës
Durrës, 174, 177, 180, 183, 184, 187, 203, 211, 276, 278, 417, 418, 420, 424, 426, 431, 432
Dyophysitism, 458, 464, 470
Dyrrachium. See Durrës
Edessa., 55, 536
Edirne, 31, 34, 41, 42, 43, 68, 83, 87, 90, 92, 95, 96, 97, 101, 102, 105, 115, 150, 187, 269, 270, 273, 280, 284, 286, 319, 329, 331, 337, 357, 359, 421, 427, 428, 584
Edmund Plantagenet ('Crouchback'), 10, 562
Edward I of England, 570
Egypt, 51, 53, 55, 131, 134, 137, 138, 145, 160, 171, 179, 188, 220, 221, 223, 226, 228, 229, 234, 237, 472, 552, 557, 558, 610, 613, 617, 618
Elba, 235, 236
Elbasan, 202, 203, 431, 432
Elbistan, 136
Eleutherius, 10, 469, 497, 498
Elizabeth of Bosnia, 10, 319, 320, 586
Emeric, 11, 305, 306
Empire of Nicaea, 67, 159, 189, 281, 418
Empire of Trebizond, 44, 67, 115, 123, 147, 148, 150, 157, 159, 160, 161, 162, 163, 171, 234
Enez, 250, 251, 252
England, 86, 149, 169, 308, 321, 324, 326, 467, 530, 543, 545, 548, 551, 554, 556, 562, 563, 570, 583, 607, 608
Enrico Dandolo, 11, 56, 61, 186
Ephesus, 90, 185, 445

Epirus, 67, 68, 69, 70, 81, 159, 187, 199, 279, 280, 281, 351, 352, 355, 418, 419
Eretnids, 133
Erik Gnupsson, 537
Ertugrul Bey, 11, 29, 569
Erzincan, 150
Estonia, 608
Euboea, 186, 187, 189, 191, 193, 196, 197, 201, 202, 203, 204, 205, 208, 209, 210, 232
  Conquest of, 205, 207, 658
Eugene I, 472
Eugene II, 489, 490
Eugene III, 11, 546, 548
Eugene IV, 11, 89, 591, 592, 593, 594
Eulalius, 448, 449
Euphrates River, 150
Euripus Strait, 204
Eustathius, 520
Făgăraș, 383, 385, 390, 396
Fajsz, 296
Famagusta, 243, 244, 250, 252
Farfa Abbey, 489
Fatimid, 185
Felix II, 11, 447, 457
Felix III, 457
Felix IV, 461, 462
Felix V, 592, 593
Ferdinand I of Aragon (Naples), 11, 430, 595, 597, 598, 599, 600, 613
Ferrara, 553, 592
Firuz Pasha, 423
Flavius Aetius, 11, 450, 451, 452, 453
Florence, 89, 90, 198, 247, 527, 528, 563, 574, 575, 578, 579, 584, 586, 591, 592, 597, 601
Foggia, 562
Formosus, 11, 500, 501, 502, 503, 504, 505, 506

France, 86, 149, 169, 211, 234, 235, 246, 251, 254, 321, 324, 326, 451, 467, 479, 490, 499, 506, 516, 518, 524, 535, 538, 540, 543, 544, 545, 547, 548, 551, 554, 556, 557, 561, 564, 569, 571, 572, 573, 575, 576, 577, 579, 580, 581, 583, 586, 587, 589, 608
Frangipani, 539, 542, 543, 546, 566
Franks, 270, 449, 467, 479, 480, 482, 484, 485, 486, 487, 488, 493
Frascati, 523, 568, 590
Frederick I 'Barbarossa', 11, 224, 229, 304, 305, 548, 549, 551, 553, 554
Frederick II, 11, 227, 228, 229, 230, 233, 311, 555, 556, 557, 558, 559, 560, 561, 574
Frederick II of Austria, 311, 312
Frederick II of Sicily, 11, 573, 574
Frederick III, 11, 328, 329, 332, 334, 337, 338, 339, 393, 593, 595
Frederick the Fair, 580
Friar Julian, 309
Friuli, 209, 210
Fumone, 572
Gaeta, 170, 427, 492, 499, 538, 587
Galata, 58, 103, 104, 109, 110, 111, 160, 186, 189, 190, 191, 234, 237, 239, 241, 242, 244, 248, 249, 250, 253
Galata Tower, 58
Gallipoli, 30, 31, 35, 82, 83, 84, 98, 104, 187, 193, 238, 242, 244, 285, 319, 353, 582, 584
Gaul, 168, 449, 451, 453, 454, 456
Gavril Radomir of Bulgaria, 11, 277, 278
Gedik Ahmed Pasha, 11, 138, 599, 600, 601, 605
Gelasius I, 457, 458
Gelasius II, 538

Gennadius Scholarius, 102, 103
Genoa, 33, 45, 46, 69, 79, 82, 84, 89, 98, 103, 110, 135, 160, 161, 167, 170, 171, 182, 188, 189, 190, 191, 192, 193, 196, 201, 219, 220, 221, 222, 223, 225, 226, 227, 228, 229, 230, 232, 234, 235, 236, 237, 239, 240, 241, 242, 243, 245, 246, 247, 248, 250, 251, 252, 254, 318, 324, 543, 553, 555, 561, 565, 586, 601
Genseric, 11, 449, 452, 453, 454, 455, 463
George I of Bulgaria, 283, 284
George II of Bulgaria, 284, 285
Georgia, 122, 146, 157, 158, 161, 163
Gepids, 383, 465
Gerard Thom (Blessed Gerard), 11, 605, 606
Germany, 149, 227, 228, 296, 297, 299, 300, 301, 314, 325, 326, 327, 329, 500, 509, 510, 512, 513, 514, 515, 516, 517, 518, 519, 520, 522, 523, 524, 525, 527, 529, 530, 532, 536, 537, 540, 541, 543, 544, 545, 547, 548, 549, 551, 554, 556, 559, 561, 562, 563, 564, 567, 570, 577, 578, 579, 580, 581, 588, 590, 593, 608
Germiyan, 134
Gertrude of Merania, 307
Géza I, 11, 300, 301, 302
Géza II, 11, 303, 304, 367, 551
Géza of Hungary, 297
Ghaznavids, 122
Ghibellines, 514, 550, 560, 563, 565, 574, 578
Giovanni Giustiniani Longo, 11, 103, 113, 114, 248, 249
Giuliano Cesarini, 12, 43, 90, 92, 329, 593, 657
Gjin Progoni, 417
Glycerius, 456

Godfrey III, 12, 527, 528, 529
Golden Horde, 190, 240, 281, 282, 283, 385, 401
Golden Horn, 33, 51, 58, 59, 60, 61, 62, 66, 70, 84, 98, 99, 103, 104, 105, 106, 107, 108, 109, 110, 111, 114, 185, 186, 187, 191, 196, 234, 241, 249
Golem, 418
Gollub War, 403
Gothia. See Theodoro
Goths, 51, 167, 168, 263, 383, 450, 461, 463, 464, 465, 466
Greece, 31, 33, 43, 44, 45, 53, 67, 68, 70, 71, 81, 82, 83, 84, 88, 91, 93, 104, 124, 132, 138, 150, 179, 184, 187, 189, 191, 193, 194, 199, 201, 204, 209, 223, 231, 263, 264, 265, 266, 267, 269, 276, 280, 319, 347, 354, 355, 376, 417, 418, 447, 449, 450, 468, 533, 594, 595, 617
Greek fire, 52, 109, 112, 473
Gregory I, 12, 467, 468
Gregory I of Tusculum, 12, 517, 518, 519
Gregory II, 12, 477, 478, 479
Gregory III, 12, 478, 479
Gregory IV, 490
Gregory IX, 559, 560
Gregory Kamonas, 418
Gregory V, 12, 516, 517
Gregory VI
    Anti-Pope, 12, 519
    Pope, 12, 184, 521, 522, 523
Gregory VII, 12, 530, 531, 532, 533, 534, 535, 536, 572
Gregory VIII
    Anti-Pope, 12, 538
    Pope, 12, 553
Gregory X, 566
Gregory XI, 584
Gregory XII, 12, 589, 590

Guelphs, 514, 550, 551, 560, 574, 575, 578
Guillaume II (William the Conqueror), 529, 530
Güneri of Karaman, 12, 131, 132
Guy II, 12, 499
Guy III, 12, 500, 501, 502
Guy of Tuscany, 12, 508
Habsburger, 567
Hadân Suleiman Pasha, 408, 409
Hagia Sophia, 60, 62, 65, 66, 102, 103, 187, 275, 526
Haifa, 190, 236
Halicarnassus, 67, 609, 610, 613, 614, 617
Halych, 305, 307
Hellespont. See Dardanelles
Henry II, 12, 298, 518, 519, 520, 551
Henry II of Bavaria, 297
Henry III, 12, 299, 522, 523, 562, 563, 564
Henry IV, 12, 184, 300, 527, 530, 531, 532, 533, 535, 536
Henry Raspe, 561
Henry V, 12, 221, 536, 537, 540, 553
Henry VI, 12, 226, 227, 535, 552, 554, 555, 556
Henry VII, 12, 239, 578, 579
Heraclea Pontica, 158, 159
Heraclius, 13, 469, 470, 471, 476
Herzegovina, 200, 348, 360, 361, 374, 377, 378
Hexamilion Wall, 86, 94, 99, 199, 200
Heyreddin Bey, 600
Hilarius, 13, 455, 458
Hohenstaufen, 540, 556, 566
Holy Land, 54, 57, 63, 160, 221, 305, 307, 519, 536, 537, 541, 542, 545, 546, 547, 548, 552, 554, 555, 559, 566, 576, 583, 605, 606, 607, 610

Holy Roman Emperor, 150, 169, 224, 227, 239, 304, 311, 320, 325, 326, 327, 328, 549, 550, 555, 556, 558, 570, 577, 578, 580, 581, 583, 592
Honorius, 13, 448, 449
Honorius I, 13, 469, 470, 471, 474
Honorius II, 576
  Anti-Pope, 13, 529
  Pope, 13, 539, 540, 542, 545
Honorius III, 13, 228, 557, 558, 559
Honorius IV, 569
Hormisdas, 13, 460, 461, 462
House of Dăneşti, 387, 389, 391
House of Drăculeşti, 387
Hugh of Arles, 508
Hugues de Payens, 606
Hunedoara. See Hunyad
Hungary, 33, 42, 46, 85, 88, 90, 93, 95, 103, 135, 149, 150, 198, 199, 200, 202, 209, 228, 244, 268, 272, 277, 279, 281, 287, 295, 297, 298, 299, 300, 301, 302, 303, 304, 305, 306, 308, 309, 310, 311, 313, 314, 315, 316, 317, 318, 319, 320, 321, 324, 325, 326, 327, 328, 329, 332, 333, 334, 335, 337, 338, 339, 341, 349, 350, 351, 352, 353, 355, 356, 357, 358, 359, 360, 367, 368, 369, 370, 371, 372, 373, 374, 375, 376, 377, 378, 383, 384, 385, 386, 387, 388, 390, 391, 392, 393, 397, 401, 402, 403, 406, 422, 451, 558, 584, 586, 587, 590, 592, 593, 595, 596, 597, 601, 608, 618
Huns, 167, 263, 449, 450, 451, 452
Hussite Wars, 326, 328
Hussites, 326, 590
Hynyad, 328
Ibrahim II of Karaman, 13, 44, 90, 91, 92, 97, 135, 136, 137, 162, 197, 331

Iconoclasm, 477, 478, 479, 485, 488, 489, 496
Iconodule, 485
Ilias I, 404
Imroz, 177, 203, 205, 218, 250, 251
Innocent I, 448
Innocent II, 13, 543, 544, 545, 556, 557, 606
Innocent III
    Anti-Pope, 13, 552
    Pope, 13, 55, 228, 555, 556, 557, 558
Innocent IV, 13, 230, 560, 561, 562
Innocent V, 567
Innocent VI, 13, 582, 583
Innocent VII, 13, 588, 589
Iraq, 145
Irene of Athens, 13, 268
Isaac II Angelos, 13, 57, 60, 62, 158
Isidore of Kiev, 13, 102, 594
Istanbul, 115, 138, 149, 150, 163, 196, 197, 198, 202, 203, 204, 205, 208, 209, 210, 251, 252, 253, 267, 360, 376, 395, 409, 477, 599, 600, 601, 613, 617

Italy, 46, 71, 115, 160, 167, 168, 169, 170, 171, 179, 183, 184, 185, 192, 197, 201, 203, 211, 220, 223, 224, 227, 229, 230, 233, 235, 239, 244, 272, 309, 314, 318, 334, 335, 375, 419, 431, 432, 433, 449, 451, 452, 453, 454, 456, 457, 458, 460, 461, 462, 463, 464, 465, 466, 467, 468, 469, 471, 472, 476, 478, 480, 484, 485, 486, 487, 488, 489, 491, 498, 499, 500, 501, 502, 503, 504, 505, 506, 507, 508, 509, 510, 513, 514, 515, 516, 518, 519, 520, 521, 522, 523, 524, 525, 526, 528, 530, 532, 533, 534, 535, 536, 537, 538, 540, 542, 543, 544, 548, 549, 550, 551, 552, 553, 554, 556, 558, 559, 560, 561, 563, 564, 565, 566, 573, 574, 575, 577, 578, 579, 580, 581, 582, 583, 584, 585, 586, 590, 594, 598, 599, 600, 601, 605, 611, 612
Iuga, 403
Ivan Alexander, 13, 285, 286, 354
Ivan Asen II of Bulgaria, 13, 68, 280, 281, 282, 284, 351
Ivan Asen III of Bulgaria, 13, 283
Ivan II of Bulgaria, 284
Ivan Šišman, 14, 286, 287, 385
Ivan Sratsimir, 14, 286, 287, 288, 385
Ivan Stefan of Bulgaria, 285
Ivan Vladislav of Bulgaria, 13, 277, 278
Ivaylo of Bulgaria, 13, 282, 283
Izmir. See Smyrna
Jahan Shah, 14, 146, 147
Jajce, 200, 338, 376, 377, 378
Jan Huus, 326
Janissaries, 32, 42, 94, 108, 113, 151, 252, 388, 395, 617

Janos Hunyadi, 14, 42, 43, 90, 92, 95, 96, 103, 106, 328, 329, 330, 332, 333, 334, 335, 336, 337, 358, 388, 389, 390, 391, 425, 595, 657
Jelena Gruba, 374
Jerusalem, 44, 53, 55, 57, 58, 63, 64, 185, 221, 228, 229, 235, 321, 322, 324, 329, 351, 445, 446, 469, 471, 526, 530, 536, 537, 542, 547, 552, 554, 557, 558, 559, 561, 583, 587, 605, 606, 607, 610
   Reconquest of, 55, 553, 606, 654
Joanna I of Naples, 14, 318, 582, 584, 585, 586
Joanna II of Naples, 14, 591, 593
Johannes Klenkoka, 584
Johannes Wildeshausen, 368, 369
John Crescentius, 14, 512, 518, 519
John I, 461
John I Tzimiskes, 14, 275, 276, 514
John II, 462
John II of France, 585
John III, 14, 465, 466, 467
John III Doukas Vatatzes, 14, 50, 67, 68, 418
John IV Laskaris, 14, 68, 69, 147, 162, 282, 470, 471
John IX, 14, 503, 505
John Kantakouzenos, 14, 80, 81, 582, 583
John of Brienne, 228
John V, 475
John V Palaiologos, 14, 30, 81, 82, 83, 84, 85, 176, 192, 193, 217, 242, 243, 244, 285, 286, 319, 584
John VI, 14, 30, 76, 81, 82, 241, 242, 285, 476
John VII, 476
John VIII, 14, 498, 499, 501
John VIII Palaiologos, 14, 88, 89, 90, 91, 92, 96, 592
John Wycliffe, 584
John X, 14, 506, 507, 508

John XI, 508, 509
John XII, 14, 509, 510, 511, 512
John XIII, 14, 512, 513, 514
John XIV, 515
John XIX, 14, 520, 521, 526
John XV, 515, 516
John XVI, 516, 517
John XVII, 518
John XVIII, 518, 519
John XXI, 568
John XXII, 14, 579, 580, 581
John XXIII, 590
Julius Nepos, 456
Justin I, 14, 460, 461, 462
Justin II, 465
Justinian I, 15, 169, 462, 463, 464, 465
Justinian II, 15, 264, 265, 476, 477
Kai Tribe, 29, 131, 306, 317
Kaliman Asen II of Bulgaria, 281, 282
Kaliman I of Bulgaria, 281
Kalona Harbour, 610
Kaloyan of Bulgaria, 279, 280
Kara Hizin Pasha, 41
Karaman, 34, 44, 88, 90, 91, 93, 97, 128, 131, 132, 133, 134, 135, 136, 137, 138, 148, 150, 161, 162, 197, 331
   Conquest of, 148, 658
Kardam of Bulgaria, 268
Karl Topia, 420
Karpathos, 611
Kasım, 15, 137, 138, 148, 149, 151
Kastellorizo, 609, 610
Kastoria, 184
Kayqubad I, 15, 29, 131
Kazakhstan, 53, 121
Kefken, 69
Kerîmeddin Karaman Bey, 131
Kilij Arslan I, 123
Kingdom of Sicily, 233, 542, 556, 562, 574

Kingdom of Thessalonica, 66, 68, 279
Kleidion, 277
Ključ, 377
Knights Hospitaller, 149, 208, 240, 311, 321, 324, 576, 577, 587, 605, 606, 607, 608, 609, 610, 611, 612, 613, 614, 615, 617, 618
Knights of Malta. See Knights Hospitaller
Knights of Rhodes. See Knights Hospitaller
Knights Templar, 237, 542, 545, 547, 554, 576, 606, 607, 608, 609
Komnena Nemanjić, 418
Konya, 123, 131, 132, 133, 137, 138
Kormesiy of Bulgaria, 266
Kormisosh of Bulgaria, 15, 266, 267
Kos, 609, 610, 614
Kosovo, 43, 84, 95, 103, 133, 317, 356, 358, 373, 374, 423, 425, 426
Kosovo Polje, 333
Kostur, 418
Koylu Hisar, 148, 150
Krak des Chevaliers, 607
Krstjani. See Bogomils
Krujë, 96, 202, 203, 209, 210, 417, 418, 421, 422, 423, 426, 429, 430, 431, 432
Krum, 15, 268, 269, 276, 295, 488
Kučevo, 355
Kulin, 15, 367, 368
Ladislaus I, 301, 302
Ladislaus II, 304
Ladislaus III, 306
Ladislaus IV, 15, 313, 314, 315
Ladislaus of Naples, 15, 320, 325, 587, 588
Ladislaus Posthumous, 103
Ladislaus V, 15, 315, 316, 328, 332, 334, 337

Lambert II, 15, 502, 503
Lando, 506
Languedoc, 557, 608
Laodicea, 221
L'Aquila, 571
Larissa, 184, 276
Lațcu, 402
Lateran Palace, 447, 470, 475, 481, 483, 484, 489, 490, 497, 508, 509, 522, 523, 524, 530, 534, 543, 568
Latin Empire of Constantinople, 124, 189, 557, 569
Laurentius, 15, 458, 459, 460
Lazar Branković, 359
Lazar Hrebeljanović, 15, 355, 356, 373
League of Lezhë, 422, 427, 432
Lecce, 600
Lemnos, 87, 200, 205, 209, 210, 242
Leo I, 15, 449, 452, 453, 455
Leo II, 474, 475
Leo III
    Emperor, 15, 266, 477, 478, 479
    Pope, 15, 486, 487
Leo IV
    Emperor, 15, 268, 485
    Pope, 15, 491, 492
Leo IX, 16, 524, 525, 526, 527, 528
Leo V
    Emperor, 15, 269, 270, 488
    Pope, 15, 504
Leo VI
    Emperor, 15, 272, 273, 295, 505
    Pope, 15, 508
Leo VII, 15, 508, 511
Leo VIII, 15, 511, 512
Leontios, 16, 264, 265
Lepanto, 198, 209, 211, 278
Lesbos, 46, 186, 201, 204, 243, 250, 252
Liberius, 447
Libius Severus, 16, 455
Lido, 245

Liguria, 219, 222, 223, 227, 228, 230, 239, 245
Ligurian Sea, 219
Limassol, 608
Little Armenia, 123
Liutprand, 16, 478, 479
Lombard League, 229, 230, 551, 558, 559, 560
Lombards, 169, 183, 188, 465, 466, 467, 468, 469, 472, 478, 479, 480, 481, 482, 483, 484, 485, 488, 498, 519, 520, 523, 528, 529, 530, 531, 534
Long Campaign, 91, 135, 330, 331, 358, 421, 657
Longobardia, 514
Lorenzo de'Medici, 597
Lothair I, 16, 488, 489, 490, 491, 493
Lothair II, 16, 540, 543
Lothair II of Lotharingia, 16, 493, 494, 495, 497
Lotharingia, 493
Louis I of Anjou, 16, 585, 586, 587
Louis I of Hungary, 16, 317, 318, 319, 320, 371, 372, 373, 384, 385, 401, 402, 582, 586
Louis II, 16, 491, 493, 494, 497, 498, 499, 503, 549
Louis II of Naples, 16, 587, 588
Louis III of Anjou, 16, 591, 593
Louis IV ('the Bavarian'), 16, 580, 581
Louis IX of France, 16, 234, 564
Louis the Blind, 16, 503, 504, 505
Louis the Pious, 16, 270, 488, 490, 491
Louis VII of France, 16, 303, 544, 545, 547, 548, 551
Lucca, 529, 578, 589
Lucius II, 545
Lucius III, 16, 552, 554

Lyon, 71, 230, 523, 561, 566, 567, 568, 569, 576, 579
Macedonia, 46, 199, 203, 209, 251, 268, 317, 352, 355, 371, 423, 425, 430, 596
Magyars, 272, 273, 274, 295, 296, 297, 309
Majorian, 454
Malamir of Bulgaria, 270
Malta, 615, 618
Mamluk, 131, 132, 134, 136, 137, 138, 145, 160, 189, 190, 209, 236, 607, 610, 617
Mandraki Harbour, 610, 611, 612
Manfred of Sicily, 16, 233, 418, 419, 562, 563, 564, 565
Mangup, 164
Manisa, 43
Mantua, 451, 595
Manuel I Komnenos, 16, 224, 304, 305, 349, 367
Manuel II Palaiologos, 16, 33, 77, 85, 86, 87, 88, 94, 194
Manzikert, 53, 122, 184, 535
Mara Brancovic, 16, 41, 356, 357, 358, 359
Maramureş, 401, 402
Marcellae, 267, 268
Maria of Antioch, 225
Maria Palaiologina Kantakouzene, 17, 282, 283
Marinus I, 17, 500, 501, 568
Marinus II, 508
Maritsa River, 355, 373
Mark, 51
Marozia, 17, 505, 507, 508, 520
Marqab, 607
Marquisates of Boudonitza, 66
Martin I, 17, 471, 472, 476
Martin IV, 17, 568, 569
Martin V, 17, 326, 590, 591, 592, 594

Mary of Hungary, 17, 319, 320, 321, 373, 374, 587
Matej Ninoslav, 17, 368, 369
Matilda of Tuscany, 17, 532, 534, 537, 540, 552
Matthew Kantakouzenos, 17, 30, 82, 242
Matthias I (Corvin), 17, 337, 338, 339, 360, 375, 377, 391, 392, 393, 396, 397, 406, 407, 595, 597
Mauretania, 449
Mecca, 469
Medina, 469
Mediterranean Sea, 33, 52, 66, 84, 131, 161, 181, 235, 248, 428, 491, 598, 610, 614
Megaskyrate of Athens and Thebes, 66
Mehmed I, 17, 34, 35, 87, 134, 135, 327, 387, 609
Mehmed I of Karaman, 131
Mehmed II, 1, 17, 41, 42, 43, 45, 46, 97, 98, 99, 101, 102, 104, 105, 106, 107, 108, 109, 110, 111, 112, 113, 114, 115, 116, 136, 137, 138, 146, 147, 148, 149, 150, 151, 152, 161, 162, 163, 164, 195, 196, 197, 198, 199, 201, 202, 203, 204, 205, 206, 207, 208, 209, 210, 211, 248, 249, 250, 251, 252, 253, 277, 298, 334, 335, 336, 337, 338, 339, 341, 342, 347, 358, 359, 360, 374, 375, 376, 377, 378, 390, 392, 393, 394, 395, 397, 404, 405, 407, 408, 409, 427, 428, 429, 430, 431, 432, 445, 593, 595, 596, 597, 598, 599, 601, 605, 610, 611, 613, 617, 618
Mehmed II of Karaman, 17, 134, 135
Meister Georg, 612
Melus of Bari, 519
Mesih Pasha, 17, 611, 612, 613

Messina, 565
Michael Asen I, 17, 281
Michael Asen II, 282, 283
Michael I, 17, 269, 526
Michael III, 17, 270, 496
Michael IV, 278
Michael IX Palaiologos, 17, 80, 238, 284, 353
Michael Shishman of Bulgaria, 17, 285, 353
Michael VII Doukas, 183
Michael VIII Palaiologos, 17, 68, 69, 70, 71, 72, 79, 231, 232, 233, 265, 282, 283, 418, 419, 563, 566, 567, 569
Mihai I, 387
Milan, 230, 239, 242, 244, 246, 247, 445, 465, 537, 540, 551, 553, 558, 560, 580, 583, 584, 586, 592, 593, 601
Miltiades, 17, 446, 447
Mircea I, 18, 32, 385, 386, 387, 388, 391, 403
Mircea II Dracula, 18, 388, 389
Misivri, 103, 334
Mistra, 70, 96, 201
Mitso Asen of Bulgaria, 18, 282, 283
Mladen I, 370
Mladen II, 370
Modon, 66, 88, 185, 187, 200, 201, 211, 242
Moldavia, 45, 163, 209, 286, 301, 317, 318, 324, 341, 360, 384, 390, 396, 397, 398, 401, 402, 403, 404, 405, 406, 407, 408, 409, 410
Monemvasia, 232
Mongols, 29, 34, 86, 121, 124, 131, 132, 160, 191, 238, 240, 252, 281, 282, 283, 284, 310, 311, 312, 314, 317, 318, 341, 351, 352, 369, 383, 385, 401, 561

Monophysitism, 457, 458, 463, 464, 470
Monothelitism, 464, 469, 470, 471, 472, 473, 474, 476, 477
Monte Cassino, 534, 540, 541
Montenegro. See Zeta
Moravia, 270
Morea, 45, 66, 70, 71, 83, 84, 86, 88, 89, 91, 93, 94, 96, 103, 104, 115, 185, 187, 195, 197, 198, 199, 200, 201, 202, 204, 210, 211, 232, 595, 617
Mount Athos, 46, 159
Mourtzouphlos, 62, 63, 64, 65
Muhammad (Abū al-Qāsim Muḥammad ibn ʿAbd Allāh ibn ʿAbd al-Muṭṭalib ibn Hāshim), 18, 271, 469, 472
Murad I, 18, 31, 32, 33, 83, 84, 95, 132, 133, 244, 355, 356, 373, 420
Murad II, 18, 36, 41, 42, 43, 44, 87, 88, 89, 90, 91, 92, 93, 94, 95, 96, 134, 135, 136, 137, 194, 195, 199, 248, 287, 326, 327, 328, 329, 330, 331, 333, 334, 357, 358, 387, 388, 390, 420, 421, 422, 423, 424, 425, 426, 427, 593
Musa, 34, 35, 86, 87, 132, 386
Mustafa Pasha, 425, 428
Mutimir, 18, 347, 348
Mytilene, 252
Nafplio, 199, 200, 201
Naples, 71, 149, 170, 233, 239, 283, 314, 318, 320, 325, 373, 427, 429, 430, 463, 466, 492, 499, 544, 555, 561, 564, 565, 566, 570, 572, 573, 574, 577, 578, 581, 582, 583, 584, 585, 586, 587, 588, 589, 591, 593, 595, 597, 599, 600, 601, 617
Naxos, 197, 204, 209
Nefise, 18, 132, 133

Negroponte, 197, 204, 206, 207, 232, 240, 252, 612
Neretva River, 181
Nero, 18, 445, 446
Nesebar, 103, 264
Nicaea, 30, 67, 69, 70, 80, 115, 123, 159, 160, 231, 281, 282, 307, 308, 351, 418, 446, 447, 485
Niccolo da Canale, 18, 205, 207, 208
Nicholas I, 18, 493, 494, 495, 496, 497, 500, 549
Nicholas II, 18, 495, 528, 529, 530, 531
Nicholas III, 568
Nicholas IV, 18, 160, 570, 571
Nicholas Mystikos, 505
Nicholas V
  Anti-Pope, 18, 580
  Pope, 18, 95, 102, 593, 594
Nicolae Alexandru, 384, 385
Nicomedia, 30, 80, 159
Nicopolis, 33, 85, 133, 288, 322, 323, 324, 329, 332, 356
Nikephoros I, 18, 268, 269, 419
Nikephoros II Phokas, 513, 514
Nikephoros III Botaneiates, 183
Niksar, 150
Niš, 330, 421
Nocera, 586
Normandy, 169, 506, 520, 529
Normans, 54, 169, 183, 184, 185, 220, 224, 278, 506, 519, 520, 522, 523, 525, 527, 528, 530, 533, 534, 535, 536, 538, 541, 543, 550, 554, 605, 606, 607, 608, 609
Norsemen, 493, 497, 506
North Africa, 462
Novo Brdo, 356, 357
Numidia, 449
Oblast Brankovića, 356
Oderisio di Sangro, 541
Odoacer, 18, 51, 167, 168, 456, 457

Oghuz Yabgu State, 121, 122
Ohrid, 430
Olybrius, 18, 455, 456
Omurtag of Bulgaria, 269, 270
Oranik, 428
Order of the Dragon, 326, 388
Oreoi, 191
Orhan, 18, 30, 31, 81, 82, 83, 97
Orleans, 451
Oryahovo, 322
Osman, 18, 29, 30, 79, 80, 81, 145, 146, 569
Ostia, 491, 492, 534, 559, 567, 572, 575, 582
Ostrogoths, 167, 168, 169, 457, 465
Otranto, 599, 600, 601
Otto I, 18, 296, 509, 510, 511, 512, 513
Otto II, 19, 513, 514, 515, 517
Otto III, 19, 298, 316, 515, 516, 517, 518
Otto IV, 19, 227, 556
Ottokar II, 312, 313
Ottoman Interregnum, 34, 86, 88, 89, 134, 194
Paderborn, 486
Padua, 244, 246
Pagan of Bulgaria, 267
Palazzo Venezia, 597
Palermo, 183, 565
Palestine, 53, 123, 131, 160, 189, 190, 209, 220, 223, 228, 229, 230, 445, 554, 558, 571, 613, 618
Palestrina, 524, 553, 570
Panagyurishte, 90
Pantheon, 469, 473

Papal States, 230, 480, 481, 482, 487, 498, 499, 500, 502, 503, 504, 506, 509, 510, 514, 519, 522, 528, 530, 535, 541, 542, 544, 552, 553, 556, 559, 560, 561, 562, 564, 565, 567, 568, 577, 578, 584, 590, 591, 592, 597, 601
Paris, 56, 506, 547, 570, 575, 576, 609
Parma, 529, 561
Paschal I, 19, 488, 489
Paschal II, 19, 536, 538, 539, 605
Paschal III, 19, 551, 552
Paul I, 19, 480, 481
Paul I Šubić, 370
Paul II
    Patriarch, 19, 471
    Pope, 19, 596, 597
Pavel Branovic, 348
Pavia, 465, 510, 515, 516, 518, 591
Pechenegs, 272, 273, 275, 295, 301, 303, 304, 383
Pelagius I, 465
Pelagius II, 467
Pellestrina, 245
Peloponnese. See Morea
Pentapolis, 478
Pepin the Short, 19, 479, 480, 481, 482, 486
Persia, 34, 52, 53, 86, 121, 122, 145, 152, 160, 468, 618
Petar Gojnikovic, 348
Petar Svačić, 19, 302
Peter Deljan of Bulgaria, 278
Peter I of Bulgaria, 19, 274, 275, 276
Peter I of Cyprus, 19, 583, 584
Peter III of Aragon, 19, 71, 235, 569, 570
Peter IV of Bulgaria, 279
Peter Orseolo, 299
Petronius Maximus, 19, 452, 453
Petru I, 402

Petru II, 19, 402
Petru III, 19, 404, 405, 406, 407
Peuce, 264
Philadelphia, 30, 80, 81, 238
Philip II, 19, 554, 556
Philip IV, 19, 571, 572, 573, 574, 575, 576, 577, 579, 608
Philip of Swabia, 19, 57, 158, 227, 556
Philip the Good, 19, 199, 596
Philip V, 19, 580
Philip VI, 581
Philippe de Villiers de L'Isle-Adam, 614
Philippikos Bardanes, 20, 265, 477
Philippopolis, 286
Phoenix, 472
Phokia, 218, 250, 251
Phokianova, 218, 250, 251
Piacenza, 54, 516, 535
Pierleoni, 539, 540, 543, 545, 546
Pierre d'Aubusson, 612
Pietro II Orseolo, 181
Pir Ahmed, 20, 137, 138, 148, 149, 151
Pisa, 170, 182, 188, 192, 220, 222, 225, 226, 227, 230, 235, 236, 241, 546, 553, 555, 565, 579, 580, 583, 589
Pius II, 20, 198, 430, 595
Pliska, 264, 267, 269
Pločnik, 287, 321, 355
Po River, 179, 502
Poland, 42, 77, 90, 149, 298, 299, 300, 301, 302, 310, 315, 316, 318, 319, 320, 328, 329, 337, 386, 388, 402, 403, 404, 405, 409, 449, 593
Pomorie, 265, 274
Pons of Melgueil, 541
Porto Pisano, 235, 236, 655
Porto Torres, 235
Portugal, 168, 547, 551

Portus, 491
Prague, 312, 337
Presian I of Bulgaria, 270
Preslav, 275
Prespa, 277
Prijezda I, 369
Prijezda II, 369
Prilep, 277
Prinkipo, 190
Pristina, 333
Procopius Anthemius, 455
Progon, 417
Provence, 222, 223, 467, 503, 504, 507
Prussia, 309, 608
Prvoslav, 348
Puglia, 517
Pylos, 192
Qara Iskander, 20, 145, 146
Qara Yusuf, 145
Radivoj, 20, 374, 376
Radu I, 385
Radu II, 20, 387, 403
Radu III (cel Frumos), 20, 389, 393, 395, 396, 397, 407, 408
Ragusa, 46, 170, 181, 201, 352, 353, 357, 369, 371, 372, 374, 377, 427
Ramon Berenguer IV, 222
Ranulf II, 544
Rasboieni, 409
Rascia, 349
Ravenna, 168, 449, 454, 456, 457, 458, 459, 461, 465, 466, 470, 471, 473, 474, 475, 476, 478, 480, 487, 495, 514, 516, 517, 532
Reggio, 463
Renaissance, 568, 594, 597
Rene of Anjou, 593
Republic of Turkey, 618
Rheims, 488, 538, 547
Rhodes, 149, 186, 583, 605, 609, 610, 611, 612, 614, 615, 618

Rhone River, 225, 582
Richard I (Lionheart), 20, 554, 555, 556, 562, 608
Ricimer, 20, 454, 455, 456
Rimnicu Sarat, 407
Robert Guiscard, 20, 183, 184, 530, 533
Robert of Anjou, 20, 239, 578, 579, 580, 581
Roger II of Sicily, 20, 542, 543, 544, 545, 546, 548, 549
Rollo, 20, 506
Roman, 406
Roman Empire, 31, 32, 51, 52, 53, 66, 121, 167, 168, 227, 229, 298, 299, 311, 314, 315, 325, 417, 433, 445, 446, 447, 448, 449, 456, 462, 487, 507, 514, 518, 555
Roman I, 402, 403
Roman II, 404
Romanos IV Diogenes, 53, 122
Romanus, 503
Romanus IV Diogenes, 120, 122

Rome, 31, 51, 52, 53, 54, 89, 160, 168, 180, 184, 192, 230, 271, 321, 326, 334, 375, 383, 417, 428, 445, 446, 447, 448, 449, 450, 452, 453, 454, 455, 456, 457, 458, 459, 460, 461, 462, 463, 464, 465, 466, 467, 468, 469, 470, 472, 473, 474, 475, 476, 477, 478, 479, 480, 481, 483, 484, 486, 488, 489, 490, 491, 492, 493, 494, 495, 496, 498, 499, 500, 501, 502, 503, 504, 505, 507, 508, 510, 511, 512, 513, 514, 515, 516, 517, 518, 519, 520, 521, 522, 523, 524, 525, 526, 527, 528, 529, 533, 534, 535, 537, 538, 539, 540, 541, 542, 543, 544, 545, 546, 547, 548, 549, 550, 551, 552, 554, 555, 556, 557, 559, 560, 561, 563, 564, 565, 566, 567, 568, 569, 570, 571, 572, 573, 574, 575, 576, 577, 578, 579, 580, 581, 584, 585, 586, 587, 588, 589, 590, 591, 592, 593, 594, 596, 597, 599, 600, 601, 611, 615
Romulus Augustus, 20, 51, 456
Rudolf I, 20, 567, 568, 570, 577
Rumelia, 30, 31, 36, 42, 44, 52, 53, 59, 61, 83, 87, 104, 124, 132, 150, 163, 209, 295, 618
Rupert, 325, 326, 588
Rus, 275, 281, 298, 303
Sabin of Bulgaria, 267
Sabinian, 468
Safavids, 152

Saladin (Ṣalāḥ ad-Dīn Yūsuf ibn Ayyūb), 20, 55, 552, 553, 554
Salep River, 554
Salerno, 183, 499, 533, 555
Salona, 66, 456, 463
Salonika, 185
Samos, 186
Samothrace, 177, 203, 250, 251
Samuel Aba, 20, 299

Samuel of Bulgaria, 20, 276, 277, 278
San Fele, 586
Saracens, 184, 219, 220, 222, 491, 492, 493, 497, 498, 499, 500, 506, 507, 518, 528, 542
Sardinia, 219, 220, 225, 235, 236, 239, 242, 450, 491
Sas, 401
Sassanids, 52, 450
Sassari, 235
Sava, 351
Sava River, 335
Savona, 230
Saxons, 94, 99, 184, 307, 309, 312, 352, 384, 385, 386, 390, 391, 467, 608
Scandinavia, 32, 44, 169, 224, 548
Scotland, 587
Sea of Azov, 190, 243
Sea of Marmara, 30, 58, 80, 84, 86, 92, 99, 103, 104, 105, 107, 123, 149, 190, 195, 196, 198, 204, 205, 232, 238, 243, 267, 473, 611
Şebinkarahisar, 150
Seleucia-Ctesiphon, 445
Selim I, 20, 617, 618
Seljuk, 122
Seljuk Empire of Rum, 124, 132, 159, 161
Serbia, 32, 35, 41, 42, 45, 46, 84, 85, 91, 95, 138, 150, 199, 209, 270, 271, 274, 277, 278, 281, 283, 285, 286, 287, 306, 318, 321, 324, 326, 328, 329, 330, 331, 333, 338, 341, 347, 348, 349, 350, 351, 352, 353, 354, 355, 356, 357, 358, 359, 360, 361, 367, 369, 370, 371, 372, 373, 374, 375, 383, 389, 392, 397, 407, 418, 424, 425, 426, 428, 595
Serbian Grand Principality, 349
Sergius I, 20, 470, 475, 476

Sergius II, 20, 491, 492
Sergius III, 21, 504, 505, 506, 508
Sergius IV, 21, 519
Sevar of Bulgaria, 266
Severin, 385
Severinus, 470, 471
Shiite, 42
Shkodër, 209, 210, 211, 418, 425, 426, 432
Shkumbi River, 202, 203, 431
Sibiu, 384, 390, 391
Sicilian Vespers, 71, 79, 170, 235, 283, 419, 567, 569, 655
Sicily, 70, 71, 107, 170, 183, 184, 189, 191, 219, 220, 223, 224, 226, 227, 233, 234, 235, 238, 239, 283, 313, 314, 418, 419, 450, 463, 472, 473, 491, 499, 518, 528, 533, 541, 542, 543, 544, 545, 546, 548, 549, 551, 553, 554, 555, 556, 559, 561, 562, 563, 564, 565, 567, 569, 570, 571, 572, 573, 574, 587, 594, 615
Sidon, 190, 236
Siege of Alessandria, 552, 654
Siege of Belgrade, 329, 337, 360, 595, 657
Siena, 547, 550, 578, 579, 595
Sighisoara, 388
Sigismund of Hungary, 21, 33, 85, 90, 319, 320, 321, 322, 323, 324, 325, 326, 327, 328, 357, 373, 374, 385, 388, 587, 590, 592
Sihabeddin Pasha, 42
Silifke, 137, 138, 149
Silistra, 275, 283
Silivri, 103, 334
Silk Route, 160
Silverius, 21, 462, 463, 464
Simeon I of Bulgaria, 21, 272, 273, 274, 295, 348
Simplicius, 21, 455, 456, 457
Sinop, 123, 148, 150, 157, 160, 163

Sinucello della Rocca, 21, 235, 236
Sipahi, 323, 421
Siricius, 448
Sisinnius, 476
Sivas, 123, 131
Sixtus III, 449
Sixtus IV, 597
Skanderbeg, 11, 21, 45, 93, 95, 199, 202, 203, 204, 330, 333, 358, 420, 421, 422, 423, 424, 425, 426, 427, 428, 429, 430, 431, 432, 595, 596, 597
Skiros, 205
Sklaviniai, 347
Skopje, 376
Slavonia, 309, 313, 315
Slavs, 31, 263, 264, 269, 270, 271, 347, 367, 383, 384, 417, 470, 496
Slovenia, 167, 360, 361
Smederevo, 90, 326, 330, 333, 357, 358, 359, 360, 375
Smilets of Bulgaria, 284
Smyrna, 67, 149, 240, 597, 609
Sofia, 51, 90, 95, 264, 268, 269, 287, 329, 338, 360, 594
Söğüt, 29, 569
Solino, 221
Solomon I, 21, 300, 301
Spain, 52, 149, 168, 219, 220, 222, 223, 296, 479, 491, 551, 561, 565
Split, 369
Spoleto, 465, 479, 486, 499, 500, 502, 503, 507, 510, 559
Srebrenica, 338
St.John Lateran, 543
St.Mark's Square, 189
St.Peter, 21, 445, 446, 460, 461
St.Peter's Cathedral, 455, 459, 473, 483, 487, 489, 491, 492, 503, 543, 548, 593, 601
St.Romanus Gate, 105, 106, 111, 112, 113

Stefan (II) Nemanjić, 21, 350, 351, 418
Stefan Dragutin, 21, 352, 353, 369
Stefan I of Hungary, 21, 298, 299, 301
Stefan I of Moldavia, 403
Stefan II of Hungary, 21, 302, 303
Stefan II of Moldavia, 404
Stefan III of Hungary, 304
Stefan III of Moldavia, 21, 390, 396, 397, 405, 406, 407, 408, 409, 410
Stefan IV, 304
Stefan Kulinić, 368
Stefan Lazarević, 21, 324, 356, 386
Stefan Nemanja, 21, 306, 350, 367
Stefan Radoslav, 351
Stefan Uroš I, 352
Stefan Uroš II Milutin, 21, 352, 353
Stefan Uroš III Dečanski, 353
Stefan Uroš IV Dušan, 22, 344, 345, 353, 354, 355, 371, 372
Stefan Uroš V, 22, 354, 355
Stefan V, 21, 312, 313
Stefan Vladislav I, 22, 351, 352
Stephen II, 22, 479, 480
Stephen III, 22, 481, 482, 483, 484, 490
Stephen IV, 488
Stephen IX, 528
Stephen V, 22, 500, 501
Stephen VI, 22, 502, 503, 505
Stephen VII, 508
Stephen VIII, 508
Stjepan Dabiša, 22, 373
Stjepan I, 22, 369, 370
Stjepan II, 22, 318, 370, 371, 372
Stjepan Ostoja, 374
Stjepan Tomaš, 22, 359, 374, 375
Stjepan Tomašević, 22, 359, 360, 365, 375, 376, 377, 378

Stjepan Tvrtko I, 22, 364, 372, 373, 374
Stjepan Tvrtko II, 374
Strumitsa, 277
Styria, 312
Suleiman I, 1, 22, 252, 339, 378, 613, 618
Sultanate of Rum, 28, 29, 34, 67, 79, 123, 124, 131, 160
Sutri, 478, 522, 537, 538
Svetigrad, 424, 425, 426
Svyatoslav I of Kiev, 275
Sylvester I, 22, 447, 460
Sylvester II, 22, 517, 521
Sylvester III, 22, 521, 522
Symmachus, 22, 458, 459, 460, 486
Syria, 52, 123, 131, 145, 185, 220, 228, 229, 237, 247, 266, 321, 552, 607, 618
Syrmia, 352, 353
Tabriz, 148, 152
Tagliacozzo, 565
Taksony of Hungary, 22, 296, 297
Tana, 190, 191, 240, 241, 243
Taranto, 220, 221, 599, 600, 601
Tarascon, 571
Târgoviște, 388, 389, 390, 391, 395
Tatars, 157, 199, 252, 309, 385, 401, 402, 408, 596
Taurus Mountains, 121, 131
Telerig of Bulgaria, 22, 267, 268
Telets of Bulgaria, 267
Telmessos, 609
Tenedos, 82, 192, 193, 205, 243, 244, 246
Tervel of Bulgaria, 22, 264, 265, 266, 476
Teutberga, 493, 494, 495
Teutonic Knights, 307, 309, 311, 403, 555, 559, 607, 608
Thasos, 177, 203
Theatre of Marcellus, 539

Thebes, 185
Theodahad, 22, 462, 463
Theodelinda, 23, 467, 468
Theodora, 23, 463, 464
Theodora Senatrix, 23, 504, 505, 506
Theodore Gabras, 157
Theodore I, 471
Theodore I Lascaris, 23, 67, 159
Theodore II, 23, 503
Theodore II Laskaris, 23, 68, 281
Theodore Komnenos Doukas, 23, 68, 280, 351
Theodore Svetoslav of Bulgaria, 23, 284
Theodoric (the Great), 23, 168, 457, 458, 459, 460, 461, 462, 486
Theodoric I, 23, 451, 453, 454
Theodoric II, 23, 454
Theodoro, 157, 158, 163, 164, 234, 252
Theodosian Wall, 249
Theodosios III, 23, 266, 477
Theodosius I, 23, 168, 447, 448
Theodosius II, 23, 99, 449
Theophanu, 23, 514, 515, 516
Theophilos, 270
Theophylact I, 23, 504, 505, 506, 507
Thessaloniki, 68, 86, 88, 194, 196, 272, 280, 281, 445
Tiber River, 492, 502, 539, 549
Tiberios III, 265
Tihomir, 349, 350
Timur (Tamerlane), 23, 34, 35, 44, 86, 87, 93, 133, 134, 145, 193, 327, 386, 589
Timurid Empire, 34, 35, 86
Tisza River, 311
Tivoli, 511, 517, 547, 548, 561
Tokat, 150
Toktu of Bulgaria, 267

Tomasina Morosini, 23, 314, 315
Tortosa, 222, 223
Totila, 464
Tower of Italy, 609, 612, 614
Tower of St Nicholas, 611
Trajan's Gate, 276, 277
Transylvania, 94, 99, 296, 298, 300, 307, 309, 312, 313, 316, 328, 332, 339, 357, 383, 384, 385, 387, 388, 390, 391, 396, 397, 398, 401, 405, 406, 407, 410, 608
Trapani, 233
Travunia. See Zeta
Treaty of Brétigny, 583
Trebizond, 44, 66, 67, 97, 123, 146, 147, 148, 150, 157, 158, 159, 160, 161, 162, 163, 595
Triarchy of Euboea, 66
Trier, 494, 495, 547
Tripoli, 55, 536
Tuğrul, 122
Turcopoles, 353
Turin, 246, 318, 493, 561
Turkmen, 122, 123, 148
Turkmenistan, 121
Tuscany, 462, 465, 504, 508, 523, 524, 528, 533, 540, 552, 579
Tusculum, 504, 521
Tycho Brahe, 44
Type of Constans, 471
Tyre, 188, 190, 231, 236
Tyrrhenian Sea, 219, 220, 225
Umor of Bulgaria, 267
Urban II, 23, 54, 55, 530, 534, 535, 536, 539
Urban III, 553
Urban IV, 23, 563, 564
Urban V, 23, 583, 584
Urban VI, 23, 585, 586
Uroš I, 24, 349, 352
Uroš II, 24, 349
Uzbekistan, 121

Valentian III, 24, 450, 451, 452, 454
Valois, 493
Vandals, 449, 450, 452, 453, 454, 455, 456, 461, 462, 463, 465
Varangian Guard, 32, 62, 184
Varna, 42, 91, 92, 93, 95, 103, 136, 195, 248, 268, 331, 358, 374, 389, 422, 423, 593
Vaslui, 408, 409
Veliko Tarnovo, 283, 286
Venice, 33, 45, 46, 56, 64, 66, 69, 79, 83, 84, 88, 89, 93, 98, 103, 135, 146, 148, 149, 151, 161, 167, 170, 171, 179, 180, 181, 182, 185, 187, 188, 189, 190, 191, 192, 193, 194, 195, 196, 197, 198, 199, 201, 203, 204, 205, 207, 208, 209, 210, 211, 219, 222, 223, 225, 226, 227, 230, 231, 232, 233, 234, 235, 236, 237, 239, 241, 242, 243, 244, 245, 246, 247, 251, 254, 277, 303, 305, 314, 318, 324, 326, 350, 354, 371, 375, 376, 417, 419, 420, 424, 425, 427, 428, 430, 431, 432, 487, 518, 552, 561, 583, 595, 596, 597, 598, 599, 611
Verona, 465, 504, 553
Vicenza, 465
Victor II, 527
Victor III, 534
Victor IV (Anti-Popes), 24, 544, 550, 551
Vidin, 264, 286, 287, 288, 322, 383, 393
Vigilius, 24, 463, 464
Vikings, 224, 493, 499, 506
Vinekh of Bulgaria, 267
Visigoths, 167, 168, 448, 449, 451, 453, 454, 455, 456, 462, 465
Vitalian, 24, 472, 473, 474
Viterbo, 546, 547, 548, 563, 564, 566, 568, 580, 588

Vitiges, 463
Vlad I ('Uzurpatorul'), 386
Vlad II Dracul, 24, 91, 92, 96, 332, 388, 389, 391
Vlad III Dracula, 1, 24, 96, 376, 389, 390, 391, 392, 393, 394, 395, 396, 397, 404, 405, 406, 409, 595, 659
Vlad IV Călugărul, 24, 391, 397, 409
Vladimir of Bulgaria, 272
Vladislav I, 385
Vladislav II, 24, 95, 96, 333, 358, 389, 390, 391
Vlastimir, 24, 270, 347
Vlorë, 599, 600, 612
Vuk Branković, 356
Vukan, 349
Vukan Nemanjić, 24, 306, 350, 367
Waldrada, 493, 494, 495
Wallachia, 32, 45, 46, 91, 92, 96, 150, 199, 209, 279, 284, 286, 287, 317, 318, 319, 321, 324, 329, 332, 341, 356, 357, 360, 376, 383, 384, 385, 386, 387, 388, 389, 390, 391, 392, 393, 396, 397, 398, 401, 402, 403, 405, 406, 407, 408, 409, 410, 595
Wenceslaus IV, 24, 325, 326

White Sheep, 44, 137, 145, 146, 147, 148, 149, 150, 151, 152, 160, 161, 162, 163, 208, 598
William I 'the Wicked', 549
William II of Holland, 24, 70, 232, 554, 561, 562, 563
Wladyslaw III, 327, 328, 329, 331, 332, 357
Wladyslaw III, 24, 42, 43, 77, 90, 91, 92
Wladyslaw III, 593
Wladyslaw III, 657
Worms, 500, 524, 538, 540
Zachary, 479
Zachlumia, 348
Zaganos Pasha, 108
Zagreb, 315
Zaharije Prvoslaviljevic, 348
Zara, 56, 57, 203, 245, 305, 306, 318, 325, 371, 557
Zeno, 24, 148, 150, 168, 245, 246, 457
Zeta, 347, 348, 349, 351, 352, 353, 354, 355, 356, 357, 360, 361, 372, 373, 420, 424
Zoltán of Hungary, 296
Zosimus, 448
Zvornik, 338

APPENDIXES

A - OVERVIEW OF KEY MILITARY ENCOUNTERS
B - CONSOLIDATED TIMELINE

Appendixes

APPENDIX A

OVERVIW OF KEY MILITARY ENCOUNTERS

This appendix outlines the key military encounters mentioned in this book. It does so in chronological order.

Battle of Catalaunum

In 451 a combined Roman and Visigoth coalition army under Flavius Aetius moved to meet marauding Huns under Attila at Catalaunum (modern day Châlons-en-Champagne in France).

The battle was indecisive and the Visigoth King Theodoric I was killed during the battle. Attila was back in western Europe the following year.

Battle of Mu'tah

In 629 the Muslim army under Muhammad for the first time faced a Byzantine army at Mu'tah in (modern) Jordan.

The battle was indecisive, though sources vary in their assessment, but it was a sign of things to come.

Battle of the Masts

In 655 a Muslim and Byzantine fleet met for the first time in sea-battle outside Phoenix (modern day Finike in Turkey).

The Muslim fleet was successful, and the battle marked the start to Muslim superiority at sea.

Battle of Ongal

In 680 the Byzantines, under Emperor Constantine IV, moved against the budding state of Bulgaria headed by Asparukh. They met a Peuce Island, an island - the size of Rhodes - in the Danube Delta which was heavily fortified.

The battle saw victory for the Bulgarians and soon after the Byzantines had to recognize the new Bulgarian state.

Appendixes

First Battle of Anchialus

In 708 the Byzantines, under Emperor Justinian II, attacked the Bulgarians, under Tervel, in order to retake territories previously ceded to the Bulgarians.

The Byzantine army camped at Anchialus (modern day Pomorie in Bulgaria), where they were surprised by the Bulgarians. The result was a rout of the Byzantines and a consolidation of the Bulgarian state.

Second Battle of Anchialus

In 763 raids by the Bulgarians, under their new Khan Telets, provoked the Byzantine Emperor Constantine V to take his army against the Bulgarians.

Telets failed to use his strategic advantage in the mountains and instead decided to meet the Byzantines in open battle outside Anchialus. The result was a resounding Byzantine victory which stopped Bulgarian progress and saw Telets murdered by his own nobles.

Battle of Boulgarophygon

In 896 the Byzantines attacked the Bulgarians, under Simeon I, as the culmination of an ongoing conflict. The armies met at Boulgarophygon (modern day Babaeski in European Turkey).

The Byzantine army was routed, and the Byzantines had to agree to pay an annual tribute to the Bulgarian Empire.

Third Battle of Anchialus

In 917 the Byzantines once again attacked the Bulgarians, this time as a direct result of their defeat in 896 at the Battle of Boulgarophygon, where they had been forced to agree to a humiliation annual tribute.

The two armies once again met at Anchialu and the Bulgarians won a decisive victory. As a result, Simeon I was crowned as Bulgarian Emperor in Constantinople, marking the zenith of the First Bulgarian Empire.

Battle of Lechfeld

In 955 the German King Otto I had consolidated his position at home, and he decided to stand against Magyar (Hungarian) raiders, who frequently raided into Germany.

The two forces met at Lechfeld (Augsburg in Germany) and the Germans were victorious despite numerical inferiority. The German King was elevated as emperor by his troops while the Hungarian Grand Prince Fajsz was replaced by Taksony. The battle ended Hungarian expansion into western Europe.

Appendix A - Overview of Key Military Encounters

Battle of Kleidion

In 1014 the Byzantine Emperor Basil II ('the Bulgar Slayer') moved to eradicate the First Bulgarian Empire under Emperor Samuel.

The two armies met at Kleidon (modern day Klyuch in Bulgaria) and the Byzantine victory was decisive. Bulgarian prisoners were sent home in groups of 100, 99 being blinded and the last only blinded in one eye so he could lead the rest.

Though it would take another four years to mop up, the battle effectively crushed the First Bulgarian Empire.

Battle of Ménfő

In 1044 King Peter Orseolo ('the Venetian') of Hungary sought the support of Emperor Henry III in retrieving his crown.

The German army met the Hungarian army at Ménfő (near Győr in Hungary) and the Germans were victorious. As a consequence, Peter Orseolo was re-crowned as king and Hungary became subject to the suzerainty of the Holy Roman Empire.

Battle of Manzikert

In 1071 the Byzantine Emperor Romanos IV Diogenes took the Byzantine army east to confront the Seljuks under Alp Arslan, who were pushing over the Byzantine border in Anatolia.

The armies met at Manzikert (modern Malazgirt in eastern Turkey) where the Seljuks won a convincing victory and captured the Emperor. The Seljuk victory opened the door for further Seljuk west expansion into Anatolia.

The First Crusade

The First Crusade was called by Pope Urban II in 1095 at Clermont. It was supposed to muster support for the Byzantine Empire's struggle against the Seljuks.

Instead, it turned into a popular movement, followed by an armed intervention, which in 1099 conquered Jerusalem and formed the kingdom of Jerusalem (and some smaller Crusader States).

Battle of Monte Porzio

In 1167 Emperor Frederick I was campaigning in northern Italy where opposing ideas of pro- or anti-imperial ideologies dominated the political scene.

Rome was at the time housing Pope Alexander III, in opposition to Anti-Pope Paschal III who was the Emperor's man. Against the Pope's advice the (anti-imperial) Senate in Rome decided to attack the town of Tusculum (now a ruin near Frascati in Italy).

The Emperor came to the town's rescue and annihilated the Roman army. He subsequently proceeded to Rome where he re-instated Anti-Pope Paschal III (for a short time).

Appendixes

Siege of Alessandria

In 1174 Emperor Frederick I came back to northern Italy. He was met by the Lombard League, a union of anti-imperial city-states strongly sponsored by Pope Alexander III.

In 1175 the Emperor laid siege to Alessandria - named after Pope Alexander III - but, despite penetrating under its walls, the imperial forces were thrown back and had to raise the siege. The event was the first real setback for the Emperor in Italy.

Battle of Legnano

In 1176, following the Siege of Alessandria and failed peace-negotiations, the armies of Emperor Frederick I and the Lombard-League met in open battle at Legnano (in northern Italy).

The battle was won by the Lombard League and led to the Peace of Venice in which the Emperor had to concede to the Pope and the League's claims for autonomy from the Empire.

Reconquest of Jerusalem

In 1187 Saladin - the Sultan of Egypt - reconquered Jerusalem, on Latin hands since the First Crusade.

Even if it was partly back on Latin hands for a short time following the Sixth Crusade, the loss of Jerusalem spelled the beginning to the end of the Crusader States in Palestine and Syria.

The Fourth Crusade

The Fourth Crusade aimed at retaking Jerusalem, but lacklustre response to the call to arms and financial difficulties resulted in the Crusaders - supported by Venice - instead, attacked Constantinople.

In 1204 Constantinople was conquered and sacked after which the Latin Empire of Constantinople was put in place to replace the Byzantine Empire.

Battle of Mohi

In 1241 the Mongol Golden Horde swept over the borders of Hungary. King Béla IV mobilized the Hungarian army, though many nobles refused his call to arms.

Abandoned also by his Cuman allies, King Béla IV and his army were defeated at Mohi (modern day Muhi in north-eastern Hungary). The battle left Hungary open to the Mongol invaders, but they left the following year leaving whole counties depopulated and devastated in their wake.

Reconquest of Constantinople

Since the Fourth Crusade the successor states to the Byzantine Empire had gradually built up strength in Nicaea and Epirus.

By a stroke of luck, partisans of Michael VIII Palaiologos managed to enter and conquer the city in 1261. It was the rebirth of the Byzantine Empire, which lasted until 1453.

Appendix A - Overview of Key Military Encounters

Battle of Benevento

After the death of Emperor Frederick II his illegitimate son, Manfred, took the throne in Naples. The Pope had charge of the legitimate heir, Conradin, but nevertheless decided to - in effect - sell the throne to Charles of Anjou, brother to the King of France.

In 1266 the armies of Manfred and Charles of Anjou met at Benevento in southern Italy. The battle was a decisive win for Charles of Anjou who took the throne of Naples.

Sicilian Vespers

The rule of Charles of Anjou in Naples was unpopular with the population and at Easter of 1282 civil unrest broke out on the island of Sicily.

What started as a brawl became a revolt and Peter III of Aragon took the opportunity - with Byzantine support - to invade the island. This put a stop to Charles of Anjou's plans to reconquer Constantinople from the revived Byzantine Empire.

Battle of Meloria

After decades of open conflict between Pisa and Genoa, the Genoese finally in 1284 took their fleet to Pisa where they lined up outside Porto Pisano. The Pisans came out to meet them but were outflanked and soundly beaten.

The battle was the catalyst to the de-facto end of Pisa's position as a leading maritime state.

Battle of Maritsa

In 1371 the Serbian Empire went on the offensive to stop the growing threat from the Ottoman Empire in the Balkans. The ensuing battle took place near the village of Chernomen on the Maritsa River (modern Ormenio in Greece).

The battle was a decisive win to the Ottomans and effectively was the end of the Serbian Empire, which was split up into smaller bits, easily overcome by the Ottomans in the years to come.

Battle of Chioggia

In 1380 Genoa, with a string of allies, laid siege to Venice itself. The Genoese fleet was blocking access to the Gulf of Venice off the island of Chioggia.

By clever use of their knowledge of local conditions the Venetians managed to trap the Genoese fleet, which was destroyed. The Battle marked the end of armed hostilities between Venice and Genoa and confirmed Venice's dominance in the Adriatic Sea.

Appendixes

First Battle of Kosovo

Serbian troops from the remnants of the Serbian Empire had fought off Ottoman expeditionary forces at Dubravnica (1381) and Pločnik (1386). In 1389 the full Ottoman army commanded by Sultan Murad I arrived in Serbia.

The Serbians gave battle at Kosovo (in the vicinity of Pristina) and the Ottomans were victorious even if Sultan Murad I was assassinated immediately after the battle.

The Ottoman victory opens up Serbia, and the last remnants of Serbian resistance were mopped up in the following years, giving the Ottomans full control over Serbia.

Battle of Nicopolis

Urged on by Pope Boniface IX, Sigismund of Luxembourg supported by French knights marched on the Ottomans in the Balkans in 1396. The project was an ambitious attempt to not only throw the Ottomans out of Europe, but indeed to march (triumphantly) all the way to Jerusalem.

While the Christian army was laying siege to Nicopolis in northern Bulgaria, Sultan Bayezid I brought his army up from Constantinople and surprised the Christians. The resulting Ottoman victory was a disaster for the Christian cause and put a stop to any concerted campaigns against the Ottomans in Europe for nearly fifty years.

Battle of Ankara

Timur's new empire in the East started to challenge the Ottoman borders in Anatolia. Sultan Bayezid I abandoned a siege of Constantinople to go and meet the new challenger.

In 1402 Timur beat the Ottomans outside Ankara. The Sultan was taken prisoner, and the Ottoman Empire started a ten year interregnum which eventually saw Mehmed I emerge as the victor in 1413.

Battle of Gallipoli

Sultan Mehmed I was well aware of the dangers caused by the need for the Ottomans to cross between the two continents of their empire across waterways they did not control. He therefore, in the deepest secret, started to build up an Ottoman fleet stationed at Gallipoli.

Ottoman pirates were commonplace and an attack against a Venetian convoy in 1416 initiated a Venetian fleet to carry ambassadors to the Ottoman court. When the fleet went into the port at Gallipoli its intentions were misunderstood and the Ottoman fleet attacked.

The result was the destruction of the Ottoman fleet, which was not rebuilt until 1453.

Appendix A - Overview of Key Military Encounters

The Long Campaign (Battle of Niš)

Encouraged by the Pope's representative, Cardinal Guiliano Cesarini, King Wladyslaw III of Hungary and Poland assembled an army of Polish, Hungarian and Serbian soldiers which in 1443 marched into the Balkans.

An extended battle took place at Niš in Bulgaria where the Christian army defeated the local Ottoman troops. The army marched on and got close to Edirne when onset of winter forced it to turn around and return to Hungary. Though all gained terrain was quickly retaken by the Ottomans, the 'Long Campaign' encouraged the Christians to attack again in the following year.

Battle of Varna

Encouraged by their relative success during the 'Long Campaign', Cardinal Guiliano Cesarini and King Wladyslaw III - despite having signed a peace agreement with Sultan Murad II - marched on Edirne again in 1444.

This time the army went along the Black Sea coast and was met by the Ottoman army at Varna in Bulgaria. The resulting battle was an overwhelming Ottoman victory which saw both Cardinal Guiliano Cesarini and King Wladyslaw III slain.

Second Battle of Kosovo

Despite the defeat at Varna, Hungarian Regent Janos Hunyadi decided to attack the Ottomans again in 1448. The army was mainly Hungarian and marched through - hostile - Serbia to face the Ottomans at Kosovo.

The resulting Ottoman victory put an end to Christian attempts to expel the Ottomans from Europe through a single battle.

Conquest of Constantinople

Constantinople had been under siege repeatedly during its millennium-long existence. The Empire had, however, survived, even when temporarily replaced by the Latin Empire following the Fourth Crusade.

When Mehmed II put the city under siege in 1453 he brought the latest in siege-technology; massive cannon specifically designed to take down the ancient walls. His conquest of Constantinople spelled the end of the Byzantine Empire and finally locked Ottoman presence onto European soil.

Siege of Belgrade

Mehmed II's siege of Belgrade in 1456 was the logical follow-up to his conquest of Constantinople three years prior. If Belgrade fell, the road into western Europe and Italy was open for the Ottoman army.

A desperate defense combined with freak luck prevented the fall of Belgrade and kept Mehmed II contained inside the Balkans.

Appendixes

Conquest of Karaman

Previous experience - not least during his father's rule - had demonstrated that the one Ottomans weakness was fighting on two fronts at the same time.

The Karamanids had been particularly active in providing unrest in the East while the Christian forces attacked in the West, so while the territorial gains achieved in Karaman were insignificant, the conquest in 1469 was of great strategic importance.

Conquest of Euboea

By 1470 Venice and the Ottoman Empire had been at war for seven years. Though skirmishes came and went, the war was expensive but not decisive.

The Ottoman conquest of Euboea, the largest Venetian enclave in the Aegean Sea, was a turning point which sent Venice into a downward spiral that only ended when they sued for peace in 1479.

Battle of Otlukbeli

The last real danger for Mehmed II in the East was the White Sheep. They had repeatedly cooperated with western parties, in particular Venice, and were a constant threat to the Ottomans' eastern border.

The Battle of Otlukbeli in 1473 once and for all crushed the White Sheep militarily and within a few years the state had killed itself off through infighting.

Conquest of Caffa

Though a rather low-scale affair in its own right, the Ottoman conquest of Caffa in 1475 was of major importance.

The loss of Caffa meant the end of Genoese dominance in the Black Sea and made the Black Sea and Ottoman lake commercially as well as physically.

APPENDIX B

CONSOLIDATED TIMELINE

Appendixes

CONSOLIDATED TIMELINE

Year	Event	Chapter
64	Persecution of Christians in Rome	16
301	Christianity becomes State Religion in Armenia	16
311	Emperor Constantine allows Christianity in Roman Empire. Miltiades is first official Bishop of Rome	16
314	Sylvester I is first officially elected Bishop of Rome	16
324	Foundation of Constantinople as a Christian city. San Giovanni in Laterano becomes the official Arch Basilica and the Lateran Palace the seat of the Bishop of Rome.	3, 16
325	Council of Nicaea	16
380	Christianity becomes only official religion of Roman Empire	16
381	First Council of Constantinople. Constantinople becomes a see	16
395	Roman Empire split into Eastern (Byzantine) and Western (Roman) part	16
410	Rome is sacked by Visigoths under Alaric, Western Emperor moves to Ravenna	16
439	Vandals establish kingdom in northern Africa with Carthage as capital	16
440	Leo I becomes pope	16
451	Battle of Catalaunum	16
452	Pope Leo I meets Attila at Mantua	16
455	Vandal sack of Rome	16
476	Odoacer becomes King of Italy	16
493	Theodoric becomes Ostrogoth King of Italy	16
494	Pope Gelasius I issues Duo Sunt letter and start questioning Monophysitism in Constantinople	16
500s	First mention of Venice in written sources. Slav migration into western Balkans	10, 14
519	Reunification of Western and Eastern churches	16
526	Felix IV becomes first politically appointed pope	16
536	John II is first pope to change his name. Byzantine invasion of Rome	16
545	Pope Vigilius is forcefully brought to Constantinople	16
550	Ostrogoth sack of Rome	16
553	Second Council of Constantinople. Compromise agreed on Monothelitism	16
568	Lombards first appear in Italy	16
638	Ecthesis is issued as an Imperial Edict	16
648	Type of Constans is issued	16
649	Lateran Council condemns Type of Constans	16
653	Pope Martin I is brought as prisoner to Constantinople	16
655	Battle of the Masts	16
663	Emperor Constans II enters Rome	16
674	Muslim siege of Constantinople	3, 16
680	Battle of Ongal forces Byzantium to recognize Bulgarian state and pay tribute. Third Council of Constantinople	12, 16
692	Quinisext Council	16

Appendix B - Consolidated Timeline

Year	Event	Chapter
Late 600s	'Bulgars' migrate into Byzantine territories south of the Danube River.	12
700s	Oguz Yabgu State develops in central Asia	5
702	Bulgarians under assist Tervel Justinian II with conquest of Constantinople	12
708	First Battle of Anchialus	12
653	Pope Martin I is brought as prisoner to Constantinople	16
655	Battle of the Masts	16
663	Emperor Constans II enters Rome	16
674	Muslim siege of Constantinople	3, 16
680	Battle of Ongal forces Byzantium to recognize Bulgarian state and pay tribute. Third Council of Constantinople	12, 16
692	Quinisext Council	16
Late 600s	'Bulgars' migrate into Byzantine territories south of the Danube River.	12
700s	Oguz Yabgu State develops in central Asia	5
702	Bulgarians under assist Tervel Justinian II with conquest of Constantinople	12
708	First Battle of Anchialus	12
710	Pope Constantine goes to Constantinople	16
717	Muslim siege of Constantinople	3
718	Bulgarian army attack Arab besiegers of Constantinople	12
719	Bulgarians assist Anastasios II in failed attempt on Constantinople	12
726	Iconoclasm in Constantinople	16
728	The Donation of Sutri	16
754	The Donation of Pepin	16
755	Bulgarian defeat at the Anastasian Wall	12
756	Byzantine attack on Bulgaria	12
759	Byzantine attack on Bulgaria ambushed at Rishki Pass	12
763	Second Battle of Anchialus	12
774	Byzantine attack on Varna	12
780	Abandoned Byzantine campaign in Bulgaria	12
787	Second Council of Nicaea	16
792	Battle at Marcellae. Byzantium agrees to pay tribute	12
800	Charlemagne becomes Emperor of the Romans	16
803	Pax Nicephori' states that Venice remains part of Byzantium. Krum becomes Khan of Bulgaria	10, 12
805	Bulgarians overrun Avars and take Sofia	12
809	Byzantine campaign burns Pliska and takes Sofia	12
811	Byzantine campaign is ambushed and Emperor Nikephoros I is killed	12
812	Pax Nicephorus	16
813	Battle at Adrianople. Assassination attempt on Krum	12
816	Thirty years peace agreement signed	12
818	Lothair I crowned as King of Italy	16
824	Constitutio Romana is issued	16
827	Clashes between Bulgaria and Frankia	12

Appendixes

Year	Event	Chapter
829	Clashes between Bulgaria and Frankia	12
830	Vlastimir mentioned as Knez ('Prince') of Sklaviniai	14
831	Byzantine attack on Bulgaria	12
837	First reports of Magyar mercenaries in Bulgarian service	13
839	War breaks out with new Serbian State	12
840	Bulgarian invasion repelled	14
846	Saracens raid St.Peter's Cathedral	16
849	Battle of Ostia. Foundation of the Leonine City	16
852	Boris I becomes Khan of Bulgaria	12
853	Bulgarian invasion repelled	14
854	Bulgaria suffers setbacks in attack on Frankia and Serbia	12
855	Bulgarians suffers setbacks against Croatia and Byzantium. Catholic Missionaries arrive in Bulgaria	12
856	Boris I secures peace with Byzantium	12
858	Nicholas I becomes pope. Emperor Louis II submits to the Pope's authority	16
863	Conflict with Byzantium. Orthodox missionaries replace catholic missionaries	12
864	Boris I is baptized	12
866	Letters exchanged between Boris I and Pope Nicolas I. Catholic missionaries arrive	12, 16
870	The Patriarch grants the Bulgarian Church status as an autocephalous archbishopric. Bulgaria becomes orthodox	12
870s	Serbia recognized as vassal state to Byzantium. Christianity adopted by Serbs.	14
891	Formosus becomes pope	16
893	Simeon I becomes Khan of Bulgaria	12
895	Byzantine and Magyar attack on Bulgaria	12, 13
896	Battle of Boulgarophygon. Byzantium pays tribute to Bulgaria. Bulgarians and Pechenegs defeat Magyars. Árpád leads the Magyars across the Carpathian Mountains to Aquincum (Buda) (known as honfoglalás)	12, 13
897	Serbian state recognized by Bulgaria. Cadaver Synod	14, 16
904	Pope Sergius II gets elected as pope. Start of the Saeculum obscurum	16
907	Árpád dies. Magyar raiders penetrate into western and eastern Europe.	13
911	Rollo is baptized	16
913	Bulgarian siege of Constantinople	12
915	Bulgarian siege of Adrianople	12
917	Third Battle of Anchialus, Bulgarian invasion	12, 14
921	Bulgarian invasion	14
924	Abandoned Bulgarian attack on Constantinople. Simeon I declared Emperor. Serbia annexed by Bulgaria	12, 14
926	Unsuccessful Bulgarian campaign in Croatia	12
928	Marozia takes Rome. Pope John X is imprisoned	16
933	Serbia reclaimed from Bulgaria. Expands to Adriatic Sea	14
935	Saracen raid on Genoa	11

Appendix B - Consolidated Timeline

Year	Event	Chapter
955	Battle of Lechfeld ends Magyar raids in western Europe. John XII becomes pope	13, 16
960	Časlav Klonimirović dies. Serbia is split up	14
962	Otto I is crowned as Roman Emperor. Diploma Otonianum is issued	16
965	Byzantium stops paying tribute. Attack by Rus allies of Byzantium	12
969	Bulgaria invaded by Rus	12
970	Géza becomes Grand Prince of the Hungarians	13
972	Byzantine attack on Rus in Bulgaria. Bulgaria becomes Byzantine province	12
973	German missionaries are allowed into Hungary	13
976	Boris II is killed. Roman becomes nominal Bulgarian Emperor	12
977	The Ghaznavids take control of Persia	5
985	The Seljuk clan converts to Islam and splits from Oguz Yabgu State	5
986	Byzantine army ambushed at Trajan's Gate	12
991	Byzantium starts years-long campaign in Bulgaria	12
995	Géza is baptized	13
998	Battle of Veszprém. Stefan I becomes King with papal blessing.	13
1000s	'Albanoi' people mentioned in historic sources	15
1000	Venice granted status as Dux Dalmatiae' by Byzantium	10, 12
1003	Hungary annexes Transylvania	13
1014	Battle of Kleidion	12
1016	Genoa and Pisa attack Saracens in Sardinia	11
1018	Final Byzantine defeat of First Bulgarian Empire	12, 13, 14
1032	Benedict IX becomes pope	16
1034	Genoa and Pisa attack Bone in Algeria	11
1041	Short-lived Bulgarian revolt. King Peter Orseolo sent into exile	12, 13
1044	Battle of Ménfő	13
1049	Leo IX becomes pope	16
1050	Genoa attacks Sardinia	11
1053	Battle of Civitate. The Pope recognizes Norman lords in southern Italy	16
1054	East-Western Schism. Break between the Eastern and Western churches	3, 16
1055	Seljuks capture Persia and ends Ghaznavid dynasty. Tuğrul becomes 'Sultan' of the Great Seljuk Empire	5
1060	Genoese traders reported in Egypt	11
1060s	Genoa at war with Pisa. Hospital of St. John established in Jerusalem	11, 17
1063	Alp Arslan becomes Seljuk Sultan	5
1066	Guillaume II conquers England under a papal banner	16
1068	Romanus IV Diogenes becomes Emperor of Byzantium	5
1069	Byzantine campaign in eastern Anatolia	5
1071	Battle of Manzikert. Seljuks capture Trebizond	3, 5, 8
1072	Malik-Shah I becomes Seljuk Sultan	5
1076	The Walk to Canossa	16

Appendixes

Year	Event	Chapter
1077	The Seljuk Sultanate of Rum splits from the Great Seljuk Empire. Ladislaus I becomes King of Hungary	5, 13
1080s	Byzantines recapture Trebizond. Theodore Gabras becomes governor.	8
1081	Alexios I Komnenos becomes emperor. Battle with Normans off Corfu	3, 10
1082	Venice given exclusive trading rights in the Byzantine Empire	10
1083	Venetian retake Durrës and Corfu from Normans	10
1084	Battle with Normans off Corfu. Norman sack of Rome	10, 16
1087	Genoa and Pisa attack Mahdia in Tunisia	11
1091	Theodore Gabras marries Mariam of Georgia. Hungarian invasion attempt in Croatia. Vukan becomes Grand Prince of Serbia	8, 13, 14
1092	Malik-Shah I die. Civil war follows	5
1095	Pope Urban II calls for 'crusade'	3
1095	Council of Clermont. Pope Urban II calls for a crusade to relieve Constantinople	16
1097	First Crusade, Genoa is early participant. Hungarian annexation of Croatia	11, 13
1098	Second expedition to the Holy Land	11
1099	First Crusade, conquest of Jerusalem	3, 5, 10, 16, 17
1100	Genoa become 'commune'	11
1101	Grand Fleet leave for the Holy Land	11
1103	Genoa barred from Egypt	11
1111	Pisa given trading rights in Byzantine Empire	10
1113	Pope Paschal II confirms the Knights Hospitallers as a religious order	16, 17
1119	War begins with Pisa	11
1122	Venetian attack on Byzantine Empire. Concordat of Worms	10, 16
1123	Trading rights in the Kingdom of Jerusalem	10
1126	Restoration of 1082 trading rights in Byzantine Empire	10
1128	Agreement hat Kingdom of Sicily is papal fief	16
1129	The Knights Templar are confirmed as a religious order	16, 17
1136	Genoese attack on Bougie in Algeria. Hungary forms Banate of Bosnia	11, 14
1137	Hungary occupies Bosnia. Roger II unifies Sicily and Naples into Kingdom of Sicily	13, 16
1139	Pope Innocent II recognizes Kingdom of Sicily	16
1140s	Knights Hospitaller build Krak de Chevalier castle	17
1144	Commune of Rome removes the Pope's temporal powers	16
1145	Pope Lucius II is killed during street battle in Rome. Pope Eugene III calls for Second Crusade	16
1146	Naval battle off Almeria	11
1147	Second Crusade. Conquest of Almeria	5, 11
1148	Conquest of Tortosa	11
1155	Frederick I becomes Holy Roman Emperor	16

Appendix B - Consolidated Timeline

Year	Event	Chapter
1156	Genoa given trading rights in Byzantine Empire. Treaty of Benevento	10, 16
1159	Genoa obtain trade rights in Byzantine Empire	11
1162	Genoese and Pisan clash in Constantinople. Byzantine coup sees Ladislaus II as King of Hungary	11, 13
1165	War breaks out with Pisa	11
1166	Byzantine coup	14
1167	Banate of Bosnia back under Byzantine control. Battle of Monte Porzio	14, 16
1171	Genoese settlement in Constantinople attacked. Venetians are arrested and attack Byzantine Empire. Venetians expelled from Constantinople	10, 11
1172	Béla III becomes King of Hungary. Stefan Nemanja in Byzantine imprisonment	13, 14
1176	Battle of Legnano	16
1179	Venetians allowed back in Constantinople in limited numbers	10
1182	Attack on Latins in Constantinople	10, 11
1183	Kulin retakes Bosnia as Hungarian vassal	14
1185	Rusudan escaped to Georgia with her sons Alexios and David Komnenos. Venice officially returns to Constantinople. Bulgarian revolt. Peter IV appointed Emperor of Bulgaria	8, 10, 12
1186	Knights Hospitaller buys Marqab castle	17
1187	Egyptian reconquest of Jerusalem. The papal bull Audita tremendi starts the Third Crusade	3, 16
1190	Battle of Tryavna. Principality of Arbanon forms around Krujë	12, 15
1191	First foreign podestà appointed	11
1192	Third Crusade	5
1194	Genoa assists Henry VI in conquest of Sicily. Battle of Arcadiopolis	11, 12, 16
1198	Teutonic Knights confirmed as a religious order. Pope Innocent III calls for the Fourth Crusade	16, 17
1200	Genoa assists Philip of Swabia with invasion of Sicily	11
Early 1200s	Kai tribe arrives in eastern Anatolia. Afshar tribe arrive at Sivas	1, 6
1202	Hungarian invasion. Fourth Crusade conquer Zara	12, 13
1203	The Pope appoints Kaloyan King of the Bulgarians. John de Casamaris conducts papal inquiry on Kistjani heresy in Bosnia	12, 14
1204	Fourth Crusade. Sack of Constantinople. Alexios and David Komnenos invade Trebizond and declare independence. Venice becomes Dominante. Genoa expelled from Constantinople. Durrës becomes Venetian	3, 8, 10, 11, 12, 15, 16
1205	Trebizond expels Seljuk attack on Sinop. Baldwin I of Constantinople killed in battle. András II becomes King of Hungary. Introduces Novæ Institutiones.	8, 12, 13
1206	David Komnenos lays siege to Nicomedia. Nicaea receives help from Constantinople. Trebizond expels Seljuk attack on Sinop	8
1207	Seljuks conquer Antalya. Boniface of Montferrat killed in battle	5, 12

Appendixes

Year	Event	Chapter
1208	Theodore I becomes Emperor of Nicaea. David Komnenos lays siege to Nicomedia. Nicaea receives help from Constantinople. Arbanon is allied with Serbia	3, 8, 15
1211	Teutonic Knights given Burzenland	13
1212	David Komnenos dies as a monk. Frederick I visits Genoa. Peace agreed with Pisa. The Pope recognizes Stefan Nemanjić as King of Serbia	8, 11, 14
1213	Arbanon suppressed by Epirus	15
1214	Seljuks conquer port-town of Sinop. Battle of Bouvines	5, 8, 16
1218	Fifth Crusade. Ivan Asen II becomes Emperor of Bulgaria.	11, 12, 13, 16
1219	Orthodox Patriarch recognizes Serbia. Serbia's first constitution (Zakonopravilo) issued	14
1221	John III Doukas Vatatzes becomes Emperor of Nicaea	3
1222	Pisans burn down Genoese quarters in Acre. Golden Bull	11, 13
1225	Teutonic Knights expelled from Transylvania	13
1226	Béla IV becomes Duke of Transylvania	13
1228	Sixth Crusade	16
1230	Battle of Klokotnitsa	12
1232	Krstjani revolt	14
1234	Crusade against Bosnia	14
1235	Alliance with Empire of Nicaea.	12
1237	Sultanate of Rum disintegrates. Imperial ban on Genoa. Emperor Frederick II defeats Lombard League at Battle of Cortenuova	1, 11
1239	Afshars revolt. Cumans allowed asylum in Hungary	6, 13
1240	Genoa besieged by imperial land troops and a Pisan navy	11
1241	Mongol invasion. Hungarian occupation interrupted by Mongol invasion	13, 14
1242	Naval battle with Pisa off Savona. Bulgaria agrees to pay tribute to Golden Horde. Knights Hospitaller, Cumans and 'Saxons' settlers given land in wake of Mongo invasion. Retreating Mongols raid Serbia and Bosnia.	11, 12, 13, 14
1243	Mongols conquer Seljuk Sultanate. Mongol invasion creates opportunity for Afshars under Kerîmeddin Karaman Bey. Innocent IV becomes pope	5, 6, 11
1244	The Pope goes into exile in Genoa	11
1246	Nicaea conquers Thessaloniki	3
1247	Crusade avoided by diplomacy	14
1250	Sacking of Venetian quarters in Acre. Hungarian invasion. Persecution of Krstjani	10, 11, 14
1254	Theodore II Laskaris becomes Emperor of Nicaea. Battle of Foggia	3, 16
1255	Venetian fleet attacks Acre and Tyre	10, 11
1257	Peace with Pisa. Constantine Tikh becomes Emperor of Bulgaria. Arbanon invaded by Naples	11, 12, 15
1258	The infant Theodore II Laskaris becomes Emperor of Nicaea. Mongols overrun Persia. Trebizond becomes endpoint on Silk Route. Venice and Genoa do battle in Acre	3, 8, 10, 11

Appendix B - Consolidated Timeline

Year	Event	Chapter
1259	Michael VIII Palaiologos becomes co-Emperor of Nicaea. Nicaea invades Arbanon	3, 15
1261	Byzantine reconquest of Constantinople. Naples retake Arbanon	3, 10, 11, 12, 15
1262	Mehmed I becomes Bey of Karaman	6
1264	Bulgarian incursion into Byzantium	12
1265	Genoa is expelled from Constantinople. Naval battle off Trapani	10, 11
1266	Independence from Naples. Battle of Benevento	15, 16
1267	Genoa is invited back to Constantinople	10, 11
1268	Venice is invited back to Constantinople	10
1270s	Autonomous barons refuse to pay tribute to Hungary	14
1270	Peace with Venice	11
1271	Krak de Chevalier is lost	17
1272	War with Charles of Anjou. Albania becomes part of Naples by agreement	11, 15
1274	Partly annexation of Morea. Reunification of the Christian Church. Mongol raids into Bulgaria start. Byzantine attack on Albania. Council of Lyon	3, 12, 15, 16
1277	Karamanids occupy Konya. Güneri becomes Bay of Karaman. Peace with Charles of Anjou	6, 11
1280	George I becomes Emperor of Bulgaria	12
1281	Osman becomes leader of Kai tribe	1
1282	Sicilian Vespers. Andronikos II Palaiologos becomes Emperor of Byzantium. War breaks out with Pisa over Corsica. Full Byzantine control of Albania	3, 4, 11, 15, 16
1284	Battle of Meloria. Genoa destroys Pisan fleet	11
1285	Dismantling of the Byzantine fleet. Second Mongol invasion repelled. Marqab is lost	4, 13, 17
1290	Pisan attack on Elba. Porto Pisano filled in, Corsica and Chios added to Genoese possessions.	11
1291	Pope Nicholas IV forbids trade with Muslims. Enclave granted to Genoa. Acre is lost to Egypt. Vandino and Ugolino Vivaldi leave to find India	8, 10, 11, 16, 17
1292	George I abdicates and flee to Constantinople	12
1294	Karamanids conquer Antalya	6
1296	Venetian attack on Constantinople. Serbian attack	10, 11, 15
1297	Genoese attack on Constantinople	10, 11
1298	Venetian attack on Constantinople. Naval battle of Curzola.	10, 11
1299	Peace settlement. Chaka becomes Emperor of Bulgaria. Serbia expands to Macedonia and northern Albania. Croatian invasion. Renewed persecution of Krstjani	10, 11, 12, 14
1300	Kai tribe becomes known as 'House of Osman'. Mahmut becomes Bey of Karaman. Chaka is murdered. Theodore Svetoslav becomes Emperor of Bulgaria. Charles Robert of Anjou lands in Croatia. Besarab I settles in Campulung as Hungarian vassal. Jubilee Year in Rome	1, 6, 12, 13, 14, 16
1302	Ottomans beat Byzantines at Nicomedia. Venetian attack on Constantinople. Treaty of Caltabellotta	1, 4, 10, 16

Appendixes

Year	Event	Chapter
1303	Genoa transports the Grand Company of Catalans to Constantinople. Pope Boniface VIII is arrested	11, 16
1304	Byzantines beat Ottomans at Philadelphia. Revolt against Serbians	1, 4, 15
1305	Pope Clement V is consecrated at Lyon	16
1307	Mongols Attack on Caffa. Peace with Byzantium. Knights Templars arrested in France	11, 12, 16, 17
1308	Karamanids conquer Konya. Genoa abandons Caffa	6, 11
1309	Curia is moved to Avignon. Knights Hospitaller conquer Rhodes	16, 17
1310	Charles I is crowned as King of Hungary. Henry VII enters Italy	13, 16
1311	Genoa ceded to Henry VII	11
1312	Serbia assists Byzantium. Knights Templar are dissolved and their assets given to the Knights Hospitaller	14, 16, 17
1313	Civil war following death of Henry VII	11
1315	The Knights Hospitaller buys Kos from Venice	17
1316	Genoa returns to Caffa	11
1319	Enclave granted to Venice	8
1322	Bosnia return to Hungarian suzerainty	14
1324	Orhan becomes leader of Ottomans. Papal ban on trade with Muslims. New peace agreement with Byzantium	1, 10, 12
1325	Venice acquires trading rights at Tana. First Florints are minted. Wallachia stops payment of vassalage to Hungary	10, 13, 14
1326	Ottomans conquer Bursa. Bosnian attacks on Serbia	1, 4, 14
1328	Andronikos III Palaiologos becomes Emperor of Byzantium. New peace agreement with Byzantium. Louis IV is crowned as Holy Roman Emperor in Rome	4, 12, 16
1329	Ottomans defeat Byzantines at Pelekanon. Chios is lost to Byzantium	1, 4, 11
1330	Unsuccessful Bulgarian attack on Serbia. Battle of Posada. Wallachia becomes independent	12, 13, 14
1331	Ottoman annexation of Nicaea. Peace agreement ends civil war. Genoa ceded to Naples. Ivan Alexander becomes Emperor of Bulgaria. Stefan Uroš IV Dušan becomes King of Serbia	4, 11, 12, 14
1335	Naples expelled from Genoa	11
1337	Ottoman annexation of Nicomedia. Byzantine control of Epirus	4
1339	Public revolt in Genoa	11
1340	Catholic missionaries allowed to operate in Bosnia	14
1341	John V Palaiologos becomes Emperor of Byzantium	4
1342	Civil war in Byzantium. Louis I becomes King of Hungary. Serbian Invasion	4, 13, 15
1343	Mongol attack on Tana and Caffa. Hungarian invasion	10, 11, 14
1344	Papal trade-ban expires	8, 10
1345	Hungarian invasion	14
1346	Mongol attack on Caffa. Black Death. Genoa retake Chios. Stefan Uroš IV Dušan is crowned as Emperor of Serbia	10, 11, 14
1347	Venetians back in Tana	10
1347	Hungarian invasion of Naples	13, 16

Appendix B - Consolidated Timeline

Year	Event	Chapter
1348	John VI Kantakouzenos becomes co-Emperor of Byzantium (end of civil war). Black Death reached Europe. Short conflict with Byzantium	4, 10, 11, 12
1350	Genoa, with Ottoman support, unleashes pirate fleet against Venice. Second Hungarian invasion of Naples. Serbian invasion attempt	11, 13, 14
1350s	Ottoman raids on Bulgaria. Bulgarian Empire starts to disintegrate. Hungary annexes Moldavia	12
1351	Venetian attack on Constantinople	10, 11
1352	Civil war in Byzantium Ottoman mercenaries are given quarters at Çimpe. Musa returns to power after long internal battle for power. Naval battle off Constantinople	1, 4, 6, 10, 11
1353	Dragoș is sent to Moldavia to create a buffer against Tatars. Papal campaign starts in Italy	14, 16
1354	Ottomans annex town of Gallipoli	1
1354	John V Palaiologos becomes Emperor of Byzantium (end of civil war). Ottoman mercenaries re-populate and rebuild town of Gallipoli after earthquake. Naval battle off Pylos. Genoa under protection of Milan. Hungarian invasion	4, 10, 11, 14
1355	Peace agreement. Genoa destroys Modon. Peace agreement. Lesbos becomes Genoese. Stefan Uroš IV Dušan. Serbia is split into smaller autonomous principalities. Charles IV is crowned as Holy Roman Emperor in Rome	10, 11, 14, 16
1356	Suleyman becomes Bey of Karaman. Milan expelled from Genoa	6, 11
1360	Bogdan I established himself as independent Voivode of Moldavia	14
1361	Murad I becomes leader of Ottomans. Alaattin Ali Becomes Bey of Karaman	1, 6
1363	Ottomans annex Adrianople (Edirne). Hungarian invasion attempts	12, 14
1364	Wallachia becomes Bulgarian vassal, then moves back to Hungary. Amlaș and Făgăraș confirmed as being part of Wallachia.	14
1365	Ottomans conquer Adrianople (Edirne)	1, 4
1366	Stand-off with Byzantium over Byzantine Emperor's passage through Bulgaria. Savoyard crusade	12, 16
1367	Urban V enters Rome	16
1368	Karl Topia conquers Durrës	15
1369	Emperor John V Palaiologos is held at Venice, offers the island of Tenedos to Venice	4, 10, 11
1370	Louis I becomes King of Poland	13
1371	Byzantium agrees to pay annual tribute to expanding Ottoman Empire. Ivan Alexander dies and the Bulgarian state split up. Battle of Maritsa, Serbian Empire disintegrates. Lațcu obtains papal acceptance of title as voivode and independent Moldavian bishopry	4, 12, 14, 15
1373	Genoese attack on Cyprus. Bulgarian Emperor accepts vassalage to Ottomans	11, 12
1376	Venice once again granted Tenedos	10, 11

Appendixes

Year	Event	Chapter
1377	Stjepan Tvrtko I proclaimed King of Bosnia	14
1378	Naval battle off Anzio. Pope Urban VI moves the Curia back to Rome	11, 16
1379	Naval battle off Pola.	11
1380	Battle of Chioggia	10, 11
1381	Battle of Dubravnica. Settlement over Tenedos. Peace of Turin	1, 10, 11, 13, 14
1382	Mary crowned as King of Hungary	13
1383	Durrës falls to Zeta	15
1385	Ottomans take Sofia. Karl Topia retake Durrës with Ottoman help	12, 15
1386	Battle of Pločnik. Murad I becomes 'Sultan'. Karamanids occupy, then lose, Beyşehir. Mircea cel Batran becomes Voivode of Wallachia	1, 4, 6, 12, 14
1387	Bulgaria cancels vassalage to Ottomans. Sigismund is crowned as King of Hungary. Moldavia becomes Polish vassal	12, 13, 14
1388	Battle of Bileća. Ottoman expeditionary force stopped. Wallachia annexation of Dobrogea	14
1389	First Battle of Kosovo. Bayezid I becomes Ottoman Sultan. Serbian Empire disintegrates	1, 4, 12, 14, 15
1390	Ottoman annexation of Philadelphia. Renewed attempt at annexing Ottoman territories	4, 6
1391	Manuel II Palaiologos becomes Emperor of Byzantium	4
1392	Durrës ceded to Venice. Rest of Albania becomes Ottoman province.	15
1393	Ottoman invasion of Bulgaria. Ottoman occupation of southern Dobrogea	12, 14
1394	Building of Anadoluhisarı. Siege of Constantinople. Bosnia returns to Hungarian suzerainty. Battle of Rovie. Ottoman invasion	1, 4, 14
1395	Ottoman mop-up operations in Bulgaria. Serbia troops serve Ottomans in Wallachia	12, 14
1396	Battle of Nicopolis. Genoa ceded to France. Bulgarian state becomes an Ottoman province. Serbian troops serve Ottomans	1, 4, 11, 12, 13, 14, 16
1397	Mircea cel Batran back in Wallachia	14
1398	Ottomans take Konya. Alaattin Ali executed	6
1399	Emperor Manuel II Palaiologos travels through Europe support. Ottoman annexation of Dobrogea. Ladislaus of Naples consolidates the Kingdom of Naples	4, 14, 16
1400	Alexandru I becomes Voivode of Moldavia	14
1402	Battle of Ankara. Beginning of Ottoman Interregnum. Mehmed II becomes Bey of Karaman. Serbian troops serve Ottomans in Battle of Ankara. Stefan Lazarević becomes Despot of Serbia. Castle at Smyrna is lost to Timurids	1, 4, 6, 14, 17
1403	Emperor Manuel II Palaiologos returns to Constantinople. Byzantium supports Suleiman in Ottoman war of succession. Last freebooter-fleet leaves Genoa. Ladislaus of Naples land in Dalmatia	4, 11, 13

Appendix B - Consolidated Timeline

Year	Event	Chapter
1404	Timur dies. Wallachia retake Dobrogea. New castle is founded at Halicarnassus	7, 14, 17
1408	Timurid attack on Black Sheep. Hungarian campaigns in Bosnia and Croatia. Sigismund forms the 'Order of the Dragon'. Conclave at Pisa elects third pope	7, 13, 16
1409	French expelled from Genoa. Hungarian invasion	11, 14
1410	Timurid attack on Black Sheep. Moldavia assist Poland	7, 14
1411	Musa defeats Suleiman and besiege Constantinople	4
1412	Mehmed I defends Constantinople and defeats Musa	4
1413	Mehmed I becomes Sultan. End of Ottoman Interregnum	1, 4
1414	Seljuks surrender former Ottoman territories. Council of Constance	6, 13, 16
1415	Rebuilding of the Hexamilion Wall. Wallachia starts paying tribute to Ottomans	4, 14
1416	Battle of Gallipoli	1
1417	Pope Martin V becomes only pope	16
1419	Sigismund becomes King of Bohemia. Hussite Wars	13
1420	White Sheep attempt to invade Black Sheep. Conflict over Corsica leads to Genoa being ceded to Milan. Ottoman annexation of Dobrogea. Moldavia repels Ottoman attack on Akkerman.	7, 11, 14
1421	Murad II becomes Ottoman Sultan. Byzantium supports Mustafa against Murad II. Seljuk attempt on Antalya. Mehmed I is killed. Bengi Ali becomes Bey of Karaman	1, 4, 6
1422	Ottoman siege of Constantinople and Thessaloniki. Moldavia assists Poland	4, 14
1423	Thessaloniki ceded to Venice	4, 10
1424	Byzantines renew annual tribute to Ottomans. Ibrahim II becomes Bey of Karaman with Ottoman support	4, 6
1425	John VIII Palaiologos becomes Emperor of Byzantium	4
1427	Đurađ Branković becomes Despot of Serbia	14
1428	Hungary and Ottomans agree on new Serbian capital at Smederevo. Vassalage is agreed with both Hungary and Ottoman Empire	13, 14
1429	Timurids put Abu Sa'id in control of Black Sheep, but Qara Iskander retain the leadership	7
1430	Byzantium takes full control of Morea. The Ottomans conquer Thessaloniki. Venice gains trade rights in Ottoman Empire. Moldavian attack on Poland	4, 10, 14
1431	Naval battle off Portofino. Vlad II Dracul becomes member of the Order of the Dragon. Council of Basel	11, 14, 16
1432	Birth of Mehmed II	2
1433	Karamanids take Beyşehir. Peace with Venice. Sigismund of Hungary is crowned as Holy Roman Emperor	6, 11, 13, 16
1435	Ottomans re-take Beyşehir. Qara Osman dies and war of succession follows in the White Sheep beylik. Milan expelled from Genoa. Mara Hatun marries Ottoman Sultan Murad II	6, 7, 11, 14
1436	Timurids put Jahan Shah in control of Black Sheep. Vlad II Dracul becomes Voivode of Wallachia. Albanian rebellion	7, 14, 15

Appendixes

Year	Event	Chapter
1437	Prince Ahmed dies. Emperor John VIII Palaiologos goes to Rome. Karamanid siege of Amasya	2, 4, 6
1438	Serbian troops serve Ottomans in raid on Transylvania. Ottoman incursion in Serbia. Wallachia supports Ottomans during raids in Transylvania	14
1439	The Christian Churches are (nominally) reunited. Ottomans annex Serbia. Đurađ Branković in exile. Council of Florence	4, 14, 16
1440	King Wladyslaw III of Poland becomes King of Hungary. Black Sheep attempt invasion of Georgia. Ottoman siege of Belgrade. Mamluk attack on Rhodes	4, 7, 13, 17
1442	Janos Hunyadi expels Ottoman raiders at the Iron Gates. Hungary invades Wallachia	13, 14
1443	Prince Ali is assassinated. The Long Campaign. Karamanids revolt. Đurađ Branković supports Hungary during Long Campaign. Ottomans reinstate Vlad II Dracul. Battle of Niš. George Kastrioti - Skanderbeg - returns to Albania	2, 4, 6, 13, 14, 15, 16
1444	Battle of Varna. Sultan Murad II abdicates. Karamanids revolt. Black Sheep attempt invasion of Georgia. Venice participates in campaign leading to Battle of Varna. Genoese ships transport Murad II's army from Anatoli before the Battle of Varna. Peace settlement sees Đurađ Branković reinstated as Despot of Serbia. Vlad II Dracul imprisons Janos Hunyadi on his return from Battle of Varna. League of Lezhë. Ottomans defeated at Torvioll	2, 4, 6, 7, 10, 11, 13, 14, 15, 16
1445	Ottomans defeated at Mount Mokra	15
1446	Sultan Murad II returns to power. Ottoman suppression of Morea. Venice and Ottomans renew trade agreement. Janos Hunyadi becomes regent. Ottoman defeat at Otonetë	2, 4, 10, 13, 15
1447	Jahan Shah tales control of all Black Sheep territories. Prolonged war starts between White Sheep and Black Sheep. Ottoman attack on Morea leaves Venetian possessions untouched. Hungarian invasion kills Vlad II Dracul. Albanian attack on Venetian Albania	7, 10, 14, 15
1448	Second Battle of Kosovo. Constantine XI Palaiologos becomes Emperor of Constantinople. Karamanid invasion of Cilicia. Venetians supply Ottomans and Albanians in Albania. Ottomans install Vlad III Dracula temporarily as voivode. Ottoman defeat at Svetigrad	2, 4, 6, 10, 13, 14, 15
1450	Venetians supply Ottomans and Albanians in Albania. Ottoman siege of Krujë	10, 15
1451	Mehmed II becomes Ottoman Sultan. Karamanids revolt. Mehmed II's first campaign in Anatolia. Karaman agrees to pay tribute. War between White Sheep and Black Sheep ends. Treaty of Gaeta	2, 4, 6, 7, 15
1452	Mehmed II cuts off Black Sea route with Boğaz Kesen castle on the Bosporus Strait. Janos Hunyadi negotiates with Byzantium. Ottoman invasion repelled. Papal support to Constantinople	4, 8, 10, 13, 15, 16

Appendix B - Consolidated Timeline

Year	Event	Chapter
1453	Ottoman conquest of Constantinople, Venetians ships and troops leave before the battle. Uzun Hasan becomes Bey of the White Sheep. Venetians granted trade rights in Ottoman Empire. Unofficial Genoese support to Byzantium during Conquest of Contantinople	4, 7, 10, 11, 13, 16
1454	Ottomans demand tribute of Caffa. Albanian defeat at Berat	11, 15
1455	Failed Ottoman attack on Chios. Ottomans conquer Phokia and Phokianova.	11
1456	Egypt re-take Cilicia. Ottoman expeditionary force at Trebizond forces annual tribute to be agreed. Ottomans conquer Enez, Imroz and Samothrace. Siege of Belgrade, Serbians harass retreating Ottomans. Vlad III Dracula returns as Voivode of Wallachia in wake of Siege of Belgrade. Ottoman defeat at Svetigrad. Pope Callixtus III calls for crusade in support of Belgrade	6, 8, 11, 13, 14, 15, 16
1457	Stefan III becomes Voivode of Moldavia. Ottoman defeat at Ujebardha	14, 15
1458	Mehmed II pays impromptu visit to Negroponte. Ottomans enforce tribute on Duchy of Naxos. Genoa under French rule. Matthias I Corvin becomes King of Hungary. Hungarian campaign in Bosnia and Serbia. Ottoman invasion of Serbia turns around at Smederevo. Stjepan Tomašević appointed Despot of Serbia under Hungarian suzerainty	10, 11, 13, 14
1459	David Megas Komnenos becomes Emperor of Trebizond. Ottomans conquer Amasra. Ottoman invasion of Serbia. Serbia annexed into Ottoman Empire. Council of Mantua	7, 8, 11, 14, 16
1460	Uzun Hasan forward ultimatum to Ottomans on behalf of Trebizond	7, 8
1461	Final Ottoman annexation of Morea. Ottomans conquer Empire of Trebizond. French expelled from Genoa. Stjepan Tomašević refuses to pay tribute to Ottomans. Vlad III Dracula attacks Ottoman Bulgaria. Albanian assistance to Ferdinand I of Naples	4, 7, 8, 11, 14, 15, 16
1462	Karamanid war of succession. Ottoman siege of Lepanto. Ottomans fortify Dardanelles. Ottomans conquer Lesbos. Ottoman invasion removes Vlad III Dracula. Moldavian attack on Chilia	6, 10, 11, 14
1463	Venice proposes alliance with White Sheep. David Megas Komnenos is executed in Istanbul. Ottomans occupy Argos. Venice declares war on Ottoman Empire. Venetians retake Argos. Ottoman counter-offensive in Morea. Hungarian attack on Bosnia. Ottoman invasion. Stjepan Tomašević captured and subsequently executed. Bosnia becomes Ottoman province. Crusader alliance is formed	7, 8, 10, 13, 14, 16
1464	Ibrahim II dies. White Sheep assist in revolt in Karaman. Ottoman counter-offensive in Bosnia. Venetian attack on Lesbos. 'Crusader' alliance breaks down when the Pope dies. Genoa loses Famagusta. Hungarians retake Jajce. Hungary and Ottomans skirmish around Jajce. Albanian victory at Ohrid	6, 7, 10, 11, 13, 14, 15, 16
1465	Pir Ahmed becomes Bey of Karaman as Ottoman vassal. Moldavian conquest of Chilia	6, 14

Year	Event	Chapter
1466	Venice takes Imroz, Thasos and Samothrace and lays siege to Athens. Ottoman siege of Krujë, Ottomans build castle at Elbasan	10, 15
1467	War between White and Black Sheep see White Sheep conquer Black Sheep territories. Ottoman siege of Durrës. Ottoman raiders in Croatia. Battle of Baia. Ottoman campaign at Krujë and Durrës. Skanderbeg dies	7, 10, 14, 15
1468	Ottoman campaign in Karaman. Genoa under Milanese rule. Krujë and Shkodër ceded to Venice	6, 10, 11, 15
1469	Ottoman campaign in Karaman. Pir Ahmet flees to the White Sheep. Ottomans annex Karaman. White Sheep provides shelter for Karamanid refugees. Ottoman raiders in Dalmatia. Venetian raids in Morea	6, 7, 10
1470	Ottomans conquer Euboea. Moldavian attack on Wallachia	10, 14
1471	Ottoman mop-up campaign in Karaman. Alliance between White Sheep and Venice. Wallachian counter-attack on Moldavia	6, 7, 10, 14
1472	Ottoman mop-up campaign Karaman. Pir Ahmet attempts invasion. White Sheep incursions in Trebizond and Karaman. Christian fleet raid in Mediterranean and Aegean Sea. Tatar attack on Moldavia	6, 7, 10, 14, 16
1473	Battle of Otlukbeli. Ottomans annihilate White Sheep army. Venetian artillery-support for White Sheep is returned to Venice. Moldavian attack on Wallachia	7, 10, 14
1474	Final purge of Karamanid nobility. Uzun Hasan's son revolts. Ottoman siege of Shkodër. Moldavian attack on Wallachia	6, 7, 10, 14
1475	Ottomans annex Theodoro in Crimea. Ottoman attacks on Lepanto, Lemnos and Naxos. Ottomans conquer Caffa and Samos. Moldavian attack on Wallachia. Wallachians assist Ottomans in Moldavia. Battle of Vaslui	8, 10, 11, 14
1476	Siege of Krujë. Wallachians assist Ottomans in Moldavia. Battle of Rasboieni. Stefan III puts Vlad III Dracula back on the throne of Wallachia.	10, 14
1477	Ottoman raiders reach outskirts of Venice. Moldavian invasion	10, 14
1478	Uzun Hasan dies. After war of succession Ya'qub becomes Bey. Ottomans take Krujë. Ottoman raiders outside Venice. Siege of Shkodër. Ottomans conquer Krujë	7, 10, 15
1479	Peace agreement between Venice and Ottoman Empire. Wallachia again becomes Ottoman vassal	10, 14, 16
1480	Ottoman army lands at Otranto. Ottoman attack on Rhodes. Albania used to launch Ottoman attack on Italy	15, 16, 17
1481	Moldavian invasion. Ottomans conquer Shkodër. Sultan Mehmed II dies. Ottoman invasion is abandoned	14, 15, 16
1482	Herzegovina annexed by Ottomans	14
1490	Ya'qub dies and the White Sheep dissolve in following war of succession.	7
1503	Moldavia agrees to pay tribute to Ottoman Empire	14
1523	Knights Hospitaller expelled from Rhodes	17
1565	Ottoman siege of Malta	17

ABOUT THE AUTHOR

In his own words:

I was an Army Officer when I was young, but I have spent more than twenty years as a leader in various software and telecoms organizations, including some blue-chip companies. Though Danish, I have spent two decades outside my native country, living and working on three different continents.
In 2011 I retired from working-life to concentrate on pursuing my life-long hobby as an amateur-historian, this book being a direct result.
In 2014 I enrolled as a mature student at University of Southern Denmark, where I currently (2015) study Classical Civilization.

In his wife's words:

Jens Ole Schwarz-Nielsen (Sir Jens) was a remarkable man.
He had many passions, of which ancient history was but one.
In 2025, he died suddenly and unexpectedly, leaving a huge void in the lives of those who loved him.
He will be forever missed by his family, friends, and those lucky enough to have entered his orbit. However, his legacy lives on in his books, and it is my sincere wish that they leave the reader feeling as excited about history as Jens intended.

Enquires directed to: https://www.facebook.com/InTheShadowOfEmpires